MARRIAGE AND FAMILY IN A CHANGING SOCIETY

MARRIAGE AND FAMILY IN A CHANGING SOCIETY

Fourth Edition

Edited by
JAMES M. HENSLIN

THE FREE PRESS
New York   London   Toronto   Sydney   Tokyo   Singapore

The Free Press
A Division of Simon & Schuster Inc.
1230 Avenue of the Americas
New York, N.Y. 10020

Printed in the United States of America

printing number

3 4 5 6 7 8 9 10

Library of Congress Cataloging-in-Publication Data

Marriage and family in a changing society / edited by James M.
  Henslin.—4th ed.
    p.   cm.
  ISBN 0-02-914475-2
  1. Marriage—United States. 2. Family—United States.
I. Henslin, James M.
HQ734.M3867   1992
306.8'0973—dc20
                                      91-34169
                                      CIP

Credits and
Acknowledgments
▼▼▼▼▼▼▼▼▼▼▼▼▼▼▼▼▼▼▼▼▼▼▼

Grateful acknowledgment is made to the authors and publishers who have granted permission to reprint the following selections:

CHAPTER
NUMBER

1. Copyright © 1985, 1989, and 1992 by James M. Henslin.

2. Reprinted by permission of the wife and daughter of David R. Mace.

3. This article appeared in the September 1989 issue and is reprinted with permission from *The World & I,* a publication of *The Washington Times Corporation,* copyright © 1989.

4. Excerpt from *The War Over the Family: Capturing the Middle Ground* by Brigitte Berger and Peter L. Berger. Reprinted by permission of Doubleday, a division of Bantam, Doubleday, Dell Publishing Group, Inc.

For
la compañera de mi alma
with whom I am privileged to share
that life-transforming experience
known as marriage

rough times
and good times
but always our times

together growing
changing with those times
in sharing more and more
the two becoming one

Contents

▼▼▼▼▼▼▼▼▼▼

Preface
▼▼▼▼▼▼▼

THE BOOK'S FRAMEWORK

I have taught the basic course in marriage and family for a good many years. Desiring to be an effective instructor in this course, which enrolls many students who are not sociology majors, I have tried several approaches in my teaching.

Of the many things that I have learned from my attempts, the following stands out: Students respond well to a developmental approach to the study of marriage and family life. Therefore, I present the course materials sequentially, from early life through such experiences as dating and mate selection, marital adjustment, divorce, and remarriage. Consequently, I have utilized a developmental framework as the organizing device for this book—a framework that received a favorable response in the first three editions.

The primary advantage of this approach is that it builds on a framework for thinking about marriage and family that students bring to the course. Building on the familiar makes it easier for the instructor to teach and the students to learn. For example, most students have already experienced love, are acutely aware of their sex roles, are involved in some form of dating, have probably considered alternatives to marriage, and anticipate what their own marriage will be like. Following their wedding, almost all expect to make the transition to marital sexuality, to balance work and marriage, and to become parents.

Two variations are worth noting, however. First, not all students who take this class find themselves at the same point in their lives. The presence of older students means that some have already experienced parenting, divorce, and so forth. Nevertheless, the developmental approach permits students to look directly at what they have already experienced, through sociological analyses to gain greater understanding of those events, and then to anticipate future experiences.

Second, it seems good to lay a broad sociological foundation before moving into the developmental sequence. Consequently, the book opens with a section in which we explore the social and historical context of marriage and family. This section allows students to see first what a *sociology* of marriage and family is—to make visible some of the interconnections between individual experiences and their sociohistorical context.

THE STRUCTURE OF THE BOOK

As an introduction to the sociological perspective on marriage and family, this book opens with an article by Henslin on how society molds expectations of intimacy, marriage, and family life. Next, Mace examines the effect of social change on four fundamental areas of marriage and family: the basis of marriage, sexual relationships, parenthood, and divorce. Then Sayres shows that the concept of "family" encompasses so many relationships that the term defies definition. Finally, Berger and Berger stress that the perception of the family as a problem is anything but new.

In Part II, we continue to lay our basic sociological foundation by focusing on the social and cultural diversity of marriage and family life. First, Rubin contrasts the sharply different realities that the working and middle classes encounter in marriage. Then Staples presents a brief history of black families and Becerra discusses the family life of Chicanos. Browder then analyzes why women are disadvantaged in cohabitation, and Harry looks at cohabiting relationships between people of the same sex. Finally, Stein examines the diverse world of single adults, and Veevers examines the process by which couples decide not to have children.

Part III highlights the cultural underpinnings of love, romance, and intimacy. This focus clarifies the vital shaping process of socialization, making more visible how "society within us" is so extensive that it influences even our intimate desires. Bumiller's discusion of arranged marriages in India throws our customary approaches to marriage and family formation into broad relief, while Collins's use of the concept of property relations casts a different light on love. Then comes Karp's and Yoels's analysis of the process by which people develop intimate relationships. Finally, Trotter contrasts different types of love.

Part IV concentrates on communication between husbands and wives. First, Sarnoff and Sarnoff look at barriers to communication that can block a love-centered marriage, as well as ways to overcome these barriers. Next, Berger and Kellner explore the process by which husbands and wives develop shared realities. Stuart and Johnson then analyze how to surmount the "secret contracts" made during courtship that impede marital communication. Mace then considers how a husband and wife can creatively use the anger that inevitably arises in love relationships, while Barbeau discusses how couples can solve communication problems that arise from their divergent sex roles.

In Part V, we turn our sociological inquiry to parenting. Eagan presents an overview of the diverse practices of childbirth during the past two centuries, and Henslin contrasts child-rearing practices through the ages. Bagne then examines how technology is creating such vast changes in conceptive practices that they are affecting our attitudes and, perhaps, even society itself. Rubenstein then focuses on sexual adjustments of couples following the birth of a child, and Bronfenbrenner analyzes the conditions that are necessary for the healthy development of children. Handel turns the focus on siblings—their rivalries, intimacies, and attempts to develop equity and loyalty in their relationships. Finally, Rubin examines the transition that mothers make when their last child leaves home, contrasting the myth of the empty nest with its reality.

In Part VI, we shift to the issue of work and marriage. First, Bernard sketches the sweeping changes in the basic provider role, emphasizing that our current arrangements are outgrowths of earlier patterns. Next, Gerson examines the hard choices that women face, comparing the satisfactions and regrets of those who have opted for children or careers. Berg then focuses on the guilt that many working mothers feel, while Roache analyzes the reluctance of husbands to share housework. Finally, Chesser looks at the advantages and disadvantages of dual-career marriages.

In Part VII, we turn our focus onto pathological relationships. First, Levine and Kanin analyze why date rape has become more common in our society. Ferraro and Johnson then discuss why battered wives remain with battering husbands. As Straus examines three primary causes of marital violence, he stresses that no single factor is the cause of family violence. Finally, Jackson focuses on families caught up in the crisis of alcoholism, looking at how they adjust their resources to meet the crisis.

In Part VIII, we look at the marital transitions of divorce, remarriage, and widowhood. First, McGoldrick and Carter analyze the major "tasks" of each stage of the family life cycle, stressing the dislocations that divorce brings. Henslin then tries to explain why there is so much divorce in today's society. As Wallerstein and Kelly look at the effects of divorce on children, they examine their stresses, adjustments, and coping devices. Kelly then turns to the reactions of adults at different points along the divorce route, while Bronfenbrenner describes the vicious cycle that divorced mothers find themselves caught up in. Weitzman analyzes gender inequalities in divorce—why the standard of living of most ex-husbands rises dramatically and that of ex-wives drops sharply. Papernow then looks at the families formed by remarriage, and DiGiulio examines the four stages of bereavement.

The book ends with a focus on lasting relationships. In Part IX, Blumstein and Schwartz look at the three major areas that couples must negotiate successfully if they are to find marriage satisfying. Lauer and Lauer then examine the qualities that couples in long-lasting, satisfying relationships have in common. Cuber and Harroff stress that there is no single model of marital success, but, rather, a variety of types of marital relating that couples develop over time. Finally, Stinnett identifies the characteristics of couples who are highly satisfied with their marriages and who have developed a strong family life.

VALUES UNDERLYING THIS BOOK

One frequently hears that sociologists should specify their value positions, since values influence the outcome of professional endeavors. As the editor of this volume, I am aware that my value positions have been instrumental in compiling this book, especially in my selection of particular articles. Which values, then, have helped to shape its contents?

First, I am convinced that the sociological perspective can make a course in marriage and family highly rewarding. I think of the sociological perspective not as merely an academic device but as a highly practical framework that allows us to integrate personal experiences with the social context within which we live. I see this interpretative tool as an effective way to view even the intimacies of life—those events that, shaping what we feel, eventually become an essential part of how we look at the world.

From this conviction, I have tried to present articles that communicate a sociological understanding of marriage and family, and that do so in an engaging way. These selections should not only stimulate provocative in-class discussion but also give students contextual understanding of life-shaping events that affect them so intimately.

Second, I am convinced that the need to form intimate relationships is part of our biological makeup and that marriage is a valuable way to satisfy this basic need. It is not for nothing that this social institution is universal. Marriage has much to offer—especially a sense of fulfillment and purpose, solace during personal crises, a challenge to personal growth, and a sense of satisfaction as you learn to please the person who has become so vital to you. Moreover, I know of no experience comparable to that of having and raising children: to hold your infant for the first time and then to participate in his or her growth and development, knowing that you are making an essential contribution to what your child will become.

These positions have not led me to be Pollyana-ish in my choice of articles—for I believe the *potential* of marriage is realizable only through struggle—in an encounter so far-reaching and intimate that it challenges even one's basic orientations to life. Nor have I rejected articles that express contrary values, for some find deep satisfaction in pursuits and relationships that lead to paths other than marriage and family.

Three emphases, then, mark the selections in this book—the sociocultural context, the potential, and the struggle of marriage and family life. To place marriage and family in a social context is essential for its adequate understanding. Mutually satisfying marital relationships simply do not come without struggle, and without a willingness to change in response to another person, who, with all his or her individualized orientations, becomes incorporated into one's own being.

From these value positions emerges a related theme that unites the selections in this book: Marriage is not a state, but a process. It is this dynamic of marriage that these articles convey—that marriage is an ongoing, developing relationship, intimately affected not only by the two individuals involved but also by the society in which they live.

It is my intention, then, to provide students with selections that communicate both the potential of marriage and a sociologial perspective on the barriers that frequently prevent that potential from being realized. The clarification of both these factors can help students increase their self-awareness and overcome the challenges they face (or will face) as they work out their own realities in marriage.

At the foundation of these values, then, is the premise that the better we understand the sociological context that both constrains and opens possibilities for us, the better we are equipped to deal with those twinned aspects of social life.

If education in the liberal arts is at all intended to provide knowledge that ultimately frees people from the various contraints with which they began their educational process, so, then, sociological knowledge holds remarkable potential for enabling freedom.

CHANGES AND EMPHASES

Users of earlier editions should find themselves at home in this edition's basic structure and, I hope, will welcome the changes. In response to their suggestions, I have added more material on problem-solving in marriage, social change, marital communication, childlessness, same-sex relationships, housework, the "not-so-empty" nest, date rape, and stepfamilies.

Following suggestions of adopters of the previous edition and because of the growing stream of literature in marriage and family, I have been able to expand the book's topical coverage. Altogether, 20 of the 49 selections are new to this edition.

APPRECIATIONS

As in previous editions, I first wish to express appreciation to my wife, Linda. The dedication page reflects years of experience in growing together—years that I hope will lengthen into several decades.

I also wish to thank the following instructors who, by sharing their teaching experiences with me, were instrumental in this edition: Laurence A. Basirico, Selma K. Brandow, Marie Tobia Deem, Melissa Deller, Heather Fitz-Gibbon, Brenda Forster, Jean C. Karlen, David Knox, Steve M. McGuire, Kenneth E. Miller, Ray Quiett, Christian Smith, Kathleen Maurer Smith, N. J. Tayani, and Carol Whithurst.

The authors and publishers of these selections also deserve my appreciation for granting permission to use their work and to edit their articles to the necessary length. I also wish to thank my students, who have borne with me as I have developed my perspective on the basic materials in marriage and family. I have learned much from them—especially from their frank and enthusiastic sharing of what is essential in their world.

Finally, I would be pleased to hear from students and teachers about their experiences, positive or negative, in using this book. I welcome suggestions for making revisions in future editions. You may contact me at the address below.

James M. Henslin
Department of Sociology
Southern Illinois University
Edwardsville, Illinois 62026

PART I
▼▼▼▼▼▼▼▼▼▼▼▼▼▼▼▼▼▼▼▼▼

Laying the Sociological Foundation

Whether they study war or a kindergarten, criminals or presidents, high school dropouts or aspiring executives, sociologists always look for *social* influences on people's lives. The sociological perspective on marriage and family is no exception, for sociologists stress that people acquire their particular marriage and family patterns from society. Because marriage and family are molded and shaped by society, they take radically different forms in different places in the world. These forms, with their accompanying expectations, give shape to what people do and how they view life.

Many examples could be used to illustrate this point. In our society, men and women are allowed to have only one spouse at a time; in some others, they are able to have more than one. We consider it the parents' duty to provide food for their children, as well as to discipline them, while in some other parts of the world these responsibilities go to someone outside the nuclear family, often the mother's oldest brother.

How extensively the social group influences people's attitudes and

1

behaviors in marriage and family is especially apparent in the case of premarital sex. In some societies, premarital sex is forbidden, and unmarried males and females are strictly kept apart; in others, such sexual relations may be tolerated, or perhaps even encouraged. In some rare instances, premarital sex may even be required: For example, in pre–World War II Samoa, to prove that she was fertile and thus would be a suitable wife, a young woman had to give birth *before* she was allowed to marry.

No matter what the particular customs, and no matter how radically they may differ from one another, they all are *predetermined* for the individual at birth. Learned early, they become a major part of the individual's assumptions of what the world is like—and of what family life *ought* to be like. These *social creations* provide the basic framework that shapes the choices we make in life. That our own particular customs are not natural, but learned, however, tends to drop from our consciousness.

At the heart of the sociological perspective of marriage and family, then, is the attempt to make this cultural framework visible. The sociological perspective stresses that our society's expectations of family life underlie the marital and familial roles that we assume. What we do in marriage and family is not what it often appears—a matter of personal choice—but the result of historical forces set in motion long ago.

That marriage and family are an essential part of the other institutions of society is a significant theme in the sociology of marriage and family. Every human group has developed basic *social institutions* to cope with recurring problems. For example, every society establishes some customary way to deal with armed threat. The social institution established to deal with this problem is the military. Similarly, each society faces the recurring problems of illness and injury. A group's customary method of handling threats to the health of its members is called the medical institution. So it is with the challenge to pass knowledge and skills from one generation to the next (education), to distribute property in an orderly fashion (the economy), to handle disputes among neighbors and deal with people who violate the rights of others (the legal system), to establish relations with the spiritual world (religion), and so on.

Another set of recurring problems facing each group includes regulating the sexual behaviors of its members, providing for the safety and security of children, helping people achieve emotional stability, and so on. Over time, each human group has developed its own customary ideas about how best to meet these needs. *The term given to the social institution that meets these universally recurring needs is marriage and family.* Although their unique histories give societies different forms of this social institution, marriage and family are universal, for they represent the solution to universal problems or needs.

All social institutions are part of the *moral* sphere of social life. That is, since they embody successful solutions to a group's basic needs that have evolved over time, these institutions bring with them ideas about the way that life *ought* to be carried on. Marriage and family are no exception to this moral precept that social institutions communicate "the proper way to do things." Perhaps because human sexuality, children, intimacy, and property are involved, marriage and family shoulder much of the responsibility of conveying morality. Consequently, violation of the expectations called for by a society's form of marriage and family is never taken lightly.

Part I provides a brief glimpse into how marriage and family are interconnected with other parts of society. The goal is to introduce the broad social context that determines our particular experiences in marriage and family. The chapters are designed to make evident the sweeping social changes that affect what we have experienced, are now experiencing, and will experience. To adopt the sociological perspective is to enlarge our vision so that we can better see the social forces that affect people's lives—including our own.

In Chapter 1, James M. Henslin stresses that marriage and family so closely interconnect the individual with society that they shape even our personal, intimate desires. Because some readers may be unfamiliar with the meaning of the term, the goal of this opening selection is to define "the sociology of marriage and family," and hence to lay the foundation for understanding the selections that appear in this book.

In Chapter 2, David R. Mace demonstrates the vital interconnection between marriage and family and the other institutions of society. He analyzes how the Industrial Revolution changed even the basis for marriage, and brought with it new ideas about premarital sex, sexual exclusivity, and expectations of parenthood. He shows how that revolution, seemingly so impersonal and remote, even affects our own chances of divorce.

In Chapter 3, William Sayres makes the point that during the course of our lives we are likely to belong to several different types of families. Indeed, families differ so greatly that it is impossible to come up with an encompassing definition. He points out that while extended families—history's most common type of family—dominate the rest of the world, nuclear families characterize the Western world. To better understand family in our own culture, he distinguishes between stepfamilies, foster families, adoptive families, communes, and group families.

In Chapter 4, Brigitte Berger and Peter L. Berger analyze why so many people think that the family is in serious trouble. They trace a brief history of the rise of the bourgeois (middle-class) family to dominance, review how the family has been portrayed in American sociology, and analyze how views of the family have changed in recent decades. They conclude that a problem must always be perceived from someone's point of view, and that the primary clashing points of view today are represented by liberals and conservatives.

1
▼▼▼

The Sociology of Marriage and Family
▼▼▼▼▼

James M. Henslin

ABSTRACT: What is meant by the phrase, "the sociology of marriage and family"? It indicates that sociologists analyze how society molds people's expectations and behaviors concerning marriage and family life.

Unlike animal behavior, human behavior is not shaped by instincts. We do not simply mate, perhaps following elaborate courting rituals that are built into our genes. Instead, our behaviors are the result of learning. Through a socialization process that begins at birth, we come to view our own society's expectations of marriage and family life as natural. Arbitrarily established by the social group, those expectations differ from one society to another. They provide cultural "directions" for what we should be like as husbands and wives and children, for how we are to relate to one another in marriage and family. Mechanisms of social control (both direct and indirect) influence even the intimate areas of our lives. The author uses an extended example to illustrate these points, and concludes by examining the issue of "social forces" versus "individual choice."

To help gain an understanding of what is meant by the term "the sociology of marriage and family," let us first look at the following event:

4

The government of China has mobilized an army of party members to enforce its birth control policies. These officials utilize a tempting carrot and a rather brutalizing stick. They offer financial, educational, and health care incentives to couples who limit their reproduction to one child, while they reduce wages and refuse promotions to couples who violate the government's wishes and have a second or third child.

Because the Chinese have a strong preference for sons, this policy has led to a sharp increase in female infanticide.

A woman who conceives a second or third time is visited by party members who try to convince her to have an abortion for the good of the country. Government officials force abortion on some who refuse, and medical personnel will sometimes inject a woman about to give birth so she delivers a stillborn.

The social control is so exacting and explicit that women must display their sanitary napkins on demand to show they are not pregnant. (Vinck, 1981; Mirsky, 1983)

In a similar manner, our society . . . but we shall return to this matter later. First, I wish to stress that the heart of the sociological perspective is that human behavior is not understandable apart from the broader sociocultural context within which that behavior occurs. Human behavior is not determined by instincts; nor do people possess other built-in mechanisms that push them into specific behaviors. Humans are not driven by internal forces that, invariably patterning their lives, make one human group quite like that of another.

Human behavior is quite the contrary. As in the illustration above, patterns of human behavior differ markedly from one human group to another. On the broader level, the customs of a group of primitive people living in Australia differ sharply from the practices of peasants in Southeast Asia. Similarly, both differ markedly from those of people living in industrialized societies. And the customs of one industrialized group can be unlike those of another, just as the way of life of one peasant group differs from another.

It is obvious that to understand these various peoples we must see their behaviors through the lens of their customs, their interrelated ideas of what is right and wrong, and their views of how one ought to go about living life. Only as we apprehend their beliefs and values (as well as their ways of organizing themselves, their environmental and technological constraints) can we make sense out of their way of life.

To interpret an individual's or group's behavior within the broader sociocultural context is also central to the sociology of marriage and family. The sociological approach is to consider the social forces that shape, direct, and otherwise influence what people do in marriage and family.

While this point also seems obvious, and hardly worth stressing—for we all know that wedding customs, for example, differ from one group to another—the implications of this position are anything but obvious. The scope of a society's influence is much more pervasive than is ordinarily visible to us. We are usually unaware of the extent to which society molds us: not only our dating practices, sexual behaviors, sex roles, and modes of child rearing, but, ultimately, even the most intimate portions of our private lives. Even our thoughts, desires, and expectations, things considered so intimately personal, are molded by the society and broader culture of which we are members.

This shaping process begins as each newborn is ushered into a preformed, ongoing, complex world. One's birth signals membership into a particular culture, one of humanity's thousands of more or less coherent shared ways of thinking and doing. To become socialized—to become a knowing or capable member of society—means that these preestablished ways of thinking and doing become a part of oneself.

Human offspring cannot survive on their own. Babies must be nourished by a caretaker in order for normal physical and emotional development to occur, and they must interact with others so they can develop language and other expected social skills. Culture channels the ways in which the family performs these basic orientational functions. These cultural constraints, this sociocultural context of learning society's basic expectations, also channel sexual expression by providing guidance for viewing one's own self, one's own body, one's spouse, and one's relationships, including rights and responsibilities within the family.

In short, this characteristic of humans not growing up alone or isolated and not depending on instincts to determine their behavior, but becoming members of a family—an ongoing sociocultural unit already embedded within a larger network of social relations—imparts to the individual a sociocultural heritage. Because the family is an intricate part of a larger network of culturally patterned ways of behavior and shared ways of looking at the world, each individual becomes immersed in shaping mechanisms that vitally affect his or her own behaviors, perceptions, and orientations toward all areas of life, including relating to the opposite sex in dating, marriage, and the family.

The focal concern in the sociology of marriage and family flows from this universal fact of cultural heritage. The ways in which human culture and social participation shape the fabric of marriage and family life, then, become basic points of sociological inquiry. For example, in what way does social membership influence how we perceive others as marriageable? As desirable? What are the mechanisms that are brought into play to channel our perception and desires into socially approved and predetermined avenues? While such orientational attitudes are ordinarily deemed a matter of "personal preference," perceptions of marriageability and desirability are, in fact, determined by a myriad of sociocultural factors.

As a quick illustration, ask yourself why you are not (or are, as the case may be) attracted to someone who has colorful scars on his or her face, hair braided in a certain manner, wears very large rings in the ears or a ring through the nose, and so on—for each of these characteristics is a sign of high attractability in some cultures.

To assure continuity over time, each society needs to exercise control over its members. This is a basic fact of social existence. The resulting social control, however, is so pervasive that it affects almost every aspect of life. To accomplish this control, both simple and complex mechanisms are brought into play. In smaller, tribal societies the techniques of social control center around face-to-face relationships, with positive and negative sanctions being given on a direct and fairly immediate basis. In larger societies the direct and face-to-face basis of sanctioning is partially replaced by more formal and sometimes indirect social control mechanisms. Regardless of the type of society into which an individual becomes socialized—whether hunting and gathering, small and agricultural, or large and industrialized—social control mechanisms are utilized to teach the individual to act, think, and believe according to already existing expectations.

In one of his more entertaining and provocative books, Freud (1930) stresses that as civilization develops, greater and greater constraints are placed on the individual. The group attempts to make its members cooperate in activities deemed important, to direct their energies, time, and other resources toward what are considered to be common goals. Even though individuals may be thinking in terms of self-interest, such as their own paycheck, their own goals, or whatever rewards they feel they are receiving from their activities, ordinarily each person comes under the direction of the larger social group.

For resources and efforts to be directed to goals larger than the individual, and in the ideal case for them to become interrelated with the welfare of others, requires restrictions on the individual. Consequently, the actions of large numbers of people become aligned with one another, forming an interrelationship of social institutions. The control that must be exerted over individuals to bring about such large-scale interrelated or cooperative activities includes control over their sex drive, their romantic involvements, and their reproduction. Allowed to operate freely, such individualizing inclinations as love and mating would upset the expected social arrangements, those, presumably, upon which the society's welfare depends (Goode, 1959).

In each society, then, mechanisms of various sorts are put into practice in order to channel dating, marriage, the expression of sexuality, and parenting into acceptable forms. Because the excessive withdrawal of some persons from the activities and interests of the larger sociocultural unit would threaten this collectivization of resources, each society attempts to control the excessiveness of paired involvements. Efforts are made to somehow make certain that people do not so greatly withdraw into dyads that they neglect those activities that ultimately affect the welfare of others. (Cf. Slater, 1963.)

The illustration with which I began this article is a striking example of *direct* social control over matters ordinarily thought quite individual and private. Yet the government of China feels so threatened by population growth that it has instituted family planning this severe.

In contrast, most social control is *indirect*. Most is based on influencing people's expectations that, in turn, affect their actions. In our own country, for example, while no one is forcing women to undergo abortions, officials are not visiting our homes to enforce their reproductive goals on us, and government agents are not inspecting sanitary napkins, we are still immersed in a myriad of sociocultural expectations concerning children. For most of us, these expectations quite effectively limit our desire to reproduce.

These indirect forms of social control, however, are largely invisible to us, yet, immersed in them, we respond unwittingly. Consequently, the sociology of marriage and family attempts to make visible the mechanisms and effects of indirect social control. As we perceive some of the sociocultural influences that act on us, we gain a better understanding of society's influences on marriage and family—and of ourselves.

In each society the mechanisms of social control, perhaps put into effect to reduce the antisocial potential of the sex drive, channel that drive into acceptable forms. This process contributes to the social order by encouraging certain forms of pairing and maximizing the likelihood that procreation will occur within the form of the family idealized within that culture. This centrality to society of the social control of the sex drive becomes apparent when we note that, among other things, marriage and family represent a means of reducing sexual competition, encouraging cooperation, providing a regularized and socially acceptable sexual outlet while reducing erotic outlets deemed unacceptable, defining the responsibilities and privileges of social relationships, and bestowing major role identities such as husband and wife, son and daughter, parent and child. (Cf. Mead, 1949:183–200; Davis, 1976).

As other social institutions are so critically significant in the process of determining marital and familial norms and roles, sociologists of marriage and family emphasize how a society's institutions affect family life. What influence, for example, does religion have on marriage? Or how do the economics of society affect the family? Or advances in medical technology? Or war, peace, or other forms of politics?

This institutional focus also leads sociologists to examine other macro (large-scale) determinants of individuals' expectations. On the societal level sociologists examine social change, while on the individual level they look at how marital happiness is affected by the forces of social change. This includes such matters as how the macro phenomenon of the state of a society's economic well-being, such as its rate of employment and changes in gross national product, influence such practical micro-level decisions as whether or not a wife goes to work outside the home. And because those economic factors do not exist in isolation, sociologists examine other broad social forces that affect such "simple" marriage and family decision making. For example, they try to decide how changing sex role expectations figure into the picture. And how these, in turn are related to education—the wife's, the husband's, or general levels in society. While the issue of a wife taking paid employment outside the home is certainly a private family matter, such individual decisions, and their conflict and resolution, are mitigated by vast, encompassing influences from the larger social system in which the family is embedded.

As they examine such questions as love, sex, and marriage and family, sociologists continually return to the part that membership in a particular culture plays in molding the basic orientations of its members. The institution of marriage and family is an essential consequence of this shaping, while it, in turn, serves to give form to much of the society of which it is a part. Consequently, basic questions include: As a consequence of their membership in a particular group within a particular society how do people view their role in the family? How do such self-views vary cross-culturally? How do they change over time? How do the patterns of marriage and family that characterize a culture reflect broader cultural characteristics—especially how those patterns of behavior are related to the other institutions of that society? In what ways do social institutions and cultural expectations channel people's orientations so they result in those particular forms or patterns of behavior? And in what ways does the playback of cultural learning, as modified by individuals and their unique life experiences in marriage and family life, in turn, affect cultural expectations?

I realize that this analysis, along with the concerns and issues that have been raised, may seem rather abstract, vague, and difficult to grasp. Perhaps the best way of moving from abstract statements about the sociology of marriage and family, in order to make them more real, is to use an extended example. While this example will not illustrate all of the above statements, it will cover the basic points and help to illustrate what is meant by a sociology of marriage and family.

I shall use an example that especially illustrates how society constrains (or channels, molds, or influences) individual choice while at the same time the individual experiences freedoms rather than constraints. To do this, let's look at a common event in our society: one individual dating another and then, eventually, marrying that person. As we focus on this rather prosaic situation, we want to keep asking: From a sociological point of view, what is occurring?

First, it is significant to note that the "choice" of date and eventually of mate takes place within highly constricted boundaries—avenues that, channeling the choice, are largely invisible to the individual. If we look at the matter more closely, we see such things as:

1. The individuals (let's give them typical names and call them Bob and Mary) made the assumption that dating was proper. That is, Bob and Mary assumed dating was a good thing and that they "ought" to date. In fact, they viewed dating as so proper that they would have thought of themselves as oddballs if they did not date.

Although they experience dating as a personal desire (as something that flows up out of themselves), what is not readily apparent to Bob and Mary is how the society is geared to making them want to date. That dating is merely an artifact of society—an arbitrary practice currently in vogue—and not some activity that spontaneously arises from within individuals, some inevitable expression of human nature, can be illustrated by noting that in many societies dating is unknown. In ours, in contrast, dating is a form of male/female interaction that is highly encouraged—at least among certain people at certain times.

2. Bob and Mary chose each other as dates. They experienced the "choice" as a natural tug from within, a part of personal desire and human freedom.

In point of fact, however, they "chose" one another from within a highly limiting range of choices—limits that were arbitrarily established by their social group membership. For example, Bob and Mary, as typical as they are, did *not* date someone from another race. They did *not* date someone too rich or too poor, or, for that matter, someone too old or too young, too tall or too short, too fat, unhealthy, or ugly. Moreover, they *did* date an unmarried member of the opposite sex.

In other words, not unlike most of us, Bob's and Mary's dating followed certain well-established social lines, demarcations set up before they were born that continue to match basic expectations of society. Growing up in this society, Bob and Mary internalized these expectations (made them a part of their thinking, actually their very being) and, as they followed these internalized expectations, they felt that they were simply "doing what was natural." The constraining effects of their socialization went largely unnoticed by them.

As far as most people are concerned, in fact, following the lines laid out by society is not what needs to be explained, for they seem so "natural." It is violations of these expectations that need to be explained—not why Bob and Mary dated within their own race, for example, but why Joe, a white, dated Ann, a black; or why Elaine, who is twenty-seven, is dating Fred, who is seventeen.

From a sociological point of view, however, both conformity to expectations *and* their violations beg explanation. *Neither* is simply some natural unfolding from within, but *both* are natural outcomes of very human and understandable social processes. Yet, in either case, those processes

largely remain invisible to those who are doing the conforming or devi-
ating. It is an essential part of the sociological perspective to make visible that which underlies the social channeling of human choice.

3. After graduating from college, Bob and Mary were married. They
had a beautiful wedding—a church, gowns, flowers, music, gifts and
guests, and so on—and each felt that the "choice" of the other as spouse
was one "freely" made.

Largely invisible to Bob and Mary were the huge shaping devices put
into effect by their society and culture, some of which we have already
mentioned. But note some of the strong influences on Bob and Mary:

  a. Their culture dictates that monogamy is the only acceptable form
     of marriage;
  b. Society has provided idealized expectations concerning the proper
     timing of marriage (for example, following specified major life
     events, such as graduation from high school or college);
  c. The peer group exercises remarkable influence, exerting social
     control over "personal choice" in matters of the height, weight,
     age, race, intelligence, social class, and popularity and reputa-
     tional qualities of prospective dates. Accordingly, the peer group
     wields great influence in channeling people toward prospective
     spouses;
  d. We have not even mentioned a variety of other sources of primary
     influence on Bob and Mary, such as their parents (whose resi-
     dence in a social class and racially segregated neighborhood lim-
     ited their choice), their religion (with its membership typically fol-
     lowing social class and racial lines, as well as its highly specific
     teachings about right and wrong in dating and marriage), and
     their education (private, public, or parochial schools—with their
     mix or lack thereof concerning social class and racial back-
     grounds).

In addition to all these influences are the broad sociohistorical factors
that become part of the "choices" that Bob and Mary make after their
marriage. For example, these influences, largely determining their basic
expectations concerning what Bob is like as a male, Mary as a female,
and their expectations of one another as a male or female, become essential in their basic roles of husband and wife. Within those broad frame-
works ("What you ought to do because you are a male—and my husband," thinks Mary, and "What you ought to do because you are a
female—and my wife," thinks Bob) Bob and Mary will play out their
roles as husband and wife.

Again, each largely experiences these roles as a matter of "personal
choice," generally remaining blind to the many pervasive cultural, social, and historical factors that shape the "choices" they make. For ex-

ample, both Bob and Mary have decided to work outside the home. They have also decided that they will share the housework and cooking and child care. Such choices simply were not options for most newly-weds some years back. Now, however, *because society has been undergoing major modifications and those changes have affected marital roles,* Bob and Mary experience that change as a matter of "personal choice."

And in many ways Bob and Mary are right: It is a matter of choice concerning what sex and marital roles they wish to adopt. Several options do lie before them. But largely invisible to Bob and Mary are the constraining forces, those broad social factors, that either make such choices an option for a married couple in the first place or that remove them from even the possibility of consideration.

The sociological perspective on marriage and family, then, is to view the world of marriage and family life in light of the social forces that operate in people's lives. Sometimes this is direct government control, as in the China example, but it usually involves more indirect forms of influence. The specifics on which sociologists focus vary widely. They could be the dynamics of socialization into sex roles, as well as how those roles operate in dating and married life, the influence of peers in mate selection, our expectations concerning sexuality and married life, or even the social factors that underlie our experience of love. Regardless of the specifics, sociologists who specialize in these fascinating activities that we call marriage and family throw the sociological spotlight on the social factors that underlie what people experience as matters of individual taste and choice.

REFERENCES

DAVIS, KINGSLEY. "Sexual Behavior." In *Contemporary Social Problems,* edited by Robert K. Merton and Robert Nisbet, fourth edition, 219–261. New York: Harcourt Brace Jovanovich, 1976.

FREUD, SIGMUND. *Civilization and its Discontents.* Translated by J. Rivière. New York: Cape and Smith, 1930.

GOODE, WILLIAM J. "The Theoretical Importance of Love." *American Sociological Review* 24 (1959): 38–47.

MEAD, MARGARET. *Male and Female: A Study of the Sexes in a Changing World.* New York: William Morrow, 1949.

MIRSKY, JONATHAN. "The Infanticide Tragedy in China." *The Nation,* July 2, 1983.

SLATER, PHILIP. "On Social Regression." *American Sociological Review* 28 (June 1963): 339–364.

VINCK, MICHELLE. "Abortion and Birth Control in Canton, China." *The Wall Street Journal,* November 30, 1981.

2

▼▼▼

Issues in Marriage

▼▼▼▼▼

David R. Mace

ABSTRACT: Marriage is a universal social institution because it is related to human survival. During their history, humans have experienced two major changes that have fundamentally altered their way of life: (1) the transition from a nomadic way of life to agriculture and (2) the Industrial Revolution. Each of these social mutations brought fundamental change to marriage and family. The effects of the Industrial Revolution are not yet over, and currently it is bringing change in four basic areas of marriage and family: (1) the basis for marriage, which now is companionship, (2) ideas about premarital sex and sexual exclusivity in marriage, (3) expectations of parenthood, and (4) the likelihood of divorce. These changes are not a sign that marriage and family are breaking down, but only that they are being modified to meet changing circumstances. Indeed, they are signs that the institution of marriage is healthy.

MARRIAGE IN THE PAST

The archaeologists tell us that we have had at least a million years of [humans]. They are not able to report with equal confidence that we have had a million years of marriage; but I strongly suspect that we have. We can be certain that, during those million years, the continuity of the race was provided for by the fact that women had babies. We know that they couldn't have had babies without first having had sexual intercourse with men. We know that the experience of motherhood makes a woman vulnerable, and in the grim struggle for existence we can assume that the woman whose man stayed with her and supported her through the experience of motherhood would have a better chance of survival than the woman left to fend for herself. The search for food and shelter and safety was probably most successfully carried out by small groups of people cooperating with one another; and the most natural nuclear grouping, in terms of mutual needs and mutual service, is a man, a woman, and their children. So it is a reasonable supposition that marriage of some sort has existed throughout the entire period of human history.

This was the view of Edward Westermarck, who wrote the classical three-volume *History of Human Marriage* [a hundred] years ago. One of his major conclusions was that marriage is a universal human institution and has been part of the social structure of all settled societies; but that it is also a very flexible institution, and has existed in many forms. He defined marriage as "a relation of one or more men to one or more women which is recognized by custom or law and involves certain rights and duties both in the case of the parties entering the union and in the case of the children born of it."

Another of the major findings of Westermarck was summarized in his famous dictum that "marriage is rooted in the family, and not the family in marriage." What he meant was that human survival depends upon providing the best possible conditions for the birth and upbringing of children, that experience has shown these conditions to be best provided in family life, and that therefore marriage must be controlled and safeguarded by the community in order to ensure the continuity of the family.

This concept of marriage as subsidiary to the family, and therefore subservient to it, has dominated human history and has never been seriously challenged until our own time. But we are living today through an era of tremendous cultural change, in which all our institutions are being severely shaken; and marriage is no exception. In fact, marriage is changing so much that it is literally being turned inside out. If you think this sounds like dramatic exaggeration, let me assure you that I mean it quite literally; and let me explain what I mean.

In the entire sweep of human history, there have been only two major changes in our way of life—changes so vast that I prefer to call them "social mutations." The first was when man stopped being a wandering hunter and food-gatherer, a puny pygmy fighting against the enormous forces of a hostile nature, and learned to cooperate with nature by growing his food and taming wild animals and enlisting them in his service. This was the change from the nomadic to the agricultural way of life. It led to a long period of relative prosperity, with people living on the land in comparative security. The family was the basic unit of society, and it was generally a large or "extended" family of one kind or another, in which the kinship groups were united in cooperating with one another for the common good. The family was a very rigid institution, resisting all change and dedicated to maintaining the *status quo* from generation to generation.

Then came what we call the Industrial Revolution, which led to the second major social mutation in human history. We are in the midst of this now, and there has never been anything like it before. It began in England with the building of the first factories, and the flocking of the people from the land to the cities. We know all about this change, because we are part of it. The enormous advances of science and technology have now given man power over nature, so that its great forces are more and more coming under his direct control. This is changing radically the entire pattern of human living. Because it is happening gradually, we are not aware how profound the change is. It is almost as if the human race were being transferred from one planet to another, and having to adapt to almost entirely new conditions.

What is important for us that our new environment is breaking up all our traditional institutions and forcing us to create new ones of quite a different kind. Professor J. K. Whitehead, the English social philosopher, expressed this very well when he said that before the Industrial Revolution, an institution could survive only if it had rigidity and stability; whereas since the Industrial Revolution, the qualities needed for survival are the opposite, namely flexibility and adaptability. These were in fact qualities that the traditional type of marriage could not tolerate. Consequently, marriage and the family as we have known them in the past, throughout most of human history, are breaking down, and must break down. There is absolutely no possibility that they will survive in the new urban-industrial culture that is taking shape everywhere in the world today.

Many people take alarm at this, because they assume that marriage and the family are themselves breaking down. It is very important to stress the fact that this is not so. The disintegration of the old rigid patterns is not something unhealthy, but something healthy. It is the inevitable prelude to the establishment of new patterns that will be much more appropriate to our new way of life. The family is changing, not breaking down. And, as Clark Vincent pointed out in a speech at a National Council of Family Relations Conference, the family is showing its fundamental health by proving, after long centuries of rigidity, that it is actually capable of considerable adaptation to our new environment.

In the process of this adaptation, marriage is being turned inside out. In the old days, the central goal in marriage was that it must fulfill certain social and familial obligations—the continuation of the family line, the family inheritance, the family tradition—while somewhere out on the periphery there was a pious hope that the couple might get along harmoniously together. But so long as the familial obligations were met, nobody cared very much whether the couple were happy or unhappy in their interpersonal life. That was quite secondary.

Today, however, the central goal in marriage is personal fulfillment in a creative relationship, and the traditional familial and social obligations have moved out to the periphery. The mood of today is that if your marriage doesn't turn out to be happy, you quit, because finding happiness in marriage is the fulfillment of its fundamental objective.

Some people consider this change of goal as a manifestation of selfishness and irresponsibility. But the change of goal actually corresponds with the change of environment. In the old rural-agricultural society, the major business of life was economic survival and physical safety, and marriage had to conform to these requirements. But in an affluent society, economic survival is taken for granted; and the police, though they have troubles, do their best to assure us of physical safety. In our urban-industrial society, many of the traditional functions of marriage and the family—education, economic production, recreation, and many others—have been taken over by the state. And now our deepest need is for *emotional* security, for the survival of our sense of personal worth and individual significance in a vast world of people in which the individual often doesn't seem to count for anything. By shifting its focus, marriage has now become the primary means by which this individual need for comfort and support and love and understanding can be met. Gibson Winter calls this the "quest for intimacy." In our study of the Soviet family, my wife and I found that in the days of Stalinist terror, marriage was sometimes the only means by which people could keep sane. Surrounded by insecurity, they found their security in the openness and the cathartic communication they could enjoy as husband and wife, when they were alone together. There is a sense in which this kind of need, though not in the same extreme sense, is pervading the whole of modern life. And if marriage can meet that need, it will simply be manifesting one of its dormant potentialities which was almost totally neglected in the past, but is highly relevant today.

MARRIAGE IN THE PRESENT

This brings us to the point at which we can look at contemporary issues in marriage. There are so many of these that it is hard to choose; but for this discussion I have selected four:

1. Marriage as Companionship

You will remember that Ernest Burgess, who might be called the father of family sociology, summarized the fundamental change that is taking place today in the title *Marriage: From Institution to Companionship.* So our focus today is upon marriage as a relationship. This is what we are concerned about; this is what more and more of what we are writing about marriage focuses upon; this is what marriage counselors are working with and trying to facilitate. So I would say that the primary issue in modern marriage is how we can make it a really creative relationship for husband and wife.

When we think of marriage in these terms, however, we begin to realize that husband and wife enter not into one relationship, but into two relationships, which coexist and interact, and yet can be clearly distinguished from each other. There is the relationship between two persons living together as partners, sharing life on an equal basis; and there is the relationship between a man and a woman, which is not equal at all, but reciprocal and complementary. In simple language, married couples have to contrive to be both good partners and good lovers. Success in one of these areas will not compensate for failure in the other. There must be a reasonable measure of satisfaction in both.

The concept of husband and wife as equal partners, sharing life in openness and intimacy, represents a radical break with tradition. Of course there have always been marriages in which good partnership was achieved; but there has never before been a time in which this was a primary criterion of success applied to *all* marriages. Indeed, traditional societies devised two means by which the concept of equal partnership, and of the two-vote marriage, was carefully avoided. First, a hierarchical distinction was made between husband and wife, the husband being acknowledged as having almost all the power, and the wife being compliant and obedient. Second, the spheres of influence of husband and wife were rigidly separated, so that there was the minimum chance that they might compete or clash with one another. These devices were highly developed, and there is no doubt that they were based on the discovery that attempts to make marriage a relationship of close sharing led to explosive consequences that must be avoided in the interest of family stability.

But in our modern world we have deliberately given a central place to this concept of the shared life; and the explosive possibilities are very much with us! It would not be too much to say that interpersonal conflict, far from being an extraneous element in modern marriage, actually represents the raw material out of which an effective marital partnership has to be shaped. Unless we clearly recognize this, and deliberately teach young people to expect conflict in marriage, and to cope with it adequately, we simply doom large numbers of them to inevitable disillusionment and even disaster. Conflict in marriage is simply the emotional manifestation of disagreement, which is an inevitable consequence of difference. And difference cannot be avoided between two people who live in continuing intimacy, because it is unreasonable to imagine that two different people would always want to do the same thing in the same way at the same time. By insisting on homogamy as a primary condition for successful marriage, we have contrived to minimize interpersonal conflict. But I am not at all sure that the marriages of people with a minimum of difference are necessarily the best marriages. There are enormous potentials for creativity and growth in two people who begin with a good deal of difference, but have the maturity to resolve it and grow together.

When we consider the other relationship in marriage, that of husband and wife as lovers, we encounter at once the fascinating but baffling question of masculine-feminine interaction. For long centuries this has been rather naively interpreted in terms of dominance and submission, or even as superiority and inferiority. One of the somewhat bizarre side effects of the emergence today of the idea of marriage as companionship is the open revolt of youth against the extreme stereotypes of masculinity as hairy-chested male aggressiveness on the one hand, and docile female compliance on the other. Modern youth has dramatized this protest in the long-haired boy who is not ashamed to identify himself with femininity by looking like a girl, and the modern girl who does not feel any loss of womanhood when she engages in activities that hitherto were reserved exclusively for men.

2. Marriage and Sex

There is an argument going on at the present time as to whether there is a sexual revolution or not. I am in no doubt whatever about this question. There is, emphatically, a sexual revolution. But the confusion is caused by the fact that people are arguing not about the revolution, but about the consequences of it. In my judgment, a revolution is by definition a complete change, a reversal of what previously was believed. But a revolution also, in my view, always takes place in the realm of ideas, and then is gradually translated into changed patterns of living. In these terms, we can say emphatically that the sexual revolution is not only here; it is now almost complete. It began about three-quarters of a century ago, and has resulted in a total change in the way we think about sex. Beginning with an attitude that considered sex essentially negatively, as unwholesome and regrettable though perhaps an unavoidable necessity, we have moved to an attitude which sees sex positively, as something essentially good and creative, though of course capable like everything else of misuse. If a change of this magnitude is not a revolution, I can think of no other radical change in human thinking that is worthy of the name.

However, this revolution has led to many consequences, and one of them concerns the relationship between sex and marriage. In the older cultures, where sex was officially recognized only as a means of procreation for married people, and unofficially as a clandestine pastime in which men exploited women with little regard for the interpersonal implications, a state of uneasy equilibrium could with a little difficulty be maintained. But our new attitude to sex has broken this up completely, and forced us to reevaluate the total situation.

What has precipitated the crisis is the change in our concepts of mate selection. So long as the parents or village elders chose your husband or wife for you, there was no need for boys and girls to be exposed to the risks of meeting socially and forming friendships. Indeed, Confucius insisted that after the age of seven a boy and girl must never even sit together in public! But once the principle was established that young people could choose each other, they naturally wanted to do so on a basis of personal compatibility, and personal compatibility has to be tested out in a period of friendship. Once this has been conceded in any culture, the flood gates are open to the free association of unmarried men and women. This means that it is henceforth impossible to confine sex to marriage by the appeal to force or fear, and sexual morality becomes a question of conscious and deliberate choice based on an acceptance of certain values, which not all men and women will necessarily accept.

Once a principle is established that a man and woman who are unmarried may respond to each other emotionally, and carry that response as far as they personally choose, it becomes impossible to exclude married people from the same privileges. Once premarital chastity has become a matter of conscious choice, marital fidelity follows suit. The consequences of infidelity for the married are of course generally more serious, and this introduces restraints, but we should not be realistic if we did not recognize that one of the major issues in marriage today, in an era where increasingly effective contraceptives are available, is the question of how far married couples generally will accept the principle of sexual exclusiveness, and what is likely to happen to marriage if they don't.

3. Marriage and Parenthood

We all recognize that there has been a radical change in our pattern of marriage, but we are not so ready to see that there has been a corresponding change in parenthood. The societies of the past were rigidly structured, and had little use for individualists who refused to accept the roles allocated to them. The son was expected to follow in his father's footsteps, or go in whatever direction the family decided was appropriate for him. The task of families was therefore to bring up children to be obedient conformists, who would do what they were told without expressing individual preferences or asking awkward questions. Parenthood was therefore essentially a task of molding human beings to accept their lot without resistance or complaint.

Today, in our open society, obedient conformists become social misfits. In a world where the individual must stand on his own feet and shape his own destiny, qualities that are desirable are the opposite of those needed in the past—namely, autonomy and self-reliance, and the capacity to handle a degree of personal freedom seldom experienced in the past. To prepare children for living in this new world, parents have to accept completely new roles. Their task now is not to mold the child into conformity, but to cooperate with him flexibly in learning to use freedom with wisdom and restraint. This is a much more difficult task, and puts a heavy strain on modern families.

One aspect of this strain is the need for a child to see in his parents the effective exercise of freedom in good relationships and cooperation. We used to accept, without critical examination, the principle that one of the child's primary needs was to be brought up in a home where his father and mother were both present. But the question is now being asked, whether the mere presence of father and mother is enough, if their relationship is vitiated by destructive conflict. We would all agree with the principle that a warm, loving relationship between husband and wife creates the perfect emotional climate for the healthy development of the child. But we have been less willing to examine what the atmosphere created by a bad marriage does negatively to the emotional life of the child. In the close and confining atmosphere of the nuclear family, a continued state of unresolved marital conflict might well be a breeding ground of psychopathology. In the old extended family, this was unlikely to happen, because there were always other family members in whom the child could find emotional compensation when his immediate parents caused him anxiety and distress.

4. Marriage and Stability

We have seen that in the past the continuity of the family was absolutely essential, and everything else had to be sacrificed to it. Today, our values are different. In the old days, the married couple were shut up in a box together and had to get on with the familial tasks that were committed to them, whether they were happy together or not. I once asked a group of Indians what an Indian wife could do if she found herself in an intolerable marital situation. Quite seriously, I was told that the correct solution for this problem was suicide! This was true throughout the Orient, and there are plenty of illustrations that it was resorted to on occasions. The stability of marriage was the primary value, and nothing else mattered in comparison.

Today the emphasis has shifted, and I believe the shift is permanent. We must face realistically the fact that in the future it will be impossible to hold marriages together by coercion from outside. They will only be held together by cohesion from within. What this means is that the principle that an unhappy marriage must be tolerated for the sake of the stability of the institution, which is an article of Catholic dogma, will be less and less readily accepted in the future. People who consider their marriages unhappy will get out of them, either to remarry or to abandon marriages as a way of life. I think we are moving to the point at which the primary value in marriage will no longer be stability, but creativity. We may not like this, or approve of it. But we can hardly suggest that the difference between stability and creativity in marriage can be equated to the difference between good and evil.

What seems to be clear from our discussion is that the case for a good marriage is overwhelming. A good marriage results in the kind of companionship that marriage is ideally fitted to provide in our modern world. A good marriage finds its own satisfactory solution of the sexual needs of the partners, and provides the atmosphere for happy and successful parenthood. But a bad marriage, or a poor marriage, or a mediocre marriage, poses problems for the persons involved, and for the society to which they belong, which can no longer be avoided or neglected.

What is clear is that marriage in contemporary culture raises all kinds of problems and questions which simply did not bother our ancestors. Those of us who are workers and specialists in this field have been facing these problems and questions. As I perceive the situation, there are three basic tasks that confront us. The first is study and research, so that we may identify the true nature and dimensions of the problems. The second is a massive program of education to enlighten people concerning what is happening to marriage today, and to give them some intelligent understanding of the task they assume when they get married. The third is to develop counseling services to tide married people through the crises that are inevitable in the close and intimate kind of relationship they are asking marriage to provide. The programs we have developed have been on the right lines, and we have made considerable headway with them. What we now need is the widespread support of the community, and the money to provide the services that are needed. This will come only when the community and the nation recognize that good marriages are their most precious asset, and that bad marriages lead to costly and destructive consequences.

MARRIAGE IN THE FUTURE

I have tried to indicate that the changes that are taking place in marriage are a healthy adaptation to the new functions marriage must serve in the altogether different environment in which our children and our children's children will have to live. In the vast, impersonal world of the future, technology will achieve miracles in ministering to human need. But what technology cannot do is to provide for that deep need in all of us that can only be met through intimate relationships in which we know ourselves to be loved and cherished, supported and sustained. There are many ways in which this need can be met, but none that can compare with the experience of a really happy marriage. None of us can predict what life will be like on this planet for distant future generations. But in the foreseeable future, I believe men and women will seek to enter marriage not less eagerly, but more eagerly, than in the past. And as our knowledge increases, and as we learn to make it available and assimilable through sound education and effective counseling, I think the chances are that people will become more mature and more creative, so that they are able to enter into the relationships in depth that make marriages truly happy and successful. In short, as I look into the future of marriage I feel rather optimistic. I do not share the gloomy forebodings that I often hear expressed by those around me. As I look ahead, my feeling is that the potentialities of marriage have not been exhausted. On the contrary, they have not yet begun to be fully developed. I think there is a good chance that what the children of today will see, in their lifetime, is not marriage sinking ignominiously into obsolescence, but blossoming and flourishing as it has never done before in human history.

3

What Is a Family Anyway?

William Sayres

ASTRACT: The forms of the family are so varied that the term defies definition. During his or her lifetime, an individual is likely to belong to several different types of families. History's most common type is the extended family. Nuclear families, however, characterize the Western world, while extended families still dominate the rest of the world. The author distinguishes between stepfamilies, foster families, adoptive families, communes, and group families.

The following two statements about the family were written at different times by the same author, Hope Jensen Leichter.

"The family is an arena in which virtually the entire range of human experience can take place. Warfare, love, violence, tenderness, honesty, deceit, private property, communal sharing, power manipulation, informed consent, formal status hierarchies, egalitarian decision making—all can be found within the setting of the family."

"The more one looks at the family, the more it isn't there."

Although they may seem to be contradictory—saying that the family is both all and nothing at all—they, in fact, underscore the two most salient features of the family. First, the family is the oldest and most

23

basic social unit. Second, it has become so variable in the forms it has assumed over the years that it defies definition in a way acceptable to all the diverse groups that consider themselves families: From their perspective, there is no such thing as "the" family.

This is why the much-heralded 1980 White House Conference on the Family became the White House Conference on *Families* and ended not with a bang but a whimper: The distinguished participants in "the endless seminars and colloquia preparing this Conference" found it "impossible to arrive at even rudimentary consensus on what 'the American family' was supposed to be. . . . The meetings and discussions . . . became a veritable battlefield of competing interests and philosophies."

Not only do family forms vary in the United States as well as in other countries, but in the contemporary world it is not at all unusual for a parent to belong to several different types of families in the course of a lifetime. Consider, for example, the hypothetical case of Marsha, who marries John. In time, they have children and become a *nuclear family*. When John's father dies, his mother and elderly sister come to live with them, and they become an *extended family*. Marsha, however, finds that living with in-laws does nothing to improve a souring marriage, and the ensuing divorce leaves her with the children and a *single-parent family*. Taking a job in a law office, she falls in love with a colleague who is a widower with children of his own, and when she marries him she becomes a stepparent in a *stepfamily*. She and her husband want to have a child together, but when they find they cannot, they take in an orphaned child and successively form a *foster family* and an *adoptive family*. All this is eventually too much for Marsha, and she runs off to join a *commune*, where she gets along so well with two other parent-child combinations that the three decide to move in together and become a *group family*.

This has elements of a soap opera, of course, but in the unsettled world of today few if any of us can say with certainty that the parental role we now have will be the only one we will ever have. Different family forms are of more than academic interest: Each change may alter the parental role in significant ways, and we may find ourselves playing unexpected parts with unfamiliar lines.

Let us review the major forms of the family, along with the prospective advantages and disadvantages of each.

THE EXTENDED FAMILY

Throughout history, in most of the world, the extended family, consisting of parents, children, and other adult relatives such as grandparents, aunts, and uncles, has been the most common household arrangement. It evidently goes back to a time when families were relatively self-sufficient economic units, with everyone pitching in as collective pro-ducers and providers of their own food, clothing, shelter, and other necessities. Large families meant more helping hands, and it was obvi-ously advantageous to have other family members available to look after the younger children while the parents and older children were busy hunting, gathering, cultivating, grinding, baking, weaving, and other-wise contributing to the family maintenance. The traditional importance of the family as an economic unit is reflected in the very origin of the term *economics*, a derivative of the Latin word *oeconomia*, which means "household management."

Today, extended families are still predominant in the non-Western world, while in Europe and North America they constitute only a small minority of permanent households. However, in Western societies they are often formed on a temporary basis: For example, a young couple with children may live with the husband's or wife's parents until they can afford a place of their own, or other relatives may come to stay for varying periods because of changing circumstances in their lives.

Perhaps extended families' chief advantage, from a parental perspec-tive, is the help they can provide in the sharing of household responsi-bilities and child care. The main disadvantage is a potential dilution or weakening of parental authority and influence over the child.

THE NUCLEAR FAMILY

Social scientists are in general agreement that the nuclear family, composed simply of parents and their children, is not a recently emergent form but in fact had predominated in Western societies for the past three centuries. While extended families tend to stress the impor-tance of *consanguineal*, or blood-kin, ties linking successive generations through maternal or paternal lines of descent, nuclear families place more emphasis on the *conjugal* tie between husband and wife.

Some social scientists have noted a "fit" between the nuclear family form, with its emphasis on conjugal bonds, and certain Western social and cultural values. William Goode, for example, argues that the nu-clear family "is best able to maximize the values of individualism and equalitarianism. The extended family system tends to subordinate the individual to the family group—family continuity is more important than individual welfare and desires."

From a parental vantage point, the degree of individual freedom and independence afforded by the nuclear family may be a plus—but at a price. In the United States, for example, the number of married mothers entering the labor force has dramatically increased over the years, and well over half of them currently have jobs outside the home. On the one hand, the trend reflects gains in freedom, choice, and opportunity. Yet on the other hand, it reflects growing economic necessity and heightened strains on marital and parent-child relationships, with attending persisting problems of finding sufficient "quality time" and adequate day-care facilities for the children.

At a more fundamental level, the very openness and flexibility that have contributed to the appeal of the nuclear family have also contributed to its instability. Divorce is known all over the world and is not at all a recent phenomenon. The United States has the highest divorce rate in the Western world, almost twice as high as that in the second-ranked country, Sweden. About half of the U.S. marriages of today are expected to end in divorce, with estimates for some sectors of the population running considerably higher.

Thus parents in the most typical form of the American family—the nuclear family—may enjoy the relative autonomy, mobility, and range of options it provides. When it works, it can work very well indeed. Yet the dynamism intrinsic to such an arrangement can loosen the marriage bond to the point where it is no longer the tie that binds. When this happens, parents—especially mothers—may find themselves, willingly or reluctantly, members of the family form that has shown the most explosive growth in recent years.

THE SINGLE-PARENT FAMILY

In Third World societies, especially those with high death rates due to malnutrition, disease, and regional conflicts, the loss of a parent is hardly uncommon. Nevertheless, in the extended families characteristic of these regions, the slack is typically taken up by other family members, and replacement marriages may be quickly arranged to ensure family continuity. In Western societies, however, and particularly in the United States, the number of single-parent families has been rising at a precipitous rate. Almost fifteen million children in the United States were living in single-parent homes in 1986, representing an increase of 250 percent since 1960 and about a quarter of the nation's children. The U.S. Census Bureau estimates that more than half of all American children born today will live in single-parent households before they reach adulthood, and more specific projections range as high as 60 percent.

Although many single-parent families are the outcome of broken marriages, many others are the result of births to unmarried women, most notably teenagers. An estimated 270,000 children are born each year to unmarried teenage mothers in the United States, and almost one-fourth of all American children born in the coming year will be born out of wedlock, with the number more than twice that among urban minority groups. It is perhaps even more startling to note that more than 30 percent of the children born to unmarried teenagers are second or third children.

On the whole, the single-parent family is understandably not the family of choice. The members of single-parent families, children as well as parents, tend to suffer socially, economically, and psychologically. Yet for many single parents, the arrangement has its advantages; It means an absence of marital bickering and strife; it can bring parent and child close together; and it can facilitate the parent's personal growth. Many single mothers from broken marriages, for example, report increased feelings of mastery over their lives and their relationships with their children as well as more positive self-images and stronger self-concepts, states Mark Hutter in his book *The Changing Family: Comparative Perspectives*. This helps to explain the most recent phenomenon of successful career women who opt for single motherhood because, frankly, they would rather have a child than a spouse!

VARIANT FAMILY FORMS

In addition to extended, nuclear, and single-parent families, there are several other family forms that may intersect or combine with them. For example, an extended family may include step kin, a nuclear family may be partly or wholly adoptive, and a single-parent family may become part of a commune or group family.

Stepfamilies

Stepfamilies (also referred to as *blended families*, *binuclear families*, and *reconstituted families*) are formed wherever and whenever parents remarry. They are accordingly found throughout the world, but are most common in the United States, where divorce and marriage occur with the greatest frequency. Each year in the United States approximately 1.5 million people remarry; most of those remarrying have children. In fact, 90 percent of divorced women with children in this country eventually remarry. At present, there are more than thirty-five million stepparents in the United States, and it is estimated that by the year 2000 there will be more children in stepfamilies than in other two-parent families.

The problems faced by stepparents have largely to do with the difficulties of building positive relationships with their stepchildren—winning their acceptance, trust, and affection—without letting the frustrations and setbacks they may encounter become disruptive to other family relationships. Nevertheless, studies show that with patience, perseverance, and the shedding of unrealistic expectations, the experience can be mutually rewarding to stepparents and stepchildren alike.

Foster and Adoptive Families

Foster families and adoptive families may seem to be somewhat similar in the sense that in both child care is provided in a family setting by nonbiological parents, and there are cases where the foster parents, in time, become the adoptive parents; nevertheless, the two family forms serve different purposes. By law and custom the foster family is a temporary arrangement, typically involving the placement of children "at risk" in the protective custody of paid caretakers until they can be returned to their parents or other responsible adults. The adoptive family, on the other hand, has the same legal and social permanency as a biological family.

By all accounts, foster parenthood offers far fewer rewards (other than monetary) than adoptive parenthood. Foster parents are not encouraged to develop such close ties to their foster children that the parting will prove traumatic on either side; they are often ill prepared to deal with any special problems the children may have, and they have few legal rights. Foster parenthood is found in other parts of the world but is particularly common in the United States, with its high incidence of broken homes. It was recently estimated that more than half a million American children are living in foster homes, and that almost half of them have lived in two or more foster homes.

Perhaps the most basic reward of adoptive parenthood is that it makes parenthood possible for couples who cannot have biological children. There is a special quality to adoptive parenthood because it necessarily entails a deliberate choice and an often prolonged effort to create a home for the homeless. There are adoptive parents throughout the world, and in those areas where natural and man-made disasters have orphaned many children, they are especially widespread. In North America, it has been estimated, adopted persons represent between 2 and 4 percent of the population and no less than one person in five is "directly and intimately linked to the experience of adoption," as a parent or child or other member of an adoptive family.

While the pluses of adoptive parenthood largely center on the distinctive closeness that can develop between a *choosing* parent and a *chosen* child, the minuses tend to be related to maintenance of the relationship if and when the growing child experiences identity problems related to the adoptive status; comes to behave in ways that cause the adoptive parents to wonder about the potential negative effects of heredity; or plays the absent biological parents against the adoptive parents ("If you were my *real* parents, you wouldn't treat me this way"). A complicating factor is a concomitant of the increasing frequency of *"mixed" families* formed through the adoption of children from other cultures, religions, and ethnic groups. When the novelty and appeal of "differentness" wear off, the family may become a forum for clashes between traditional allegiances.

Communes and Group Families

Finally, there are family forms involving more than two parental figures. In communes, the primary commitment is to the group as a whole, whereas in group families the dominant bond is among the multiple partners, in what has been termed a "multilateral marriage." A variant of the group-family arrangement is the family based on a *polygamous* marriage, in which a man has more than one wife (*polygyny*) or a woman has more than one husband (*polyandry*). Such a "marriage" may be extralegal (as among some Mormon families that still practice it in the United States) or quite legal, as in the Islamic world, where a man is permitted to have up to four wives.

Communes are found in various parts of the world, such as the *kibbutzim* in Israel and the *ashrams* established by Hindus in India and elsewhere: In the United States, ashrams and their Hindu leaders have attracted considerable attention in recent years. Most communes are relatively short-lived and unstable. Described by Peter and Brigitte Berger in their book *The War Over the Family*, a typical communal philosophy is "to produce a new kind of human being, freed from the egoism deemed to be intrinsic to the bourgeois way of life and ready to live in collective structures of mutual affection and shared responsibility." While many parents undoubtedly find what they are looking for, in other instances studies have shown widespread disillusionment among the parents and negative effects on the communally raised children, effects evidently related to the loss of control by parents over their children and the difficulties of subordinating the individual will to the collective imperative.

While there are group families in other cultures, most studies have focused on their emergence as a kind of counterculture among comparatively well-off sectors of Western societies like the United States. In group families, contrary to much of the media hype, the predominant theme is not swinging sex but the search for an alternative life-style characterized by the development of multiple personal relationships and growth through interaction within an expanded (*i. e.*, less limiting) family structure. Nevertheless, the "swinging" label persists, and a fundamental problem with parenting in such groups stems from the social stigma attached to "deviant" life-styles. There are obvious difficulties in raising children in a social environment so extensively criticized or condemned, especially when the parents realize that their children may grow up alienated either from them or from the mainstream culture to which they eventually will be called on to adapt.

CONCLUDING NOTE

Recognition of the heterogeneity of the many living arrangements regarded as families by their members leads us to this conclusion: Although there may be no such thing as "the" family, in the sense of a single form with designated members, the family as a concept is a very powerful one, indeed. It is a way of thinking about that social unit, whatever form it may take, that speaks most persuasively to our need to bond with others.

The two family forms that have prevailed the longest from East to West are nuclear and extended families. With their broad support systems and commitment to continuity, they are clearly the families of choice to most peoples of the world. Looking ahead, we can also see that within these family forms there is a growing recognition that effective parenting involves both mothering and fathering. The themes of "Leave it to mother" or "Father knows best" are giving way to an increasing appreciation of the need for more active complementarity, cooperation, and sharing in the responsibilities as well as the rewards of parenting. The children involved in healthy nuclear or extended families are very fortunate indeed.

4

▼▼▼▼▼

The War Over the Family

▼▼▼▼▼

Brigitte Berger
Peter L. Berger

ABSTRACT: Many Americans are concerned that today's family is in trouble. Such a view is not unique to our period, however. After the bourgeois (middle-class) family became dominant in the Western world, practices of lower-class families that differed from the dominant form came to be seen as a problem. Always, what is perceived as a problem represents a particular vantage point.

Perceptions of the American family have ranged from the viewpoint of sociologists in the 1930s and 1950s that the family was suffering from the disintegrative forces of modernization to seeing it as a success story (the "ideal" family of the 1950s). A significant change in perception occurred during the 1960s when critics came to see the American family itself, along with its ideals, as a problem. In recent years, conservatives and liberals have held opposing views of what is problematic about the family.

"The family has become a problem."

This observation is widely made today, in America as well as in other societies, to the point where it has become a commonplace. Needless to say, people who make the observation differ among themselves about the nature of the problem and about possible solutions; indeed, what is

a solution to some appears as yet another facet of the problem to others.
. . . It may be useful to . . . ask what it means in the first place that
something is seen to be a "problem"—or, in more precise language,
that some phenomenon in human experience that used to be taken for
granted becomes "problematized." And then it will be important to ask
how the family, of all things, came to be seen in this light—an institution, after all, that has been around since the dawn of history, that was
taken for granted for millennia, and that is surely the leading candidate
for the status of [the] basic institution in human society.

To say that any object of experience is a "problem" implies at least
two perceptions: First, there is the cognitive implication that this object
"sticks out" from the rest of experience, that it invites attention, and
that it does so because there is something not fully understood and perhaps not quite right about it. Thus any part of our own bodies or of our
natural environment can become a problem if it interferes with what we
have come to regard as the normal course of events. We pay no attention to our breathing, say, until we have breathing difficulties; we do
not perceive a particular tree as a problem until we develop anxieties
that it may fall in on our roof. Human institutions are not the same as
bodily or natural phenomena, but their problematization in the minds
of individuals follows roughly the same logic—that is, an institution becomes the object of attention and concern because some difficulty arises
in its role in the flow of social life. At least in modern times, however,
there is a second implication to a declaration that this or that has become
a "problem"—namely, that we ought *to do* something about it. In this
sense (a specifically modern sense) death is not a problem, but illness
is—because we believe, at least in principle, that science has given us
the means to seek a cure for any particular illness even if death remains
our ultimate fate. This practical, activist implication is especially important when an institution is declared to be a problem, since one peculiarly
modern assumption is that society (unlike the body and the natural environment) is a human construction and therefore may be *re*constructed
if enough people think it should be.

The family has a history, as all human institutions do, and there have
been instances in earlier times when the family has come to be seen as a
problem, sometimes abruptly and dramatically. Still, the basic relations
between the sexes and the generations have often gone undisturbed for
centuries, indeed have remained undisturbed even through periods of
great turbulence in other areas of social life. And since these basic relationships constitute, for most people, the most intimate core of their
lives, there is a specially shocking quality to their sudden redefinition
as public issues. . . .

The French historian Philippe Ariès has argued persuasively that
childhood as we now understand it was invented by the rising bourgeoi-

sie of Europe. As the bourgeoisie triumphed as a class, so did its ideals of child-raising. And as these ideals became institutionalized—in the law, the educational system, and in the thinking of individuals—a particular vision of childhood came to be taken for granted. What "stuck out" as a "problem," then, was any treatment of children that failed to conform to this vision. Such treatment, of course, was mostly meted out to the children of *non*-bourgeois parents, and a vast amount of energy was expended by well-meaning bourgeois men and women in attacking this problem, first through private charities and then through public policies. It is not much of an exaggeration to say that the origins of both social work and the welfare state lie in the missionary efforts by which the bourgeoisie sought to propagate its family ethos among the lower classes. . . .

We may assume that there have always been individuals for whom the family became a problem, be it because they were the sort who always see problems where other people see none (the Socrates sort, as it were) or because they lived through difficult times (war, foreign conquest, natural catastrophes, or more personalized mishaps, all conducive to putting in question what had previously been taken for granted). But, on the level of ideas, a plausible time to take as the start of the currently operative problematization of the family is the Enlightenment of the eighteenth century. The central goal of the Enlightenment was to free human beings from the shackles of tradition. Not surprisingly, the family was perceived as a problem for the realization of this project—it is, undoubtedly, one of the most traditional of institutions. For most Enlightenment thinkers—such as Locke, in England; Rousseau, in France; and Paine, in America—the project certainly did not include abolition of the family but, rather, its reform in the spirit of the new humanity to be brought about. The new political order that the Enlightenment sought to bring about was to be a great liberating agency, and education (still perceived as mainly taking place within the context of the family) was to provide training for the liberated citizens. . . .

In the nineteenth century, both in Europe and in America, the hopes for a liberating education were increasingly concentrated on the school, an institution outside the family. In one sense, this entailed a loss of function for the family. But it would be quite mistaken to think that, therefore, the bourgeois family ethos lost ground. Quite the opposite was the case. Not only did the school itself become a powerful instrument for the propagation of bourgeois values—an instrument, however, which, after the passage of compulsory education laws, had behind it the full force of governmental coercion. But the bourgeois family itself gave birth to new ideological configurations, to further developments of its distinctive values. The nineteenth century, rather than the eighteenth, saw the full flowering of the new bourgeois sensibility—not acci-

dentally, since the nineteenth century saw the triumph of the bourgeois class in one Western country after another. Here, then, was the ideal bourgeois family come into its own, called by various names—"Victorian" in England, "Biedermeier" in Germany, and so on—but everywhere manifesting similar characteristics: an emphasis on high moral standards, especially in sexual matters; an enormous interest in the welfare of children, especially in their proper education; the inculcation of values and attitudes conducive to economic success as well as civic peace; at least the appearance of religious faith; a devotion to the "finer things" in life, especially the arts; and last but not least, a sense of obligation to redress or alleviate conditions perceived as morally offensive.
. . .

Now [it is] clear from the above considerations . . . [that it] is not enough to say that a problem has arisen; one must also ask *whose* problem it is. One person's taken-for-granted reality is another's problem, and vice versa. Thus it is safe to say that the working-class objects of all this bourgeois benevolence did not understand why their family life was supposed to be a problem—at least in the beginning, before the missionary indoctrination had begun to take hold in some proletarian minds. Then, as now, when one hears the proposition that "the family [or this or that type of family] has become a problem," one ought immediately to ask, "*Says who?*" Very likely, one will find that those who say so come from a specific class location in society. And often one will also find . . . that some of them have very concrete, indeed crude, vested interests in the matter: . . . There are people who make a living from allegedly solving certain problems—and who therefore have a vested interest in propagating the notion that these problems are very serious, very urgent, and (most important) insoluble without their own expert assistance.

. . . But there also developed in the nineteenth century an important viewpoint in which the family is seen as a more or less passive reflection of broader historical forces. In its Marxist form, this viewpoint is very much alive today. Marx himself did not write extensively on the family, but his disciples Friedrich Engels and August Bebel did. In this view, the family always takes on specific forms due to the forces and relations of production. The family here becomes a sort of barometer for the state of the class struggle at any given moment of history. Thus the bourgeois family reflects the objective class situation of the bourgeoisie, the working-class family the situation of the working class. The Marxists, to be sure, found much fault with both the bourgeois and the working-class family—the former an embodiment of all the vices of the exploiting class, the latter a victim of the same exploitation—but, by the nature of their theory, they could not be bothered with reforms in this area. The woes of family life could be cured only by the revolutionary transformation of society as a whole. . . .

In America, the period after World War I was marked by the rise of sociology as a new and (everyone thought) highly promising tool for the solution of social problems. . . . American sociology, in the 1920s, and to some extent still in the 1930s, was dominated by the department at the University of Chicago, and the so-called Chicago School produced a still astounding volume of books, articles, and dissertations about every aspect of American society but especially about the dynamic social reality of American cities. The family was not the principal interest of the Chicago School, but it entered into most of the School's analyses. The Chicago School viewed the family in the context of the urbanizing transformations of social life and in this context spoke about the increasing isolation of the nuclear family—the term referring to the shrunken unit of spouses and children deprived of the supports supposedly characteristic of the older, extended family. The emphasis was on rootlessness. . . . The problem, in other words, was not the bourgeois family but the process by which it was weakened through the loss of the old kinship and communal supports.

In its specific American situation, the Chicago School took up once more what had been one of the basic themes of classical European sociology: that transformation of society which we usually refer to today as modernization. In France, Émile Durkheim described this as the passage from "mechanical" to "organic" solidarity; in Germany, Ferdinand Tönnies analyzed the same historical process as the change from *Gemeinschaft* to *Gesellschaft*. Both pairs of concepts contrast an earlier form of society, in which human beings were tied to each other by an absolute and unquestioned sense of belonging, with modern society, in which relationships are limited, open to revision, and increasingly specified through legal contracts. If one compares this view with the pre-sociological notions of nineteenth century family reformers, it becomes apparent that the definition of the problem has expanded. It is not just the working-class family that is seen as the problem now (though this type of family may have peculiar problems of its own), but the middle-class family, too, is problematized because of its subjection to the disintegrative forces of modernization. . . .

After World War II, the importance of the Chicago School in American sociology greatly diminished, though many of its concepts continued to be of influence and merged with newer approaches. In the 1950s, the dominant school was that of so-called structural-functionalism, of which Talcott Parsons was the most prominent theorist. . . . Like the Chicago sociologists, the structural-functionalists were not primarily interested in the family as such, but they paid a good deal of attention to the family as one important case in point of the larger societal processes they wanted to understand. . . . Compared to the Chicago School, Parsons' view of the family was certainly more upbeat. The emphasis was not on loss but on new functions understood in a basically positive way. . . .

The argument runs something like this: The family has been greatly changed as a result of various modernizing processes. The most important effect of modernization is institutional *differentiation*—a key concept of Parsons', which means that functions earlier performed by one institution are now distributed among several institutions. Thus the family has indeed *lost* functions, notably economic and educational ones. This very loss, however, has *freed* the family for taking on new functions, some of which never existed before. These new functions centered particularly on the individuals in the family, their rights and their potential for self-realization. Thus marriage, while no longer essential for economic production (the modern economy functions independently of kinship structures) and for the socialization of children (largely taken over by the educational institutions), now becomes the locale for highly complex and emotionally demanding interaction between the spouses. . . .

. . . The rearing of children frequently appears as a kind of afterthought in this sociological literature. Parsons himself believed that the specialization of child-rearing functions was beneficial to children, because it increased efficiency. Indeed, child-rearing became more and more of a professional task outside the family—part of the institutional differentiation of modernity—and this process, supposedly in a benign way, acted back upon the family itself. One phrase of Parsons', the "professionalization of parenthood," came to be widely used. It aptly described, and at the same time legitimated, what was going on in society anyway. . . .

. . . The 1950s in America was marked by what came to be called a family renascence. Undoubtedly there were many reasons for this: the desires of the war veterans returning home, the new affluence of the postwar period, the heightened mobility (geographical as well as social) of large portions of the population, the rise of the new suburbs, perhaps even a new accessibility of birth-control techniques. Whatever the reasons, the 1950s fostered a positive view of the American family—or, at any rate, of its ideal or normative form. This view, of course, was, once again, a middle-class view, but it percolated down to other strata as well. . . . The family became increasingly child-centered—and that was supposed to be good. Women were to find their mission at home, as mothers and as the intelligent, emotionally sensitive companions to their husbands—and if they did not accept this mission, the psychologists were ready to treat this reluctance as a neurotic ailment. . . .

Already in the 1950s, however, there were some who questioned the success story. The new functions of the family, liberating and emotionally rich as they may have been, were also filled with a lot of anxiety.

Especially the women, celebrated as mothers, wives, and "home-makers," were thrown back upon themselves into a kind of social vacuum. This was especially the case in the new, middle-class suburbs, where women were separated geographically as well as socially from the non-"homemaking" activities of their husbands and frequently experienced a sort of cage effect. Suburbia, and by extension middle-class existence as a whole, [was] soon interpreted as [a] problem. . . .

The critical voices, still relatively few and far between in the 1950s, turned into a crescendo of denunciation in the 1960s. This [new radicalism, a] . . . historically unprecedented explosion of cultural self-criticism, even self-laceration, . . . [turned] the definition of the problem . . . upside down: No longer were deviations from the norm seen as the problem, but the norm itself—that is, the normative American family—was perceived and denounced as the real problem. In other words, the problem was not maladjusted individuals or social groups but, rather, the "sick society," of which the "sick family" was an integral part.

If one were to identify one book that crystallized this new sensibility, it would be Betty Friedan's *The Feminine Mystique*, first published in 1963. . . . Friedan captured a spreading mood with great acumen and, having given it literary form, helped to diffuse and legitimate it. There was now a widespread rebellion against the family ideals of the preceding decade, against their "privatism" (Friedan coined the apt phrase of the "cult of domesticity") and their "repressiveness." Most of the social and cultural movements of the 1960s fed into this anti-family mood: the new feminist movement itself, of course, but also other movements of sexual liberation (including the gay and lesbian movements), the various cults of sensitivity and personal self-realization (subsumable under the heading of the "California syndrome"), the New Left (which was highly critical of American society as a whole and the normative American family along with the rest), and the rising black cultural self-consciousness (which rejected prevailing family norms as white impositions). . . .

. . . The 1960s was the decade in which the American welfare state underwent its greatest extension, dwarfing the 1930s in its growth rate. Perhaps inevitably, this included a redefinition of miscellaneous private woes as public ones—and that means as problems to be dealt with politically. Many of the ideas proposed as radical innovations in the 1960s, at least in the area of the family, were really not all that new. What was new was, first, their embodiment in intense social movements, and second, their politicization. Thus the New Politics, finding a (so far) rather stable home in the left wing of the Democratic Party, included many of the radical ideas of the 1960s in its agenda. In the process, of course, the ideas had to be toned down and modified, but they retained enough of their original fervor to give continuing satisfaction to large numbers of erstwhile "movement people"—and this has remained so until today. Finally, insofar as some of the same ideas were adopted by the "helping professions," they, too, were now diffused into the lower classes of society. . . .

If one wishes to look upon the radical movements of the 1960s as a cultural revolution, then one may say that in the 1970s, efforts were made to institutionalize that revolution. There were well-organized demands for sweeping changes in the family's social context through legislation and public policy. These demands were no longer made by radicals alone, but were supported or even initiated by other elements in society: activist sectors of the religious community, politicians and, most important, the professional combines regarding the family as their field of expertise. Now the "helping professions" not only claimed jurisdiction over the family, but they wanted to be put on the public payroll in the exercise of this jurisdiction. A new and large constituency for "family policy" began to take shape. By and large, the political results of this have been disappointing to this constituency, but successful in at least one respect: thoroughly alarming and mobilizing an opposition. . . .

What also happened in the late 1970s . . . was the appearance of a strong, increasingly well-organized countermovement, the so-called "pro-family" camp. Like its radical counterpart, it, too, was an agglomeration of people of differing interests: anti-feminists, people concerned with the alleged evils of homosexuality and of pornography, people concerned with the official secularism (or what they perceived as such) in American public life (the Supreme Court decision banning prayer in the public schools continues to be a powerful issue here), parents just plain disgusted with the intellectual and social failures of public education, and, a core ingredient of this new coalition, the "pro-life" (read: anti-abortion) movement. As with the radicals, the heterogeneous interests in this camp sometimes ran in various directions and could not always be coordinated for political purposes. Nevertheless, this camp has gained remarkable coalescence around several issues affecting the family and family policy, and it continues to exercise a powerful political influence. . . .

As we come to the present time, then, we can discern three major alignments on family issues in America: the radical-to-reformist coalition rooted in the movements of the 1960s, moderated somewhat by middle age and by the compromises of political horse trading but still marching under the old banners of liberation; the new "pro-family" camp, more brash and uncompromising by its very youth, marching in step with the general veering toward conservatism in the national mood; and . . . the combines of professionals, academics, and bureaucrats who make the family their field of expertise, advocacy, and management, more sympathetic on the whole with the first, rather than the second, movement, but inevitably more pragmatic because of both their alleged scientific spirit and their institutional interests. All these people share the very formal proposition that the family has "problems" or even *is* a "problem," but, of course, they vary sharply in their understanding of what it is that is problematic and what should be done about it. Indeed, the "solutions" of the first camp are an essential part of what the second camp sees as the "problem," and vice versa, while the family experts often have "problems" that nobody else on the scene is capable of perceiving. But such are the exigencies of pluralism and of democratic politics. . . .

PART II
▼▼▼▼▼▼▼▼▼▼▼▼▼▼▼▼▼▼▼▼▼▼▼▼▼

Social and Cultural Diversity

*I*f anything characterizes American society, it is *diversity*. We are fragmented into countless groups, each with at least somewhat different ways of going about life.

The largest of our groups are known as *social classes*. Social classes are composed of tens of thousands of families who are similar to one another in their level of education, occupational prestige, and annual family income. Sociologists typically divide Americans into upper, middle, and lower classes. They then subdivide each class into two divisions. Thus sociologists tend to look at American society as being made up of an upper-upper class, a lower-upper class, an upper-middle class, a lower-middle class, an upper-lower class, and a lower-lower class. The particular distinctions between the classes are not relevant here—except for the upper-middle and the upper-lower classes, which are the foci of the opening chapter.

In Chapter 5, Lillian Breslow Rubin analyzes significant differences in marriage and family patterns in these two social classes. As is apparent in her findings, early socialization in a particular social class establishes our basic orientations to life, including our ideas and attitudes. Those ideas and attitudes, in turn, are played out in marriage. They shape the way we look at the world and what we expect out of life—including what we expect from a wife or husband.

Our attitudes, ideas, and behaviors are also shaped by our membership in other groups. One of the most significant of these other groups is a *subculture*, a group that shares the primary orientations of the overall society, but is set apart by distinctive *values* (what their members hold dear in life), *norms* (their rules for living and getting along), *beliefs* (what they think is true about the world), and *life-style* (the general approach that they take to living in society). Their distinctions also include *appearance* (what they look like), *conduct* (what they do), and *manner* (the attitudes they "give off" when they do things). It is around these distinctive characteristics of subcultures that people bond with others, orient themselves toward life, and learn their personal identification—the answer to that perennial question, "Who am I?"

A large society such as ours has thousands of subcultures. Some, such as those of cabdrivers, construction workers, and physicians, are based on unique occupational experiences. Others, such as those centering around adolescence and old age, are based on one's stage of life. Regardless of its basis, which are practically endless, each subculture has features that set its members apart from most other members of society.

Some subcultures are distinctive because they are built around specific interests and activities. For example, stamp collectors and runners are similar to most other people in most ways: Most of their values, norms, beliefs, and life-styles match those that are dominant in our culture. Except for particular role-playing, such as when a runner dresses in racing attire, neither their appearance, conduct, nor manner sets them apart. Consequently, one is ordinarily hard pressed to identify the stamp collectors or runners in a crowd of people.

In contrast, some subcultures are much more encompassing: A unique history provides group experiences that give their members a distinctive approach to life. Raised in a specific group, an individual becomes part of that common history, participates in its current life-style, learns common orientations to life, and identifies with members of the group. One major way in which such groups are distinctive is their family customs. It is to the analysis of family life among African Americans and Mexican Americans, the two largest racial-ethnic-cultural groups in American society, that Robert Staples and Rosina M. Becerra address themselves in Chapters 6 and 7, respectively.

To gain a sense of other significant differences that characterize our society, we also look at diversity of life-styles. Here the differences from the majority do not arise from socialization in social class or racial-ethnic groups, as they did in Chapters 5, 6, and 7. Rather, the people who follow these life-styles come from all social classes and all racial-ethnic groups.

In Chapter 8, Sue Browder focuses on cohabitation, which has become increasingly common not only in our society but also throughout the Western world. With the easing of our double standard and greater acceptance of premarital sex, cohabitation is seen by many as an acceptable option to marriage. When they begin to cohabit, many couples believe that they have the best of two worlds: They retain much of the independence that they highly value and that being single allows, and yet they can have sexual relations with a caring partner. Men and women, however, often experience cohabitation quite differently, and, as Browder points out, the greater intimacy that most female cohabitants feel puts them at a disadvantage.

In Chapter 9, Joseph Harry turns to a highly controversial life-style when he places the focus on same-sex relationships, explaining that they tend to be more egalitarian than heterosexual ones. His contrast of gay and lesbian relationships illustrates that early socialization into the broader gender orientations of our culture carries over into homosexual relationships.

In Chapter 10, Peter J. Stein examines the pushes and pulls toward and away from marriage experienced by people who choose singlehood as a life-style. He examines some of their primary adaptations to being single—their choosing to live in an urban environment and their search for personal satisfaction and meaning in life within an extended, rather amorphous network of singles.

In Chapter 11, Jean E. Veevers looks at couples who choose to remain permanently childless. Using the metaphor of a game, the author analyzes four stages through which such couples go. Veevers also identifies factors that accelerate the commitment to childlessness—or "childfreeness," as many social analysts are now calling it, indicating that such couples now face less stigma.

The value of looking at diversity in marriage and family is that such an examination can help us attain a sociological perspective, an essential goal of this book. To examine marriage and family among different groups in American society can broaden our focus, helping us overcome the narrow perspective that our individuating experiences in marriage and family produce. This helps us gain a comparative base from which to view and understand our own experiences, as well as an appreciation of the diversity of marriage and family in our pluralistic society.

5

▼▼▼

Worlds of Pain
▼▼▼▼▼

Lillian Breslow Rubin

ABSTRACT: Rubin compared working- (upper-lower-) class families with professional (upper-middle-class) families. She found that the arrival of a child soon after marriage complicates the adjustment of working-class husbands and wives. Reactions to the birth usually are bewilderment, anger, discontent, fear, a sense of loss of the past, and jealousy by the husband. Young working-class parents rely heavily on their relatives for child care. Working-class wives commonly find that the mother-in-law interferes on behalf of her spoiled son.

The financial problems of most [working-class] couples [were exacerbated by] the fact that the children were born just months after the wedding. The modal time between marriage and the birth of the first child was seven months, the average, nine months—leaving little time for the young couple to stabilize their financial position before assuming the burdens of parenthood. Unlike the professional middle-class families I met where, on the average, the first child was born three years after they were married and where most wives worked during that time, the working-class families were forced almost at once to give up the wife's

44

earnings. The professional families thus are doubly advantaged. Their jobs pay more and offer career patterns that are more stable than those in the blue-collar world. And by deferring childbearing, young wives are able to work while the men are becoming established.

Other investigators, observing the same phenomena, have theorized that it is precisely those differences that account for professional success—that is, that putting off marriage and childbearing is a symbol of the middle-class ability to defer immediate gratifications in the interest of future rewards. Conversely, the early marriage and childbearing of the working class allegedly is symptomatic of their inability to defer gratifications and the cause of their low status in the society. If one examines the facts through a less self-righteous and self-congratulatory prism, however, we can see instead that it is those at the lower ends of our socioeconomic order who are forced to delay gratifications, while those at the upper levels usually manage to have their cake and eat it. For example, among the college-educated middle class, premarital sexual behavior is not only more widely held to be legitimate but the opportunities for engaging in such behavior are more readily and comfortably available. In the [past two decades], even dormitories—those last bastions of parietal regulations—largely have given up the attempt to control the sexual activities of their student residents. For those young people, a bed and privacy are easily found; sex can be undertaken in leisure—a sharp contrast from the stories told by most working-class youth who still must resort to the back seat of a car or a dark corner in a park.

Similarly, for highly educated middle-class women to delay childbearing may simply be to defer one pleasurable activity in favor of another since they often do some kind of interesting and rewarding work that pays substantially more than the low-level clerical, sales, or factory work available to most high-school-educated working-class women. Most of the middle-class women I talked to, for example, worked at interesting jobs that they liked—social worker, freelance editor, writer, teacher, accountant, office manager, personnel manager, calligrapher. Those who either did not enjoy working or who had jobs they found dull and unrewarding often had their first child in considerably less than the three years cited as the average—a decision that can be made in professional families without the enormous economic costs exacted in the working class.

Indeed, children born just months after the wedding added emotional as well as economic burdens to the adjustment process. Suddenly, two young people, barely more than children themselves, found their lives irrevocably altered. Within a few months—too few to permit the integration of the behaviors required by new roles in new life stages, too few to wear comfortably even one new identity—they moved through a series of roles: from girl and boy, to wife and husband, to mother and father.

They often responded with bewilderment, filled with an uneasy and uncomprehending sense of loss for a past which, however difficult, at least was known:

> I was so depressed and I felt so sad all the time. I felt like I'd fallen into a hole and that I could never climb out of it again. All I wanted was to be a little girl again, real little, so that somebody would take care of me.

. . . an angry and restless discontent with an uncomfortable present:

> I don't know why but I was just angry all the time. Everything she did would make me angry—crazy angry.

. . . and an enormous well of fear about an unknown future:

> All of a sudden, you couldn't tell what would happen tomorrow. I was scared out of my wits half the time; and when I wasn't scared, I was worried out of my mind.

As with all of us, however, such a welter of feelings are rarely recognized, let alone understood. At best, we are aware only that we're experiencing turmoil without knowing what it's about. One young mother expressed it well:

> All I knew was that I was churning up inside all the time.

Most immediately, both wives and husbands knew that the fun and good times that had brought them together were gone—replaced by a crying, demanding infant, and the fearsome responsibilities of parenthood. No longer were they free to run around with the old crowd, to prowl the favored haunts, to go to a movie, bowling, or partying whenever the mood struck. Both wives and husbands were shaken as it quickly became clear that the freedom they had sought in marriage was a mirage, that they had exchanged one set of constraints for another perhaps more powerful one. They felt stuck—thrust abruptly into adulthood, unexpectedly facing the fear that their youth was behind them.

The struggle to adapt simultaneously to so many new situations was complicated by young husbands who were jealous of their wives' suddenly divided time and attention. Before they had a chance to adapt to a twosome in marriage, they became a threesome, with the third member of the household a noisy, demanding, helpless infant. The young wife, anxious about her capacity to be a good mother, became absorbed in the child. Between household and baby-tending chores, both days and nights were full, leaving little time and energy for companionship or lovemaking. The young husband, until then accustomed to being the center of her life, felt excluded and deprived. Each time he made a move toward her that was rebuffed, the situation worsened. He became more hurt and jealous; she became more angry and defensive. The conflict escalated—both husband and wife acting out their frustration in painful and hurtful ways. Typical of such interactions is the story told by this couple, both twenty-nine, married ten years. The husband:

> Our first kid was born less than a year after we were married. By the time he came, it seemed like she'd either been pregnant or with the baby the whole time we were married.

> When we were first married, I'd come home from work and she'd be kind of dressed up and fixed up, you know, looking pretty for me. Then she kept getting bigger and bigger, and she'd be tired and complaining all the time. I could hardly wait for her to finish being pregnant. And when that was over, she was too busy and too tired to pay me any mind.

> I used to get mad and holler a lot. Or else I'd stay out late at night and get her worried about what I was doing. We had nothing but fights in those days because all she wanted to do was to take care of the baby, and she never had any time for me. It sounds dumb when I talk about it now— a man being jealous of a little kid, but I guess I was.

The wife:

> It felt like I was going crazy. There I was with a new baby and he was all the time nagging at me for something or other. Instead of helping me out so that I wouldn't be so tired, he'd just holler, or else he'd run out and stay out all night. Then he'd come home and expect me to be friendly and loving. Why should I? What was he doing for me? I didn't like being stuck with all those dirty diapers any more than he did, but somebody had to do it and he sure wasn't.

> We used to have the most terrible fights after my son was born; it was just awful. I couldn't understand how he could be jealous of a little, tiny baby, but he was. It made me mad, I just didn't know what to do. But I sure didn't feel much like loving him.

Parents in professional middle-class families have a sense of their own success, of their ability to control their world, to provide for their children's future, whatever that might be. For them, the problem is not how to support the children through tomorrow, not *whether* they can go to college or professional school, but *which* of the prestigious alternatives available to them ought to be encouraged. For working-class parents, however, the future is seen as uncertain, problematic. For them, the question is most often *whether*, not *which*—and that "whether" more often asks *if* children will finish high school; *if* they will grow up without getting "into trouble"; *if* even with maximum vigilance, they—the parents—can retain some control over their children's future.

Complicating the matter still further, the men and women of these families are not at ease with most of the public or private institutions that share responsibility for socializing young children. They can't do

much about the public schools with their mandatory attendance requirements and their "too liberal" teachers, although in recent years they
have been trying. But they *can* keep their children at home with them
as long as possible. Thus, where nursery school attendance is a commonplace among the children of middle-class families, it is rare among
those of the working class—not primarily for financial reasons, nor because working-class parents value education less, but because they look
with question and concern at the values that are propagated there:

> I think little kids belong at home with their mothers not in some nursery
> school that's run by a bunch of people who think they're experts and
> know all about what's good for kids and how they're supposed to act. I
> saw some of those kids in a nursery school once. They act like a bunch of
> wild Indians, and they're dressed terrible, and they're filthy all the time.
> [Twenty-seven-year-old housewife,
> mother of two, married seven years.]

So strong are these feelings that even in those families where mothers
work part- or full-time, institutional child-care facilities are shunned in
favor of arrangements with grandmothers or neighbors—arrangements
that keep children close to home and in the care of people who share
parental values. Typical are these comments from one young couple.
The twenty-five-year-old wife, mother of two, married seven years, who
works part-time as a file clerk, says:

> I don't want my kids brought up by strangers. This way it's just right. My
> mother-in-law comes here and stays with them and it's family. We don't
> have to worry about what kind of stuff some stranger is teaching them.
> We know they're learning right from wrong. I'd be afraid to leave them
> in a school or someplace like that. I'd worry that they might get too far
> away from the family.

Her husband, a twenty-seven-year-old refinery worker, agrees:

> I wouldn't let Ann work if we couldn't have my mother taking care of the
> kids. Even though it helps out for her to work, I wouldn't permit it if it
> meant somebody I didn't know was going to raise my kids and tell them
> how to act and what to think. With my mother, I know it's all okay; she
> teaches them the way she taught me.

Thus, both husbands and wives agree on the primacy of their parental responsibilities. But the costs to a marriage of ordering priorities thus
can be heavy. For the demands of parenting often conflict with the
needs of the wives and husbands who are the parents—needs for privacy, for shared adult time and leisure, for companionship, for nurturance from a husband, a wife.

Finally, these early years bring with them the inevitable in-law problems. Despite the prevalence of mother-in-law jokes that focus on the
wife's mother, it is not the men but the women who complain most

regularly and vociferously about mothers-in-law, especially in the beginning years of the marriage. Fully half the working-class women spoke
of problems with mothers-in-law as second only to the financial one; a
few even put the in-law problems first. The primary struggle was over
"who comes first"—wife or mother:

> That first year was terrible. He called her every single day when he came
> home from work. As soon as he'd walk through the door, he'd go to the
> telephone to talk to his mother. And then, a few times he went to see her
> before he ever even came home. That really did it. I said, "Listen buster,
> this has to stop. I'm not going to take that anymore. Either I'm going to
> come first or you can go live with your mother."
> [Twenty-four-year-old typist,
> mother of four, married five years.]

> He was so used to helping out around his mother's house that he just
> kept right on doing it after we were married. Can you imagine that? He'd
> go there and help her out with the yard work. Here our yard would need
> trimming, and he'd be over there helping his mother.
> [Thirty-eight-year-old housewife,
> mother of four, married twenty years.]

> He used to stop off there on his way home from work and that used to
> make me furious. On top of that, they eat supper earlier than we do, so
> a lot of times, he'd eat with them. Then he'd come home and I'd have a
> nice meal fixed, and he'd say he wasn't hungry. Boy, did that make me
> mad. We were always having these big fights over his mother at first.
> [Thirty-two-year-old housewife,
> mother of three, married thirteen years.]

This is not to suggest that conflicts around in-laws do not exist in
other strata in society. But no professional middle-class wife or husband
talked of these problems with the heat and intensity that I heard among
the working-class women. Partly, that may be because few of the
middle-class couples had families who lived close by at the time of the
marriage which often took place when husbands were still in professional schools far from their hometowns. This gave these young couples
a chance to negotiate the initial adjustment hurdles without interference
from either family. Equally important, however, even when they live in
the same city now, most of these professional couples do not have the
kinds of relationships with parents that keep them actively intertwined
in their lives. No grandparent in a professional family, for example,
baby-sits with young children while their mother works—a common arrangement among working-class families, one which makes it difficult
for the young couple to insist upon their autonomy and independence,
to maintain their privacy.

Adding to the in-law problems, many of the women were aggrieved
because their mothers-in-law had spoiled their sons—waiting on them,
tending their every need, always sacrificing self for the men and boys

in the family—thus making the lives of their wives more difficult. For men like these expected similar "services" from their wives—services most modern young women of any class are not so willing to perform:

> His mother was like a maid in the house, and he wanted me to do the same kinds of things and be like her. I know it's my job to keep the house up, but wouldn't you think he could hang up his own clothes? Or maybe once in a while—just once in a while—help clear the table?
>
> [Twenty-eight-year-old housewife,
mother of three, married ten years.]

Again, obviously, it is not only working-class mothers who spoil their sons. Still, no middle-class wife offered this complaint—a fact that, at least in part, may be because the professional men all had lived away from home for several years before they married. Without a mother or wife to do things for them, these men had to learn to care for themselves—at least minimally—in the years between leaving the parental home and getting married. In contrast, the working-class men generally moved from parental home to marriage, often simply transferring old habits and living patterns, along with their wardrobe, to a new address.

Indeed, overriding all these reasons why more working-class than professional middle-class women had complaints about mothers-in-law may be the simple fact that most working-class men lived with their families and contributed to the support of the household before they were married. Their departure from the family, therefore, probably is felt both as an emotional and an economic loss. Mothers, already experiencing some panic over the loss of maternal functions which have provided the core of their identity for so long, suffer yet another erosion of that function—a problem women in professional middle-class families deal with when children leave for college rather than when they marry. And the family economy, relying on income from all its working members, suffers the loss of his dollar contribution:

> His parents didn't accept me at all. Tim was a devoted son and his mother needed that; she couldn't bear to give him up to anyone. Then, he also helped out a lot when he was living there. They needed the money and he turned his paycheck over to his mother. They made me feel like I was taking a meal ticket from them when we got married.
>
> [Thirty-year-old file clerk,
mother of four, married twelve years.]

These, then, were the beginning years—the years when illusions were shed along with childhood; the years when the first disappointments were felt, the first adjustments were made; the years of struggle for stability economically and emotionally—both so closely tied together; the years during which many marriages founder and sink. Some of these couples had already had that experience once; they were determined not to let it happen again.

6

African American Families

Robert Staples

ABSTRACT: Although African Americans could not legally marry during slavery, the family was the center of their nonworking life. Whenever masters wished, however, they could sell their slaves, thus separating husbands and wives and children. After emancipation, during a period of severe deprivation, African Americans achieved family stability. In contrast with this period, the African American family today is facing a crisis due to a large proportion of single adults, out-of-wedlock births, divorce, and single-parent families. Although these patterns reflect broader changes in American culture—greater sexual permissiveness, alternative family life styles, and increased divorce—at their heart lies the institutional decimation of African American males.

INTRODUCTION

As the United States' largest visible minority, the black population has been the subject of extensive study by behavioral scientists. Its fam-

51

ily life has been of particular concern because of the unique character of this group, as a result of a history that is uncharacteristic of other ethnic groups. There are four cultural traits of the black group that distinguish it from other immigrants to the United States: (1) blacks came from a country with norms and values that were dissimilar to the American way of life; (2) they were from many different tribes, each with its own language, culture, and traditions; (3) in the beginning, they came without women; and, most importantly, (4) they came in bondage (Billingsley, 1968).

The study of black family life has, historically, been problem-oriented. Whereas the study of white families has been biased toward the middle-class family, the reverse has been true in the investigation of black family patterns. Until relatively recently, almost all studies of black family life have concentrated on the lower-income strata of the group, ignoring middle-class families and even stable, poor black families. Moreover, the deviation of black families from middle-class norms has resulted in them being defined as pathological. Such labels ignore the possibility that although a group's family forms may not fit into the normative model, it may instead have its own functional organization that meets the needs of the group (Billingsley, 1970). . . .

HISTORICAL BACKGROUND

The Slave Family

In attempting to accurately describe the family life of slaves, one must sift through a conflicting array of opinions on the subject. Reliable empirical facts are few, and speculation has been rampant in the absence of data. Certain aspects of the slave's family life are undisputed. Slaves were not allowed to enter into binding contractual relationships. Because marriage is basically a legal relationship that imposes obligations on both parties and exacts penalties for the violation of those obligations, there was no legal basis for any marriage between two individuals in bondage. Slave marriages were regulated at the discretion of the slaveowners. As a result, some marriages were initiated by slaveowners and just as easily dissolved (Genovese, 1975).

Hence, there were numerous cases in which the slaveowner ordered slave women to marry men of his choosing after they reached the age of puberty. The slave owners preferred marriages between slaves on the same plantation, because the primary reason for slave unions was the breeding of children who would become future slaves. Children born to a slave woman on a different plantation were looked on by the slaveholder as wasting his man's seed. Yet, many slaves who were allowed to get married preferred women from a neighboring plantation. This allowed them to avoid witnessing the many assaults on slave women that occurred. Sometimes, the matter was resolved by the sale of one of the slaves to the other owner (Blassingame, 1972).

Historians are divided on the question of how many slave families were involuntarily separated from each other by their owners. Despite the slaveholder's commitment to keeping the slave families intact, the intervening events of a slaveholder's death, his bankruptcy, or lack of capital made the forceable sale of some slave's spouse or child inevitable. In instances where the slavemaster was indifferent to the fate of slave families, he would still keep them together simply to enforce plantation discipline. A married slave who was concerned about his wife and children, it was believed, was less inclined to rebel or escape than would an unmarried slave. Whatever their reasoning, the few available records show that slaveowners did not separate a majority of the slave couples (Blassingame, 1972).

This does not mean that the slave family had a great deal of stability. Although there are examples of some slave families living together for 40 years or more, the majority of slave unions were dissolved by personal choice, death, or the sale of one partner by the master. Although individual families may not have remained together for long periods of time, the institution of the family was an important asset in the perilous era of slavery. Despite the prevalent theories about the destruction of the family under slavery, it was one of the most important survival mechanisms for African people held in bondage (Blassingame, 1972; Fogel and Engerman, 1974).

In the slave quarters, black families did exist as functioning institutions and as models for others. The slave narratives provide us with some indication of the importance of family relations under slavery. It was in the family that the slave received affection, companionship, love, and empathy with his sufferings under this peculiar institution. Through the family, he learned how to avoid punishment, cooperate with his fellow slaves, and retain some semblance of his self-esteem. The socialization of the slave child was another important function for the slave parents. They could cushion the shock of bondage for him, inculcate in him values different than those the masters attempted to teach him, and represent another frame of reference for his self-esteem besides the master (Abzug, 1971).

Much has been written about the elimination of the male's traditional functions under the slave system. It is true that he was often relegated to working in the fields and siring children rather than providing economic maintenance or physical protection for his family, but the father's role was not as insignificant as presumed. It was the male slave's inability to protect his wife from the physical and sexual abuse of the master that most pained him. As a matter of survival, few tried, because the consequences were often fatal. However, it is significant that tales of their intervention occur frequently in the slave narratives. There is one story of a slave who could no longer tolerate the humiliation of his wife's sexual abuse before his eyes by the master. The slave choked him to death with the knowledge that it also meant his own death. He said he knew it would mean his death, but he was unafraid of death, so he killed him (Abzug, 1971:29).

One aspect of black family life frequently ignored during the slave era is the free black family. This group, which numbered about one-half million, was primarily composed of the descendants of the original black indentured servants and the mulatto offspring of slaveholders. For this minority of black families, the assimilation and acculturation process was, relatively, less difficult. They imitated the white world as closely as possible. Because they had opportunities for education, owning property, and skilled occupations, their family life was quite stable. Some of them even owned slaves, although the majority of black slave-holders were former slaves who had purchased their wives or children. It is among this group that the early black middle-class was formed (Frazier, 1932).

After Emancipation

There has been a prevailing notion that the experience of slavery weakened the value of marriage as an institution among black Americans. Yet, the slaves married in record numbers when the right to the freedom to marry was created by governmental decree. A legal marriage was a status symbol, and weddings were events of great gaiety. In a careful examination of census data and marriage licenses for the period after 1860, Gutman (1976) found that the typical household was a simple nuclear family headed by an adult male. Further evidence that black people were successful in forming a dual-parent family structure is the data that show that 90 percent of all black children were born in wedlock by the year 1917.

The strong family orientation of the recently emancipated slaves has been observed by many students of the reconstruction era. One newspaper reported a black group's petition to the state of North Carolina asking for the right "to work with the assurance of good faith and fair treatment, to educate their children, to sanctify the family relation, to reunite scattered families, and to provide for the orphan and infirm"

(Abzug, 1971:34). Children were of special value to the freed slaves, whose memories were fresh with the history of their offspring being sold away.

It was during the late nineteenth century that the strong role of women emerged. Men preferred their wives to remain at home, because a working woman was considered a mark of slavery. However, during the period, which has been described as the most explicitly racist era of American history (Miller, 1966), black men found it very difficult to obtain jobs and, in some instances, found work only as strikebreakers. Thus, the official organ of the African Methodist Episcopal church exhorted black families to teach their daughters not to avoid work, because many of them would marry men that would not make on the average more than 75 cents per day (Abzug, 1971:39). In 1900, approximately 41 percent of black women were in the labor force, compared with 16 percent of white women (Logan, 1965).

What was important, then, was not whether the husband or wife worked, but the family's will to survive in an era when blacks were systematically deprived of educational and work opportunities. Despite these obstacles, black families achieved a level of stability based on role integration. Men shared equally in the rearing of children; women participated in the defense of the family. As Nobles (1972) comments, a system in which the family disintegrates because of the loss of one member would be in opposition to the traditional principles of unity that defined the African family. These principles were to be tested during the period of the great black migration from the rural areas of the South to the cities of the North.

The rise of black illegitimately born children and female-headed households are concomitants of twentieth century urban ghettos. Drastic increases in these phenomena strongly indicate that the condition of many lower-class black families is a function of the economic contingencies of industrial America. Unlike the European immigrants before them, blacks were disadvantaged by the hard lines of northern segregation along racial lines. Furthermore, families in cities are more vulnerable to disruptions from the traumatizing experiences of urbanization, the reduction of family functions, and the loss of extended family supports.

In the transition from Africa to the American continent, there can be no doubt that African culture was not retained in any pure form. Blacks lacked the autonomy to maintain their cultural traditions under the severe pressures to take on American standards of behavior. Yet, there are surviving Africanisms that are reflected in black speech patterns, esthetics, folklore, and religion. They have preserved aspects of their old culture that have a direct relevance to their new lives. Out of the

common experiences they have shared, a new culture has been forged
that is uniquely black American.

CHANGING PATTERNS OF BLACK FAMILY LIFE

Recent years have brought about significant changes in the marital
and family patterns of many Americans. Americans have witnessed an
era of greater sexual permissiveness, alternate family life-styles, increased divorce rates, and reductions in the fertility rate. Some of these
changes have also occurred among black families and have implications
for any public policy developed to strengthen black family life.

The sexual revolution has arrived, and blacks are very much a part
of it (Staples, 1981). By the age of 19, black women were twice as likely
as white women to have engaged in intercourse. Although the percentage for white females was lower, they were engaging in premarital coitus more often and with a larger number of sexual partners. However,
a larger number of sexually active black females were not using reliable
contraceptives, and 41 percent had been, or were, pregnant (Zelnik and
Kantner, 1977).

One result of this increased premarital sexual activity among blacks
is the large number of black children born out of wedlock. More than
[six hundred] of every 1,000 black births were illegitimate in the year
[1990]. Moreover, the rate was higher in this period for blacks than in
the most recent earlier periods. The racial differences in illegitimacy
rates also narrowed in the last 20 years (U. S. Bureau of the Census,
1983). One reason for the continued racial differential is the greater use
by white women of low-cost abortions. In one study, 26 percent of pregnant black women received an abortion, compared with 41 percent of
white women (Cummings, 1983). In all probability, the black out-of-
wedlock birth rate will continue to increase as a higher percentage of
black children are born to teenage mothers.

When blacks choose to get married, the same economic and cultural
forces that are undermining marital stability in the general population
are operative. In the last decade, the annual divorce rate has risen 120
percent. For white women under the age of 30, the chances are nearly
two out of four that their marriage will end in divorce. Among black
women, their chances are two out of three. In 1981, 30 percent of married black women were separated or divorced, compared with 14 percent for white women. The divorce rate of middle-class blacks is lower,
because the more money that a family makes and the higher their educational achievements, the greater are their chances for a stable marriage
(U. S. Bureau of the Census, 1983).

A combination of the aforementioned factors has increased the percentage of black households headed by women. The percentage of female-headed families among blacks increased 130 percent in the last decade, from 21 percent to 47 percent. One-third of these female household heads worked and had a median annual income of only [$10,017] in [1987]. The percentage of black children living with both parents declined in the last decade, and currently, only 42 percent of children in black families are residing with both parents. It is apparently the increasing pressures of discrimination, urban living, and poverty that cause black fathers to leave their homes or never marry. At the income level of $20,000 and over, the percentage of black families headed by a man is similar to that for white families (U. S. Bureau of the Census, 1983). . . .

MALE-FEMALE RELATIONSHIPS

Relationships between black men and women have had a peculiar evolution. Unlike the white family, which was a patriarchy and sustained by the economic dependence of women, the black dyad has been characterized by more equalitarian roles and economic parity in North America. The system of slavery did not permit black males to assume the superordinate role in the family constellation because the female was not economically dependent on him. Hence, relationships between the sexes were ordered along social-psychological factors rather than economic compulsion to marry and remain married. This fact, in part, explains the unique trajectory of black male-female relationships.

Finding and keeping a mate is complicated by a number of social-psychological factors, as well as structural restraints. Social structure and individual attitudes interface to make male-female relationships ephemeral rather than permanent. The imbalance in the sex ratio will continue to deny large numbers of black women a comparable mate. Furthermore, there are only a limited number of ways to deal with that irreversible fact of life. At the same time, there exists a pool of black males who are available to this group of women, and the tension between them builds barriers to communicating and mating. This is a complex problem, and there is no easy solution. Although there are some black men who are threatened by the successful black woman, further investigation reveals other underlying forces. Men are torn between the need for security and the desire for freedom, the quest for a special person to call their own and the temptation of sexual variety. They see marriage as a way of establishing roots but are seduced by the enticement of all the attractive, possibly "better" women in their midst. . . .

One should not be deluded by the ostensible reluctance of many black single adults to enter the conjugal state. When a person has not been able to develop a lasting, permanent relationship with a member of the opposite sex, he or she must play it off and make the best of whatever it is they have at the moment. Although the industrial and urban revolution has made the single life more a viable way of life, it has also made the need for belonging more imperative. The tensions of work and the impersonality of the city have created a need to escape the depersonalization by retreating into some sort of an intimate sanctum. This is especially imperative for blacks in the middle class who have their selfhood tested daily by a racist society and who must often work and live in isolation. In modern society, individuals are required to depend on each other for permanence and stability, which is a function previously served by a large familial and social network.

It is the fear that even marriage no longer provides that permanence and stability that causes people to enter and exit their relationships quickly. It is the fear of failure that comes from failure. Until black single adults develop a tenacity to work as hard at a relationship as they did at their schooling and jobs, we will continue to see this vicious cycle repeated again and again. Marriage and the family continue to be the most important buffer for blacks against racism and depersonalization. When one looks at the strongest predictors of happiness in America, it is inevitably such social factors as marriage, family, friends, and children. Across the board, married people tend to be happier than those who are unmarried. The best confirmation of this fact is that most people who divorce eventually remarry. Before anyone can find happiness in a marriage, they must form a strong basis for marriage. It is that task that continues to perplex black single adults.

There is a growing trend toward single life among American blacks. A majority of black women over the age of 18 years are no longer married and living with a spouse (Staples, 1981). Although the institutional decimation of black males is the primary factor in this unprecedented number of singles, other sociocultural forces have an impact on the relationships between black men and women. Among them are the changes in black institutions and values. Franklin (1984) traces the conflict between black men and women to incompatible role enactments by the two sexes. The societal prescription that women are to be passive and men dominant is counteracted by black women who resist black men's dominance and black men who wish to be accorded the superior male role but cannot fulfill the economic provider role, which supports the dominance of men in American society.

Husbands and Wives

Marriages are very fragile today. Fewer people are getting married, and the divorce rate in the United States is at an all-time high. There are many forces responsible for this changing pattern including changing attitudes and laws on divorce, changing and conflicting definitions of sex roles and their functions in the family, economic problems, and personality conflicts. Although divorce is on the rise and its increase cuts across racial and class lines, it is still more pronounced among blacks. Only one out of every three black couples will remain married longer than 10 years.

It is not easy to pinpoint unique causes of black marital dissolution because they are very similar to those of their white counterparts. In some cases, it is the severity of the problems they face. Economic problems are a major factor in marital conflict [for the poverty rate is three times as high among blacks as whites]. The tensions blacks experience in coping with the pervasive incidents of racism often have their ramifications in the marital arena. One peculiar problem blacks face is the imbalanced sex ratio, which places many women in competition for the available males. Too often, the males they compete for are not available, and this places serious pressure on the marriages of many blacks.

At the same time, many blacks are involved in a functional marriage at any given point in time. Many adult blacks are married and have positive and loving relationships with their spouses. Unfortunately, practically no research exists on marital adjustment and satisfaction among blacks. What little research does exist indicates that black wives are generally less satisfied with their marriages than white wives. However, the source of their dissatisfaction is often associated with the problems of poverty and racism.

The last decade witnessed a significant increase in interracial dating and marriage. Among the reasons for this change in black-white dating and marriage was the desegregation of the public school system, the work force, and other social settings. In those integrated settings, blacks and whites met as equals, which facilitated homogenous mating. There were, of course, other factors such as the liberation of many white youth from parental control and the racist values [that] they conveyed to them.

Not only has the incidence of interracial relations increased but their character has changed as well. Over 25 years ago, the most typical interracial pairing was a black male and a white female with the male partner generally being of a higher status. This pattern was so common that social theorists even developed a theory of racial hypergamy. In essence, it was assumed that the higher-status black male was exchanging his socioeconomic status for the privilege of marrying a woman who belonged to a racial group that was considered superior to all members of the black race. Contemporary interracial relations are much more likely to involve people with similar educational background and occupational status.

Although no research studies have yet yielded any data on the subject, there appears to be a change in interracial unions toward a decline in black male/white female couples and an increase in black female/white male pairings. Several factors seem to account for this modification of the typical pattern. Many black women are gravitating toward white men because of the shortage of black men and disenchantment with those they do have access to. In a similar vein, some white men are dissatisfied with white women and their increasing vociferous demands for sex-role parity. At the same time, there is a slight but noticeable decrease in black male/white female unions. One possible reason is that it is no longer as fashionable as it was a few years ago. Also, much of their attraction to each other was based on the historical lack of access to each other and the stereotype of black men as superstuds and white women as forbidden fruit. Once they had had extensive interaction, the myths exploded and the attraction consequently diminished (Poussaint, 1983).

We should be fairly clear that there are relatively normal reasons for interracial attractions and matings. At the same time, it would be naive to assume that special factors are not behind them in a society that is stratified by race. Given the persistence of racism as a very pervasive force, many interracial marriages face rough sledding. In addition to the normal problems of working out a satisfactory marital relationship, interracial couples must cope with social ostracism and isolation. One recent phenomenon is the increasing hostility toward such unions by the black community, which has forced some interracial couples into a marginal existence. Such pressures cause the interracial-marriage rate to remain at a very low level. Less than 5 percent of all marriages involving a black person are interracial (Poussaint, 1983).

CHILDHOOD AND CHILD REARING

One of the most popular images of black women is that of "Mammy," the devoted, affectionate nursemaids of white children who belonged to their slavemaster or employer. This motherly image of black women probably has some basis in fact. Motherhood has historically been an important role for black women, even more meaningful than their role as wives (Bell, 1971). In the colonial period of Africa, missionaries often observed and reported the unusual devotion of the African mother to her child. The slave mother also developed a deep love for, and impenetrable bond to, her children (Ladner, 1971). It would appear that the bond between the black mother and her child is deeply rooted in the African heritage and philosophy that places a special value on children because they represent the continuity of life (Brown and Forde, 1967).

Many studies have conveyed a negative image of the black mother because she does not conform to middle-class modes of childrearing. Yet, black mothers have fulfilled the function of socializing their children into the multiple roles they must perform in this society. They prepare them to take on not only the appropriate sex and age roles but also a racial role. Children must be socialized to deal with the prosaic realities of white racism that they will encounter daily. Black females are encouraged to be independent rather than passive individuals because many of them will carry family and economic responsibilities alone (Iscoe et al., 1964). Taking on adult responsibilities is something many black children learn early. They may be given the care of a younger sibling, and some will have to find work while still in the adolescent stage. The strong character structure of black children was noted by child psychiatrist Robert Coles (1964) who observed their comportment under the pressure of school integration in the South during a very volatile era.

The black mother's child-rearing techniques are geared to prepare her children for a kind of existence that is alien to middle-class white youngsters. Moreover, many white middle-class socialization patterns may not be that desirable for the psychological growth of the black child. The casual upbringing of black children may produce a much healthier personality than the status anxieties associated with some rigid middle-class child-rearing practices (Green, 1946). Using threats of the withdrawal of love if the child fails to measure up to the parent's standards is much more common among white parents than black parents of any class stratum. One result of the black child's anxiety-free upbringing is a strong closeness to his parents (Nolle, 1972; Scanzoni, 1971).

Although black parents are more likely to use physical rather than verbal punishment to enforce discipline than white parents, this technique is often buttressed by the love they express for their children. Moreover, as Billingsley (1969:567) has noted, "even among the lowest social classes in the Black community, families give the children better care than is generally recognized, and often the care is better than that given by white families in similar social circumstances." One indication of the decline in this attitude is found in the statistics, which show that child abuse has become more common in black families than in white families (Gil, 1971). Some of the racial differences can be attributed to reporting bias, but much of it reflects the effect of poverty and racism on black parent-child relationships. . . .

Problems in child development are alleged to be a function of the father's absence or ineffectiveness. There has yet to be found a direct relationship between the father's absence and child maladaptation (Hare, 1975; Rubin, 1974). In part, the black child continues to have male role models among the male kinsmen in his extended family network, and the mother generally regards her children's father as a friend of the family who she can recruit for help rather than as a father failing his parental duties. However, one must be careful not to overromanticize the single-parent family as a totally functional model. They are the poorest families in the United States and are overrepresented among the society's failures in education, crime, and mental health.

The ineffective black father has been assumed to be pervasive among black families. Much of the more recent literature suggests that black fathers have warm, nurturing relationships with their children and play a vital role in their children's psychology and social development (Lewis, 1975; Scanzoni, 1971). How well they carry out the paternal role may be contingent on the economic resources available to them. Hence, we find better patterns of parenting among middle-class black fathers who have the economic and educational resources, and, consequently, participate more in child care, are more child-oriented, and view their role as different from the mother's (Cazanave, 1979; Daneal, 1975). As far as the male child's sexual identity is concerned, Benjamin (1971) discovered that black male youth had a better conception of the male role when their father had one or more years of college education, indicating a strong relationship between the opportunity to play a role and the actual playing of that role. . . .

CHANGE AND ADAPTATION

The last 30 years have culminated in the gradual disintegration of the black nuclear family. Changes in the black family structure are in tune with the changes in American families. A number of social forces account for the increase in the number of single adults, out-of-wedlock births, divorces, and single-parent households. As women have become economically and psychologically independent of men, they have chosen to remain single or leave marriages they regarded as not satisfying their needs. Simultaneously, the growing independence of women and the sexual revolution . . . have allowed men to flee from the responsibility attendant to the husband and father roles (Ehrenreich, 1983).

Although these sociocultural forces have an impact on the marriage and family patterns of many Americans, they are more pronounced among blacks because of one critical etiological agent: the institutional decimation of black males. As an Urban League report concluded, "the attrition of Black males . . . from conception through adulthood finally results in an insufficient number of men who are willing and able to provide support for women and children in a family setting" (Williams, 1984). Thus, many black women are denied a real choice between monogamous marriage or single life. Most do choose to bear and raise children because that is deemed better than being single, childless, and locked into dead-end, low-paying jobs. Although many would prefer a monogamous marriage, that is no longer possible for the majority of black women. The same forces that drive many black men out of social institutions also propel them out of the family.

Those forces have their genesis in the educational system. Black women are more educated than black men at all levels except the doctoral level. This, again, is in the overall direction of change in American society. White men have also been losing ground to white women in educational achievements. The reasons for the ascendency of women in the school system are unclear. Some speculate that because teachers are disproportionately female, the behaviors tolerated and most encouraged are those that are more natural for girls (Hale, 1983). The higher educational level of black women endows them with educational credentials and skills that make them more competitive in the job market. The changing nature of the economy has placed women at an advantage. While the industrial sector has been declining, the service and high-technology sectors of the economy have been expanding. Black women are more highly concentrated in the expanding sector of the economy whereas black men are overrepresented in the shrinking industrial jobs. . . .

The crisis of the black family is, in reality, the crisis of the black male and his inability to carry out the normative responsibilities of husband and father in the nuclear family. The family's disintegration is only a symptom of the larger problem, that problem being the institutional decimation of black males. One should be clear that the institutional decimation of black males represents the legacy of institutional racism. . . .

REFERENCES

ABZUG, ROBERT H. 1971. "The Black Family During Reconstruction," in Nathan Huggins, et al. (Eds.), *Key Issue in the Afro-American Experience.* New York: Harcourt, Brace and Jovanovich, 26–39.

BELL, ROBERT. 1971. "The Relative Importance of Mother and Wife Roles Among Negro Lower-Class Women," in *The Black Family: Essays and Studies.* Belmont, CA: Wadsworth, 248–256.

BENJAMIN, R. 1971. *Factors Related to Conceptions of the Black Male Familial Role by Black Male Youth.* Mississippi State University Sociological-Antropological Press Series.

BILLINGSLEY, ANDREW. 1968. *Black Families in White America.* Englewood Cliffs, NJ: Prentice-Hall.

——. 1969. "Family Functioning in the Low-Income Black Community," *Social Casework,* 50(December):563–572.

——. 1970. "Black Families and White Social Science," *Journal of Social Issues,* 26(November):127–142.

BLASSINGAME, JOHN. 1972. *The Slave Community.* New York: Oxford University Press.

BROWN, A. R. RADCLIFFE, and DARRYLE FORDE. 1967. *African Systems of Kinship and Marriage.* New York: Oxford University Press.

CAZANAVE, NOEL. 1979. "Middle-Income Black Fathers: An Analysis of the Provider Role," *The Family Coordinator,* 28(November).

COLES, ROBERT. 1964. "Children and Racial Demonstrations," *The American Scholar,* 34(Winter):78–92.

CUMMINGS, JUDITH. 1983. "Breakup of Black Family Imperils Gains of Decades," *New York Times* (November 20):1–2.

DANEAL, JEALEAN EVELYN. 1975. "A Definition of Fatherhood as Expressed by Black Fathers." Ph.D. diss., University of Pittsburgh.

EHRENREICH, BARBARA. 1983. *The Hearts of Men: American Dreams and the Flight from Commitment.* Garden City, NY: Doubleday.

FOGEL, WILLIAM, and STANLEY ENGERMAN. 1974. *Time on the Cross.* Boston: Little, Brown.

FRANKLIN, CLYDE W. 1984. "Black Male-Female Conflict: Individually Caused and Culturally Nurtured," *Journal of Black Studies,* 15(December):139–154.

FRAZIER, E. FRANKLIN. 1932. *The Free Negro Family.* Nashville, TN: Fisk University Press.

GENOVESE, EUGENE. 1975. *Roll, Jordan, Roll.* New York: Pantheon.

GIL, DAVID. 1971. Violence Against Children. *Journal of Marriage and the Family,* 33(November):637–648.

GREEN, ARNOLD. 1946. "The Middle-Class Male Child and Neurosis," *American Sociological Review,* 11(February):31–41.

GUTMAN, HERBERT. 1976. *The Black Family in Slavery and Freedom, 1750–1925.* New York: Pantheon.

HALE, JANICE. 1983. *Black Children.* Provo, UT: Brigham Young University Press.

HARE, BRUCE R. 1975. "Relationship of Social Background to the Dimensions of Self-Concept." Ph.D. diss., University of Chicago.

ISCOE, IRA, MARTHA WILLIAMS, and JERRY HARVEY. 1964. "Age, Intelligence and Sex as Variables in the Conformity Behavior of Negro and White Children," *Child Development,* 35:451–460.

LADNER, JOYCE. 1971. *Tomorrow: The Black Woman.* Garden City, NY: Doubleday.

LEWIS, DIANE R. 1975. "The Black Family: Socialization and Sex Roles," *Phylon,* 36(Fall):221–237.

LOGAN, RAYFORD. 1965. *The Betrayal of the Negro.* New York: Collier.

MILLER, ELIZABETH. 1966. *The Negro in America: A Bibliography.* Cambridge: Harvard University Press.

NOBLES, WADE. 1972. "African Root and American Fruit: The Black Family," *Journal of Social and Behavioral Sciences,* 20(Spring):52–64.

NOLLE, DAVID. 1972. "Changes in Black Sons and Daughters: A Panel Analysis of Black Adolescent's Orientation Toward Their Parents," *Journal of Marriage and the Family,* 34(August):443–447.

POUSSAINT, ALVIN. 1983. "Black Men-White Women: An Update," *Ebony,* 38(August):124–131.

RUBIN, ROGER H. 1974. "Adult Male Absence and the Self-Attitudes of Black Children," *Child Study Journal,* 4:33–44.

SCANZONI, JOHN. 1971. *The Black Family in Modern Society*. Boston: Allyn and Bacon.

STAPLES, ROBERT. 1981. *The World of Black Singles: Changing Patterns of Male/Female Relations*. Westport, CT: Greenwood Press.

U. S. Bureau of the Census. 1983. *America's Black Population, 1970 to 1982: A Statistical View, July 1983*. Series P10/POP83. Washington, DC: U. S. Government Printing Office.

WILLIAMS, JUAN. 1984. "Black Male's Problems Linked to Family Crises," *The Washington Post*, August 1, p. A-6.

ZELNICK, MELVIN, and JOHN KANTNER. 1977. "Sexual and Contraceptive Experience of Young Unmarried Women in the United States, 1976 and 1971," *Family Planning Perspectives*, 9(May/June):55–59.

7

Mexican American Families
▼▼▼▼▼

Rosina M. Becerra

ABSTRACT: Because of continuous emigration from Mexico, first-generation immigrants reinforce traditional values in the Mexican American community. Extended families—characterized by mutual support, sustenance, and interaction among family members during both work and leisure hours—are rooted in the agrarian and craft economies of Mexico. The stereotype of male dominance is more ideology than reality; that of rigid sex and age grading comes closer to reality, while the stereotype of a strong familial orientation is true. With a low divorce rate, Mexican Americans are likely to live in two-parent families. Assimilation is moderate, intermarriage high, education low, and unemployment high. The Mexican American family is an emergent form that combines elements of the cultures of Mexico and the United States.

CONTINUITIES WITH THE PAST

Mexican American families consist largely of individuals who are descended from or who are themselves unskilled immigrants who come to the United States to work in low-wage sectors of the southwestern economy (McWilliams, 1968; Grebler, Moore, and Guzman, 1970). Unlike the members of some other Hispanic groups, very few Mexicans entered the United States as professional people.

Because of the Southwest's geographic proximity to Mexico and its demand for low-wage labor, the Mexican population is highly concentrated in the southwestern states. In fact, in [1989], 76 percent of Mexican Americans lived in one of two states: California or Texas. From 1870 through 1980, these two states have always been home to between 70 percent and 80 percent of the Mexicans in the United States (Jaffe, Cullen, and Boswell, 1980). During most of their time in the Southwest, Mexicans have been the victims of prejudice and discrimination, varying in intensity from time to time and place to place but always present (Grebler, Guzman, and More, 1970; Hoffman, 1974; Estrada et al., 1981).

Because of their long history of settlement in the United States and continuous emigration from Mexico, the Mexican American population is far more generationally diverse than other Hispanic groups. In 1970, 16 percent were first-generation immigrants (i.e., foreign born), 34 percent were second generation, and 50 percent were third or later generations (Jaffe, Cullen, and Boswell, 1980). The generational diversity of the Mexican American people implies a corresponding diversity of social and economic statuses within the population.

What makes the situation of the Mexican American any different than that of other immigrating groups, who with the passage of time have been acculturated into mainstream America? Although change and, presumably, acculturation are taking place, Mexican Americans have more continuous interaction with first-generation immigrants and proximity to their original homeland. First-generation community members constantly reinforce traditional values. The rate and direction of acculturative change are thus greatly influenced and cause some cultural values to remain unchanged. The proximity of Mexico to the United States, regardless of the amount of flow back and forth, reinforces the familial ties—and the family values—that span the two countries (Becerra, 1983).

Heterogeneity and Homogeneity

Because family socialization takes root in the economic and political forces of society, the history of the Mexican American family must be anchored in the context of the American economy (Saragoza, 1983). Mexican Americans are a highly heterogeneous population. An important factor accounting for this variability is history. Mexican groups in the United States have different histories of immigration and settlement. Some trace their roots to the Spanish and Mexican settlers who first settled the Southwest before the arrival of the pilgrims, whereas others are immigrants or children of immigrants who began to arrive in large numbers by the beginning of the twentieth century (Martinez, 1985). Saragoza (1983) points out that this history supports the fundamental cultural variation and social differentiation among Mexican American families. Crucial factors are variability across region (including Mexico) and changes over time. Mexican American families in different historical periods have adapted differently to economic and political forces, and family socialization patterns have responded differently to societal pressures (Baca-Zinn, 1983).

The traditional structure of the Mexican family grew out of the socioeconomic needs dictated by the agrarian and craft economies of Mexico. For the traditional Mexican, the word *familia* ("family") meant an extended, multigenerational group of persons, among whom specific social roles were ascribed. By dividing functions and responsibilities among different generations of family members, the family was able to perform all the economic and social support chores necessary for survival in the relatively spartan life circumstances of the rural Mexican environment. Mutual support, sustenance, and interaction among family members during both work and leisure hours dominated the lives of persons in these traditional Mexican families (Becerra, 1983).

After the conquest of the Southwest, Mexican families who remained or moved to the United States out of necessity tended to work and live in ethnically homogeneous settings. Minimally influenced by Anglo American culture, these communities supported the maintenance of Mexican familial structures as they might have been practiced in rural Mexico. The male took the role of authority figure and head of the household, and the female took the role of childbearer and nurturer (Sanchez, 1974). This family form was a response to particular economic and political forces, as are all family forms, that resulted in the Mexican American family carrying both these ideals and values and the need for modification under the new economic and political circumstances in the United States.

Traditional Family Structure

Much has been written about the traditional structure of Mexican American families. Depending on the author, these structures appear rigid, cold, and unstable on one end of the continuum or warm, nurturing, and cohesive on the other end. The three main characteristics of the Mexican American family that are addressed by these polar views are the following: (1) male dominance, (2) rigid sex and age grading so that "the older order the younger, and the men the women", and (3) a strong familial orientation (Mirande, 1985:152).

Male Dominance

Of all the popular stereotypes surrounding the Mexican American family, none has become so much a part of American usage as the concept of *machismo*. Machismo is often equated with male dominance. Male dominance is the designation of the father as the head of the household, the major decision maker, and the absolute power holder in the Mexican American family. In his absence, this power position reverts to the oldest son. All members of the household are expected to carry out the orders of the male head.

The concept of machismo has various interpretations. For many, machismo is equated with excessive aggression, little regard for women, and sexual prowess. The macho demands complete allegiance, respect, and obedience from his wife and children. Madsen (1973:20) states that "ideally the Latin male acknowledges only the authority of his father and God. In case of conflict between these two sources, he should side with his father."

In contrast, genuine machismo is characterized by true bravery, or valor, courage, generosity, and a respect for others. The machismo role encourages protection of and provision for the family members, the use of fair and just authority, and respect for the role of wife and children (Mirande, 1985).

Although male dominance is a Mexican American cultural entity, as well as a structural component, its counterpart, the self-sacrificing, virtuous, and passive female, is no more true than the selfish, sexually irresponsible, and aggressive male. In fact, since 1848, many men have, for economic reasons, had to leave the family home to search for work, leaving the woman behind to head the household. Mexican American history is full of examples of women who have deviated from the submissive role. The ideals encompassed in the patriarchal tradition were often contradicted by the circumstances of day-to-day life. The types of jobs available to Mexican American men kept them away from their families for long periods of time working as teamsters, wagon drivers, miners, and farm workers. Over time, more and more women who were heads of households (even temporarily) were forced into the job market, further changing the expected roles of women (Griswold del Castillo, 1984).

Patriarchal values did not disappear under the impact of economic and political changes. Mexican American men continued to expect women to be submissive, but in this respect, they were no different from other men. Family life became a mixture of the old and new values regarding paternal authority and the proper role of women. Increasing poverty and economic insecurity intensified the pressures on Mexican American nuclear families and led to increased matriarchy and more working, single mothers. As a result, the ideology of patriarchy found less confirmation in everyday life. As a system of values and beliefs, however, the ideology of patriarchy continues to exist (Griswold del Castillo, 1985:39).

Sex and Age Grading

Complementing the concept of male dominance is the concept of sex and age subordination, which holds that females are subordinate to males and the young to the old. In this schema, females are viewed as submissive, naive, and somewhat childlike. Elders are viewed as wise, knowledgeable, and deserving of respect.

To some degree, these designations were derived from division of labor. Women as childbearers and childrearers did not perform the so-called more physically difficult jobs and therefore needed to be more protected by the man. If the women needed protection, the man took the role of overseeing the family. Nonetheless, the power of the male was more apparent than real. Respect for the breadwinner and protector rather than dominance was more key to the family. Roles within the familial network were stressed so that the constellation of the minisystem operated to the betterment of the individual and the familial system (Mirande, 1985).

In the isolated rural areas where many of the Mexican American families lived, the coordination of role expectations facilitated survival on the frontier. Each person behaviorally and institutionally carried out those roles that would ensure family survival.

The female child learned the roles and skills of wife and mother early, because she would carry them out both in the absence of the mother and as a future wife and mother. The eldest female child was expected to oversee the younger children so that the mother could carry out her tasks in the upkeep of the family. The eldest male, after puberty, had authority over the younger children as well as his elder sisters, because he would take on the responsibility for the family in his father's absence and for his own family as a future father.

The older family members, after they physically could no longer work, assumed the role of assuring family continuity. They were the religious teachers, family historians, nurturers of small children, and transmitters and guardians of accumulated wisdom. Their accumulated wisdom and numerous years of labor for the family were repaid by the respect given to them for their years (Becerra, 1983).

Thus, although particular role expectations are based on gender and age, and these dictate relationships and interactions, these roles were originally developed in response to a means for family maintenance and survival.

Familistic Orientation

The Mexican American family form was a result of a style that was brought from Mexico, modified in the United States, and adapted to fit a pattern of survival in the isolated, rural areas of the Southwest. Because of this history, there is an assumption that the Mexican family and the Mexican American family are isomorphic, allowing one to evaluate the Mexican American family from knowledge of the Mexican family, which is, in fact, fallacious (Montiel, 1970). However, the importance of the familial unit continues as a major characteristic among Mexican Americans to this day.

The familistic orientation continues because the family is viewed as a warm and nurturing institution for most Mexican Americans. It is a stable structure, in which the individual's place is clearly established and secure (Mirande, 1985). The family, as Murrillo (1971:99) indicates, offers "emotional security and sense of belonging to its members," and offers support throughout the individual's lifetime. The family is a major support system, a unit to which the individual may turn for help when in stress or in other types of need. Key to the family system is the value of sharing and cooperation.

Extended kinship ties assume a prominent place within the Mexican American culture. The extended family may include godparents and/or very close friends. Studies show that Mexican families tend to live near relatives and close friends, have frequent interaction with family members, and exchange a wide range of goods and services that include babysitting, temporary housing, personal advice, nursing during times of illness, and emotional support (Muller et al., 1985:67).

In sum, numerous studies (Ramirez 1980; Ramirez and Arce, 1981) demonstrate that familial solidarity among Mexican Americans is not just a stereotypical ideal, but a real phenomenon. Although expressed differently today because of changing cultural values and socioeconomic pressures, the pattern of a strong familistic orientation continues. It appears that Mexican Americans continue to have more cohesive family support systems than other groups (Griswold del Castillo, 1984).

THE CONTEMPORARY MEXICAN AMERICAN FAMILY

Marriage and Divorce

Marriage patterns among Mexican Americans are similar to those of other groups. Among those individuals ages 15 and over, 59.6 percent of Mexican Americans are married, compared with 59.2 percent for the total United States population. Interestingly, the percentage of never-married Mexican Americans is larger than that for persons of non-Hispanic origin (31 percent compared with 25.8 percent). This could be accounted for by the large proportion of younger persons in the Mexican American population (U.S. Bureau of Census, 1983).

Mexican Americans have a divorce rate of 5.4 percent, the lowest rate of all groups, compared with the United States population average of 7.2 percent (U. S. Bureau of Census, 1983).

With respect to family stability among Mexican American families, 75.7 percent are headed by married couples, compared with 52 percent for Puerto Rican families, 80.9 percent for non-Hispanic families, and 80.3 percent for the total population. Furthermore, 18.6 percent of Mexican American families are female-headed households, compared with a high of 44 percent for Puerto Rican families and a low of 16 percent for Cuban families. Interestingly, of male-headed (no wife present) families, Mexican males are more likely (5.8 percent) to take on the single parent role than any other group (compared with 3.6 percent for the entire population of the United States). Thus, Mexican families generally appear to be stable, two-parent families with a relatively lower rate of divorce than other ethnic families. The men seem to take over the household more often when there is no mother present.

Assimilation and Intermarriage

Assimilation is a multidimensional process in which ethnic groups begin to blend into a total community. One major dimension in this process is structural integration (Yinger, 1985). Considering the structural dimension, Yinger (1985:32) defines integration as the ''degree to which members of a group are distributed across the full range of associations, and regions of a society in a pattern similar to that of the population as a whole.'' According to this definition, Mexican Americans are only moderately assimilated. They are beginning to be a political strength, a voting bloc sought after, and a strong enough constituency to promote and elect their own politicians (e.g., nine of the 13 Hispanics in the House of Representatives are Mexican Americans). In this arena, it appears that this political force will continue to increase.

In other areas, however, considerable inequities prevail. Economically, Mexican American family income is still only 73 percent of the median income for all United States families, Mexican American unemployment rates are 60 percent higher than for non-Hispanic whites, and Mexican Americans continue to be concentrated in blue-collar jobs and underrepresented in white-collar jobs. Educationally, only approximately two out of five Mexican Americans complete high school. Although there has been some progress in these areas, as indicated by the higher proportion represented in colleges and universities, greater numbers in white-collar jobs, and increased incomes, the gains are only moderate.

Intermarriage is often considered one major measure of integration, reflective of the degree of other assimilative processes (Yinger, 1985). Intermarriage in this context usually means marriage between a Mexican American and an Anglo American. Murguia (1982) has compiled one of the most extensive studies on Mexican American intermarriage. His findings suggest that among the three most populous southwestern states (which have high concentrations of Mexican Americans), the intermarriage rates range from 9 to 27 percent in Texas, from 27 to 39 percent in New Mexico, and from 51 to 55 percent in California. Intermarriage rates are greatly influenced by the forces that influence integration. As educational levels increase, residential segregation decreases, and social-class mobility increases with decreases in discrimination, intermarriage should probably increase accordingly. Furthermore, as the Mexican American socioeconomic profile moves closer to the socioeconomic profile of the population as a whole, the assimilation process should move accordingly.

CHANGE AND ADAPTATION

Today's Mexican American family is a unique culture in American society in that it is fully characterized by neither the Mexican culture nor the American culture—it maintains elements of both. The Mexican family has been modified by the social and economic pressures of American life, yet the proximity of the Mexican border provides a continual influx of Mexican nationals that serve to maintain the familial and emotional ties to Mexico and to enhance the Mexican culture values.

One key element encouraging change has been the increased movement of families from rural to urban life. Today, 85 percent of all Mexican American families reside in the urban centers of the southwestern and midwestern United States. This factor has had a profound impact on the familial structure. Although a familial orientation remains, Mexican American families today are less likely to be composed of extended kin residing in the same household than to be residing nearby, which still facilitates more frequent interaction. The supportive family system is much more characterized by voluntary interaction than by the necessity for economic survival that characterized the rural environment of their forefathers.

Because of the various patterns of immigration, there exists much heterogeneity among the Mexican American population. Mexican American families span the continuum of acculturation and assimilation, depending on the conditions of their immigration, length of time in the United States, and their sense of relatedness to Mexico.

Since the advent of the Chicano movement, Mexican American families have increasingly become more involved in the political process. For example, [Mexican Americans in] Los Angeles, the home of the largest concentration of persons of Mexican origin outside of Mexico City, have shown their political strength by electing the first Mexican American state senator to the California legislature, the first Mexican American female assemblywoman, the first Mexican American city councilman in many years (California's Ed Roybal was the first), several other state assemblymen, and another member of the House of Representatives. This show of political strength is becoming more apparent throughout the nation.

Although there continues to be a disproportionate number of Mexican American families in the lower socioeconomic levels, there has been increasing social and economic mobility, as characterized by a growing number of Mexican American students in colleges and universities, an increase in Mexican Americans in professional and managerial positions, and a stronger Mexican voice in all aspects of society.

As has been true of all women in society, more Mexican American women are entering the labor force. There are greater numbers entering professions and participating more fully in various walks of life.

These factors come together to continually modify the Mexican American family by changing roles and expectations of all family members. As more opportunities emerge, social forces affect family life, and responses to an economic and political structure occur, the Mexican American family will continue to change and adapt to the forces around them. However, although the traditional Mexican American family has changed and will continue to change, there will continue to be a family form among Mexican Americans that fuses the culture of its roots and that of its American homeland.

REFERENCES

ACUNA, R. 1981. *Occupied America: A History of Chicanos* (2nd ed.). New York: Harper and Row.

BACA-ZINN, M. 1983. "Ongoing Questions in the Study of Chicano Families," in A. Valdez, A. Camarillo, and T. Almaguer (Eds.), *The State of Chicano Research on Family, Labor, and Migration.* Stanford, CA: Stanford Center for Chicano Research.

BEAN, F. D., R. M. CULLEN, E. H. STEPHEN, and C. G. SWICEGOOD. 1984. "Generational Differences in Fertility among Mexican Americans: Implications for Assessing the Effects of Immigration," *Social Science Quarterly,* 65(June):573–582.

BECERRA, R. M. 1983. "The Mexican American: Aging in a Changing Culture," in R. L. McNeeley and J. L. Colen (Eds.), *Aging in Minority Groups*. Beverly Hills: Sage Publications, pp. 108–118.

ESTRADA, L. F., F. C. GARCIA, R. G. MACIAS, and L. MALDONADO. 1981. "Chicanos in the United States: A History of Exploitation and Resistance," *Daedalus*, 110:103–131.

GREBLER, L., J. W. MOORE, and R. C. GUZMAN. 1970. *The Mexican American People*. New York: Free Press.

GRISWOLD DEL CASTILLO, R. 1984. *La Familia: Chicano Families in the Urban Southwest, 1848 to the Present*. Notre Dame: University of Notre Dame Press.

HOFFMAN, A. 1974. *Unwanted Mexican Americans in the Great Depression*. Tucson: University of Arizona Press.

JAFFE, A. J., R. M. CULLEN, and T. D. BOSWELL. 1980. *The Changing Demography of Spanish Americans*. New York: Academic Press.

MADSEN, W. 1973. *The Mexican-Americans of South Texas* (2nd ed.). New York: Holt, Rinehart, and Winston.

MARTINEZ, M. A. 1985. "Towards a Model of Socialization for Hispanic Identity: The Case of Mexican Americans," in P. San Juan Cafferty and W. C. McCready (Eds.), *Hispanics in the United States: A New Social Agenda*. New Brunswick, NJ: Transaction Books, pp. 63–85.

McWILLIAMS, C. 1968. *North From Mexico*. New York: Greenwood Press.

MIRANDE, A. 1985. *The Chicano Experience: An Alternative Perspective*. Notre Dame: University of Notre Dame Press.

MONTIEL, M. 1970. "The Social Science Myth of the Mexican-American Family," *El Grito: A Journal of Contemporary Mexican-American Thought*, 3(Summer):56–63.

MULLER, T., et al. 1985. *The Fourth Wave: California's Newest Immigrants*. Washington, DC: Urban Institute Press.

MURGUIA, E. 1982. *Chicano Intermarriage: A Theoretical and Empirical Study*. San Antonio, TX: Trinity University Press.

MURRILLO, N. 1971. "The Mexican-American Family," in N. N. Wagner and M. J. Haug (Eds.), *Chicanos: Social and Psychological Perspectives*. St. Louis: C. V. Mosby, pp. 97–108.

RAMIREZ, O. 1980. "Extended Family Support and Mental Health Status among Mexicans in Detroit," *La Red*, 28 (May).

RAMIREZ, O., and C. ARCE. 1981. "The Contemporary Chicano Family: An Empirically Based Review," in A. Barton, Jr. (Ed.), New York: Praeger.

SANCHEZ, P. 1974. "The Spanish Heritage Elderly," in E. P. Stanford (Ed.), San Diego: Campanile Press.

SARAGOZA, A. M. 1983. "The Conceptualization of the History of the Chicano Family," in A. Valdez, A. Camarillo, and T. Almaguer (Eds.), *The State of Chicano Research on Family, Labor, and Migration*. Stanford, CA: Stanford Center for Chicano Research.

U. S. Bureau of the Census. 1983. *General Social and Economic Characteristics: United States Summary*. Washington, DC: U. S. Government Printing Office, 1985.

YINGER, J. M. 1985. "Assimilation in the United States: The Mexican Americans," in W. Conner (Ed.), *Mexican Americans in Comparative Perspective*. Washington, DC: Urban Institute Press, pp. 30–55.

8

▼▼▼

Is Living Together Such a Good Idea?

▼▼▼▼▼

Sue Browder

ABSTRACT: Only a small proportion of cohabitants marry one another. Those who do have unhappier marriages and are more likely to divorce than those who do not live together before marriage. Living together means different things for men and women: usually commitment for women, but sex for men. Male cohabitants wield more power than their partners and are less considerate than husbands. Breaking up can be as devastating as divorce.

You've been seeing him for six months. You can't believe you've met someone you're so attracted to and so comfortable with. He's equally smitten with you. One evening, after a romantic dinner and wonderful lovemaking, he smiles boyishly and pops the question: "Why don't you move in with me? We're already practically living together."

Well, maybe it's not *the* question, but you could use a little more time to be sure you're ready for marriage. Or, if you think that he is the man you want to marry, its reassuring to see that he's getting ready and opening the door to greater intimacy.

Many of us in this situation would pack our bags and move in without batting an eye. In fact, millions of women already have: between 1970 and 1980, the number of live-in couples in the United States more than tripled to 1.6 million. And according to the 1988 U.S. Bureau of the Census figures, about 2.6 million unmarried American couples are currently cohabiting. As Allan Bloom, Ph.D., notes in *The Closing of the American Mind*, ''The kind of cohabitations that were dangerous in the twenties, and risqué or bohemian in the thirties and forties, have become as normal as membership in the Girl Scouts.''

How has this great social experiment turned out? Is living together really a good idea? Is it as emotionally fulfilling as most women hope it will be? Does living together usually lead to marriage? If it does, will your marriage be better because you practiced first?

Sociologists and psychologists have been studying couples who've lived together in order to find answers to these questions. The verdict: for many women, living together has turned out to be less than ideal.

IF YOU'RE INTERESTED IN MARRIAGE, KEEP IN MIND THAT MOST LIVE-INS NEVER MARRY

While living together can provide you with all the warmth and companionship you need for a short time, if you're interested in a long-term commitment, cohabitation is probably not a good bet. Of course, you might be living with your mate precisely because you *don't* want to marry him now; you're still not sure and need more time to weigh the relationship. Or you may not be interested in marriage at all—you may prefer staying officially single. But if you crave greater commitment and have settled for a live-in deal because that's all the man you love offers— if you harbor hopes that he'll suddenly walk in one night and pop *the* question—you would be wise to reexamine your decision to live together. Living with a marriage-shy lover is not the best way to coax him to the altar.

In 1977, sociologists at the University of Kentucky concluded that only about one in three cohabiting couples ties the knot. A 1985 Columbia University study suggests your odds of marrying a live-in lover in the eighties may be even slimmer: only 26 percent of the women surveyed—and a scant 19 percent of the men—married the person with whom they were cohabiting.

IF YOU DO MARRY, DIVORCE MAY BE THE PRICE OF HAVING LIVED TOGETHER FIRST

According to a surprising new study, couples who live together before marrying have nearly an 80 percent *higher* divorce rate than those who do not. The National Bureau of Economic Research in Cambridge, Massachusetts, surveyed nearly 5,000 women in Sweden (Sweden was chosen because it tends to prefigure American social trends by 10 to 15 years). Neil Bennett, Ph.D., who teaches sociology at Yale University and is one of three authors of the bureau's report, says, "It appears that people who cohabit premaritally are less committed to the institution [of marriage] and are more inclined to divorce than people who don't live together [first]."

This research calls into question the popular argument that cohabiting can help a couple test the marital waters, iron out their differences, and make their future marriage more blissful.

A 1983 study by the National Council on Family Relations of 309 recently married couples, finds that couples who live together before marriage are less happy in their marriages. Women who have lived with their mates before marriage are especially unhappy with the quality of communication with their spouses after the wedding. Of course, you would think that couples who've lived together would have had more time to learn how to talk to each other. Why then are these women so disappointed?

One possible explanation is that live-in lovers' communication skills were lacking during courtship; that's why they hesitated more about their decision to marry. Another, as Bennett points out, is that people who cohabit tend not to believe in living "happily ever after"; they don't give marriage the gung-ho commitment it needs to grow strong.

A third possibility may be that, because they're just living together, live-ins are often afraid to complain about each other's annoying faults (after all, if you gripe too much about his working late, he may just walk out the door). As a result, they set up faulty communication patterns, which they find tough to break after saying "I do."

MEN COHABIT MOSTLY FOR SEX, WOMEN COHABIT FOR COMMITMENT

In 1973, when 139 Northeastern University students were asked why they were living with a lover, the number one reason women cited was that they wanted to get married. One young woman surveyed said, "It's a first step toward marriage, and if I don't grab him, somebody else will." For cohabiting males, the number one motive was sex. Male responses to the question included, "It's less of a hassle to get laid," and "Sex—when you want it, where you want it."

Certainly, not all men enter live-in arrangements just to have sex. And simply because a man lists sex as his *top* reason for living with a woman doesn't preclude that his other reasons could be love and friendship. Besides, many women say that they want to live with their lovers because *they* want sexual adventure or more frequent lovemaking. But the bottom line is this: before agreeing to duplicate apartment keys, you should have a heart-to-heart talk to make sure you both have the same goals in mind concerning what your relationship should be now and where you want it to go.

LIVE-IN ARRANGEMENTS FAVOR MEN

Only you can know exactly how the balance of power feels in your relationship, but among live-in couples it generally tips in the man's favor. A 1985 Columbia University study suggests that the man is more often the first one to get antsy and want to break up in a live-in relationship. What's more, sociologist Paul Newcomb, Ph.D., in a 1979 article in the *Journal of Marriage and Family*, cited a 1973 study that found that live-in males sleep around more than their partners do. Thus, if these figures hold true today, live-in males, as a group, put their partners at higher risk for AIDS, herpes, and other sexually transmitted diseases than their partners put them.

Emotionally, of course, the one who is least committed to making the relationship work holds the most power. The more involved partner may become insecure and feel continually forced to compromise and cater to the mate's needs in order to make sure the partner will stick around. Among the women who responded to the 1986 *New Woman* Sex Survey, more cohabiting women felt insecure about their love relationships than did other women. Interestingly, the uncertainty a woman feels about her mate's feelings for her may even *cause* her to move in with him. Lara, a New York City public relations employee currently living with a work-addicted real estate developer, says, ''Eric's so busy with his career that I *have* to live with him if I want to see him.'' (Eric told me he also felt it was the only way they would see each other. But it never occurred to him to say he would have to cut back on his work load if he wanted to see more of Lara.)

LIVE-IN MALES ARE LESS CONSIDERATE
THAN HUSBANDS ARE

Live-in love is often romantically portrayed as a beautiful experience between two free and independent people who feel secure enough to grant each other unjealous love without succumbing to the neurotic need to possess each other. That may be how living together should be, but that's not usually how it works out.

Like some marriages, some live-in arrangements are rife with hostility. The 1986 *New Woman* Sex Survey found that a whopping 40 percent of cohabiting women had endured a kind of sex they didn't want or enjoy. Not even as many divorced and separated women (35 percent) felt they had been as mistreated or intimidated sexually.

We tend to picture live-ins as lovers who are in the early stages of courtship and are infatuated with each other. But why would a love-struck man be more likely to force unwanted sex on his mate than would a (possibly) sexually bored husband? Josh, 32, a happily married Los Angeles screenwriter who cohabited with another woman for three years, offers this crass but candid explanation: "The main reason you start living with a woman is for sexual adventure. You figure, 'Well, if we have oral sex and she doesn't like it, tough. She'll get over it. And if she doesn't, I'll just leave.' When you're married, you hope you'll be with this woman years from now, so you're more considerate of her feelings. You don't want to screw up the relationship."

If you're living with a man (or even if you're not), you may find Josh's attitude appalling. Can he be typical? "He very well *could* be," says Pasadena, California, sociologist Jack Balswick, Ph.D., "The main problem is, as Josh says, there is no *commitment* in a live-in relationship. It's all for immediate payoff, immediate gratification. So the man figures, 'If I don't get what I want now, then I'll just get out of the relationship.' A falsehood many people who buy in to temporary relationships believe is the notion that they can build a meaningful relationship *without* full commitment."

LIVE-IN BREAKUPS CAN BE AS DEVASTATING AS DIVORCES

When you move in with a man, you may reassure yourself that, if the relationship fails, you can just shake hands and part as friends, thereby avoiding the messy histrionics and legal hassles of divorce. While some couples achieve this ideal, others find the human heart—and the legal system—less predictable.

When Kathy, a fashion photographer, was told by her live-in lover Jim to move out after they'd been together five years, she says that she was so devastated she temporarily "lost it" and went into a frenzy, slashing all Jim's suits to ribbons and throwing the shreds out the window. There is no way, she says, that "being a live-in lover rather than a wife made our breakup more bearable to me."

Joleen, a 21-year-old freelance photographer, cried nightly for three months after her live-in lover left. "Divorce is simpler," she says. "It's a legally certified tragedy that causes sympathetic friends, co-workers, and relatives to rally around you. When you break up with a man you 'simply live with,' your parents may actually be relieved. And if you mope too much around friends, you're seen as overreacting."

Frederick G. Humphrey, Ed.D., past president of the American Association for Marriage and Family Therapy, says, "Unmarried couples may cherish the pseudointellectual belief that they are free to leave. But when they split up, the emotional pain and trauma is often virtually identical to that experienced by married couples getting divorced."

Nor is living together any guarantee that you'll avoid legal or financial hassles when you break up. Donald Schiller, president of Schiller, DuCanto & Fleck, a law firm in Chicago specializing in divorce, notes that since many states still have laws declaring unmarried cohabitation illegal, your rights when you live with a man are iffy at best. Let's say, for example, that you and your lover buy a condo together. Both your names are on the mortgage, so you figure your property is safe. But if your lover dies with no will, you may suddenly find half of *your* condo now belongs to *his* mother.

There is no way you can avoid the emotional pain of a breakup, and you can only avoid legal hassles in a live-in relationship by keeping all your possessions separate or by seeing a lawyer and drawing up a cohabitation agreement before you move in. . . .

9

Same-Sex Relationships

Joseph Harry

ABSTRACT: There is little evidence to support the "butch-femme" hypothesis (that of a masculine, dominant partner and a feminine, submissive partner). Because the incomes of persons in same-sex relationships tend to be similar and there usually is no "houseperson," same-sex relationships usually are more egalitarian than heterosexual ones. If there is an age gap, older partners usually dominate the relationship. In contrast to lesbians, male homosexuals are more likely to visit gay bars and tend to be less sexually exclusive. Many male and female homosexuals have children from heterosexual marriages. No courts have recognized homosexual marriages.

GAY COUPLES

The Butch/Femme Hypothesis

Tripp (1975:152) has observed that persons unfamiliar with gay male relationships often tend to heterosexualize them by viewing one partner as masculine (i.e., doing the masculine household chores, being dominant in sexual activities and decision making, and financially supporting the partner) and the other as engaging in complementary feminine activities. However, the one thing that the literature most clearly shows about intimate gay relationships is that they infrequently approximate this version of husband and wife roles. Bell and Weinberg (1978:323–325) found specialization in sex-typed tasks to occur in fewer than 10 percent of their 686 interviews of gay male respondents in San Francisco. Westwood (1960:119), in a study of 127 English homosexuals, reported little evidence that masculine and feminine gay men were mutually attracted to each other and found that the large majority preferred masculine partners. Similarly, Saghir and Robins (1873:74–75), in a study of 89 homosexual males, found that few gay couples pattern their relationships according to a traditional husband/wife model. Although a few gays may organize their relationships in a "butch/femme" manner, the literature strongly indicates that gay relationships are more likely to be patterned after a "best friends/roommates" model than after a heterosexual sex role model. . . .

. . . Further evidence that the butch/femme hypothesis may hold only for a small minority of gay relationships is reflected in findings from Harry's (1982a:213) study of 1556 gay men in Chicago who responded by mailback questionnaire. Gay men who rated their hypothetical preferred erotic partners as "very masculine" were about 40 percent more likely to agree that "it is very important for me to look masculine." Thus masculinity when valued in the self appears to be also valued in erotic partners. Since masculinity of appearance is positively evaluated by many gay men, it is suggested that a butch/butch pattern may be the more dominant pattern.

Equality in Relationships

Peplau and her associates (Peplau, 1981; Peplau and Cochran, 1981) have compared the values and relationship expectations of 128 gay men, 127 lesbians, and 130 unmarried heterosexual men and women. Of their gay male respondents 92 percent said that both partners to a relationship should "have exactly equal say," although only 37 percent of the currently coupled reported that their relationship was exactly equal. Peplau (1981) found that, regardless of sexual orientation, women were somewhat more likely than men to value equality, emotional expressiveness, and similarity of attitudes between partners. . . .

Peplau and Cochran (1981) also indicate that a large majority of persons value equality in relationships regardless of sex or sexual orientation, although in practice there often may be departures from equality. A common reason for departure from equality in relationships is differential access to resources outside of the relationship (Blood and Wolfe, 1960:29–30). This also seems to hold in gay relationships, since it has been found that income differences between gay partners are associated with self-reported differences in decision making (Harry and DeVall, 1978b: 99). However, in gay and lesbian relationships such incomes differences seem to be considerably less than in the case of heterosexual couples. Housepersons in gay relationships are quite rare, and most couples are dual-worker, dual-career units. Harry (1979; 1982b) found that only 1 percent of his Detroit gay respondents and none of his Chicago respondents were economically supported by another man. Since the analogue of a housewife is unusual among gay couples, and typically both parties work, the economic basis for inequality in relationships is virtually absent. Income differentials in gay or lesbian relationships are also reduced due to the fact that both parties are of the same sex and hence likely to be subject to the same degree of sex discrimination in jobs and income. In contrast, working wives in heterosexual couples are likely to earn considerably less than their husbands and hence are more likely to be somewhat economically dependent on them. These two factors—the general absence of housepersons and the approximate similarity of incomes—suggest that gay relationships often may be more egalitarian than heterosexual ones.

A major source of potential inequality in relationships is age difference between partners. Blood (1972:526) has reported that older partners in heterosexual relationships tend to be dominant in decision making, although the age difference must be fairly large, e.g., ten or more years, to have an effect. Harry (1982a:209) also reports that older partners in both past and present gay relationships say they were more likely to make the decisions in the relationship. He summarizes, (1982a:209): "If a gay relationship is inegalitarian in decision making, it is likely to be one between age-different persons, although age difference predicts less well to decision making.". . .

Sexual Exclusivity

The literature clearly shows that gay male relationships are considerably less sexually exclusive then heterosexual ones or lesbian relationships. Peplau (1981) found that 46 percent of her coupled gay males had been sexually exclusive during the last six months compared to 87 percent of the lesbian counterparts. Schafer (1977) reported similar findings when comparing West German gay and lesbian couples. Harry and De-Vall (1978b:88) found that a quarter of their coupled gay males had been exclusive during the last year, a finding that supports figures reported by Saghir and Robins (1973:57). Sexual exclusivity has been found to be negatively related to the duration of a relationship. Harry and DeVall (1978b:92) found that 46 percent of their coupled gay men in relationships of less than three years duration had been exclusive during the last year versus 16 percent of those in longer-term relationships. The Chicago data replicate this finding and show complete exclusivity to have been the case for 39 percent of persons in relationships of one to less than five year's duration, and 9 percent of those in relationships of five or more years duration. Apparently, exclusivity is more common during the honeymoon stage of gay relationships.

Hoffman (1968:154–177) has interpreted the common nonexclusivity of gay relationships as a major problem, often leading to jealousy and termination of relationships. However, Warren (1974:72–76) has suggested that exclusivity may be nonnormative and problematic principally in the heterosexual community. She has suggested that, although it may be characteristic of the honeymoon stage of gay relationships, nonexclusivity often becomes accepted as the most common expectation for "mature" relationships and represents an adjustment to reality. Harry and DeVall (1978b:91–92) found support for Warren's hypothesis in that in longer-term relationships there was greater agreement between partners on *either* fidelity or infidelity, while disagreement decreased with length of relationships. Couples in relationships of three or more years duration were divided into three roughly equal groups; those who were agreed on exclusiveness, those who agreed on nonexclusiveness, and those who disagreed. It would seem that since gay couple relationships lack the conventional cultural guidelines that govern heterosexual relationships, they develop in more diverse directions and exclusivity may be either approved or disapproved. Since Peplau (1981) found that sexually exclusive coupled gay men did not differ from nonexclusives on measures of relationship intimacy or satisfaction, both of these adaptations seem workable. . . .

GAY FATHERS

Because a percentage of gays have been heterosexually married, many gay men are also fathers. The percentages of gays who have ever married, as reported in the literature, are: 25 percent (Dank, 1972); 18 percent (Saghir and Robins, 1973:11); 17 percent (Weinberg and Williams, 1974:128); 20 percent (Harry and DeVall's Detroit data); 19 percent (Bell and Weinberg, 1978:374); 16 percent (Harry, 1982a:42); 14 percent (Robinson et al., 1982). Thus it is safe to say that about 20 percent of gay men have been heterosexually married. Of these marriages, about half (52 percent) resulted in children (Bell and Weinberg, 1978:391); a similar percentage (56 percent) was found for lesbians who have been married (Bell and Weinberg, 1978:391). In a few cases children have been adopted by gay or lesbian couples through marginally legitimate channels (Miller, 1979).

The reasons that gay men have married include a lack of awareness of their own homosexuality, a belief that their homosexuality was a peripheral part of their lives, or an assumption that marriage would help them overcome their homosexuality (Dank, 1972). In a third of the cases it appears that the spouse was aware of the gay man's homosexuality before the marriage but believed that the marriage would eliminate the husband's homosexuality (Bell and Weinberg, 1978:386). The marriages, which lasted three or four years (Bell and Weinberg, 1978:388), were typically full of problems, especially sexual problems. In over half of the cases the men fantasized about other men during sexual relations with the wife (Bell and Weinberg, 1978:384). The majority of gay men who either have been or currently are married tend to give negative descriptions of these marriages (Ross, 1971). Reporting on thirteen currently married gay men, Ross (1971) found many of these marriages filled with resentment and bitterness over the infrequency of sexual relations, the nonexclusivity of the husband due to his search for male sexual partners, and the feeling that the husband had deceived the wife at time of marriage.

During the course of the marriage, as the husband's need for sexual fulfillment through sex with other men became more conscious and pressing, most resorted for a period to furtive sexual encounters in a variety of places. Many such encounters are described in Humphreys' classic study, *Tearoom Trade* (1970). Of the men who had had sex in restrooms, 54 percent were heterosexually married (Humphreys, 1970:112). This period of their lives was one in which the husbands engaged in quick sex at the sleazy periphery of the gay world, hated themselves for doing it, and lied to their wives about where they had been and what they had been doing. Men in occupations permitting greater freedom in their movements and control over their time commitments appear to have managed this phase with less worry and more grace. Movement from this lifestyle to an acceptance of one's own homosexuality, becoming socially active in the gay world, and, usually, getting a divorce, was motivated principally by coming to see gay men and homosexuality in a more positive light and falling in love with another man (Miller, 1978).

All of the forty gay fathers interviewed by Miller (1979) feared disclosure of their homosexuality to their children and most feared disclosure to their wives. When they did disclose to their wives, the wives, after a period of initial shock, sometimes agreed to arrangements that permitted the marriage to continue while allowing the husband to pursue homosexual activities outside of the marriage (Bozett, 1981). These included allowing a "night out with the boys," understanding that the husband would only have sex with other men when in other cities, and an occasional *menage à trois* (Bozett, 1981; Ross, 1971). While Bozett (1981), reporting on eighteen gay fathers, has described these arrangements as mutually consensual "permission giving," they also appear to have been last-minute attempts to keep a marriage that was near collapse together. Virtually all of the gay fathers studied stated that the principal reason they remained in their marriages as long as they did was because they loved their children (Miller, 1979; Bozett, 1980).

Those gay fathers who disclosed to their children, either before or after a divorce, reported that, after the initial surprise, the children generally responded quite acceptingly. Although the numbers involved in the various studies are small, there is the suggestion that acceptance by female children is more forthcoming than by male children. Both Miller (1978) and Bozett (1980) report that relationships with children tended to improve after disclosure. "Children who showed the greatest acceptance were those who, prior to full disclosure, were gradually introduced by their parents to homosexuality through meeting gay family friends, reading about it, and discussing the topic informally with parents" (Miller, 1979). . . .

LESBIAN COUPLES

Lesbian partners are somewhat more likely to live together than are gay male partners (Bell and Weinberg, 1978: 319; Schafer, 1977; Cotton, 1975) and to value the importance of living together (Bell and Weinberg, 1978:322). Approximately three-quarters of lesbian couples live together compared with somewhat more than half of all gay male couples. Lesbian couples are also more likely to be sexually exclusive than are gay couples (Peplau et al., 1978; Peplau, 1981; Cotton, 1975). Exclusivity seems to be characteristic of 75 to 85 percent of the cases. The differences in degree of exclusivity between lesbians and gay men have been attributed by Simon and Gagnon to their respective gender role socialization and are said to parallel the differences in exclusivity among heterosexual males and females (Kinsey et al., 1948: 585; Hunt, 1974: 257–258; Kinsey and Gebhard, 1953: 435–438). Males are socialized to engage in sexual behaviors both with and without affection while women are more expected to combine the two. As a result, when two men enter a partnership, nonexclusiveness can be expected, while when two women enter a relationship, exclusiveness could be expected. Aside from exclusivity, men and women do not seem to differ in the values, e.g., romanticism, that they bring to a relationship (Peplau, 1981). Laner (1977) reported great similarity among student samples of gay men, lesbians, heterosexual men, and heterosexual women in what they expect in a partner. The great majority (89 to 92 percent) of all four groups wanted a permanent partner with little difference among groups. It thus seems that the principal sex difference is not in relationship values but in how sexuality is combined with those values.

The butch/femme hypothesis has also been applied to lesbian couples (Jensen, 1974). While a small minority of lesbian couples do play gender roles, role playing is relatively rare (Tanner, 1978:99–101; Ponse, 1978:114–116; Wolf, 1979:49–43). The division of household tasks is typically done by turns or by talent and both parties to the relationship are usually employed. Both Ponse and Wolf report that role playing seems to have been more common in the 1950s and 1960s and is somewhat more common among older lesbian couples. This seems supported by the one study that found gender-typed division of household tasks in the large majority of the seventeen couples studied (Jensen, 1974). It should be noted that these seventeen couples were interviewed in the mid-1960s and the majority were Mormons living in Salt Lake City and Denver, highly gender-conservative environments.

Role playing as a relationship style has become quite unpopular in lesbian circles, probably due to the fact that a large percentage of lesbian women became affiliated with the women's movement of the late 1960s and the 1970s (Wolf, 1979:85). One goal of the lesbian/feminist movement has been to create identities as women rather than in relationship to men. Toward this end, one fairly large segment of the lesbian world advocates and practices separatism from men. Such separatism sometimes extends to advocating that lesbian mothers should give up their male children to the father, although the voluntary practice of this is rare (Wolf, 1979:156–158). The rise of the women's movement and of feminist theory has had the effect of creating a quite varied spectrum of lesbian circles, ranging from traditional and often closeted role players on the "right" to lesbian/feminists in the "center" to lesbian/feminist/ separatists on the "left." At the left may be found communal households containing one to three pairs of lovers plus a few single women (Wolf, 1979:98–101). Household boundaries tend to coincide with political boundaries and having the proper political credentials may be a condition for admission to a household.

While gay couples tend to interact within such gay institutions as the gay bar, the gay church, and gay organizations, lesbian couples tend to live within social networks of lesbians, although there is some overlap between the gay world and that of lesbians (Ponse, 1978:89–90; Tanner, 1978:66–70). The lesbian bar plays a much smaller role in the world of lesbians than does the gay bar in the gay world (Tanner, 1978:67–68). The principal forms of socializing in the lesbian world include inviting other lesbian couples to one's home, attendance at lesbian coffee houses and theater, and participation in women's organizations. The lesbian bar seems somewhat more significant in the lives of unattached women (Tanner, 1978:67; Cotton, 1975), although some lesbians disparage lesbian bars as places for socializing because of the "role-playing, fighting, or drug use" that may occur there (Chafetz et al., 1974). Since roughly three quarters of lesbians are currently coupled compared to 40 to 50 percent of gay men (Bell and Weinberg, 1978: 318; Shafer, 1977; Harry and DeVall, 1978b: 85; Peplau and Amaro, 1982), the social world of lesbians tends to be a world of couples whereas the world of gay men is one of singles *and* couples.

Lesbians tend to meet their partners through lesbian friendship networks (Tanner, 1978: 66–71). There subsequently follows a period of courtship lasting from one to nine months. In contrast, the courtship period for gay men is considerably truncated and may be preceded by sexual relations. Thus among lesbians a sexual relationship usually arises out of a developing affectional relationship while among gay men affection may develop out of a sexual relationship. . . .

LESBIAN MOTHERS

Lesbian households are considerably more likely to contain children than are gay households. This is largely due to the fact that a higher percentage of lesbians have been heterosexually married: approximately one-fifth of gay men have been married versus one-third of lesbians (Bell and Weinberg, 1978: 374; Saghir and Robins, 1973: 255; Cotton, 1975; Schafer, 1977). Also contributing to the greater presence of children in lesbian households is the tradition of the courts awarding custody to the mother *as long as the mother's homosexuality is not an issue in the divorce* (Maddox, 1982). A further reason for the greater presence of children is that lesbians tend to "come out" a few years later than gay men. While gay men usually come out during late adolescence at approximately 18 or 19 years of age (Dank, 1971; Harry and DeVall, 1978b: 65; Saghir and Robins, 1973: 67), lesbians do so during their early 20s (Schafer, 1977; Saghir and Robins, 1973: 232). One effect of this is that lesbians are at risk of marriage for a longer time than are gay men, particularly at the age when a large percentage of their heterosexual peers are getting married. . . .

Like gay fathers, lesbian mothers often advise their children to be guarded in providing information about the home life to neighbors and school teachers (Wolf, 1979:153). It appears that in those cases in which a gay father has disclosed his gayness to a child a common tactic has been for the father to suggest that the child practice discretion (Bozett, 1980). For example, the father's live-in lover is referred to as an "uncle" in the presence of other children. The evidence suggests that, while the lives of the children of gay and lesbian parents are not problem free, harrassment is not common and seems typically manageable.

Because of the court's strong propensity not to accord custody of children, and especially male children, to lesbian mothers, these mothers are often fearful of losing their children and attempt to conceal their homosexuality from exhusbands, grandparents, welfare workers, landlords, neighbors, and school personnel (Pagelow, 1980). In a study of 20 lesbian and 23 nonlesbian single mothers, Pagelow (1980) reported that lesbian mothers may be somewhat more likely to live in houses rather than apartments since the former housing permits greater privacy. They were also more likely to be self-employed, thus permitting a greater measure of both privacy and freedom. . . .

CONCLUSION

. . . Although there have been a number of attempts by gay and lesbian couples to obtain legal marriages, no court to date has recognized such unions (Rivera, 1979). The acquisition of legal marriages by gays and lesbians would bring with it the advantages of symbolic equality, spouse social security benefits, spouse health insurance benefits, lower car insurance, family membership in various organizations, and inheritance rights. In the case in which there are children in the lesbian or gay household, the lack of these benefits also accrues to these children. However, there are also disadvantages to the acquisition of legal marital status. The termination of the relationship would obligate the parties to undergo the bother and expense of legal and financial disentanglements. A legal marital status would also grant to the state a right to regulate relationships that are essentially private, and a major thrust of the gay/lesbian movement has been to get the state out of the bedroom. . . .

REFERENCES

BELL, A. and M. WEINBERG (1978) *Homosexualities*. New York: Simon & Schuster.

BLOOD, R. (1972) *The Family*. New York: Macmillan.

BLOOD, R., and D. WOLFE (1960) *Husbands and Wives*. New York: Macmillan.

BOZETT, F. (1981) "Gay fathers: evolution of the gay-father identity." American Journal of Orthopsychiatry 51: 552–559.

——(1980) "Gay fathers: how and why they disclose their homosexuality to their children." Family Relations 29: 173–179.

CHAFETZ, J., P. SAMPSON, P. BECK, and J. WEST (1974) "A study of homosexual women." Social Work 19: 714–723.

COTTON, W. (1975) "Social and sexual relationships of lesbians." Journal of Sex Research 11: 139–148.

——(1972) "Role playing substitutions among male homosexuals." Journal of Sex Research 8: 310–323.

DANK, B. (1972) "Why homosexuals marry women." Medical Aspects of Human Sexuality 6: 14–23.

——(1971) "Coming out in the gay world." Psychiatry 34: 180–197.

HARRY, J. (1982a) Gay Children Grown Up: Gender Culture and Gender Deviance. New York: Praeger.

——(1982b) "Decision making and age differences among gay couples." Journal of Homosexuality.

——(1979) "The marital liaisons of gay men." Family Coordinator 28: 622–629.

——(1974) "Urbanization and the gay life." Journal of Sex Research 10: 238–247.

HARRY, J., and W. DEVALL (1978a) "Age and sexual culture among homosexually oriented males." Archives of Sexual Behavior 3: 199–209.

——(1978b) The Social Organization of Gay Males. New York: Praeger.

HOFFMAN, M. (1968) The Gay World. New York: Bantam.

HUMPHREYS, L. (1970) Tearoom Trade. Chicago: Aldine.

HUNT, M. (1974) Sexual Behavior in the 1970s. New York: Dell.

JENSEN, M. (1974) "Sexual differentiation in female quasi-marital unions." Journal of Marriage and the Family 36: 360–367.

KINSEY, A., W. POMEROY, and C. MARTIN (1948) Sexual Behavior in the Human male. Philadelphia: W.B. Saunders.

KINSEY, A. W., and P. GEBHARD (1953) Sexual Behavior in the Human Female. Philadelphia: W. B. Saunders.

LANER, M. (1977) "Permanent partner priorities: gay and straight." Journal of Homosexuality 3: 21–39.

MADDOX, B. (1982) "Homosexual parents." Psychology Trade 16: 62–69.

MILLER, B. (1979) "Unpromised paternity: the life-styles of gay fathers," pp. 240–252 in M. Levine (Ed.) Gay Men. New York: Harper & Row.

——(1978) "Adult sexual resocialization." Alternative Lifestyles 1: 207–232.

PAGELOW, M. (1980) "Heterosexual and lesbian single mothers." Journal of Homosexuality 5: 189–204.

PEPLAU, L. A. (1981) "What homosexuals want in relationships." Psychology Today 15: 28–38.

PEPLAU, L. A., and H. AMARO (1982) "Understanding lesbian relationships," in J. Weinrich and W. Paul (eds.) Homosexuality: Social, Psychological, and Biological Issues. Beverly Hills, CA: Sage.

PEPLAU, L. A. and S. COCHRAN (1981) "Value orientations in the intimate relationships of gay men." Journal of Homosexuality 6: 1–19.

PEPLAU, L. A., K. ROOK, and C. PADESKY (1978) "Loving women: attachment and autonomy in lesbian relationships." Journal of Social Issues 34: 7–27.

PONSE, B. (1978) Identities in the Lesbian World. Westport, CT: Greenwood.

RIVERA, R. (1979) "Our straight-laced judges: the legal position of homosexual persons in the United States." Hastings Law Journal 30: 799–955.

ROBINSON, B., P. SKEEN, C. HOBSON, and M. HERRMAN (1982) "Gay men's and women's perceptions of early family life and their relationships with parents." Family Relations 31: 79-83.

Ross, L. (1971) "Mode of adjustment of married homosexuals." Social Problems 18: 385-393.

Saghir, M. and E. Robins (1973) *Male and Female Homosexuality*. Baltimore: Williams & Wilkins.

Schafer, S. (1977) "Sociosexual behavior in male and female homosexuals." Archives of Sexual Behavior 6: 355-364.

Tanner, D. (1978) The Lesbian Couple. Lexington, MA: D. C. Heath.

Tripp, C. A. (1975) The Homosexual Matrix. New York: Signet.

Voeller, B. and J. Walters (1978) "Gay Fathers." Family Coordinator 27: 149-157.

Warren, C. (1974) Identity and Community in the Gay World. New York: John Wiley.

Weinberg, M. and C. Williams (1974) Male Homosexuals. New York: Viking.

Westwood, G. (1960) A Minority. London: Longmans.

Wolf, D. (1979) The Lesbian Community. Berkeley: University of California Press.

10

▼▼▼▼

The Diverse World
of Single Adults

▼▼▼▼

Peter J. Stein

ABSTRACT: In recent years, the proportion of Americans in their twenties who have never married has increased dramatically. Most young single persons have not given up on marriage, just postponed it. Moving in disproportionate numbers to large urban areas, they seek meaningful work, living arrangements, and friends. To them, age thirty appears to mark a transition point, a time for reevaluating their life-styles and life goals. Single women who are successful in attaining higher education and income are not as likely to marry as are women with less education and lower incomes. Single women are better adjusted than are single men. All singles experience pushes and pulls toward marriage, but for a variety of reasons some remain single, even in their elderly years.

Until recently, it was assumed that all single persons wanted to marry, were waiting for the "right" person to come along, were relatively unhappy, and were alike. Recent research by social scientists indicates that there is a great diversity among single adults, that there are several distinct single life-styles, and that single people face different

The author is grateful to James Henslin for his suggestions in the revision of this chapter.

life chances, depending on their education, income, occupation, health, race and ethnicity, age, residence, and parental status.

Some single persons are older and others are younger; some have already been married and others never will marry; some would prefer marriage if only the "right" person came along, while others enjoy their single state; some are well educated, earn good incomes, and enjoy comfortable lives, while others struggle economically, support aging parents, and have a limited social life; some live alone and others live with roommates or parents; most are heterosexual in their preferences, but others prefer same-sex partners; and some are parents, while others prefer to remain childless (Adams, 1976; Austrom, 1984; Barkas, 1980; Cargan and Melko, 1982; Hass, 1983; Peterson, 1982; Shostak, 1987; Simenauer and Carroll, 1982; Staples, 1981; Stein, 1981).

Yet all single people, like all married people, face certain key issues of adulthood that require decisions and actions—education; work and career; living arrangements; friendships, intimacy, and sexuality; emotional and physical health; relations with parents; aging; and whether to become parents themselves. But the social context within which they deal with these issues is different from the situation of married people. Single people often have no significant other with whom to make such decisions. Because they have to rely more on themselves in dealing with issues of adulthood, some develop great resourcefulness and personal strength while others are subject to stresses and strains that are unrelieved by social supports.

The normative strength of marriage in the United States is reflected in the fact that single people are seen as immature adults. That is, an adult is someone who is married; to remain single, therefore, is to be less than an adult. This cultural stereotype of singles is supported and spread by the major social institutions and the mass media. It shapes how married people respond to single people and influences how single people see each other and how they interpret their own experiences. This article seeks to present a more accurate portrait of single adults.

BRIEF DEMOGRAPHIC OVERVIEW

More than 38 million Americans over age 18 are unmarried. That number represents 25 percent of all men and 19 percent of all women. The largest proportion of single persons are the never-married. The increasing tendency for young adults to delay marriage is reflected in the median age at first marriage, which increased from 22.5 years in 1970 to 25.3 years in 1987 for men and from 20.6 years in 1970 to 23.6 years in 1987 for women. Since 1970, the proportion of women and men in their late twenties and early thirties who have never married has more than doubled.

Although a majority of Americans expect to marry and have lasting marriages, future projections suggest that the proportion of Americans who never will marry will increase from 5 percent to 8 or even 10 percent (Thornton and Freedman, 1983). As more and more women and men postpone marriage and experience single life, some find it sufficiently satisfying and rewarding to remain single. Others who remain single, particularly women, find the number of eligible partners depleted, and thus remain single not so much by choice as by circumstance. Both groups, joined by those who are single again after divorce or the death of a spouse, swell the ranks of single adults.

THE LIFE CYCLE AND LIFE SPIRAL
OF SINGLE ADULTS

Erik Erikson developed an influential model of life stages and ego development, termed the "life cycle." He extended the stages of personality growth and change to cover the entire span of one's life (1959). By proposing that the life course is composed of a series of challenges that require reorganization of the ego, he opened to our consideration the possibility of continual personal change and growth. Erikson (1964) described eight stages, each of which involves a person's ability to adapt to life changes. Although his model is grounded in psychology, his major transition points coincide with major changes in the person's social environment and the sequence of roles one is culturally expected to perform. Those eight stages are: from infant to child, from child to student, from student to worker, from single to married, from nonparent to parent, and from full involvement with work and the community to retirement. These changes provide the opportunity to reorganize the self because in each stage the person interacts with different role partners who present new expectations.

Levinson (1978, 1986) proposed that we compare the various stages of adult life to the seasons of a year. He suggested that development occurs in predictable segments that follow each other in chronological order.

Erikson's and Levinson's models of life passing through orderly stages assume that development is hierarchical, sequenced in time, and cumulative. The implications of these models of life stages are that (1) every "normal" adult must pass through the stages, (2) each stage has distinctive tasks that must be accomplished during that stage, (3) an individual is more or less successful in negotiating these crises, (4) successful resolution of a previous stage is necessary for the successful resolution of subsequent stages, and (5) each stage is tied to chronological age (Brim, 1977).

Etzkowitz and Stein (1978) suggest that life has many seasons and that a spiral more accurately represents life's configuration. Development is not necessarily related to chronological age, and themes of development may be resolved at one age only to need reevaluation later on. Developmental stages may overlap; one may never resolve certain issues. Life is an ongoing process with themes and patterns which repeat. It is less like the seasons of a single year than like a panorama of seasons.

For adults whose lives follow traditional patterns of development, the life cycle, with its stages and seasons, may accurately represent their lives. Less traditional lives may be more accurately described by the spiral model. There may be changes over the span of one's life: the spiral may be more accurate at one period, the cycle more accurate at another. This paper will consider first the cycle and then the spiral models of single adulthood.

THE YOUNG NEVER-MARRIEDS

We can identify various stages of the adult life cycle. The years from the early twenties to about twenty-eight are the period of "getting into the adult world," when the focus of one's life shifts from "family of origin to a new home base in an effort to form an adult life of one's own" (Levinson et al., 1974, p. 246). It is a time of exploratory searching and provisional choices and a time for assessing the correctness of initial choices and increasing the commitment to choices.

The sixteen-year period from 1970 to 1986 brought a dramatic increase in the proportion of men and women who remain single (Table 10.1). Over this period, the percentage of both women and men aged 25 to 34 who remained single more than *doubled*. The increase has been the greatest among women between the ages of 25 and 29 and men between 30 and 34.

The greatest increase in the number of singles has been among women ages 20 to 34 and among men ages 25 to 39. As indicated in Table 10.1, there were 2.8 times as many single women between the ages of 25 and 29 in 1988 as in 1970 and 2.6 times as many single women between the ages of 30 and 34. There were 2.3 times as many single men in the 25-to-29 age group in 1988 as in 1970 and 2.7 times as many in the 30-to-34 age group. Overall there has been an increase in the proportion of both women and men who remain single for every age group except for men age 45 to 54. This dramatic increase in the number and proportion of single adults has many social ramifications.

Table 10.1 **Women and Men Remaining Single in the United States, 1970–88**

	1970 (percentage)	1980 (percentage)	1988 (percentage)	Change from 1970 to 1988 (percentage)
Women				
20–24	35.8	50.2	61.1	71
25–29	10.5	20.9	29.5	181
30–34	6.2	9.5	16.1	160
35–39	5.4	6.2	9.0	67
40–44	4.9	4.8	6.2	27
45–54	4.9	4.7	5.1	4
Men				
20–24	54.7	68.8	77.7	42
25–29	19.1	33.1	43.3	127
30–34	9.4	15.9	25.0	166
35–39	7.2	7.8	14.0	94
40–44	6.3	7.1	7.5	19
45–54	7.5	6.1	5.6	− .25

SOURCE: *Statistical Abstract*, 1990: Table 52.

With the increase of young adults who remain single has come the tendency to establish their own households. However, the patterns of the 1970s changed in the 1980s. Although the number of persons under age 35 who were living alone more than trebled between 1970 and 1980, increasing from 1.4 to 4.8 million, recently there has been a decline among the youngest singles who live alone. While in 1980 54 percent of men and 43 percent of women between the ages of 18 and 24 were living with their parents, by 1988 the percentages increased to 61 for men and 48 for women. However, in the 25-to-34 age group, 73 percent of the men and 84 percent of the women maintained or shared their own households, though even in this age group more lived with their parents than was the case in 1970. Overall, men are more likely to live with their parents than are women.

Background factors that increase the tendency to remain with parents include the postponement of first marriage, divorces, greater emphasis on college and postcollege education, employment problems, and the higher costs of housing. Single persons who do establish their own households are more likely to live in urban areas and big cities. They are concerned with finding meaningful employment, satisfying living arrangements, congenial friends, and an entertaining social life. Large cities provide the occupational and social structures to satisfy these concerns. Adjustment to the world of work and patterns of forming friendships provide crucial connections and supportive social structures.

THE AGE-THIRTY TRANSITION

The men whom Levinson interviewed experienced considerable turmoil and confusion and struggled with societal pressures, their families, and themselves during their late twenties and early thirties. For others, these years involved a reevaluation of goals and values and an intensification of efforts to achieve such goals. Similarly, many men and women who remain single into their thirties also report that the mid-to-late twenties and early thirties was a period of great difficulty (Stein 1981). There is about a 44 percent decrease in the proportion of women and men who (from their late twenties) remain single into their early thirties and about another 44 percent decline among those who stay single into their late thirties. These men and women experience intense societal and parental pressures to marry and at that time of their lives, some work hard to find prospective spouses. Yet, many derive little intrinsic satisfaction from the search for a mate and some report negative experiences and a decline in self-esteem.

A major source of difficulty during the age-thirty transition is work related. This transitional period marks a deeper commitment to an occupation for some, but for others it involves a rejection of earlier occupational choices as too constricting and not meeting initial expectations of satisfaction. More women than men lack clear occupational goals on graduation from college and view their occupations as temporary, unsatisfactory, and noninvolving. Similarly, living arrangements are seen as temporary, often with a same-sex roommate, to be changed with marriage. Schwartz (1982) found that "as these singles approached 30, many became critical of those patterns and began to reevaluate their lives . . . [recognizing] the possibility that they might never marry and that they themselves had the responsibility for designing meaningful lives." The single people Schwartz studied reexamined earlier occupational decisions, weighed the possibilities of starting or returning to graduate or professional schools, reevaluated living situations and improved living places, developed new interests, started new activities, and expanded and reinforced circles of friends.

THE MIDDLE YEARS: HIS AND HER SINGLE LIFE

The number of persons who have never married continues to decline in the middle-years of life. In 1988, only about 6 percent of the women and about 8 percent of the men aged 40-to-44 had not married. (In the 45-to-54 age group, about 6 percent of the men and 5 percent of the women had never married.)

What are the experiences of these single men and women? In a summary of many studies of the state of marriage, Bernard (1982) concluded that although "his" marriage is physically, socially, and psychologically good, "her" marriage more likely involves frustration, dissatisfaction, and other problems. The situation with respect to singlehood is quite the opposite—long-term singlehood tends to be a more positive experience for women and a more negative experience for men. This situation is particularly true for older never-married singles.

Bernard reported that women who completed college and postgraduate education, who are in one of the professions, and earn high incomes are more likely to remain single than are women with less education and lower incomes. Doudna and McBride (1981) asked, "Where are the men for the women on top?" and found that the men are either already married, playing the field, or intimidated by successful women. Studies have found that many of the women who remain single are superior to single men in education, occupation, and income. Moreover, the demographics of big cities indicate a dramatic shortage of single men.

In contrast to single women, older never-married men are more likely to show mental health problems, including depression, neurotic symptoms, and fears. In summarizing a number of studies, Bernard (1982) reported that among the unmarried, men have mental health problems more often than women. It is not known whether the experience of single life is more stressful for men than for women or whether the men who remain single have more problems to begin with. Bernard suggested, however, that single women tend to represent the "top" of the marriage market while single men are more likely to be at the "bottom" of the market—not a good fit for either group. Columnist Ellen Goodman asked, "Is it success that makes a 35-to-50 year old woman unmarriage material, or is staying single what makes her successful?"

THE PUSHES AND PULLS OF SINGLE LIFE

My study of voluntary single people revealed that complex factors enter into the decision to remain single, to live with a lover, to marry, or to separate. These factors may be considered a series of pushes and pulls and are so presented in Table 10.2.

Pushes represent negative factors in a situation; pulls represent attractions to a potential situation. The strength or weakness with which a person experiences these pushes and pulls depends on a number of variables, including one's life course, sexual identification, extent of in-

Table 10.2 **Pushes and Pulls toward Marriage and Singlehood**

Marriage	
Pushes *(Negatives in Present Situations)*	*Pulls* *(Attractions in Potential Situations)*
Pressure from parents	Approval of parents
Desire to leave home	Desire for children and own family
Fear of independence	Example of peers
Loneliness and isolation	Romanticization of marriage
No knowledge or perception of alternatives	Physical attraction
	Love, emotional attachment
Cultural and social discrimination against singles	Security, social status, social prestige
	Legitimation of sexual experiences
	Socialization
	Job availability, wage structure, and promotions
	Social policies favoring the married and the responses of social institutions

Singlehood	
Pushes *(To Leave Permanent Relationships)*	*Pulls* *(To Remain Single or Return to Singlehood)*
Lack of friends, isolation, loneliness	Career opportunities and development
Restricted availability of new experiences	Availability of sexual experiences
Suffocating one-to-one relationship, feeling trapped	Exciting life style, variety of experiences, freedom to change
Obstacles to self-development	Psychological and social autonomy, self-sufficiency
Boredom, unhappiness, and anger	Support structures: sustaining friendships, women's and men's groups, political groups, therapeutic groups, collegial groups
Poor communication with mate	
Sexual frustration	

Source: Stein, 1976.

volvement with parents and family, availability of friends and peers, and perception of choice. For some, dating patterns, pressures from parents, and acceptance of the cultural script led them to marry early. At a later time in their lives, these same people found greater pulls toward satisfying careers, work colleagues, and developing friendships, all of which seemed more possible outside marriage.

Others never married and found the single state satisfying. These men and women offered many positive reasons, or pulls, for remaining single. They spoke of freedom, enjoyment, career opportunities, developing friendships, economic self-sufficiency, enjoyable sexual experiences, and personal development. They experienced the factors Adams (1976) cited as making singleness a viable life-style: economic independence, social and psychological autonomy, and a clear intent to remain single by preference.

Without marriage and a spouse, the single men and women I interviewed spoke of the importance of substitute networks of human relationships that met their needs for intimacy, sharing, and continuity. For all the adults, a major source of intimacy was friends, both men and women (Stein, 1986). Friends and support networks, such as women's and men's groups, political groups, social groups, therapy groups, and organizations formed around specialized interests, helped validate the single life-style and the decision not to marry. Although these groups were not restricted to singles, they were cited as helpful in legitimating new roles and patterns and providing support during critical life events.

With respect to work, the adult life course of these men and women involved experimenting with job and career possibilities; exploring vocational and avocational activities between the completion of school and their full-time entry into the labor force; and a returning, for some, to school in their middle and late twenties.

For some of the women and men in the sample, the rejection of earlier, more tentative occupational choices did not crystallize until their late twenties and early or middle thirties. About 40 percent postponed "entry into the adult world" because they were unable to break economic and psychological ties with their family of origin until their early thirties; their lives fit a pattern typified by experimenting with different life-styles, searching for career orientations, and wanting to keep their options open.

For these men and women, issues of intimacy and work do not surface "on time" but appear earlier or later than suggested by Levinson's model. Moreover, even when issues are resolved during the expected age period, they may reappear at later times and in different settings.

CONCLUSION

We have looked at the diverse world of single adults, compared the life cycle and life spiral models of single adulthood, and focused in greater depth on the major groups of singles including the young never-marrieds, the age-thirty transition, the middle years, and the complex factors influencing singles' decisions to marry or remain single. The interviews suggest that single life can contribute to a developed personality. Single people are highly adaptive. Without clear role models or the support of society as a whole, they shape their lives by taking risks and forging into uncharted territory. Without the support of a marital partner and with various degrees of social and cultural support, adults who choose singlehood can be understood as pioneers of an emergent cultural life-style.

REFERENCES

ADAMS, M. *Single Blessedness.* New York: Basic Books, 1976

AUSTROM, D. *The Consequences of Being Single.* New York: Longman, 1984.

BARKAS, J. L. *Single in America.* New York: Atheneum, 1980.

BERNARD, J. *The Future of Marriage.* New Haven, Conn.: Yale University Press. 1982.

BRIM, O., JR. "Remarks on Life Span Development." Paper presented at the American Institute on Research, 1977. Mimeographed.

CARGAN, L., and M. MELKO. *Singles: Myths and Realities.* Beverly Hills, Calif.: Sage Publications, 1982.

DOUDNA, C., and F. McBRIDE. "Where Are the Men for the Women at the Top?" In P. J. Stein, Ed., *Single Life,* pp. 21–33. New York: St. Martin's Press, 1981.

ERIKSON, E. H. *Identity and the Life Cycle.* New York: International Universities Press, 1959.

ERIKSON, E. H. *Childhood and Society,* rev. ed. New York: W. W. Norton & Co., 1964.

ETZKOWITZ, H., and P. STEIN. "The Life Spiral: Human Needs and Adult Roles." *Alternative Lifestyles.* 1: 4, 1978, pp. 434–446.

HASS, A. *Love, Sex and the Single Man.* New York: Franklin Watts, 1983.

LEVINSON, D. "A Conception of Adult Development." *American Psychologist,* 41:1, 1986, pp. 3–13.

LEVINSON, D., et al. *Seasons of a Man's Life.* New York: Alfred A. Knopf, 1978.

LEVINSON, D., et al. "The Psychosocial Development of Men in Early Adulthood and the Mid-Life Transition" in D. F. Ricks, A. Thomas, and M. Roff, Eds., *Life History Research in Psychopathology.* Minneapolis: University of Minnesota Press, 1974.

PETERSON, N. L. *The Ever Single Woman.* New York: Quill, 1982.

SCHWARTZ, M. A. "The Career Strategies of the Never Married." Paper presented at the American Sociological Association meetings, 1982.

SHOSTAK, A. "Singlehood: The Lives of Never-Married Employed Americans." In M. B. Sussman and S. K. Steinmetz, Eds., *Handbook of Marriage and the Family.* New York: Plenum Publishing Corp., 1987.

SIMENAUER, J., and D. CARROLL. *Singles: The New Americans.* New York: Simon & Shuster, 1982.

STAPLES, R. *The World of Black Singles: Changing Patterns of Male/Female Relations.* Westport, Conn.: Greenwood Press, 1981.

STEIN, P. J. *Single Life: Unmarried Adults in Social Context.* New York: St. Martin's Press, 1981.

STEIN, P. J. "Men and Their Friendships" in R. Lewis and R. Salt, Eds., *Men in Families,* pp. 261–270. Beverly Hills, Calif.: Sage Publications, 1986.

THORNTON, A., and D. FREEDMAN. *The Changing American Family* (Population Reference Bureau) 38: 4, October 1983.

U.S. BUREAU OF THE CENSUS. "Marital Status and Living Arrangements: March 1986." *Current Population Reports*, Series P-20, No. 418. Washington, D.C.: U.S. Government Printing Office, 1987.

11

Permanent Postponement

Jean E. Veevers

ABSTRACT: By Interviewing married couples who were childless by choice, Veevers identified four stages in becoming permanently childless: (1) postponement for a definite (specific) time; (2) postponement for an indefinite time; (3) deliberating the pros and cons; and (4) accepting permanent childlessness. Three factors can accelerate commitment to permanent childlessness: pregnancy scares, aging and the possibility of adoption, and ambivalence toward achievement.

More than two-thirds of the couples interviewed remained childless as a result of a series of decisions to postpone having children until some future time, a time which never came. Rather than explicitly rejecting parenthood prior to marriage, they repeatedly deferred procreation until a more convenient time. These temporary postponements provided time during which the evaluations of parenthood were reassessed relative to other goals and possibilities. At the time of their marriages, most couples who became postponers had devoted little serious thought to the question of having children, and had no strong feelings either for

104

or against parenthood. Typically, they simply made the conventional assumption that, like everybody else, they would probably have one or two children eventually.

The transition from wanting to not wanting children typically evolves through four separate stages, which will be described in some detail. Although it is convenient to discuss each stage separately, it must be realized that in reality the stages are not discrete and discontinuous categories, but represent overlapping foci of the marriage at various times. Movement from one stage to the next is facilitated, or in some instances retarded, by various career contingencies which will be outlined and illustrated.

Postponement for a Definite Time

The first stage in the postponement route to childlessness involves deferring childbearing for a definite period of time. At this stage, the voluntarily childless are difficult to distinguish from the conventional and conforming couples who will eventually become parents. In most groups, it is not necessarily desirable for the bride to conceive during her honeymoon. It is considered understandable that, before starting a family, a couple might want to achieve certain goals, such as graduating from school, traveling, buying a house, saving a nest egg, or simply getting adjusted to one another. The reasons for waiting vary, but there remains a clear commitment to have children as soon as conditions are right. For example, one wife had formulated very definite fertility plans very early in her marriage. It was her intention to work until her husband completed graduate school. His graduation was scheduled for a specific date, to be followed, if all went well, by a satisfactory job offer. When these two conditions had been met, her intentions were to conceive as soon as possible, to quit her job sometime in the middle of her pregnancy, and thereafter to devote herself full time to raising children.

During Stage One, childless couples practice birth control conscientiously and continuously. If the couple manage to postpone pregnancy deliberately for even a few months, they have established a necessary but not a sufficient condition to voluntary childlessness, namely the habit of effective birth control within marriage. Once this has occurred, habit and inertia tend to make them continue in the same behavior. The couple must now decide whether or not they wish to stop using birth control so as to have a child. Although for the first few months of marriage the postponement of pregnancy is widely accepted, even at this stage the permanently childless are somewhat different from their preparental counterparts. Many conventional couples, even those who approve of birth control and have access to it, do not seriously try to control their own fertility until they have had at least one child.

Postponement for an Indefinite Time

The second stage of the postponement route involves a shift from postponement for a definite period of time to an indefinite one. The couple often cannot recall exactly when they shifted into this second stage. They continue to remain committed to being parents, but become increasingly vague about when the blessed event is going to take place. It may be when they can "afford it" or when "things are going better" or when they "feel more ready." For example, one immigrant couple had recently experienced a rapid series of changes in country of residence, in cities within Canada, and in occupations, some of which were terminated involuntarily and some of which were terminated because they were unsatisfactory. They had very limited savings and felt that, without any family in Canada, there was no one on whom they could rely in an emergency. After nearly five years of marriage, they still wanted to remain childless until they felt financially and occupationally secure.

A more conventional couple postponed parenthood until they were "ready" and had "had some fun" in their adult, married lifestyle. The husband summed up their situation during this stage as follows:

> We were very happy and satisfied the way things were— our jobs, friends, new house, vacation trips—and we didn't want to change it just then. Our ambivalence about kids began to grow during this time, but we still assumed that someday we'd be parents just like everybody else.

Some couples postpone parenthood until they feel that they can give children all the things they think children should have. Under these circumstances, Stage Two of the postponement process closely parallels the reticence felt by many parents who do not want children too soon. A common concern is not having children until one is living in a "large enough" space, which might be defined as a two-bedroom apartment or as a three-bedroom house. Often, couples are concerned with being able to spend enough time with their children, a condition which may depend upon the woman's readiness to quit work, and/or the couple's readiness to manage on one salary. These kinds of reasons are generally relatively acceptable, in that they are attempts to maximize the advantages available to children, rather than to minimize the disadvantages that accrue to parents. A common consequence of such reasoning, however, is that the standards to be achieved before one is truly "ready" to have a child can escalate indefinitely, resulting in a series of successive "temporary" postponements.

Deliberating the Pros and Cons of Parenthood

Stage Three involves a qualitative change in the thinking of childless couples, in that for the first time there is an open acknowledgement of the possibility that, in the end, the couple may remain permanently childless. In this phase of the career, the only definite decision is to postpone deciding until some vague and unspecified time in the future. For example, a nurse reported a typical progression from Stage One to Stage Three:

> When we were first married, we had long discussions about children. He wanted four and I only wanted two at the most, but it was no problem because it was still at the intellectual level because we were still discussing whether we wanted children and if we did, how many we would have. But we didn't want them then, we wanted to enjoy each other. Later on, we were trying to save to buy a house, the down payment anyway, and we did, not this one but another we have sold since. Then my husband decided to go back to school, and he talked me into going back, too. So that meant no kids for several years. We had been married I guess about three years when we really started to think that maybe we wouldn't have kids at all. We still haven't definitely decided never-never; it is a very hard decision to make, really. But a pregnancy now would just disrupt our whole way of life. Maybe later. He is thinking of a vasectomy, has been for a year or so. Maybe later; or maybe we might adopt or—I just don't know yet.

. . . [H]usbands are often less articulate about their rationale for avoiding parenthood because they have tended to think about it considerably less than have their wives. Since wives most often raise the issue of the advantages of a childfree lifestyle, the husband often ends up in the role of the devil's advocate, articulating the advantages of children in order to encourage his mate to consider both sides of the issue. One husband reported:

> It really became silly for a while there. She would give the routine that kids would tie us down, that they would be a big pain in the ass, etc. Then I chime in with all the ''howevers'' and ''buts,'' supporting the notion of being parents and the joys of watching our own kid grow. I wasn't all that [crazy] about the idea, but wanted to be sure she was seeing both sides of the issue. . . .

. . . Most couples who follow the normal moral career of parenthood cope with these questions [of the disadvantages of having children], in part by keeping them below the level of awareness. They do not have to decide to become parents because they have never questioned the inevitability of parenthood, or if they have questioned it, they have remained committed to the idealized and romanticized notions of what it will be like. A significant step in the moral career of childlessness is simply questioning the inevitability of parenthood and considering negative as well as positive aspects.

Acceptance of Permanent Childlessness

The fourth stage involves the definite conclusion that childlessness is a permanent rather than a transitory state. For most couples, there is never a direct decision made to avoid having children. Rather, after a number of years of postponing pregnancy until some future date, they become aware that an implicit decision has been made to forego parenthood. One wife reported a typical sequence:

> Our decision not to have children was a very gradual thing. When we first got married, we decided we were going to do a little bit of traveling before we had a family. We went to England first of all for a holiday. We decided we definitely wanted to do that before we settled down. And then when we came back from England, we decided we couldn't stand not having a car any longer; we wanted to be able to go out for drives and so on, so we figured we could wait another year and buy a car instead. And it kept getting postponed and the more we postponed, the less I really wanted to have children. Actually, I don't know that I ever really did want to have children; it was sort of a matter of this is what you do. I was never really wild about the idea. It was always going to be two at the most, and then it went down to one. We decided we would have one and if it was a girl, we would adopt a boy, and if it was a boy, we would adopt a girl. And then after that it went down to none and maybe adopt one. Or maybe just adopt one and we went to see the agency, like I told you. And then we just dropped it altogether.

The process is one of recognizing an event which has already occurred, rather than of posing a question and then searching or negotiating for an answer. At first, it was "obvious" that "of course" the couple would eventually have children; later it became equally "obvious" that "of course" they would not.

> Every couple of years we'd discuss whether to have a child or not, not because we really wanted children, but because the time seemed to be right. And then we'd look at the bank balance and put if off for another two years. After five years, we sort of stopped discussing it. We just decided let's let it ride, we're really not that keen on it anymore. If he really wanted to have a family, I'd go along with it wholeheartedly. Of the two of us, I'm the wishy-washy one. I would do it just because it wouldn't destroy any preconceived ideas I had about being married; you know, you get married and have children—that was already set. This is more of an unfamiliar terrain at this point, to say you are not going to. He was the one who made the decision. I never really disputed the preconceived notion that married people have children. I never even thought about it much one way or the other.

Two years later, at the age of thirty-six, the husband decided to get a vasectomy and the wife agreed it was a good decision. . . .

COMMITMENT TO CHILDLESSNESS

The degree of certainty attached to the acceptance of permanent childlessness varied among the respondents interviewed. All of the persons who were early articulators, and who had demanded a childlessness clause in their marriage contracts, felt that not wanting children was an immutable characteristic of themselves. Together with some persons who were involved in the postponement process, they felt that "becoming a parent is not the right thing for me." Such persons are "independents" (Cooper et al., 1978) in that they make their decision to parent or not independently of the attitudes of their spouse. In discussing the extent to which childless persons were committed to childlessness, and the extent to which that commitment did or did not relate to their current marriage, respondents were asked: "What would you do if you (or if your wife) got pregnant?" Most immediately protested that such a thing could not happen accidentally, but were then persuaded to consider the consequences if, hypothetically, the "impossible" did occur. As an illustration of the extent to which some persons are committed to childlessness as an immutable personal attribute, rather than merely as a decision reflecting their current circumstances, one young husband replied concisely:

> Well, in that case, my wife could have three choices. One, she could have an abortion. I hope she would do that, but I guess I couldn't make her do it. If not, two, she could have the baby and place it for adoption. Or three, she could have a divorce. . . .

In contrast to persons who characterize themselves as irrevocably childless by choice, more than half of our respondents related their decision not to have children to their present marriages. They acknowledged that, if they had happened to marry someone else, they might well have decided to have a child. Moreover, they often speculate that, if in the future they were to be married to someone who did want children, they might very well be persuaded to change their minds. Such persons feel that not wanting children reflects not their own nature *per se* so much as the situation in which they find themselves. After a period of negotiation, they and their mates came to agree that "becoming parents is not the right thing for us" or more likely "becoming parents is not the right thing for us right now." This does not imply a lack of consensus or a lack of satisfaction, but it does imply an openness to the potential for sometime living differently. One husband, who resisted the idea of sterilization, explained:

> Right now, I'm totally happy. We have a good marriage, we don't need kids. But who knows? Suppose we got a divorce. Suppose she got killed? I'd remarry, I know I would, and if my next wife wanted a baby, I would

not automatically be opposed to it. That would be a different marriage, I'd be a different kind of husband married to a different kind of wife. If she wanted to be a mother, I'd be a father, I suppose. But now, here, for us? No way!

MOVING FROM STAGE TO STAGE: SOME FACTORS ACCELERATING COMMITMENT

Couples who know before they marry that they will never have children are not troubled by decisions, other than by choosing how they will avoid pregnancy. However, couples who remain childless through continued postponement, and who in doing so progress through four rather distinct phases, tend to have considerable variation in the ease and speed with which they move from one step to the next. Some circumstances tend to push couples rapidly on to the next stage; others tend to provide ample opportunity for continued delay.

Pregnancy Scares

One traumatic event which may serve to accelerate a couple's movement from one state of postponement to the next is a pregnancy scare. When the wife's menstrual period is late, or even worse, when a period is missed entirely, the possibility of pregnancy may serve to crystallize hitherto vague and unrecognized feelings about parenthood. Irregular periods, or even amenorrhea, may have many causes other than conception, but for sexually active woman pregnancy is the explanation which comes most readily to mind. The abstract idea of a child is quite different in its psychological impact from the concrete idea of a child's forming and growing day by day. For example, in response to the question of when she first knew she did not want children, one woman replied very emphatically and precisely: "The first moment I knew, and I was absolutely certain about it, was the first moment I knew I was pregnant." In fact, although she "knew" she was pregnant, her menstrual period was simply delayed and started spontaneously ten days later. During that time, she had been involved in an intense search for a competent abortionist, a search which she described as discouraging and humiliating. She was greatly relieved to discover that she was not pregnant after all, but by that time, the decision had been crystallized, and she and her husband were weighing the relative advantages of vasectomy versus tubal ligation.

The husband of another couple in a similar position stated:

When we thought she was pregnant we found ourselves desperately try-ing to look on the positive side of it—that it will be fun being parents—but we weren't fooling ourselves, though we *thought* we were being nice guys and fooling each other. When her period came, we knew we'd made our decision never to risk pregnancy again.

Aging and the Decline of Fecundity: The Adoption Alternative

One of the problems of opting for the postponement model is the biological fact that childbirth cannot be postponed indefinitely. . . . Three interrelated problems are involved. In the first place, fecundity is known to decline with advancing age. Although it is theoretically possi-ble for a woman to bear a child until her menopause is completed, in actuality her fecundity tends to decline with each year, as to a lesser extent does her husband's. Couples who could have had a child in their twenties but who chose to wait until their thirties may find that their fecundity has declined, or has been lost, during the intervening decade and that conception is no longer possible. In the second place, many childless couples perceive that once the wife is in her late thirties or early forties, the chances of having a defective child are much increased and that it therefore would be dangerous to do so at that late date.* Third, it must be realized that a larger part of the definition of how old is "too old" to have children is social, rather than biological in origin (Rindfuss and Bumpass, 1976). When the mother's age is too advanced, it is believed that her tolerance of young children is reduced and that the family situation would not be "good" for the child. Moreover, since couples tend to associate with persons their own age, a late birth would place them in the unusual situation of coping with toddlers while their friends were coping with teenagers.

As a consequence of these three factors, as the age of the wife ap-proaches thirty, the decision to postpone deciding whether or not to have a child becomes less comfortable. In order to avoid the stress of having to make an imminent decision, one strategy is to redefine the maximum age at which reproduction would still be safe and desirable. Interestingly, this age seems to recede in time, depending upon the age of the woman, with a tendency to leave a margin of about two years. Thus, women of twenty-eight report they feel they must make a deci-

---

*The increased medical risks associated with late pregnancies are more important relative to other women at younger ages than they are in absolute terms. For example, Down's syndrome is a congenital malformation which clearly increases in risk with advancing maternal age, especially after the age of forty. However, among births to women aged forty to forty-four, the incidence of Down's syndrome is less than one per cent (Nortman, 1974:7). In other words, a childless woman of this age has a better than 99 per cent chance of not having a Mongolian idiot. "Clearly, in the absence of a personal history to the contrary, older women run only a small risk of producing a congenitally malformed child, al-though their risk is much higher than that faced by younger women" (Nortman, 1974:7).

sion by the time they are thirty; women of thirty-four say they must do so by thirty-six; and women of thirty-eight vow to make up their minds by forty. Although such stalling defers immediate pressure, it is inevitably a temporary solution. When a forced choice appears imminent, a more practical solution is to include the vague possibility of adoption as a satisfactory "out" should one be needed. One wife makes a typical comment when she trails off her discussion of children by concluding: "If we've left having children too late, we might adopt one." An ex-nurse of twenty-nine, who believes that if you are going to have children, you should have them before you are thirty, suggests that: "If at fifty we decide we did miss something after all, we will adopt an Indian kid, or maybe a homeless teenager."

When we examined our childless couples closely on this subject of future adoption, however, it became clear that, in most instances, talk about adoption is unlikely to be a precursor of actually becoming adoptive parents. Although many of the childless couples referred at least once to the possibility of someday adopting a child, their discussions of this eventuality were exceedingly vague. They had apparently given no thought to the kind of child they might like to adopt, not even in terms of such obviously important traits as sex, age, or race. They had no information regarding the conditions under which adoption would be possible or what steps it would entail. It is noteworthy that it apparently never occurred to any of the couples who discussed adoption that, if they wanted to adopt, a suitable child might not be available. Nor did it occur to them that, if a child were available, he or she might not be placed with them. Although adoption is seldom a pragmatic option for voluntarily childless couples, it does have considerable symbolic importance in that it allows postponers to remain indefinitely at the third stage of debating endlessly the pros and cons of parenthood.

Ambivalence Toward Achievement

Couples in the first stage of postponement, who hold out other goals as "excuses" for not starting a family, may find themselves feeling quite ambivalent when they do finally achieve their goals. Such achievement is intrinsically desirable and presumably satisfying, but at the same time, it removes one of the most readily acceptable reasons for avoiding parenthood. Thus, one can be happy about graduating from college or about getting a good job, and at the same time be apprehensive about the attendant responsibilities that may come with it. For example, one husband reflected:

I remember we were out celebrating the fact that we would both be finished with school and would graduate from college a full semester sooner, but when it dawned on us that now we didn't have any excuses left to postpone a family, we got a sinking feeling inside. Neither of us wanted that now. We found ourselves agreeing that it wouldn't be a good idea to have kids yet. We still acted the same way, but after that, it was a lot harder to explain. It was like our days of grace had run out, like on a mortgage or something.

Similarly, if couples have postponed having children until they are "out of debt," or until they can "afford to buy a house," their achievement of these goals necessitates a reevaluation of their parenthood aspirations. Thus, removing the once-perceived obstacles to "being ready" for parenthood accelerates the couples more quickly toward a resolution of their dilemma and their inevitable entrance into either parenthood or a childfree life-style. . . .

REFERENCES

COOPER, PAMELA E., BARBARA CUMBER, and ROBIN HARTNER, 1978. "Decision-making patterns and postdecision adjustment of childfree husbands and wives," *Alternative Lifestyles*, 1 (February):71–94.

NORTMAN, DOROTHY, 1974, "Parental age as a factor in pregnancy outcome and child development," *Reports on Population/Family Planning*, 16 (August):1–51.

RINDFUSS, RONALD R., and LARRY L. BUMPASS, 1976. "How old is too old? Age and the sociology of fertility," *Family Planning Perspectives*, 8 (September/October):226–230.

PART III

▼▼▼▼▼▼▼▼▼▼▼▼▼▼▼▼▼▼▼▼▼▼▼▼▼▼▼

Love, Romance, and Intimacy

*A*s was stressed in Part I, our birth marks our entrance into a pre-formed world, one whose set of ideas and way of life shape what we become. During its unique history, each society has met many challenges. Those ways of coping with problems that have worked in the past then become part of the taken-for-granted assumptions about the way the world is and ought to be.

From childhood on, our socialization centers on learning the basic assumptions of our culture. As infants, we are introduced to these assumptions through the acquisition of language and through seeing people's behavior—from the primary role models of our parents and siblings to the roles portrayed on television. As we grow older, our socialization continues, and each new experience is a refinement of our earlier learning. Eventually, we become more or less full-fledged members of society; that is, we come to the point that we have adopted the basic assumptions of our culture and are able to pass on significant aspects of it to others.

If our socialization is successful, most of us will think in roughly the same terms when it comes to such broad aspects of social life as war and peace and what is desirable and undesirable in life; to more specific aspects of group life, such as money, cars, taxes, education, and work; and even to such a highly focused matter as "good" and "bad" words, and when they should and should not be used.

By no means, however, does this statement imply that we all think alike or that we are robots. Our culture provides for individual choice of behavior and of ideas. Although few seem to grasp the irony, that provision is one of our culture's basic assumptions! Although we take great pride in our intense individuality, as we grow up in American society, we inevitably learn to think "like an American." Among the most easily recognizable features of our American-like thinking are the high value we place on individuality, personal freedom, and equality, and the power of what we, as Americans, refer to as the "almighty dollar."

From birth, we are immersed in these American orientations and the related behaviors that such views of life indicate—for each orientation contains the assumption that certain behaviors match the orientation and are therefore right, while others veer away from it and thus are wrong. We are constantly influenced by our cultural assumptions of the way the world ought to be, including the ways in which we conceptualize and use space, time, money, work, property, leisure, and sex. Essential to these orientations are ideas of what is considered proper among people because of how the culture designates their relationships to one another. Owing to their position in life, certain relationships are deemed proper and others wrong. This assumption includes not only our ideas about what is right for employers and employees, teachers and students, customers and clerks, but what is especially significant for our purposes here, friends with friends, wives with husbands, and parents with children.

Most of our culture's basic ideas are learned at such a young age and are so consistently taught and reinforced that we seldom question them. Moreover, they become so fundamental to our orientation to social life that they also are invisible to us. We usually simply assume that this is what people are naturally like and how everyone ought to experience life.

As is true of people in all societies, it is impossible to escape the influences of our culture. Those socially inherited boundaries of thought shape our fundamental expectations of life--not only how we ought to act toward others, but also our underlying assumptions about who we are and, therefore, how others ought to regard and act toward us. We might say that cultural assumptions of relationships become rooted in our social being, that they become an essential part of the influences that make us social creatures.

When it comes to marriage, from childhood we learn that the romantic ideal is its proper basis. We are taught to expect to "fall" in love at some point in our lives. We learn that love is the inevitable and natural outcome of dating and the appropriate basis for marrying and having children.

But what love is remains undefined and somewhat confusing. Beyond being one of the most talked-about and longed-for human experiences in the Western world, what is love? We all speak and act as though we know exactly what love is, but when we attempt to pin it down, it turns out to be elusive—almost impossible to put into words. Although we all "know" what love is, our "knowing" falls flat when it comes to defining the specifics of love. It is bound to be that way, for we are dealing with a basic and encompassing human emotion. Any definition of love must fall short of the deep experiences that it attempts to describe.

Why are sociologists and other social scientists interested in the topic of love? The primary reason is that to understand societies in which love is a significant experience is to comprehend better how men and women relate to one another. Let us see how a topic that first appears to belong exclusively to the realm of poets and lyricists has deep sociological significance.

When we look at the situation cross-culturally, we find that "love" is not simply a natural, biological experience of some sort, for expectations concerning love vary tremendously from one society to another. Ours is at one extreme: our assumption that love should be the *essential* ingredient that underlies every marriage; our failure to comprehend why people would marry if they were not "in love;" and our suspicions that if people marry for something other than love, they somehow border on the immoral—if they have not already crossed that boundary.

In contrast, in some societies love is *separated* from marriage. Some other element—commonly respect for parents' wishes or duty to the kin group—is considered the essential basis for a good marriage. If love develops after a couple is married, that is fine, but respect for family, custom, and spouse is essential. If respect is not present, then something is fundamentally wrong—again something bordering on immorality.

In Chapter 12, Elisabeth Bumiller focuses on marriage in one such society, India, in which respect for family and tradition is the proper basis of marriage. Looking at the culture from its own framework helps make apparent how these assumptions are rational and functional. The Indian approach to marriage is so fundamentally distinct from ours—and so "natural" for them—that this contrast should help make more visible the culturally arbitrary nature of *our* assumptions about marriage.

No matter what factors are considered to be the essential bases for marriage, however, in all societies marriage means a changed set of relationships. Marriage "relates" an individual not only to a husband or a wife, but also to a *group* of other persons. (In our society, we term those people "in-laws.") In one sense, then, one marries not only a spouse, but also the spouse's family (or, in some societies, the spouse's clan or tribe).

By establishing relationships between groups of people, marriage also changes property relationships. For example, because of marriage, people who previously had no right to inherit the property of others gain that right. Indeed, marriage itself can be seen as a form of property, as Randall Collins shows in Chapter 13, in which he looks at marriage as a cultural form of defining sexual access.

For both the bride and groom and their families, the new relationships that marriage establishes bring with them new rights, duties, and privileges. How these changed relationships are calculated depends on how the particular society is set up. Marriage may mean the right to be supported, or the obligation to support someone. Marriage may specify who owns what property and how it is to be used. Marriage may mean the obligation to visit, the right to be visited, or even that one must refrain from visiting. These rights and obligations may be governed by informal rules, such as those concerning the show of respect and deference, and by formal rules, such as those that govern property and inheritance.

If we peer beneath the surface, then, we see that marriage vitally affects the welfare of many people other than the bride and groom. Because the fundamental rights and relationships of many are at stake, each society tries to make certain that the "right" people marry one another. "Passionate love," however, poses a threat to these efforts to "channel" the "right" people to one another, for it can propel a couple to one another in spite of the consequences. By leading people to violate the fundamental expectations into which they have been so carefully socialized, love threatens to disrupt the orderly social relations on which social groups attempt to perpetuate themselves.

Sociologists are vitally interested in what keeps societies together. In their attempts to understand what they call *social control* (efforts to keep people in line) sociologists analyze factors that support and maintain the *social structure* (the usual arrangements among the members of a group). This characteristic of love—that it leads people to disregard the expectations of others and propels them into relationships that others do not consider right, proper, or wise—makes love a significant sociological topic. If love can upset social relationships, it is important for the members of a society to control it—and for sociologists to understand how they attempt to do so.

Almost every teenager dreams of meeting the "right" person and "falling in love." And at some point, almost all of us Americans do find ourselves attracted to another person, experience feelings of love, and get married. Although some may think the process of attraction and love mysterious, as sociologists David A. Karp and William C. Yoels analyze in Chapter 14, the development of intimacy can be abstracted and analyzed. Its elements are remarkably similar from one situation to another.

We still face the thorny question, however, of what "love" is. Despite the difficulty of answering this question, we would do less than justice to the topic if we did not attempt to define it. Accordingly, in Chapter 15, Robert J. Trotter looks at the meaning of love. Actually, he analyzes its *meanings,* for the three essential components of love—intimacy, passion, and commitment—result in a variety of forms.

Although these chapters are only a brief introduction to the cultural background of love, romance, and intimacy, they should provide a better understanding of the sociological complexities of love—its interconnections to ideas of proper relationships and property, the process of its development, and its many meanings.

12
▼▼▼▼

First Comes Marriage—Then, Maybe, Love
▼▼▼▼▼

Elisabeth Bumiller

ABSTRACT: In India, marriages are typically arranged by the parents of the bride and the groom. Despite social change, including greater education for women, the movement of women into nontraditional occupations, and even educational and dating experiences in the United States and Europe, arranged marriages continue to be the dominant pattern. Why do Indian men, who have been educated in the Western world, and Indian women, who play leading roles in politics and law, still consent to their parents' wishes when it comes time to marry? In this selection, the author sets out to answer that question.

New Delhi, India—A story of marriage and love in modern India:

Arun Bharat Ram had come home to New Delhi after graduating from the University of Michigan when his mother announced she wanted to find him a wife.

Her son was prime marriage material—27 years old, an heir to one of the largest fortunes in India, a sophisticated man who had gone to prep school with Prime Minister Rajiv Gandhi, and who was soon to start work in the family's textile business.

But Bharat Ram had dated American women in Ann Arbor, and the idea of an arranged marriage, though expected in India, "did not seem quite right to me." He finally agreed to see a prospective bride so his mother would stop pestering him.

Manju, the prospect, was no less reluctant. She was 22, a recent graduate of a home economics college, from a conservative, middle-class family.

She had always known that her marriage would be arranged but still shuddered when she remembered how a relative had been asked to parade before her future in-laws—"like a girl being sold."

Arun and Manju met over coffee with their parents at a luxury hotel in New Delhi. Manju was so nervous that she dropped her cup, but everyone assured her this was a sign of good luck.

Arun found Manju pretty and quiet; she was impressed that he didn't boast about his background. There were four more meetings, only one with the two alone. Then it was time to decide.

"If Arun wants to marry you," Manju's parents asked their daughter, "will you agree to marry him?"

Manju had no major objections. She liked him, and that was enough. A few days later Arun's mother came to the house. "We want her," she said. Then Prime Minister Indira Gandhi and 1,500 others came to the wedding.

"I didn't love him," Manju recalls of the days after the engagement. "But when we talked, we had a lot of things in common."

Today, almost 18 years and three children later, the Bharat Rams are a model of domestic contentment. They are the first to say it hasn't always been easy, but their friends marvel at how well the marriage has worked.

"I've never thought of another man since I met him," Manju says, "and I also know I would not be able to live without him."

"It wasn't something that happened overnight," Arun adds. "It grew, and became a tremendous bond. It's amazing, but in arranged marriages people actually make the effort to fall in love with each other."

Few areas separate the East more from the West than their attitudes toward love, marriage and sex.

In India sociologists estimate that 95 percent of all marriages are still arranged, including the majority of those among the educated middle class. This is changing among the urban, Westernized elite, but not entirely.

An Indian man will still come home after years of dating American girls to marry someone he hardly knows. The Sunday newspapers continue to be filled with pages of matrimonial ads.

Many Indian college women still want their parents to find husbands for them and are so sure of the wisdom of their elders that some say yes to a prospective groom after a half-hour meeting.

The tradition survives in part because a new kind of arranged marriage has emerged among the growing middle class, broadly estimated as 10 percent of India's 750 million people. It is particularly prevalent in the upper-middle class.

A generation ago, even among the richest families, a bride and groom rarely spoke to each other before the wedding. They had no veto power over their parents' choice, and if the marriage was miserable, so be it.

But now couples are allowed to meet several times before making a decision, and a few can go out alone. Some engagements last six months and more. Women can reject the choice of their parents, and many do. This is considered a breakthrough.

"Frankly, I don't think it's such a bad system," says Leila Seth, who is one of only 10 women high-court judges of the 400 in India. As a socially progressive mother, Seth has told her daughter that she can make her own decision but will also help her find a husband if that's what she wants.

Since most Indian teenagers are still not allowed to date, parents think their children will be unprepared to make choices of their own. The big parental fear is that a daughter will fall for the first man who comes along. This kind of passion is considered dangerous.

"Love is traditionally blind," says Sudhir Kakar, a prominent New Delhi psychoanalyst. "So if you fall in love, you'll be marrying blindly."

In America a young woman can simply move on when that first intense love affair fizzles, but an Indian woman risks gossip that might ruin her chances of a good husband later.

When she falls in love, she usually has to marry the man. If it doesn't work out afterward, her friends will cluck that her love was immature and foolish. . . .

In the Indian view, American marriages fail because of the inevitable disappointment that sets in after the first few years of romantic love wear off.

Most Indians believe true love is a more peaceful emotion, based on long-term commitment and devotion to family. Few in the West would quarrel with that.

But Indians also think they can "create" love between two people by arranging the right condition for it, which is a marriage of common backgrounds and interests.

Americans know that common interests are essential but see love as a mysterious force that exists on its own. In the West one of the favorite themes is of star-crossed lovers like Romeo and Juliet, whose passion defies the forces of society.

But in India love is believed to flow out of social arrangements and is actually subservient to them. In the West love must come before marriage, but in India it can only come after.

Yet there is something universal about what the Indian arranged marriage seeks to accomplish. Even though it is a concept that makes sense primarily on its own terms, and even though it is often disastrous in practice, it can still tell the West something about the relationship between marriage and love.

Meeta Sawhney is 20, a student in economics at Delhi University, an attractive, bright woman who plans on a doctorate and a business career.

She got engaged in August to a man her parents found for her. He is 25 and works in his father's business. His family has known Sawhney's for generations. She saw him often while they were growing up but never considered him marriage material.

"Then one day my mother just sat down with me," Sawhney recalls, "and said, 'We have this boy in mind.'" She had reservations but agreed to see him. They met numerous times last year and sometimes went out to movies and restaurants alone.

But there was no fire between them, at least on Sawhney's part. Then last summer the man proposed, and Sawhney said yes. "He's very understanding, and not like normal Indian men," she says. "He doesn't want me to sit at home. He says whatever I want to do with my life is all right." . . .

Does she love him? "That's a very difficult question," she says. "I don't know. This whole concept of love is very alien to us. We're more practical. I don't see stars, I don't hear little bells. But he's a very nice guy, I get along with him fine and I think I'm going to enjoy spending my life with him. Is that love?"

Even Indians who live in the West preserve their own ideas of love. Rama Rajakumar, a Brahman from south India, is a 34-year-old supervisor at the World Bank in Washington.

In 1971, at a friend's house, she met a man who was a Brahman from her part of India. He was studying at the University of Texas. She didn't hear from him again until two years later, when the man wrote to the mutual friend and said he wanted to marry Rama.

The friend quickly took on the role of marriage broker and wrote to both sets of parents in India.

First, the horoscopes of the prospective couple were exchanged. "They matched perfectly," says Rama, talking during a recent visit to New Delhi.

The parents exchanged further details on family background and education. Then photos were mailed. A few months later Rama's parents declared themselves pleased.

Rama, who was 22 and had not had a date with anyone in the four years she'd been living in America, told them she'd marry the man. She had not seen him since the meeting two years before.

"From the very beginning, my mind was set that my parents would choose the right person for me," she says. Marrying an American was out. "Just to cook for a nonvegetarian husband would have been horrible."

The marriage was in May 1973 in Madras, India. Rama recalls that she wasn't concerned about how the two strangers might get along for the rest of their lives. "I still think he's a much better husband than anyone I could have asked for," she says.

But wasn't she worried that she wouldn't fall in love with him?

The question makes no sense to her. "No," she says. "I just thought, 'He is my husband, and I love him.'"

Hindu marriage is considered sacred, but in the ancient religious texts it is based on the devotional worship of a wife for her husband, much like the love for a god. The two partners were not regarded as equals.

A woman lived her life through her husband and often died with him too, sometimes committing suttee by throwing herself on his funeral pyre. Suttee was outlawed in 1829, although there have been rare cases reported in recent years.

The Hindu religious tradition continues to have a strong hold on middle-class families today. Girls are told from childhood that they will love the man their parents choose. Only in exceptional circumstances, like wife-beating, will a mother listen to a daughter's complaints about her husband.

Divorce between two Hindus has been legal only since 1955 and is still rare even among the urban elite. Since most women are still raised to be submissive, they usually say these rules suit them fine. . . .

Arranged marriage is a perplexing custom in a country that has one of the world's richest traditions of love and passion.

The *Kamasutra* is perhaps the most famous poem ever written on the finer points of lovemaking, and the erotic sculptures at Khajuraho still startle even forward-thinking Westerners today. The Indian gods copulate blissfully across the pages of the great epics, and every Indian schoolchild knows the love story of the god Krishna and the beautiful milkmaid, Radha.

As described in the ancient religious texts, their love-making was so intense that Radha's jewelry" was torn from her body . . . the chignon dislocated . . . she nearly lost her reason and could not distinguish day from night."

But this greatest of Hindu love stories also happens to be about an adulterous affair, not marriage. Radha eventually went back to her husband. Krishna later married Rukmini, more for duty than love, and then turned his attention to fighting demons.

Historically, devotion and duty have been more important than passion in Indian marriage, at least among the middle class. Yet middle-class parents are well aware of the lust that can rage between a young bride and groom who have never had sex before.

So parents often make sure that the bride spends some time away from her husband during the first year of marriage, usually in long visits to her family.

Mahatma Gandhi, the revered leader of India's independence movement, says in his autobiography that it was this custom that helped keep him from drowning in sexual obsession during the first year of his marriage, when he and his wife were 13.

Every few months his wife's parents would summon her home. "Such calls were very unwelcome in those days," Gandhi wrote, "but they saved us both."

Theoretically, in the first phase of an arranged marriage in India a woman has a tremendously seductive power over her husband. When sexual passion cools as expected, the couple supposedly settle down to the everyday business of life.

"Love is fine," says Usha Seth, a 41-year-old, well-to-do New Delhi housewife who agreed to marry the man her parents selected three days after she met him. "But after the first few years, that's when you realize how important it is that a person is considerate and kind." . . .

In the end, the relationship between love and marriage is so different in India and the West that there appears to be little common ground. Americans may not have figured out marriage and love, but the Indians don't seem to have found perfect answers, either.

"Both in the East and the West we have very little knowledge of what marriage is," says Promilla Kapur, a New Delhi sociologist who is also a family and marriage counselor.

"Young people either think it will be heaven, or that it will be the end of their freedom. It's neither. In marriage one has to go on practicing. And if you enter into it with the determination that you are going to make it a success, then there are more chances for that success than if you have the casual attitude of 'If it works, fine, and if it doesn't, I'll just get out of it.'"

. . . Says Arun Bharat Ram, the University of Michigan graduate who had an arranged marriage 18 years ago, . . . "I do think people adjust to a difficult situation much easier in India than they do in the West. I think we are far more tolerant and giving."

13

Love and Property

▼▼▼▼

Randall Collins

ABSTRACT: Family and sexual relations are not part of some natural ordering of things, but are part of a society's system of stratification. The author conceptualizes family relations as a type of property. Because it grants and denies sexual access, he says that marriage is a form of property rights over human bodies *(erotic property)*, while the rights of parents over children are also a form of property rights *(generational property)*. As societies change, so do property systems. Consequently, our particular form of sexual stratification is undergoing change.

. . . The family and sexual relations are not just natural but exist as part of a system of stratification. The theory of sexual stratification is . . . now in the process of being developed, and there is a good deal of discussion over just how it works. But certain basic, and nonobvious, points can be made.

The guiding idea that I will follow here is that family relations are relations of property. This property is of [two] kinds: (1) property rights over human bodies, which we might call *erotic property* [and] (2) property rights regarding children—let us call this *generational property*. . . .

126

. . . Once we can understand these forms of property, it becomes important to see that they are not static. Property systems, including sexual ones, are not natural and immutable forever. They are produced by certain social circumstances, and they change with those circumstances. If we understand these conditions, we can predict the rise and fall of various kinds of sexual stratification. The current type of family structure, and of sexual domination, has not existed forever, and it will not continue indefinitely into the future. . . .

EROTIC PROPERTY

How can people be property? Except for slavery, which hardly exists anymore, people cannot be bought and sold. Human beings have no monetary value; we regard ourselves as beyond money. People are not things; they are ends in themselves. Hence, it would seem that people are not property, at least not in the modern world.

The mistake, though, is to think of property as a thing, and especially as a thing that can be bought and sold for money. Property is not actually the thing itself, a physical object. Property is a social relationship, *a way in which people act toward things.* What does it mean, for instance, that a piece of land "belongs" to someone? It means that person can use it, live on it, go on it when he or she likes, and that other people must stay off unless they are given permission. If they don't, the owner can call the police or go to court to keep others off. Property is a relationship among people regarding things; it is some kind of enforceable agreement as to who can or cannot do what with certain things, and who will back others up in enforcing these actions. It is the society that makes something property, and not some inviolable relationship between one individual and the soil. . . .

If property is a social relationship, then, rather than the thing itself, it makes sense to look at love and sex as forms of property. The key aspect of property is the right of possession, the right to keep someone else from possessing it, and the willingness of society to back up those rights. The very core of a marriage is property in just that sense.

What makes people married? It is not primarily the marriage vow, nor the civil or religious ceremony. A couple who live together and have sexual intercourse exclusively with each other are for all intents and purposes married. If this goes on for several years, in many places they are thereby legally married, as a "common law" marriage. On the other hand, a couple who are legally married but never have sexual intercourse is said not to have "consummated" the marriage. This is grounds for legal annulment, since the implicit terms of the marriage contract are not put into effect. In our society, marriage is a contract for exclusive rights to sexual access between two people. Socially speaking, they are exchanging their bodies as sexual property to each other.

This sexual property is the key to the family structure; it is the hinge on which everything else turns. Marriages are created by establishing the sexual tie. The old traditions of the wedding night and the honeymoon point directly to this fact. The more traditional the marriage, the more ceremony there was surrounding the first act of sexual intercourse. This went on whether or not people sensed the fact that they were establishing a form of erotic property. Traditionally, before the legal reforms of recent decades, the only way one could get divorced was by proving adultery. This has been true [until recently] in conservative, Catholic-dominated countries such as Italy. Why is adultery so crucial? Because it is a breaking of the central property right, exclusive sexual access.

Similarly, in traditional societies, heavy emphasis was placed upon the bride being a virgin at marriage. The husband's property rights over her body would have been sullied if she had had intercourse with another man. That these same societies tended not to regard male virginity at marriage as very important implies that the property system was much more one of males owning women's bodies than vice versa. . . .

The erotic property system is especially visible when we look at the points at which it is violated. There has long been a sort of unwritten law, which condoned spouses taking violent action when their sexual property was abused. A judge or jury usually would not convict a man of murder for killing his wife's lover, or even his wife, when he discovered her having an adulterous affair. . . . The custom of allowing [an] unpunished killing to take place in these circumstances has declined somewhat in contemporary times. Why this is so also reveals something about the sexual property system.

The practice of adultery-killing was strongest in places where marriage was regarded as most inviolate and divorces were least common. Why should this be so? Because this traditional marriage system meant that a woman would have only one sexual partner in her lifetime; her body was the exclusive sexual property of her husband. Such arrangements have usually had a rather sexist tone in that men were more likely to be allowed to have extramarital affairs or access to prostitutes; so, although a marriage was in principle unbreakable, the man had more opportunities for compensating for erotic and emotional incompatibility. With the rise of the divorce rate, though, in many communities it is generally expected that most people will have more than one marriage, and hence more than one sexual partner in their lifetime. For this reason, sexual property is no longer taken as such an absolute, something that if tarnished once is forever gone. This is not to say that sexual property no longer exists. But it has shifted into a different modality: one might say, from absolute long-term property to a series of short-term property arrangements. People still get angry about adultery, but the result is more likely to be a divorce instead of a violent death.

Laws and customs about violence tell us other things concerning erotic property. Virtually everywhere, a rape within a marriage is not a crime. According to the law in most countries, and all but a [few] American states, a man has the right of sexual access to his wife, and she cannot use the power of the state for protection against his forcing himself upon her. Implicitly, the marriage contract gives away the right of sexual resistance once and for all. The fact that the issue is now being raised, and that some places have made a crime out of marital rape, indicates the extent to which the sexual property system is being challenged today. But the resistance to such a legal change continues to be strong. To some extent it is balanced by the prevalent right to divorce that has emerged in recent decades, which makes it easier for a woman to escape from an undesirable husband.

All of this discussion seems to imply that marriage is simply a matter of sex, and that there is no affection, no love, involved. But this is certainly not so. Erotic relations are the key to the marriage contract, both legally and in the unwritten laws of customary belief. But this is by no means exclusive of emotional ties. In fact, the emotional ties now usually go along with the sexual ones. Love and sex, from a sociological viewpoint, are part of the same complex. At least this is so in the modern marriage system, which places a great deal of emphasis on an ideal expression of love. One might even refer to modern marriage as a ritual-love system of erotic property . . . in which love is a crucial element in establishing a sexual tie.

There are several ways in which we can show that the emotions of love are tied to the erotic property system. For starters, look at the language of romance. Aside from ''I love you'' the most common sorts of love-expressions are phrases like ''Will you be mine?'' ''Take me,'' ''I'm yours forever.'' Popular songs are full of this terminology, and so is the way people ordinarily converse about their loves, both among themselves and to other people. It is the language of property. ''My,'' ''mine,'' ''his,'' ''hers,'' ''yours'' are probably the most common words in love talk, even more than the word ''love'' itself.

All this possession-talk, moreover, refers simultaneously to affection and to sex. A lover possesses the other's body and affections at the same time. One is usually the symbol of the other. The man who says he loves a woman but will not have intercourse with her (''make love to her,'' in the telling phrase), either inside or outside a marriage tie, is certainly going to be doubted in his expression of affection. The same is of course true (perhaps even more so) the other way around, concerning the woman's behavior.

We can look at the same thing from the negative side. The kinds of things that make a lover jealous apply both to sexual behavior and to affections. A woman who professes to love a man but sleeps with someone else is more than likely to make him jealous, and at least to make him doubt whether she is sincere when she says she loves him. In the same way, she could make him jealous by sleeping with him but declaring that she loves someone else. People expect that love and sex will go together: at a minimum, they feel that truly strong love ties result naturally in sexual intercourse. Many people (though men more than women) will openly say that sex can be enjoyed without love, although this usually means that some degree of affection should be there. This seems to imply at least a short-term emotional tie, if not one of the "I'm yours forever" form.

The comparative study of jealousy gives a neat illustration of the social basis of emotions. Whom one feels jealous toward is relative to how sexual property is arranged. In our society, where erotically exclusive male-female pairs are the predominant form of sexual exchange, each partner is jealous of anyone who threatens to impose on the affections, or the genitals, of [the] partner. In polyandrous societies, however, the situation is quite different. This is a type of system, found for example in some of the mountain tribes of India and Tibet, in which a woman has several husbands. Usually it is a group of brothers who have the same wife. They are not jealous of each other, and all are expected to have a share in the woman's body and attentions. This does not mean such people are so broad-minded as to be incapable of jealousy. On the contrary, they can be quite jealous of outsiders who are not part of the polyandrous situation. Similarly, Eskimo men frequently share their wives, on a temporary basis, with visitors who come their way on long hunting expeditions. At the same time, Eskimo societies have had a very high incidence of fights and murders, often over possession of a woman. It makes a tremendous difference whether a guest is invited to share a woman (implicitly in return for some later reciprocity) or if he simply helps himself. Property, in short, is not given up when it is given away. In fact, the giving of a gift (in this case, a loan of a woman's body) reaffirms the sense of property, precisely because it makes clear to everyone involved that someone is doing something with *their* property and that they expect it to be received in a proper way.

These kinds of polyandrous or wife-lending situations actually are rather rare on the world scene. Somewhat more common are marriage systems in which a man has several wives. Such polygynous systems are especially prominent in tribal Africa. There, again, we find jealousy turned in quite different directions than in our own society. The various co-wives are usually not jealous of one another, although they may be jealous of outside women who are not part of the family situation. There is usually a chief wife, who has certain rights and powers over the other wives. In such a situation, a woman contemplating marriage may be more concerned about whether she will be moving into a family in which she gets on well with the co-wives than with how well she likes the husband himself.

This kind of anthropological comparison lets us see that the emotions we usually associate with sexual relations are variable, but not at all random. Just how much affection there is, and how much jealousy, and at whom it is directed, depends on the typical structure of sexual property relations. In our own society, erotic relationships are heavily imbued with romance, and emotions of affection and love are a crucial part of this. I am not saying that people fall in love because they feel they are supposed to. It is true that our popular culture tends to make people expect that this will happen, but the widespread experience of love is by no means simply the result of indoctrination by the media. Rather, it follows naturally from the type of negotiating that people must do in order to find a sexual partner in a situation of free individual bargaining. . . .

. . . The sexual-bargaining process . . . tends to generate feelings of anxiety, hope, fear, and also happiness and excitement. Hence, there is usually an emotional buildup when people find someone that they like, and joy if they find that this person, out of all the contacts they have tried, likes them too. Just how much a couple likes each other, even in these circumstances, may be a matter of degree. Each may still be eyeing the field, to see if there is someone they like better who might be attracted to them. A courtship thus can be somewhat uneasy for a while, until a couple finally settles down to a commitment to each other as the most favorable person they know. But this very uneasiness is what makes love affairs dramatic and arouses emotions. A couple that never goes through little reverses and potential breakups likely will not have as strong emotional feelings about each other as a couple that does.

I am suggesting, then, that the negotiating process itself tends to create strong emotions and that these feelings of tension and excitement, when they are finally resolved into a strong commitment to each other, are what turn into love. Moreover, the "language" by which a personal commitment is negotiated is likely to be to a large extent nonverbal: it is the language of sexual intimacy itself. A courtship is carried out not only by conversation but by a series of moves toward increasing physical intimacy. Touching, holding hands, kissing goodbye, necking, petting, intercourse—these are a typical progression, which sometimes may be drawn out at considerable length. The reason a couple does not usually go straight to the erotic climax is, in fact, because these various kinds of sexual contacts are heavily symbolic. They are not just pleasures in themselves. Sometimes they aren't necessarily even that: holding hands, for example, is not much of a physical pleasure, although it can be a highly emotional one. One could even suggest that many forms of much more intimate sexual contact, such as oral-genital contact, are also largely symbolic of a type of emotional relationship. They probably represent total intimacy, and perhaps total domination and submission, rather than simply physical pleasure.

The progression of physical intimacies, rather, is more like a ritual by which a man and woman indicate just how much commitment they have to each other. In general, they are bargaining their way into a tie, through various gradual steps that represent their tentativeness and the possibility that they might still pull back from the relationship. By the time the negotiation gets to full sexual intercourse, usually the couple has made some commitment to each other that involves a good deal of sexual exclusiveness, and along with this goes the emotion of love. This is, in fact, the way most modern marriages have been negotiated. . . .

The emotion of love arises from the process of negotiating an exclusive and relatively permanent sexual contract among free individuals. It is a natural part of the drama that [all people go] through as they try to manage their own fate in a world where everyone else is simultaneously trying to do the same. From the ups and downs of the dating game come the ritualized establishing of the intense, private world of a new couple. It should not be surprising, then, that the emotion is strongest when the bond is first made, and during the period when it is confirmed as true and strong.

. . . The ingredients of a ritual are all there, and in a very intense form. The couple is constantly in each other's presence and tends to exclude or ignore everyone else. Their love-talk and their kissing, hand-holding, and other erotic play have the patterned, repetitive form of ritual behavior. The emotions they bring to their encounters are intensified by being shared, just as any successful ritual revs up the feelings of the group. We can say, then, that lovers are carrying out a ritual that forms a very small, solidarity-group: a group of two, to be exact. This group has a very strong tie and very strong boundaries toward the outside. . . .

GENERATIONAL PROPERTY

In an important respect, children are property too. Parents have certain rights over them, and they act to defend those rights in the same way as they protect other kinds of property. Children are not, however, sexual property. All societies are very strict about this. The incest taboo within the nuclear family is virtually universal; sexual intercourse between parents and children, or among siblings, and sometimes among other relatives, too, is regarded with particularly strong revulsion. The incest taboo ought to be considered part of the generational property system; it is one of the principle *negative* rules as to what people *cannot* do with their generational property. (There are equivalent negative rules about physical property, too; zoning ordinances forbidding certain kinds of modifications of your house or land are instances of this.)

The incest taboo cannot simply be taken for granted, though. It is not a natural or instinctual revulsion; if so, no one would ever commit incest, whereas in fact the incest taboo is violated to a surprising extent. Rather, it is enforced above all from *outside* the family, by other people who look upon incest as improper and prosecute it as illegal. Why outsiders do this has largely to do with the general system of sexual bargaining that takes place in that society. People expect the children of other families to be available as sexual partners to outsiders, not to be monopolized within the family. It is possible to demonstrate this because different societies vary as to just what they count as incest, and these variations are tied to the kind of marriage system that prevails.

In some societies, like our own only a few generations ago, marriage with cousins was prohibited as incestuous, and people were expected to marry further afield. In many tribal societies, on the other hand, certain cousins are expected to marry each other whenever possible. This is because there is a system of regular alliances among families, and the continuous intermarriages of cousins (especially what are called "cross-cousins") is what keeps the families tied together generation by generation. Such examples, incidentally, prove that the reason for the incest taboo is not because people are concerned about possible genetic defects from inbreeding; societies practicing regular cousin marriage are obviously following the opposite of such a policy. Moreover, these same societies have incest rules that are in some respects much more extreme than our own; they prohibit large categories of people from marrying because they belong to the wrong lineage, even though we would consider them not very closely related biologically at all.

The reasons for the incest taboo are not biological but are part of the larger system of sexual property exchange. In our own society, wholesale alliances of families are no longer important, and our incest taboos have shrunk to the bare minimum that will still require children to leave their own family to find sexual partners in the larger marriage market.

The incest taboo, then, is a negative rule of the generational property system. It regulates what parents cannot do with their children, as well as what children are not allowed to do with each other. The positive aspects of generational property include a number of things. Parents have a certain physical property right over their children: the power to keep them in their houses, send them to school, and whatever else they wish to do with them. Parents have rights to direct their children's behavior in many respects: to determine how they dress; what religious training they are to be given, if any; whom they should associate with; and many other things. These rights are not necessarily very much enforced these days. We have come a long way from the Roman family in which the father could punish his children any way he wished, and even put them to death. . . .

14

From Strangers to Intimates

David A. Karp
William C. Yoels

ABSTRACT: How do people who do not know one another become intimates? Before we begin to answer this question, we need to note that people are not left on their own. Rather, their culture provides guidelines for developing intimacy. In our society, people learn not only that they "ought" to "fall in love" but also the most appropriate time to do so.

Love, say the authors, is like a slowly turning wheel: It gradually emerges through a process of rapport, self-revelation, mutual dependency, and the fulfillment of needs. Rapport and self-revelation involve meeting one another, physical attraction, continued interaction, idealized images, and an information game of self-disclosure. Mutual dependency and commitment center on the development of intertwined lives, a public identity as a couple, and a commitment to the relationship.

We want to explore the process through which strangers become intimates. Such persons must meet, typically date one another, gradually become committed to each other, experience falling in love, and usually marry. So, while the specifics of the process through which strangers are transformed into intimates may vary widely, the socially prescribed

135

benchmarks or stages of our respective relationships look much alike. In the following pages we will examine some of the available literature describing the central points in the intimacy process. . . .

We expect to "fall in love," have sex, and get married within well-recognized time frames. Adults typically define teenagers' first attempts at establishing an intimate relationship as infatuation or "puppy love." Teenagers are, after all, too young to experience the "real thing." At the other extreme, persons who remain unmarried past their late twenties may be considered "problems" by parents, relatives, and friends. . . .

In America the completion of formal education seems to be a key point in our intimacy time conceptions. High school students who do not go on to college frequently marry soon after graduation. For many others the college years are thought an appropriate time to fall in love. Indeed, because college students constitute a readily accessible sample of persons for researchers, most of the generalizations concerning the process through which persons fall in love come from studies of college students. To understand this process, we must first appreciate the conception of love that guides the construction of our intimate relations.

THE ROMANTIC IDEAL

Some years ago one of the authors had as a friend a Korean graduate student who became visibly distressed and depressed as she neared the completion of her master's degree work. When questioned about it, she answered that she had been receiving letters from her parents indicating that she would be married upon her return to Korea. Throughout her several years of undergraduate and graduate education in the United States she knew that she would eventually be expected to marry the person her parents had chosen for her. At this point, she did not want to return to Korea and she certainly did not want to marry someone she had never met. She knew, however, that it would be a breach of cultural tradition to refuse her parents' wishes. Had she not adopted American values which hold the idea of arranged marriages archaic and silly, she probably would not have experienced strain or tension. She would have considered her arranged marriage as inevitable and reasonable as we consider "love" the inevitable basis for marriage.

The tenets of the romantic love ideal, first formulated in France and Germany during the twelfth century, gradually filtered down from the nobility to the lower classes. Today, the elements of the romantic love ideal are captured in the lyrics of popular songs and in greeting card verses. In its pure form the ideal of romantic love involves the notion that there is only one person in all the world that we are meant to love; that, although "love is blind" we will recognize our "true love" at first sight. The role of *fate* is an important strong feature of the romantic ideal. We are, after all, expected to "fall" in love, and the lyrics of songs have us believing that "you were meant for me." Don't we all wait from adolescence on for that moment when "That old black magic [has us] in its spell?" While we celebrate the pure romantic ideal in movies, literature, and song, we interpret it liberally in our own lives. Kierkegaard points this out when he says:

> The proposition that the first love is the true love is very accommodating and can come to the aid of mankind in various ways. If a man is not fortunate enough to get possession of what he desires, then he still has the sweetness of the first love. If a man is so unfortunate as to love many times, each time is still the first love. . . . One loves many times, and each time one denies the validity of the preceding times, and one still maintains the correctness of the proposition that one loves only once. [Kierkegaard, 1959:252]

[It is significant to note here that there] are studies indicating differences between men and women in the weight given to love as a condition for marriage. Contrary to popular belief, men are more likely than women to hold to the romantic ideal. In other words, women are *less* romantic than men (Waller, 1938:243). Women's traditional dependence on men has made the process of mate selection of much greater consequence to women, and, for this reason, women have been less idealistic and more rational and cautious than men. In one study, many of the female respondents made such comments as the following: "I don't think I ever felt romantic about David—I felt practical. I had the feeling that I'd better make the most of it" (Hill, Rubin, and Peplau, 1977).

You all no doubt know someone who claims to have fallen in love "at first sight." For most couples, however, the development of a love relationship is a gradual process. One researcher, Ira Reiss (1960), has described the steps in what he calls the "wheel theory of love." The four central stages of a relationship are represented by the spokes of the wheel (see Figure 14.1). They are: rapport, self-revelation, mutual dependency, and need fulfillment. According to Reiss, persons must proceed through these stages one at a time and in order. The theory suggests that, before we are willing to reveal deep identity information about ourselves to others, we must first have achieved a certain level of rapport with them. Self-revelation, in turn, sets the stage for persons' sense of mutual dependency. The final stage in this process is the belief that another person fulfills our basic needs.

Much research (see Davis, 1973; Rubin, 1973) has been conducted on various aspects of the process leading to mate selection and marriage. This literature suggests that there is, indeed, considerable regularity and rationality to the process. Using Reiss's wheel theory as a general guide, we can more fully analyze the movement from rapport to self-revelation

Figure 14.1 **Graphic Presentation of the Wheel Theory of the Develop-ment of Love**

Source: Ira Reiss, "Toward a Sociology of the Heterosexual Love Relationship," *Marriage and Family Living* 22 (May) 1960, p. 143.

to commitment and marriage as well as the factors that sometimes hinder such movement.

RAPPORT AND SELF-REVELATION
("You think you know me, but you don't know me.")

We all have had the experience of meeting a stranger at a party, through the introduction of mutual friends, at bars, and the like. Such meetings typically begin with casual conversation and the exchange of superficial biographical information. College students meeting at a party engage in fairly ritualistic conversation: "What year are you in? What is your major? Where are you from?" If one of the persons has no desire to continue the conversation, this incipient relationship is easily ended. If, however, the individuals wish to pursue the relationship, the conver-sation will necessarily become progressively less superficial and more far-reaching, as each person seeks to learn more about the other.

[Most people are aware that] physical attractiveness is a critically im-portant factor determining whether persons will want to see each other again after an initial meeting. Additional studies support the importance of physical attractiveness, but these studies also note the differential sig-nificance attached to it by men and women. In one study (Byrne, 1970) persons were asked to rank a variety of factors concerning their attrac-tion to others, and 90 percent of the male respondents ranked physical attractiveness as most important. This was not true for women. Although they certainly ranked attractiveness high, they considered it more important that the males with whom they develop an ongoing relationship share their attitudes and values. Ninety-two percent of the female respondents ranked value and attitudinal similarity as more important than physical attractiveness. Such a finding supports Bertrand Russell's contention that "On the whole, women tend to love men for their character, while men tend to love women for their appearance."

Typically, once persons have begun to interact, their primary goal is to determine the issues on which they agree and disagree and to assess the significance of their similarities and differences. . . . One of the factors inevitably complicating the information assessment process during the initial stage of a relationship is the purposive impression-management engaged in by both parties. Individuals may be so intent on establishing a relationship that they systematically present attitudes and values that they believe accord well with the others' values and attitudes. Each will be careful early in a relationship to "feel out" the other person before expressing an opinion that he or she might dislike enough to end the relationship. All of us manipulate identity information to present the proper first impression. Let us acknowledge that deliberate identity manipulation early in a relationship frequently leads at some point to the declaration: "I thought I knew him/her, but I didn't." In their book *Pairing*, Bach and Deutsch (1970) offer several examples of couples who learn later in their relationship that the other had deliberately manipulated original presentations of self. Many of you are likely to find parallels in your own relationships to the following exchange:

DOUG: I don't understand why you don't want to take the weekend backpack trip with Hal and Gwen. You know it's been three months since we've been in the woods or the mountains? I really miss it.

HELEN: Well, I was never that much of an outdoor woman after all. I mean, I love the scenery, but camping out is pretty hard on a woman. It's different for a man.

DOUG: But don't you remember what you said when we met on that Sierra Club Hike?

HELEN: What did I say? That I loved the scenery? That I loved nature? Of course, I do. But carrying a pack is really exhausting for me.

DOUG: It seems so much like part of us—being alone in the wilderness. Remember how we slipped away, the two of us? Cooked our meals together?

HELEN: Well, what do you want me to say?

DOUG: I don't know. You seem different now, somehow. It just isn't the same. That's why I want to get into the mountains with you again, bring it back, bring you back. [Bach and Deutsch, 1970:175]

Throughout the whole period of courtship persons tend to offer idealized images of themselves and largely to accept the idealized images others offer. An interesting study (Knafl, 1975) related to the idea of information control during the early stages of a relationship suggests that one of the best predictors of eventual marital success is the extent of conflict and its management by couples as they plan for their weddings. The author contends that this is the first time during the idyllic and fantasy-like period of courtship that the couple must make some of the practical social and economic decisions that will later typify their married life.

> With regard to the experience of preparing for the wedding, without exception, the couples interviewed reported difficulties surrounding the planning and execution of this event. They associated the staging of the wedding with an explicit shift in the nature of their relationship. While respondents typically described courtship as an essentially carefree time characterized by numerous shared, pleasurable experiences, questions concerning their wedding plans elicited a very different kind of response. Typically the respondent's tone of voice changed and comments focused on the multitude of problems being faced. [Knafl, 1975:8]

We have been suggesting that during the early stages of a relationship the participants engage in what might be termed an "information game." Persons manage impressions of themselves by systematically concealing information they consider potentially damaging in the encounter. At the same time, they seek out information about the other. Our examples indicate that it is relatively easy for persons to manipulate information about their attitudes and values. Other items of identity information, however, are difficult to hide or conceal, such as the ascribed attributes of ethnicity, race, religion, and social class. These "master attributes" also serve as relationship "filters." If persons discover that another's ethnic, religious, or class affiliation is very different from their own, they are likely to end the relationship at an early stage.

Whatever might be the unique elements involved, we can say that during the early stages of a relationship, individuals make presentations of themselves and the symbols defining their worlds. Supplied with this information, individuals decide whether the social worlds they respectively inhabit are close enough that they will eventually be able to produce and sustain a common reality as a couple. The literature that stresses class, value, and attitudinal similarity as initial filtering mechanisms implies that if persons' biographies are too dissimilar they will likely be unable to produce a viable joint reality. As an illustration of this point, we may see that it is the obvious disparity in biography that forms the substance of such fairy tales as *Cinderella*. *Cinderella* is a fairy tale precisely because it expresses the highly unlikely story of an ongoing relationship forged between persons with widely different biographies. It is the success of the relationship despite the incongruity of the individuals' biographies that gives the story its fairy-tale quality.

If a relationship endures beyond the point of self-disclosure and individuals have begun to date each other "seriously," they begin to interpret seriously their level of commitment to the relationship. "Intimates, like college professors, want tenure. And in order to guarantee that their relationship will continue, they must make a commitment to each other. After [a] probationary period, intimates, again like academics, go 'up or out'" (Davis, 1973:192). As one single friend has put it, "You reach a crossroads in the relationship where you either have to break it off or continue it and probably get married."

MUTUAL DEPENDENCY AND COMMITMENT
("All I ever need is you.")

You may be involved or know others who are involved in a relationship that has reached the point where persons' everyday lives are much intertwined. Most significant at this juncture in the relationship—the stage of mutual dependency—is that the couple's relationship has ceased to be their private affair. At this point, the individuals have likely been *publicly defined* as a couple. This public definition is critically important because, once it occurs, the exclusivity of their relationship becomes more inevitable. The couple now finds itself embedded in a complex and constraining system of expectations. Not only do the participants in the relationship have new expectations of each other, so also do their friends and family. The couple is now issued joint invitations, each person is expected to accompany the other to social gatherings, and when they are apart, each partner is expected to be able to account for the other's ideas, attitudes, and whereabouts. The partners signal the seriousness of their relationship to each other, family, and friends by engaging in a variety of activities generally understood to indicate a growing level of commitment. Such symbolic gestures may include: spending time together every day rather than just on weekends, introducing the partner to relatives, bringing the other to such important family events as weddings and annual gatherings, and the purchase of expensive gifts for each other.

As those of you who have seen your relationship with another progress to the point of mutual dependency know, it is a time when the relationship may undergo severe tensions and stresses. These difficulties are often related to the growing intensity of commitment that is occurring. Given the set of expectations described above, one or another of the partners may feel smothered by the pressure to make a permanent commitment. We should mention here that the meaning attached to commitment has, in the past, been different for men and women. Traditionally, males have viewed the acceptance of a long-term relationship as a surrender of their freedom and independence. Women, on the other hand, have been socialized to seek the security of a permanent commitment. More and more, however, women also are becoming wary of losing their identity in a relationship. Many women today refuse to subordinate their interests to those of their male friends and are increasingly willing to dissolve a relationship in which they are treated as [an] "appendage" to the male.

Another threat to a relationship at this stage may be the negative evaluation of an individual's dating partner by parents and friends. If, for example, a woman's friends, upon meeting her companion, demand to know what she sees in him, she may be inspired to reconsider and possibly end the relationship. In college, as in high school, students turn to their friends for advice on personal and academic matters. Many college students form friendships with slightly older persons such as seniors, graduate students, or young faculty members who frequently offer guidance in loco parentis. Students may also experience conflicts with parents that threaten a developing relationship. Consider the father who has dreamed of sending his son to medical school. If the father perceives his son's intimate relationship as a potential threat to this plan, he may demand: "Stop seeing her or I will stop paying for your education." Parents' control over students' financial welfare can extend as well to control over their love lives.

For many students, graduation from college precipitates a "commitment crisis." Time and again students come to our offices with much the same problem:

> "I think that I am in love with him, but he has been accepted to graduate school and I don't want to go there. I have my own career to think about. But I am pretty sure that if we go our separate ways now, it will in all likelihood spell the end of our relationship. This whole situation is driving me crazy and I don't know what to do."

In years past, many women in this situation would have subordinated their own career plans in order to sustain the relationship. Today, many relationships founder at this point unless arrangements can be made for both persons to pursue their own career goals in the same geographic area.

In their study of breakups before marriage, Hill, Rubin, and Peplau (1977) [found] it useful to speak of "his breakup" and "her breakup." Contrary to commonly accepted stereotypes, these investigators found that breakups are much harder on men. Men find it more difficult to

believe that they are no longer loved. As we have noted, this sex difference might be explained by women's greater practicality in love relationships. In general, these investigators found support for the view that
the partners in a lasting relationship are likely to share equal commitments to it. Their data indicate that only 23 percent of equally involved
couples broke up compared to 54 percent of those relationships in which
one person was more committed than the other.

Because the couples they studied were college students, Hill, Rubin,
and Peplau found that relationships tended to break up at clear demarcations in the school year: May-June, September, December-January.
Understandably, the person interested in terminating the relationship
found it easier to suggest just before vacation that "It might not be a
bad idea for us to date others while we are apart." Also, as might be
expected, individuals' conception of the relationship differed according
to whether they acted in the role of "breaker-upper" or "broken-up-
with." Both women and mean felt considerably "less depressed, less
lonely, freer, happier, but more guilty when they were the breaker-
uppers than when they were the broken-up-with" (Hill, Rubin, and
Peplau, 1977:324). Moreover, there is a tendency for each partner to
claim that he or she initiated the breakup. It is obviously preferable to
define the situation as one in which you have exercised power and,
therefore, largely controlled another's behavior.

Many relationships end in the face of the kinds of pressures we have
described. Alternatively, it does frequently happen that persons develop a commitment to a relationship because it has continued over a
long time period. Intimate relationships often develop a momentum as
a result of sheer endurance. Investing time and energy in their own
relationship while foregoing others commits people; often they remain
in the relationship even when it becomes a painful one (see Becker,
1960). . . .

Relationships are not static, thing-like entities. Rather, they are continually being interpreted and reevaluated by the participants. Such
interpretation and evaluation does not occur randomly. We described
the process through which strangers are transformed into intimates as
constituting a "career" with discernible stages. Relying on current literature, we analyzed the "typical" movement of a relationship from the
participants' achievement of rapport to self-revelation to mutual demonstration of commitment. . . .

REFERENCES

BACH, G., and DEUTSCH, R. *Pairing: How to achieve genuine intimacy.* New York: Avon
Books, 1970.

BECKER, H. "Notes on the Concept of Commitment." *American Journal of Sociology*, 1960, 66, 32–40.

BYRNE, D. "Continuity between the Experimental Study of Attraction and Real-Life Computer Dating." *Journal of Personality and Social Psychology*, 1970, 16, 157–165.

DAVIS, M. *Intimate relations*. New York: The Free Press, 1973.

HILL, C., RUBIN, Z., and PEPLAU, I. "Breakups Before Marriage: The End of 103 Affairs." In A. Skolnick and J. Skolnick (Eds.), *Family in transition*. Boston: Little, Brown, 1977.

KIERKEGAARD, S. *Either/or*. Garden City, N.Y.: Doubleday Anchor, 1959.

KNAFL, K. "Preparing for Marriage: A Case of Misrepresentation." Paper presented at the *American Sociological Association Annual Meetings*. San Francisco, California, 1975.

REISS, IRA. "Toward a Sociology of the Heterosexual Love Relationship." *Marriage and Family Living*, May 1960, 22, p. 143.

RUBIN, Z. *Liking and loving*. New York: Holt, Rinehart & Winston, 1973.

WALLER, W. *The family: A dynamic interpretation*. Hinsdale, Ill.: Dryden Press, 1938.

15

▼▼▼

The Three Faces of Love

▼▼▼

Robert J. Trotter

ABSTRACT: Robert J. Sternberg and Susan Grajek have developed a triangular model of love consisting of emotions, motivations, and cognitions. The emotional side of the triangle is intimacy or a feeling of closeness, the motivational side is passion, and the cognitive is commitment. A love relationship can be analyzed according to the significance that each of these elements plays. With time, different elements become more important, and as levels of intimacy, passion, and commitment change so does the love relationship.

Brains and sex are the only things in life that matter. Robert J. Sternberg picked up that bit of wisdom from a cynical high school classmate and appears to have taken it to heart. "I spent the first part of my career studying brains, and now along comes sex," he says, claiming to be only partly facetious.

Sternberg, IBM Professor of Psychology and Education at Yale University, has, in fact, made a name for himself as one of the foremost theoreticians and researchers in the field of human intelligence (see "Three Heads are Better than One," *Psychology Today*, August 1986), but

145

in recent years he has turned a good deal of his attention to the study of love. Why? Because it's an understudied topic that is extremely important to people's lives. "It's important to my own life," he says. "I want to understand what's happening."

Sternberg began his attempt to understand love with a study for which he and graduate student Susan Grajek recruited 35 men and 50 women between 18 and 70 years old who had been in at least one love relationship. Participants rated their most recent significant love affair using the well-tested scales of loving and liking developed by psychologist Zick Rubin and the interpersonal involvement scale developed by psychologist George Levinger. The participants also rated their love for their mothers, fathers, siblings closest in age and best friends of the same sex.

Sternberg and Grajek found that men generally love and like their lover the most and their sibling the least. Women tend to love their lover and best friend about the same, but they like the best friend more than they like the lover. Sternberg thinks he knows why. "Women are better at achieving intimacy and value it more than do men, so if women don't get the intimacy they crave in a relationship with a man, they try to find it with other women. They establish close friendships. They can say things to another woman they can't say to a man."

Sternberg and Grajek concluded that, while the exact emotions, motivations and cognitions involved in various kinds of loving relationships differ, "the various loves one experiences are not, strictly speaking, different." In other words, they thought they had proved that love, as different as it feels from situation to situation, is actually a common entity. They thought they had discovered the basis of love in interpersonal communication, sharing and support.

This research generated a lot of publicity in 1984, especially around St. Valentine's Day, and earned Sternberg the appellation "love professor." It also generated a lot of phone calls from reporters saying things like, "You mean to tell me the way you love your lover is the same as the way you love your 5-year-old kid? What about sex?" Sternberg had to rethink his position.

He analyzed various relationships to figure out what differentiates romantic love from companionate love, from liking, from infatuation and from various other types of love. He finally concluded that his original theory accounted for the emotional component of love but left out two other important aspects. According to Sternberg's new triangular theory, love has motivational and cognitive components as well. And different aspects of love can be explained in terms of these components (see "How Do I Love Thee?" at the end of this chapter).

Sternberg calls the emotional aspect of his love triangle intimacy. It includes such things as closeness, sharing, communication, and support. Intimacy increases rather steadily at first, then at a slower rate until it eventually levels off and goes beneath the surface. Sternberg explains this course of development in terms of psychologist Ellen Berscheid's theory of emotions in close relationships.

According to Berscheid, people in close relationships feel increased emotion when there is some kind of disruption. This is common early in a relationship primarily because of uncertainty. Since you don't know what the other person is going to do, you are constantly learning and experiencing new things. This uncertainty keeps you guessing but also generates new levels of emotion and intimacy. As the other person becomes more predictable, there are fewer disruptions and less expressed, or manifest, intimacy.

An apparent lack of intimacy could mean that the relationship and the intimacy are dying out. Or, says Sternberg, the intimacy may still be there in latent form. The relationship may even be thriving, with the couple growing together so smoothly that they are hardly aware of their interdependence. It may take some kind of disruption—time apart, a death in the family, even a divorce—for them to find out just how they feel about each other. "Is it any wonder," Sternberg asks, "that some couples realize only after a divorce that they were very close to and dependent on each other?"

The motivational side of the triangle is passion, which leads to physiological arousal and an intense desire to be united with the loved one. Unlike intimacy, passion develops quickly. "Initially you have this rapidly growing, hot, heavy passion," Sternberg says, "but after a while it no longer does for you what you want it to—you get used to it, you habituate."

Passion is like an addiction, Sternberg says. He explains it according to psychologist Richard Solomon's opponent process theory of motivation, which says that desire for a person or substance involves two opposing forces. The first is a positive motivational force that attracts you to the person. It is quick to develop and quick to level off. The negative motivational force, the one that works against the attraction, is slow to develop and slow to fade. The result is an initial rapid growth in passion, followed by habituation when the more slowly developing negative force kicks in. "It's like with coffee, cigarettes or alcohol," Sternberg says. "Addiction can be rapid, but once habituation sets in, even an increased amount of exposure to the person or substance no longer stimulates the motivational arousal that was once possible.

"And then when the person dumps you, it's even worse. You don't go back to the way you were before you met the person," Sternberg explains. "You end up much worse off. You get depressed, irritable, you lose your appetite. You get these withdrawal symptoms, just as if you had quit drinking coffee or smoking, and it takes a while to get over it."

The slow-starting, slow-fading negative force is still there after the person or the substance is gone.

The cognitive side of Sternberg's love triangle is commitment, both a short-term decision to love another person and a long-term commitment to maintain that love. Its developmental course is more straightforward and easier to explain than that of intimacy or passion. Essentially, commitment starts at zero when you first meet the other person and grows as you get to know each other. If the relationship is destined to be long-term, Sternberg says, the level of commitment will usually increase gradually at first and then speed up. As the relationship continues, the amount of commitment will generally level off. If the relationship begins to flag, the level of commitment will decline, and if the relationship fails, the level of commitment falls back to zero. According to Sternberg, the love of a parent for a child is often distinguished by a high and unconditional level of commitment.

Levels of intimacy, passion and commitment change over time, and so do relationships. You can visualize this, says Sternberg, by considering how the love triangle changes in size and shape as the three components of love increase and decrease. The triangle's area represents the amount of love and its shape the style. Large amounts of intimacy, passion, and commitment, for example, yield a large triangle. And in general, Sternberg says, the larger the triangle, the more love.

Changing the length of the individual sides yields four differently shaped triangles, or styles of love. A triangle with three equal sides represents what Sternberg calls a "balanced" love in which all three components are equally matched. A scalene triangle (three unequal sides) in which the longest leg is passion represents a relationship in which physical attraction plays a larger role than either emotional intimacy or cognitive commitment. A scalene triangle with commitment as its longest leg depicts a relationship in which the intimacy and passion have waned or were never there in the first place. An isosceles triangle (two equal sides) with intimacy as its longest leg shows a relationship in which emotional involvement is more important than either passion or commitment. It's more like a high-grade friendship than a romance.

Sternberg admits that this triangle is a simplification of a complex and subtle phenomenon. There can be a variety of emotions, motivations, and types of commitment in a loving relationship, and each would have to be examined to completely diagnose a relationship. Beyond that, he says, every relationship involves several triangles: In addition to their own triangles, both people have an ideal triangle (the way you would like to feel about the person you love) and a perceived triangle (the way you think the other person feels about you).

Sternberg and graduate student Michael Barnes studied the effects these triangles have on a relationship by administering the liking and loving scales to 24 couples. Participants were asked to rate their relationship in terms of how they feel about the other person, how they think the other person feels about them, how they would feel about an ideal person, and how they would want an ideal person to feel about them. They found that satisfaction is closely related to the similarity between these real, ideal, and perceived triangles. In general, the closer they are in shape and size, the more satisfying the relationship.

The best single predictor of happiness in a relationship is not how you feel about the other person but the difference between how you would ideally like the other person to feel about you and how you think he or she actually feels about you. "In other words," Sternberg says, "relationships tend to go bad when there is a mismatch between what you want from the other person and what you think you are getting.

"Were you ever the overinvolved person in a relationship? That can be very dissatisfying. What usually happens is that the more involved person tries to think up schemes to get the other person up to his or her level of involvement. But the other person usually sees what's going on and backs off. That just makes the overinvolved person try harder and the other person back off more until it tears the relationship apart. The good advice in such a situation is for the overinvolved person to scale down, but that advice is hard to follow."

An underlying question in Sternberg's love research is: Why do so many relationships fail? Almost half the marriages in the United States end in divorce, and many couples who don't get divorced aren't all that happy. "Are people really so dumb that they pick wrong most of the time? Probably not," he suggests, "What they're doing is picking on the basis of what matters to them in the short run. But what matters in the long run may be different. The factors that count change, people change, relationships change."

Sternberg can't predict how people or situations will change, but he and his assistant Sandra Wright recently completed a study that suggests what will and won't be important in the long run. They put this question, what's important in a relationship, to 80 men and women from 17 to 69 years old, and divided them into three groups according to the length of their most recent relationship. The short-term group had been involved for up to two years, the mid-term group between two and five years, the others for more than five years.

Among the things that increase in importance as a relationship grows are willingness to change in response to each other and willingness to tolerate each other's imperfections. "These are things you can't judge at the beginning of a relationship," Sternberg says. "In the beginning," he explains, "some of the other person's flaws might not seem important. They may even seem kind of cute, but over the long term they may begin to grate on you. You both have to be willing to make some changes to make the relationship work and you both have to be willing to tolerate some flaws.''

Another thing that becomes increasingly important is the sharing of values, especially religious values. ''When you first meet,'' says Sternberg, ''you have this love-overcomes-all-obstacles attitude, but when the kids come along you have to make some hard decisions about the religion issue. All of a sudden something that wasn't so important is important.''

Among the things that tend to decrease in importance is how interesting you find your partner. ''In the beginning,'' Sternberg says, ''it's almost as if the other person has to keep you interested or the relationship will go nowhere. Later on, it's not quite as critical because there are other things in your life that matter.''

In addition to asking what is important at different times, Sternberg and Wright asked how much of these various things people had at different times in their relationships. The answers were not encouraging. The ability to make love, for example, often goes just at the time when it is becoming more important. In fact, Sternberg says, almost everything except matching religious beliefs decreased over time. The ability to communicate, physical attractiveness, having good times, sharing interests, the ability to listen, respect for each other, romantic love—they all went down. ''That may be depressing,'' says Sternberg, ''but it's important to know at the beginning of a relationship what to expect over time, to have realistic expectations for what you can get and what is going to be important in a relationship.''

And Sternberg feels that his triangular theory of love can help people in other ways. ''Just analyzing your relationship in terms of the three components can be useful,'' he says. ''Are you more romantic and your partner more companionate? It's helpful to know where you and your partner are well-matched and where you are not and then start thinking about what you can do to make yourselves more alike in what you want out of the relationship.''

If you decide to take steps to improve a relationship, Sternberg offers a final triangle, the action triangle. ''Often there's quite a gap between thought or feeling and action,'' he explains. ''Your actions don't always reflect the way you feel, so it could help to know just what actions are associated with each component of love.''

Intimacy, he suggests, might be expressed by communicating inner feelings; sharing one's possessions, time, and self; and offering emotional support. Passion, obviously, is expressed by kissing, hugging, touching, and making love. Commitment can be expressed by fidelity, by staying with the relationship through the hard times that occur in any relationship, or by getting engaged or married. Which actions are most important and helpful will vary from person to person and from relationship to relationship. But Sternberg feels it is important to consider the triangle of love as it is expressed through action because action has so many effects on a relationship.

Citing psychologist Daryl Bem's theory of self-perception, Sternberg describes how actions can affect emotions, motivations and cognitions. ''The way we act shapes the way we feel and think, possibly as much as the way we think and feel shapes the way we act.'' Also, he says, certain actions can lead to other actions; expressions of love, for exam-

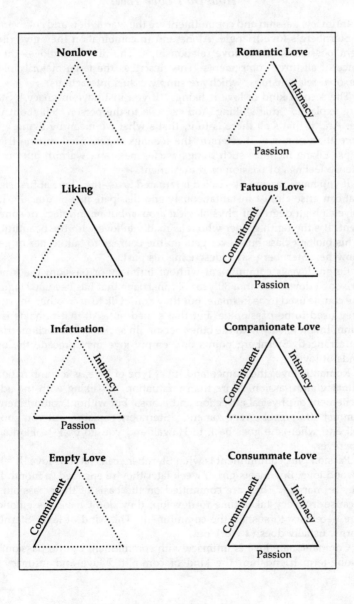

ple, encourage further expressions of love. Furthermore, your actions affect the way the other person thinks and feels about you and behaves toward you, leading to a mutually reinforcing series of actions.

"The point," Sternberg concludes, "is that it is necessary to take into account the ways in which people express their love. Without expression, even the greatest of loves can die."

How Do I Love Thee?

Intimacy, passion and commitment are the warm, hot, and cold vertices of Sternberg's love triangle. Alone and in combination they give rise to eight possible kinds of love relationships. The first is nonlove—the absence of all three components. This describes the large majority of our personal relationships, which are simply casual interactions.

The second kind of love is liking. "If you just have intimacy," Sternberg explains, "that's liking. You can talk to the person, tell about your life. And if that's all there is to it, that's what we mean by liking." It is more than nonlove. It refers to the feelings experienced in true friendships. Liking includes such things as closeness and warmth but not the intense feelings of passion or commitment.

If you have passion, it's called infatuated love—the "love at first sight" that can arise almost instantaneously and dissipate just as quickly. It involves a high degree of physiological arousal but no intimacy or commitment. It's the tenth-grader who falls madly in love with the beautiful girl in his biology class but never gets up the courage to talk to her or get to know her, Sternberg says, describing his past.

Empty love is commitment without intimacy or passion, the kind of love sometimes seen in a 30-year-old marriage that has become stagnant. The couple used to be intimate, but they don't talk to each other any more. They used to be passionate, but that's died out. All that remains is the commitment to stay with the other person. In societies in which marriages are arranged, Sternberg points out, empty love may precede the other kinds of love.

Romantic love, the Romeo and Juliet type of love, is a combination of intimacy and passion. More than infatuation, it's liking with the added excitement of physical attraction and arousal but without commitment. A summer affair can be very romantic, Sternberg explains, but you know it will end when she goes back to Hawaii and you go back to Florida, or wherever.

Passion plus commitment is what Sternberg calls fatuous love. It's Hollywood love: Boy meets girl, a week later they're engaged, a month later they're married. They are committed on the basis of their passion, but because intimacy takes time to develop, they don't have the emotional core necessary to sustain the commitment. This kind of love, Sternberg warns, usually doesn't work out.

Companionate love is intimacy with commitment but no passion. It's a long-term friendship, the kind of committed love and intimacy frequently seen in marriages in which the physical attraction has died down.

When all three elements of Sternberg's love triangle come together in a relationship, you get what he calls consummate love, or complete love. It's the kind of love toward which many people strive, especially in romantic relationships. Achieving consummate love, says Sternberg, is like trying to lose weight, difficult but not impossible. The really hard thing is keeping the weight off after you have lost it, or keeping the consummate love alive after you have achieved it. Consummate love is possible only in very special relationships.

PART IV
vvvvvvvvvvvvvvvvvvvvvvvvvvvvv

Communicating with
One Another

*H*ow beautiful it would be if the dream became the reality—if after
the marriage ceremony, the couple could ride into the sunset and
be blissfully happy and forever content with one another. Marriage, of
course, is not like the dream. No magnificent sunset enfolds us into a
magical world. Instead of transporting us into fantasy, marriage confronts us with a world that sometimes is all too real. Unlike the dream,
the reality of married life has its own harsh constraints and demands to
which newlyweds must adjust.

Those constraints and demands hold the disturbing potential to destroy love—as so many couples who began marriage with beautiful feelings and excellent intentions have sorrowfully discovered. Essential in
overcoming the many forces that tend to pull couples apart is communication, for to maintain love a couple must share how they feel about
their experiences. As Irving Sarnoff and Suzanne Sarnoff point out in
Chapter 16, however, we humans have a built-in barrier to communication: Although we yearn for love, we simultaneously resist the closeness
of love. As the Sarnoffs also indicate, an understanding of the stages of

marriage can enable a couple to overcome this tendency to self-destruct and help them build love into their married life.

To match our cultural ideal of marriage, often termed *companionate marriage,* in which friendship is seen as the essential relationship between a husband and wife, the newlyweds must form common perceptions. At least to some extent, their identities must merge. Their different backgrounds, however, impede this unifying process. As Peter L. Berger and Hansfried Kellner analyze the matter in Chapter 17, the key to jointly constructing marital reality is conversation. As they talk with one another, a husband and wife generate shared perceptions—ideas and attitudes that grow increasingly similar over the years. It is not simply that the two experience more in common as the years pass, but, rather, their very talk merges their ideas, allowing them to see things from increasingly closer perspectives.

A mutuality of perceptions occurs only after years of association. Such closeness may remain elusive, however, as many couples discover. Indeed, husbands and wives whose separate realities conflict tend not to stay together. The contrasts between the ways in which they view the world are too painful for their ideals, which often makes it attractive to seek satisfaction elsewhere. Those who remain together and reconcile their points of view construct a world in common (one that, perhaps curiously, is based primarily on conversation, or "linguistic perception").

A major barrier to the communication that merges a couple's separate worlds is the benevolent self-deception of courtship. In Chapter 18, Richard B. Stuart and Barbara Jacobson analyze how couples unwittingly make "secret contracts" that sabotage marriage: Each tends to take the other's behavior during courtship as a promise about how he or she will act after marriage. Yet each tends to think of his or her own behavior as not implying such a promise. Shortly after marriage, then, most couples experience problems in communication; some, unpleasantly surprised at the "real" husband or wife who has unexpectedly emerged, even wonder what happened to the person they thought they were engaged to.

Although no couple manages to overcome all the barriers to communication and make their worlds entirely one, most desire harmony and manage at least to shorten the distance between their perceptions. Attempts to live in harmony occasionally fail, however, no matter how much a couple may love one another and try to get along. The very fact of closeness in living is bound to result in at least occasional frustration. And frustrated desire produces anger. Anger, in turn, is deadly to a love relationship. Consequently, since it is inevitable that marriage will produce anger, a husband and wife must learn how to deal with it. In Chapter 19, David R. Mace presents practical suggestions for doing so.

Of the many sources of frustration and anger in marriage, our sex (or gender) roles rank toward the top. Differences in the socialization of males and females pose a primary impediment to successful marital communication. Perhaps the chief culprit is our culture's emphasis on males thinking of themselves as superior to females. Since equality is essential to our newly emerged ideal form of marriage, this contradiction contains built-in tension that leads to recurring marital problems. In Chapter 20, Clayton Barbeau analyzes how disparities of sex-role socialization underlie our chief failures in marital communication. He also indicates that negative communications are so serious that they even interfere with a husband's and wife's sexual relations—which themselves can be viewed as an essential form of marital communication. Fortunately, as Barbeau indicates, a couple can take steps to overcome this obstacle to successful communication.

16

▼▼▼▼

Love-Centered Marriage

▼▼▼▼

Irving Sarnoff
Suzanne Sarnoff

ABSTRACT: Love-centered marriage holds the promise of expanding the boundaries of individuality, increasing interdependence, providing pleasures of love-making, and transcending differences in gender. Two primary barriers to love-centered marriage are a natural fear of the closeness of love and competitive occupational striving. To overcome these hindrances, couples can institute a plan to achieve six objectives (or dialectical stages) in marriage. The dual names indicate the tension essential to each stage: (1) coupling and concealing, (2) reproducing and retreating, (3) nurturing and negating, (4) focusing and fragmenting, (5) renewing and regressing, and (6) deepening and drifting.

Everyone is born with a need to love and be loved; to give and receive affection, sexual pleasure, and care. When a man and a woman take their wedding vows, it is this deep desire for love that they hope to fulfill in marriage. What many sense only dimly, if at all, is that just as deeply rooted in human nature is a basic inhibition against loving, a fear that the union they yearn for menaces their personal survival. We struggle back and forth between these two forces all our lives—striving desperately to enjoy fully the love we find, yet fearing the merger it inevitably requires.

This normal conflict has been exacerbated in recent years by society's increasing emphasis on individual achievement. Our self-centered world incites both men and women to unceasing competition in the workplace, making them uncertain exactly where to place love on their scale of values.

Faced with these pressures of nature and nurture, how can husbands and wives preserve and deepen their love? Our answer is a new, love-centered model of marriage that makes cultivation of their relationship the couple's top priority. When a couple makes the commitment to put love first, everything else—work, child-rearing, recreation, community activities—becomes another opportunity to reach their full potential for loving.

This concept of love-centered marriage is based on the extensive research available on love and marriage, on interviews with couples who have been married for varying lengths of time—and on our own married lives, in which we have tested all the ideas presented here. We used a dialectical method of exploration—learning by doing and changing what we did in light of what we learned.

Contrary to prevailing stereotypes, we found that the quality of a couple's marriage is not defined by similarities or differences in their individual backgrounds and personalities. Rather, a marital relationship is a shared conception of how mates agree to love one another and to express their fear of loving. Spouses jointly and equally create these agreements in the here-and-now of their direct interactions, and they can always decide to make relational changes for their common good.

We also discovered that the affectionate and sexual wholeness of love contains four promises: expanding the boundaries of individuality; increasing interdependence; immersion in the pleasures of lovemaking; and transcending differences in gender. By redeeming these promises, spouses joyfully build their romance—the mental representation of the love they share. Neither trivial nor illusory, a couple's romance is the dynamic stimulant of energy that sustains their morale for a lifetime.

In fulfilling each promise, however, spouses invariably experience a dire threat, evoking fear for their very existence. So they covertly construct complicities—interpersonal defenses—to protect themselves. Yet by deceitfully fighting and fleeing, they deplete their energy and block the flow of their love.

These ideas are especially useful in coping with the stress marriage has been under in recent years as the principal field for tension between the sexes. Traditional marriage has accorded more status and power to husbands than to wives. This institutionalized sexism puts significant strain on many modern couples who seek the unique rewards of marriage without giving up the chance for both partners to live full lives that allow room for the exercise of their talents and interests.

A love-centered marriage is an egalitarian relationship, one that offers both men and women the conditions for a twin transcendence: freedom from socially learned gender roles, but also freedom to accept and enjoy fully their biological differences.

Many couples have already loosened the shackles of inequality; adding zest to their romance while expressing the entire spectrum of abilities and traits that characterize the common humanity of both sexes. But even with these intentions, couples still may fall into the ideological trap of judging their relational equality by their individual standing in society's hierarchy of wealth, prestige, and power. Sprinting in separate lanes on a fast track, neither partner is spared the strains husbands used to bear alone. While readily sympathizing with each other's stresses, they still may find it difficult to switch from being hard-driving and hard-nosed all day to being tender and compassionate lovers at night.

Commitment to a love-centered marriage gives a couple a philosophical perspective for avoiding this misery. Since the social structure is blatantly unjust, why bring its injustice into marriage? Their relative success in the marketplace has no inherent relevance to their marital happiness. Realizing this can help couples resist the pressure to emphasize occupational striving at the expense of their marriage and devote maximal time to being together.

THE SIX STAGES OF MARRIAGE

Spouses develop their capacity to love by adopting a *relational life plan* for meeting six desirable objectives. Because each objective is the main challenge of a marital era, that interval constitutes a stage. These stages do not unfold automatically, like the passing seasons. Mates create the stages by deciding to do what is best for their relationship at a particular period of time.

During the six stages, a couple fulfills the promises of love in new ways by accomplishing the tasks specific to each objective. But at every stage, they are vulnerable to fresh jolts from the threats of love and respond by forming new conflicting complicities to reduce their fears.

Couples play out this conflict in different ways as they meet each objective. The essence of these differences is conveyed in the dual names we've given each stage: The first stands for the *joint action* the man and woman take to attain an objective: the second expresses the quality of their *mutual defensiveness*. Recognizing both the goals of each stage and the defenses these goals evoke can enable a couple to derive the maximum pleasure and satisfaction from their marriage as they change and deepen it over time.

Stage 1: Coupling and Concealing

Newlyweds begin by establishing their romance as the most important ingredient in their relationship. They do this by coupling—making love frequently, talking openly about how they feel, and spending as much time as possible together. Through lovemaking, they attain an incomparable union of body and mind—equality at the most profound existential level. Inside his wife's vagina, a husband is as privy as he can ever be to how she perceives her erotic functioning. Surrounding his organ with her vagina, a wife gets as close as a woman can to knowing how it feels to have a penis.

Such intense intimacy, physical and emotional, stirs up all the threats of love. Most newlyweds feel obliged to protect themselves in various ways—perhaps by throwing themselves more completely into their jobs, by spending more time with their own parents, siblings, or friends, or by hiding their innermost thoughts from each other.

Stage 2: Reproducing and Retreating

Spouses expand their opportunities for love by deciding to have children and by participating as equally as possible in pregnancy and birth. Unquestionably equal in their contribution to conception, they at first revel in their natural differences. But the awesome female power of gestation and birth can eventually lead him to feelings of envy and inadequacy. Conversely, she may come to covet his freedom from the discomforts and dangers of birth. In a sense, he resents his wife because she is pregnant. She resents him because he is not.

There are ways to offset such defensiveness. She can suggest that they go together to the obstetrician and to classes on childbirth. He can encourage her to remain at work as long as possible. Participating together in all aspects of the pregnancy, they reach the pinnacle of transcendence in sharing the climactic episode of delivery.

Stage 3: Nurturing and Negating

After their child is born, spouses enhance their relationship further by raising a loving child or children and earning a living for the enlarged family. But while they reap the rewards of nurturing, they also may succumb to its threats. Many spouses aim for flexibility and equality in dealing with the demands of parenting, homemaking, and work—but then start to fear being too much alike. She's afraid of losing her female prerogatives, so she ends up doing most of the housekeeping and child rearing, even if she holds a job. Afraid of becoming an emasculated wimp, he refrains from offering his help and becomes totally absorbed in his career.

Some couples take these sexist patterns into bed with them: The husband always initiates lovemaking, trying hard to convince his wife, and himself, that he's a paragon of virility. She acquiesces to his demands, ever the docile "lady in waiting" whose attractiveness is proven by his coming on to her. He's afraid of being rejected as unmanly and losing his potency if he enacts his fantasies of letting her make the advances. She fears being rebuffed as wanton, aggressive, and unfeminine if she unleashes the intensity of her erotic appetite.

In this *pas de deux*, couples undermine their sexual enjoyment. Envying the social power symbolized by her husband's penis, the wife is loath to admit she needs it for her pleasure and won't let go enough to have a satisfying orgasm. With similar spite, disaffection, and frustration, he rushes through foreplay and "gets his rocks off" quickly. He envies her ability to just "lie back" instead of having to get and maintain an erection.

Some parents use children as pawns in their complicities. Threatened about losing their individuality, a rivalrous couple may compete for their children's affection and disagree bitterly over how they should be raised. One parent opts for strict discipline, the other for permissiveness. In all these ways, spouses negate their potentials for loving as well as those for their children.

Stage 4: Focusing and Fragmenting

As their children grow, couples may vacillate about the ultimate size of their family. Conditioned to rigid gender preferences and the ethos of "having it all ways," many couples are dissatisfied with offspring of only one sex. Pushing themselves to have at least one child of each gender, they risk fragmenting their relationship just when they could benefit themselves—and their present child or children—by being satisfied with what they have.

Other couples decide not to have any more children and to devote more time to each other, as they did when they were younger. Converging toward greater equality, they depart from traditional gender roles. Ironically, by focusing more on each other and less on having and rearing children, couples arouse their fear of loving. So they find ways of

fragmenting their relationship. He may try to sabotage her new assertiveness, while she derides his inept attempts to work around the
house.

Other husbands and wives—afraid of which activities should be
"his" and which "hers"—get involved separately in recreational pursuits with members of their own sex. By excluding one another in this
way, they block the growth of their social equality. But by airing their
fears and standing fast to tolerate them, the couple can avoid locking
themselves into sexual segregation.

Stage 5: Renewing and Regressing

Middle-aged couples get another chance to renew the vitality of their
marriage after their children leave. Relieved of contraceptive hassles and
fear of pregnancy, many women celebrate by enjoying their erotic capacities to the fullest. The physiological slowing of the man's ejaculatory
response helps give his wife enough stimulation for a fulfilling orgasm.
He is no longer the pounding Bull of the Pampas nor she the seething
Tigress of the Serengeti. But with their cumulative familiarity, they
know the exact places to touch and kiss and the right pace for cresting
the tide of their passion.

For many couples, unfortunately, their children's departure seems
like the end of marriage. With the children gone, a couple loses the
daily satisfactions—and challenges—of parenting. And without children
around as a barrier to their intimacy, couples may feel at a loss, at least
temporarily, about how to relate exclusively as husband and wife. They
may even be haunted by a sense that something is missing in their relationship—although there is actually more going on between them in
terms of direct interaction.

At the same time, many couples must deal with the negative effects
of aging. The wife's menopause may cause depression and trigger hor-
monal changes that result in vaginal dryness. The husband, struck by a
decline in sexual potency, may also experience depression. The double
loss—no longer having any children at home and their own physical
decline—makes love even more threatening than it had been in earlier
stages.

Reacting defensively, some couples behave like toddlers clinging to a
security blanket and resist any change in their lives. Others take the
opposite tack and flee into activity reminiscent of their early married
years. They quit their jobs, sell their houses, move to another state,
away from family and friends. Both extremes work against the
strengthening of love.

Stage 6: Deepening and Drifting

Spouses who reach the age of 65 or 70 have a wonderful opportunity for deepening the gratifications of their relationship—even in the face of growing physical problems and the imminence of death. Doing everything together, couples can resolve to love each other as much as possible in the time left to them. They can also maximize their interdependence by taking care of whatever unfinished business remains in settling the details of their estate, the living arrangements for whoever survives the other, and any misunderstandings that still exist between themselves and their children.

Too often, this enriching objective is threatening by their joint fear of death and the ambiguity of not knowing who will go first. Afraid of depending too much on someone who may soon be gone, they find ways to drift apart well before death separates them.

CHOOSING LOVE OVER FEAR

Unless they realize the dialectical nature of their relationship—the constant struggle between the deep need for love and the equally deep fear of it—spouses are likely to blame each other for the conflicts and tensions no couple can avoid. Understanding the inevitability of such problems permits them to appreciate more the progress they do make in loving, to be less harsh with themselves about their defensiveness and more motivated to overcome it. In this way, couples can learn to tip the balance of their ambivalence in favor of love over fear at every stage of a lifelong marriage.

Building your life around a loving relationship is not really a selfish act. What it takes to be a loving and equal spouse is exactly what it takes to live as a balanced, mature adult in the outside world. Spouses carry these individual benefits of their relational development into more humane and honest relationships with their children, their friends and their co-workers. Thus, by centering their marriage on love, couples can contribute to change for a better world.

17

Marriage and the Construction
of Reality

▼▼▼▼▼

Peter L. Berger
Hansfried Kellner

ABSTRACT: People need a sense of order (*nomos*) in their lives. Reality, however, does not come with a ready-made sense of order. Consequently, people construct order for themselves by jointly deciding how to look at things (*the social construction of reality*). Contemporary marriage functions as a primary means of providing this sense of order (its *nomos-building* function), of giving common meaning to life events. A husband and wife construct a new reality as their conversations alter their ideas of others and themselves (*definitions of reality*).

Key terms for understanding this chapter are

anomie: normlessness; a sense of not belonging, or losing one's bearing or
         sense of order
definition of reality: the ideas or views that someone has of something
endogamy (endogamous): marrying within one's group
exogamy (exogamous): marrying outside one's group
nomos: a sense of order and of belonging; the opposite of anomie
social construction of reality: the process, based on conversation, by which
                       people determine their understanding of life
                       events—their views of what is
typifications: the categories that people use to classify their experiences

validation: gaining a sense of agreement from others concerning one's views
or definitions of reality

Ever since Durkheim, it has been a commonplace of family sociology
that marriage serves as a protection against anomie for the individual.
Interesting and pragmatically useful though this insight is, it is but the
negative side of a phenomenon of much broader significance. If one
speaks of *anomic* states, then one ought properly to investigate also the
nomic processes that, by their absence, lead to the aforementioned
states. If, consequently, one finds a negative correlation between marriage and anomie, then one should be led to inquire into the character
of marriage as a *nomos*-building instrumentality, that is, of marriage as
a social arrangement that creates for the individual the sort of order in
which he can experience his life as making sense. . . .

Marriage is obviously only *one* social relationship in which this process of *nomos*-building takes place. It is, therefore, necessary to first look
in more general terms at the character of this process. . . .

The process that interests us here is the one that constructs, maintains, and modifies a consistent reality that can be meaningfully experienced by individuals. In its essential forms this process is determined
by the society in which it occurs. Every society has its specific way of
defining and perceiving reality—its world, its universe, its overarching
organization of symbols. This is already given in the language that
forms the symbolic base of the society. Erected over this base, and by
means of it, is a system of ready-made typifications, through which the
innumerable experiences of reality come to be ordered. . . .

The socially constructed world must be continually mediated to and
actualized by the individual, so that it can become and remain indeed
his world as well. The individual is given by his society certain decisive
cornerstones for his everyday experience and conduct. Most importantly, the individual is supplied with specific sets of typifications and
criteria of relevance, predefined for him by the society and made available to him for the ordering of his everyday life. This ordering or
. . . nomic apparatus is biographically cumulative. It begins to be
formed in the individual from the earliest stages of socialization on, then
keeps on being enlarged and modified by himself throughout his
biography. . . . Every individual requires the ongoing validation of his
world, including crucially the validation of his identity and place in this
world, by those few who are his truly significant others. Just as the individual's deprivation of relationship with his significant others will
plunge him into anomie, so their continued presence will sustain for
him that *nomos* by which he can feel at home in the world at least most
of the time. Again in a broad sense, all the actions of the significant
others and even their simple presence serve this sustaining function. In
everyday life, however, the principle method employed is speech. In

this sense, it is proper to view the individual's relationship with his significant others as an ongoing conversation. As the latter occurs, it validates over and over again the fundamental definitions of reality once entered into, not, of course, so much by explicit articulation, but precisely by taking the definitions silently for granted and conversing about all conceivable matters on this taken-for-granted basis. Through the same conversation the individual is also made capable of adjusting to changing and new social contexts in his biography. In a very fundamental sense it can be said that one converses one's way through life.

If one concedes these points, one can now state a general sociological proposition: the plausibility and stability of the world, as socially defined, is dependent upon the strength and continuity of significant relationships in which conversation about this world can be continually carried on. Or, to put it a little differently: the reality of the world is sustained through conversation with significant others. This reality, of course, includes not only the imagery by which fellowmen are viewed, but also includes the way in which one views oneself. . . .

With these preliminary assumptions stated we can now arrive at our main thesis here. Namely, we would contend that marriage occupies a privileged status among the significant validating relationships for adults in our society. Put slightly differently: marriage is a crucial nomic instrumentality in our society. We would further argue that the essential social functionality of this institution cannot be fully understood if this fact is not perceived.

We can now proceed with an ideal-typical analysis of marriage, that is, seek to abstract the essential features involved. Marriage in our society is a *dramatic* act in which two strangers come together and redefine themselves. The drama of the act is internally anticipated and socially legitimated long before it takes place in the individual's biography, and amplified by means of a pervasive ideology, the dominant themes of which (romantic love, sexual fulfilment, self-discovery and self-realization through love and sexuality, the nuclear family as the social site for these processes) can be found distributed through all strata of the society. The actualization of these ideologically predefined expectations in the life of the individual occurs to the accompaniment of one of the few traditional rites of passage that are still meaningful to almost all members of the society. It should be added that, in using the term "strangers," we do not mean, of course, that the candidates for the marriage come from widely discrepant social backgrounds—indeed, the data indicate that the contrary is the case. The strangeness rather lies in the fact that, unlike marriage candidates in many previous societies, those in ours typically come from different face-to-face contexts—in the terms used above, they come from different areas of conversation. They do not have a shared past, although their pasts have a similar structure.

In other words, quite apart from prevailing patterns of ethnic, religious, and class endogamy, our society is typically exogamous in terms of nomic relationships. Put concretely, in our mobile society the significant conversation of the two partners previous to the marriage took place in social circles that did not overlap. With the dramatic redefinition of the situation brought about by the marriage, however, all significant conversation for the two new partners is now centered in their relationship with each other—and, in fact, it was precisely with this intention that they entered upon they relationship.

It goes without saying that this character of marriage has its root in much broader structural configurations of our society. The most important of these, for our purposes, is the crystallization of a so-called private sphere of existence, more and more segregated from the immediate controls of the public institutions (especially the economic and political ones), and yet defined and utilized as the main social area for the individual's self-realization. It cannot be our purpose here to inquire into the historical forces that brought forth this phenomenon, beyond making the observation that these are closely connected with the industrial revolution and its institutional consequences. The public institutions now confront the individual as an immensely powerful and alien world, incomprehensible in its inner workings, anonymous in its human character. If only through his work in some nook of the economic machinery, the individual must find a way of living in this alien world, come to terms with its power over him, be satisfied with a few conceptual rules of thumb to guide him through a vast reality that otherwise remains opaque to his understanding, and modify its anonymity by whatever *human relations* he can work out in his involvement with it. . . . The private sphere . . . is mainly where . . . the individual will seek power, intelligibility and, quite literally, a name—the apparent power to fashion a world, however Lilliputian, that will reflect his own being: a world that, seemingly having been shaped by himself and thus unlike those other worlds that insist on shaping him, is translucently intelligible to him (or so he thinks); a world in which, consequently, he is *somebody*. . . . In sum, it is above all and, as a rule, only in the private sphere that the individual can take a slice of reality and fashion it into his world.

. . . Unlike an earlier situation in which the establishment of the new marriage simply added to the differentiation and complexity of an already existing social world, the marriage partners now are embarked on the often difficult task of constructing for themselves the little world in which they will live. . . .

The attempt can now be made to outline the ideal-typical process that takes place as marriage functions as an instrumentality for the social construction of reality. The chief protagonists of the drama are two individuals, each with a biographically accumulated and available stock of experience. As members of a highly mobile society, these individuals have already internalized a degree of readiness to redefine themselves and to modify their stock of experience, thus bringing with them considerable psychological capacity for entering new relationships with others. Also, coming from broadly similar sectors of the larger society (in terms of region, class, ethnic, and religious affiliations), the two individuals will have organized their stock of experience in similar fashion. In other words, the two individuals have internalized the same overall world, including the general definitions and expectations of the marriage relationship itself. Their society has provided them with a taken-for-granted image of marriage and has socialized them into an anticipation of stepping into the taken-for-granted roles of marriage. All the same, these relatively empty projections now have to be actualized, lived through and filled with experiential content by the protagonists. This will require a dramatic change in their definitions of reality and of themselves.

As of the marriage, most of each partner's actions must now be projected in conjunction with those of the other. Each partner's definitions of reality must be continually correlated with the definitions of the other. The other is present in nearly all horizons of everyday conduct. Furthermore, the identity of each now takes on a new character, having to be constantly matched with that of the other, indeed being typically perceived by people at large as being symbiotically conjoined with the identity of the other. In each partner's psychological economy of significant others, the marriage partner becomes the other *par excellence*, the nearest and most decisive co-inhabitant of the world. Indeed, all other significant relationships have to be almost automatically reperceived and regrouped in accordance with this drastic shift.

. . . By definition, then, marriage constitutes a nomic rupture. In terms of each partner's biography, the event of marriage initiates a new nomic process. Now, the full implications of this fact are rarely apprehended by the protagonists with any degree of clarity. . . . What typically is apprehended are certain objective and concrete problems arising out of the marriage—such as tensions with in-laws, or with former friends, or religious differences between the partners, as well as immediate tensions between them. These are apprehended as external, situational and practical difficulties. What is *not* apprehended is the subjective side of these difficulties, namely, the transformation of *nomos* and identity that has occurred and that continues to go on, so that all problems and relationships are experienced in a quite new way, that is, experienced within a new and ever-changing reality.

Take a simple and frequent illustration—the male partner's relationship with male friends before and after the marriage. It is a common observation that such relationships, especially if the extramarital partners are single, rarely survive the marriage, or, if they do, are drastically redefined after it. This is typically the result of neither a deliberate decision by the husband nor deliberate sabotage by the wife. What rather happens, very simply, is a slow process in which the husband's image of his friend is transformed as he keeps talking about this friend with his wife. Even if no actual talking goes on, the mere presence of the wife forces him to see his friend differently. This need not mean that he adopts a negative image held by the wife. Regardless of what image she holds or is believed by him to hold, it will be different from that held by the husband. This difference will enter into the joint image that now must needs be fabricated in the course of the ongoing conversation between the marriage partners—and, in due course, must act powerfully on the image previously held by the husband. Again, typically, this process is rarely apprehended with any degree of lucidity. The old friend is more likely to fade out of the picture by slow degrees, as new kinds of friends take his place. The process, if commented upon at all within the marital conversation, can always be explained by socially available formulas about "people changing," "friends disappearing" or oneself "having become more mature." . . .

Marriage thus posits a new reality. The individual's relationship with this new reality, however, is a dialectical one—he acts upon it, in collusion with the marriage partner, and it acts back upon both him and the partner, welding together their reality. . . . Thus the new reality is not posited once and for all, but goes on being redefined not only in the marital interaction itself but also in the various maritally based group relationships into which the couple enters. . . .

The reconstruction of the world in marriage occurs principally in the course of conversation, as we have suggested. The implicit problem of this conversation is how to match two individual definitions of reality. By the very logic of the relationship, a common overall definition must be arrived at—otherwise the conversation will become impossible and, *ipso facto*, the relationship will be endangered. Now, this conversation may be understood as the working away of an ordering and typifying apparatus—if one prefers, an objectivating apparatus. Each partner ongoingly contributes his conceptions of reality, which are then "talked through," usually not once but many times, and in the process become objectivated by the conversational apparatus. The longer this conversation goes on, the more massively real do the objectivations become to the partners. In the marital conversation a world is not only built, but it is also kept in a state of repair and ongoingly refurnished. The subjective reality of this world for the two partners is sustained by the same conversation. The nomic instrumentality of marriage is concretized over and over again, from bed to breakfast table, as the partners carry on the endless conversation that feeds on nearly all they individually or jointly experience. Indeed, it may happen eventually that no experience is fully real unless and until it has been thus "talked through."

This process has a very important result—namely, a hardening or stabilization of the common objectivated reality. It should be easy to see now how this comes about. The objectivations ongoingly performed and internalized by the marriage partners become ever more massively real, as they are confirmed and reconfirmed in the marital conversation. The world that is made up of these objectivations at the same time gains in stability. For example, the images of other people, which before or in the earlier stages of the marital conversation may have been rather ambiguous and shifting in the minds of the two partners, now become hardened into definite and stable characterizations. A casual acquaintance, say, may sometimes have appeared as lots of fun and sometimes as quite a bore to the wife before her marriage. Under the influence of the marital conversation, in which this other person is frequently "discussed," she will now come down more firmly on one *or* the other of the two characterizations, or on a reasonable compromise between the two. In any of these three options, though, she will have concocted with her husband a much more stable image of the person in question than she is likely to have had before her marriage, when there may have been no conversational pressure to make a definite [choice] at all. The same process of stabilization may be observed with regard to self-definitions as well. In this way, the wife in our example will not only be pressured to assign stable characterizations to others but also to herself. Previously uninterested politically, she now identifies herself as a liberal. Previously alternating between dimly articulated religious positions, she now declares herself an agnostic. Previously confused and uncertain about her sexual emotions, she now understands herself as an unabashed hedonist in this area. And so on and so forth, with the same reality—and identity—stabilizing process at work on the husband. Both world and self thus take on a firmer, more reliable character for both partners.

Furthermore, it is not only the ongoing experience of the two partners that is constantly shared and passed through the conversational apparatus. The same sharing extends into the past. The two distinct biographies, as subjectively apprehended by the two individuals who have lived through them, are overruled and reinterpreted in the course of their conversation. Sooner or later, they will "tell all"—or, more correctly, they will tell it in such a way that it fits into the self-definitions objectivated in the marital relationship. The couple thus construct not only present reality but reconstruct past reality as well, fabricating a common memory that integrates the recollections of the two individual pasts. The comic fulfilment of this process may be seen in those cases when one partner "remembers" more clearly what happened in the other's past than the other does—and corrects him accordingly. Similarly, there occurs a sharing of future horizons, which leads not only to stabilization, but inevitably to a narrowing of the future projections of each partner. Before marriage the individual typically plays with quite discrepant daydreams in which his future self is projected. Having now considerably stabilized his self-image, the married individual will have to project the future in accordance with this maritally defined identity. This narrowing of future horizons begins with the obvious external limitations that marriage entails, as, for example, with regard to vocational and career plans. However, it extends also to the more general possibilities of the individual's biography. To return to a previous illustration, the wife, having "found herself" as a liberal, an agnostic, and a "sexually healthy" person, *ipso facto* liquidates the possibilities of becoming an anarchist, a Catholic, or a Lesbian. At least until further notice she has decided upon who she is—and, by the same token, upon who she will be. The stabilization brought about by marriage thus affects the total reality in which the partners exist. In the most far-reaching sense of the word, the married individual "settles down"—and *must* do so, if the marriage is to be viable, in accordance with its contemporary institutional definition.

It cannot be sufficiently strongly emphasized that this process is typically unapprehended, almost automatic in character. The protagonists of the marriage drama do *not* set out deliberately to recreate their world. Each continues to live in a world that is taken for granted—and keeps its taken-for-granted character even as it is metamorphosed. The new world that the married partners, Prometheus-like, have called into being is perceived by them as the normal world in which they have lived before. Reconstructed present and reinterpreted past are perceived as a continuum, extending forwards into a commonly projected future. . . . Typically, the reality that has been "invented" within the marital conversation is subjectively perceived as a "discovery." Thus the partners "discover" themselves and the world, "who they really are," "what they really believe," "how they really feel, and always have felt, about so-and-so." . . .

. . . If one conceives of the marital conversation as the principal drama and the two partners as the principal protagonists of the drama, then one can look upon the other individuals involved as the supporting chorus for the central dramatic action. Children, friends, relatives, and casual acquaintances all have their part in reinforcing the tenuous structure of the new reality. It goes without saying that the children form the most important part of this supporting chorus. Their very existence is predicated on the maritally established world. The marital partners themselves are in charge of their socialization *into* this world, which to them has a preexistent and self-evident character. They are taught from the beginning to speak precisely those lines that lend themselves to a supporting chorus, from their first invocations of "Daddy" and "Mummy" on to their adoption of the parents' ordering and typifying apparatus that now defines *their* world as well. The marital conversation is now in the process of becoming a family symposium, with the necessary consequence that its objectivations rapidly gain in density, plausibility, and durability.

In sum: the process that we have been inquiring into is, ideal-typically, one in which reality is crystallized, narrowed and stabilized. Ambivalences are converted into certainties. Typifications of self and of others become settled. Most generally, possibilities become facticities. What is more, this process of transformation remains, most of the time, unapprehended by those who are both its authors and its objects. . . .

. . . Put simply: marriage involves not only stepping into new roles, but, beyond this, stepping into a new world. The *mutuality* of adjustment may again be related to the rise of marital equalitarianism, in which comparable effort is demanded of both partners.

Most directly related to our considerations are data that pertain to the greater stability of married as against unmarried individuals. Though frequently presented in misleading psychological terms (such as "greater emotional stability," "greater maturity," and so on), these data are sufficiently validated to be used not only by marriage counselors but in the risk calculations of insurance companies. We would contend that our theoretical perspective places these data into a much more intelligible sociological frame of reference, which also happens to be free of the particular value bias with which the psychological terms are loaded. It is, of course, quite true that married people are more stable emotionally (i.e. operating within a more controlled scope of emotional expression), more mature in their views (i.e. inhabiting a firmer and narrower world in conformity with the expectations of society), and more sure of themselves (i.e. having objectivated a more stable and fixated self-definition). *Therefore* they are more liable to be psychologically balanced (i.e. having sealed off much of their "anxiety," and reduced ambivalence as well as openness towards new possibilities of self-definition) and socially predictable (i.e. keeping their conduct well within the socially established safety rules). All of these phenomena are concomitants of the overall fact of having "settled down"—cognitively, emotionally, in terms of self-identification. . . .

. . . The prevalence and, indeed, increasing prevalence of divorce might at first appear as a counter-argument to our theoretical considerations. We would contend that the very opposite is the case, as the data themselves bear out. Typically, individuals in our society do not divorce because marriage has become unimportant to them, but because it has become so important that they have no tolerance for the less than completely successful marital arrangement they have contracted with the

particular individual in question. This is more fully understood when one has grasped the crucial need for the sort of world that only marriage can produce in our society, a world without which the individual is powerfully threatened with anomie in the fullest sense of the word. Also, the frequency of divorce simply reflects the difficulty and demanding character of the whole undertaking. The empirical fact that the great majority of divorced individuals plan to remarry and a good majority of them actually do, at least in America, fully bears out this contention.
. . .

. . . We have used the case of marriage for an exercise in the sociology of knowledge, a discipline that we regard as most promising. . . . The sociology of knowledge must not only be concerned with the great universes of meaning that history offers up for our inspection, but with many little workshops in which living individuals keep hammering away at the construction and maintenance of these universes. In this way, the sociologist can make an important contribution to the illumination of that everyday world in which we all live and which we help fashion in the course of our biography.

18

▼▼▼

Uncovering Secret Contracts
▼▼▼

Richard B. Stuart
Barbara Jacobson

ABSTRACT: Courtship is a time of benevolent self-deception—of taking our partner's behavior as a promise to continue courtship behavior after marriage, while
making no such promise ourselves. These "secret contracts"—assumptions of
what marriage will be like made on the basis of courtship behaviors—often create problems that sabotage marriage, for they have little to do with marital realities. Suggestions for identifying and negotiating secret contracts are provided.

Courtship is the time of maximum human deception. Never during
the course of human development do we overstate our virtues to conceal our vices as skillfully as we do when we try to convince someone
to share our lives.

We are not alone. Many animals put on exaggerated displays in order
to gain an opportunity to reproduce. Like these animals, humans engage in courtship rituals to attract attention and win favor. But we differ
from other animals in two important ways. Rejected animals seem to
turn immediately to courting another prospective partner, while we are
more likely to go into mourning. And while animals rarely have contact
with one another after fertilization, courtship is just an early stage of a

long-term relationship for humans. Only people allow courtship to affect their self-esteem and their expectations for the future.

Our forefathers were very suspicious of courtship. In 1647, the Massachusetts legislature believed that courtship should be regulated by law, claiming that it was a process in which "young men . . . watch all advantages for their evil purposes, to insinuate [themselves] into the affections of young maidens. . . ." Others did not see courtship as an evil, but they believed it had little to do with the realities of marriage. William Congreve warned that "courtship is to marriage as a very witty prologue is to a very dull play" and Alexander Pope observed "they dream in courtship, but in wedlock wake."

"To court" means "to allure, to tempt . . . to seek to attract by attentions and flatteries . . . leading to engagement and marriage." The definition of the word makes it clear that courtship is not intended to provide a couple with a realistic picture of a lifetime together, but simply to increase the likelihood that the couple will marry. It's only natural, then, that men and women who are courting present themselves in the most positive light.

· Courtship patterns have changed through the ages, and many people nowadays try very hard to "be themselves" as they get to know a prospective mate. If we've been married before, we're particularly skeptical about those appealing images we see in courtship. One major disappointment is enough to convince us that courtship promises may have little to do with marriage realities. But most of us eventually find dating more disappointing than fulfilling, and we long for the comfort and security of a more permanent and stable relationship. So we are willing to set our doubts aside, idealizing what we can, rationalizing flaws we can't deny, and doing our best to convince ourselves that *this* person is the *right* person.

As soon as we decide that we want this relationship to work, we start trying harder to please. We do our best to create a good impression, trying to earn as much affection, respect, and trust as we can. We display table manners that may never be seen again. We bone up on books and current events that will never earn our notice in the future. We take pains to laugh at our dates' jokes, no matter how corny they may seem. And we feign interest in anything from basketball games to ballet just to show that we like the same things. We don't want to lie, but neither do we want to emphasize our liabilities. Since we are trying to sell ourselves, we carefully choose what to reveal about our past. When we talk about our first marriages, we describe our heroic efforts to make things work and our spouses' failure to do anything to help. And we talk more about how well our children did in school than how much trouble they have caused at home. Everything we do is intended to create an aura conducive to "I will" rather than "How could you even ask?"

Since many people no longer trust the dating process, they choose to live together in an attempt to get a more accurate idea of what the future would hold. Unfortunately, couples who live together before marriage are no less likely to divorce than those who don't. This suggests that even twenty-four-hour contact for months or even years is insufficient to convey the truth about life after marriage.

People live together in good faith, without deliberately planning to deceive. But cohabitation is different from marriage in important ways. Palimony suits notwithstanding, cohabiting couples have fewer legal and social ties than those that bind married couples. Families, friends, and religious leaders who often pressure a married couple to stay together may actually feel relieved when a cohabiting pair splits up. And the partners agree to stay together only as long as both are happy. Because they know that the relationship can be ended as soon as either loses interest, both are motivated to make a constant effort to keep the satisfaction level high.

Marriage offers a very different commitment. We speak vows that are unconditional, promising to maintain the bond "as long as we both shall live" not "as long as we both are happy." This unconditional promise often allows married couples to feel less obligation to continue to work on the relationship. Once the goal is reached and the marriage vows exchanged, attention can be turned to other concerns. All too often, we unwittingly rely upon social, religious, and legal forces to preserve the marriage. Unfortunately, while outside forces may be strong enough to keep the marriage intact, only the partners' efforts can make it happy.

Assumptions made on the basis of courtship behaviors, with or without cohabitation, often create problems that can eventually sabotage marriage. We naively interpret courtship behaviors as promises that our partners will be as eager to please us after marriage as before. We engage in a bit of benevolent self-deception in which we assume that our partners plan to continue to deliver, but we never check out our assumptions. We want so much to believe all is well that we decide to act as if it is.

As a result, we think we have our partners' promise to continue courtship behavior even though we realize that we have made no such commitment ourselves. The commitment is assumed and never verified, but we act as though it were as binding as a formal vow. Unfortunately, because these expectations are never discussed, they may be false. For example, during courtship he may regularly prepare gourmet meals for her, leading her to expect more of the same when they marry. Imagine her surprise and disappointment when he comes home with carry-out fast foods on his nights to cook.

Since most of us consider courtship to be a preview of the coming marriage, why aren't we more open about our expectations? Often, we are too embarrassed to discuss our wishes in detail. For example, we may be reluctant to prescribe the way we want our partners to express affection, approach us sexually, or manage their personal hygiene. We would rather just assume that our desires will be met. Unfortunately, the fact that we never asked for the things we didn't get does not minimize our disappointment when they aren't delivered.

Many of us are also reluctant to create a debt that has to be repaid. As long as we don't ask for what we want, we can feel less responsible for reciprocating when we get it. Although we operate on a pay-for-what-you receive basis in business, we expect good behavior from our spouses as a matter of right, whether or not we meet their desires in return. This belief inevitably causes problems.

Finally, we often fail to discuss important issues before we marry simply because it never occurs to us to do so. We are so taken up with the romantic excitement of courtship that we don't consider details like who will be bringing home the bacon, or who will clean the refrigerator in which it is kept.

We pay a heavy price for not discussing what we have and what we want. Whether we realize it or not, *everything that we do in courtship is understood to be an implicit promise to continue to act the same way throughout the marriage*. Our expectations of marriage are based much more upon behavior than intent.

How binding can these premarital secret agreements be? Life does not stand still, and we can't be expected to act on our silver anniversaries the same way we did on our wedding nights. Change in behavior over the years is not only unavoidable, it is even desirable. But when a behavioral change implies a change in basic values, the marriage can be threatened.

While it's expected that we will handle the details of our lives differently over time, we have a responsibility to base any changes in behavior on a consistent set of principles. We *should discuss* any plans to change our behavior, but we *must negotiate* any shift in values.

Values are the superstructure of our lives, the general principles that guide our answers to the important questions we face throughout the years. Value decisions relevant to marriage might include: the relative importance of home and work, the importance of a sexually exclusive relationship, the amount of openness and sharing desired, concern for a healthy way of living, the role of religion in the couple's life, and expectations concerning independence versus interdependence. It's reasonable for courting couples to hold one another accountable for the values expressed before marriage, although the ways in which these values are acted upon may vary according to the constraints and opportunities that emerge over time.

Let's see how this looks in the example of one couple. Ken's first marriage had been a traditional one. His wife stayed home and raised the children while he worked hard to provide the financial support. As the years went by, Ken felt more and more oppressed. It seemed that no matter how much money he made, his family always wanted more. He also felt that any time he wasn't at work, he was expected to do something for one child or the other. In his opinion, he was not appreciated as a person, but only as a breadwinner, tutor, and chauffeur.

Then Ken met June at a friend's party, and he was immediately entranced. June was young, dynamic, divorced, and powerfully attracted to him. She had been married for three years and had a child who was living with his father. As the story so often goes, Ken eventually divorced his first wife and married June. He was exhilarated at having the opportunity to recapture some of his lost youth, and he luxuriated in the freedom of not being a full-time parent.

His ecstasy with June continued for about a year. Then, on her thirty-second birthday, June told Ken that she wanted her son to live with them, and she also wanted to move from the city to the suburbs. She intended to continue to work part-time, but she planned to combine work with motherhood.

Ken felt his new lease on life had been cruelly shattered. He had already put in his time as a father, and he didn't want another cycle of hours behind the wheel and endless struggles to find excuses for not being a Little League coach, assistant scout master, debate judge, or host for the graduation beer-bust. Even more important, he feared that June, like his first wife, would neglect him in favor of her son.

For her part, June had always believed that Ken was a man who basically enjoyed fatherhood but who just needed to experience it with a more appreciative spouse. Her work was important, but she expected to feel complete only after she became a full-time mother again. The ensuing struggle between Ken and June left them both with very bad feelings as each held the other accountable for deliberate deception.

How is it that Ken and June managed to avoid discussing this crucial issue before they decided to marry? Certainly each must have had some idea that the issue of child custody could arise again. But in order to keep each other happy, as courting couples must do, they avoided detailed discussions about issues where they feared disagreement. They spoke less often and less emphatically about their own expectations, and they interpreted each other's messages in the most positive way. For example, when Ken heard June describe her pleasure at being alone with him, he felt sure she was saying that she was happy to devote all of her attention to him. When June saw the pride Ken took in her son's accomplishments, she was sure he wouldn't mind having him live with them. The process of drawing self-serving conclusions from our partners' words and actions almost guarantees a troublemaking secret contract.

Ken and June could have guarded against this misunderstanding by an early discussion of their long-term expectations about work, children, and where to live. Talking about these issues was not without its risks: they might have decided not to marry, because being free of children now was as important to Ken as reuniting with her son was to June. But if neither was willing to negotiate on this issue, they should have tried to make that clear before they married.

Another couple had a different problem involving mismatched expectations. Ted and Ellen met when they were both management trainees, soon fell in love, and started to live together. They lived together very well, with equal sharing of nearly every aspect of their lives. Ellen cooked during the week and Ted cleaned up. Ted cooked weekend meals or arranged for dinner out. He took care of the laundry and garbage; she serviced their cars. She found and paid someone to clean their apartment; he paid the bills and prepared their taxes.

When Ted was offered a good job in another state, they decided to marry and make the move together, even though Ellen knew she might not be able to find a job. Soon after they married, they started arguing over who should do the grocery shopping, who should mow the lawn, who should prepare the meals and clean up afterward. Ellen maintained that they should share the chores as they had done before, but after marriage Ted seemed to think that fresh vegetables grew in the refrigerator and dishtowels were designed to fit only a woman's hands. Ted said he had been brought up to believe that the wife should take care of the home when the husband is the primary wage-earner. Ellen felt she had already sacrificed a good job to the relationship, and she had no intention of adding the responsibilities of a full-time housewife to her burden.

Neither Ted nor Ellen was acting in bad faith, although each accused the other of having made false promises about marriage while they were living together. They were eventually able to negotiate an agreement about household responsibilities, but if they had done it before they married, they could have prevented months of bickering.

Bargaining done before marriage helps both partners make informed decisions about whether to marry. When it occurs after marriage, the process is made more complicated by the anger that often develops when expectations haven't been met. Still, the uncovering of secret contracts can be useful at any stage of a relationship.

The secret contract is as powerful as it is unknown. We can start by defining it as precisely as we can:

A secret contract is the belief by courting partners that each will continue to act after marriage in accordance with the values and patterns established at the time they agreed to wed. It is understood that the values will prevail throughout their life together, while the daily patterns will continue until circumstances or open discussion necessitate change.

Why is it that so many of us break these implicit promises and change for the worse after we marry? After all, people can't be so devious as to deliberately put on an act only until they have "caught" a mate. And yet, it does seem that we often stop trying to please once the knot is tied.

One reason may be that courtship, though wonderful, takes tremendous effort. If courtship is to be successful, the relationship usually has to come first. Work, family, friends, and personal development may be neglected while we focus on our prospective spouses. Once married, we often tend to drift back to business as usual; consequently, the new spouses get less attention than courtship would have led them to expect.

Also, after we have formally made a lifetime commitment to another person, a question that we seldom ask while courting comes to mind, namely: "Do I want to live with this behavior for the rest of my life?" Many actions that seemed trivial or only mildly annoying during courtship become oppressive when we think in terms of living with them for a lifetime. And yet, it's easy to understand the anger that can result from having your spouse suddenly tell you that many of the things you thought were acceptable are annoying and ought to be changed.

We also change because circumstances change. People move, change jobs, make new friends, have children, get sick, and undergo the normal transitions of aging. It's foolish to expect that patterns established at age 25 will be equally feasible or even as desirable at age 55.

Let's look at a brief example of how secret contracts can change in response to new opportunities. During the time they lived together, Dan was a student and had many hours to spend with Liz. She worked full-time, but didn't really enjoy her job and rarely took work home from the office, so her evenings were also free. After they were married, Dan landed a well-paying job which kept him busy from early morning until at least nine most nights. When Dan's income increased, Liz decided to cut back and work part-time. But Dan's free time was at a premium, just when Liz expected to see more of him. He felt that she had become demanding and insensitive, while Liz felt that Dan had become self-absorbed and indifferent. Each accused the other of breaking courtship promises, when they were really both adapting to a change in circumstances. What they needed to do was find new ways to give each other caring and attention that didn't depend on large amounts of shared time.

As if the normal complications aren't bad enough, remarrying couples have a special problem. We sometimes expect our second spouses to act the same way our first partners did. We're as likely to expect the good things as the bad, and both expectations can lead to trouble. For example, Brenda's first husband reacted with fury when she talked to other men at parties they attended together, but he never cared who she saw when they were apart. Without ever asking, Brenda assumed that her second husband had similar views. During their courtship, she always stayed by his side at parties, but she made lunch "dates" with friends of both sexes. After they were married, her husband began to complain about her lunches with male friends. Brenda was initially dismayed, and she accused him of being jealous and possessive. But further discussion revealed that there were many areas in which he was not the least bit jealous. For example, he didn't care at all who she talked to at parties, and in fact preferred that they mingle separately. Her misunderstanding was not over the rules of the game, but about which players were in the game.

Whatever the cause, partners feel angry when secret agreements are broken. The anger is inappropriate, because there never was an explicit agreement, so there could not be a deliberate violation. But frustration over the inability to talk about a concern will eventually lead to anger. And the arguments that result are hard to resolve because the partners invariably have two very different ideas of the terms of the initial agreements.

When the content of these implicit agreements is revealed, each person can offer to act in certain ways and can request the kinds of responses he or she desires in exchange. When the agreement is explicit, further discussion and amendment are possible.

The list below can help you and your partner record the details of the promises you think you heard or know you want from each other. A written document has the advantage of making it easier for both partners to be sure of what is and is not expected. It's also easier for some people to put expectations in writing rather than talk about them.

Nothing should be censored from this list: include everything that is important to you. Very often, the things you are most self-conscious about discussing are the ones you are the least willing to do without. Answer these questions separately and then discuss each expectation with your partner, agreeing to those that are acceptable and negotiating compromises for those that are not.

Bear in mind that this exercise is not risk free: you may discover differences that seem alarming. Those who are considering marriage can use the exercise to discover and openly resolve differences before marriage. Those who are already married can use this exercise to uncover unstated expectations that may be at the core of recurring conflicts.

SECRET CONTRACT EXPECTATIONS

In what ways do you think you and your partner have agreed to handle the following issues?

1. Ownership of property and other assets
2. Management of household responsibilities
3. Deciding how to spend money
4. Use of free time
5. The role of religion in your lives
6. The role of relatives in your lives, including parents, siblings, former spouses, and children by former marriages
7. Your plans to have, or not to have, children
8. Management of the use of alcohol and other drugs
9. Management of personal health and appearance
10. Development of independent and mutual personal interests
11. The role and importance of friends in your lives
12. Ways of expressing affection
13. Details of sexual expression
14. Extramarital sex
15. Education and professional development
16. Any other important issues (specify)

When you have both identified your expectations, compare your lists. You should give each other precise descriptions of each item you list. For example, "Talk to my mother when she calls on Sundays" is much less ambiguous than "Be nice to my family." Then each of you should describe the extent to which you are willing to meet the other's expectations.

During this discussion, you will find many areas in which you accurately understand each other's desires, and are happy to meet them. You may also find some areas of disagreement. It's worth taking the time and risk needed to negotiate your differences, because after secret contracts have been revealed, they can be replaced by realistic expectations.

Let's look at an example of how one couple we saw benefitted from this exercise. Karen and Todd met each other when they were both unhappily married to other people. Eventually, they ended their marriages and began to discuss a formal commitment to each other. When they saw us for premarital counseling, they were both clearly under the spell of new love, but they also wanted to make sure that their second marriage would be more rewarding than the first.

As they completed the secret contract exercise, they were surprised to discover a number of issues they hadn't thought about. They knew they agreed about the importance of religion, family, and attention to personal fitness, but they had never discussed the way they would manage money or free time after marriage. Todd was still recoiling from his divorce settlement, and he favored the idea of keeping his remaining assets in his name only. Since Karen was successfully self-employed (and had given her ex-husband a large share of her assets in order to be free of the relationship), he assumed that she, too, would prefer separate ownership. Karen, as it turned out, believed in sharing everything, and she had interpreted Todd's generosity during courtship as a statement that he felt the same way.

This couple's expectations about free time also differed. Before they married, it was difficult for them to see each other, and they took advantage of every opportunity. Todd expected Karen to continue to spend as much time with him as possible, while Karen believed that too much time together would create the same unhealthy dependency she had in her first marriage.

Because Todd and Karen were eager to please each other and to make the relationship work, and because they had never argued about time or money, they were able to discuss their differences and work out compromises that suited them both. They decided to share most, but not all, of their assets, and they agreed to an amount of time together that each felt was acceptable though not ideal. Each felt more confident about entering a second marriage once they had worked out some of the potentially difficult details. . . .

. . . The differences that you find between yourself and your future spouse should be seen as a challenge, for meeting them is an excellent way of strengthening your marriage. Developing the ability to understand each other's views and reach mutually satisfying compromises is the best guarantee that you'll like what you get in your . . . marriage.

19

The Deadly Love-Anger Cycle

David R. Mace

ABSTRACT: The fundamental cause of marital failure in our time is the inability to resolve the anger that is inevitably generated in an intimate relationship. The author examines the nature of anger, its impact on a love relationship, and its constructive management in marriage. He rejects the concept of "marital fighting" in favor of a three-step procedure for managing anger in companionship marriage.

. . . I have been a marriage counselor for nearly forty years, and have seen the inside workings of thousands of marriages in trouble. During the past thirteen years, as a result of sharing with my wife the leadership of many marriage enrichment retreats, I have in addition seen the inside workings of hundreds of marriages that were not in trouble.

Thinking over what was happening in all these marriages, I have asked myself some basic questions. What is it, above all else, that prevents so many marriages from achieving the warm, loving, mutually creative experiences the partners hope and long for? Some say it is sexual maladjustment. Others say temperamental incompatibility, or poor role functioning, or inadequate communication, or adverse environ-

185

mental pressures. There are many theories. I have considered them all—
and rejected them all in favor of something that is hardly ever mentioned. My conclusion is that what causes marriages to fail, over and
over again, is the incapacity of the couple to cope with their own and
each other's anger.

COMPANSIONSHIP MARRIAGE
AND THE QUEST FOR LOVE

Let me at once explain what kind of marriage I am talking about. I
take the view, shared widely by others, that the traditional marriage,
with its rigid institutional character, cannot survive in our new, open
society. It is rapidly being replaced by an alternative form, clearly recognized by Ernest Burgess in 1945, and described by him as the companionship marriage. In describing the new emerging form, Burgess uses
such terms as "interpersonal relationships, mutual affection, sympathetic understanding, comradeship." The popular terminology would
describe it as being based less on duty than on love.

In the course of a generation, millions of couples have turned away
from traditional marriage and chosen companionship marriage as their
preferred life-style. But in doing so they have fallen into a trap. They
have not understood (and we have not enlightened them) that the companionship marriage does indeed offer them the interpersonal fulfillment they are seeking; but that to achieve it they must learn new skills
which their forefathers didn't need to learn. These new skills are
summed up in Nelson Foote's term "interpersonal competence." Without those skills, they will be very likely to end up on the rocks. And the
most dangerous rock of all, responsible for untold multitudes of marital
wrecks, is the destructive force of anger.

Imagine a typical couple moving into marriage. What they want is
love. In order to get it, they seek intimacy. As they move closer to each
other, something happens. Differences between them, which may have
seemed unimportant or even attractive when viewed from a distance,
now become threatening and cause disagreement. This happens inevitably when people enter into the shared life. They are now in a dilemma.
Should they move away from each other to ease the disagreement? No,
because they want intimacy, and that means moving closer. So they
move closer. Then the disagreement becomes more painful. It heats up
and becomes conflict. The loving couple find a flood of negative feelings
being stirred up—hostility, resentment, irritation, disillusionment, all of
which create anger. These negative feelings destroy the warm loving
feelings with which they approached each other. They feel cheated.

They have put their quarter in the slot machine to get out a package of love—and out comes a package of anger instead!

What do they do next? If they move still closer, the anger tends to get hotter and burn up their love. If they move away, the anger dies down; but they have to give up, for the time being, their quest for intimacy. There seems to be no solution.

This interaction process is what I have called the "love-anger cycle." You seek intimacy to get love. As you do so, the inevitable differences between you become disagreements and then heat up into conflict. This releases a flood of anger which destroys love. Shocked and hurt, you back away and abandon the quest for intimacy. This process is instantly recognized by most married couples. A few have been able to work through it. The vast majority, baffled and beaten, have finally given up and settled for a relatively superficial relationship. The dream of love is shattered, and they are secretly or openly disillusioned.

This deadly and destructive cycle is the great wrecker of companionship marriages. It existed, of course, in traditional marriages too. But it did not wreck them, for several reasons. They were based on duty, and did not need love to keep them intact. The couple did not seek or expect intimacy as we define it today. Husbands were allowed, even encouraged, to vent anger, which was viewed as a proof of their masculinity. But wives were sweet and patient, and swallowed their anger. Thus the head-on collision that is so devastating to love was avoided.

THE NATURE OF ANGER

If we are to find any solution to this serious problem, we must take a close look at anger. The first step is to recognize it as a healthy emotion. It is the biological survival kit issued to all of us, to enable us to survive in crisis situations.

The physiology of anger is fascinating—the outpouring of adrenalin, the increase in the heart-rate, the tensing of muscles, the withdrawal of anticoagulants in the blood, the constriction of external arteries, and much besides. A general alert goes out to all body systems, like the calling up of all reserves in a country threatened with war.

Of course, in civilized society, we seldom need all those elaborate preparations; because our lives are not likely to be threatened. But they are all there, part of our inheritance from the days when life was a constant struggle for survival.

It seems, however, that anger is not a primary emotion. It is triggered off by other emotions, and two in particular—fear and frustration. The relationship between fear and anger is obvious. Fears warns us of danger; and we react by preparing to fight with all our resources, or if necessary to run away at a phenomenal speed. These are the things we can do when, as we express it, our "blood is up."

For our purpose, however, the frustration reaction is more important. The animal gets angry not only when danger threatens. He also gets angry when food is out of reach, and he must jump high or tear down a barrier to reach it. He can perish equally by being attacked and by being deprived. So anger musters all his resources to grasp the food that seems to be out of reach.

Our civilized society reduces danger but increases frustration. So for most of us, anger is triggered off when we can't get what we want and need. That happens very often when, after long years of living independently, we enter into an intimately shared life with another person. Marriage probably produces more frustration and more anger than any other human situation in which we are likely to find ourselves. We are told that a great deal of the violence in our society today is family-related. . . .

LOVE AND ANGER

. . . Those who seek intimacy find themselves, again and again, in states of strong emotion. The emotions concerned are both positive and negative—that must be accepted as natural and inevitable. Love and anger prompt them to actions that are opposites—to stroke or to strike. One way to avoid striking is to stop stroking too—some couples do that. Another way is to accept the impulse to stroke but reject the impulse to strike. Some couples try to do this; but it usually is not very successful, because it is hard on a relationship to allow one kind of emotion to arise and forbid the other kind. In a good marriage the couple should be open to recognize all emotions that develop between them—only so can they feel safe and secure in cultivating intimacy.

Most of us seem now to agree that suppressing anger in marriage is unhealthy and counterproductive. So the cult of our time is to allow, and even to encourage, the venting of anger at least within limits. I have come to the conclusion that this is having devastating results in our family life. Observers tell us that in most families today a great deal of communication is taking place; but that most of it is negative communication. This is sometimes explained by saying that it is easier for us to get over our inhibitions about expressing negative feelings than it is to get over our inhibitions about positive feelings. I cannot accept this explanation. What is much more likely is that with so much striking going on, the impulse to stroke is simply being crushed.

I do not, therefore, accept George Bach's concept of "marital fighting" as being natural and healthy. I have read his writings carefully, and am impressed by his profound studies of the subject. Oddly enough, I suspect that he does not really accept the concept of marital fighting himself! By the time his couples have learned all the rules, they are not fighting at all! He says, for example, that it is sometimes best to go into a fight with the intention of losing; and that in the best fights, both win! This seems to me to be stretching the meaning of the word "fighting" beyond all reason. I have a suspicion that the term "marital fighting" and "intimate enemy" may have seemed so intriguing to George Bach, or to his publisher, that he mislabeled what he had to say in order to use a catchy title that would sell the book. This seems a great misfortune, because I find that large numbers of people who talk about "marital fighting" have to admit that they have not really read the book.

The position at which I have finally arrived is that the venting of anger is inappropriate in a love relationship. In such a relationship of intimacy, two people, in order to be open to each other's feelings, must make themselves vulnerable. But this cannot be done with any real sense of security if one's trust can be exploited by a sudden and unexpected invitation to a fight. My own relationship to my mother, in my childhood years, never became close because she had an explosive temper. She considered this harmless, because her explosions were "soon over," after which she "felt better." Alas, I could not open my heart to her under those conditions, and remained at a safe distance.

I think it is not unreasonable to liken the venting of anger to spitting—throwing out something that is venomous and not wanted. I would consider it inappropriate at any time to spit at my wife; and I would likewise consider it inappropriate to vent my anger on her. Vented anger is simply incompatible with love, and therefore out of place in a relationship in which people are seeking intimacy.

MANAGING ANGER
IN A COMPANIONSHIP MARRIAGE

The inevitable question therefore confronts us: If the quest for love through intimacy inevitably produces anger, and if vented anger destroys love, what can we do about it? I have found in the literature several suggestions about this. None of them satisfy me. Let me comment on three of them.

One is the contention that vented anger is a helpful form of nonverbal communication, which says in effect to the partner, "Look out—I'm on the warpath." some instructive parallels are given from animal behavior. I admit I am an animal, but I also have the advantage of being able to use speech. I see no reason why I should have to startle my wife with a roar of rage in order to tell her I'm angry when I am perfectly capable of saying to her simply, "Look. I'm getting angry. Let's do something about it."

Another theory is that intimate relationships can be restrictive, and that people need to withdraw at times and put distance between them. This they do by having fights, then later they come back together and renew their intimacy. I agree about the occasional need for assistance; but again, since husband and wife can communicate, I see no reason why these periods of solitude cannot be negotiated between them when necessary, without the need for a fight to tear them apart.

A third theory is that some couples value their intimacy more when they have been through a period of alienation; for example, it is said that making love is particularly satisfying after a fight. If fighting really enhances love for some couples, by all means let them make war as an aid to making love. I suspect, however, that such couples are in the minority. Venting anger, according to my observation, is for most couples a painful and hurtful experience, damaging to their intimacy. It is for these couples that we need to find a solution.

The solution I have found involves training couples to deal with anger in three successive steps. Training is absolutely necessary, because all three steps are opposed to the instinctual or cultural mechanisms with which we have been endowed.

1. *Acknowledge your anger.* What this means is simply learning to say to your spouse, "I'm getting angry with you" instead of communicating this indirectly with a cutting comment or a burst of rage. It has simply never occurred to most husbands and wives to do this; but once they've tried it out, they're amazed at how much more constructive it can be. Often the trouble is that they think being angry is wicked, and they're ashamed or embarrassed to admit it. But why not say, "I'm angry," just as you would say "I'm frightened," "I'm hurt," "I'm tired," or "I'm depressed"; and just as you would say "I'm happy," "I'm feeling affectionate," "I'm excited," or "I'm grateful." In a good companionship marriage, all states of feeling can and should be communicated—at the time they occur.

2. *Renounce your anger as inappropriate.* This does not mean you do not have a right to be angry. In an appropriate situation, your anger could be a life-saver. Anger enables us to assert ourselves in situations where we should. Anger exposes antisocial behavior in others. Anger gets wrongs righted. In a loving marriage, however, these measures are not necessary. My wife is not my enemy. She is my best friend; and it does not help either of us if I treat her as an enemy. So I say, "I'm angry with you. But I don't want to be angry with you. I don't like myself in this condition. I don't want to want to strike you. I'd rather want to stroke you." This renouncing of anger on one side prevents the uprush of retaliatory anger on the other side, and the resulting tendency to drift

into what I call the "artillery duel." If I present my state of anger against my wife as a problem I have, she is not motivated to respond angrily. . . . Instead of a challenge to fight, it is an invitation to negotiate.

3. *Ask your partner for help.* This third step is the clincher. Without it, not much progress can be made. The anger may die down, but that is not enough. Both partners need to find out just *why* one got made with the other. If they do not, it could happen again, and again, and again. A request for help is not likely to be turned down. It is in your partner's best interests to find out what is going on, and correct it, if a loving relationship is going to be maintained. When the request for help is accepted too, the stimulus that caused the anger is usually completely neutralized, and the negative emotion dissolves away. Then the work can begin right away if possible, or at some agreed future time. The whole situation can thus be calmly examined, and some solution found. In fact, conflicts between married people are not really destructive. Rightly used, they provide valuable clues that show us the growing edges of our relationship—the points at which we need to work together to make it richer and deeper.

CONCLUSION

I have described the love-anger cycle, which I think is the root cause of most failures to achieve a companionship marriage. And I have described a simple form of training which can help couples to break out of the cycle. My wife and I have tested this out, very successfully, in our own marriage; and I have used it to train other couples to deal with their conflicts, again with gratifying success. It is my impression that the fundamental barrier to growth in most marriages is the inability of the couple to cope effectively with anger. Once they have learned to do this, and are no longer afraid of anger in themselves and in each other, they become free to grow in love and intimacy. It is as if they had broken through the sound barrier; and now—the sky is the limit!

Finally, I need to add a few extra comments:

1. Hearing about this way of dealing with anger is in itself of little use. It has to be *applied*. This means that a couple must *make a contract* that they will learn together the three necessary steps. This will probably be quite difficult at first, because established habits will tend to reassert themselves. But with guidance and help from a counselor, couples can in time make progress, and the encouraging results when they succeed will give them the motivation to continue.

2. Individuals have widely differing anger thresholds. Some become angry at the slightest provocation, others do so only under heavy pressure. These variations seem to depend on stimulus response. People

who are insecure and prone to fear develop anger more often than those who are strong and self-confident. Type A persons also develop anger more easily and more often than those with low motivation for achievement. . . .

3. The procedure I have described applies not only to married couples. It can be used in parent-child relationships, where a lot of anger is stirred up. It can also be effective in other relationships—among friends and between colleagues, for example. . . .

20

▼▼▼▼

The Man-Woman Crisis

▼▼▼▼▼

Clayton Barbeau

ABSTRACT: Although the traditional man-woman relationship has been rendered obsolete by technology, our socialization continues to perpetuate male-female inequalities. Men's basic feelings of superiority, combined with their economic power, create resentment in women. Because our obsolete sex roles continue to dominate male-female relationships, they continue to engender resentments. Consequently, husbands and wives struggle against one another—with one result being incompatible approaches to sex. To solve this basic man-woman crisis requires that individuals break out of the stereotypical roles into which they have been thrust—not an easy thing to do, but not impossible either.

[F]or most of human history and for most of humankind, the respective roles of men and women have been determined by the needs for maintenance and survival of the family and tribe or nation. Whatever we may think of such roles as they were worked out in different cultures in different eras, the fact is that they were usually clearly defined. In times previous to ours, most men and women conformed to patterns of behavior toward each other that were taught by their society. It was left

193

to our current century—with its newborn industrialism, its rapid shift of population from farms to cities, its sudden access to cross-cultural information, its universal education, its advances in communication and personal mobility—to shatter the old functional roles. Add to the list the new demands of a technological society, the enormous increment of scientific research, the advances in knowledge of human behavior, the provision of means of having sexual pleasure without fear of pregnancy, and we have the elements that dramatically render obsolete previously hallowed patterns of the man-woman relationship.

Despite this, much of our acculturation of boys and girls for their adult man-woman roles persists in educating them for patterns of sexual relating that are no longer functional. This cultural lag appears to be a major factor in the current almost palpable tension between men and women in our society. . . . [W]e still tend to educate the majority of boys in modes of behavior that place the masculine label upon toughness, the suppression of tender emotions, the notion of masculine dominance over women. . . .

Often enough, the only area in which a particular man can feel or assert his power over women is in the economic sphere. Many men define their roles in family life solely in terms of being the "breadwinner." Thus they are threatened when their wives decide to earn an income of their own, and even some of the most "liberated" men are unwilling to see their wives earn an income larger than their own. More than one professional woman has turned down a job promotion with increased income because it would mean that she would be making more money than her husband and she didn't think he would be able to adjust to that. At the same time, some women who are totally economically dependent upon their husbands have very negative feelings about their own situation. A former client [expressed it this way]:

> I remember the freedom I felt when I got my first paycheck for a part-time job. I had earned this money. I could buy those things (a new lamp, fix the kitchen floor, etc.) that Peter said we couldn't afford. He was making $34,000 a year. I never could understand why we couldn't afford nicer furniture, etc. It was two months after I took the part-time job that he said he was leaving me to marry another woman (or should I say "mother"?). All I cared about, he said, was a career. He told people I wasn't satisfied with my home life; that is was obvious I was really messed up.
>
> My earning power was very subtly sabotaged. All counseling fees were to be paid by me—"You're the one who wanted this!" Any time we had dinner out other than for social or business reasons, I paid. After all, if I didn't have that job, I wouldn't be too tired on Friday night to make dinner, right?

For many men, not only does economic power continue a superior-inferior notion of the male-female relationship; many men expect it to be understood as an expression of their love. "I don't know what in hell more she can want from me," one client shouted. "She can write a check for any damned thing she needs." His wife was asking for intimacy. She phrased it as "consideration for my feelings," "a willingness to listen to me," "sharing his feelings with me." He countered such declarations with angry assertions of his economic strength, flexing his money muscles. "You ought to see the home I've bought her. And she's got her own car."

The male mystique works in other ways to destroy healthy relationships between men and women. One man had ignored his wife's feelings for years. He had had more than one affair, which, while not overtly boasting about, he made little attempt to conceal from his male friends. His wife confronted him one day with the news that she was getting a divorce in order to marry a man to whom she had turned for intimacy. The husband went on a furniture-breaking rampage, threatened murder, stormed out for a three-week binge, flirted with suicide, then sobered up and promptly moved into the apartment of one of his former bedpartners. He incorporated into that behavior much of the male mystique: He subscribed to the double standard; he threatened aggression against others and himself as a solution to his problem; he then sought out another woman to be dependent upon him, thereby reassuring himself of his masculine power. Informative as is his reaction to the crisis, it is a reaction rooted in the same male mystique that led to his marital breakup. . . .

The symptom of adultery on the part of wives has been, in my counseling experience, most often caused by a searching for intimacy with a man who cares and who demonstrates his caring, for a personal relationship that the husband is not supplying. One woman having an affair with an impotent man stated, "My husband is a stud in bed, but my lover is just that, a romantic lover who listens to me, who shares with me." Adultery on the part of a husband, on the other hand, is often a flight from the very demands of intimacy his wife is making. "She wants too much. I can't take all that closeness," one wandering husband disclosed. Particularly in one-night stands, he finds he can have some sexual activity without love, without self-revelation. And therein he hopes to find reassurance of his masculinity. The very fact that he needs such constant reassurance signals the location of his personal difficulties. The misnamed "great lovers" Don Juan and Casanova were likewise afflicted: Because their last conquest had not proved to them that they were adequate, they had to find another.

In reality, the sexual act itself—and the male orgasmic response—is closely tied to these problems. It is not uncommon for both husbands and wives to express dissatisfaction with their sexual lovemaking: she because of the lack of positive emotional content, of tenderness or true intimacy in their relationship; he because he finds her basic dissatisfaction, or her demands, a hindrance to his sense of "good performance." Her lack of response and his sense of failure often lead to a diminishing, even disappearance, of sexual lovemaking in marriage.

One client, separated for over a year, said, "Initially I begged him for some understanding. He simply tossed a sex manual at me. When I suggested counseling he said no. He said the problem was mine, not his. For the last ten years of our marriage, we lived like good friends, brother and sister, good parents. To the outside world, we were a lovely couple. Then I decided life must offer something more. Our separation was amicable. Then I met a man. He courted me, paid attention, listened, understood, responded to me as a person. When we finally, months later, made love, I discovered there was nothing wrong with me; I loved it. I think it was because he touched me emotionally, spiritually, personally, long before he ever touched me physically."

Because the male tends to think of the sexual act as an adequacy test, a performance equivalent to the strong swing of the hammer that will ring the gong at the state fair, he may not understand the causes of his wife's dissatisfaction. If he is one of those who is focused on "providing" an orgasm for his wife as a means of showing his prowess, he may himself get little pleasure from the activity. And if he fails to "provide" an orgasm, he too is dissatisfied. . . .

I have been present in group therapy sessions where . . . I've heard a veritable chorus of voices saying, "I'm tired of being his mother. I want a husband. I want a man to husband me, not a big boy who alternates between boasting to his friends, getting into angry rages with me or the kids and then coming with whimpering requests for sex, like it was some sort of candy I dole out when he's been a good boy for the last hour."

Coupled with complaints that "he's the oldest boy in the family" and "he won't talk to me of anything that really matters" (i.e., won't talk of their relationship or what's really happening with him or them) is the plaint that "he's more in love with television sports than with me." The television program "Love American Style" once had a skit which illustrated this syndrome. The husband was totally caught up in watching a football game, while the wife tried every seductive wile she knew to distract him from the ongoing competition to her presence. Failing every effort, she finally shouted, "You love football more than you love me!" He turned for the moment to announce, "Yes, but I love you more than I love baseball," and returned to watching the game.

Humorous as the sketch was, it is less than humorous when seen in the life of the women who know its truth. . . . In such cases it seems apparent that sports are being used merely to avoid intimate contact with the spouse. One athlete whose wife had left him wept over his loss. "I sent her two dozen roses. She refused them, saying, 'Last year a single rose might have done. It's too late now.' She smashed the television set one day with a beer bottle, during a game I was watching. I said she was crazy and went to a buddy's house to watch the game.'' Significantly, he admitted to neglecting his daughter also, while he devoted full attention to his ''jock'' son and to the boy's progress as a young athlete.

These examples of typical problems in the man-woman relationship are directly related to the miseducation of the American male. They are outcroppings, on the adult level, of the masculine mystique inculcated from birth. Another example is the astonishing level of drug addiction, especially alcoholism, among males. In adolescence, drinking is seen as a sign of manliness. One of the rites of initiation into the cult of the big-boys peer group when I was growing up was the ability to chugalug a pint or so of hard liquor. . . .

Because drinking hard liquor is touted as masculine, many men in our society promptly run for the bottle when they feel their adequacy threatened. They prefer it as a form of escape from women who demand that they meet them on a more adult ground. . . .

''What does woman want?'' Freud plaintively asked, and left us without the hint of an answer, having his own problems with women. It is a question on the minds of many men today. Surely everyone knows what women do not want: They do not want to be considered as receptacles for male sperm; they do not want to be servants to men; they do not want less pay for the same work that some man is doing; they do not want discrimination in job promotions; they do not want.
. . . But what *do* they want? More specifically, what do they want from the men or the man in their life? Perhaps as a man I am being terribly presumptuous when I essay some possible responses to the question. Yet I sally forth like Don Quixote because I'm afraid we've had all too many explorations of what's wrong in the man-woman relationship, where the problems originate, and how dreadful things are, with too few people offering even a hint of positive steps that might be taken to turn this crisis into a moment of true growth in understanding between men and women. . . .

What they really want, if I hear them at all correctly, is that their men grow up. Single or married, the articulate, self-possessed, self-supporting woman finds herself too often confronting the tender ego of the male who wants a woman who will look up to him (which implies his elevated status and her genuflection at his shrine), and who will be, or appear to be, dependent upon him in those ways (emotionally or financially or intellectually) that will make him feel strong. If she doesn't play this game, he may feel uncomfortable with her, threatened by her, ill at ease in her company. Or, he may want her to meet all his needs—emotional, physical, nurturing, supportive—as his mother did, without his paying much attention to any of her needs. In either case, then, what she wants of the man in her life is that he be a grown-up person.

But what do we mean by grown-up? . . . If the men of our time are to live up to the women of our time, then I think that they must take a long, hard look at their upbringing and their assumptions as men. How much of my life is lived as a role I am playing, trying to "be a man" in the eyes of other men rather than having the courage to be myself? Consider for a moment a simple, tiny example of this sort of thing. One of my favorite before-dinner drinks is a sweet vermouth with a twist of lemon. Yet, on more than one occasion when ordering this, I've had men who were ordering a scotch or "double martini, very dry" exclaim, "Why don't you have a man's drink?" I've often wondered how many men really would have preferred a daiquiri, or even a soft drink, but were afraid of losing esteem as "real men" for ordering less than hard liquor. . . . Sometimes the assertion of oneself takes such simple forms as rejecting pressures of that sort.

The courage to be myself and not play roles implies, of course, the courage to examine myself and find out who I am. If the criteria for manliness are uncertain in our time, it is because too few men have had the courage to reexamine the attitudes inculcated in them in their early years and to question the validity of such conditioning today. While many men are ready to pay lip service to the notion of women's equality as persons, even to agree on the important aspects of man-woman relationships, men continue to lag behind women in doing the hard work of digging into themselves and seeing what historical baggage they can jettison, what chains from the past they can saw off, to bring themselves greater emotional freedom.

That introspective look into ourselves to confront what we consider masculinity to be for us is the first task for any man who wishes to begin the process of growth. . . .

Freud left the popular impression that we are unfree creatures, victims of our unconscious drives and instincts. Marx claimed we were economically determined creatures, victims of the system. Darwin argued, as did Spencer, that we were biologically determined. Too many of us men today seem to have accepted this status of victimhood; but we do that at our own peril. The fact is that we are responsible creatures, free to choose our own course. No one need remain a victim of his or her upbringing or of unexamined assumptions. We really can open ourselves up to the questioning that leads to growth. . . . Furthermore, we men might begin to pay attention to what the women in our lives are trying to tell us. . . .

I personally do not hear my female clients telling their husbands to define themselves only in terms of wifely needs or to dedicate their lives simply to serving their wives' desires. I do hear them calling for us to have the courage to drop our masks and our role-playing and to begin to search for new and more authentic ways of treating ourselves and of relating to them.

Perhaps most crucial to our growth as men is that we learn to take the risks of disclosing ourselves to those we love. For there can be no authentic loving that does not involve self-revelation. It is only in authentic love relationships—ones in which we are openly listening to one another, in which we are touching one another on ever-deepening levels of personal awareness—that we begin to gain a sense of personal fulfillment. . . .

Women who complain of the men in their lives as ''not caring for my feelings, not listening, always walking all over me, talking down, treating me like a child, not giving a damn about me'' are describing a male victim of the masculine mystique. If we have heard those remarks directed at us, we ought to examine ourselves carefully for the cause. Usually, in my own case, the cause was the same: a lack of respect for the woman's personhood. The comment was a warning signal that I was not living up to my own ideals. The mature man, in touch with his own personhood, has the ground for appreciating and reverencing the personhood of others. The basic sign of this lack of respect is not paying attention to the other. Paying attention is a profound sign of love for another. My attentiveness to you tells you that you are important to me. The fact that I am truly listening to you, not interrupting or discounting what you say, but seeking to hear it, to empathize with it, tells you that you are as important to me as my own self—perhaps even more important, for I've laid down my preoccupations in order to let your thoughts, your feelings, enter into me. . . .

Manliness, the sort of manliness that may enable men to cope more effectively with the man-woman crisis in our times, is not a set of trophies to be won and put on a shelf. There is no classroom in which it can be learned. Most men and women today find manliness difficult to define, for many of the qualities found admirable in men are equally admirable in women. Yet I do think that the beginning of a definition of masculinity can be found in those men who listen to their own feelings and to those of the women in their lives. In both sets of feelings we have sources of insight into what we might do to rid ourselves of the oppression of the male-female stereotypes that are so often the source of conflict between men and women today. . . .

PART V

▼▼▼▼▼▼▼▼▼▼▼▼▼▼▼▼▼▼▼▼▼▼

Parenting: Choices and Challenges

*O*ur socialization into the orientations of society is so pervasive—it includes so much, at such a young age, and continues for all our lives—that sociologists sometimes refer to it as "society within us." This means that our social learning becomes an essential part of us, that our thoughts and acts are a response to what we have learned. Much of our learning is so thoroughly internalized that we fail to see that our thinking and acting are a consequence of social learning. We tend to think of them as "natural," a basic part of our biological makeup.

That our acts, and even thoughts, are so far removed from "natural" becomes more apparent when we look at how socialization affects even our biology. Because we live in society, what we otherwise would do as "natural acts"—if we somehow lived in a wilderness by ourselves— become "social acts." That is, society enshrouds our biology with so many expectations that we are unable to separate biological acts from social learning.

Childbirth is an example. Certainly childbirth is a biological act. It is as natural a part of humanity as anything could be. Women have given birth to children for as long as humans have inhabited the earth. If anything is natural in life, it is childbirth.

Let us suppose, for example, that as a social experiment a male and a female—let's call them Bob and Mary—were raised apart from others and dropped in a wilderness to live by themselves. They would respond to biological forces. Let us assume that sex is among those biological forces. If Mary became pregnant, would she have a baby? Of course. Under these circumstances, having a baby would be a pure biological act. Mary would not even have seen a child, much less have witnessed childbirth. She would not know what was happening to her as her stomach became distended, nor would she know that she was about to deliver. Biological facts would take over in the absence of social learning.

But now, let's look at Mary and Bob apart from that imaginary wilderness setting. They are members of some social group. And each social group has its own ideas about childbirth. For each person raised in a social group (and that means all of us), the group's "childbirth culture" becomes part of the person's orientations. Giving birth, then, takes place within the framework of a group's beliefs and attitudes about childbirth.

No longer, then, do we have a pure biological fact, some in-and-of-itself "natural" act. Rather, biological acts occur within the context of our socialization. It can be no other way. All of us are raised in social groups. And our socialization is so thorough that it does not leave even our biology untouched.

Similarly, society transforms child raising from a "natural" to a "social" act by enshrouding this aspect of marriage and family with its expectations. Theoretically, we might be able to conceive of raising children as a "natural" act. But raising children always occurs within the context of social learning—especially the group's ideas of what the nature of children "is," what children ought to "become," and the best way of bringing the "is" and the "become" together. And those are social ideas, held by a social group and transmitted to its members.

After the birth of their first child, a couple is no longer just husband and wife. They are socially transformed into "father" and "mother," terms that indicate whole new sets of expectations. Indeed, the changes in roles and relationships are so distinct that social scientists use a different term to define the newly formed unit. Before children, the couple is a married *couple*, a husband and wife. But technically, *they are not considered a family*. Social scientists generally reserve the term *family* for the marital unit that contains children. One can quarrel with this position, of course, for terms are a matter of arbitrary definition.

Perhaps the most awesome task that anyone can have is to be responsible for the entire welfare of another person. To become a parent is to face that task. It is to take responsibility for a baby's nurturance and well-being, to take care of his or her basic biological and social needs—and, if your background allows it, also his or her basic spiritual needs.

That child quickly passes through infancy to become a toddler and then, as we divide matters up in our culture, a preschooler, a grade-schooler, a preadolescent (at times called a "tween"), an adolescent (or teenager), a postadolescent (or young woman or young man), and, finally, an adult.

The responsibility is awesome—especially because we are taught in our culture that parents are responsible for the type of people that their children become. If a child becomes a thief or drug addict, it is due to bad parenting. If a child becomes a valedictorian, it is because of good parenting.

Not that personal responsibility is accounted for in the same way in every culture. Indeed, it has not always been counted this way in our own culture. In the past, children were thought to develop like beautiful flowers or nasty weeds. There was not much you could do about it—just provide for your children's basic needs and see what you got.

But now, our culture has developed a different perspective on what children are and the responsibilities of parents in "maximizing" their children's potential. That change is awesome. And we are not even at the end of this cultural cycle. For example, we are now finding out that we can change children's intelligence by the way we treat them. When the implications of this finding-in-process trickle down through television, "how-to" parenting books, and "pop" psychology talk shows and become a common cultural "fact," another huge area of responsibility is likely to be laid at the feet of parents.

In spite of the enormous responsibilities for the outcomes of parenting that our culture dictates, the vast majority of husbands and wives decide to become parents. Most couples apparently find that the benefits of parenting outweigh its disadvantages. Many parents appear to derive immense satisfactions from significant participation in their children's intricate development from birth to maturity. The potential pleasures outweigh the cultural responsibilities.

In this Part, we examine the choices and challenges that contemporary parents face. To set the stage, in Chapter 21 Andrea Boroff Eagan surveys Western childbirth practices of the past two hundred years, and in Chapter 22 James M. Henslin surveys childraising practices through the ages. The sociological significance of their reports is that childbirth and child raising differ from society to society, and even from one historical period to another within the same society. In Chapter 23, Paul Bagne explores technological advances that are changing conception, advances that portend huge implications for humanity.

In Chapter 24, Carin Rubenstein looks at how a couple's sex life changes after a baby arrives, and in Chapter 25 Urie Bronfenbrenner identifies essential conditions for a child's healthy development. In Chapter 26, Gerald Handel identifies factors that create equity and loyalty between siblings during childhood, and in Chapter 27 Lillian Rubin looks at the waning years of parenting, how parents react when their children leave home.

21

▼▼▼▼

200 Years of Childbirth

▼▼▼▼

Andrea Boroff Eagan

ABSTRACT: The author traces practices in childbirth from seventeenth-century England to twentieth-century America. She covers the transmission of disease, the use of chloroform, cesarean section, confinement, twilight sleep, and the movement for natural childbirth, specifically the methods of Lamaze and Leboyer. As she traces this history, she stresses social attitudes toward women and women's reactions to repressive medicine.

A woman begins to feel the first pangs of labor. Her husband or perhaps one of her older children is dispatched to alert the midwife and probably several other women in the community, who rapidly gather. The women remain with their laboring friend, talking and praying, helping with household and farm chores, as long as necessary. The labor, like most, is painful and uneventful. Eventually the baby is born, the mother rests. The midwife and one or more of the other women stay to attend the new mother and to help for a few days or even a few weeks.

This was childbirth in America until the nineteenth century. Women attended women at childbirth, and the death of a woman in childbirth, as far as we can determine, was a very uncommon event. The babies, of course, were more fragile, and it is not unusual to read of a family in which only one or two of eight or more children survived to adulthood.

Things changed by the mid-nineteenth century. Childbirth, for many women, became something to be feared as an unbearably painful and quite often fatal event. Victorian morals and the growth of cities made women, at least middle-class women, less active than their rural grandmothers had been. A woman whose diet was probably seriously deficient (the Victorians were not much for eating vegetables), who had no exercise at all, whose knowledge of the processes of labor and delivery was very limited if not nonexistent, and who had kept herself tightly corseted throughout her pregnancy, then faced birth without even the comfort that her eighteenth-century grandmother would have had of a knowledgeable midwife and probably several other older, more experienced women. A respectable, middle-class woman was likely to be delivered in her home by a doctor, one of the new breed of "scientific practitioners" who promised to employ the latest advances—forceps and other instruments and bloodletting—to speed labor.

Advances in the management of childbirth always come as a reaction to the standard practices and problems of the times. And, for that reason among others, what is an improvement for one age often turns out to be a major problem of the next. Thus, many people who were considered heroes at the time they practiced later became symbols of interference, mismanagement, and disaster.

FORCEPS

In England, where by the seventeenth century the population was more urbanized (and less healthy) than in colonial America, the midwives' custom was to call in the barber-surgeon when a normal delivery appeared impossible. These men had a number of instruments that they used to extract the infant, living or dead, from the mother when all else had failed.

Early in the seventeenth century, a surgeon named Peter Chamberlen developed an instrument, called the forceps, which was shaped like two large spoons, to be inserted one at a time into the birth canal around the infant's head. The handles were then joined, and the infant could be extracted. To protect this very lucrative practice, the design of the forceps was kept secret. The instruments were carried about in a huge, carved, locked wooden box. When a member of the Chamberlen family arrived to attend a birth, the patient was blindfolded and the door was locked. One of the family would make noises, ringing bells and such, to cover the clanking sound of the instruments. The Chamberlen family kept the design of their device secret for over a century, becoming famous for successful deliveries in difficult cases, and rich in the process.

Eventually, the secret was stolen, and forceps gradually came into wide use in England, Europe, and America. As their use increased, however, untrained practitioners or doctors in a hurry damaged or killed a great many babies, as they were saving others. As a result, forceps developed a bad reputation with midwives, but retained their popularity with doctors. As the training of doctors improved in the twentieth century, their use of forceps became less dangerous. Nonetheless, the development, in the 1970s, of suction devices for delivering a baby who is stuck in the birth canal, was seen by some as a significant advance in safety, since forceps, even in skilled hands, can still cause injury to both the infant and the mother.

PUERPERAL FEVER

In America in the nineteenth century, members of the middle class were born and died at home; hospitals were considered to be places for the fallen and the destitute. The death rate in many hospitals from puerperal (or childbed) fever was high—20 percent of the patients in one Boston hospital died of the disease in 1883, according to historians Richard and Dorothy Wertz. The fact that puerperal fever was contagious had been deduced by Alexander Gordon, M.D., of Aberdeen, as early as 1793, but the medical texts of the nineteenth century made no mention of contagion. Oliver Wendell Holmes, a doctor practicing in Boston (and the father of the Oliver Wendell Holmes who later became a Justice of the Supreme Court), knowing of Gordon's theory, published an eloquent paper in the *New England Quarterly Journal of Medicine and Surgery* in 1843, laying out the horrors of the disease and the evidence for its extreme contagiousness. Holmes believed that the disease-causing agent was carried from one woman to another on the unwashed hands of the attending physician. Holmes was ridiculed and attacked: one prominent Philadelphia physician, Dr. Charles D. Meigs, wrote furiously that doctors, being gentlemen, could not possibly have dirty hands. In 1855, Holmes published another monograph on the subject, which eventually, and fortunately, had widespread influence, especially after Pasteur's discovery of germs in the 1880s.

But the preventive measures taken against the contagion were truly horrendous, even to read, and must have been unbearable for the poor women subjected to them. Holmes' very simple suggestion that the hands be thoroughly washed between patients might have been rejected, but repeated injections of carbolic acid into a woman's genitalia were acceptable. The increased use of instruments and surgical intervention, which caused easily infected wounds, made puerperal fever a continuing problem into the 1930s and 40s, when it finally came under control as a result of better sterile procedures, improved general health, and antibiotics. But were it not for Holmes and some of his European colleagues, the death rate from this terrible scourge would undoubtedly have been even higher than it was.

CHLOROFORM

The discovery of an apparently safe way to spare women the agonies of childbirth seemed to some a tremendous advance in its time. . . .

Dr. James Simpson, a Scot, who first used chloroform for anesthesia in childbirth in 1847, argued that God himself had put Adam to sleep before removing his rib. In 1853, because of one woman who used chloroform, it became acceptable, even fashionable, to be put to sleep during labor. Queen Victoria accepted chloroform from one of her doctors, John Snow, M.D., during her eighth confinement, at the birth of Prince Leopold. Though the Palace tried to keep it quiet, the news rapidly spread. Women were assured that suffering was not inevitable, though, of course, it was subsequently learned that chloroform was dangerous for both mother and infant.

CESAREAN

Cesarean section (named for the myth that the Roman Emperor Julius Caesar was delivered by surgery) was performed for centuries when it became necessary to try to deliver a live baby from a mother who had already died. It was not performed on living women, because it was always fatal. Some historians believe that the first cesarean in which both mother and baby survived was performed by an eighteenth-century Irish midwife named Mary Dunally. The first successful cesarean section that is documented, however, was performed in 1882 by a German physician, Max Sänger, who had the good sense to attempt to use sterile techniques and to sew up the uterine wall as well as the abdomen. The death rate from cesarean section remained high until after the first quarter of the twentieth century, when the timing and the techniques for the procedure were properly developed.

CONFINEMENT

A middle-class woman in 1900, pregnant for the first time, had no way of confirming the pregnancy. When she was reasonably certain that she was indeed pregnant—missed periods (assuming she understood the significance of that), nausea, a spreading middle, and perhaps the baby's first stirrings—she would, with some embarrassment, confess the news to her husband and female relatives and thereupon be ''confined'' until well after the baby was born. ''Confinement'' was not a figure of speech: pregnant women did not leave their homes or even receive any but the most intimate visitors. Some health experts denounced the inactivity and the wearing of corsets during pregnancy, but most women felt there was little alternative to hiding their state. With the turn of the twentieth century, women began taking a more public role, and confinement during pregnancy became more and more onerous. In 1904, a young dressmaker was asked by a client to make a gown which she could wear for entertaining at home during her pregnancy. The seamstress, Lena Bryant, produced a tea gown, which had an accordion-pleated skirt attached to an elastic band at the waist. It was an instant hit. More clothing—loose and concealing, but still fashionable—including some that could be worn *out of doors*, followed. A change in Bryant's first name from ''Lena'' to ''Lane'' resulted from a mistake made in filling out a check by the nervous and newly successful young designer. The chain of Lane Bryant retail stores was built on this line of maternity clothes.

INTERVENTION

Joseph DeLee is scarcely a hero. His patients qualify better than he does for heroism. But as a shaper of modern obstetrics, he is unparalleled. DeLee, a prominent Chicago obstetrician, did as much as anyone to promote the idea that childbirth is ''decidedly pathologic'' and to popularize routine intervention.

In 1920, DeLee spoke at a meeting of the American Gynecological Society, and his paper was subsequently published in the *American Journal of Obstetrics and Gynecology.* DeLee believed that modern women were too ''nervous'' and inefficient to withstand childbirth. Therefore, he recommended a regimen that included ''twilight sleep'' (which was already becoming very popular) for early labor, general anesthesia for the second stage, along with an extensive episiotomy and the use of forceps to extract the infant from its unconscious mother. Although twilight sleep, accomplished by giving the woman a combination of morphine to suppress pain and scopolamine to make her forget everything that happens, has fallen out of favor, anesthesia and forceps for the actual delivery remain standard procedure in many hospitals today. And, as any woman who has delivered in a hospital knows, episiotomy remains an almost inevitable part of every American birth.

DeLee argued that normal labor was harmful not only to the mother, who would suffer unbearable pain and exhaustion and risk tearing of the tissues, but that it was perhaps even more dangerous for the baby whose head was subjected to "prolonged pounding" during delivery. The large and repeated doses of drugs necessary to maintain twilight sleep were eventually, of course, found to be dangerous to the baby. The routine use of forceps, especially in unskilled hands, could and often did cause brain damage resulting in retardation, cerebral palsy, and other conditions. The episiotomy was necessary because the woman, then as now, usually delivered lying on her back with her legs in high stirrups, a position which made the forceps delivery easier for the doctor. This position stretches the perineum, making it virtually impossible to deliver the baby's head without tearing or cutting. DeLee, however, like many doctors since, argued that the cut had an advantage, because its repair would restore the mother to "virginal conditions.". . .

NATURAL CHILDBIRTH

By the late 1930s, some women had begun to object to the routine intervention they faced in childbirth. When *Childbirth Without Fear*, by the British obstetrician Grantly Dick-Read, was published, it rapidly became enormously popular. Read, as a young doctor, had been taught that childbirth was always unbearably painful and that every woman needed relief. But not long into his practice, he was startled while attending a birth to have the woman refuse chloroform. Asked why, she replied, to Read's amazement, "It didn't hurt. It wasn't meant to, was it, Doctor?"

Read came to believe that pain in childbirth resulted primarily from fear and that, if women were taught to look upon birth as a natural process, to understand the process of labor, to exercise to strengthen the muscles and to breathe through contractions, they would suffer little (or at least less) pain than their unprepared sisters. Although Read had great success with his own patients, the method never really caught on in the United States. One requirement of Read's method was that every woman have emotional support, preferably from someone close to her, throughout labor. Read recommended that this be the husband, but it would be years before American hospitals were willing to have anyone but regular hospital personnel present during labor and delivery. Hospitals also rarely had sufficient staff to permit someone to stay with an unmedicated woman in labor, and American doctors had long since given up staying with a patient through labor. A woman all alone through many hours of labor was less troublesome (and may have been better off) if she was medicated. Read's work, however, planted the idea in the minds of American women that childbirth could be something natural, normal, satisfying, and even joyful. It would take a woman, however, to really start the revolution.

THE LAMAZE METHOD

Russian doctors were the first to apply Pavlov's principles of conditioned reflex, combined with some old midwives' tricks, to the problem of labor pain, in a technique they called psychoprophylaxis. In 1951, two French doctors, Fernand Lamaze, M.D., and Pierre Vellay, M.D., visited the Soviet Union, and on their return began applying the method with their patients at a metalworkers' clinic near Paris. The method stressed the woman's control over the birth process. As most Americans now know, the Lamaze method teaches a series of breathing techniques designed to block the sensation of pain. The method had been in use in France for about five years when it was discovered by an American, Marjorie Karmel (who was living in France and looking for someone to deliver her baby by the Read method), whose first child was delivered by Dr. Lamaze. On her return, she wrote *Thank You, Dr. Lamaze*, which described the birth of her first child and Lamaze's method. The book was immensely popular, and Karmel, with several others, founded the American Society for Psychoprophylaxis in Obstetrics, which led the battle to get American doctors and hospitals to accept the method.

Most significant perhaps, for American women, Karmel's book described her struggle to deliver her *second* baby in an American hospital as she had delivered the first in France. American doctors resisted the Lamaze method for the same reasons that they didn't like Read: they preferred to be in charge. However, as the Lamaze method became adapted to the American hospital, the doctor *was* able to remain in charge. While in France the woman had a trained *monitrice* with her for aid and encouragement, the American woman had her husband. While he might also give support and encouragement, he had, as American couples rapidly discovered, no standing in the hospital; he was there only as long as he and his wife behaved themselves.

American women fought hard for the Lamaze method. Eventually, it became widely accepted by doctors because it reduced the need for drugs, which everyone was coming to understand were harmful to babies. Nonetheless, most Lamaze patients continue to receive some medication, and delivery is rarely accomplished without local anesthesia and episiotomy. The Lamaze method also makes women more cooperative and less noisy in childbirth, with the doctor still in control. The most popular American text on the Lamaze method counsels: "If your doctor himself suggests medication, you should accept it willingly—even if you don't feel the need for it.''

FULL CIRCLE: LEBOYER

In 1975, Frederick Leboyer, M.D., another French obstetrician, published *Birth Without Violence*, which has had a tremendous impact on the way that we in America think about newborns, although its effect on hospital practice has been less than profound. Recognizing the newborn's ability to see, hear, and feel, Leboyer argues that ordinary delivery-room conditions and practices—air conditioning, bright lights, shouted orders, clanking equipment, and seizing the just-emerged infant, holding her upside down by the feet and slapping her on the buttocks—provides a rather shocking entry into the world.

Leboyer's techniques, which include very low light, quiet, warmth, and a body-temperature bath, undoubtedly provide not only a smoother transition for the newborn but probably also a more relaxed atmosphere for the mother. The Leboyer ''method'' is now frequently offered to parents whose babies are delivered in hospital birthing rooms and in many out-of-hospital birth centers. With the exception of the bath, the Leboyer techniques, of course, resemble the ordinary conditions of that eighteenth-century birth, where bustling staff, operating-room lights, and scissors clinking in a metal basin were not a problem.

Leboyer's sensitivity to the feelings of the newborn is counterbalanced a bit, in the minds of some critics, with his apparent obliviousness to the mother. He is the infant's deliverer. Instead of the mother being given the baby to hold, the infant is taken by the doctor or the father to be bathed. But Leboyer has educated us, more than anyone else, to look at the effects of our practices on the child as it is born.

BACK TO NATURE

In the face of rising rates of intervention, routine use of electronic fetal monitors, and the rocketing increase in cesarean section, Michel Odent, another Frenchman, may become a hero of obstetrics in the future. The proponent of what he himself calls anti-obstetrics, Michel Odent brings us full circle, back to nature. His goal, in his own words, is to ''give birth back to women.''

At the maternity clinic he runs in Pithiviers, outside Paris, women of all ages and classes deliver in a dark, warm room, with a cushioned platform to sit or lie on. A pool of warm water is also available for relaxing in during labor, and some women deliver in the water. Many, however, seem to prefer to deliver in a semi-squatting position, supported from behind by the midwife, the doctor, or their husband.

What is revolutionary about Odent is that he insists that the woman be in charge. It is she who decides to walk or to lie down, to eat or to drink, to scream or to moan. No one directs her; the doctor and the midwife accede to her wishes. Odent believes that women need no preparation for birth, that we instinctively know how to do it. The midwife and the doctor are there for encouragement, to help the woman relax, to be a comforting presence, and in case of the rare emergency. Pain is expected; so is joy.

The cesarean-section rate at Pithiviers is under 7 percent, in a population of women that is *not* selected (compared to 19 percent in the United States, 15 percent in France, by Odent's estimate); many women come to Pithiviers because they have been told that the birth will be complicated or that they are at high risk. Episiotomies, which are common practice in most United States hospitals, are performed on only 7 percent, usually when the baby is in the breech position, to allow it to be born more quickly. The safety record at Pithiviers is impressive, and the satisfaction of the women who deliver there is reported to be considerable.

THE PARENTS

The history of obstetrics is, by and large, one of establishment resistance to change and of ongoing tension and struggle for control, between women and doctors and between doctors and midwives. Pregnant women still find themselves caught between the philosophy articulated by most midwives and a few doctors, like Odent, that birth is a completely natural process that under the vast majority of circumstances requires no intervention at all, and the present direction of American obstetrics, which prescribes the utmost in technological interference, from routine ultrasound examination to determine pregnancy to surgical delivery at term.

Whether the ideas of Odent and the midwives will ever be accepted, even in modified form, by American doctors and hospitals will depend on those who can, if they wish to, really shape American obstetrics: the parents whose choices, made with their feet and their pocketbooks, can be the key influence on the future of childbirth in America.

22

▼▼▼▼

Centuries of Childhood
▼▼▼▼

James M. Henslin

A century or so ago, a nurse was amusing herself with a gentleman. Working for a noble family, she had charge of the future Count, the Comte de Marle. She and the gentleman-in-waiting were throwing the swaddled infant back and forth through an open window. In the midst of their play, one of them fumbled, dropping him onto the stone steps. No longer was there a future count.

To the royal family about this same time was born Louis XIII. To help him nurse better, and to prevent the future king from stuttering, the royal surgeon cut the "fiber" under the newborn's tongue.

—McCoy, 1985, p. 386

Why should we be interested in childhood? Is not childhood simply a universal condition, a stage that all of us go through? Is not growing merely physical maturation—something that the body does by itself, genetic programming in control?

I wish to express my indebtedness to Philippe Ariès, whose title I have unabashedly lifted.

Actually, childhood is much more than a "condition" or "stage of growth." It always takes place within some specific social context; that is, every child lives in some society at some historical point in time. And that social context cannot help but influence the outcome—not only what happens to children psychologically and socially, but even to their genetic imprinting. For example, second- and third-generation Japanese-Americans are taller than are Japanese people who are raised in Japan. The genetics are the same, but the social environment changes even body height.

This chapter does not examine physical maturation: rather, it looks at family life in the past, focusing on the social influences on childhood. After introducing the scholarly endeavor called family history, I shall compare our mythical images with what childhood was like in the past. I shall then ask you to think about this question, "What if *you* had been born in the past?"

FAMILY HISTORY

Sometimes the things that are closest to us are the most difficult to see. Their very closeness makes us take them for granted. Being accustomed to their presence, we tend to not ask questions about them.

Childhood is like that. Every teenager and adult around us was once a child. With childhood fondly or not so fondly ensconced into our memories and common to everyone, we tend to take childhood for granted.

Historians have not been immune to this tendency. Although they looked at the more dramatic aspects of social life—wars, depressions, revolutions, and the like—they took childhood for granted. After all, what could be significant about childhood? Historians wore the same blinders as the rest of us; they did not see what was closest to them.

But about two or three decades ago, historians began to question and investigate family life. Some of their findings from the historical records are helping to shed light on present practices. (See Bailyn, 1960; Gillis, 1974; Graff, 1987; Hawkes and Hiner, 1985; and Kett, 1977.)

This recent development in historical research is known as family history. Lawrence Stone, director of Princeton University's Shelby Cullom Davis Center for Historical Studies (quoted in McCoy, 1985, p. 387), calls family history "the most explosive field of history today." He points out that in the 1930s, only about ten books and articles on childhood and the family in history were published a year. Now, hundreds of such scholarly works are published each year and two scholarly journals are devoted to exploring what past family life was like.

Why have historians become interested in family life? There seem to be four primary reasons. First, there is only so much that historians can say about the "big events" of history. Spending years trying to dig up clues that will add to our understanding of those events yields less each year. The ground has been overworked. In contrast, a focus on ordinary life opens up vast areas of uncharted territory.

Second, historians are attempting to "round out" their understanding of the past. Although one certainly gains an understanding of the past by looking at the doings of royalty, in the past (as today) almost everyone was a common person—a peasant or some such thing. Consequently, studying only elites, such as royalty, gives us a lopsided understanding of the past—one that excludes most people who lived during earlier periods.

Third, family history is part of a broader trend known as psychohistory—the attempt (in my estimation, usually a failure) to use psychological concepts to interpret people's motivations and experiences in the past. A major figure in this subfield is Lloyd deMause, founder of a journal on childhood and psychohistory. DeMause (1974) is convinced that the understanding of childhood is the key to comprehending the historical events that shape society. Although few historians take such a statement seriously, deMause claims that "child-rearing practices have been *the* central force for change in history." He says that "if you want to understand the causes of historical events like the growth of Nazism, you have to look at how the children who became Nazis as adults were treated as children" (quoted in McCoy, 1985, p. 388).

As a sociologist, I find this a gross overstatement. Although the child-rearing practices that are common in a society can contribute to the characteristics, traits, or tendencies of adults in that society, I do not believe that child-raising practices underlie the rise of Nazism or any other "ism." The extent to which patterns of child raising contribute to such events is at best doubtful. Such "isms" take place within a broad socio-cultural context of economic trends, specific political events, international relations, relations between social classes, religious and philosophical orientations, generalized expectations and frustrations, and the like. These broader social forces create the more significant social context that gives shape to social movements and their various "isms."

Fourth, today's generalized anxiety about family life has aroused interest in this topic. As Stone suggested (quoted in McCoy, 1985, p. 387), Americans feel:

> general anxiety about the state of the family and whether it is breaking down, concern about the rising divorce rate, anxieties about current permissiveness in raising children, and concern about what effects women's liberation will have on children, the family, and society. And underlying all of these anxieties are two questions: Are we really doing so badly? Was it better in the past?

Well, was it?

OUR MYTHICAL IMAGES

Our ideas of the past are driven by mythical images. As we grow up, we hear bits and pieces about past life. Those little anecdotes impart an image of what life was like. We also learn something about history at school. In our minds, we bring those fragments together, and a picture of the past emerges. This picture of an earlier life, accompanied by scenes that we play back in our memories, form what I refer to as mythical images.

Our mythical images are always inadequate. They never accurately represent the past, only our pieced-together ideas of what life used to be like.

So it is with our ideas of past family life. Our mythical images picture an extended family, almost a clan when they all get together. There is the mother, the father, and their eight or ten children, as well as an unmarried brother or sister. Grandma, who lost her husband a few years back and now lives contentedly with her children, is always central to this image.

And everyone is happy. The father smiles because he has sired a brood of happy children. The mother smiles because she is surrounded by love and devotion. The children smile because they feel so good being an integral part of this large, loving, warm, devoted, contented family.

And the grandma, of course, smiles because everything is just right. She bakes cakes and apple pies and beams when she sees her grandchildren's faces light up at the delectable goodies that await them.

The family may be poor, but that means little in the face of their togetherness. They all work hard, yet they somehow manage to find much time to spend together, just sitting around and smiling a lot.

When we think about it, of course, we *know* our mythical images cannot be right. At least on examination, something should strike us as unrealistic.

Although I purposely have overdrawn this portrait, we all carry around images of a past, idyllic family life. Although our grandparents may not match the image or even come close to it, we *know* that if we just go back far enough, we will see our image merging with social reality. The scene may not represent the 1950s, but it certainly does depict the 1850s and probably 1900.

CHILDHOOD IN THE PAST

Has the research of the new family historians confirmed such images? How should we modify our mythical images to bring them more in line with historical reality?

Several modifications are in order. First, the average family was much smaller than we generally assume it to have been. Families of eight or ten children were the exception.[1] Some researchers say that even in the 1700s, the typical American family consisted of only a husband, a wife, and approximately three children (Blumstein and Schwartz, 1985). Although the historical record is too fragmented for us to pinpoint exact averages, it appears that small families have been a "cultural consistency" in our society and the large, extended families of the past were the exception (Hareven, 1982). Yet the atypicality of large families has not prevented them from becoming the stuff from which mythical images are made.

Second, families were not all alike. For example, in the 1800s, most families lived on farms, and, on average, rural families were somewhat larger than urban families, even as they are today.

Families also differed by social class. Just as our society has its rich and poor and those in between, so it did in the past. And, like today, a family's economic circumstances were the main factor that dictated what family life was like. It should come as no surprise that the rich had life a lot better. As now, the children of the wealthy avoided much of the hoi polloi by being sent to private schools. But life for such children was not as easy as it might appear. In the private schools, the curriculum was difficult and the discipline harsh (Kett, 1971).

Furthermore, the type of wealthy family one was born into also made a profound difference. For example, mill owners and manufacturers apparently did not think much of education. In spite of their wealth, they made child laborers of their sons by putting them to work in the family factories at age eight or nine (Kett, 1971).

In the 1800s, childhood was not a tender period of being protected from work. Rather, it was considered a time to learn to shoulder the heavy burdens of labor. Children were likely to be thought of as little adults, "unable as yet to take up all the duties of their elders, but nonetheless bound to do so as much as they could" (Stansell, 1982).[2] Poor families were likely to do anything that helped them survive the rigors of daily life. And the correct word is families, not fathers, for mothers and children also did what they could to produce food and clothing. If the women and children did not work as servants, they helped on the farm, raising chickens, milking cows, making butter, growing and canning vegetables, and so on.

Children were expected to "earn their keep," as the common phrase

[1]For example, my own father, born in 1910, came from a family of ten children. But my mother, born in 1917, came from a family that had only four children, still larger than the average family today but considerably smaller than our mythical images—and closer to the average of 1917.
[2]Basing his research on French historical records, Philippe Ariés (1965) indicates that earlier generations in the Western world did not recognize childhood as a separate period of life. This pathbreaking analysis of historical evidence has been challenged, however, and is undergoing modification. See Davis (1975), Vann (1982), and Wilson (1980).

of the period so pointedly indicates. Urban children often engaged in scavenging and street selling. Children sold newspapers, fruit, candy, hot corn and sweet potatoes on street corners, and food and household supplies door to door. Children scoured the garbage for bits of rags, nails, bottles, paper, kitchen grease, bad meat, and bones, and searched the neighborhoods for any loose bit of fuel to take home or to peddle to neighbors. On occasion, children's street hustling slid gradually into theft and prostitution (Stansell, 1982).

Street peddling and scavenging were everyday activities of poor city children—families who barely made ends meet. But, like today, many families lived in abject poverty. Some families, evicted from their homes, found themselves traveling from one city to another seeking work or a handout. Others lived under bridges and in abandoned buildings. Then there were families in which the parents, usually the husband-father, were addicted to alcohol. In those troubled families, the wife and children were likely to be beaten and everyone to be miserable. Clothing was relatively expensive in past eras, and poor families were likely to wear rags. With no central heating and the uncertainty about getting food (much less balanced diets), their hygiene and health suffered.

When we think about life in earlier eras, for some reason the slave family does not come into the minds of most of us. But those families were also part of our past scene. What was life like for their children? The significant difference, of course, was control by masters, who could beat them, or without warning could sell them to strangers who might live hundreds of miles away (Sterling, 1984). In general, however, their living conditions were similar to those of most poor rural folks of the time. Slave children (what an oxymoron!) were put to work at an early age, especially the girls, who at the age of seven or younger might be assigned to help care for infants and young children in the plantation's nursery. Living in drafty cabins made of chinked logs, with mud-and-stick chimneys that sometimes caught fire, most children wore a one-piece garment, fitted like a long shirt or slip reaching to the ankles. Few of those children had shoes or underclothing, which meant that they were exposed to the cold during winter, especially when they fetched water from the spring, barefoot on the frozen ground or in the snow (Webber, 1978).

What was childhood like in the past, then? Just like today, it all depended on what kind of family you came from. If you had chosen your parents wisely, life was good. If not, it could be miserable.

As you well know, there is no typical contemporary family. Instead, there are many, many different types of families in our society. Family life in a contemporary professional's home (lawyer, dentist, professor) is as radically different from life in a welfare home in the ghetto as both are from home life in today's ruling class (the wealthy and political elite, such as the Kennedys, Fords, and Vanderbilts).

So it was in the past. So it is today. And so it will be tomorrow.

IF YOU HAD BEEN BORN IN THE PAST . . .

After reviewing the literature on family history, McCoy (1985) asked what childhood would have been like in the past.[3] Let's take a look at what we can reasonably conclude.

Perhaps you would not have wanted your children. Pregnancy was a frightening prospect because of the high risk of dying from childbirth and related conditions. Today, less than 1 percent of American women die from causes related to childbirth, but two hundred years ago, the maternal death rate was over *twenty* times as high. When about one in five women died of causes related to giving birth, pregnancy was indeed terrifying. Consequently, it is assumed, rightly or wrongly, that a woman was not likely to have wanted the children to which she gave birth (McCoy, 1985).

One can interpret the risk of death in the past in a different light, however. Although a woman might have been ambivalent about her pregnancy, if she risked her life to have children, might she not have had an even greater love for them?

In the past, people practiced birth control primarily by sexual abstinence (which did not work well because husbands and wives seemed to ignore it from time to time) and lactation, nursing a child until he or she was about two years old (which apparently worked well because nursing makes a woman less fertile). Their nontechnological attempts at birth control, largely ineffective, meant that a husband and wife could neither control the number of children they had nor space them, as people do today. Consequently, since most people were poor, another child meant another mouth to feed.

This factor of past life is also interpreted to mean that people did not really want their children. I find this argument weak—a failure to move out of one's current environment and to view people in light of the times in which they lived.

> I shall never get the image of Celia out of my mind. Only about thirty years old and living in a remote area of Mexico, Celia had already given birth to twelve children. With her swollen, varicose veins and blackened and missing teeth, Celia looked like an old woman.

[3]The listing in this section is structured after McCoy (1985).

She beamed as she pointed to her distended stomach, indicating that since our last visit she was now expecting her thirteenth child. Looking at her smiling face, it was evident that Celia could not have been happier, as was her husband Angél. She was eagerly looking forward to another "gift from God."

We tend to judge things from our own perspective. (If *we* were poor and already had twelve children, *we* certainly would not be looking forward to a thirteenth!) What we fail to grasp is the point of view of the people who experience a phenomenon—a perspective that may contrast sharply with our own (Henslin, 1990).

Your baby would have a good chance of dying before his or her first birthday. There is no question about the high risk of dying at a young age. On the basis of historical records, it is estimated that in medieval England and seventeenth-century France, 20 to 50 percent of all babies died during their first year. Those were times that preceded the development of public sanitation such as sewers, much less waste treatment, and exposure to raw sewage, especially in drinking water, created chronic, severe health problems. Infants had an especially difficult time surviving plagues, diseases, and the generally unsanitary living conditions.

Life in the American colonies appears to have been somewhat healthier for newborns. In Plymouth Colony, infant mortality was about 10 to 15 percent. Although this rate was considerably lower than that in Europe, it is approximately *ten* times higher than our current rate (McCoy, 1985).

Although no one doubts that the death rate was high, its interpretation is another matter. Some family historians suggest that this rate of infant mortality discouraged parents from lavishing affection on their children, that parents stood their emotional distance from infants until they determined that the child was going to make it through his or her critical first year. Perhaps. But one could just as easily interpret high infant mortality as evidence of a *greater* affection for infants. After all, the parents might soon lose their child, so they had better love it while they had the chance.

This, of course, is a perennial problem with drawing conclusions from so-called social facts: as with maternal mortality, the same information can be interpreted in different, even opposite, ways.

If you were well-off, your baby probably would have been breast-fed by someone else. For about 1,800 years, women had an interesting custom called wet-nursing. If a woman could afford it, she sent her baby to be nursed by another woman. Freeing the mother from what was apparently considered an onerous responsibility, the custom provided a partial livelihood for poorer women who were able to continue to produce milk and were willing to sell this service. If the wet nurse were one of the household servants, the baby remained at home. If not, the infant would be sent away to live with a wet nurse and would not see his or her parents and siblings for a couple of years. At the end of that time, the child would be returned to his or her mother—a total stranger.

The Puritans broke with this pattern in the seventeenth century. In the eighteenth century, a movement favoring maternal breast-feeding developed in both the United States and England. The popularity of breast-feeding evidently waxes and wanes from one historical period to another, and only in recent decades has such a movement (La Leche among others) again grown to counteract our tendency to bottle-feed infants.

Your infant would have been swaddled from birth to about eight months. Swaddling was the practice of tightly wrapping cloths around an infant. This custom can be traced back to biblical times, since Jesus was swaddled upon his birth (Luke 2:7). It continued into the eighteenth century in England, the nineteenth century in France, and the twentieth century in Russia.

With their hands and legs wrapped tightly against their bodies, the babies could not even suck their thumbs. After about four months, they gained some freedom when their legs were unbound.

Perhaps swaddling served a good purpose at the time, for houses, including castles, were damp and drafty. Maybe swaddling helped keep infants warm. Certainly convenience was one of the reasons for swaddling. Supposedly, swaddled infants slept more and cried less, allowing their mothers to leave them alone while they worked. Swaddling also made infants easier to carry, and sometimes a swaddled baby would even be hung on a peg on the wall, where he or she was neatly kept out of the way.

Your discipline would have been harsh. In earlier centuries, a primary goal of child raising was to "break the child's will." This phrase refers to the attempt to instill complete obedience by crushing all assertiveness. Depending on the family and the place and time in history, this could mean mild treatment at the hands of adults or what today we would call child abuse. For example, as McCoy (1985, p. 392) noted:

> Louis XIII was whipped every morning, starting at the age of two, simply for being "obstinate," and was even whipped on the day of his coronation at the age of nine. . . . It was considered the duty of parents to use physical harshness and psychological terrorization—locking children in dark closets for an entire day or frightening them with tales of death and hellfire. . . .

And it was not only tales of death and the macabre that were used to instill discipline. Sometimes children were forced to witness real-life examples to terrify them into submission. For example:

> A common moral lesson involved taking children to visit the gibbet [upraised post on which executed bodies were hung by chains], where

they were forced to inspect rotting corpses hanging there as an example of what happens to bad children when they grow up. Whole classes were taken out of school to witness hangings, and parents would often whip their children afterwards to make them remember what they had seen (deMause, 1975, p. 86).

Your childhood would have been a lot shorter. We have seen that American children in the 1800s learned to work at an early age. This was a continuation of past trends. In medieval England, for example, boys were apprenticed at about seven years. With no say in the matter, a boy would be sent to live in the household of a craftsman, such as a clock maker, a broom maker, or a stonemason. There, for a period of some ten years, he learned how to make a living. The master exercised complete control over him, including the right to discipline him for disobedience or laziness. And discipline legitimately included beating.

A girl was likely to remain at home. There was no reason to send a girl away, since she was expected to learn the womanly duties, which centered on caring for the house, a husband, and children. As it was for her mother, so it would be for her.

Young girls from some of the poorer families, however, might be sent to live with a family that had more money (sometimes not a wealthy family, but a poor family that produced enough food to take on an additional member). There, they served as "servant girls," performing household chores in exchange for bed and board. If they were lucky, they worked for a caring family in which they were treated as one of the family's children. If not, they might be verbally abused, work at hard duties from morning to dark, and go to bed hungry. There were no eight-hour days served under a union contract.

And we ought to keep in mind that the sexual abuse of children is not a new phenomenon. Because they were often in the presence of men who were strangers, and without family supervision, those conditions certainly would have fostered such abuse.

At some point, your child would likely have lived with only one parent. One of the major negative consequences of our current rates of unwed parenthood, desertion, and divorce is that one of every five children now lives with only the mother (*Statistical Abstract*, 1990: Table 69). Furthermore, it is estimated that at some point in their lives about 60 percent of all American children will live with only one parent (Weitzman, 1985).

Part of our countervailing mythical imagery is that in the past, families were not only happy but intact. However, although there was practically no divorce, a large proportion of families (the exact number is unknown) were broken because of the death of one of the parents. Although figures are scant, we know that life was precarious and mortality at all ages was much more common than it is now. We can gain some idea of how frequently death broke up marriages and forced children into stepfamilies by noting that, of all marriages in Plymouth Colony, between one-fourth and one-third were of people who remarried after the death of a spouse (Demos, 1970).

CONCLUSION

Customs in raising children come and go. As with the practice of swaddling, a particular custom may become so ingrained in a culture that it lasts for centuries. At any given time, each society has its own ideas about how best to raise children. Adults pass those ideas on to one another, and parents pass them on to their children. The ideas become entrenched as they are reinforced by other aspects of the culture, such as "morality stories" about parents who fail to do what their culture prescribes and whose children come to a bitter end.

Although such stories are still told, today our techniques of child raising are more likely to be reinforced by the mass media, especially by television. Any orientations to child raising that become popular or are promulgated by some supposed psychological guru of child raising will be transmitted to the masses by television and received as the "correct" way to bring up children. It is likely, however—no matter how enlightened we may think we are—that our currently "correct" ways of child raising, culturally originated and culturally transmitted, are no more right or wrong than were those of the past.

I am pleased that we no longer swaddle infants, beat children as much as at some earlier periods, or allow so many young children to run the streets. At the same time, I must add that abandoning children of only a few weeks or months to impersonal, intermittent strangers in child care centers is no masterly stroke of cultural genius in child raising, nor is abandoning them at home to television, the "electronic socializer," whose programming, although masterfully conceived and implemented, may contain morals and values that sharply conflict with what the parents, apparently too lazy or too misinformed, desire for their children.[4]

REFERENCES

ARIÈS, PHILIPPE. *Centuries of Childhood.* R. Baldick, trans. New York: Vintage Books, 1965.

BAILYN, B. *Education in the Forming of American Society.* Chapel Hill: University of North Carolina Press, 1960.

[4]For an insightful analysis of children and television, see Meyrowitz (1984), who says that the widespread use of television "is equivalent to a broad social decision to allow young children to be present at wars and funerals, courtships and seductions, criminal plots and cocktail parties [and that] television exposes children to many topics and behaviors that adults have spent several centuries trying to keep hidden from them."

BLUMSTEIN, PHILIP, and PEPPER SCHWARTZ. "The American Couple in Historical Perspective." In James M. Henslin, ed., *Marriage and Family in a Changing Society*, pp. 34–42. New York: Free Press, 1985.

DAVIS, N. Z. "The Reasons of Misrule." In *Society and Culture in Early Modern France*. Stanford, Calif: Stanford University Press, 1975.

DEMAUSE, LLOYD. *The History of Childhood*. New York: Psychohistory Press, 1974.

DEMAUSE, LLOYD. "Our Forebears Made Childhood a Nightmare." *Psychology Today*, 8(11), April 1975, pp. 85–88.

DEMOS, JOHN. *A Little Commonwealth: Family Life in Plymouth Colony*. New York: Oxford University Press, 1970.

GILLIS, J. R. *Youth and History: Tradition and Change in European Age Relations, 1770–Present*. New York: Academic Press, 1974.

GRAFF, HARVEY J., ed. *Growing Up in America: Historical Experiences*. Detroit: Wayne State University Press, 1987.

HAREVEN, TAMARA. "American Families in Transition: Historical Perspectives on Change." In Froma Walsh, ed., *Normal Family Processes*, pp. 446–466. New York: Guilford Press, 1982.

HAWKES, JOSEPH M., and N. RAY HINER, eds. *American Childhood: A Research Guide and Historical Handbook*. Westport, Conn.: Greenwood Press, 1985.

HENSLIN, JAMES M. *Social Problems*. Englewood Cliffs, N.J.: Prentice Hall, 1990.

KETT, JOSEPH F. "Growing Up in Rural New England, 1800–1840." In Tamara K. Hareven, ed., *Anonymous Americans*, pp. 1–16. Englewood Cliffs, N.J.: Prentice-Hall, 1971.

KETT, JOSEPH F. *Rites of Passage: Adolescence in America, 1790 to the Present*. New York: Basic Books, 1977.

McCOY, ELIN. "Childhood Through the Ages." In James M. Henslin, ed., *Marriage and Family in a Changing Society*, 2nd Ed., pp. 386–394. New York: Free Press, 1985.

MEYROWITZ, JOSHUA, "The Adultlike Child and the Childlike Adult: Socialization in an Electronic Age." *Daedalus*, 113, (1984), pp. 19–48.

STANSELL, CHRISTINE. "Women, Children, and the Uses of the Streets: Class and Gender Conflict in New York City, 1850–1860." *Feminist Studies* 8:2 (1982), pp. 309–35.

STERLING, DOROTHY. *We Are Your Sisters: Black Women in the Nineteenth Century*. New York: W. W. Norton & Co., 1984.

VANN, RICHARD T. "The Youth of *Centuries of Childhood*." *History and Theory*, 21 (1982), pp. 279–297.

WEBBER, THOMAS L. *Deep Like the Rivers: Education in the Slave Quarter Community, 1831–1865*. New York: W. W. Norton & Co. 1978.

WEITZMAN, LENORE J. *The Divorce Revolution: The Unexpected Consequences for Women and Children in America*. New York: Free Press, 1985.

WILSON, ADRIAN. "The Infancy of the History of Childhood: An Appraisal of Philippe Ariès." *History and Theory*, 19 (1980), pp. 132–53.

23

▼▼▼▼

High-Tech Breeding

▼▼▼▼

Paul Bagne

ABSTRACT: Artificial insemination, now a highly developed technology, has become increasingly significant for modern life. With the ability to preserve sperm for a long time and the development of a capitalist market, specialized sperm banks have come into existence. Competitive clinics, some specializing in sperm from specific types of donors, make it possible for a customer to specify what she wants in a donor—and then to purchase it. The current situation raises serious questions about the role of science in social biogenics, especially the potential to create a population along predetermined, select biological lines.

Sensing she had ovulated, Afton Blake reached for the phone and called Paul Smith. He agreed to meet her that evening after work.

As he left his office, Smith took with him a tiny vial, which he carefully placed in an insulated tank stowed in the back seat of his Volkswagen Rabbit. The vial contained the frozen sperm of an anonymous Nobel laureate who Afton Blake hoped would become the father of her first child.

When Smith arrived, he thawed the semen and placed a small sample under a microscope. Most of the spermatozoa were dead. A few pathetically wagged their tails but were clearly going nowhere. Blake was deeply disappointed. She had seen a photo of the donor when he was young, and "he seemed to have such character."

Smith stayed late into the night. Together he and Blake pored over a catalogue from the Repository for Germinal Choice, where Smith works. After studying traits, values and characteristics of these anonymous men, Blake selected a new donor, not a Nobel Prize winner. She conceived but miscarried. Several more months of insemination followed before she conceived again. A year ago Afton Blake gave birth to a healthy boy she named Doron.

Doron Blake's father is a computer scientist and an accomplished classical musician—a kind of man Afton says she "might have married." She calls him "28." Doron is the second of five children produced by the Respository for Germinal Choice, in Escondido, California, a relatively small, specialty sperm bank dedicated to the improvement of the human species. Its founder, retired lensemaker and millionaire Robert Graham, told *Mother Jones*, "We provide the finest germinal material we can get our hands on." Paul Smith is Graham's employee. He travels around the country by bus and plane to fetch the sperm of the six men Graham has decided are superior. He delivers specimens to women who hope that the seed of an accomplished man will help them give birth to a brilliant and talented child.

The five Germinal Choice offspring join 300,000 other children conceived in the United States since 1960 by artificial insemination. The number of such births is expected to rise dramatically in the coming years as more and more gynecologists begin to perform artificial insemination regularly: several sources estimate that 1.5 million more Americans will be created this way by the year 2000. As the practice grows more popular and the demand for sperm increases, sperm bankers are refining the methods of selecting, concentrating, freezing and even genetically altering the samples. Along the way, artificial insemination—with its accompanying technology—has come to mean different things to different people.

- To infertile couples it simply means babies.
- To single women it means children without having to find Mr. Right.
- To lesbians it means conception without being sexually intimate with men.
- To geneticists it means control of inherited disorders such as diabetes and cystic fibrosis.
- To clinical ecologists it provides an opportunity to preserve the sperm of young men who are likely to be exposed to chemical and radioactive mutagens in the environment and the workplace.

- To advocates of selective breeding, like Graham and Smith, insemination is the method that has been sought since it was first proposed to improve the human race by encouraging the fit to multiply.
- And to genetic engineers, who each day get closer to restructuring the DNA molecule, artificial insemination is just about the simplest of many procedures that will create people designed by science rather than nature.

SHOPPING FOR DADDY

Doron Blake lives in a quiet neighborhood in a house crammed with books and art. He is a robust and happy child. His mother, Afton, rushes through ideas with contagious energy. "It was time to have a child," she says. "I was secure emotionally and not in a steady relationship with a man." She thought first of asking a friend to coparent with her, but she feared that such a setup could turn into an awkward triangle. That left insemination.

She went first to the Tyler Medical Clinic in nearby Westwood. "It was huge and commercial and took so much away from the wonders of conception," she says. "They were more interested in assuring me the donor was Caucasian than in telling me what kind of person he was." To Blake, who had once considered having an interracial child, the Tyler pitch was repulsive. She then contacted Southern California Cryobank, a firm she found much more appealing and personal, but she felt it offered too little information about its donors. She finally turned to the Repository for Germinal Choice. "From the first day they were just what I had hoped for. They were extremely involved and obviously dedicated to helping in every way."

Blake, a psychologist interested in child development, believes that intelligence is both acquired and inherited. She chose a donor described as "brilliant." But it was not only intellect she sought. "It's something beyond that," she says. "More like soul. And I think genes play a part in this too." In the catalog, she found the kind of person she wanted to father her child: "someone who treasures the world and everything in it."

The psychologist who tested No. 28 as part of the repository screening process said the donor was creative in all directions, suggesting that in another age he might have been a painter or composer. Professionally, the man works in computers, but he has won acclaim as a pianist.

"Music is very important to me," Blake says. Just after bringing her infant home from the hospital, she placed him between the speakers of her stereo for a quick test of his musical aptitude. "I put Chopin on,

---

Donor No. 28: Doron Blake's Father

Summary: Good intellectual and musical ability, charismatic personality and very good looks, with cataract risk.

Ancestry: Northwest European. Born: 1950s.

Eye color: Hazel. Skin color: Fair.

Hair: Blond (straight but thinning).

Height: 1.8 m (6'0").

Weight at 24: 77 kg. (170 lb).

General appearance: Normal with narrow face. Very handsome.

Personality: Good presence, very charismatic, friendly and highly creative. Interests include swimming, bicycle riding and hiking.

Achievements: He teaches a hard science at a major university. He has won many prizes and fellowships.

I.Q.: Not known, scored 800 in Math on SAT.

Music: He has won prizes performing classical music.

Athletics: No achievement, but two first-degree relatives were track champions.

Manual dexterity: Excellent.

General health: Excellent.

Defects: Impacted wisdom teeth. Slight hemorrhoids. Two grandparents developed cataracts in their 60s.

Blood type: O +. Pressure: 122/80.

Comment: The estimated recurrence risk is 30 percent for hemorrhoids, 40 percent for impacted wisdom teeth and 22 percent for cataracts developing after age 60.

Each donor to the Repository for Germinal Choice is given a random number. Children must remember their father's number to keep from marrying their own siblings.

and he started to go like this.'' She swayed and moved her hands in gentle circles, fingers open. ''When I turned it off, his hands went down. Turn it on, he'd do this again. It never ceased to amaze me and everybody else.''

The sperm bank that begat Doron the musician was inspired by the late American geneticist Hermann Muller, who suspected that traits like brotherliness, loving kindness, and humility were linked to genes. He proposed gathering and freezing ''copious reserves of the most precious of all treasures: the germinal material that has formed the biological basis of those human values that we hold in highest regard.'' Donors would be outstanding men with such values: they would be healthy, vigorous and bright. Couples would have a choice of ''material [sperm] likely to embody" the traits they personally admired, such as "infectious sociability," "physical agility" or "the gift of song."

Muller won a Nobel Prize for research that proved that X-rays cause mutations. In 1961, he proposed that men likely to confront the unassessed hazards of modern life should store their semen in underground repositories. Future generations, he wrote, would regard our failure to take this precaution as gross negligence. He envisioned great banks of human semen containing "stocks [which] might become recognized as especially worthy." He predicted that widespread procreation by "conscious selection of germ cells" would begin after the sperm of superior men was available. He even dreamed of a democratic, eugenic republic, where all would be born genetically improved.

In 1964, Muller began recruiting some forty colleagues and sympathizers to promote genetic improvement through sperm-banking. Respected biologists, physicians, and psychologists were contacted, as were famed British biologist Julian Huxley and two self-described disciples of Muller: Robert Graham and Paul Smith, who later founded the Repository for Germinal Choice. The repository has "changed the face of sperm-banking forever," says Dr. Charles Sims, codirector of the Southern California Cryobank. Recipients are no longer satisfied with terse donor descriptions listing favorite sport, academic achievements and other interests. Women who used to go to sperm banks and say "I just want a baby" are now more likely to say "I want a baby and it had better be the best." . . .

Chemists made the long-term preservation of sperm possible in the early 1960s, when they turned to liquid gases. The temperatures of some liquid gases can be more than a hundred degrees colder than dry ice—solid carbon dioxide—which had been used in previous experiments in cryobiology, the study of how living matter responds to low temperatures. Liquid nitrogen, at $-196°C$, will vitrify sperm (hold it in a glass-like state): biochemical reactions cease and molcules stop moving. "We are in the dark ages of cryobiology," said [Dr. Cappy] Rothman [a specialist in male fertility]. "It's a whole new science that we are just now getting familiar with."

One of the country's leading cryobiologists is Armand Karow, Ph.D., director of Xytex, a sperm bank in Augusta, Georgia. "Theoretically, when you lower sperm to this temperature, assuming the cell is not damaged, there is no reason it will not remain viable indefinitely," he says. Although with current techniques, many cells are killed in freezing, a recent study calculated that sperm, if properly frozen, could be thawed and used in 10,000 years—a figure Karow regards with skepticism. But as research progresses, he says, the recovery rate, now about 50 percent, will improve dramatically. Red blood cells can be frozen and thawed with a 95 percent recovery, Karow says. "There is no reason this cannot be done with sperm cells."

Some sperm banks, however, attempt to improve marginal semen samples by concentrating and freezing the best swimmers of several ejaculates. At Gametrics Ltd., a biotech research firm in Sausalito, California, Dr. Ronald Ericsson has developed ways to separate good sperm from bad. He can even separate X-chromosome sperm from Y, so that his clients can choose the sex of their baby. He has licensed this technique to physicians in the United States, Egypt, Italy, Taiwan, Singapore, Malaysia, and Korea. The sex selection process is especially popular in Asia, Ericsson says, where boy babies are much preferred.

Medical science is also making rapid advances in understanding conception, says Cappy Rothman optimistically. "With better technology, we'll be able to use very few sperm and get conception," he says. "If you freeze two ejaculates—800 million sperm—that's all a man will need to store for the rest of his life." Other researchers may take the same technology and use it for more nefarious purposes, Rothman says, but, "what we are doing in clinical medicine is simply helping people have babies."

THE DOCTOR AS DONOR

The sperm count of the average American male has dropped to what some believe is an all-time low. Men who have not contributed to this decline, some of whom can deliver an ejaculate twice as potent as others, are popular at sperm banks. One of them, No. 17, visits a doctor's office once or twice each week to impregnate women he will never meet. He arrives just before the patient, slips into a bathroom with a copy of *Penthouse* or *Playboy*, locks the door and exits a few minutes later with a small cup of semen. "If there is a way to help women have babies, I don't think they should be denied it," he told *Mother Jones* anonymously over the phone. "I saw the look on my wife's face after she had given birth. I know how much it meant to her." No. 17's wife approves of what he does, even though to keep his sperm count high they must abstain from sex for two days before he contributes.

For every five donors who apply to sperm banks, four are rejected after genetic screening and physical exams. Others are rejected because of poor semen quality or a bad attitude. "A donor must be able to drop a sample into a black box and never care what happens to it," says one physician. Of the sperm banks surveyed for this article, at only one, the Repository for Germinal Choice, can donors restrict the use of their semen in any way. Just as money bankers decide what will be done with your cash, so will sperm bankers decide what will be done with your seed.

One Saturday morning I visited an insemination clinic—part of a fertility study—at a medical school; two donors, who avoided making eye contact with me, waited at the door of a storage closet to do their duty for science (and a $50 fee). In a small lab near exam rooms down the hall, five little cups of semen sat in a row on a stainless steel table, awaiting the ovulating women who were scheduled to arrive, 15 minutes apart.

Despite advances in techniques of freezing sperm, most doctors still use the fresh stuff, and most of their donors are medical students or hospital residents. A 1979 study by University of Wisconsin researchers found that 62 percent of doctors used men training to be physicians as donors. That computes to some 186,000 pre-med tots born in the past two decades. "They are selecting what they consider superior genes and they have chosen to reproduce themselves," said George Annas, professor of health law at Boston University School of Medicine.

But the director of the medical school insemination clinic said that getting fresh semen to a woman at the right time would be an "impossible logistics problem" without students as donors.

They do it for convenience, I told Annas on the phone.

"Seems like it would be just as handy to use the janitor," he responded.

Do you think it's a plot to spread their genes? I asked.

"I don't think it's a conscious thing, but given the choice, doctors choose doctors. If law professors were doing it, they would pick attorneys. If the military were doing it, they'd pick their favorite generals."

THE CHASE MANHATTAN

"You need a Malaysian donor?" asks Joseph Feldschuh, director of Idant Fertility Laboratories in New York City. "We have several." Idant is the Chase Manhattan of American sperm banks.

Feldschuh is proud of the ethnic diversity of his bank, which has so far produced 11,000 babies. Idant sends catalogs and ships semen to physicians across the United States, as well as in South America, Canada, and Europe. In Idant's tanks are 40,000 specimens. Some were stored by men who have since had vasectomies; others by cancer patients who were later made sterile by chemotherapy. Some were reserved by mothers who want another child by the same donor. About half are for sale.

Idant, a commercial venture, was set up in 1971 to store the ejaculates of men about to have vasectomies or undergo chemotherapy. By 1974, investors had put $1.2 million into its facilities, but only a small percentage of vasectomy patients were storing their sperm. Feldschuh, who by that time had begun working at Idant, arranged a merger with Daxor, a

New York corporation that designs and sells electronic medical equipment. Feldschuh expanded the donor program with an eye on the growing market for artificial insemination—half of the estimated three million American couples who are trying and failing to conceive a child, each couple needing an average of half a dozen inseminations at $40 per specimen. Feldschuh predicts steady growth for Idant, particularly as the technology of freezing semen improves and as more and more doctors give up the notion that for specimens, fresh is best.

The Idant people say they go to great lengths to recruit donors of above-average intelligence. "Anybody who thinks intelligence is not partly inherited is just silly," says Feldschuh. They also offer donors with specific desired traits. Women are asked to list the characteristics they are seeking in descending order of importance. Ask for a medium-built Mediterranean type with math skills and a love of the outdoors, and chances are Idant will find one for you. Feldschuh is developing computer software to track the permutations. . . .

Scientist as Creator

Insemination by frozen sperm is the most primitive of the new reproductive technologies. Down the road are far more exotic practices: transplanting fresh and frozen embryos, bringing the human fetus to term in artificial wombs, and redesigning the DNA of human cells.

"Mankind is on the verge of modifying life," says Dr. Richard Seed, a specialist in embryo transplants at Chicago's Reproduction and Fertility Clinic. "You'll be able to sit down and specify a DNA sequence associated with intelligence and put that in the embryo. We're talking about manipulation. We're talking about control."

When I spoke with Seed, he had just transplanted a fertilized embryo in a human uterus. He was waiting to see if it would take. The procedure would soon be routine, he said.

Will you have a few hundred embryos frozen in liquid nitrogen to sell someday? I asked.

"Maybe in five or ten years. Just as semen is for sale today."

Somewhere on this trek through the Brave New World of high-tech procreation, near this milepost of the frozen embryo, distinctions began to blur between physician as healer and scientist as creator.

What happens when something goes wrong in the course of transplanting genes into an embryo?

"That's where we are, my friend," answered medical ethicist Paul Ramsey, professor of religion emeritus at Princeton University. "In a quiet moment you can get a scientist to admit they may have to practice infanticide. The child may be regarded as not human enough; just a mishap—something which falls below the standard for entering the world.''

Gifts for the Führer

In December 1935, in Nazi Germany, S.S. Commander Heinrich Himmler launched a selective breeding program called Lebensborn. Pornographic films and military decrees encouraged elite German troops to impregnate carefully selected Aryan women both in German and in occupied countries. The women, once they had been certified as racially pure, were placed in special homes so that they could give birth under the most advantageous conditions. The Lebensborn were to become the first-generation leaders of Hitler's Thousand-Year Reich. Before the end of World War II, the Lebensborn project created 12,000 blond, blue-eyed babies. Himmler called them ''gifts to the Führer.''

One architect of Nazi race policies, Dr. Hans Endres, predicted that one day the young German male would be the most desired in Europe. ''He will make the women shiveringly submissive wherever he appears. Radiant, tall and vigorous, he will conquer and embrace them.'' Women, he said, would consider his sexual advances an honor—helping to ''procreate men of his kind.''

Lebensborn (''Well of Life'') was only part of the Nazi program of eugenics (human improvement through genetic control). Cash grants and loans were awarded to acceptable couples who wanted children. Laws prohibited intercourse between Jews and Aryans. Anyone who was ''hereditarily ailing'' was sterilized. Later, certain undesirables were put to death and, finally, Jews were exterminated.

Before Lebensborn and the Holocaust, eugenic ideas had gained a large measure of acceptance here in the United States. By 1932, laws in 27 states permitted public health officials to sterilize institutionalized ''defectives and subnormals,'' in some cases without consent. In 1935, Dr. Clarence Campbell, the only American speaker at the Berlin Population Congress, endorsed the concept of Nordic supremacy. In February 1937, Earnest Hooton, a Harvard University anthropologist, proposed that ''morons, criminals and social ineffectuals'' be purged through compulsory sterilization. And in December of that year, the National Education Association formally proposed ''the improvement of the national stock'' through government subsidies that would encourage the intellectually superior to procreate.

—P.B.

24

▼▼▼▼

Is There Sex After Baby?

▼▼▼▼▼

Carin Rubenstein

ABSTRACT: Following the birth of a child, couples have less sex. Three-quarters of the married couples surveyed showed a dramatic decrease for six months. A year later, their frequency of sex was about the same as that of couples over 60. The primary reasons for this decline are the new mother's fatigue and lack of desire. Part of the problem is that the arrival of a baby produces a triad, which complicates the couple's relationship. Husbands tend to feel sexually frustrated, for their sexual desires do not diminish. Eventually, the sexual relationship returns to normal.

The sexual revolution, like most revolutions, has come to an ironic and unforeseen end. Men and women who were merrily changing partners and trying new sexual techniques are now married and changing diapers and trying new brands of baby powder. For better or worse, it's the era of Baby Comes First.

This is just one of the conclusions to be drawn from the deluge of responses to the *Parenting* survey on sex and parenthood (November 1987). Other key findings:

235

- After the birth of a baby, many parents go into a sexual hiatus that lasts at least a year. For the majority of new mothers, sex is not as much fun as it was or seems like something from a former life. Yet most fathers say that sex is as enjoyable as it was before. But because it takes two to tango, there are a great many teeth-gritting, sexually frustrated new dads out there.
- Sex may be down, but for many respondents, love is up. Four in ten who are new mothers and 55 percent of new fathers are more in love than ever with their mates.
- A lot of parents have yet to cut the cord. Two-thirds have never spent a weekend away together, without their baby.
- New mothers are especially likely to manifest baby-on-the-brain syndrome. There's widespread agreement—91 percent of women, 83 percent of men—that the mother of a young child often pays more attention to the baby than to her husband.

SAYS WHO?

Nearly 6,000 people responded to the *Parenting* survey, two-thirds of them women. On average, the women are 30 years old and the men are 32. Most of the fathers, 87 percent, work more than 40 hours a week. Only 20 percent of the mothers work that many hours; half do not work outside the home. Most of the couples are in their first marriage and have been together about six years. They have one or two children. Eighty-six percent have a child younger than two years old, including half who have a baby under 12 months old. One in five mothers is still nursing; 15 percent are pregnant or trying to conceive.

Female respondents range from a 33-year-old mother in Harrisburg, Pennsylvania, who has an 11-month-old child and works more than 50 hours a week as a business manager, to a 21-year-old wife of a Texas truck driver. The men who replied include a 45-year-old businessman in Baltimore with a newborn baby from a second marriage and a 24-year-old father from New York City. Although we cannot generalize from this sample about all American families with young children, the findings provide a glimpse into the lives of a special group of contemporary parents—and what they say about parenthood and sexuality applies to many similar couples with children.

SEX? WHAT'S THAT?

About 80 percent of both husbands and wives agree that "after they become parents, most couples' sex lives suffer." Sex expert Dr. William

Masters, of the Masters and Johnson Institute, is not at all surprised. "A new mother's very low sex steroid level hardly prepares her to be excited in bed," he says. Also, "a new baby is demanding and saps strength," he adds. "Women should expect a reduction in interest and responsiveness to sex for at least two months."

Respondents agree. Three-quarters say that in the first six months after the baby was born, the frequency of their sexual intercourse decreased dramatically. A year later, sex is still at a low ebb for at least 50 percent. Right now, half of the respondents make love only once a week or less—a level of sexuality usually associated with men and women over 60. In *American Couples* (Morrow, 1983), sociologists Philip Blumstein and Pepper Schwartz examined the sex lives of couples who had been married between two and ten years, the majority of whom did not have children. They found that only half as many (27 percent) had sex as infrequently as once a week or less.

"Before childbirth, I was like a cat in heat," says a 40-year-old mother responding to the *Parenting* survey. "After, I can take sex or leave it. I have no particular complaints; I just feel a marked lack of interest." A 35-year-old mother of a two-year-old admits that "before children, sex was great and spontaneous, on the kitchen floor, in the bathroom, wherever, whenever." Now, she adds, "we are lucky if we can get together once a week."

A 37-year-old father of a two-year-old says that "the quality of my sex life has diminished with the decline in intercourse from four times a week to once per week (if I'm lucky)." He adds that "sex is not as much raw fun as it was before our two-year-old's birth."

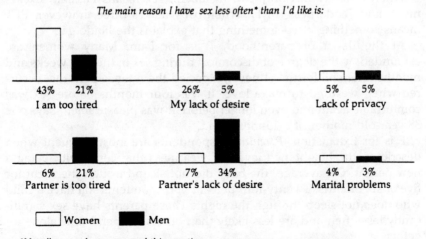

The main reason I have *sex less often** than I'd like is:

43% 21%	26% 5%	5% 5%
I am too tired	My lack of desire	Lack of privacy
6% 21%	7% 34%	4% 3%
Partner is too tired	Partner's lack of desire	Marital problems

☐ Women   ■ Men

*Not all respondents answered this question.

Figure 24.1 **Sexual Stumbling Blocks: Worse Than a Headache**

New parents say they have sex less often than they would like—mostly because of the new mother's fatigue or lack of desire. Quite simply, many women enjoy sex less during the first six or even twelve months of motherhood. More than half of the new mothers and 40 percent of the fathers say that sex is "not as much fun as it used to be" or that it's "something from my former life." Fewer husbands than wives, however, say that their potential for sexual enjoyment decreased in the six months after a child's birth. Indeed, the majority of husbands say that they are as sexually eager as ever. Perhaps as a result, husbands masturbate more often than wives during this time: In the six months after the birth of a child, 27 percent say they masturbate more than before, compared with only 8 percent of the wives. (Indeed, 30 percent of the wives say they masturbate less during this time.)

"Since the pregnancy, our sex life has come to a virtual standstill," complains a 30-year-old father of a newborn. "The typical reasons are she's too tired, too sore, too sick, too et cetera. I am, essentially, on my own. This makes me feel sorry for myself and left out of the picture."

He is typical of many new fathers, all left out of the same picture. In the year after the birth of a baby, a woman's hormones tend to suppress her sexual desire—especially if she is nursing. She sees herself as a nurturing, asexual creature. Her husband, the new father, feels neglected and sexually frustrated. Both parents think that they are the only ones who have ever felt this way.

THE PET FACTOR

When a family has only two members, sex means Passion, Excitement, and Tenderness (PET). When baby makes three, however, PET means something else—something that explains the libido gap.

At the dawn of parenthood, P is for Pain. Many women are astounded by the degree of discomfort during sex in the first weeks and months after childbirth. "I never expected the intense pain that occurred when we tried to make love. It was four months before sex was comfortable again and even longer before it was pleasurable," says one 38-year-old mother of a 15-month-old.

E is for Exhaustion. *Parenting* respondents are most eloquent when describing the heightened levels of weariness that come with being a new parent. On average, the baby did not sleep through the night for five or six months. Twenty-four percent of respondents still have a child who does not sleep through the night. These parents have sex significantly less often and are less likely than others to spend time alone together.

One mother of an insomniac baby gets through her day by "daydreaming of sleep." Another says that if she had to describe herself in one word for the year, that word would be "fatigued." If given the choice, says a 32-year-old mother of a three-month-old, "I'd rather sleep than eat. I'd rather sleep than do anything." A mother of two who is an intensive-care-unit nurse reports that both she and her husband "can fall asleep at the drop of a hat." In sum, one mother writes, fatigue is the "slayer of our sex life."

T is for no-Togetherness, the third sexual saboteur. Half of the respondents did not spend even three waking hours alone together until more than two months after the birth of the baby, and the majority rarely or never dine without their children. Two-thirds have not yet spent a weekend away from their child. Mothers are more likely than fathers to notice the lack of togetherness, although the majority of both perceive the difference. And the time couples do spend together tends to be more quarrelsome than gratifying: One-half of the wives and one-third of the husbands say that they argue more since the arrival of the baby.

A woman who had been married for seven years before she had a child wrote that she misses the "intimacy in our everyday lives" that made good sex possible. "Long car trips when we sometimes conversed nonstop for two or three hours, late weekend nights in bed laughing over 'Star Trek' reruns—that's what's missing." She adores her three-month-old baby, but admits that she fell in love with her husband "through talk and lots of it." For now, she confesses, that kind of communication has vanished.

WHAT'S LOVE GOT TO DO WITH IT?

Sex and love are usually inextricably linked. But the love-sex bond can be both enriched and diminished by the addition of a new baby. A child, in many ways the third spouse, inspires a fierce new love, and alters forever the nature of parental sexuality.

Since becoming parents, 44 percent of the wives responding and 55 percent of the husbands say that they are more in love with their partner. A 37-year-old father of two says of his wife, "I understand and care more for her in recognition of her qualities as a mother as well as her qualities as a friend, wife, and person."

Marital love may intensify, but the baby often competes with Dad for Mom's attention. A nursing mother usually has very little physical and emotional energy left over for the new father. Almost all respondents (91 percent of mothers, 83 percent of fathers) agree that the mother of a young child pays more attention to the baby than to her husband. "Even though I feel a much greater love for my husband than I ever have," confesses one mother, "I still love my baby more. This saddens me. . . ."

Many fathers are aware that they take second place, at least for a while. About half of husbands say that they received less love and affection from their wives in the first six months after their child was born.

Some mothers do not realize that they neglect their mates because of the baby. A 30-year-old mother recalls that before her son was born, she and her husband "would sometimes have sex two or three times a day." Now, they make love barely once a week. After her husband told her that he thought she no longer loved him, she realized what had happened. "Since the baby was born," she told him, "I guess I put you on the back burner. All I think about 24 hours a day is our son. I guess it is time I started paying you more mind. Both of you can be part of the main course."

BABY LOVE

The love triangle that a new baby creates turns many marriages emotionally inside-out and upside-down. Some women are surprised by the depth and intensity of the love they feel for their baby. One new mother describes the tie as an "emotional umbilical cord that can't exist between two unrelated adults."

Yet some marriages thrive after the birth of a baby. Why? Couples whose parenthood makes them feel more in love than ever spend more time together. Compared with partners who are less in love, loving couples go out to dinner and visit friends more often. They are apt to do chores and run errands together. And more of them feed, bathe, and put their child to sleep together.

One mother who is more in love with her husband claims that he is now "more helpful with both the children and the housework. This leaves both of us less tired and irritable at the end of the day. We always take time for ourselves as a couple and surprise each other with special dinners or small presents. We appreciate what we have and try very hard to keep that special spark."

A 28-year-old mother of three, still nursing a two-month-old baby, says that although she and her husband have sex less often than they did before having children, when they do it is "much more romantic and enjoyable." She believes that her children have intensified her attachment to her husband "in ways not possible when we were only a couple. To share the love of three children and to parent, befriend, discipline, and teach them really has made us appreciate each other and love each other more deeply."

This is not to say that couples who are more deeply in love also have better sex than before—most don't. Their problem is not lack of desire, but simply fatigue. A 30-year-old mother of a newborn admits that "there are times I run on little sleep, but I always look forward to beginning and ending the day with a dose of my husband's touch, smell, and taste." And, she adds, "the first time I saw my husband hold our son against his bare chest, it was very sexy to me. After all, it was one of our moments of great passion that brought our baby into this world."

THE WORKING MOM BLUES

"By the time we get home from work, pick up the kid from daycare, give him a snack, make and eat dinner, feed *him* dinner, bathe and put him to bed," says a 32-year-old working mother, "I feel like I've been beaten with a stick." Her attitude toward sex: "Okay, but try not to wake me up while you're doing it."

Another working mother compares sex to "another wifely chore, like cleaning the bathroom." Not all of the mothers who are working 30 hours a week or more (28 percent) are quite that cynical, but their overwhelming exhaustion shows. Mothers who do not work outside the home are happier with their marriages and more likely to say that sex is fun. A year after the birth of a baby, mothers who don't work are more in love with and spend more time with their husbands, have renewed interest in sex, and enjoy it more.

A 34-year-old mother and teacher writes that she is "so exhausted from working full time, fulfilling family needs, and giving to everyone that the last thing I want to do is give in bed!" A 34-year-old mother who takes her infant son to work with her says that "I put a lot into being a good mom and good business partner and trying to provide a clean home and meals for my husband." She confesses, in a sentiment that may be inevitable, "it all seems so overwhelming."

SEXUAL REAWAKENING

Eventually, life does get back to normal—pain disappears, exhaustion diminishes, sexual desire returns. Just how long it takes before this sexual reawakening occurs, though, depends on a number of factors: the type of birth, the temperament of the parents and child, the availability of childcare, and the amount of paternal support and participation. "Sex is a natural appetite," as Dr. Masters points out, and simply needs to be stimulated after a period of abstinence. Getting back into the sexual habit requires a conscious effort. Or, as one mother put it, "just a combination of talk and K-Y Jelly."

Sometimes, however, deeper problems complicate the process of getting back on the postpartum sexual track. The perception of sex for procreation and not recreation may dampen sexual ardor. "I once felt that enjoyment of regular sex was the God-given right of every adult," says a 36-year-old mother of three. "But because of my constant physical contact with the pure, unwavering love of an infant, now I view sex differently. With the end product of my sexuality in my arms day and night, intercourse strikes me more as a means to an end."

Sex therapists advise parents to rid themselves of the notion that mommies and daddies should not be sexual creatures. Once a baby sleeps regularly and a couple begins to spend more time together, there's no reason not to resume an active sex life. One mother's solution is to schedule sex two nights a week because, she says, "I find that having it on the calendar helps me to gear up for it mentally, as if I were single again and planning for a date."

Rekindling the sexual flame after a baby's birth requires a new spirit of cooperation and empathy between partners and a recognition that a baby irrevocably alters both love and sexuality. For better or worse, say *Parenting* respondents, after baby arrives, life and sex change in more ways than anyone could have imagined.

25
▼▼▼▼

Principles for the Healthy Growth and Development of Children
▼▼▼▼

Urie Bronfenbrenner

ABSTRACT: The author develops seven propositions to "sum up everything that scientists know for sure about the necessary and sufficient conditions for the healthy growth and development of children." They are (1) enduring irrational emotional involvement, (2) participation of adults by both sexes, (3) enduring rational emotional involvement, (4) support by third parties, (5) a variety of people, (6) consensus, connection, and accommodation between settings, and (7) public policies, belief systems, and practices that provide for opportunity, status, resources, encouragement, example, stability, and time.

In this chapter I presume to sum everything that we scientists know for sure about the necessary and sufficient conditions for the healthy growth and development of children. . . . That's a lot to cover in a limited frame, but we'll make it because of a clause that I cleverly inserted in the small print above. I promised I'd describe *all that we scientists know for sure*. That's not very much. . . .

SEVEN ESSENTIALS
FOR CHILDREN'S DEVELOPMENT

What has science shown to be the conditions essential for human development? The findings can be condensed into seven propositions.

Proposition I

In order to develop physically, intellectually, emotionally, socially, and morally—any and all of those—a child needs the enduring irrational emotional involvement of one or more adults in care and in progressively more complex joint activity with that child.

What do I mean by "irrational emotional involvement"? I mean somebody has to be crazy about that kid.

What do I mean by "progressively more complex joint activity"? I mean a Ping-Pong game where you start off slowly and simply but when you have the right partner the game gradually grows faster and more complex. Soon you're having to go to the backhand, and the ball often gets away from you. If your partner is your son (or daughter), he may take pity on the old man and slow it up a little so you can catch up, but as soon as you think you're OK, he puts on the heat again. That's progressively more complex joint activity.

Notice that in this situation each side is teaching the other new tricks. That happens from the first moment of birth. The newborn in our species teaches its caregiver a very complicated game. There is nothing more challenging intellectually than having to take care of an infant. It's the most complex and captivating activity we're capable of. Once you begin it, you get hooked. You begin to become irrational about that little creature, and it becomes irrational about you. That irrationality is very important, because without it, the little creature can't become competent. For example, it can't, years later, take SAT tests very successfully unless it experienced that irrational commitment years before. We're very interesting organisms, we humans. We are indeed social animals, evolved so on a biological basis. Accordingly, development begins and continues as a Ping-Pong game between people who are crazy about each other. That's how we become human, and how we remain human as adults (if we do).

This first principle is grounded in a substantial body of research accumulated over the past half century. Of course, mothers and teachers have known it from the beginning of recorded time. It took us scientists some time to catch up, but now we're beginning to. The remaining principles are of more recent vintage, having emerged from investigations conducted during the last two decades.

Proposition II

The development power of emotionally involved care and progressively more complex joint activity is enhanced by the participation of adults of both sexes in the joint process. Isn't science wonderful!

Proposition III

This has only one word different from Proposition I: In order to develop physically, intellectually, emotionally, socially, and morally, a child needs the enduring *rational* involvement of one or more adults in progressively more complex activity.

You need both kinds of involvement: rational and irrational. First, you need somebody who thinks you're the most wonderful creature in the world. The primacy of this need is illustrated by the quip of a Russian colleague when I asked him why the Soviets gave up their boarding schools. There was a time, some years ago, when the Russian leaders decided that things weren't quite right in their society because the people who had status and power were getting all the benefits and those who didn't have status and power weren't. That wasn't right by the communist principles. So they planned to give bennies to everybody by sending kids to boarding school, where the best teaching methods and materials known to science would be provided to all. Some years later, this practice was discontinued. I asked why. My colleague's unpublished answer: "You can't pay a woman to do what a mother will do for free." As you see, the Soviet Union is a very male-chauvinist society, but the general point is still valid. One of the essential conditions for human development requires having people who are crazy about children.

It's not easy to find many people like that, but there's one group on which you can count almost 100 percent. You can count on parents to care about their children irrationally. It's much more difficult to find somebody else who's that crazy about you. You can approach it with relatives, friends, occasionally teachers. But the only ones you can really be sure of to be irrationally committed are parents.

You also need somebody who is *not* irrational about you; who values you as a child but considers you no more wonderful than another child. Such a person works for your development in a fair, rational manner. If you don't have somebody like that in your life, it is very difficult to become a full human being. Another problem is that the same person can't play both roles. You really can't be crazy and fair at the same time. So we're beginning to answer our second question. What are the things that only parents can do?

One of the things we have been doing in our mistaken notion that there are no limits, that everything is possible, is to try to make teachers out of parents and parents out of teachers. It doesn't work. Each type of adult is different and vitally important. They need each other: as colleagues, companions, and friends. Yet we seem to be building a world in which parents and teachers are being defined as adversaries: "I can't teach these kids because of those parents." "I can't do anything with my kid because of that school." Any time you have that situation, you risk having children with reading problems, children who can't write and don't care, children who cop out and engage in vandalism and violence. You can't have effective education unless there's consensus. That brings us to our fourth principle.

Proposition IV

The effectiveness of the Ping-Pong game depends on the extent to which third parties support or undermine the activities of those actually engaged with the child.

We have recently found the third party to make a powerful system. Before that, right after World War II, there was a big social-science breakthrough, when psychologists, teachers, counselors, and everybody else discovered the *dyad*. First they discovered the mother/child dyad, and that was terrific. Then things got really advanced, and they discovered the father/child dyad. It turns out that anything she can do he can do, from the first moment of birth. At first nobody believed that. We thought men couldn't be sensitive and nurturant to babies. Well, they can't be, if you don't give them a baby to hold. If you don't, they have no chance to become sensitive until they get married and have their own child, and then it may be too late. But if they start early, they can do it; but differently. The infant needs the difference, needs to be cared for by both men and women. Moreover, how well the Ping-Pong game is played by mother and child depends on father; and how well the father/child game is played depends on mother. Each one can make it or break it; and nowadays it's often being broken. It's very difficult to make it work without that third party, especially if that third party is working to unmake it. And that isn't all.

Proposition V

In order for a child to develop physically, intellectually, emotionally, socially, and morally, it takes a variety of people in a variety of Ping-Pong games.

You can't just stay home and do it. As we grow up, we need to get different strokes from different folks in different settings to become sentient, capable, competent, and compassionate human beings. But for those strokes in different settings to be effective, they have to be coordinated.

Proposition VI

For successful child rearing, there must be consensus, connection, and mutual accommodation between the different settings in which the child lives: home, day care center, school, work place, peer group, and neighborhood.

The people in these settings can't be at odds with each other. You can't say, "I don't know what they're doing, and I don't care. That's their business." Don't ask for whom the bell tolls, whether it's the school bell or the doorbell. It's ringing for you because it's ringing for your child. Even what happens in an office, shop, or factory has almost as much effect on the Ping-Pong game as what happens at home. Unless there's some mutual accommodation, connection, and consensus, the process gets wobbly, and the mechanism runs down.

Proposition VII

This is the most important, especially in modern industrialized societies. The involvement of adults in care, joint activity, and support of child rearing requires public policies, belief systems (ideologies), and practices that provide opportunity, status, resources, encouragement, example, stability, and above all, time: time for child rearing, primarily by parents but also by all other adults in the child's environment and in the environment of those who deal with children.

That's a tall order. But that tall order must be filled for a society to thrive. We are accustomed to measuring the success of a society by its gross national product. We are now discovering that the gross requires the fine. The material requires the spiritual. That's what science is now discovering. The first president of Cornell University, Andrew Dickson White, wrote a book called, "The War between Science and Theology." We're about to visit his gravestone and say, "Andy, they've signed the peace."

Critical Age

Based on an analysis of the available research evidence, these seven propositions define the critical conditions for making, and keeping, human beings human. At this juncture you may well ask, "How old is the child referred to in these propositions?" That point is debatable. I would suggest anyone under the age of say, 89! For if you examine these propositions, you will discover that they speak to the human condition throughout our lives. As human biologists remind us, one of the distinguishing features of our species, *Homo sapiens,* is that we are social animals. Sooner or later, and usually sooner, we need each other. It's because that need has been met for us, for you and me, that we are here. We couldn't read, we couldn't think, we couldn't function, we couldn't relate to each other if somebody hadn't made the investment I've been describing. When I was a kid my father used to say to me, "Little One, always remember, you are the people in your life." . . .

WHAT IS TO BE DONE?

Some things are obvious. Why aren't they being done? Not because we don't know what to do, but for some reason we don't have the will. What we are experiencing is an erosion of the social fabric that sustains the primary institutions in which human development takes place. Families can't function when they are not receiving adequate health care, when there's not enough money to buy food, when there's no one to take care of your child if you're lucky enough to get a job, and where neither the neighborhood, the school, nor world of work show any understanding or support for you or your family. The family can't function without that support. Even those superhumans, the mothers of this country, can't do it alone.

Our task is to reweave the unraveled social fabric. We have to rebuild the connections between the home, the school, the work place, the community, and the neighborhood. We have to recognize the fact that families are not self-sufficient. We have to provide recognition and resources at the concrete level, at the local community level. . . .

To begin with, somebody's got to be crazy about you. Remember Harlow's marvelous experiment years ago, in which infant monkeys were separated from their mothers and given terry-cloth mothers, soft cuddly creatures. At first it looked as if all the terry-cloth kids were OK. But when they grew up, they rejected their own children, pushed them away. But those children didn't know that. They'd keep coming back, coming back, coming back, until the mothers killed them. Of course that's child abuse in another species. Or is it just another species? Does it also furnish a clue to the rising rate of child abuse among our own kind? Perhaps we need to teach terry-cloth kids how to be real mothers rather than terry-cloth mothers. . . .

There is a principle that sums up all seven propositions. It comes from a world far worse than our own. A Soviet friend once said to me, "We're going to outlive you as a society, and do you know why? Because with all our horrors, one thing we never forget: the family." The Soviet Union had a huge national problem after the Revolution: Tens of thousands of children and youth were roaming the countryside, stealing, vandalizing, and murdering. They went to a schoolteacher-social psychologist named Makarenko. He was a genius. He solved the problem at a national level. He established communities for the homeless youth, and many of those children today hold leadership positions in Soviet society. They are very talented human beings. When people asked Makarenko, ''How did you do it?'' he stated a simple principle, simple, but difficult to do: ''The maximum of support and the maximum of demand.'' You say to people, ''Here are the resources. We expect you to do a terrific job and we'll help. But if the job is sloppy, we say, 'Do it over.'''

The need is to create formal systems of challenge and support that generate and strengthen informal systems of challenge and support, which in turn reduce the need for the formal system. The place to do it is at the local level, and the time to begin is now!

26

▼▼▼▼

Equity and Loyalty
Among Brothers and Sisters

▼▼▼▼

Gerald Handel

ABSTRACT: Four conditions cause problems in the relationships of brothers and sisters: (1) shared parentage, (2) differences in ages, (3) psychosociobiological individuality, and (4) differences in sex. The most fundamental issue in sibling relationships is equity, establishing a sense of fairness. Problems of equity arise because parents treat their children differently in matters of (1) unequal performance, (2) the application of rules of conduct, (3) the resolution of disputes, and (4) scarcity. A second vital issue is loyalty, which involves availability, sharing, handling information, and protection.

The social sciences (including . . . psychology and psychiatry) have focused the greatest attention on the hostility between siblings. The most fully developed concept pertaining to sibling relationships is sibling rivalry. The long established psychological focus on sibling rivalry has in recent years been supplemented by sociological investigations of violence between siblings, part of a larger inquiry into violence in families. The leading students of violence in families inform us that sibling

Note: This selection presents two of the four issues that the author defines as central. Readers interested in the full statement of the issues and their interrelationships are referred to the original source.

violence is the most frequent type of family violence; it occurs more often than either violence of parents toward children or violence between spouses. They report that 53 of every 100 children attack a brother or sister in a year by kicking, biting, punching, hitting with objects or "beating up." "That means well over 19 million attacks which would be considered as assault if they occurred outside the family" (Straus et al., 1980, p. 82). . . .

When we consider the powerful Biblical stories of hatred between brothers, together with the psychological and sociological studies of sibling rivalry and violence, we may wonder how it was possible for an ideal of brotherhood or sisterhood to develop at all. Are these ideals pure fantasies, without foundation in any real families?

Anthropologist David Schneider and sociologist Elaine Cumming argue that sibling solidarity is a characteristic of the American kinship system. In their study of aging adults 50 to 80 years old, perhaps they came upon one of the foundations of the ideal of brotherhood. They found that among aging men, morale is higher among those who have siblings nearby than among those who do not. Among women, the situation is more complicated, but what can be said is that among married women, the presence of siblings ameliorates low morale (Cumming and Schneider, 1961). Marvin B. Sussman (1974) found, in a sample of lower middle- and working-class adults, that about 47 percent of them had given some form of help to a sibling in the preceding month and 49 percent had received some kind of help from a sibling in the preceding month. . . .

In a study of 75 adults (but not of their siblings), investigators found that "the most powerful contributor to feelings of closeness between individual siblings was the framework of the family in which siblings grew up. The sense of belonging to the family, and of being close to particular siblings, was, for most subjects, permanently affected by experiences shared in childhood. . . . Participants who felt close to their families and to their siblings recalled an emphasis on family unity and believed that democratic child-rearing practices further encouraged its development. Especially important among these recollections were practices which stressed expectations for harmony, absence of favoritism, recognition of individual talents and accomplishments and—less frequently—the teaching of strategies for getting along and using conflict constructively" (Ross and Milgram, 1982, p. 229). This is a useful exploratory study, but it raises many questions that must be answered before closeness can be understood. To cite just one or two: Does an emphasis on unity always lead to it? Could not siblings develop a unity among themselves though their parents were mired in discordant conflict?

Cicirelli (1982, p. 281) reports that ". . . most siblings feel close affectionally to each other, with the least closeness between brothers and the most between sisters. It is clear that siblings are capable of true intimacy and extraordinary understanding of one another's problems, although most sibling relationships do not attain this level. . . . Overt sibling rivalry appears to diminish in intensity as people get older. . . . However, there is evidence that rivalry may be dormant and can be reactivated in such situations of adulthood as caring for aging parents, questions of inheritance, and so on." . . .

Surely the ground that we have covered thus far points to some issues that call for deeper probing into the nature of sibling relationships. We live with an ancient heritage of brotherhood as an ideal, one that has inspired cohesive action under some circumstances. The modern women's movement has been animated by an ideal of sisterhood. Yet although we know that some adults benefit in some ways from continuing sibling relationships, we have only very fragmentary knowledge of how cohesive sibling relationships are constructed in actual families. Our most profoundly understood and most fully documented aspect of sibling relationships is sibling rivalry. We understand a great deal about jealousy, envy, and hatred among siblings. We don't know much about how some children solve these problems more easily than others. We do not know why some siblings not only help each other in adult life but are close friends, while others grow up to be indifferent or inimical. . . .

In the balance of this paper I propose to begin to construct a framework for analyzing sibling relationships in childhood. I suggest an initial series of issues in childhood sibling relationships that have emerged from [the] study of interviews of parents and children in 33 families. . . . The issues I have identified will be illustrated with brief quotations from the interviews. . . .

PROBLEMATIC CONDITIONS
IN SIBLING RELATIONS

There are essentially four conditions that make for problematic relations between or among brothers and sisters. The *first* and most fundamental is the fact of shared parentage. There is a general social expectation that parents have an obligation to give care to the children they have begotten and that each of their children has a rightful claim upon this care. The children who have the same mother and father come to know that they have a relationship with each other that they do not share with children who have other mothers and fathers. They learn this from their parents who usually teach it, and they learn it from outsiders who define them as brothers and sisters.

Shared parentage is problematic for two reasons: (1) because each child sees the same person as vital for providing the resources the child wants and requires from others [and] (2) because the parents define the children's shared parentage as a basis for solidarity between or among the children. Thus, children of the same parents come to find themselves under pressure to feel affection and/or to act with consideration or moderation in relation to someone who is also competitive for parental affection and time and other benefits.

The *second* condition that makes the relations of siblings problematic is that they are of different ages. Thus, a second basis of strain is found in the contrast between pressures toward solidarity that derive from shared parentage and the differences in social expectation directed toward children of different chronological ages.

A *third* condition that makes the relations of siblings problematic is that each has a psycho-socio-biological individuality along with [his or her] shared parentage. Each newborn presents himself or herself as a unique configuration of characteristics. Each evokes a somewhat individualized response from each parent. The extent of one sibling's perceived differences from an earlier-born may be great or small, but some consequential difference is likely to be perceived by parents who may later try to eradicate, minimize, or foster it. In any event, these perceived differences will enter into the interactive histories of the family members. The significance of the differences will become part of the ground for interaction and establishment of relationships within the family.

Finally, if siblings are of different [sexes], this fact becomes a *fourth* condition that makes the relationships among them problematic. The difference in sex is met with different expectations concerning sex roles. Brothers and sisters learn to deal with each other in ways that are conditioned by the fact of their being of opposite [sexes], while also expecting that as children of the same parents they have the right to be treated "equally" by their parents.

The issues that arise among siblings and in parental handling of the sibling situation derive from these problematic conditions built into [the] family structure in our culture. The conditions that make sibling relationships problematic in intact families exist in somewhat modified form in blended or reconstituted families composed of remarried parents with children possibly from . . . earlier marriages as well as from the current one. . . .

ISSUES IN SIBLING RELATIONS

Equity

Perhaps the most pervasive, most fundamental issue in sibling relationships is the issue of equity. . . . Commonly, children are sensitive to the way parents treat them and their siblings. They will be attentive to and make comparisons between rewards and punishments distributed to self and sib. Parents will ordinarily feel some obligation within themselves to be fair to their children, to reward and punish in ways that satisfy both themselves and their children that they are neither excessively harsh nor excessively indulgent toward one as compared to the others. When parents do show favoritism, they may be under some external pressure from the adversely affected child if from no other to modify this unfairness. The child who feels treated persistently unfairly and who feels defeated in efforts to modify the practice of inequity may become troublesome in ways that cause him to be diagnosed as emotionally disturbed (Vogel and Bell, 1960).

Parents must deal with the problem of equity in a number of different contexts:

1. *Unequal Performance.* When two children perform differently in relation to some parental expectation, the parents must work out some strategy for dealing with the problem. They may reward good performance and punish unsatisfactory performance; they may reward only; they may only punish the unsatisfactory, or they may construct a more complex strategy. Mrs. GG wrestles with this problem in relation to the school performance of her two children. Grace, age eight, gets good grades; Gregory, age seven, does not. Asked, "Did you do anything about it?" Mrs. GG answers:

> No, we tried. . . . I mean, it was difficult because we wanted to praise Grace because she did, and yet we could see the reasons for Gregory's low grades so what we made more of an issue of was the fact that he'd get checks for talking and not keeping profitably busy and things like that. We made more of that point than of his low grades. And then we tried to give him any incentive to do better.

The dilemma Mrs. GG is here wrestling with is how to be fair to one child without having a damaging impact on the performance of the other. Related is the issue of whether similar performance can in fact be expected from both children. Each child is an audience for the interaction between parent and sibling. As parents wrestle with questions of expecting similar performance from different children and with [the] consequences of responding to differential performances, the children are engaged in defining the parental behavior as fair or unfair.

2. *The Application of Conduct Rules and Standards.* A second context in which issues of equity arise is in the application of conduct rules and standards. A particularly candid recognition of this problem was provided by Mr. GG. When the interviewer asked, "Which of the children do you find it easiest to handle, would you say?" he responded:

> Well, I think that, . . . in most cases . . . the girl has a certain, . . . preference as far as my tenderness is concerned. She's the firstborn, and the

fact she's a girl, I know I give her the benefit of a lot of doubts. I've been inclined at times to be more severe on the boy, only to look at him later that night or something and realize that, . . . he's only a little fellow and . . . maybe I shouldn't have been mean to him. And the fact that he idolizes me so, it only makes it that much harder.

Grace clearly recognizes her father's disposition:

> Interviewer: What kind of person is your father?
>
> Grace: Very nice and kind. . . . When I'm in trouble he takes care of the other person I'm in trouble with and that person is usually my dear little brother.

Her seven-year-old brother's interview does not yield a clear comment that bears on this issue of equity. It would be a mistake, however, to assume that the differential treatment is without impact on him; the absence of relevant data is more likely due to difficulty in eliciting statements that are specifically informative on this point.

There is some evidence to suggest that a perception of being equitably treated contributes to a feeling of solidarity between siblings. Consider the R family with two sons, Ralph, 15, and Russell, 12. In the course of a series of questions relating to other members of the family, Ralph was asked, "Do your parents treat Russell any different from you?" Ralph answers, "We both get a fair break." During an earlier interview Ralph was asked, "What do you like to do best?" His answer:

> There's three things, fishing, dating, and camping. I like to spend as much time outdoors as I can. And then Russell and I like to have a vision. He wants to be a naturalist of some kind and live in a small town. I'm going to be a lawyer, and as soon as I have my degree I'm going to the same town. And then when my dad retires they will come out there, too. We can do a lot of fishing and hunting together.

Ralph's vision should not be interpreted to mean that the brothers never fight or feel antagonism; the interviews provide abundant evidence of fighting and anger between them. But the vision of a shared future accommodating disparate occupations bespeaks a feeling of solidarity, and I suggest as a reasonable hypothesis that the sense of being fairly treated by parents is one of the factors—perhaps a necessary factor—that contributes to that sense of solidarity.

Parents are considered to be unfair when they are perceived to apply rules or standards unevenly. Thus, in the Q family, 14-year-old Quentin says that he gets mad at his mother because she sticks up for his sister when she's wrong. His sister, in turn, complains that her brother is allowed to get away with things that she does not get away with.

From the examples cited, it is evidence that a certain amount of the work that goes on in families is work to arrive at interpretations of fairness and unfairness. Is this event equivalent to that? Does it call for the same or different handling? Is this way of handling situation X equal in meaning to the handling of earlier situation W? What allowance does fairness demand should be made for a girl that is not made for a boy? Why do you treat my brother/my sister more leniently than you treat me? Why don't you notice the error of his/her ways as consistently as you notice mine?

3. *Resolution of Disputes.* A third context in which the issue of equity arises is in the resolution of disputes. These situations are of various kinds. In one type, a parent intervenes to break up a quarrel or fight. Both children receive the same treatment, but one may feel this is unfair because the other started it. To this child, the equal treatment (based on a parental presumption that both are culpable) is unequal.

Another type of situation is one that two siblings may want to control themselves. In the P family, 12-year-old Paul says of his older sister, "If she wouldn't tease me, I wouldn't tease her." For him, fairness necessitates retaliation. He must make his sister uncomfortable if she makes him uncomfortable. Otherwise, he would allow himself to be treated unfairly by her. Equity here means "getting even." A related type of situation is one in which getting even is not handled by the siblings alone but draws the parents in as punishers. Thus, in the Z family, 14-year-old Zachary reports his 8-year-old sister's misdoings to their parents. He explains, "I tell on her because she has told on me." Equivalent victimization in Zachary's solution to the fairness problem presented by Zelda's initiatives.

4. *Scarcity.* A fourth context in which the issue of equity arises is the context of access to scarce resources. An obvious type of instance is when two children, with one TV set, want to watch different programs at the same time. How can this scarce resource be apportioned so that both children feel fairly treated? . . .

In some families, equal access to parents' time and attention becomes an issue of enduring significance. In the L family, an interviewer with 16-year-old Larry elicits his views of his father's treatment of him and his 12-year-old sister Lisa. Toward the end of a series of questions on ideal family members, he is asked what an ideal son is and how he feels he measures up. He answers:

> I don't suppose I measure up either, but that's because they aren't ideal parents. . . . (How about Lisa?) Depends on what you consider ideal. If it's someone who does everything you are told to do and never grunt, then she's ideal. Of course, I think they have been more ideal with her than with me. She's gotten more attention, usually what the younger child gets. (Have you ever felt jealous?) I don't anymore. I used to feel jealous of the attention she'd get. I'm satisfied now.

Although Larry says he is no longer jealous, he also believes that the inequity in attention made him a less ideal son that he might have been.

[Interviews of parents and children show that] issues of equity are clear in some families [and] less clear in others. . . . Nevertheless, it seems useful to assume that every family in which there are at least two children must deal with such issues. Pressure toward fairness emanates from several sources, while the structure of life presents challenges to realizing such a standard. Fairness is a norm in Western culture, and parents are likely to experience some inclination to live up to it with regard to their children. But when that inclination is minimal or non-existent, one or more of the children themselves are likely to press toward such a norm, or despair that it is attainable. In any event, the equity issue presents itself and is consequential. At the same time, equity is necessarily elusive. Children of different ages, [sexes], and potentiality present their parents with ambiguities and uncertainties that must be translated into equivalencies that will satisfy all concerned: this punishment of this misdeed is equivalent to that other punishment of the sibling's misdeed. This reward is equal to that other reward and is not a sign of favoritism. The siblings themselves must work out some kind of modus vivendi. They may or may not agree that each is being fair to the other or being fairly treated by parents, but one way or another they will confront the issue of fairness between or among themselves. . . .

Loyalty

Membership in a family imposes on its members multiple and conflicting loyalties. All the members are expected to be loyal to the family, and each is expected to be loyal to each other member. But these loyalties cannot remain fixed in place all the time. They are subject to stresses, so that one loyalty may be temporarily weakened by another. A child may prefer the way something is done in a friend's family over his own. A sibling may make a demand that conflicts with a parental demand. Family members have conflicting claims on each other; responsiveness to one claim strengthens the loyalty in that relationship. Disregarded claims loosen loyalty. The strengthening and loosening of loyalties are continuing processes. . . .

1. *Availability.* Even as siblings pursue their own individual interests and form individual associations with playmates or friends outside the family, they also often want the other sibling(s) to be available on demand. This availability is desired for support in a particular situation, for advice, or, particularly among younger children, for companionship in play. . . .

A . . . version of availability is provided in the GG family. In response to the opening interview question, "What are the important things about your family?" eight-year-old Grace answers:

Like my mother, father and brother and my other relatives, our house and our care and all that stuff. We couldn't live without my mother. She sews and washes and changes our beds, and my father makes the money and if we didn't have a car he couldn't make any money. And my brother, well he's important to play with just to have someone around when I need him.

Later in the same interview, Grace gives an illustration of the value of *her* availability to her brother:

Sometimes on Sunday I like to watch TV instead of looking for new houses. I like to go but I like to watch TV. And one time when my brother was sick I was forced to stay home and they said they'd be home at four-thirty and they didn't come home until six-thirty. He was crying and everything but I finally made him some crackers and cheese and calmed him down.

In distress, or perplexity, or boredom, siblings turn to each other for or with appropriate manifestations of loyalty.

They do not always respond. In the W family, when 16-year-old Wendy is asked about her 13-year-old brother, "Do you ever get mad at Walter?" she says, "Sometimes, like when I get home from work and I want to go out and he won't help with the dishes. He just won't do a thing." Wendy clearly makes the unspoken assumption that, as members of the same family, she has a justified claim on her brother's support. Loyalty to the family ought to obligate him to assist her with her chore when she is short of time, but he does not live up to her expectation. . . . "He acts like a baby sometimes and runs to Pop, but he's young anyway. I'd much rather have an older brother." Her volunteered comment expressing a wish for an older brother suggests the hypothesis that sibling relationships tend to generate expectations of sibling loyalty, and when those expectations are not fulfilled, fantasies of a more idealized sibling relationship to replace the disappointing one are produced. Here, then, may be another clue to the ideals of brotherhood and sisterhood: these ideals may partly represent compensatory fantasies for disappointing sibling relationships, the disappointment being grounded in expectations of loyalty more or less inevitably intrinsic to the relationship.

2. *Sharing.* One child in a family may have possession of an item the other values. If feasible, there will often be an expectation by at least one of the siblings that it should be shared. A certain amount of interaction among siblings is devoted to constructing rules for sharing. These rules are often incomplete or ineffectual, and a fairly frequent complaint in these interviews is that one sibling takes or borrows something from another without asking. The taker or borrower is almost certainly acting on a presumption that the taking or borrowing is justified by shared family membership; it is unlikely that most of the borrowers would bor-

row equally freely from friends, without asking. Shared family membership imposes on siblings an obligation to share possessions that is pre-
sumptively more compelling than obligations to share with outsiders.

When an expectation of sharing is not fulfilled, the disappointed sibling can become aggressive and evoke an aggressive response. This happened in the K family, with 11-year-old Kenneth, as his 13-year-old
brother Karl tells it:

> My little brother is fat and jolly. He's too jolly. Couple nights ago I had a
> piece of candy in my jacket and he kept nagging, "Give me some," and
> I told him "No," and he kept trying to get in my pocket and we were
> wrestling around and he got in and so I hit him.

3. *Handling Information Appropriately.* At some early age—it is not clear
just when—children begin to understand the importance of information
as something that can be managed. They recognize that information
management has some significant dimensions and that it has diverse
consequences, depending on the nature of the information and the persons who have it.

One dimension is incrimination. Information can be incriminating. A
child may find himself or herself in a situation in which he or she feels
that such information that may be known to a sibling should, for loyalty's sake, not be shared with the parents. In short, one's brother or
sister should not tattle to one's parents about something one has done.
That information in the hands of parents can lead to unpleasant consequences. A sibling ought to understand and respect the consequences
of information mismanagement. In the C family, 12-year-old Caroline
expresses her exasperation with her 6-year-old sister:

> My mother is more often on Cynthia's side because both of us (Caroline
> and 10-year-old brother) are against Cynthia and Cynthia is such an inno-
> cent angel. If you ask her to promise not to tell my mother and father
> something, she promises and then she tells. . . .

Another dimension of information is its status value. At some unknown age children become aware of secrets, and they come to recognize that those who share in a secret have more status than those who
are excluded from it. The self is enhanced when one is deemed fit by
others to be entrusted with a secret. Thus, in the B family, in specifying
what she likes best about each member of her family, 12-year-old Barbara says of her 10-year-old sister, "My sister, if anything happens, she
always tells me about it. She doesn't keep anything from me."

4. *Protection.* Sibling loyalty is often put to a test outside the family,
when one child is in conflict with peers. When neighborhood children
give a child a hard time, that child is fortunate who has an older,
tougher sib to back him [or her] up. Nine-year-old Doreen makes clear
that she is the protector of her eight-year-old brother:

(Who do you usually go to when you feel worried or get into trouble?) Nobody, I worry about my own troubles, but if I did something—. I beat up my brother for fighting two little girls. I settled it. I did not tell my mother. I'll probably end up telling her if she is in a good mood. And if my little brother gets into trouble or if somebody is beating him up, he'd come to me. He said, "Boy, my sister can beat you up." I can beat him up so he thinks I can beat everybody. I can.

Doreen evidently sees herself as a protector of the underdog, which sometimes makes her an enforcer against her brother, but when he is in the underdog role she is his loyal protector. . . .

Sibling relations have yielded enduring metaphors of human aspiration. Brotherhood and sisterhood are ideals that have called forth great human effort. Yet the kinship relations to which these ideals metaphorically refer are scarcely known and understood. No social scientist today of any persuasion can tell us why some siblings develop the kind of loyalty that leads to enduring trust and friendship among them while other siblings do not. Few have even asked the question. Yet if rivalry is an aspect of relations between or among siblings in all families, it surely seems worth knowing why it is overcome in some and not in others, or even among some sibs but not others in the same family.

REFERENCES

CICIRELLI, VICTOR. Sibling influence through the life span. In Michael E. Lamb and Brian Sutton-Smith (Eds.), *Sibling relationships*. Hillsdale, New Jersey: Lawrence E. Erlbaum Associates, 1982.

CUMMING, ELAINE, and SCHNEIDER, DAVID. Sibling solidarity: A property of American kinship. *American Anthropologist*, 1961, *63*, 498–507.

ROSS, HELGOLA G., and MILGRAM, JOEL I. Important variables in adult sibling relationships: A qualitative study. In Michael E. Lamb and Brian Sutton-Smith (Eds.), *Sibling relationships*. Hillsdale, New Jersey: Lawrence E. Erlbaum Associates, 1982.

STRAUS, MURRAY, A., GELLES, RICHARD J., and STEINMETZ, SUZANNE K. *Behind closed doors: Violence in the American family*. Garden City, New York: Doubleday Anchor, 1980.

SUSSMAN, MARVIN B. The isolated nuclear family: Fact or fiction? In Marvin B. Sussman (Ed.), *Sourcebook in marriage and the family* (4th ed.). Boston: Houghton Mifflin, 1974.

VOGEL, EZRA F., and BELL, NORMAN W. The emotionally disturbed child as the family scapegoat. In Norman W. Bell and Ezra F. Vogel (Eds.), *A modern introduction to the family*. Glencoe, Illinois: Free Press, 1960.

27

▼▼▼▼

The Empty Nest

▼▼▼▼

Lillian Rubin

ABSTRACT: After interviewing 160 middle-aged women from varied backgrounds whose children had left home for college, marriage, or jobs, the author concludes that the stereotype of a painful empty nest is a myth. Most women look at their transition as a source of freedom, relief from responsibilities, and time for themselves. Feelings of loss or sadness are short-lived. The differences between working-class and middle-class women are slight, but the transition is somewhat easier for middle-class women. Differences show up between men and women: mothers fear that their children will leave before they're emotionally ready and fathers before they're financially ready.

> Lonesome? God, no! From the day the kids are born, if it's not one thing, it's another. After all those years of being responsible for them, you finally get to the point where you want to scream: "Fall out of the nest already, you guys, will you? It's time."

It's time—an urgent cry that wells up from deep inside, an impassioned plea that rises from the knowledge that too soon there will be no more time.

Time for what? Almost universally, the answer is:

Time, finally, for me. Time to find out who I am and what I want. Time
to live for me instead of them. All my life I've been doing for others. Now,
before it's too late, it's time for me.

Until quite recently, this stage of women's lives was the province of
clinicians. If a woman became depressed after her children left home,
the relationship was assumed to be one of cause and effect. Children's
leavetaking, they said, causes depression, a particular kind of depression that even warranted its own name. The empty-nest syndrome, they
called it. Nothing to worry about, they assured us. It's a loss like any
other. And as with any loss, the normal process of grief and mourning
would produce their healing effect. Although the healing didn't always
come, few questioned the theory. Instead, such women were characterized as neurotic-pathological in their inability to separate from their children, in their incapacity to manage internal conflict without breakdown.

As consciousness heightened about the nature of the life problems
women face, as more women moved into the social sciences where such
theories are born, ideas about the empty-nest syndrome underwent a
reinterpretation. Now, the pathology was located *not* in the woman, but
in the system of social roles and arrangements that makes it always difficult, sometimes impossible, for a mother to develop an identity that
rests on alternative roles.

An important shift in understanding, this. But not yet enough. For,
in fact, these new explanations still rest on the same unspoken assumptions as the old ones—assumptions that depression in midlife women is
linked to the departure of their children, that it is the loss of the mothering role that *produces* the sadness and despair. Like the old ideas, these
new ones too often still take as given the belief that a woman is little
more than the builder of the nest and the nurturer of the young, that
her reason for being is in that nesting and nurturing function.

Think about the language we unquestioningly use to characterize this
period of life: *the empty nest*. Not *the awakening*, not *the emergence*, not
words that might suggest that inside that house all those years there
lived someone besides a mother; no, we say *the empty nest*. And think,
too, about the associations to those words. Do we picture a father filled
with sadness because his children have left the home? Of course not,
because the nest is so intimately associated with mother that it is difficult to separate the two. . . .

That's the stereotype which permeates the culture, dominates our
image of women at midlife. It's so consonant with our view of Woman-
as-Mother—a view so widely shared and, until recently, so unconsciously held—that the phrase *empty-nest syndrome* has slipped into the
language as if it speaks to an eternal and unvarying truth. Since we have

failed to take heed of the assumptions that underlie the words, however, we also have not noticed that most of the ideas we have about depression in midlife women comes from research done on hospitalized patients.

Does this sad creature of the stereotype exist in the larger world where women live their lives and dream their dreams? Not among the women I met.

It's true that some are sad, some lonely, some are even depressed. It's true also that some are hesitant, some unconfident, and most are frightened as they face an uncertain future. But except for one, none suffers the classical symptoms of the empty nest syndrome. . . . *Almost all the women I spoke with respond to the departure of their children, whether actual or impending, with a decided sense of relief.*

Among those whose children already are gone, almost everyone is unequivocal in those feelings.

> I can't tell you what a relief it was to find myself with an empty nest. Oh sure, when the last child went away to school, for the first day or so there was a kind of a throb, but believe me, it was only a day or two.

Even those most committed to the traditional homemaker role— women who have never worked outside the home in the past and say they don't intend to in the future—speak in the same vein.

> When the youngest one was ready to move out of the house, I was right there helping him pack. We love having the children live in the area, and we love seeing them and the grandchildren, but I don't need for any of them to live in this house ever again. *I've had as much as I ever need or want of being tied down with children.*

A few—generally those who are a little closer to the time of the transition—are more ambivalent.

> It's complicated; it doesn't just feel one way or the other. I guess it's rather a bittersweet thing. It's not that it's either good or bad, it's just that it's an era that's coming to an end and, in many ways, it was a nice era. So there's some sadness in it, and I guess I feel a little lost sometimes. But it's no big thing; it comes and goes. [Suddenly straightening in her chair and laughing.] Mostly, it goes. . . .

Even women who have not yet watched a child leave home speak passionately of their readiness to turn their attention to their own lives.

> I'm ready to feel some freedom; I'm just itching for it. I'm looking forward, finally, to having a life of my own again. It's been such a long time.

But what about women who are divorced? Wouldn't women who have no husbands around to claim their attention—perhaps no prospect of marriage in sight—find the departure of the children more troubling? Surprisingly, the answer is *no*. Like their married sisters, they're relieved to be freed of the responsibilities of mothering, glad to be able to call their lives their own.

A little more than one-fifth of the women I met are divorced—some for almost a decade, some for only a few weeks or months. Those for whom divorce is relatively new are still in the process of adjustment—a few suffering acutely because the rupture in the marriage came as an unexpected blow; most grappling with the fear, the loneliness, the sense of loss that are almost always part of the immediate aftermath of divorce. But whatever the issues a divorced woman suffers, the departure of the children is not high among them.

It's true that some of those who are recently divorced are frightened at the prospect of a lifetime alone. But having the children at home does nothing to still those fears.

> It's hard to face that I might have to live alone forever.

Is it harder now that the last of your children has just married?

> No. I thought it would be, but it's not. I was talking to a friend about it just yesterday, and she said, "Why should it make a difference if the kids are home or not? They don't warm up the bed."

Women who have lived longer with divorce are simply and plainly relieved to be freed from the daily burdens of single parenting.

> It was hard not to be in a marriage when the children were smaller. During those years, I felt it was incumbent upon me to provide a full family life for them—I mean, to provide them with a two-parent home where there was at least a substitute father. I guess I blew that one because I didn't remarry, and felt pretty guilty and uncomfortable about it for years. But now that the children are grown, there's no compelling reason to be married. [Interrupting the flow of her words for a thoughtful moment.] What I'm saying is that it's great not to have to worry about them anymore. Now if I decide to get married, it'll be for me, not for them, which, of course, is the only way it ought to be anyway.

Whether married or not, it seems as if there's a kind of revolution of rising expectations among midlife women. With children in the teenage years, they have more freedom than ever before, but it's not enough to satisfy. Instead, a taste of freedom opens up the hunger for more—not just for more time to themselves, but for the opportunity, finally, to claim themselves.

> You know, when the kids get a little older, you can actually go away for a weekend by yourselves, and that's great. But somehow, your head is still at home worrying about what's going on there. I'm ready to be able to go away and have all of me away. I'm *ready*. [Groping for words to express the depth of her feeling.] Oh hell, it's not just going away that I care about. I want all of me. It's as if I want to take myself back after all these

years—to give me back to me, if you know what I mean. Of course, that's providing there's any "me" left.

Are there no women, then, who experience feelings of loss at their children's departure, none who feel the grief and sadness that inevitably accompanies such loss? Of course there are. Most women do. But there's wide variation in the duration of those feelings—some speaking of days, some weeks, much more seldom, months. And whatever their intensity, such feelings rarely devastate women, rarely leave them depressed and barely functional.

Sometimes the leave-taking is more problematic for working-class than for middle-class mothers. But notice *first* the word *sometimes*. And notice also that this says nothing about depression. In fact, in those instances where such problems exist for working-class women, they are almost always short term and of limited intensity. Still, there is a difference—a difference related to the *process* by which the children of each class generally leave home.

Almost from birth, most middle-class parents know when the big break will come—at eighteen, when the child leaves for college. There's plenty of warning, plenty of time to get ready. But in working-class families, college attendance is not taken for granted—often these days not even desired—and children are expected to live at home until they marry. Even among those working-class girls and boys who are college bound, most know they will live at home during those years—both because it's part of the family expectations, and because generally they cannot afford to do otherwise. Since the age of marriage is not clearly fixed, that means the time of departure is also indefinite—for both parents and children, somewhat like living with an indeterminate sentence rather than a firm release date that's agreed upon and understood by all. That difference alone—the unpredictability of the departure date— makes preparation for separation more difficult in working-class families.

Indeed, often middle-class mothers speak of the child's senior year in high school as the year in which much of the separation work is done—what sociologists call "anticipatory socialization."

> By the time my daughter left for college, I had really dealt with the issues. From time to time in her senior year in high school, I'd get a pang thinking about what was coming. I must admit, though, that by the time it actually happened, even I was surprised at how easy it was. I guess I had just grown accustomed to the idea by then.

But for the working-class woman, there is no such clear marker, no date known years in advance when she can expect a child's departure. For her, therefore, preparation is different, separation perhaps more difficult for some brief period of time. But almost always the difficulty certainly is brief, and it surely does not approach anything that rightfully could be called a depression. . . .

How then can we account for the persistence of the myth that inside the empty nest lives a shattered and depressed shell of a woman—a woman in constant pain because her children no longer live under her roof? Is it possible that a notion so pervasive is, in fact, just a myth? No simple questions, these; and no easy answers. For they touch the deepest layers of social structure and personality, and the interconnections between the two.

To start, let's grant that, as with all stereotypes, there's a kernel of truth in this one. The midlife transition is, in fact, a difficult one for most women—a time often filled with turmoil and self-doubt, a time when old roles are being shed and the shape of new ones not yet apparent; a time of reordering long-held priorities, of restructuring daily life. From that small truth, however, has grown a large lie—a fabrication based on the one-sided and distorted view of women and womanhood; a view that insists that womanhood and motherhood are synonymous, that motherhood is a woman's ineluctable destiny, her sacred calling, her singular area of fulfillment. Until quite recently, this view has remained largely unchallenged—one of the accepted verities on which our social and economic system was built. Man worked outside the home, woman inside. Her biological destiny was to nurture, his to provide the safety within which she could do it. . . .

Still, everyone knows there's more talk now about such issues, more public discussion, more critical examination of long-cherished ways of thinking about women and feminity. If the new feminist movement has done nothing else, it has raised these issues and forced us into a national dialogue about them. And, indeed, often enough women now say that they know others who feel relief at the departure of the children. But whether speaking of self or friends, rarely is it said without some sign of distress. Always there's the sense that maybe it's true that other women share these feelings, but no one can be quite certain that it's all right. Thus, when discussing the subject, women often look about uncertainly, lower their voices, and generally give signals of discomfort—as if they fear being overheard. Typical is this forty-five-year-old who leaned forward in her chair as if to bestow an important confidence, dropped her voice to just above a whisper, and said:

> To tell you the truth, most of the time it's a big relief to be free of them, finally. I suppose that's awful to say. But you know that, most of the women I know feel the same way. It's just that they're uncomfortable saying it because there's all this talk about how sad mothers are supposed to be when the kids leave home.

"Most of the women I know feel the same way." How is it, then, that this woman, like so many others, doesn't really know what she knows? Why the discomfort with her own feelings? Why the guilt? Some women respond to those questions by labeling themselves and their friends as deviant or aberrant, assuming that the rest of the world is different.

> I don't think my friends are typical or representative, or anything like that. I think most women still are in very traditional places, and most women really do miss their children terribly when they go. It's as if their lives just end. I'm different and so are my friends. That's because I picked them, I suppose. . . .

All this, then, suggests the enormous complexity in the interaction between cultural expectations, their internalization, and personal experience. For what I have been saying here is that, at one level, it's no big news to women who live it that the empty-nest syndrome doesn't exist for most of them. At another level, however, they are so mystified by the ideology of motherhood that they deny their own inner experience as well as the evidence their eyes and ears bring to them from the outer world.

In fact, it should come as no surprise to anyone that the end of the active mothering function is greeted with relief. Only someone who has never been a mother would fail to understand how awesome are the responsibilities of motherhood as they are presently defined in our culture.

> You know, you love them, but there's times you wish they didn't exist, too. It's frightening to feel like whatever they're going to do or whatever they're going to become is up to you. . . .

So what? one might ask: Don't fathers also feel keenly their parental responsibilities? We all now men who are burdened with the need to plan for death as well as for life—men who struggle, not only to make a living today, but to provide for tomorrow as well. Insurance companies grow fat and rich as they offer to protect against those fears—fears that are the price men pay for their unquestioning acceptance of the present division of labor in the family. With a wife and children wholly, or even largely, dependent upon him, a man works all his life partly, at least, to ensure their support in the event of his death. A few women spoke compassionately about this issue.

> My husband is seven years older than I am. And that means he's probably going to die before I do. Then what'll happen to me if he hasn't been able to provide for me? I simply couldn't make it on my own. So he has to carry a terrible burden. All these years, he not only has to worry about supporting all of us now, but he has to worry about my future. It's no wonder he's so snappish.

Of course fathers worry. But there's a crucial difference. A mother fears leaving her children before they're emotionally ready, a father before they're financially ready.

This is not to suggest that mothers feel more deeply about their children than fathers, nor that the differences in their responses—in the nature of their concerns—belong to natural differences between women and men. There's nothing natural about mothers being the care givers and fathers being the money givers. Rather, those are social arrangements—both women and men responding to long-established, socially defined roles and functions within the family. As a consequence of that family structure, however, a father can feel he has fulfilled his responsibility if he leaves enough dollars behind him. But what replaces mother? What can she plan to leave behind to help her children until they become emotionally independent adults?

They carry with them heavy costs, these social arrangements—burdening both women and men in painful, if different, ways. . . . Contrary to all we hear about women and their empty-nest problems, it may be fathers more often than mothers who are pained by the children's imminent or actual departure—fathers who want to hold back the clock, to keep the children in the home for just a little longer. Repeatedly women compare their own relief to their husbands' distress.

> For me, it's enough! They've been here long enough—maybe too long. It's a funny thing, though. All these years Fred was too busy to have much time for the kids, now he's the one who's depressed because they're leaving. He's really having trouble letting go. He wants to gather them around and keep them right here in his house. . . .

While mother has been feeding, tending, nurturing, teaching, watching, and sharing inside the home, father has been working outside. Sometimes he spends so much time at work because it is, in fact, the major emotional commitment in his life; sometimes, simply because it's his job to ensure the family's economic stability. More often, it's probably some mix of the two—his work being both a source of satisfaction and oppression.

But whatever his feelings about his work, he generally spends most of his life at it—most of his emotional and physical energy being spent in the pursuit of economic security for the family. Consequently, he's not there when his children take that first step, when they come home from school on that first day. He's not there to watch their development, to share their triumphs and pains. . . . and besides, he never quite knew how to relate to them, what to say—how to play with them when they were little, how to talk with them as they grew.

Over and over, women—ironically, even those married to child psychiatrists and psychologists—tell of being the interpreter between father and children, the buffer, the mediator, the one whose task it is to explain each to the other.

I always felt as if I had a foot in two different worlds, as if I was the one who walked across that no man's land that always seemed to exist between them. Oh, it was better at some times than others; I mean, they were able to talk to each other some of the time. But even at its best, I was always there as mediator and explainer, the one who knew what the other wanted and tried to explain it.

It's true that women complain a good deal about this.

I hated always to have to explain the kids to him. They're his kids, too. Why couldn't he take the trouble to get to know them?

And it's true also that, with all their complaints, it's a role they often hold onto because it gives them a sense of power, of control, of mastery in a world where, in fact, they have little. . . .

On the surface, it looks like a functional division of labor—both parents get what they want or need at the moment. She gets to feel important; he gets left alone to do his work. But the cost, especially for the father, is high. Just when he has more time, just when they're old enough to be talked to like real people, just when he's beginning to notice what he's missed—his children are gone. . . .

Since mothers usually don't miss any part of the process, the end of active mothering doesn't come with any sudden wrench. Indeed, for women who can look at their children and think "There's a job well done," the sense of accomplishment transcends any feelings of loss; the relief is unequivocal. For those who suffer disappointment, the relief is mixed with painful feelings of failure. And yet, not one of those women yearned for another chance. For good or ill, they were glad the job was done, ready to move on to the next stage of life.

That doesn't mean that are no problems at this life transition, only that they lie in the contemplation and confrontation with the next stage of life, only that they have to do with anxieties about the future, not with nostalgia for the past. . . .

It isn't that I want to hold the children here, it's just that I worry about what our life will be like. I don't know what we'll talk about, just the two of us, after all these years.

But alongside those fears, there's also excitement—the feelings vying with each other as women contemplate an unknown future. For many families, especially those in the working class, there's some financial freedom for the first time in their years together; for some, for the first time in life.

It's a whole different ball game, really, to live without having the boys as our first responsibility. We always lived on a very tight budget worrying about them, you know, always trying to do for them. Now we have money to spend on ourselves for the first time in our lives. Even if I just want to blow a few dollars on myself, I can do it now. That's like a whole new life for us—just to go on and do things for yourself. . . .

All these possibilities—exciting, yet frightening. How will it be? What kind of changes will it require—in him, in her, in their marriage? For her, the greatest unknown—and her central problem in this period—is what the next thirty or forty years of her life will look like. What will be its shape and texture? What will be its daily flavor?

> The children's leaving hasn't been traumatic at all. What has been and still is traumatic is trying to find the thing I want to do, and being able to pursue it to a successful conclusion. I'm an artist—a good one, I think. But it's hard to make the kind of commitment that real success requires. I'm afraid of what it'll do to my marriage, and also to the rest of my life. And I suppose I'm afraid to really try and fail. But that's the stuff that's so hard and painful right now; it's not knowing what I'll be doing, or even what I *can* do. And from forty-five to seventy-five is a lot of years if I don't have something useful to do.

The ending, then, is difficult, not because the children are gone, but because it brings with it a beginning. The beginning has the potential for adventure and excitement, but it brings with it also the possibility of failure. Some will negotiate it successfully, some will not. Sometimes the failure will be theirs; more often it will lie in the social constraints by which women's lives have been, and continue to be, hemmed in. But for all women whose central life task has been bearing and raising children, one question is heard like an urgent demand: "What am I going to do with the next thirty years of my life?"

PART VI

▼▼▼▼▼▼▼▼▼▼▼▼▼▼▼▼▼▼▼▼▼▼▼▼▼▼

Work and Marriage

A mong almost all couples in our society, at least one partner works for pay outside the home. In more and more cases, both the husband and wife are part of the paid labor force.

Neither situation has always been true. It is obvious that the employment of the wife-mother is a recent event, but it is less obvious that this is also true of the husband-father. Yet for *almost all of human history neither husband nor wife worked for wages outside the home.*

In most societies, both husbands and wives engaged in subsistence work, together contributing to the family's survival by activities such as hunting, food gathering, or farming. Each helped provide the direct substance from which the family survived. Ever since the invention of money, there has been some labor exchanged for it, of course. But for most of human history, most people have exchanged their labor for direct objects, such as food or tools; or as part of reciprocal arrangements, such as work that someone else would later return; or to fulfill obliga-

271

tions to the group (duty to the king or chief, social expectations of friends and relatives, and the like).

Working for wages as a common economic arrangement is, historically, a recent phenomenon. For the most part, it is a consequence of the Industrial Revolution of the eighteenth and nineteenth centuries. Working for wages outside the home did not become widespread until that time—and then only for the husband-father, who left his pursuits at home in exchange for the wages available in factories.

In contrast, except perhaps for a brief period when the Industrial Revolution first began, few women have worked for wages outside the home on a regular basis. This, the most recent economic change affecting the family, may prove to be the most far-reaching of the labor-for-wage exchanges. When men left their household pursuits to work outside the home, both women and children were left behind. Although the husband-father had participated in home routines because he was in and out of the home during the day, the mother had been the children's primary caregiver. When the father left home to work for wages, the mother was still there to care for the children.

Today's situation stands in sharp contrast. When a wife-mother leaves the home to participate in the paid work force, who is left at home to care for the children? Seldom do grandparents live in the household, and only rarely are other nonworking adults a part of our small nuclear families.

Consequently, we are in the midst of what is one of the most far-reaching social changes that we have ever experienced. We do not know the effects of women's participation in the work force—on their relationships with their husbands, on the development of their children, or even on themselves.

We do know that working for wages alters the fundamentals of family relationships. At a minimum, a working wife and a working husband have different power bases than do a nonemployed wife and an employed husband. A child whose mother is at home from the time he or she is born and is present when he or she comes home from school has a different relationship with her than does a child whose mother works full time and who is cared for by sitters and at day care centers from an early age or is home alone after school until his or her parents arrive.

It is obvious, of course, that relationships are altered by the wife's employment and her absence from the home. The consequences of those changed relationships, however, are not obvious. Will they harm children, perhaps making them more fearful or distrustful? Will they make it more difficult for children to establish in-depth commitment to others in later life? Or will this change benefit children, making them more independent and self-reliant? More than likely, there will be both gains and costs in personal development. Could it be that the various benefits and costs will cancel each other out, so that there will be no essential differences in the long run?

In many ways dual employment helps a couple adjust to married life. Studies consistently show, for example, that husbands and wives who have an adequate income get along better with one another and express greater satisfaction with their marriage. By reducing the strain of making ends meet, higher income tends to reduce tension between husbands and wives. In addition, when both participate in the world of paid employment they share more mutual experiences. By yielding a more common perceptual base, employment helps a couple to jointly construct a more satisfying reality.

In addition to the economic necessity that drives millions of women to paid work, what other reasons make the second paycheck so common in our society? In brief, women are drawn into the paid work force by the advantages that they see accruing from their participation. High among those positive features are increased income and self-satisfaction. The higher family income allows a higher standard of living—better cars, more exotic and luxurious vacations, a larger home in a better neighborhood, more fashionable clothing, better furniture, more factory-prepared meals at home, more meals out, and so on. The self-satisfactions primarily derive from personal involvement in a sphere of influence, from regular association with people with whom one shares common activities and orientations, and from attaining a sense of purpose from those associations and activities.

There is also the matter of when luxuries become necessities, of when options become requisites. Sociologists use the term *relative deprivation* to refer to what happens. All of us judge ourselves by comparing our own situation in life with the situations of others. How we evaluate our situation depends largely on how we think it stacks up with those of other people we know. For example, if a few people in society have two cars, but none of our friends do, although we might like to own two cars we do not feel deprived if we have only one. It is similarly the case with a new car versus a car eight years old, with a new house versus a house thirty years old, with an eight-room house versus a house with five rooms, with having or not having a jacuzzi, swimming pool, membership at the Y or country club, clothing with designer labels, and so on.

Because our sense of relative deprivation determines what we feel that we need, a luxury at one period in time becomes another period's necessity. Our definition of necessity depends, then, on an ongoing series of socially constructed, relative definitions. In short, our standards undergo constant modification.

In Chapter 28, Jessie Bernard analyzes changes in the basic provider role. She stresses that the "traditional" family form in which the husband-father is the provider and the wife-mother a housewife is only about 150 years old. As "providing" increasingly became measured by cash derived from participation in the labor force, the provider role grew in powers and prerogatives, while those of the housewife declined. Due to the large numbers of married women in today's labor force, the powers and prerogatives of the good-provider role have been diluted, creating a fundamental realignment of the relationships between males and females.

In Chapter 29, Kathleen Gerson stresses that women, working alongside men in the home, have always played an essential role in economic production. The rise of the factory system during the nineteenth century promoted the separation of work from the home, culminating in an ideology of female domesticity in the 1950s. In terms of birth rate and women in the labor force, the 1950s are an exception to the long-term historical trend in the United States. With our current increase of women workers and a decline in their fertility, the historical trend has now resumed. She emphasizes that a recent trend is for women to be more committed to the workplace.

The chapters that follow this historical background focus on the adjustments that couples make to work. In Chapter 30, Barbara Berg examines the guilt that many mothers feel when they leave their children to go to work. She indicates that this guilt encourages self-defeating behaviors, produces a "double bind" by creating stress and then preventing activities that might alleviate that stress, and harms marriages.

In Chapters 31 and 32, Joel Roache explores implications of work arrangements in which husbands achieve a sense of fulfillment from their work, while their wives obtain self-esteem through their husbands' accomplishments. He shows how the male's greater sex-role privileges isolate husbands from their wives, create emotional distance between them, hinder communication, and affect personality and perception. He also indicates that males tend to hide from housework by claiming an inability that they do not have.

In Chapter 33, Barbara Chesser examines issues that dual-career couples face: extra demands on the couple's time and energy, timing of children, child care, spending decisions, changing sex roles, women being judged by how they succeed in the homemaking role, relative earnings, unrealistic expectations, inadequate models for working out satisfying marital roles, and the myth of the superwoman.

28

The Good-Provider Role

Jessie Bernard

ABSTRACT: The "traditional" family form in which the husband-father is the provider and the wife-mother is the housewife is only about 150 years old. It lasted from the 1830s to 1980. As "providing" increasingly became mediated by cash derived from participation in the labor force, the provider role grew in powers and prerogatives, while those of the housewife, who lacked cash income, declined. As affluence grew, the provider role escalated into the good-provider role. As more and more married women entered the labor force and assumed a share of the provider role, the powers and prerogatives of the good-provider role became diluted. Because of these shifts, men and women are now undergoing a fundamental realignment of their relationships.

The Lord is my shepherd, I shall not want. He sets a table for me in the very sight of my enemies; my cup runs over (23rd Psalm). And when the Israelites were complaining about how hungry they were on their way from Egypt to Canaan, God told Moses to rest assured: There would be meat for dinner and bread for breakfast the next morning. And, indeed, there were quails that very night, enough to cover the camp, and in the morning the ground was covered with dew that proved to be bread (Exodus 16:12–13). In fact, in this role of good provider, God is sometimes almost synonymous with Providence. Many people, like Micawber, still wait for Him, or Providence, to provide.

Granted, then, that the first great provider for the human species was God the Father, surely the second great provider for the human species was Mother, the gatherer, planter, and general factotum. Boulding (1976), citing Lee and deVore, tells us that in hunting and gathering societies, males contribute about one fifth of the food of the clan, females the other four fifths (p. 96). She also concludes that by 12,000 B.C. in the early agricultural villages, females provided four fifths of human subsistence (p. 97). Not until large trading towns arose did the female contribution to human subsistence decline to equality with that of the male. And with the beginning of true cities, the provisioning work of women tended to become invisible. Still, in today's world it remains substantial.

Whatever the date of the virtuous woman described in the Old Testament (Proverbs 31:10–27), she was the very model of a good provider. She was, in fact, a highly productive conglomerate. She woke up in the middle of the night to tend to her business; she oversaw a multiple-industry household; *her* candles did not go out at night; there was a ready market for the high-quality linen girdles she made and sold to the merchants in town; and she kept track of the real estate market and bought good land when it became available, cultivating vineyards quite profitably. All this time her husband sat at the gate talking with his cronies. . . .

In a subsistence economy in which husbands and wives ran farms, shops, or businesses together, a man might be a good, steady worker, but the idea that he was *the* provider would hardly ring true. . . .

I have not searched the literature to determine when the concept of the good provider entered our thinking. The term *provider* entered the English language in 1532, but was not yet male sex typed, as the older term *purveyor* already was in 1442. Webster's second edition defines the good provider as "one who provides, especially, colloq., one who provides food, clothing, etc. for his family; as, he is a good or an adequate provider." More simply, he could be defined as a man whose wife did not have to enter the labor force. The counterpart to the good provider was the housewife. However the term is defined, the role itself delineated relationships within a marriage and family in a way that added to the legal, religious, and other advantages men had over women.

Thus, under the common law, although the husband was legally head of the household and as such had the responsibility of providing for his wife and children, this provision was often made with help from the wife's personal property and earnings, to which he was entitled:

> He owned his wife's and children's services, and had the sole right to collect wages for their work outside the home. He owned his wife's per-

sonal property outright, and had the right to manage and control all of his wife's real property during marriage, which included the right to use or lease property, and to keep any rents and profits from it. (Babcock, Freedman, Norton, and Ross, 1975, p. 561)

So even when she was the actual provider, the legal recognition was granted the husband. Therefore, whatever the husband's legal responsibilities for support may have been, he was not necessarily a good provider in the way the term came to be understood. The wife may have been performing that role.

In our country in Colonial times women were still viewed as performing a providing role, and they pursued a variety of occupations. Abigail Adams managed the family estate, which provided the wherewithal for John to spend so much time in Philadelphia. In the 18th century "many women were active in business and professional pursuits. They ran inns and taverns; they managed a wide variety of stores and shops; and, at least occasionally, they worked in careers like publishing, journalism and medicine" (Demos, 1974, p. 430). Women sometimes even "joined the menfolk for work in the fields" (p. 430). Like the household of the proverbial virtuous woman, the Colonial household was a little factory that produced clothing, furniture, bedding, candles, and other accessories, and again, as in the case of the virtuous woman, the female role was central. It was taken for granted that women provided for the family along with men.

The good provider as a specialized male role seems to have arisen in the transition from subsistence to market—especially money—economies that accelerated with the industrial revolution. The good-provider role for males emerged in this country roughly, say, from the 1830s, when de Tocqueville was observing it, to the late 1970s, when the 1980 census declared that a male was not automatically to be assumed to be head of [the] household. This gives the role a life span of about a century and a half. Although relatively short-lived, while it lasted the role was a seemingly rock-like feature of the national landscape.

As a psychological and sociological phenomenon, the good-provider role had wide ramifications for all of our thinking about families. It marked a new kind of marriage. It did not have good effects on women: The role deprived them on many chips by placing them in a peculiarly vulnerable position. Because she was not reimbursed for her contribution to the family in either products or services, a wife was stripped to a considerable extent of her access to cash-mediated markets. By discouraging labor force participation, it deprived many women, especially affluent ones, of opportunities to achieve strength and competence. It deterred young women from acquiring productive skills. They dedicated themselves instead to winning a good provider who would "take care of" them. The wife of a more successful provider became for all intents and purposes a parasite, with little to do except indulge or pamper herself. The psychology of such dependence could become all but crippling. There were other concomitants of the good-provider role.

EXPRESSIVITY AND THE GOOD-PROVIDER ROLE

The new industrial order that produced the good provider changed not so much the division of labor between the sexes as it did the site of the work they engaged in. Only two of the concomitants of this change in work site are selected for comment here, namely, (a) the identification of gender with work site as well as with work itself and (b) the reduction of time for personal interaction and intimacy within the family.

It is not so much the specific kinds of work men and women do—they have always varied from time to time and place to place—but the simple fact that the sexes do different kinds of work, whatever it is, which is in and of itself important. The division of labor by sex means that the work group becomes also a sex group. The very nature of maleness and femaleness becomes embedded in the sexual division of labor. One's sex and one's work are part of one another. One's work defines one's gender.

Any division of labor implies that people doing different kinds of work will occupy different work sites. When the division is based on sex, men and women will necessarily have different work sites. Even within the home itself, men and women had different work spaces. The woman's spinning wheel occupied a different area from the man's anvil. When the factory took over much of the work formerly done in the house, the separation of work space became especially marked. Not only did the separation of the sexes become spatially extended, but it came to relate work and gender in a special way. The work site as well as the work itself became associated with gender; each sex had its own turf. This sexual "territoriality" has had complicating effects on efforts to change any sexual division of labor. The good provider worked primarily in the outside male world of business and industry. The homemaker worked primarily in the home.

Spatial separation of the sexes not only identifies gender with work site and work but also reduces the amount of time available for spontaneous emotional give-and-take between husbands and wives. When men and women work in an economy based in the home, there are frequent occasions for interaction. . . . When men and women are in close proximity, there is always the possibility of reassuring glances, the comfort of simple physical presence. But when the division of labor removes the man from the family dwelling for most of the day, intimate relationships become less feasible. . . .

. . . Emotional expressivity was not included in the role. One of the things a parent might say about a man to persuade a daughter to marry him, or a daughter might say to explain to her parents why she wanted to, was not that he was a gentle, loving, or tender man but that he was a good provider. He might have many other qualities, good or bad, but if a man was a good provider, everything else was either gravy or the price one had to pay for a good provider.

Lack of expressivity did not imply neglect of the family. The good provider was a "family man." He set a good table, provided a decent home, paid the mortgage, bought the shoes, and kept his children warmly clothed. He might, with the help of the children's part-time jobs, have been able to finance their educations through high school and, sometimes, even college. There might even have been a little left over for an occasional celebration in most families. The good provider made a decent contribution to the church. His work might have been demanding, but he expected it to be. If in addition to being a good provider, a man was kind, gentle, generous, and not a heavy drinker or gambler, that was all frosting on the cake. Loving attention and emotional involvement in the family were not part of a woman's implicit bargain with the good provider.

By the time de Tocqueville published his observations in 1840, the general outlines of the good-provider role had taken shape. It called for a hard-working man who spent most of his time at his work. In the traditional conception of the role, a man's chief responsibility is his job, so that "by definition any family behaviors must be subordinate to it in terms of significance and [the job] has priority in the event of a clash" (Scanzoni, 1975, p. 38). This was the classic form of the good-provider role, which remained a powerful component of our societal structure until well into the present century.

COSTS AND REWARDS OF THE GOOD-PROVIDER ROLE FOR MEN

There were both costs and rewards for those men attached to the good-provider role. The most serious cost was perhaps the identification of maleness not only with the work site but especially with success in the role. "The American male looks to his breadwinning role to confirm his manliness" (Brenton, 1966, p. 194). To be a man one had to be not only a provider but a *good* provider. Success in the good-provider role came in time to define masculinity itself. The good provider had to achieve to win, to succeed, to dominate. He was a bread*winner*. He had to show "strength, cunning, inventiveness, endurance—a whole range of traits henceforth defined as exclusively 'masculine'" (Demos, 1974,

p. 436). Men were judged as men by the level of living they provided. They were judged by the myth "that endows a money-making man with sexiness and virility, and is based on man's dominance, strength, and ability to provide for and care for 'his' woman" (Gould, 1974, p. 97). The good provider became a player in the male competitive macho game. What one man provided for his family in the way of luxury and display had to be equaled or topped by what another could provide. Families became display cases for the success of the good provider. . . .

. . . If a married woman had to enter the labor force at all, that was bad enough. If she made a good salary, however, she was "co-opting the man's passport to masculinity" (Gould, 1974, p. 98) and he was effectively castrated. A wife's earning capacity diminished a man's position as head of the household (Gould, 1974, p. 99). . . .

But just as there was punishment for failure in the good-provider role, so also were there rewards for successful performance. A man "derived strength from his role as provider" (Komarovsky, 1940, p. 205). He achieved a good deal of satisfaction from his ability to support his family. It won kudos. Being a good provider led to status in both the family and the community. Within the family it gave him the power of the purse and the right to decide about expenditures, standards of living, and what constituted good providing. "Every purchase of the family—the radio, his wife's new hat, the children's skates, the meals set before him—all were symbols of their dependence upon him" (Komarovsky, 1940, Mpp. 74–75). . . .

A man who was successful in the good-provider role might be freed from other obligations to the family. But the flip side of this dispensation was that he could not make up for poor performances by excellence in other family roles. Since everything depended on his success as provider, everything was at stake. The good provider played an all-or-nothing game.

DIFFERENT WAYS OF PERFORMING
THE GOOD-PROVIDER ROLE

Some men resented the burdens the role forced them to bear. A man could easily vent such resentment toward his family by keeping complete control over all expenditures, dispensing the money for household maintenance, and complaining about bills as though it were his wife's fault that shoes cost so much. He could, in effect, punish his family for his having to perform the role. Since the money he earned belonged to him—was "his"—he could do with it what he pleased. Through extreme parsimony he could dole out his money in a mean, humiliating way, forcing his wife to come begging for pennies. By his reluctance and resentment he could make his family pay emotionally for the provisioning he supplied.

At the other extreme were the highly competitive men who were so involved in outdoing the Joneses that the fur coat became more important than the affectionate hug. They "bought off" their families. They sometimes succeeded so well in their extravagance that they sacrificed the family they were presumably providing for to the achievements that made it possible (Keniston, 1965). . . .

Sometimes the resentment of the good provider takes the form of simply wanting more appreciation for the life-style he provides. All he does for his family seems to be taken for granted. Thus, for example, Goldberg (1976), a psychiatrist, recounts the case of a successful businessman:

> He's feeling a deepening sense of bitterness and frustration about his wife and family. He doesn't feel appreciated. It angers him the way they seem to take the things his earnings purchase for granted. They've come to expect it as their due. . . . He'd like to tell them to get someone else to support them but he holds himself back. (p. 124)

The disaffection of the good provider is directed to both sides of his role. With respect to work, Lefkowitz (1979) has described men among whom the good-provider role is neither being completely rejected nor repudiated, but diluted. These men began their working lives in the conventional style, hopeful and ambitious. They found a job, married, raised a family, and "achieved a measure of economic security and earned the respect of . . . colleagues and neighbors" (Lefkowitz, 1979, p. 31). In brief, they successfully performed the good-provider role. But unlike their historical predecessors, they in time became disillusioned with their jobs—not jobs on assembly lines, not jobs usually characterized as alienating, but fairly prestigious jobs such as aeronautics engineer and government economist. They daydreamed about other interests. "The common theme which surfaced again and again in their histories, was the need to find a new social connection—to reassert control over their lives, to gain some sense of freedom" (Lefkowitz, 1979, p. 31). . . . Most of them did not want to desert their families. Indeed, most of them "wanted to rejoin the intimate circle they felt they had neglected in their years of work" (p. 31).

Though some of the men Lefkowitz studied sought closer ties with their families, in the case of those studied by Sarason (1977), a psychologist, career changes involved lower income and had a negative impact on families. Sarason's subjects were also men in high-level professions, the very men least likely to find marriage and parenthood burdensome and restrictive. Still, since career change often involved a reduction in pay, some wives were unwilling to accept it, with the result that the marriage deteriorated (p. 178). Sometimes it looked like a no-win game. The husband's earlier career brought him feelings of emptiness and alienation, but it also brought financial rewards for the family. Greater work satisfaction for him in lower paying work meant reduced satisfaction with life-style. . . .

WOMEN AND THE PROVIDER ROLE

The present discussion began with the woman's part in the provider role. We saw how as more and more of the provisioning of the family came to be by way of monetary exchange, the woman's part shrank. A woman could still provide services, but could furnish little in the way of food, clothing, and shelter. But now that she is entering the labor force in large numbers, she can once more resume her ancient role, this time, like her male counterpart the provider, by way of a monetary contribution. More and more women are doing just this.

The assault of the good-provider role in the Depression was traumatic. But a modified version began to appear in the 1970s as a single income became inadequate for more and more families. Husbands have remained the major providers, but in an increasing number of cases the wife has begun to share this role. Thus, the proportion of married women aged 15 to 54 (living with their husbands) in the labor force more than doubled between 1950 and 1978, from 25.2 percent to 55.4 percent. The proportion for 1990 is estimated to reach 66.7 percent (Smith, 1979, p. 14). Fewer women are now full-time housewives. . . .

Smith (1979) calls the great trek of married women into the labor force a subtle evolution—revolutionary not in the sense of one class overthrowing a status quo and substituting its own regime, but revolutionary in its impact on both the family and the work roles of men and women. It diluted the prerogatives of the good-provider role. It increased the demands made on the good provider, especially in the form of more emotional investment in the family, more sharing of household responsibilities. The role became even more burdensome. . . .

For some men the relief from the strain of sole responsibility for the provider role has been welcome. But for others the feeling of degradation resembles the feeling reported [fifty] years earlier in the Great Depression. It is not that they are no longer providing for the family but that the role-sharing wife now feels justified in making demands on them. The good-provider role with all its prerogatives and perquisites has undergone profound changes. It will never be the same again. Its death knell was sounded when, as noted above, the 1980 census no longer automatically assumed that the male member of the household was its head.

THE CURRENT SCENE

Among the new demands being made on the good-provider role, two deserve special consideration, namely, (1) more intimacy, expressivity, and nurturance—specifications never included in it as it originally took shape—and (2) more sharing of household responsibility and child care.

As the pampered wife in an affluent household came often to be an economic parasite, so also the good provider was often, in a way, a kind of emotional parasite. Implicit in the definition of the role was that he provided goods and material things. Tender loving care was not one of the requirements. Emotional ministrations from the family were his right; providing them was not a corresponding obligation. Therefore, as de Tocqueville had already noted by 1840, women suffered a kind of emotional deprivation labeled by Robert Weiss "relational deficit" (cited in Bernard, 1976). Only recently has this male rejection of emotional expression come to be challenged. Today, even blue-collar women are imposing "a host of new role expectations upon their husbands or lovers. . . . A new role set asks the blue-collar male to strive for . . . deep-coursing intimacy" (Shostak, 1973, p. 75). It was not only vis-à-vis his family that the good provider was lacking in expressivity. This lack was built into the whole male role script. Today not only women but also men are beginning to protest the repudiation of expressivity prescribed in male roles. . . .

From the standpoint of high-level pure-science research there may be something bizarre, if not even slightly absurd, in the growing corpus of serious research on how much or how little husbands of employed wives contribute to household chores and child care. Yet it is serious enough that all over the industrialized world such research is going on. Time studies in a dozen countries—communist as well as capitalist— trace the slow and bungling process by which marriage accommodates to changing conditions and by which women struggle to mold the changing conditions in their behalf. For everywhere the same picture shows up in research: an image of women sharing the provider role and at the same time retaining responsibility for the household. Until recently such a topic would have been judged unworthy of serious attention. It was a subject that might be worth a good laugh, for instance, as when an all-thumbs man in a cartoon burns the potatoes or finds himself bumbling awkwardly over a diaper, demonstrating his—proud— male ineptness at such female work. But it is no longer funny.

The "politics of housework" (Mainardi, 1970) proves to be more profound than originally believed. It has to do not only with tasks but also with gender—and perhaps more with the site of the tasks than with their intrinsic nature. A man can cook magnificently if he does it on a hunting or fishing trip, he can wield a skillful needle if he does it mending a tent or a fishing net; he can even feed and clean a toddler on a camping trip. Few of the skills of the homemaker are beyond his reach so long as they are practiced in a suitably male environment. It is not only women's work in and of itself that is degrading but any work on female turf. It may be true, as Brenton (1966) says, that "the secure man can wash a dish, diaper a baby, and throw the dirty clothes into the washing machine—or do anything else women used to do exclusively— without thinking twice about it" (p. 211), but not all men are that secure. To a great many men such chores are demasculinizing. The apron is shameful to a man in the kitchen; it is all right at the carpenter's bench. . . .

A considerable amount of thought has been devoted to studying the effects of the large influx of women into the work force. An equally interesting question is what the effect will be if a large number of men actually do increase their participation in the family and the household. Will men find the apron shameful? What if we were to ask fathers to alternate with mothers in being in the home when youngsters come home from school? Would fighting adolescent drug abuse be more successful if fathers and mothers were equally engaged in it? If the school could confer with fathers as often as with mothers? If the father accompanied children when they went shopping for clothes? If fathers spent as much time with children as do mothers? . . .

REFERENCES

BABCOCK, B., FREEDMAN, A. E., NORTON, E. H., & ROSS, S. C. *Sex discrimination and the law: Causes and remedies.* Boston: Little, Brown, 1975.

BERNARD, J. Homosociality and female depression. *Journal of Social Issues,* 1976, *32,* 207–224.

BOULDING, E. Familial constraints on women's work roles. *SIGNS: Journal of Women in Culture and Society,* 1976, *1,* 95–118.

BRENTON, M. *The American male.* New York: Coward-McCann, 1966.

DEMOS, J. The American family in past time. *American Scholar,* 1974, *43,* 422–446.

GOLDBERG, H. *The hazards of being male.* New York: New American Library, 1976.

GOULD, R. E. Measuring masculinity by the size of a paycheck. In J. E. Pleck & J. Sawyer (Eds.), *Men and masculinity.* Englewood Cliffs, N.J.: Prentice-Hall, 1974, (Also published in *Ms.,* June 1973, pp. 18ff.)

KENISTON, K. *The uncommitted: Alienated youth in American society.* New York: Harcourt, Brace & World, 1965.

KOMAROVSKY, M. *The unemployed man and his family.* New York: Dryden Press, 1940.

LEFKOWITZ, B. Life without work. *Newsweek,* May 14, 1979, p. 31.

MAINARDI, P. The politics of housework. In R. Morgan (Ed.), *Sisterhood is powerful.* New York: Vintage Books, 1970.

SARASON, S. B. *Work, aging, and social change.* New York: Free Press, 1977.

SCANZONI, J. H. *Sex roles, life styles, and childbearing: Changing patterns in marriage and the family.* New York: Free Press, 1975.

SHOSTAK, A. *Working class Americans at home: Changing expectations of manhood.* Unpublished manuscript, 1973.

SMITH, R. E. (Ed.), *The subtle revolution.* Washington, D.C.: Urban Institute, 1979.

TOCQUEVILLE, A. DE. *Democracy in America.* New York: J. & H. G. Langley, 1840.

29
▼▼▼▼

Hard Choices
▼▼▼▼

Kathleen Gerson

ABSTRACT: The author contrasts the perspectives and experiences of two groups of women who have made difficult choices in the face of structural ambiguities. The first, the domestic, have chosen children ahead of a career; the second, the nondomestic, have chosen a career ahead of children. The domestic and nondomestic disparage each other's choice, which has led to deep political divisions between them.

. . . Women who chose to place family and children before other life commitments confronted the dilemmas of how to overcome the isolation that homemaking can impose and how to defend their choices against the growing social devaluation of domestic pursuits. In contrast, women who established committed ties to the workplace faced dilemmas about whether and how to integrate children into their lives. Although each group faced a different set of obstacles and central concerns, both confronted dilemmas that lacked established, institutionalized solutions. Both faced different forms of *structural ambiguity* in which they were forced to choose between mutually exclusive but equally problematic alternatives. As Oakley (1974:81) puts it, domestic and nondomestic women alike confronted

a contradiction between alternatives [that] are mutually exclusive, because
the achievement of both calls for more time, energy, and commitment than
one person can reasonably supply, and because . . . "the full realization
of one role threatens defeat in the other." . . .

Structural ambiguity, as used here, thus refers to the uncertainties
within and contradictions between the various work and family structures women confront, and not to the functions these structures might
serve. These contradictions and uncertainties promote not only psychological ambivalence within individuals and social conflict between opposing social groups, but also creative individual and social responses.
. . . [This chapter contrasts the experiences and attitudes in this regard
of women in domestic and nondomestic orientations.]

THE PERSISTENCE OF DOMESTIC PATTERNS

. . . Many respondents decided their best chance for a secure, satisfying life remained centered in the home and depended on a traditional,
"patriarchal" family structure. These women retained a vested interest
in maintaining arrangements that support and justify female domesticity. The attractions of a traditional sexual division of labor when compared to the experience of paid work led them not only to reproduce
patterns in their own lives but also to fear and oppose emerging alternatives to these patterns. . . .

. . . Although work remained an option for domestically oriented
women, careers—in the sense of full-time, continuous, committed labor-
force attachment with advancement as a goal—did not. Thus, 53 percent
of this group were committed to full-time homemaking, and the remaining 47 percent had erratic work histories and planned to work outside
the home either part-time or intermittently for the foreseeable future.
The part-time, intermittent, and generally limited nature of their labor
force participation meant, however, that their ties to the workplace did
not compete with their family responsibilities or their male partners'
positions as primary breadwinners. . . .

. . . Work commitments were carefully subordinated to family commitments. By defining work as a secondary commitment—and distinguishing it from career as a primary one—this mother and part-time
worker avoided a perceived conflict between work and family:

A: I wouldn't have gone into a career, not with [my children] little. That's
what I liked about the work. The hours were flexible. I didn't feel guilty
quitting whenever I wanted to. A career, to me anyway, means full-time work
and maybe work at home even. I don't want work to have to come home. I
really didn't have to get all that involved; I felt like a career *would* get over-
involving. . . .

The simple fact of working thus does not by itself entail significant social change. Women who maintain tentative, vague work commitments represent neither a significant departure from past patterns nor a significant force for change in the future. Instead, they remain committed to a traditional family structure and dependent on a male breadwinner who leaves them responsible for child rearing and housekeeping. . . .

Whether or not a domestically oriented woman worked, a traditional sexual division of labor was reinforced in the home. The female partner not only participated in but actively supported these arrangements because she had little to gain by upsetting the marital balance of exchanges. This homeworker explained:

Q: On the whole, do you prefer raising your children to working outside the home?

A: Oh, yes. I never plan to go back. I'm too spoiled now. I'm my own boss. I have independence; I have control; I have freedom, as much freedom as anyone is going to have in our society. No job can offer me those things.

No one in the traditionally oriented group expressed either the desire or the expectation that her spouse should or would participate equally in child care. More specifically, none of these women wished to trade her responsibilities for those of the male breadwinner. After their generally sour work experiences, all agreed with this part-time nurse that, whatever it costs, domesticity compared favorably with the task of economically supporting a family:

Q: How would you feel about working while your husband stayed home to care for the children?

A: There might be a little bit of jealousy in there—his being able to be home and my having to go off to work. . . .

This preference for a traditional sexual division of labor did not mean that homemaking held no frustrations or drawbacks. Traditional women accepted the costs of domesticity as the price they had to pay for an otherwise preferred alternative. . . .
. . . Traditional women engaged in a process of "discounting," or minimizing the importance of, the costs associated with the domestic option. Perceived costs such as social isolation and devaluation diminished in the eyes of this ex-secretary as she compared them with the perceived costs of returning to work:

Q: Is there anything you dislike about staying home?

A: Yes. There are times when it gets lonely, because most women work. There are times when it's boring, but that's true of any job. Sometimes I think, "I have to clean the house again because it's Monday," and that upsets me. But I think, if I were working, I'd be doing such and such number report every Monday; so it really doesn't matter what you do. And . . . I suppose there are times when I have some trouble with *my* identity; *that* has to do with being a mother. Because of society, sometimes the recognition or lack of it bothers me. . . .

Finally, traditional women were also motivated to reproduce the ideology that supports traditional family patterns. . . . This group thus continued to espouse two principles that have historically served to reinforce the domestic choice—that a child (and therefore its mother as well) suffers from an absentee mother and that, as a consequence, a woman can have children or a career, but not both. . . . Even when help with child rearing was readily available, these women were reluctant to trade mothering for committed work. This clerk, who was trying to get pregnant, spoke for the group when she expressed her determination to be her child's primary caretaker:

Q: What about getting regular babysitting help:

A: It's important to us that we raise our children the way *we* want to, not as our neighbors or someone else could do it. Both my sisters-in-law have said, if the situation were to arise and if I wanted to continue working, they would be more than happy to take care of the baby. It would be fine, maybe a couple of hours a day, something like that. But for me to go back full-time knowing that someone else was raising my child, I'm not too keen on the idea, and I can't really say why.

. . . Domestically oriented respondents perceived that new alternatives threatened their interests, and many expressed their resentment toward the growing social pressure to eschew domesticity. An ex-nurse lamented:

A: I have been feeling lately a lot of pressure . . . there's a lot of pressure on women now that you should feel like you want to work. Sometimes it's hard to know what you feel, because I really don't feel like I want to [work] but I think I *should* feel like I want to.

The development of nondomestic pathways posed a dilemma for domestically oriented respondents. Threatened with the erosion of the structural and ideological supports for domesticity, they struggled to justify choices they could have taken for granted only a short time ago. Most responded to this challenged by holding tightly to a set of beliefs that has historically served the cause of female domesticity while some simultaneously made limited, tentative movements toward part-time work.

In contrast, nondomestic respondents felt threatened by traditional beliefs and domestic behavioral patterns. Their coping strategies were reactions not only to structural dilemmas, but also to traditional patterns that they opposed. . . .

NONDOMESTIC RESPONSES

Those who rejected domesticity, whether by preference or necessity, faced a "motherhood dilemma." This dilemma hinged on a simple yet intractable aspect of the alternatives facing nondomestic women. On the one hand, neither their social environment nor the prevailing ideology provided institutionalized supports for combining committed work with child rearing. On the other, most had difficulty embracing the historically unpopular option of forgoing children altogether. Given a choice between two unattractive alternatives, they struggled with the questions of whether and how to integrate children into lives already defined by established commitments to work.

The considerable costs that children threatened to exact often overshadowed the potential rewards of parenthood for nondomestic women. Caught between the perceived costs of parenthood and the perceived costs of childlessness, these respondents reacted with ambivalence. At thirty, this childless executive . . . felt paralyzed by the negative consequences of *both* options:

A: I'm hung up on the negative things, on the responsibility and the problems and the loss of freedom and everything else. But I keep hoping that, when the time comes for me to have a family, I'll just automatically get ready. I think it would be nice if I were looking forward to it. I really hope that I will be a happy mother someday. I would like to have it work out that way because it's so much of a hassle to make a decision *not* to have a family . . . in terms of pressure and psychological feelings of having failed or not fulfilled myself that I anticipate I would feel later in life.

The structural contradictions between career and motherhood produced ambivalence toward childbearing. Most upwardly mobile women could not decide whether children would be more a benefit or a detriment. This ambivalence was often so deep that some, such as this twenty-nine-year-old, upwardly mobile, childless office manager, openly expressed contradictory stances toward the motherhood dilemma:

Q: How do you think you'd feel if you had children right now?

A: Extremely unhappy. It's taken everything I have to get to where I am now—to help myself. I couldn't imagine having someone depend on me. If [a child] said, "I need you," it would make me go bananas.

Q: Then what are the main reasons you want a child?

A: This sort of contradicts what I said before, but having someone who needs you. I eventually want someone who needs me and whom I can help, but not right now. But if I could have one at fifty, I'd probably wait till I'm fifty. I hope I'll be ready for it when it's time.

Ambivalence toward motherhood was expressed in contradictory and conflicted behavior as well. Because nondomestic women perceived children as both rewarding *and* costly, approach *and* avoidance marked their decision-making processes. Their fertility behavior in particular was hesitant and uncertain, leading to the selection of different options at different times. Ambivalence led to an abortion in one instance, but to pregnancy in another. Although she had aborted two previous pregnancies, this thirty-seven-year-old executive still planned to have a child:

Q: You said you had two therapeutic abortions. What was going on at the time?

A: It was *very* emotional. I was absolutely freaked out. Consciously, I was thinking how our life would have to change. We'd never be able to have a house like this, never be able to travel together again. Just the impact of having a small child around, the nuisance, and the bother—that's what I consciously thought. I was so upset. I'm sure there was a lot more going on in my head. . . .

With or without the ambivalence, these women had to decide about childbearing, if only by default. With their prime childbearing years slipping by, decision-making deadlines were nearing. . . .

For those not oriented toward domesticity, the process of deciding for or against motherhood involved assessing the potential costs of having a child and of not having a child and weighing these alternative costs against each other. . . . Those who concluded that parenthood had substantially higher costs than childlessness decided to reject motherhood. In contrast, those who perceived the denial of parenthood as more costly than parenthood itself did not enthusiastically embrace motherhood, but they were less inclined to reject childbearing altogether. . . .

Although a perspective that views children as "costs" may seem one-sided, such an analysis presumes that there are intrinsic "benefits" to parenting as well. If children were not in some sense desirable and desired, the question of whether or not to have them would not be problematic. The difficulty arises precisely because children appeared both rewarding *and* costly to nontraditional women. Because domestically oriented women did not attach the same costs to parenthood, they were able to choose more easily in accordance with motherhood's perceived rewards. . . .

CHOOSING TO STAY CHILDLESS

Those who decided against motherhood concluded over time that children would entail greater costs than rewards. [I shall discuss three of those costs, those centering on careers, the potential children, and identity.]. . . .

Perceived Consequences for Career. Childless respondents believed, above all, that children would threaten their chances for success at work. . . . When the struggle to advance at work had been hard fought, as it usually was, motherhood threatened to undo all earlier efforts in one critical step. Childbearing seemed at odds with the logic of previous adult development. Bearing a child became too dangerous for this thirty-two-year-old divorced administrator:

Q: Why do you think you won't have children?

A: It's getting into whether I'm willing to sacrifice where I've gotten in my career, which I've done really well for my age and training. That would be quite a sacrifice, I think. I'm not sure I'm willing to do that at this stage. . . . I feel real badly as I hear myself say that. But if I had a kid, I don't know what I'd do. Somewhere along the line, I would make a decision that family or job mattered more. And since I wouldn't want to be a goofy mother, I guess I would decide okay, I decided to have the child and that's *my* responsibility to do the best I can. If it means only going to level "A" instead of level "C," then that's where I am. . . .

Perceived Consequences for Children. The possibility of raising a damaged child loomed as a second, and equally discouraging, fear to work-committed women. They reasoned that, just as children would undermine success at work, so work would undermine success in child rearing. . . . Respondents feared not simply that the child would suffer, but also that this result would rebound on the mother in terrible ways. This childless physician concluded that the conflict between her needs as a worker and her child's needs would negatively affect both:

A: As a mother, I tend to worry about becoming a harsh disciplinarian, impatient, frazzled, uninterested, uninteresting. . . . And I think women who do both don't end up doing either one well or doing only one well.

Q: And you'd rather not have a child than do a bad job of it?

A: Right. There's no undoing it. . . . At least in my career, I have a lot more confidence, a lot more experience. And I'd feel awful if I had three kids who all turned out to be rotten. To say, "Well, I *never* should have had children" is the most defeating thing that can ever happen to a parent. . . .

These fears did not result from a casual attitude toward child rearing. To the contrary, these women adhered to high standards in all they did, including their approach to mothering. Aspiring workers . . . expressed a belief that children would require the same attention, care, and energy that they gave to their jobs. These high standards were in fact their undoing, for they could find no way to do both tasks well. These women decided to remain childless rather than alter their standards at home or at work. . . .

Perceived Consequences for Identity and Personal Well-Being. Women [who were] committed to childlessness also saw children as a threat to their identity. Some even concluded that rearing a child in the context of their work commitments would undermine their sanity and their physical health. Because committed work was not a negotiable choice, childlessness seemed the only way to avoid personal breakdown. This childless secretary explained:

Q: Is work a factor in your decision not to have a child, the fact that you don't think you could do both at the same time?

A: I *could* do both at the same time, but I wouldn't want to. It would drive me nuts to come home to a baby to take care of. When I come home, I want to sit down; I want it to be quiet. So I guess work is a factor, but it sounds awful.

Those with declining [occupational] aspirations focused on the liberating, nurturing, and fulfilling aspects of mothering, but . . . upwardly mobile women stressed instead its potentially negative consequences.

Coping with Childlessness

Nondomestic respondents who opted for childlessness concluded that, despite its potential pleasures, childbearing threatened to be too costly. . . . Yet these women did not find it easy to opt for childlessness. The social and psychological importance placed on childbearing remains enormous. Opting for such an unpopular choice meant weathering social disapproval and personal doubt. These women did so by developing coping strategies that provided social and emotional insulation from the worst consequences of childlessness.

. . . Childless women mustered network support for their choice.

One single professional in her mid-thirties described her efforts to sustain her decision for childlessness amid the pressures to procreate:

> A: Consciously or unconsciously, I surround myself with single women. I have very few married female friends, and I have almost no female friends with children. So my coterie of women confidantes are either childless or single, and we're a big support group. To some degree, we're all a bit frustrated about finding appropriate partners.

Childless women thus had each other. In an earlier historical period, they would have faced far greater difficulty finding peers to reinforce their personal rejection of motherhood. . . . Today, however, growing numbers of similarly situated women provide the means for voluntarily childless women to insulate themselves from the wider social expectation that any woman past thirty should have a child. Indeed, traditional women face increasing difficulty finding social support for having and caring for children. . . .

To accept childlessness, most respondents grieved for what would never be and let go of old hopes and expectations. They also struggled to defend and justify their choice against others' expectations and their own self-doubts. An upward mobile secretary committed to childlessness explained:

> A: When you get into your late twenties, people start questioning what you're doing and what your plans are, why you're not getting married. I give people a stock answer that I'm still waiting for somebody to wash dishes. It is an outright lie, but it shuts people up. That's what a man says, somebody to take care of him. I'm looking for somebody to take care of me. It took me a long time to get to that point.

Similarly, they rejected the argument that their identities, as women or human beings, would be jeopardized by childlessness or that they were denying themselves the possibility of meaningful human relationships. They emphasized, instead, their pride in their own independence.

> Q: Is there anything about never having children that bothers or worries you?
>
> A: No. I don't think I'm less of a woman, or a human being, or have not done my part for society or anything. No. I don't have any bad feelings about not having children, no fears about my old age. And I think that is just a rotten reason to have children, and put that on them. I will take care of myself until I die. I'll die with a checkbook in my hand!

With few supports to ease the integration of work and parenthood, these respondents concluded that the demands and rewards of work, personal accomplishment, and autonomy superseded whatever relational pleasures child rearing might bring. . . .

Sharply contrasting positions thus form the lines along which political constituencies have already emerged. Nondomestic women, and especially those determined to integrate work and motherhood, challenged old ideas and patterns. Domestically oriented women responded by reaffirming traditional arrangements, as well as the beliefs that legitimate them. These responses deepened the gulf between the two groups. Members of each found themselves denigrating the other's orientations and choices. . . .

. . . Full-time mothers looked with varying degrees of disdain, pity, and angry concern upon those who eschewed motherhood or remained at the workplace while their children were young. This homemaker and mother of two, for example, resented working mothers who, in her eyes, put their own needs before their children's needs:

Q: How do you respond to a woman with a young baby who goes to work every day?

A: I have a neighbor like that. She works just because she wants to. I get sort of angry. What I don't like is, you can't have everything! I think what I get angriest at is some of the justifications I hear: "Well, I spend quality time with my child." I reject that. I think I resent the unfairness to the child. . . .

Other domestically oriented women pictured the working mother not as selfish but as an unenviable victim:

Q: How do you feel about women with young children working?

A: Most of the time all I hear from them is griping, and they're tired, and they're frantic to get everything done. It's a shame. . . .

Not surprisingly, nondomestic women, both with and without children, responded with similar aversion to their more domestic peers, whom they viewed with a mixture of superiority and horror:

Q: What is your response when you see other women about your age staying home to care for young children?

A: I feel a little superior in a way. It's terrible, but I have the stereotype—here's this lady jiggling the handles of toilets that aren't flushing.

Nondomestic women projected the costs they attached to domesticity onto those who had chosen the path they rejected:

A: To me, they tend to be kind of mentally underdeveloped and not too interesting. Let's face it, it's kind of boring. I guess I don't consider having children as doing something. . . .

Thus, in order to justify their own embattled positions, domestic and nondomestic women denigrated each other's choices. This process has created deep ideological schisms between the two groups that point to two important aspects of women's current social position.

First, whether domestic or nondomestic, all women face an ambiguous set of alternatives in which to some extent they are "damned if they do and damned if they don't." Structural ambiguity ensures that there are few, if any, unambiguously legitimate paths for women. Whatever a woman's choice, she faces social disapproval and significant obstacles to achieving her goals.

Second, ideological conflicts among women are based on deeply rooted structural divisions. No matter how much each group discounts the costs of its own choices and inflates the costs of other choices, both domestic and nondomestic women must make their choices in response to a specific and contrasting set of alternatives and constraints. Ideological schisms will persist as long as the structural conditions that create them persist.

The deepening political conflicts among women reflect and spring from the social and psychological divisions in women's experiences. As long as domestic and nondomestic women face different dilemmas and contradictions, but a shared challenge to the legitimacy of their various choices, each group also retains an interest in opposing the other in order to protect its own social position. Because neither group is likely to disappear or concede defeat, the political ramifications of this conflict will shape the nature of American political life until the legitimacy and viability of both groups are guaranteed.

REFERENCE

OAKLEY, ANNE. 1974. *Woman's Work: The Housewife, Past and Present.* New York: Random House.

30

▼▼▼▼

The Guilt That Drives Working
Mothers Crazy

▼▼▼▼▼

Barbara Berg

ABSTRACT: Many women feel guilty about leaving their children to go to work, even though their children may be well-adjusted. This guilt encourages self-defeating behaviors, produces a "double bind" by creating stress and then preventing activities that might reduce that stress, and is harmful to the marital relationship. Suggestions are provided for decreasing the social bases of this guilt.

My attaché case was always the catalyst. For almost a year, when my children were both toddlers, they would sit or play quietly as I washed up, ate breakfast, and put on my coat. But as soon as I reached for my briefcase, they would burst into inconsolable tears. "Please don't go. Please don't leave us," they could chorus pitifully, sometimes wrapping their little bodies around my legs in an effort to keep me at home.

It made no difference if I explained to them in advance, over breakfast, that Mommy would be leaving for work when I finished my coffee, or if I attempted to sneak out of the door wordlessly, or even if I made four or five trips back from the elevator (which I did all too frequently) to reassure that I loved them and would be home later. Their reaction was always the same. And so was my response: gut-wrenching guilt—excruciatingly intense when the children were sick or having other problems, a bit lighter when things were going smoothly, but always lurking in the recesses of my mind, its shadowy presence darkening my day.

In my early years of struggling to combine my career and my mothering, I assumed that I was the only one who felt this kind of anguish. Certainly my husband, Arnie, didn't feel any guilt. He was dumbfounded by the suggestion that he could. For him, being both a father and a wage earner are synonymous with being a man. When he had to work late or travel, he missed the children, but guilt entered into neither his vocabulary nor his emotions. And his inability to understand why it pervaded mine was the cause of much friction between us.

Time and again, he would point out all the "certifiable" signs of my good mothering—"the children seem happy," "they love nursery school," "they have lots of friends." Time and again, I tried to explain my guilt to him, but in truth I couldn't comprehend it either, and, ironically, the way guilt ruled my life made me at least as frustrated and resentful as it made him. It prevented me from doing things that I wanted to do, like going out to dinner with a friend, and it compelled me to do things I *didn't* want to do, like making intricate Halloween costumes on one day's notice. If one of the children was having a problem, I was sure it was because I was working too much; if my writing faltered, it had to be because I was spending too much time with the children. An improvement in one area of my life filled me with worry that I was neglecting another. Like my marriage. Why did the evening conversation between Arnie and me resemble nothing more than two radio dispatchers? "You check the lamb chops," "I'll change the baby," we would shout from opposite ends of the apartment. What happened to *our* quality time? I began to truly need to know if I was the only woman who felt so torn and pulled, who underneath her staunch, unshakable commitment to having children and a career worried that both were being shortchanged.

A GENERATION OF GUILTY MOTHERS

After two years of interviewing nearly 1,000 women of varying backgrounds across the nation, I learned that guilt was their greatest emotional problem. My findings both saddened and surprised me. It saddened me to realize that the present generation of working mothers,*

---

*"Working mother" is not really a satisfactory description of women who work outside the home, since mothers who are at home work also, although in different ways. I use the term here because it has become the generally accepted way of referring to mothers who hold paying jobs.

the beneficiaries of so much hope and striving, were haunted by such conflict. "The guilt feels deep and almost physical," was how one mother put it, while another labeled it "the most painful experience of my life."

Self-reproach was high and wide: for going back to work, for taking a leave of absence, for leaving the office early to attend a school play, for working late and missing dinner, for being in too pressured a job, for not earning enough, for being short-tempered with the children, for not disciplining more. Whether a woman wanted to work outside the home or was forced to work, whether she loved her job or hated it, whether she was dissatisfied with her children's caregivers or delighted with them, she still felt guilty.

Like me, these women could recognize the gnawing, uneasy feeling guilt brings, but were not *aware* of the real toll it is taking. I had not been *aware*, for example, of the extent to which guilt is responsible for the often self-defeating ways in which we organize our lives. It can affect us at work, making some women stay in low-level jobs too long and others feel that they must be workaholics to justify their working at all. Joyce, for example, a copy chief at a large publishing house for many years, yearned for a promotion. But when she was finally offered a position as head of the department, she didn't accept it, much to everyone's astonishment. "I couldn't bear to leave my daughter," she concluded, "despite the fact that she would be in school all day and I would only get home about one and a half hours later than she."

We end up feeling as though no place is the right place to be. When we are at work, we worry that we should be with our children. When we are with our children, our minds wander to those unfinished reports on our desks. Raima Larter, Ph.D., an assistant professor of chemistry at Purdue University, expressed it this way: "I feel guilty about (a) not spending enough time with my children, (b) not spending enough time at work, but usually (c) guilty about both."

Clearly nothing has changed in the decade since renowned sociologist Jessie Bernard wrote in *The Future of Motherhood* that a "prime requisite for success of the professional mother . . . [was] mastering her feelings of guilt with regard to her children."

MARTYRDOM

Guilt can also hurt our relationships with our husbands or live-in partners. Many of us feel that we must "atone" for our working by doing the bulk of child care and housekeeping. Such martyrdom eventually backfires and we become angry at our mates for not helping more. In fact, in my study, the unequal division of household chores emerged as a major cause of arguing between couples, sometimes even leading to a divorce.

Some women feel so guilty that when their husbands do help out, they find themselves undermining their spouses' efforts. "Why did you let her go outside in such a light sweater?" "How do you allow them to make such a mess in the kitchen?" are our all-too-familiar responses to assistance. I found myself engaging in this kind of criticism when I was on a recent out-of-town book tour—a time when my guilt level soars. Each morning I would call home to say hello to the children. On one occasion, my husband told me that they were running late. "No time to make breakfast," he said. He'd pick up some doughnuts for them on the way to school.

"Doughnuts for breakfast?" I screamed into the telephone. "They can't start the day like that!"

Later, when I had time to reflect on my exaggerated response (I should note that in my eight years of mothering there have been times when I, too, have given my children doughnuts for breakfast), I realized that my guilt had made me feel competitive with my husband over who was the better parent—a phenomenon that also can occur between women and their housekeepers or baby-sitters.

"WHAT SEX LIFE?"

Guilt can also lead to competitive arguing over such things as money and work, and—it should come as no surprise—all this can erode emotional and sexual intimacy. With pathos, wit, and piercing honesty, an overwhelming majority of the women interviewed confided a loss of sexual spontaneity and closeness in their relationships. "What romance? What sex life?" asked one, while another quipped, "At this rate we will never have to use birth control again." And a third admitted, "I wish it weren't so, but my love life is a fond memory relegated to my fantasies."

Dr. Merle S. Kroop, associate director of the Human Sexuality Teaching Program at the New York Hospital–Cornell Medical Center, has observed that the lack of desire is common in working mothers. We may attribute diminishing sexual fervor to fatigue, but as Sharon Nathan, Ph.D., also with the Human Sexuality Teaching Program, noted, many of us who are too tired to have sex are not too tired to stay up until midnight watching television. So where is the exhaustion coming from?

Nathan and others suggested that it comes from emotional sources even more than physical ones. Anger can certainly generate feelings of fatigue, says Nathan, who calls anger the flip side of guilt. Our guilt is often expressed in anger toward our partner and against ourselves.

Dr. Alvin Blaustein, who teaches at the Mount Sinai Hospital Human Sexuality Program in New York City, added: "If women are feeling inadequate in the job they are doing as mothers, if they are feeling that they are not living up to their ideals from childhood, or if their husbands or mothers are making them feel guilty, they may feel that they don't deserve much sexual satisfaction."

The feeling of nonentitlement also makes working mothers reluctant to take any time for themselves. When I asked various groups of women, all of whom are very attentive to the details of their families and their jobs, why their own needs had become the "expendable luxury" of their hectic lives, they answered as in one voice: "Guilt." We hardly ever do things just for our own enjoyment or for sheer relaxation, either. And as for attending to our own care, we do it later or not at all. Said one woman, "If I could take an hour for myself, I'd be able to shave both my legs on the same day."

SHORTCHANGING YOURSELF

Haircuts and buying new clothes get put off until they are beyond the necessity stage, and although we may joke about our out-of-style winter jacket or our unruly locks, the long-term effects of our self-neglect are no laughing matter.

When I asked women about their physical and emotional health, working mothers cataloged a list of ailments that rivaled those in *The Merck Manual*, that vast compendium of human ills. Gastrointestinal complaints, back pains, insomnia, and migraine headaches all plague working mothers, though not as severely as women who stay home. Dr. Morton Leibowitz, as associate professor at the New York University School of Medicine and an internist with a large practice, has observed an increase over the past five years of working mothers who come to him for stress-related complaints.

It seems as though we are really in a double bind. First of all, guilt, which is internal and ongoing, is *itself* a powerful stressor. Second, this guilt prevents us from taking the time to go for a run, spend an hour in the bath, visit with a friend, or just do nothing—all of which could reduce our stress.

MIXED MESSAGES TO THE KIDS

The most vivid way that guilt affects us, however, is in relationships with our children. Strong is our sense of apology. We feel we need to "compensate" for our jobs, and do this in different ways.

"I found myself coming back from business trips loaded with presents for my son," said Susan Hayes, a vice president of marketing from Maryland. Other women told me they tried to make up for being at work by attempting to cram a day's worth of activities—building blocks, doing puzzles, playing games, reading books—into the few hours ("quality time") between the time they got home and their children's bedtime.

Quality time originally began as a concept that was reassuring to working mothers—how we spend our time with our youngsters is obviously more important than the amount of time we are around them—but our guilt has turned the idea of quality time into a rigid imperative, which we must achieve on a daily basis. Women told me that they rated the success or failure of their day according to whether or not they had achieved quality time with their youngsters.

Many working mothers feel that they are too indulgent with their children at home. Psychologist Alan Roland, coeditor of *Career and Motherhood,* found that guilt over working "gives a woman an impulse to do as much as possible for the children." Carolyn, an insurance executive, confessed, "I find myself picking up after them more often when I should be teaching them." Ellen, a private-school director, admits: "I tend to be lax in making them participate in household chores."

In my house, getting my children off to sleep became an incredibly stressful event. I found myself always giving in to their repeated requests for more juice, more stories, more hugs. As their demands increased, so I must confess did my resentment. I was tired; I wanted some time to unwind. But the more resentful and irritable I became, the guiltier I felt. And the guiltier I felt, the more difficulty I had turning off the light and leaving the room.

The children, for their part, became overtired and confused. Did I mean it when I said it was bedtime or didn't I? They weren't sure, and frankly neither was I.

Listening to other women explain their confusion, it seemed to me that however much we may believe in women's right to work in general, and our right to work in particular, however much we may know that our family needs our paycheck, somewhere deep within us is a prohibition against combining both roles. I was struck by the frequency with which they used phrases like, "I feel as though I am breaking with tradition" and "It doesn't feel quite natural to work with young children at home."

Our ambivalence is understandable. The strong pull of our personal pasts (so many of us having been raised by mothers who didn't work), combined with the tenacious grip the cult of traditional motherhood has on the national psyche, makes it easy to forget that *American mothers have always worked.*

DID ROSIE THE RIVETER FEEL GUILTY?

With the exception of the 1950s, when most middle-class women did not hold jobs, mothers have been working throughout our history. In fact, when female labor was required to keep the economy going, as it was in the Colonial period and during the major wars, women—the majority of them mothers—were encouraged to work.

During World War II, for example, the number of women in the work force rose from about 12,500,000 to about 18,500,000, and while almost all said they planned to quit when the men came home, by the end of the war more than 80 percent preferred to continue working. What's especially interesting is that they do not appear to have felt guilty. (At least no studies have turned up to indicate they did, and women's magazines of the time didn't cover the question.) There are a few good reasons why. First of all, 90 percent of them had the comfort of knowing that their children were being watched by relatives or friends (or, in some cases, paid baby-sitters) in their own homes. Day care, both federal and local, existed, but it was too scarce to accommodate more than a fraction of the families in need of such services. Second, the women were told that they were "indispensable to national survival." The government, along with the media, lauded the efforts of the "girls left behind." Columnist Max Lerner, referring to the legions of women in factories, wrote, "For all of them, slacks have become the badge of honor."

A 1942 ad for Sanforized clothing came up with the rhyme:

They're running farmers' tractors
They're at a factory bench
The hands that rock the cradle
Wield a nifty monkey wrench.

The situation for today's working mother is quite different. With relatives scattered and friends likely to be as busy as she, the majority have to rely on strangers to watch their children. While many hired caregivers are superb, some are not, particularly those who are themselves underpaid and given the responsibility for watching more children than can be adequately supervised by any one human being. (There are no federal standards regulating the staff-child ratio at day-care centers.). . .

When we think about how quickly and creatively the consumer sector has responded to working *families* with take-out food services, special clothing stores just for the business woman, children's birthday party services, and the like, we can begin to appreciate just how slow and noninnovative our communities, companies, and government have been in respect to child care.

Why, for example, don't corporations sponsor pools of backup child-care people? (Most organizations have pools of temporary office help.) Why can't there be more visiting-nurse services to care for the sick children of employees like the one that the 3M Corporation is presently experimenting with? Why is our typical school day from nine to three? Why aren't more flextime or part-time positions available? Why do only a fraction of our nation's employers offer on- or near-site child-care facilities? Why do we have some states that allow one caregiver to watch as many as 12 toddlers? Why are we still the only industrialized nation without some form of parenting leave?

And why aren't more of us angry about all this instead of misdirecting our anger at our spouses, our children, and mostly ourselves? Why haven't we coalesced around child-care issues? Lack of time and energy must surely be part of the answer, but our guilt and self-recrimination may well be another part of it.

So we need first to pull ourselves out of the vicious cycle. Getting rid of the superwoman myth and the many demands she makes on us is a good place to begin. Just how unrealistic that mythical creature is becomes clear when we talk with other women and learn that none of us is able to be all things to all people all the time.

It isn't surprising that those working mothers who have a chance to discuss their common problems with one another at their jobs find themselves less conflicted. A woman who is a member of Financial Mothers, one of the support groups for working mothers being formed within different companies and professions, told me that just knowing how many others share her concerns and doubts has helped her to feel less guilty.

These organizations, important as they are, affect only a small number of working mothers. For the kinds of structural changes we need, women must join together with men to strive for corporate and public policies sensitive to our needs. Only then will we be freed from the tyranny of guilt.

31

▼▼▼▼

Confessions of a Househusband

▼▼▼▼

Joel Roache

ABSTRACT: Based on his experience as a househusband, the author explores implications of the male's greater sex-role privileges. He analyzes how they tend to isolate husbands from wives, create emotional distance, hinder communication, distort personality and perception, and lead to a husband achieving a sense of fulfillment from his work, while his wife obtains her self-esteem through his accomplishments. Achieving equality will require the transformation of society's institutions.

Many men are coming to realize that sex-role privilege inflicts enormous damage on them, turning half of humanity into their subordinates and the other half into their rivals, isolating them and making fear and loneliness the norm of their existence. That ponderous abstraction became real for me in what many men consider a trivial realm: housework.

Every movement produces its truisms, assumptions that very soon are scarcely open to argument. The Women's Movement is no exception, and one of its truisms is that the home is a prison for women, trapping them in housework and child care, frustrating them and distorting their need for fulfillment as whole persons. Whatever reality lies behind many situation comedy stereotypes—the nag, the clinging wife, the telephone gossip—is rooted in this distortion. Only after *I* had assumed the role of househusband, and was myself caught in the "trap of domesticity," did I realize that the reality behind those stereotypes is a function of the role, not the person.

Two years ago, my wife Jan and I tried to change (at least within our own lives) society's imposed pattern of dependent servant and responsible master by deciding to share equally the responsibility of housework. We made no specific arrangement (a mistake from which I was to learn a great deal); it was simply understood that I was going to take on roughly half of the domestic chores so that she could do the other work she needed to do.

There was something of a shock for me in discovering the sheer quantity of the housework, and my standards of acceptable cleanliness fell rapidly. It became much easier to see my insistence on neatness as an inherited middle-class hang-up now that I had to do so much of the work myself. One of the long-standing sources of tension between Jan and me was almost immediately understood and resolved. What's more, I enjoyed it, at first. When not interrupted by the children I could, on a good day, do the kitchen and a bedroom, a load of laundry, and a meal in a little over two hours. Then I'd clean up after the meal and relax for a while with considerable satisfaction. So I approached the work with some enthusiasm, looking forward to seeing it all put right by my own hand, and for a while I wondered what all the fuss was about.

But within a few weeks that satisfaction and that enthusiasm began to erode a little more each time I woke up or walked into the house, only to find that it all needed to be done again. Finally, the image of the finished job, the image that encouraged me to start, was crowded out of my head by the image of the job to do all over again. I became lethargic, with the result that I worked less efficiently; so that even when I did "finish," it took longer and was done less well, rendering still less satisfaction. At first I had intellectual energy to spare, thinking about my teaching while washing dishes; pausing in the middle of a load of laundry to jot down a note. But those pauses soon became passive daydreams, fantasies from which I would have to snap myself back to the grind, until finally it was all I could do to keep going at all. I became more and more irritable and resentful.

Something similar happened even sooner and more dramatically to my relationship with our three children. I soon found myself angry with them most of the time, and I almost never enjoyed them. Then I watched myself for a couple of days and realized what was going on. They were constantly interrupting. I had tried simply to be available to them in case they needed me while I went on reading, writing, cleaning, or watching television. But of course with a six-year-old, a four-year-old, and a one-year-old, *someone* would need me every five to fifteen minutes. Just enough time to get into something, and up Jay would come with a toy to be fixed, or Matthew would spill his juice, or Eric would get stuck between the playpen bars and scream. In everything I tried to do, I was frustrated by their constant demands and soon came, quite simply, to hate them; and to hate myself for hating them; and at some level, I suspect, to hate Jan for getting me into this mess. My home life became a study in frustration and resentment.

I soon reached the conclusion that if I was going to keep house and take care of the children, I might as well give up doing anything else at the same time if I hoped to maintain any equilibrium at all. So I deliberately went through my housekeeping paces in a daze, keeping alert for the children but otherwise concentrating on whatever was before me, closing down all circuits not relevant to the work at hand. I maintained my sanity, I think, and I ceased to scream at the children so much, but neither they nor anyone else got the benefit of any creative energy; there just wasn't any. In half a day I could feel my mind turning into oatmeal, cold oatmeal, and it took the other half to get it bubbling again, and by then it was bedtime; and out of physical exhaustion I would have to go to sleep on whatever coherent ideas I might have got together in my few hours of free time.

Things went on this way for quite some time, partly because I couldn't think of an acceptable alternative, and partly because I was on a kind of guilt trip, possessed by the suicidal notion that somehow I had to pay for all those years Jan was oppressed. After a while I began to "adjust"; even cold oatmeal has a certain resilience. I began to perceive my condition as normal, and I didn't notice that my professional work was at a standstill. Then Jan became involved in community organizing, which took up more and more of her time and began to eat into mine, until finally I found myself doing housekeeping and child care from eight to sixteen hours a day, and this went on for about eight weeks. The astonishing thing now is that I let this masochistic work load go on so long. I suppose my guilt trip had become almost equivalent to a woman's normal conditioning, in reducing my ability to resist effectively the demands of Jan's organizing. And the excitement of her newly discovered self-sufficiency and independence (after eight years of her struggle to make me recognize what I was doing to her) functioned in the same way as the normal assumption of the superior importance of a male's work as provider.

I can pinpoint the place in time when we saw the necessity for a more careful adjustment of responsibilities, defining duties and scheduling hours more precisely and adhering to them more faithfully. It was at a moment when it became clear that Jan's work was beginning to pay off and her group scored a definite and apparently unqualified success. I went around the house for a full day feeling very self-satisfied, proud of her achievement, *as if it were my own,* which was fine until I realized, somewhere near the end of the day, that much of that sense of achievement resulted from the fact that I had no achievement of my own. I was getting my sense of fulfillment, of self-esteem, *through her,* while she was getting it *through her work.* It had happened: I was a full-fledged househusband.

A similar moment of illumination occurred at about the same time. Jan had spent the afternoon with a friend while I took care of the children and typed a revision of the bibliography for the book I was trying to finish at the time, the kind of drudgery more prosperous authors underpay some women to do. By the time Jan got home I was in a state of benumbed introversion, and when she began to talk about the substance of her afternoon's conversation, I was at first bored and finally irritated. Before long I was snapping at her viciously. She sat there looking first puzzled, then bewildered, and finally withdrawn. In a kind of reflexive self-defense she cut me off emotionally and went on thinking about whatever was on her mind. As I began to run down, I realized that what she had been trying to talk about would normally be interesting and important to me, yet I had driven her away. Then I looked at her and suddenly had the really weird sensation of seeing myself, my own isolation and frustration when I used to come home and try to talk to her. I realized that I was in her traditional position and felt a much fuller understanding of what that was. In that moment, on the verge of anger, an important part of what we had been doing to each other for all those years became clearer than it had ever been to either of us.

Another problem was suddenly clear to me also. The loneliness and helplessness I had felt before we traded responsibilities had been a function of my own privilege. My socially defined and reinforced role as *the* responsible party to the marriage had cut me off from Jan's experience; had made inevitably futile our attempts to communicate with each other from two very different worlds. Since she has a strong sense of herself as a responsible adult, Jan was bound to resist the limits of her role as dependent and (though we would never had said it) subordinate. When I found myself muttering and bitching, refusing to listen, refusing to provide any positive feedback on her experience in the outside world, I realized that her preoccupation, her nagging and complaining, her virtual absence from my psychic world, had not been neurotic symptoms but expressions of resistance to my privilege and to the power over her life that it conferred.

Jan's failure to force a real change in our life together for so long is a grim tribute to the power of socialization, and to my ability to exploit that power in order to protect myself from reality. When Jan realized how really minimal were the satisfactions of housework, there was also a voice within her (as well as mine without) suggesting that perhaps she was just lazy. If she began to hate the children, she knew that it was because they were helping to prevent her meeting real and legitimate personal needs, but the voices were always there hinting that the real trouble was that she was basically a hateful person and thus a poor mother. If her mind became sluggish, she knew at some level that she was making an adaptive adjustment to her situation, but those voices whispered in a thousand ways that she might be going crazy, or perhaps she was just stupid. And when she became sullen and resentful toward me, the voices were always there to obscure her perception that I had it coming. They even encouraged her to feel guilty, finally, when she did not feel my success as her reward, the payoff for all her drudgery. They kept her from realizing that such a payoff cost her a sense of her independent selfhood; that it was at best the pittance of exploitation: shit wages for shit work.

Those voices, within and without, kept reminding us both that Jan's real destiny was to keep me comfortable and productive and to raise "our" children. The feelings I'd come to experience in a few months had for years made Jan feel lazy, selfish, and egotistic; unable to empathize with the needs of the family (read: my need for success). Just as importantly, her knowledge that the sources of her troubles were not all within herself could not have received any reinforcement in the social world. I was her only link with that world; my affection and "respect" were her only source of assurance that she was real. To the extent that identity depends on recognition by others, she depended on me for that as surely as she depended on me for grocery money. The result was that she was afraid to share with me huge areas of her life, any areas which might threaten my regard for her. She could not afford, psychologically or economically, to challenge me overtly. And when she managed to make any suggestion that her discontent was a function of what was being done to her, it was battered down, by my recriminations, into a quagmire of guilt.

I had had some inkling of all this before I ever committed myself to cooking a meal or washing a single pair of socks (as my responsibility, rather than a favor to her). But at every stage of our experiment in role reversal (or rather our attempt to escape roles) my understanding of her position became more real. I had got a lot of domestic services but I had been denied real contact with a whole human being, and hard upon my guilt came anger, rage at what had been done to us both.

I don't have space here to go on and extend our experience into the world outside the family. It is enough to say that when someone has concrete power over your life, you are going to keep a part of yourself hidden and therefore undeveloped, or developed only in fantasy. Your identity becomes bound up in other people's expectations of you—and that is the definition of alienation. It did not take long for me to make connections between the alienating ways in which Jan had to deal with me in the early years of our marriage and the way that I was dealing with my "senior colleagues," the men and women who had power to fire me and did.

Our experience also helped me to understand the distortions of perception and personality that results from being the "superior" in a hierarchical structure. The nuclear family as we know it is one such structure, perhaps the crucial one. But the alienation which results from privilege pervades all our experience in a society which values human beings on the basis of sex, race, and class and which structures those standards into all its institutions. Housework is only a tip of that iceberg, but for Jan and me it has helped to make the need to fundamentally transform those institutions a gut reality.

32

The Myth of Male Helplessness

Joel Roache

ABSTRACT: In this follow-up on his experiences as a househusband (Chapter 31), Roache reflects on how he had to overcome his gender socialization in order to adjust to being a single parent.

About twenty years ago, I wrote an article for *Ms.* entitled "Confessions of a Househusband." It was my fifteen minutes of fame, my historical nanosecond as a hero of the women's movement. I appeared on radio (and television!) talk shows, lectured on college campuses, and generally became a minor celebrity, a bona fide novelty. Of course, I soon retreated into obscurity, and now househusbands seem almost commonplace, appearing regularly in the Style sections of newspapers all over the country.

On the other hand, if the media are still interested in us, then we are still unusual enough to be news, and for many people, bad news. Not long ago my wife, during a break at the school where she teaches, happened to mention the flounder amandine I had prepared the night before. Conversation stopped abruptly, until someone finally asked, "You mean you actually leave him in your kitchen *alone?!*"

Although woman's place is no longer in the home for our culture, the home remains woman's place, her domain, to be vigilantly protected against male ineptness; and this attitude is not some atavistic aberration confined to backwater provinces, as an evening or two of television commercials will show.

One ad features a helplessly flu-ridden housewife, and a voiceover warning us that she "is not the only one to suffer," followed by a child's voice lamenting, "Mom! Dad's *ironing!*" In another spot, Mom has left a microwavable dinner and a taped message. Her husband needs the message to do it right, of course, but the underlying pitch is that the meal is so easy that even a man can prepare it. Or can he? Witness the bit starring a famous and venerable baseball player who, at the end of the commercial, confuses the microwave oven with the refrigerator.

My favorite example takes place in a laundromat, presenting a young adult male who doesn't know that you need detergent to launder your clothes. An elderly woman has to instruct him. Finally a much younger woman (in perfectly fitted examples of the advertiser's jeans) offers the poor guy some of her detergent, since he is apparently too dumb to ask for it.

Twenty years ago the explanation of all this incompetence was simple: only female genes carried homemaking traits. The myth of male helplessness was just the flip side of the myth of female as domestic servant, and for generations men deferred cheerfully to this "natural" superiority, evading a great deal of drudgery. Today, of course, the rationale has been updated, substituting nurture for nature: our parents did not raise us for this sort of work, and so we lack the necessary skills. Thus we find men who follow the daily fluctuations of the yen and the deutschmark but cannot master the complexities of a green salad or a grilled cheese sandwich, or muster the patience needed to work a sponge mop. Women all across America, furthermore, are being told that it will be more trouble to teach us than to do it themselves. Just try and we'll show you.

It is apparently a compelling argument. The Madison Avenue wizards have done their homework, and probably predicted the success of "Three Men and a Baby," where three grown men can barely manage to care for one infant. They read the studies showing that, excluding such traditional male domains as yard work and appliance repair, women still do more than 80 percent of the housework.

For a lot of us, then, the old mythology still works.

As one of those who has given it up, though, I resent it. I was reared the same way as most men of my generation. For most of my life I didn't know the difference between an egg whisk and a garlic press. But I am not stupid. I can learn.

I will admit that like most men I had to be persuaded to learn, a task that my first wife pursued with a variety of inducements until I grudgingly and gradually came around. Then, when that marriage dissolved, I spent ten years as a single father and learned a great deal more, very quickly.

One try will teach anyone not to dry cotton T-shirts on high heat. When the children get sick of scrambled eggs, you learn to crack them without breaking the yolks. Looking at the kitchen floor every day generates a sincere interest in commercials about wax buildup. And surely even the most cloddish male will be sensitized by the political intricacies of PTA meetings.

I did not have to learn everything the hard way. A particularly fastidious bachelor neighbor taught me to fold fitted sheets, and my mother quickly persuaded me of the merits of large casseroles sufficient for two or three meals. I also turned the women I work with into teachers. I began to feel chagrined, even deprived, when I realized that, besides being as competent as I professionally, they also knew all sorts of important secrets of shopping, cooking, etc., that had been kept from me when I was growing up.

Mothers (and sometimes grandmothers) in the neighborhood, on the other hand, helped me to learn skills specific to parenting, from quick breakfasts to the delicate balance between encouragement and correction in helping with my boys' homework.

I even began accosting strangers in supermarkets, dawdling around produce sections, for instance, until I spotted someone selecting her potatoes or cucumbers with special care. Then I would descend on her with questions about her choices, until she was convinced that I really wanted to know.

Although most of the tutors I recruited in such ways were married, my domestic interests often became relevant to my social life. Few women feel threatened by a man who wants to know how to hard-boil an egg so that the shell doesn't stick. In fact, one of my most important relationships during those years was with the woman who taught me to can tomato sauce. And there are many less interesting ways to spend an afternoon than in exploring the mysteries of *coq au vin* with someone you really like. If you don't start early in the day, finally, real croissants may keep you sociably busy far into the night. I especially remember the young woman who taught me, near the end of my second bachelorhood, to make the best cheesecake around.

After mastering the recipe in only two tries, I married her.

One day soon we will invite her colleagues over for dinner, and as they sit around and chat over drinks and dip, maybe she can steer the conversation around to sex roles in TV commercials. Meanwhile, I'll put the finishing touches on the meal, in the kitchen.

Alone.

33

▼▼▼▼

Making Your Dual-Career Marriage Successful

▼▼▼▼

Barbara Chesser

ABSTRACT: Because of their double work load, dual-career couples face several pressing issues. Among them are extra demands on the couple's time and energy, the timing of children, child care, how to spend earnings, changing sex roles and decision making, women being judged by how they succeed in the homemaking role, relative earnings, unrealistic expectations, lack of models for working out satisfactory marital roles, and the superwoman myth. Thirteen advantages of dual-career marriages are listed, as well as ten recommendations for making them better.

Because of the increasing number of dual-career families, all family life education efforts should deal with issues arising in dual-career families. Whether the efforts are preventive, enrichment, or interventional in nature, the marriages of the participants will be strengthened as they become more aware of the issues that arise in dual-career marriages. An increased awareness of these issues and possible ways to handle them constructively will increase the couple's coping skills and problem-solving abilities, thereby building family strengths.

314

Dual-career family as used in this paper means both husband and wife are pursuing careers and maintaining a family together. The word "career" usually refers to a job which requires a high degree of commitment and a fairly continuous developmental life. A career is different from a job or work, for work may involve any kind of gainful employment. Work may be full-time, part-time, and periodic over the years so that it can be easily changed to accommodate marital and child-rearing responsibilities. Obviously the line of demarcation between a career and a job is not always clear. A career might be placed at one end of a continuum with higher levels of commitment, responsibilities, educational and emotional investment, whereas a job is at the other end of the continuum with lower levels of all these characteristics. The closer one comes to the career end of the continuum, the more likely the issues discussed in this paper will indeed be problematic within the marriage because of the higher level of commitment characteristic of a career as opposed to a job. The closer one approaches the job end of the continuum, the easier, relatively speaking, the issues will be to resolve because of less commitment and investment. . . .

ISSUES

To work or not to work outside the home may be an issue arising before the couple is married. Many variables will feed into this decision, but for the decision for the wife to work outside the home to be successfully carried out, the wife must really want or need to work. *Want* and *need* may be difficult to differentiate for some persons. For the two million women who head families, there is no choice: they *need* to work. Because of inflation, some wives with working husbands may also feel that they have to work to help pay the rent, buy groceries, and to rear their children. For other women, working may be a way to raise the family's standard of living. Others may work mostly to be with other people. In a society that often measures human worth by how much money you can make or what you do, many women want to feel better about themselves. . . . Being able to sort out why each works may seem too trivial or too philosophical to be practical. But many of the practical decisions in a two-career marriage often rest on why each partner works. Why a farmer's wife works during a drought year may be quite different from why a wife who is a college professor works year after year. Issues and problems may develop on the homefront for each of these couples. And each may require different solutions to keep the marriage on an even keel.

But most couples describe common problems regardless of why they say the wife works. Extra demands on time and energy seem to plague every two-career marriage. The wife may try to do all the housework as well as meet the rigorous demands of a job or career. The husband traditionally views housework as female's work and may have trouble helping with it. He may feel clumsy, or housework may make him feel unmanly, or he may be exhausted from his career. His wife may not want him to help her. She may doubt her own value if he can do "her" work.

Another issue many dual-career couples grapple with is whether or not to have children. An increasing percentage are opting for a childfree marriage, but many career couples merely are postponing the birth of their first child. And most career families have fewer children than couples which include a nonworking wife.

Determination of the "best" time for having a child rests on considerations such as educational plans and establishment of a career and the effects of time-off on these two considerations. Also the availability of maternity leaves may determine the "best" time.

For dual-career couples who have a child, child care becomes a concern. Adequate childcare facilities are still not widely available. Finding a reliable baby-sitter to stay in the home may be a challenge. The financial cost of child care is usually another concern. When the child is older and in school most of the day, child care may not be such a problem. Problems may come when a child does not follow the usual schedule, for example, when he or she is sick. Who stays home? Who takes the child to the doctor? To the dentist? Who leaves work to go to the parent-teacher conference? To the Christmas play? To weekly music lessons? In a traditional marriage, the decision is easy: the mother's job always gives in to the demands of the children. As women increasingly express commitment to their careers, couples are compelled to establish new criteria for decisions regarding child care.

Obviously these criteria are increasingly complicated if a child requires extra care and supervision because of a health problem or a handicap of some kind. Working out satisfactory child care and supervision may also be complicated if the career of one or both of the partners in a dual-career marriage requires travel.

How to handle career relocation if one spouse is offered a promotion which requires moving is another issue confronting some couples at one time or another in their careers. Decision making in this situation may be extra perplexing if it is the wife being offered the promotion. Our culture supports relocations made on the basis of the husband's promotion, not the wife's.

The issue of how to spend the combined earnings of a dual-career marriage confronts most couples. Should the discretionary income be spent on luxuries or travel, or should it be saved or invested? Dual-career families come face to face with this question. Other couples may find that there is no discretionary income. Taxes may take an extraordinary portion of their combined earnings. Transportation expenses for two careers eat up an unreasonable amount of money. Wardrobe demands may gnaw insidiously at the combined earnings. Child care may take its unfair portion. Eating meals out or the purchase of convenience foods may require an undue portion of the paychecks. This is when the couple must scrutinize the value of two careers in one marriage, or they may be challenged to search for desirable ways to economize.

Survival of a two-career family may depend upon the ability of husband and wife to make decisions satisfying to both. Some marriages thrive on the husband making all the major decisions and others depend upon the wife to make them. But partners in most dual-career marriages have to work at learning how to make decisions together. Traditionally, the man made the money, therefore he had the authority to make the decisions. If both husband and wife work to make the money, both have the right to make decisions. Deciding *who* is going to decide and *how* the decisions are made is often more critical than the decisions. Couples able to decide mutually with occasional compromise seem to survive two-career marriages.

Some males egos may be too fragile to survive a two-career marriage. A working wife may signal his failure to make enough money to be considered ''successful.'' Or a wife who makes more money than the husband may threaten a weak male ego. Husband and wife in similar careers may compete too keenly. A wife may occasionally put her husband in a double bind. She may pressure him to succeed in his job while pressuring him to be a terrific husband and father.

Some women may be uncomfortable out of a traditional homemaker role. Society still judges a man by his job and a woman by her homemaking, as a companion, mother, and hostess. Some women may be frustrated if they do better in the work world than their husbands. All husbands and wives it seems are pressured to do more and to do it better. Tensions may really mount in dual-career families if these issues are not dealt with realistically and constructively.

If two-career marriages survive these first few hurdles, they still have not completed the obstacle course. Careers make rugged demands on a husband's and wife's time and energy. So do the children's schedules. Little time and energy remain for friends or recreation. Most couples cannot maintain friendships with all they would like to. So they must make choices—a few friends from his acquaintances, a few from hers, or maybe a few from church, or from parents of their children's friends. Couples need skills in learning to say no to some activities so they can say yes to those they want to do.

Individual partners need to know what they expect of themselves as well as from their mates. They need to examine what they expect of the marriage itself. Couples must communicate these expectations to each other. One husband whose first two-career marriage ended in divorce but who was managing well in a second one shared: "You gotta have lots of heart-to-heart talks of what you want out of marriage and what you are willing to do to accomplish what you want." He explained that not only husband and wife but the kids must have a good understanding of what everyone wants out of the family and the responsibilities each is willing to assume. "Otherwise," he went on, "the family becomes like an explosion in a mattress factory: they never get it all together."

Marriage may be unsafe at any speed, but having unrealistic and unreasonable expectations may be the speed that kills. If this were true for the traditional marriage in which the husband is the breadwinner and the wife is the hearth-warmer, then it certainly is truer for the two-career marriage. Other survival tactics may help, but realistic expectations of self and partner are essential, as one college professor with three young children pointed out:

> You have to be realistic in what you expect of yourself and your marriage partner. It's impossible for one person to be terrific on the job, a terrific husband, a terrific father, and to keep the grass mowed all the time.

An enormous obstacle to two-career couples is the paucity of models of successful two-career marriages. And each two-career couple works through these issues in fairly unique ways that seem best for them. Their solution for a particular problem may not work for another couple.

Another complication is that many couples think other couples have solved most of these problems. Flashes of a superwoman haunt most women. This superwoman who knits marriage, career, and motherhood into a satisfying life without dropping a stitch is overwhelming and gives others miserable feelings of failure.

The foregoing discussion of some of the issues confronting most dual-career marriages may create a foreboding, ominous aura about the dual-career marriage. The marriages of those who do not work successfully through these issues, in fact, may be threatened. However, those who do at least to some extent successfully resolve some of the issues may enjoy some tangible benefits or advantages. Professionals should clearly outline these just as they teach about the issues that usually arise in a dual-career family.

ADVANTAGES

Some of the advantages which dual-career families may enjoy are briefly outlined as follows:

1. Dual-career families may enjoy some financial advantages. They may enjoy a higher standard of living. They may be able to accumulate savings. They may be able to provide financial security against possible disasters.
2. The wife may enjoy greater levels of creativity, self-expression, achievement, and recognition. She may enjoy being herself, not an appendage to her husband. This may help her be a better mother and wife.
3. Dual-career marriages provide a greater range of role models for children of both sexes.
4. The husband may be relieved of some of the pressures to succeed and to make money. Thus, he will be able to function more effectively as a husband and/or father.
5. The husband may enjoy his wife more since she will have outside activities and interests to share.
6. Sexual interest in the marriage may heighten in an unstereotyped, dual-career marriage.
7. Parent responsibilities can be shared. Husbands can enjoy their children more, and children can profit from having an available father.
8. Children may learn to be more responsible and more resourceful when their mothers work outside the home. This may reinforce their feelings of achievement, pride, and self-esteem.
9. Children may learn to respect their parents more, especially their mothers, as individuals.
10. The empty-nest syndrome which affects some in later years may be avoided somewhat if the wife is engaged in a meaningful career outside the home.
11. Coping with widowhood may be somewhat easier for the woman who has had a meaningful career in addition to her marriage career.
12. Increased empathy with the demands of the roles of each other may foster mutual respect and facilitate communication.
13. The increased sharing of roles may create feelings of equality, thus strengthening the family.

RECOMMENDATIONS

. . . [G]eneral recommendations that all could work on which would strengthen the American family are as follows:

1. There should be increased knowledge throughout the educational career about role flexibility and/or change. In other words,

rigid or stereotyped sex roles should be avoided in textbooks and
other learning materials.
2. Mass media should avoid perpetuating stereotypes.
3. Stereotypic assumptions about sex roles should be avoided (for
example, "women are absent more from work").
4. Better parent education should be available for all people.
5. There should be more high-quality child care for working parents. Perhaps more neighborhood child care provisions as well
as industrial child care should be explored.
6. Business and government could provide more flexible working
conditions, including more flexible working hours, sharing of positions, and more part-time positions without discrimination of
benefits, promotions, etc. Increased flexibility would reduce conflict between the demands of parents' employment and the needs
of their families. Flexible working hours would also help in bat-
tling the war against the traditional 8 to 5 schedule that is based
on the assumption that the wife is at home and free to take care
of business matters within this time frame.
7. More equitable provisions should be provided for taking time off
for childbearing and child care.
8. An integrated network of family services should be developed
more fully. All families need easily available preventive services.
9. Marriage and family counseling should continually be developed
into a more effective resource for helping members of two-career
marriages cope with their stresses and strains.
10. More research is needed on the effects of two-career families. For
example, the effects of long-distance marriages on the partners
and the children might be explored.

Two-career families are probably a testing ground of things to come
as sex roles become more flexible and interchangeable, as inflation continues, and as more careers are open to women. Professionals who are
directly involved in activities to help build strengths in families must
energetically carry out all of the foregoing suggested recommendations,
and they must continue to be supportive and empathic in whatever
ways will help strengthen two-career families. And we as professionals
need to cherish our own family relationships to provide a model of ways
to build strengths in the two-career family.

PART VII

▼▼▼▼▼▼▼▼▼▼▼▼▼▼▼▼▼▼▼▼▼▼▼▼▼

When Nightmares Become Reality

The world is filled with catastrophes—from famine and flood to war and economic depression. Against many of these, the family is unable to serve as a refuge. The catastrophe may overwhelm the family as it sweeps over a region or even part of the globe.

Against many of the distresses and adversities of social life, however, the family is able to serve as a buffer. In periods of unemployment, for example, the members of a family are able to pull together—to cut expenses, to explore alternative resources, and, above all, to encourage the unemployed member of the family. That encouragement is most significant, for it assures the individual that he or she is not facing the problem alone—and this, after all, is one of the primary benefits that people expect from their families.

It is perhaps worth noting that a feeling of *social support* (or *interpersonal solidarity*)—of people standing together—is one of the essential elements of mental health. Indeed, that feeling of support, of not facing problems alone, is also important for physical health. Both the body and the mind function better when, in confronting crises, the individual knows that he or she is not facing them alone.

One of the most poignant stories to come out of the Vietnam war concerns a high ranking officer who had been taken prisoner (Julius Segal, *Winning Life's Toughest Battles*, McGraw-Hill, 1986:

> The guards dragged Navy Vice Admiral James B. Stockdale from his North Vietnamese prison cell to an unshaded courtyard. There, for three days, they would not let him sleep. His hands were cuffed behind his back, his legs weighed down with heavy irons. There also, for three days he was forced to remain sitting under the blistering sun. The guards beat him repeatedly.
>
> After one such beating, Stockdale heard a towel snapping out prison code. As he listened, Stockdale heard a message he would never forget, the letters G B U J S. It was, "God Bless You, Jim Stockdale."

It was social support like this that allowed some of the prisoners to survive and, after even years of suffering such inhumane treatment, to return to society and to again pick up the pieces of their lives.

Just like the fellow prisoner snapping out support in code—simply letting the other know that he was there, in sympathy and understanding—so the family serves that vital function. Because we belong to a family, we know that others care. "What happens to me *does* make a difference to them." That feeling of being important to one another, of standing behind one another in times of crises, underlies the personal significance of the family.

Part VII focuses on situations of crises. In Chapter 34, Edward M. Levine and Eugene J. Kanin analyze date rape, which, unfortunately, many of the females who are reading this book have personally experienced. In surveys of my own classes, I have been shocked to find that the proportion is higher than that reported in the literature. The authors place date rape in its social context, identifying social changes that have made it more common—changes in sex roles, sexual behaviors, the double standard, the entertainment media, images of females, and basic expectations of males and females.

In Chapter 35, Kathleen J. Ferraro and John M. Johnson report on why battered women stay in abusive relationships. They found that battered women use six techniques to rationalize the violence: They appeal to the salvation ethic and to higher loyalties, and they deny the victimizer, injury, victimization, and options. These researchers also found six reasons why some battered women come to view themselves as true victims of abuse: changes in the level of violence, the resources, the relationship, or the visibility of the violence, as well as despair and external influences.

In Chapter 36, Murray A. Straus reports that each year 12 of every 100 husbands attack their wives and the same number of wives attack their husbands; violence directed by parents toward children and by siblings to one another is much higher. He identifies three primary causes of marital violence: the unintentional teaching of violence by parents who use physical punishment, cultural norms that tolerate violence in the family, and sexual inequality that both creates violence and forces women to put up with it. No one factor is *the* cause of family violence, however, and other causes include poverty, unemployment, social isolation, and various stresses.

In Chapter 37, Joan K. Jackson analyzes how wives adapt to alcoholic husbands. She found that after their first attempts to deny and to eliminate the problem, they become disorganized, attempt to reorganize, and then try to escape the problem. Finally, they reorganize the family, and if the alcoholic recovers, they eventually reincorporate him back into the family.

34

Date Rape

▼▼▼▼▼

Edward M. Levine
Eugene J. Kanin

ABSTRACT: To understand why date rape has increased, we must examine the changed social context in which it occurs. Before the 1960s, traditional sex standards helped to protect adolescent and adult females from male sexual aggression and violence. The sexual revolution and the Women's Movement challenged traditional standards, leading to fundamental changes in values, attitudes, and behaviors. These changes include the decline of the double standard, media portrayal of nude females in sexually explicit poses, and women gaining greater social and occupational equality and becoming more sexually active prior to marriage. Two consequences are a changed image of females and the higher expectations that males have of gaining sexual gratification on casual dates. A net result appears to be diminished inhibitions against forced sex.

INTRODUCTION

In recent years the crime of rape has received unprecedented attention and, as with other serious offenses, keen interest has developed

324

regarding this trend. However, the rise in incidence that has been reported in the *Uniform Crime Reports* and in select cities in recent years has been largely discredited as real, largely because the increase in the rates of reported rape reflect a greater willingness of victims to report their having been victimized. And this has been variously attributed to the influence of the women's movement, the modification of rape statutes, and to the increase in the general level of education regarding the rights of rape victims.

While it would be difficult to make a definitive case for a real increase in the rate of official forcible rape, rape among intimates—date and acquaintance rape—is another matter. Evidence can now be gathered to show that serious sexual violence (termed date rape) has increased dramatically during the last thirty years. Although the questionnaire studies of the late 1950s dealing with sexual aggression did not focus on rape, per se, case material collected at the time from the sample populations shows rape to have been an exceptional occurrence.

For example, from one study in which 82 cases were collected, only three cases of rape were identified, all of them date rapes (Kirkpatrick and Kanin, 1957). Another study of the experiences of high school seniors examined 91 case studies among whom only four date rape victims were found (Kanin, 1957). From 1957 to 1961, Kanin requested his female undergraduate students to report anonymously on their victimization experiences, and of the 372 reports of female victimization, 13 cases of forcible rape were found (3.5 percent), 11 of which were readily identified as date rape, the remaining 2 being acquaintance rape victims. Thus, investigations revealed a date rape incidence of only 3.8 percent.

In contrast, recent studies of female college students revealed strikingly higher figures. Koss and Oros (1982) found that 8.2 percent of their sample of female college students reported having had forced sex; Wilson and Durrenberger (1982) reported 15 percent in their study; Parcell (1973) found 14.6 percent; and Rapaport (1984) reported 14 percent. And more recent data from a study of 727 college females found that slightly more than 15 percent of them had been victims of date rape (Kanin, 1985). In addition, Korman and Leslie's (1982) research found that there was a higher rate of sex aggression at the genital level experienced by college females, a trend that had been detected somewhat earlier by Kanin and Parcell (1977), who found that the incidence of sex aggression experienced by college females was shifting dramatically from stranger to date and acquaintance rape.

Other evidence pertinent to our case that serious sexual aggression has become more commonplace for university women in their dating-courtship relations can be culled from the sex aggression studies from the mid-1950s to the late 1970s. This has increased from 13 percent in the early 1970s to 20 percent in the late 1970s (Kirkpatrick and Kanin,

1957; Kanin and Parcell, 1977; Korman and Leslie, 1982). Korman and Leslie (1982) also noted that "sexually exploitative attempts are becoming more coitally direct and that more women are experiencing these attempts." . . .

Although this survey of evidence should be viewed with a degree of caution, since the studies from which they are drawn represent certain problems in sampling and contrasting populations from different institutions, there is nevertheless a preponderance of and a consistency in the evidence from the past thirty years indicating that the college female is increasingly finding herself a target of sexual victimization and violence. This is now also true for female high school seniors (and perhaps even younger teenagers). In addition, males much more frequently resort to sexual aggression with no preliminary erotic intimacies than they did three decades ago.

Because such fear-inducing experiences may engender profoundly troubling emotional problems among sexually victimized females with regard to their attitudes toward marriage and family, the purpose of this study is to describe certain of the sociocultural changes that have occurred during the past generation and that appear to be largely responsible for the emergence of these trends in aggressive sexual behavior among younger males.

TRADITIONAL SEX STANDARDS

The human desire for sexual gratification is not governed by an instinct, an autonomous force that compels men and women to seek sexual gratification irrespective of their wishes. Instead, human sexual feelings and behavior are stimulated by the sex drive or impulse which becomes most intense and powerful during adolescence and young adulthood, after which its influence over human behavior gradually diminishes. Furthermore, its expression is greatly limited by the constraining influence of the moral values of tradition and religion, norms, and individual preferences that are inculcated in children by their parents, as well as emphasized by society through social institutions such as the schools. Historically, these standards have generally served to protect females against the predatory sexual propensities of males.

These values were part of the same tradition that upheld a double standard of sexual rights and responsibilities for postpubertal males and females. That is, adolescent and young adult males were generally free to enjoy such sexual pleasures as they found or that were offered them by sexually congenial women. Once married, they were expected to observe marital fidelity, although their extramarital affairs were not exceptional.

By contrast, females were expected to remain chaste until marriage and be completely faithful to their husbands thereafter. Economically dependent on their husbands, who regarded them as the weaker sex, women were also envisaged as the guardians of sexual and other moral standards that were considered as being centrally important for the stability of the family and for human well-being. Thus, modesty was a cardinal virtue of unmarried females, while the sexual posturing and dalliances of bachelors were taken for granted and commonly overlooked.

After that point in history when parents arranged their children's marriages, single, young (and even older) women who worked were obliged to live at home until they married, while their male counterparts were free to come and go as they pleased. Teenage girls were expected to introduce their dates to their parents at home so the latter could learn something about their character and their families. Parents also knew where their daughters were going, and when their dates would bring them home. The most difficult choice then confronting most adolescent girls was whether or not to give a boy a goodnight kiss on the first date, for to do so might lead him to consider her forward and improperly interested in his amorous advances which might undermine her defenses against them. While these standards still hold for some adolescent females, they have weakened considerably during the past generation, and have been rejected or abandoned by numbers of them.

WOMEN'S INDEPENDENCE AND THE NEW SEXUAL FREEDOM

The use of the contraceptive pill and the concomitant erosion of traditional values related to marriage and family and sexual behavior by the cultural revolution of the late 1960s (Levine, 1981, 1985) were major factors leading to the fundamental changes in intersexual relationships that are so prevalent today. These changes gained considerable momentum from the successes of the Women's Movement in breaking down the barriers to women's social and economic inequality, with the result that the double sexual standard collapsed for ever-growing numbers of females. Many assertive young women contend that it relegated them to a subordinate status in their relationships with men and was, therefore, a completely outmoded standard that had lost its relevance.

Armed with college and professional degrees and enjoying the satisfaction of having jobs and careers and the financial independence this provided them, increasing numbers of young women went on to claim much the same social rights and options that men have traditionally enjoyed. For example, it is no longer unconventional for working women to pay for their luncheons and dinners when dating, to invite men to be their guests for an evening date, and to engage in premarital sex almost as freely and unperturbedly as do men. In brief, women's occupational and social independence has been translated into a sexual freedom that begins to approximate that which men have had throughout the ages.

These transforming changes in women's occupational and social roles, as well as in their values and attitudes concerning their social and sexual relationships with men, have led to corresponding changes in the lives of adolescent females. That is, once women attained equality with men, the next logical step was for them (and their husbands) to raise their daughters to become fully independent, with the schools and the mass media affirming and exemplifying female equality in all important spheres of life. Consequently, steadily growing numbers of young women have been attending college for a generation and more, but especially since the early 1970s. And adolescent girls, more than ever before, anticipate working several years before they marry, are much freer in deciding when and whom to date, and are generally much less limited by their parents' regulations. Furthermore, numbers of adolescent girls are unhesitant about calling boys for dates or merely to talk with them, and are also sexually active—alarmingly so for those who become pregnant in their early teens, which is no longer uncommon among white, middle-class high school girls.

Today, adolescents are well aware that even if their parents understandingly and helpfully counsel them to remain sexually abstinent, they are also resigned, however ruefully, to their children being sexually active during their teen years. Adolescent boys guiltlessly ignore parental pieties about their behaving responsibly toward girls, and easily find girls as willing as they are to engage in sexual intercourse. The confluence of the equalized social relationships between the sexes, the sexual freedom so widely enjoyed today by adolescents and young adults, and females' greater willingness to engage in coitus make them more vulnerable to being raped.

The changing context within which the sexual victimization of females occurs is illustrated by earlier studies that provide substantial data indicating that aggressive sexual behavior followed after consensual sexual activity, such as kissing, petting, and more intensely erotic behavior (Kirkpatrick and Kanin, 1957; Kanin, 1957). However, female college students today report a surprisingly large percentage of both sexual aggression and rape that were spontaneously initiated by their male companions without any antecedent consensual, erotic activity. Approximately 44 percent of these sexual aggressions were not preceded by any form of consensual sex play (Kanin and Parcell, 1977). More explicitly, this phenomenon involved the males attempting to engage in sexual intercourse at once, rather than their engaging in a sequential seductive order involving kissing, fondling, and the like in order sexually to arouse the female.

The apparently growing tendency of males to dispense with such sexual preliminaries prior to seeking coercively to gain sexual gratification from their female companions may be partly due to the influence of the entertainment media. That is, these media often portray sexual settings in which males and females are intimately involved, but with the amorous or courtship sequences that might properly lead to this being seldom, if ever, depicted. Thus, the trend in contemporary sexual behavior of date and acquaintance rapists suggests an equivalence of male and female sexuality in the sense that such males are heedless of females' rights when the former are highly sexually aroused, behavior that is partly legitimized by the entertainment media.

It may also be the case that adolescent and college males now have far higher expectations of gaining sexual gratification from casual dates because of the changes in the roles and attitudes of their female counterparts, and are, therefore, much less willing to allow them to frustrate their sexual desires. To the extent that young women are viewed as being uninhibited by traditional standards governing female sexual behavior, and are regarded as being equally knowledgeable about and interested in sex as their dates, then males holding these views may expect females to treat coitus as casually as they do in thought and behavior. Consequently, the unwillingness of females to comply with their dates' demands for sexual intercourse may lead to sexual aggression or rape—which males may increasingly consider acceptable because they no long find clear-cut, generally respected standards ruling out such reactions. What they deem to be wholly unjustifiable is the refusal of their dates to accede to their demand for sexual gratification, since this is seen as a completely arbitrary response. In their eyes, sexual freedom for females does not countenance sexually frustrating their dates. Sex on demand on one-night stands has become normative among many young males for whom a kiss good night or even mild petting are hopelessly juvenile responses.

A study that tends to affirm this interpretation found that numbers of adolescents of both sexes now believe that extenuating circumstances limit females' right to preserve their sexual integrity. In a sample of 432 adolescents, 54 percent of the males and 42 percent of the females agreed that forced sexual intercourse *is* permissible if the girls led the boy on, sexually excited him, or agreed to have sex with him and then changed her mind (Ehrhart and Sandler, 1985). Attesting to how greatly dating norms and environments have changed are data from another study reporting that 75 percent of the female college students in its sample said that they had experienced sexual aggression, that these incidents most often occurred during their senior year of high school or their first year of college—and that they had taken place on the *first* date in either their rooms or the room of their dates (Burkhardt, 1983). Other research mentioned in the *Chronicle of Higher Education* (1983) involving United States and Canadian male college students stated that 35 percent of the sample said that they might commit rape if they could be certain that they would not be apprehended. Although this probably reflects their fantasy life more than their inclination, it is nonetheless symptomatic of negative changes in young men's attitude toward young women, and a worrisome sign of the times.

THE CULTURE OF SEX AND THE EQUALIZATION OF WOMEN

The attenuation of the traditions and norms that protected adolescent and adult females against male sexual aggression and violence has been paralleled by the popularity of magazines that feature nude females in sexually explicit poses. Paradoxically, while these magazines have prospered by exploiting young women who are deliberately portrayed as sex objects, numbers of college women regard them as unobjectionable, partly because sex has become a common subject for social and public discussion, as well as because exposing oneself to the public, if not condoned, is considered by them to be a matter of individual choice, and its legitimacy a matter of personal opinion.

Insofar as opinions are based on personal choice and right, then they tend to be equalized, for all have rights to their opinions, however dubious or slanted others may judge them to be (Levine and Ross, 1977). This relativistic standard, in tandem with the growing educational, familial, and occupational equalization of females, has modified younger men's image of women. That is, inasmuch as adolescent and older females generally want to be regarded and dealt with primarily as individuals who are on an equal footing with males, and since the media flood the public with both suggestive and explicit sexual themes, images, and fantasies that demean and degrade female sexuality, males increasingly seem to view females primarily as asexual competitors, and secondarily in terms of their gender. Consequently, males may increasingly believe that bargaining, pressuring, and threatening are acceptable, if not truly legitimate, means to employ in attempting to induce women to be sexually compliant. Thus, male aggressiveness in intersexual relationships appears to become more prevalent the more closely the females' way of life and degree of sexual freedom approximate those of males. Indeed, while Janet Chafetz (1985) found that equality in marriages had a positive effect on spouses' intimacy, her insightful comment that intersexual equality also generated more marital disputes and conflict and increased the difficulty of resolving them is also pertinent here. . . .

CONCLUSION

An accumulating body of evidence indicates that the last thirty years have witnessed a disturbingly high increase in the sexual victimization of teenage and college females by dates and acquaintances. This trend seems to be partly the result of young females having much the same degree of freedom in their social and sexual relationships that their male counterparts enjoy. It is also attributable to the largely unrestrained ways in which human sexuality is featured in the mass media and popular culture, and which have diminished young people's inhibitions about seeking and gaining sexual gratification increasingly during their adolescent years. This is very likely facilitated by their widespread and growing use of alcoholic beverages.

Given this set of conditions and the declining influence of the standards that once protected unmarried females against male sexual predations, there is a strong likelihood that younger females, and perhaps older ones as well, will increasingly constitute an at-risk population with regard to being raped by dates and acquaintances, a trend that is all the more disconcerting in view of its ramifications for the well-being of marriage and family.

REFERENCES

Burkhart, B. (1983, December.) Presentation at Acquaintance Rape and Rape Prevention on Campus Workshop, Louisville, Ky.

Chafetz, J. (1985). Marital intimacy and conflict: Irony of spousal equality. *Free Inq. Creative Sociol.* 2: 191–199.

Chronicle of Higher Education (1983, August 31). p. 9.

Kanin, E. (1957). Male aggression in dating-courtship relations. *Am. J. Sociol.* 63: 197–204.

Kanin, E. (1985). *Rape among Intimates,* Paper presented at the Annual Meeting of the American Society of Criminology.

Kanin, E., and Parcell, S. (1977). Sexual aggression: A second look at the offended females. *Arch. Sexual Behav.* 6: 67–76.

Kirkpatrick, C., and Kanin, E. (1957). Male sex aggression on a university campus. *Am. Sociological Rev.* 22: 52–58.

Korman, S., and Leslie, G. (1982). The relationship of feminist ideology and date expense sharing to perceptions of sexual aggression in dating. *J. Sex Res.* 18:114–129.

Koss, M., and Oros, C. (1982). Sexual experiences survey: A research instrument investigating sexual aggression and victimization. *J. Consult. Clin. Psychol.* 50: 455–457.

Levine, E. (1981). Middle class family decline. *Society* 1: 72–78.

LEVINE, E. (1985). The plight of the middle class family. *J. Fam. Cult.* 1: 29–41.

LEVINE, E., and KANIN, E. (1986). Adolescent drug use: Its prospects for the future. *J. Fam. Cult.* 1: 4.

LEVINE, E., and ROSS, N. (1977). Sexual dysfunctions and psychoanalysis. *Ame. J. Psychiatr.* 234: 646–651.

RAPAPORT, K. (1984). Quoted in: A disturbing look at rape. *National on-Campus Report.*

WILSON, W., and DURRENBERGER, R. (1982). Comparison of rape and attempted rape victims. *Psychological Rep.* 50: 198.

35

▼▼▼▼

Battered Wives

▼▼▼▼

Kathleen J. Ferraro
John M. Johnson

ABSTRACT: Why do battered women stay in abusive relationships? The authors'
interviews with battered women and participant observation at a shelter for
abused women disclose that battered women rationalize violence by (1) appeal
to the salvation ethic, (2) denial of the victimizer, (3) denial of injury, (4) denial
of victimization, (5) denial of options, and (6) appeal to higher loyalties. Battered
women come to view themselves as true victims of abuse for six reasons: (1) a
change in the level of violence, (2) a change in resources, (3) a change in the
relationship, (4) despair, (5) a change in the visibility of violence, and (6) external
definitions.

. . . Why do battered women stay in abusive relationships? Some observers answer facilely that they must like it. The masochism thesis was
the predominant response of psychiatrists writing about battering in the
1960s (Saul, 1972; Snell et al., 1964). More sympathetic studies of the
problem have revealed the difficulties of disentangling oneself from a
violent relationship (Hilberman, 1980; Martin, 1976; Walker, 1979).
These studies point to the social and cultural expectations of women

and their status within the nuclear family as reasons for the reluctance of battered women to flee the relationship. The socialization of women emphasizes the primary value of being a good wife and mother, at the expense of personal achievement in other spheres of life. . . . Economic conditions contribute to the dependency of women on men. . . .

Material and cultural conditions are the background in which personal interpretations of events are developed. Women who depend on their husbands for practical support also depend on them as sources of self-esteem, emotional support, and continuity. This [chapter] looks at how women make sense of their victimization within the context of these dependencies. . . .

THE DATA

. . . We were participant observers at a shelter for battered women located in the southwestern United States. . . . During the time of the research, 120 women passed through the shelter; they brought with them 165 children. The women ranged in age from 17 to 68, generally had family incomes below $15,000, and did not work outside the home. The characteristics of shelter residents are summarized in Table 35.1.

We established personal relationships with each of these women, and kept records of their experiences and verbal accounts. We also tape-recorded informal conversations, staff meetings, and crisis phone conversations with battered women. . . . Finally, we taped interviews with ten residents and five battered women who had left their abusers without entering the shelter. All quotes in this [chapter] are taken from our notes and tapes. . . .

Rationalizing Violence

Marriages and their unofficial counterparts develop through the efforts of each partner to maintain feelings of love and intimacy. In modern, Western cultures, the value placed on marriage is high; individuals invest a great amount of emotion in their spouses, and expect a return on that investment. The majority of women who marry still adopt the roles of wives and mothers as primary identities, even when they work outside the home, and thus have a strong motivation to succeed in their domestic roles. . . . Levels of commitment vary widely, but some degree of commitment is implicit in the marriage contract.

When marital conflicts emerge there is usually some effort to negotiate an agreement or bargain, to ensure the continuity of the relationship (Scanzoni, 1972). Couples employ a variety of strategies, depending on

Table 35.1 **Demographic Characteristics of Shelter Residents During First Year of Operation (N = 120)**

Age		Education	
–17	2%	Elementary school	2%
18–24	33%	Junior high	8%
25–34	43%	Some high school	28%
35–44	14%	High school graduate	43%
45–54	6%	Some college	14%
55+	1%	College graduate	2%
		Graduate school	1%

Ethnicity		Number of Children	
White	78%	0	19%
Black	3%	1	42%
Mexican-American	10%	2	21%
American Indian	8%	3	15%
Other	1%	4	2%
		5+	1%
		Pregnant	7%

Family Income		Employment Status	
–$5,000	27%	Full time	23%
$ 6,000–10,000	36%	Part time	8%
$11,000–15,000	10%	Housewife	54%
$16,000+	10%	Student	5%
No response*	17%	Not employed	8%
		Receiving welfare	2%

*Many women had no knowledge of their husbands' income.

the nature and extent of resources available to them, to resolve conflicts without dissolving relationships. . . .

In describing conflict-management, Spiegel (1968) distinguishes between "role induction" and "role modification." Role induction refers to conflict in which "one or the other parties to the conflict agrees, submits, goes along with, becomes convinced, or is persuaded in some way" (1968:402). Role modification, on the other hand, involves adaptations by both partners. Role induction seems particularly applicable to battered women who accommodate their husbands' abuse. Rather than seeking help or escaping, as people typically do when attacked by strangers, battered women often rationalize violence from their husbands, at least initially. . . . In a U.S. study of 350 battered women, Pagelow (1981) found the median length of stay after violence began was four years; some left in less than one year, others stayed as long as 42 years.

. . . Despite the development of the international shelter movement, changes in police practices, and legislation to protect battered women since 1975, it remains extraordinarily difficult for a battered woman to escape a violent husband determined to maintain his control. At least one woman, Mary Parziale, has been murdered by an abusive husband while residing in a shelter (Beverly, 1978); others have been murdered after leaving shelters to establish new, independent homes (Garcia, 1978). When these practical and social constraints are combined with love for and commitment to an abuser, it is obvious that there is a strong incentive—often a practical necessity—to rationalize violence.

Previous research on the rationalizations of deviant offenders has revealed a typology of "techniques of neutralization," which allow offenders to view their actions as normal, acceptable, or at least justifiable (Sykes and Matza, 1957). A similar typology can be constructed for victims. Extending the concepts developed by Sykes and Matza, we assigned the responses of battered women we interviewed to one of six categories of rationalization: (1) the appeal to the salvation ethic; (2) the denial of the victimizer; (3) the denial of injury; (4) the denial of victimization; (5) the denial of options; and (6) the appeal to higher loyalties. The women usually employed at least one of these techniques to make sense of their situations; often they employed two or more, simultaneously or over time.

1. *The appeal to the salvation ethic:* This rationalization is grounded in a woman's desire to be of service to others. Abusing husbands are viewed as deeply troubled, perhaps "sick," individuals, dependent on their wives' nurturance for survival. Battered women place their own safety and happiness below their commitment to "saving my man" from whatever malady they perceive as the source of their husbands' problems (Ferraro, 1979). The appeal to the salvation ethic is a common response to an alcoholic or drug-dependent abuser. The battered partners of substance-abusers frequently describe the charming, charismatic personality of their sober mates, viewing this appealing personality as the "real man" being destroyed by disease. They then assume responsibility for helping their partners to overcome their problems, viewing the batterings they receive as an index of their partners' pathology. Abuse must be endured while helping the man return to his "normal" self. One woman said:

> I thought I was going to be Florence Nightingale. He had so much potential; I could see how good he really was, and I was going to "save" him. I thought I was the only thing keeping him going, and that if I left he'd lose his job and wind up in jail. I'd make excuses to everybody for him. I'd call work and lie when he was drunk, saying he was sick. I never criticized him, because he needed my approval.

2. *The denial of the victimizer:* This technique is similar to the salvation ethic, except that victims do not assume responsibility for solving their

abusers' problems. Women perceive battering as an event beyond the control of both spouses, and blame it on some external force. The violence is judged situational and temporary, because it is linked to unusual circumstances or a sickness which can be cured. Pressures at work, the loss of a job, or legal problems are all situations which battered women assume as the causes of their partners' violence. Mental illness, alcoholism, and drug addiction are also viewed as external, uncontrollable afflictions by many battered women who accept the medical perspective on such problems. By focusing on factors beyond the control of their abuser, women deny their husbands' intent to do them harm, and thus rationalize violent episodes.

> He's sick. He didn't used to be this way, but he can't handle alcohol. It's really like a disease, being an alcoholic. . . . I think too that this is what he saw at home, his father is a very violent man, and alcoholic too, so it's really not his fault, because this is all he has ever known.

3. *The denial of injury:* For some women, the experience of being battered by a spouse is so discordant with their expectations that they simply refuse to acknowledge it. When hospitalization is not required—and it seldom is for most cases of battering—routines quickly return to normal. Meals are served, jobs and schools are attended, and daily chores completed. Even with lingering pain, bruises, and cuts, the normality of everyday life overrides the strange, confusing memory of the attack. When husbands refuse to discuss or acknowledge the event, in some cases even accusing their wives of insanity, women sometimes come to believe the violence never occurred. The denial of injury does not mean that women feel no pain. They know they are hurt, but define the hurt as tolerable or normal. Just as individuals tolerate a wide range of physical discomfort before seeking medical help, battered women tolerate a wide range of physical abuse before defining it as an injurious assault. One woman explained her disbelief at her first battering:

> I laid in bed and cried all night. I could not believe it had happened, and I didn't want to believe it. We had only been married a year, and I was pregnant and excited about starting a family. Then all of a sudden, this! The next morning he told me he was sorry and it wouldn't happen again, and I gladly kissed and made up. I wanted to forget the whole thing, and wouldn't let myself worry about what it meant for us.

4. *The denial of victimization:* Victims often blame themselves for the violence, thereby neutralizing the responsibility of the spouse. Pagelow (1981) found that 99.4 percent of battered women felt they did not deserve to be beaten, and 51 percent said they had done nothing to provoke an attack. The battered women in our sample did not believe violence against them was justified, but some felt it could have been avoided if they had been more passive and conciliatory. Both Pagelow's

and our samples are biased in this area, because they were made up almost entirely of women who had already left their abusers, and thus would have been unlikely to feel major responsibility for the abuse they received. Retrospective accounts of victimization in our sample, however, did reveal evidence that some women believed their right to leave violent men was restricted by their participation in the conflicts. One subject said:

> Well, I couldn't really do anything about it, because I did ask for it. I knew how to get at him, and I'd keep after it and keep after it until he got fed up and knocked me right out. I can't say I like it, but I shouldn't have nagged him like I did.

As Pagelow (1981) noted, there is a difference between provocation and justification. A battered woman's belief that her actions angered her spouse to the point of violence is not synonymous with the belief that violence was therefore *justified*. But belief in provocation may diminish a woman's capacity for retaliation or self-defense, because it blurs her concept of responsibility. A woman's acceptance of responsibility for the violent incident is encouraged by an abuser who continually denigrates her and makes unrealistic demands. Depending on the social supports available, and the personality of the battered woman, the man's accusations of inadequacy may assume the status of truth. Such beliefs of inferiority inhibit the development of a notion of victimization.

5. *The denial of options:* This technique is composed of two elements: practical options and emotional options. Practical options, including alternative housing, source of income, and protection from an abuser, are clearly limited by the patriarchal structure of Western society. However, there are differences in the ways battered women respond to these obstacles, ranging from determined struggle to acquiescence. For a variety of reasons, some battered women do not take full advantage of the practical opportunities which are available to escape, and some return to abusers voluntarily even after establishing an independent lifestyle. Others ignore the most severe constraints in their efforts to escape their relationships. For example, one resident of the shelter we observed walked 30 miles in her bedroom slippers to get to the shelter, and required medical attention for blisters and cuts to her feet. On the other hand, a woman who had a full-time job, had rented an apartment, and had been given by the shelter all the clothes, furniture, and basics necessary to set up housekeeping, returned to her husband two weeks after leaving the shelter. Other women refused to go to job interviews, keep appointments with social workers, or move out of the state for their protection (Ferraro, 1981b). Such actions are frightening for women who have led relatively isolated or protected lives, but failure to take action leaves few alternatives to a violent marriage. The belief of battered women that they will not be able to make it on their own—a belief often

fueled by years of abuse and oppression—is a major impediment to [acknowledgment] that one is a victim and taking action.

The denial of *emotional* options imposes still further restrictions. Battered women may feel that no one else can provide intimacy and companionship. While physical beating is painful and dangerous, the prospect of a lonely, celibate existence is often too frightening to risk. It is not uncommon for battered women to express the belief that their abuser is the only man they could love, thus severely limiting their opportunities to discover new, more supportive relationships. One woman said:

> He's all I've got. My dad's gone, and my mother disowned me when I married him. And he's really special. He understands me, and I understand him. Nobody could take his place.

6. *The appeal to higher loyalties:* This appeal involves enduring battering for the sake of some higher commitment, either religious or traditional. The Christian belief that women should serve their husbands as men serve God is invoked as a rationalization to endure a husband's violence for later rewards in the afterlife. . . . Other women have a strong commitment to the nuclear family, and find divorce repugnant. They may believe that for their children's sake, any marriage is better than no marriage. One woman we interviewed divorced her husband of 35 years after her last child left home. More commonly women who have survived violent relationships for that long do not have the desire or strength to divorce and begin a new life. When the appeal to higher loyalties is employed as a strategy to cope with battering, commitment to and involvement with an ideal overshadows the mundane reality of violence.

CATALYSTS FOR CHANGE

Rationalization is a way of coping with a situation in which, for either practical or emotional reasons, or both, a battered woman is stuck. For some women, the situation and the beliefs that rationalize it, may continue for a lifetime. For others, changes may occur within the relationship, within individuals, or in available resources which serve as catalysts for redefining the violence. When battered women reject prior rationalizations and begin to view themselves as true victims of abuse, the victimization process begins.

There are a variety of catalysts for redefining abuse; we discuss six. . . .

1. *A change in the level of violence:* . . . What [seems] to serve as a catalyst is a sudden change in the relative level of violence. Women who suddenly realize that battering may be fatal may reject rationalizations

in order to save their lives. One woman who had been severely beaten by an alcoholic husband for many years explained her decision to leave on the basis of a direct threat to her life.

> It was like a pendulum. He'd swing to the extremes both ways. He'd get drunk and beat me up, then he'd get sober and treat me like a queen. One day he put a gun to my head and pulled the trigger. It wasn't loaded. But that's when I decided I'd had it. I sued for separation of property. I knew what was coming again, so I got out. I didn't want to. I still loved the guy, but I knew I had to for my own sanity. . . .

2. *A change in resources:* Although some women rationalize cohabiting with an abuser by claiming they have no options, others begin reinterpreting violence when the resources necessary for escape become available. The emergence of safe homes or shelters since 1970 has produced a new resource for battered women. . . . One 55-year-old woman discussed this catalyst:

> I stayed with him because I didn't want my kids to have the same life I did. My parents were divorced, and I was always so ashamed of that. . . . Yes, they're all on their own now, so there's no reason left to stay.

3. *A change in the relationship:* Walker (1979), in discussing the stages of a battering relationship, notes that violent incidents are usually followed by periods of remorse and solicitude. Such phases deepen the emotional bonds, and make rejection of an abuser more difficult. But as battering progresses, periods of remorse may shorten, or disappear, eliminating the basis for maintaining a positive outlook on the marriage. After a number of episodes of violence, a man may realize that his victim will not retaliate or escape, and thus feel no need to express remorse. Extended periods devoid of kindness or love may alter a woman's feelings toward her partner so much so that she eventually begins to define herself as a victim of abuse. One woman recalled:

> At first, you know, we used to have so much fun together. He has kind've, you know, a magnetic personality; he can be really charming. But it isn't fun anymore. Since the baby came, it's changed completely. He just wants me to stay at home, while he goes out with his friends. He doesn't even talk to me, most of the time. . . . No, I don't really love him anymore, not like I did.

4. *Despair:* Changes in the relationship may result in a loss of hope that "things will get better." When hope is destroyed and replaced by despair, rationalizations of violence may give way to the recognition of victimization. . . .

5. *A change in the visibility of violence:* Creating a web of rationalizations to overlook violence is accomplished more easily if no intruders are present to question their validity. Since most violence between couples occurs in private, there are seldom conflicting interpretations of the

event from outsiders. . . . If violence does occur in the presence of others, it may trigger a reinterpretation process. Battering in private is degrading, but battering in public is humiliating, for it is a statement of subordination and powerlessness. Having others witness abuse may create intolerable feelings of shame which undermine prior rationalizations.

> He never hit me in public before—it was always at home. But the Saturday I got back (returned to husband from shelter), we went Christmas shopping and he slapped me in the store because of some stupid joke I made. People saw it, I know, I felt so stupid, like, they must all think what a jerk I am, what a sick couple, and I thought, "God, I must be crazy to let him do this."

6. *External definitions of the relationship:* A change in visibility is usually accomplished by the interjection of external definitions of abuse. External definitions vary depending on their source and the situation; they either reinforce or undermine rationalizations. Battered women who request help frequently find others—and especially officials—don't believe their story or are unsympathetic (Pagelow, 1981; Pizzey, 1974). . . . One young woman discussed how lack of support from her family left her without hope:

> It wouldn't be so bad if my own family gave a damn about me. . . . Yeah, they know I'm here, and they don't care. They didn't care about me when I was a kid, so why should they care now? I got raped and beat as a kid, and now I get beat as an adult. Life is a big joke.

Clearly, such responses from family members contribute to the belief among battered women that there are no alternatives and that they must tolerate the abuse. However, when outsiders respond with unqualified support of the victim and condemnation of violent men, their definitions can be a potent catalyst toward victimization. Friends and relatives who show genuine concern for a woman's well-being may initiate an awareness of danger which contradicts previous rationalizations.

> My mother-in-law knew what was going on, but she wouldn't admit it. . . . I said, "Mom, what do you think these bruises are?" and she said "Well, some people just bruise easy. I do it all the time, bumping into things". . . . And he just denied it, pretended like nothing happened, and if I'd said I wanted to talk about it, he'd say, "life goes on, you can't just dwell on things". . . . But this time, my neighbor *knew* what happened, she saw it, and when he denied it, she said, "I can't believe it! You know that's not true!" . . . and I was so happy that finally, somebody else saw what was goin' on, and I just told him then that this time I wasn't gonna' come home!

CONCLUSION

Shelters for battered women serve not only as material resources, but as sources of external definitions which contribute to the victimization process. They offer refuge from a violent situation in which a woman may contemplate her circumstances and what she wants to do about them. Within a shelter, women meet counselors and other battered women who are familiar with rationalizations of violence and the reluctance to give up commitment to a spouse. In counseling sessions, and informal conversations with other residents, women hear horror stories from others who have already defined themselves as victims. They are supported for expressing anger and rejecting responsibility for their abuse (Ferraro, 1981a). The goal of many shelters is to overcome feelings of guilt and inadequacy so that women can make choices in their best interests. In this atmosphere, violent incidents are reexamined and redefined as assaults in which the woman was victimized. . . .

No systematic research has been conducted on the influence children exert on their battered mothers, but it seems obvious that the willingness of children to leave a violent father would be an important factor in a woman's desire to leave.

The relevance of these catalysts to a woman's interpretation of violence vary with her own situation and personality. The process of rejecting rationalizations and becoming a victim is ambiguous, confusing, and emotional. . . .

REFERENCES

BEVERLY. 1978. "Shelter resident murdered by husband." Aegis, September/October:13.

FERRARO, KATHLEEN J. 1979. "Hard love: Letting go of an abusive husband." Frontiers 4(2)16–18.

———.1981a. "Battered women and the shelter movement." Unpublished Ph.D. dissertation, Arizona State University.

———.1981b. "Processing battered women." Journal of Family Issues 2(4):415–438.

GARCIA, DICK. 1978. "Slain women 'lived in fear'" The Times (Erie, Pa.) June 14:B1.

HILBERMAN, ELAINE. 1980. "Overview: The 'wife-beater's wife' reconsidered." American Journal of Psychiatry 137 (11):1336–1347.

MARTIN, DEL. 1976. Battered Wives. San Francisco: Glide.

PAGELOW, MILDRED DALEY. 1981. Woman-Battering. Beverly Hills: Sage.

PIZZEY, ERIN. 1974. Scream Quietly or the Neighbors Will Hear. Baltimore: Penguin.

SAUL, LEON J. 1972. "Personal and social psychopathology and the primary prevention of violence." American Journal of Psychiatry 128 (12):1578–1581.

SCANZONI, JOHN. 1972. Sexual Bargaining. Englewood Cliffs, N.J.: Prentice-Hall.

SNELL, JOHN E., RICHARD ROSENWALD, and AMES ROBEY. 1964. "The wifebeater's wife: A study of family interaction." Archives of General Psychiatry 11 (August): 107–112.

SPIEGEL, JOHN P. 1968. "The resolution of role conflict within the family." Pp. 391–411 in N. W. Bell and E. F. Vogel (eds.), A Modern Introduction to the Family. New York: Free Press.

SYKES, GRESHAM M., and DAVID MATZA. 1957. "Techniques of neutralization: A theory of delinquency." American Sociological Review 22 (6):667–670.

WALKER, LENORE E. 1979. The Battered Woman. New York: Harper & Row.

36

▼▼▼▼

Explaining Family Violence

▼▼▼▼

Murray A. Straus

ABSTRACT: A nationally representative sample of 2,143 families shows that each year 12 of every 100 husbands attack their wives, and the same number of wives attack their husbands. Wives are more likely to be injured. Violence by parents to children, and siblings to one another, is much higher. Three primary causes of marital violence are the unintentional teaching of violence by parents who use physical punishment, cultural norms that tolerate violence in the family, and sexual inequality that both creates violence and forces women to put up with it. Other causes include poverty, unemployment, social isolation, and various other stresses. No one factor is *the* cause of family violence.

We hear so much about violence in the family these days that it may not be necessary to start out by detailing how much there is. In fact, I was going to skip doing so. But I changed my mind because on the way to this conference I was reading a book by one of my most esteemed colleagues in sociology of the family—one of the best known people in the country. In commenting on the findings concerning physical aggression he says, "The frequency of wives' violence [this was a study of women only] is relatively modest among our respondents. Eighty-six percent state that they never hit their husbands.''

What do you think of that? Would you call it a ''modest'' amount of violence if I said that 86 percent of this audience never hit one another during the time that they are here at this conference? I think you would realize that 14 percent of you hit one of the other people, and you would be shocked. The point is that there are implicit cultural norms or rules which make violence in the family more acceptable, less wrong, if you will, than violence outside the family. A 14 percent rate of violence in any group would be intolerable.

This discrepancy points to a very important part of the explanation for the high rate of family violence. It suggests that there are implicit cultural norms tolerating violence within families. In the case of parents and children there are also implicit norms in the form of the legal right of parents to hit kids. Ironically, if a child is sent to reform school he or she is safer from the risk of being assaulted by an adult than at home. Reform-school personnel do not have the legal right to hit children, but you and I do. And I did. I don't mean that I was a big hitter, but I used physical punishment when my kids were little. We've found that almost everyone in our society does—for example, 97 percent of parents of three-year-olds. Between husbands and wives, the toleration of violence by the people involved and the society make the marriage license a hitting license. Of course, it is not an unlimited license. Nevertheless, there is an implicit, unrealized, but nevertheless widely followed rule, which says that it is ''understandable'' or less wrong for husbands and wives to hit each other than the same act would be in other settings.

THE STATISTICS

How much violence do we as a society license in families? Before our research at New Hampshire we really only knew this at two ends of a continuum. Murder statistics provide the evidence at the high violence end of the continuum. It has been known for years that the most frequent category of relationship between murderer and victim is that of a member of the same family. That is true in a great many societies. I tracked down the data from 18 different societies, including European, American, African, and a province in North Central India.

At the other extreme is physical punishment. Most people do not consider that to be violence. Let us compare physical punishment with the definition of violence used in the Family Violence Research Program: An act carried out with the intention of causing physical pain or injuries to another person. There is no part of physical punishment that does not fit that definition. The pain is there, even if it is usually supposed to be light. But if a child does not indicate that it hurts, a typical parent's reaction is to hit harder. Why don't we consider that violence? Because it is legitimate; i.e., it is socially acceptable to hit your own child. A kind of moral alchemy converts what in any other circumstances would be considered "violence" to something which is not violence. Aside from these two extremes—ordinary physical punishment and murder—there were no good statistics on family violence; for example, nothing dependable on husbands hitting wives, child abuse, serious violence between children, or children hitting their parents.

A NATIONAL STUDY

To fill this gap, we set out to do a study of a nationally representative sample of American families.* The study included 2,143 families in all parts of the country and all walks of life. They were selected by random processing so that they were truly representative. We have compared it with every bit of available census data. Our sample ties in precisely.

Although the sample is representative, it does not necessarily mean that we got the right information. It does not mean that everyone told all. When you knock on someone's door and, in effect, ask: "When did you stop beating your wife?" there are certain problems in getting that information which took us several years to work out. As you can well understand, when we started out, eight of ten people did not grant an interview. By the time we did this survey the figure was reversed. Eight out of ten agreed to participate. I don't have time to tell you the techniques that we used to do that, but they are described in an article called "The Conflict Tactic Scales," which appeared in *The Journal of Marriage and the Family*.

Although the pretest interview went well, we were still worried because the interviewing was done by a national survey organization, Response Analysis Corporation. Even though they are an excellent organization, and even though we trained their interviewers in our techniques, it is still not the same thing as when you and people you work with do it. I was rather concerned all the time the field work was going on that we would end up with a stack of some 2,000 interviews, all neatly filled out, in which no one said they ever lifted a finger. When the first tabulations were done I had the somewhat funny feeling of saying, "Hurray, there is all that violence out there!" Indeed, there is.

*This article summarizes some of the work carried out by the Family Violence Research Program at the University of New Hampshire. There have been nine books and over 100 articles in the decade since the beginning of that program. A program bibliography and order form for reprints will be sent on request. The work has been supported by the Graduate School of the University of New Hampshire and by grants from the National Institute of Mental Health.

HUSBAND-WIFE VIOLENCE

Let us start with violence between husband and wife. Our survey showed that each year about 16 out of every 100 couples experience a violent incident. "Violent incident" means anything from a slap, push, or shove, on up to an attack with a knife or gun.

There are a lot of people who say these figures are wrong because most of it is slaps and pushes and not "really violence." That again illustrates the different standards we have for the family. We would never tolerate slaps and shoves from our colleagues.

Sixteen percent means that each year seven and one-half million couples experience a violent incident. However, to deal with critics who say they are interested in "real violence," we separated out just those acts which carry a high risk of injury—those that go beyond pushing, slapping, shoving, and throwing things. The lists includes punching, kicking, biting, hitting with objects, repeated acts of beating up, and attacks with a knife or gun. Out of that 16 percent, 6 percent experienced one or more severe assaults, roughly equivalent to an aggravated assault if it were outside the family. Or putting it in terms of the number of families, each year almost three million American couples experience a serious injury-threatening assault from a spouse.

This makes assault statistics published by the FBI miniscule. The FBI figures are rates per one hundred *thousand*. These are rates per *hundred*. If the same denominator is used, severe assaults between spouses occur 33 times more often than other assaults. It is figures like these that lead me to say that a typical citizen walking down the most dangerous street in Lincoln, Omaha, or Chicago is safe compared to being in an average American home. Statistically, there is simply no doubt about it. But we don't realize it because the moral alchemy that I mentioned before converts the attack from violence into something else.

Husbands versus Wives

Another interesting thing which has important implications for strengthening families and preventing violence is revealed by comparing family violence rates according to who does it—the husband or the wife. Twelve out of every 100 husbands attack their wives each year, and the rate is almost identical for wives. This came as a great surprise and a considerable source of embarrassment to me. In fact, at first I didn't believe the figures. But we've replicated it five times with five different samples. And other investigators have, also. Consequently, I am absolutely convinced that is a true figure, although it masks something very important.

The Short End

What it masks is that, even though women are just as violent as their husbands, they are the predominant victims. Women end up on the short end of things overwhelmingly. I can illustrate this by one of the very first interviews I ever did on violence in the family. I was very hesitant in those days about "popping" the question. I finally got around to asking a young man whether anyone, either he or his wife, had ever pushed, shoved, slapped, or thrown something at one another when they had an argument or hassle. He said, "Yes, I was running around with another woman and I wouldn't listen to her. She had gotten angrier and angrier over a period of time. One morning she threw a coffee pot at me." He then went on to something else. Luckily, I came back to it because, later in the interview, it turned out that *she* was the one who ended up black and blue. That is a typical scenario.

Women are also the main economic victims of family violence. If the marriage breaks up because of violence, studies of the economic consequences of marriage disruption show that women suffer much greater financially than men. In over 90 percent of the cases, the children stay with the mother. Yet women earn only about half of what men earn. Child support payments rarely help because almost all men default wholly or partially on child support payments within a couple of years.

Women are also the main victims psychologically. If the marriage goes wrong, we tend to wonder what *she* did wrong. Women, especially, tend to blame themselves for what went wrong in the marriage, even though at the same time they are protesting what a so-and-so he is.

PARENTAL VIOLENCE

Any violence toward a child is so universal I didn't even give the statistics in Table 36.1. For infants and children under four, any departure from 99 percent is mostly measurement error. So the data in Table 36.1 are restricted to severe violence—anything that went beyond spanking, slapping, shoving, pushing, or throwing things. The rate for more severe violence by parents shows that 14 out of every 100 children, or six and one-half million children every year, minimum, are "abused" seriously, i.e., assaulted, by their parents.

These are truly underestimates of the amount of child abuse in the United States. The true figures are probably double. The highest risk age of child abuse is infancy, but for reasons I don't have time to explain, the study excluded children under three. We also excluded single-parent families because we were interested in studying violence be-

Table 36.1   How Violent Are American Families?*

	Annual Incidence per 100 Couples or Children	Number of Couples or Children
Violence Between Husband and Wife		
Any violence during the year	16	7,500,000
Severe violence (high risk of injury)	6	2,900,000
Any violence by the husband during the year	12	5,700,000
Severe violence by the husband during the year	4	1,800,000
Any violence by the wife during the year	12	5,500,000
Severe violence by the wife during the year	5	2,200,000
Violence by Parents		
Any violence against a child during the year	Near 100% for young children	
Severe violence (high risk of injury)	14	6,500,000
Very severe violence by parent	3.5	1,700,000
Any violence against 15–17 year-olds	34	3,200,000
Severe violence against 15–17 year-olds	6	600,000
Very severe violence against 15–17 year-olds	3.4	400,000
Violence by Children		
Any violence against a brother or sister	80	37,600,000
Severe violence against a brother or sister	53	25,000,000
Any violence against a parent	18	8,300,000
Severe violence against a parent	9	4,300,000
Violence by Children Age 15–17		
Any violence against a brother or sister	64	6,000,000
Severe violence against a brother or sister	36	3,400,000
Any violence against a parent	10	1,000,000
Severe violence against a parent	3.5	400,000

*Data from a nationally representative sample of 2,143 families.

tween the parents as well as by the parents. This could also lead to an underestimate because it is widely believed that child abuse is higher in single-parent families due to the difficulty and stress and strain of the parent bringing up kids without the aid of a partner.

Some people object to these figures because the acts used to compute the rate of child abuse include hitting with an object. They are willing to consider that abuse if it is done by a husband against a wife or a wife against a husband, but for many people, hitting a child with an object is not abuse. They might call it "strong discipline," but not "abuse." To satisfy these people, I recomputed the child abuse rate without "hitting with an object." Even this produces a rate of 3.5 out of every 100 who are severely assaulted, or a total of 1,700,000 every year. That is several times higher than the figures published by the National Center on Child Abuse and Neglect. The difference is mostly because the National Center deals with officially reported cases, and most cases of child abuse never get into the official reporting system.

"Or Else"

One of the things that got me started in family violence research was discovering that half of the high school seniors I was studying for another purpose had been hit or seriously threatened with being hit ("do this or else") by their parents during the year they were seniors in high school. I found that very hard to believe, because I thought physical punishment was for little kids. But, it keeps coming out that way. For example, Table 36.1 shows that in this national sample of 15- to 17-year-olds, the parents themselves reported hitting 34 out of every 100 of those kids. That is when the parents reported it. In other studies, we asked the kids, and the figure is much higher—roughly double.

VIOLENT CHILDREN

Let me skip down Table 36.1 now to violence by children. Any violence against a brother or sister—you can see that it is 80 out of a 100. Kids will fight. Fifty-three out of that 80 are severe attacks. Of course being punched or bitten by a four-year-old is different than being punched or bitten by a fourteen-year-old, although one lays the groundwork for another. Therefore, just taking the 15- to 17-year-olds, 64 percent were reported by their parents as having hit a brother or sister during the previous year, and 36 out of this 64 severely attacked a brother or sister during the year. What this boils down to is that children are the most violent people of all in American families. Since these are the future spouses and parents, that has a lot to say about why there is child abuse and wife abuse.

Kids also attacked their parents. Eighteen out of 100 hit their parents during the year. Nine of those 18 attacks, or half of them, were severe violence. Of course we again have to consider the difference between an attack of a four-year-old versus a 17-year-old. However, taking just 15- to 17-year olds, 10 out of every 100 were reported by their parents as having hit them. About a third of these instances involved a severe assault on the parent.

WHY SO MUCH VIOLENCE
IN AMERICAN FAMILIES?

These figures should make clear that the family is preeminent in all kinds of violence. At the same time, the family is also the most loving and supportive institution. Unraveling that paradox is what we have been working on in the Family Violence Research Program for the past ten years.

Family Training in Violence

There are many reasons for the high rate of violence in families. One of the most fundamental reasons is that families actually train people to be violent. The training is partly intentional, but for the most part unwitting. Another fundamental factor is the sexist structure of the family and society. Family violence is not going to suddenly end if we change these two factors, but it will almost certainly be reduced.

Physical Punishment

Physical punishment of children is extremely important in accounting for the high level of family violence. The training in violence provided unintentionally by physical punishment has a life-long effect. Let us look at what goes on in physical punishment. It typically starts in infancy. When I talk to parents, I am frequently greeted with incredulous looks. They say, "Well the child can't talk, can't understand." Large numbers of parents think that is the time when you have to slap.

One irate father said to me once, "What am I going to do? Give them a lecture on the germ theory?" I had given the example of an infant crawling on the ground, picking up stuff, and putting it in his or her mouth as infants do to find out about the world. Mommy or daddy says,

"Don't do that, you'll get sick." Of course the child does not understand the concept of getting sick. He or she only understands about finding out about all the wonderful things in the world and proceeds to do it again. At this point, mommy or daddy comes over and says, "No, no, you'll get sick," and gives the child a gentle tap on the hand. This is an act of love and concern, no question about it.

But it also lays the basis for child abuse and wife-beating. Why does it do this? How can that act of love and concern teach violence? Let us assume (even though it is not necessarily true) that slapping the child's hand helps the child to learn to avoid putting a dirty object in the mouth. The catch is that some other things are also being learned. One of them is that those who love you are those who hit you. In fact, they are the only ones who hit you. Who else is going to slap an infant except mommy or daddy, or maybe brother or sister? That helps establish the link between love and violence that is so pervasive in our society and, indeed, in most societies, because most societies use physical punishment.

Freud and many others believe that the link between love and violence is a biological linkage. I happen to believe that it is a deeply *learned* pattern. It is so ingrained because people get 18 years of training in the linkage between love and violence—starting before speech in infancy and not ending for half of all American children until they physically leave home. That is 18 years of intensive training in the link between love and violence.

Even more damaging, ironically, is the fact that physical punishment is usually an act done out of love and concern. Consequently, it teaches not only that those who love you are going to hit you, but also that it is morally right, because they are doing it for your own good. I can't tell you how many husbands and wives I've interviewed who have said to me, in effect, like this guy and the coffee pot, "I deserved it." That is how the man whose wife threw a coffee pot at him felt. He said, "I was running around with this other woman and I wasn't listening to reason and I deserved it." You may think this guy is being two-faced because the wife ended up black and blue, but he was simply following another rule about violence in the American families.

IMPLICIT CULTURAL NORMS PERMITTING
FAMILY VIOLENCE

In fact, there are many rules about violence, as about most aspects of life. One very important rule that most parents teach their children is "if hit, hit back," I got into some considerable trouble with my neighbors when we taught our kids the opposite: "If hit, do not hit back. Try to settle it some other way and if that doesn't work, just leave.'' Our neighbors, however, were concerned with what one called, ''John's moral development.'' Another had less polite terms that we found out about in a roundabout way. That was not just a peculiarity of my neighborhood. A national survey found that 75 percent of all Americans felt it is good for boys to get in fist fights when they are growing up.

So the family also engages in explicit training in violence. It teaches us the whole script for violence: that love and violence go together, that it is morally right, and when and how to do it.

When I said the marriage license is a hitting license, I also said it is not an unlimited license. It has limitations like a driver's license. You can't go 90 miles an hour down 33rd street. Similarly, there is a speed limit on the hitting license. The national speed limit, so to speak, is that you can't hit anyone hard enough to send him or her to a doctor. There are local and family differences in the upper and lower limits. There are also certain rules that you have to follow in order to use the license at all. One rule is that hitting can only be done if another family member is doing wrong, and that it is something really important, and that ''they won't listen to reason.'' Then you can hit, not that it is good, but it is understandable and right. Both the speed limit and these rules are learned through physical punishment. For example, the rules I just listed are the adult version of the ''Johnny, I have told you ten times rule'' that almost all of us have learned as kids.

That may seem like an appropriate rule, but ironically it is that very rule, that very set of restrictions on the hitting license, that makes violence in the family and between spouses so widespread. The reason is that restrictions imply that there are circumstances when hitting *is* permitted or at least tolerated. That makes the family unique among civilian institutions in our society. Every other group operates on the opposite set of rules, namely, that under no circumstances can one person hit another. If other groups, such as departments in a university, used the same rules as the family, the hall of academe would be literally, not just figuratively, bloody, because academic life, like family life, is full of strong beliefs and attachments and bitter disagreements.

In every family, and in every university department, sooner or later someone is going to be ''unreasonable'' about an important issue. In the family that is likely to result in violence, whereas in academic life, physical violence is extremely unlikely. The reason, as I said before, is that the two institutions operate on fundamentally different sets of implicit cultural norms about violence. In academic departments, the use of physical force is prohibited and violations are not tolerated, even if the wrongs committed are felt to be truly outrageous. One of my department colleagues, for example, has felt this way about me ever since we had a major disagreement nine years ago. He thinks I have done horrible moral wrongs. For the last nine years he won't even get in the same elevator with me. The first time this happened, I said to myself, "I'm glad I'm not married to him." Fortunately, the rules of the game are different than in the family so I am in no danger.

ALTERNATIVES

Is it possible to change the rules so that, in the family as elsewhere, no one has a right to hit anyone? Yes, but making the new rules stick is another matter. We had prohibition and people continued to drink. The rules do need to be changed, along with other aspects of the family that are even more fundamental. Consequently, reducing violence in the family is going to be a long-term effort. A high priority part of that effort should be directed toward reducing the amount of physical punishment used by parents. The importance of this can be seen from the findings on physical punishment in our national sample. They show clearly that the more a respondent was hit as a child, the higher the rate of wife-beating (Straus, 1982).

Unfortunately, just urging parents not to spank is more likely to arouse resentment than to change parents' behavior. The reason is, quite simply, that most parents don't know what else to do. We, as family life educators, must be able to offer parents practical alternatives before they are going to give up physical punishment. Parents have an obligation to train, control, and instruct. We have an obligation to teach them how to do it without unintentionally teaching the virtues of violence. There are few things that can make a more positive contribution to strengthening families.

SEXIST STRUCTURE OF THE FAMILY

A large part of the violence that goes on is because men can draw on their average greater height, weight, and better-developed muscles to have the final say, to be the "head of the family." If we could move to a true equalitarian family, that would help a great deal. As in the case of eliminating physical punishment, such a move will not be easy. It requires eliminating the built-in disabilities that women suffer from in our society, especially the economic disadvantages that make women dependent on men and therefore account for so much of why women stay and put up with it.

Women who are employed full-time—leaving out the half of married women who are full-time housewives and those who are employed part-time—only earn 59 cents on the dollar (i.e., 59 percent of what men earn). If they are being physically attacked by their husbands, they have some pretty miserable economic choices. At the back of their mind, most women know that they cannot depend on child support payments, and that they will have to support the children despite earning far less. Consequently, for many women it boils down to a choice between putting up with the violence or living in poverty.

One of the most important things that we can do is move toward a more equalitarian society. This will strengthen the family in many other ways. For example, in our nationally representative sample of American families, child abuse is lower in equalitarian families, among women who have jobs outside the home. One reason why the rate of child abuse and wife beating is higher in male-dominant families is because a hierarchical organization tends to legitimize the use of force and coercion. There is a principle in sociology growing out of conflict theory, which says that the more unequal a social system is, i.e., the greater the inequality there is, the more coercion it takes to keep the people at the bottom on the bottom. The people at the bottom are trying to get a better shake; they are trying to crawl out from the bottom. So the farther down they are, the more coercion it takes to keep them there. The principle alone says something very important about preventing violence and strengthening families.

THE LARGER PICTURE

Because time was limited, I had to concentrate on just three of the many causes of family violence—the unintentional teaching of violence by parents who use physical punishment, cultural norms which tolerate violence in the family, and sexual inequality which both creates violence and forces women to put up with it because of economic dependence on their assailants.

Important as each of these three factors may be, they are far from the whole story. Actually, each of these three factors, by themselves, accounts for only a small part of family violence. The results of the last ten years of research on family violence still leave many questions to be answered. But two things are clear.

First, these studies show that there is no single, or even no one predominant cause. If you hear someone say that "X" is *the* cause of child abuse or of wife-beating, you can be almost certain he or she is wrong (no matter what factor is pointed out), because study after study has shown that no one factor accounts for very much of the violence.

Second, although no one factor is crucial, the last decade of research has identified a great many factors, and together they add up. The results from our study of a nationally representative sample of 2,143 families (see Straus, Gelles, and Steinmetz, 1980) show how this works. We studied the potential effect of 25 causative factors, including the factors discussed in this article and other factors such as poverty, unemployment, other stresses, and social isolation. In families where none or only one or two of the factors existed, there were no incidents of wife-beating during the year studied. On the other hand, among families with twelve or more of these factors, 70 percent experienced an incident of wife-beating that year.

These findings show that we have gone a long way toward explaining the paradox of family violence. Moreover, the practical steps to be taken on the basis of these findings are encouraging for families because almost all involve actions that, even aside from their effects on family violence, are steps which will improve the quality of family life.

REFERENCES

STRAUS, M. A. Ordinary violence, child abuse, and wife beating. What do they have in common? In D. Finkelhor et al. (Eds.), *Issues and controversies in family violence research.* Beverly Hills: Sage, 1982.

STRAUS, M. A., & HOTALING, G. T. *The social causes of husband-wife violence.* Minneapolis: University of Minnesota Press, 1980.

STRAUS, M. A., GELLES, R. J., & STEINMETZ, S. K. *Behind closed doors: Violence in the American family.* New York: Doubleday/Anchor, 1980.

37

Alcoholism in the Family

Joan K. Jackson

ABSTRACT: On the basis of research with the Alcoholics Anonymous Auxiliary, the author analyzed how wives adapt to alcoholic husbands. She found that they and their families typically go through seven stages of reaction: (1) attempts to deny the problem, (2) attempts to eliminate the problem, (3) disorganization, (4) attempts to reorganize, (5) attempts to escape the problem, (6) reorganization by the family, and (7) recovery and reorganization of the whole family.

. . . Over a three-year period, the present investigator has been an active participant in the Alcoholics Anonymous Auxiliary in Seattle. This group is composed partly of women whose husbands are or were members of Alcoholics Anonymous, and partly of women whose husbands are excessive drinkers but have never contacted Alcoholics Anonymous.

. . . Verbatim shorthand notes have been taken of all discussions, at the request of the group, who also make use of the notes for the group's purposes. Informal contact has been maintained with past and present members. In the past three years 50 women have been members of this group. . . . In addition, in connection with research on hospitalized alcoholics, many of their wives have been interviewed. The interviews with the hospitalized alcoholics, as well as with male members of Alcoholics Anonymous, have also provided information on family interactions. Further information has been derived from another group of wives, not connected with Alcoholics Anonymous, and from probation officers, social workers and court officials. . . .

The families represented in this study are from the middle and lower classes. The occupations of the husbands prior to excessive drinking include[d] small business owners, salesmen, business executives, skilled and semiskilled workers. Prior to marriage the wives [were] nurses, secretaries, teachers, saleswomen, cooks, or waitresses. The economic status of the childhood families of these husbands and wives ranged from very wealthy to very poor. . . .

Statement of the Problem

For purposes of this presentation, the family is seen as involved in a cumulative crisis. All family members behave in a manner which they hope will resolve the crisis and permit a return to stability. Each member's action is influenced by his previous personality structure, by his previous role and status in the family group, and by the history of the crisis and its effects on his personality, roles, and status up to that point. Action is also influenced by the past effectiveness of that particular action as a means of social control before and during the crisis. The behavior of family members in each phase of the crisis contributes to the form which the crisis takes in the following stages and sets limits on possible behavior in subsequent stages.

Family members are influenced, in addition, by the cultural definitions of alcoholism as evidence of weakness, inadequacy, or sinfulness; by the cultural prescriptions for the roles of family members; and by the cultural values of family solidarity, sanctity, and self-sufficiency. Alcoholism in the family poses a situation defined by the culture as shameful but for the handling of which there are no prescriptions which are effective or which permit direct action not in conflict with other cultural prescriptions. . . . Thus, in facing alcoholism, the family is in an unstructured situation and must find the techniques for handling it through trial and error.

STAGES IN FAMILY ADJUSTMENT
TO AN ALCOHOLIC MEMBER

The Beginning of the Marriage

At the time marriage was considered, the drinking of most of the men was within socially acceptable limits. In a few cases the men were already alcoholics but managed to hide this from their fiancées. They drank only moderately or not at all when on dates and often avoided friends and relatives who might expose their excessive drinking. The relatives and friends who were introduced to the fiancée were those who had hopes that "marriage would straighten him out" and thus said nothing about the drinking. In a small number of cases the men spoke with their fiancées of their alcoholism. The women had no conception of what alcoholism meant, other than that it involved more than the usual frequency of drinking, and they entered the marriage with little more preparation than if they had known nothing about it. . . .

Stage 1. Attempts to Deny the Problem

Usually the first experience with drinking as a problem arises in a social situation. The husband drinks in a manner which is inappropriate to the social setting and the expectations of others present. The wife feels embarrassed on the first occasion and humiliated as it occurs more frequently. After several such incidents she and her husband talk over his behavior. The husband either formulates an explanation for the episode and assures her that such behavior will not occur again, or he refuses to discuss it at all. For a time afterward he drinks appropriately and drinking seems to be a problem no longer. . . .

Eventually another inappropriate drinking episode occurs and the pattern is repeated. The wife worries but takes action only in the situations in which inappropriate drinking occurs, as each long intervening period of acceptable drinking behavior convinces her that a recurrence is unlikely. As time goes on, in attempting to cope with individual episodes, she runs the gamut of possible trial and error behaviors, learning that none is permanently effective. . . .

. . . On the whole, a man reacts to his wife's suggestion that he has not adequately controlled his drinking with resentment, rebelliousness, and a display of emotion which makes rational discussion difficult. The type of husband-wife interaction outlined in this stage has occurred in many American families in which the husband never became an excessive drinker.

Stage 2. Attempts to Eliminate the Problems

Stage 2 begins when the family experiences social isolation because of the husband's drinking. Invitations to the homes of friends become less frequent. When the couple does visit friends, drinks are not served or are limited, thus emphasizing the reason for exclusion from other social activities of the friendship group. Discussions of drinking begin to be sidestepped awkwardly by friends, the wife, and the husband.

By this time the periods of socially acceptable drinking are becoming shorter. The wife, fearing that the full extent of her husband's drinking will become known, begins to withdraw from social participation, hoping to reduce the visibility of his behavior, and thus the threat to family status. . . .

Attempts to cover up increase. The employer who calls to inquire about the husband's absence from work is given excuses. The wife is afraid to face the consequences of the [loss] of the husband's pay check in addition to her other concerns. Questions from the children are evaded or they are told that their father is ill. The wife lives in terror of the day when the children will be told by others of the nature of the "illness." She is also afraid that the children may describe their father's symptoms to teachers or neighbors. . . .

During this stage, husband and wife are drawing further apart. Each feels resentful of the behavior of the other. When this resentment is expressed, further drinking occurs. When it is not, tension mounts and the next drinking episode is that much more destructive of family relationships. The reasons for drinking are explored frantically. Both husband and wife feel that if only they could discover the reason, all members of the family could gear their behavior to making drinking unnecessary. The discussions become increasingly unproductive, as it is the husband's growing conviction that his wife does not and cannot understand him. . . .

. . . All attempts to stabilize or structure the situation to permit consistent behavior fail. Threats of leaving, hiding his liquor away, emptying the bottles down the drain, curtailing his money, are tried in rapid succession, but none is effective. Less punitive methods, as discussing the situation when he is sober, babying him during hangovers, and trying to drink with him to keep him in the home, are attempted and fail. . . . Long-term goals . . . become secondary to just keeping the husband from drinking today.

There is still an attempt to maintain the illusion of husband-wife-children roles. When [the] father is sober, the children are expected to give him respect and obedience. The wife also defers to him in his role as head of the household. Each drinking event thus disrupts family functioning anew. The children begin to show emotional disturbances as a result of the inconsistencies of parental behavior. During periods when the husband is drinking the wife tries to shield them from the knowledge and effects of his behavior, at the same time drawing them closer to herself and deriving emotional support from them. In sober periods, the father tries to regain their favor. Due to experiencing directly only pleasant interactions with their father, considerable affection is often felt for him by the children. This affection becomes increasingly difficult for the isolated wife to tolerate, and an additional source of conflict. She feels that she needs and deserves the love and support of her children and, at the same time, she feels it important to maintain the children's picture of their father. She counts on the husband's affection for the children to motivate a cessation of drinking as he comes to realize the effects of his behavior on them. . . .

Stage 3. Disorganization

The wife begins to adopt a "What's the use?" attitude and to accept her husband's drinking as a problem likely to be permanent. Attempts to understand one another become less frequent. Sober periods still engender hope, but hope qualified by skepticism; they bring about a lessening of anxiety and this is defined as happiness. . . .

The children are increasingly torn in their loyalties as they become tools in the struggle between mother and father. If the children are at an age of comprehension, they have usually learned the true nature of their family situation, either from outsiders or from their mother, who has given up attempts to bolster her husband's position as father. The children are often bewildered but questioning their parents brings no satisfactory answers as the parents themselves do not understand what is happening. Some children become terrified; some have increasing behavior problems within and outside the home; others seem on the surface to accept the situation calmly. . . .

When the wife looks at her present behavior, she worries about her "normality." In comparing the person she was in the early years of her marriage with the person she has become, she is frightened. She finds herself nagging and unable to control herself. She resolves to stand up to her husband when he is belligerent but instead finds herself cringing in terror and then despises herself for her lack of courage. If she retaliates with violence, she is filled with self-loathing at behaving in an "unwomanly" manner. . . . She is confused about where her loyalty lies, whether with her husband or her children. She feels she is a failure as a wife, mother and person. She believes she should be strong in the face of adversity and instead feels herself weak.

The wife begins to find herself avoiding sexual contact with her husband when he has been drinking. Sex under these circumstances, she feels, is sex for its own sake rather than an indication of affection for her. Her husband's lack of consideration of her needs to be satisfied leaves her feeling frustrated. The lack of sexual responsiveness reflects her emotional withdrawal from him in other areas of family life. Her husband, on his part, feels frustrated and rejected; he accuses her of frigidity and this adds to her concern about her adequacy as a women. . . .

In Stage 3 all is chaos. Few problems are met constructively. The husband and wife both feel trapped in an intolerable, unstructured situation which offers no way out. The wife's assurance is almost completely gone. She is afraid to take action and afraid to let things remain as they are. Fear is one of the major characteristics of this stage: fear of violence, fear of personality damage to the children, fear for her own sanity, fear that relatives will interfere, and fear that they will not help in an emergency. Added to this, the family feels alone in the world and helpless. The problems, the behavior of family members in attempting to cope with them, seem so shameful that help from others is unthinkable. They feel that attempts to get help would meet only with rebuff, and that communication of the situation will engender disgust. . . .

Stage 4. Attempts to Reorganize in Spite of the Problems

Stage 4 begins when a crisis occurs which necessitates that action be taken. There may be no money or food in the house; the husband may have been violent to the children; or life on the level of Stage 3 may have become intolerable. At this point some wives leave, thus entering directly into Stage 5.

The wife who passes through Stage 4 usually begins to ease her husband out of his family roles. She assumes husband and father roles. This involves strengthening her role as mother and putting aside her role as wife. She becomes the manager of the home, the discipliner of the children, the decision maker. . . . She either ignores her husband as much as possible or treats him as her most recalcitrant child. Techniques are worked out for getting control of his pay check, if there still is one, and money is doled out to her husband on the condition of his good behavior. . . . Where her obligations to her husband conflict with those to her children, she decides in favor of the latter. . . .

In this stage the husband often tries to set his will against hers in decisions about the children. If the children have been permitted to stay with a friend overnight, he may threaten to create a scene unless they return immediately. He may make almost desperate efforts to gain their affection and respect, his behavior ranging from getting them up in the middle of the night to fondle them to giving them stiff lectures on children's obligations to fathers. Sometimes he will attempt to align the males of the family with him against the females. He may openly express resentment of the children and become belligerent toward them physically or verbally.

Much of the husband's behavior can be conceptualized as resulting from an increasing awareness of his isolation from the other members of the family and their steady withdrawal of respect and affection. It seems to be a desperate effort to regain what he has lost, but without any clear idea of how this can be accomplished—an effort to change a situation in which everyone is seen as against him; and, in reality, this is becoming more and more true. As the wife has taken over control of the family with some degree of success, he feels, and becomes, less and less necessary to the ongoing activity of the family. There are fewer and fewer roles left for him to play. He becomes aware that members of the family enjoy each other's company without him. When he is home he tries to enter this circle of warmth or to smash it. Either way he isolates himself further. He finds that the children discuss with the mother how to manage him and he sees the children acting on the basis of their mother's idea of him. The children refuse to pay attention to his demands: they talk back to him in the same way that they talk back to one another, adding pressure on him to assume the role of just another child. All this leaves him frustrated and, as a result, often aggressive or increasingly absent from home. . . .

Often [the wife] has had a talk with an Alcoholics Anonymous member and has begun to look into what is known about alcoholism. If she has attended a few Alcoholics Anonymous meetings, her sense of shame has been greatly alleviated as she finds so many others in the same boat. . . . She learns that her husband is ill rather than merely "ornery," and this often serves to quell for the time being thoughts about leaving him which have begun to germinate as she has gained more self-confidence. She learns that help is available but also that her efforts to push him into help are unavailing. . . .

Stage 5. Efforts to Escape the Problems

Stage 5 may be the terminal one for the marriage. In this stage the wife separates from her husband. Sometimes the marriage is reestablished after a period of sobriety, when it appears certain that the husband will not drink again. If he does revert to drinking, the marriage is sometimes finally terminated but with less emotional stress than the first time. If the husband deserts, being no longer able to tolerate his lack of status in his family, Stage 6 may be entered abruptly.

The events precipitating the decision to terminate the marriage may be near-catastrophic, as when there is an attempt by the husband to kill the wife or children, or they may appear trivial to outsiders, being only the last straw to an accumulation of years. . . .

The wife must come to terms with her own mixed feelings about her husband, her marriage, and herself before she can decide on such a step as breaking up the marriage. She must give up hope that she can be of any help to her husband. She must command enough self-confidence, after years of having it eroded, to be able to face an unknown future and leave the security of an unpalatable but familiar past and present. She must accept that she has failed in her marriage, not an easy thing to do after having devoted years to stopping up the cracks in the family structure as they appeared. Breaking up the marriage involves a complete alteration in the life goals toward which all her behavior has been oriented. It is hard for her to rid herself of the feeling that she married him and he is her responsibility. Having thought and planned for so long on a day-to-day basis, it is difficult to plan for a long-term future. . . .

Some events, however, help her to arrive at a decision. During the absences of her husband she has seen how manageable life can be and how smoothly her family can run. She finds that life goes on without him. The wife who is working comes to feel that ''my husband is a luxury I can no longer afford.'' After a few short-term separations in which she tries out her wings successfully, leaving comes to look more possible. Another step on the path to leaving is the acceptance of the idea that, although she cannot help her husband, she can help her family. . . .

Stage 6. Reorganization of Part of the Family

This wife is without her husband and must reorganize her family on this basis. Substantially the process is similar to that in other divorced families, but with some additions. The divorce rarely cuts her relationships to her husband. Unless she and her family disappear, her husband may make attempts to come back. When drunk, he may endanger her job by calls at her place of work. He may attempt violence against members of the family, or he may contact the children and work to gain their loyalty so that pressure is put on the mother to accept him again. Looking back on her marriage, she forgets the full impact of the problem situation on her and on the children and feels more warmly toward her husband, and these feelings can still be manipulated by him. The wide circulation of information on alcoholism as an illness engenders guilt about having deserted a sick man. Gradually, however, the family becomes reorganized.

Stage 7. Recovery and Reorganization of the Whole Family

Stage 7 is entered if the husband achieves sobriety, whether or not separation has preceded. It was pointed out that in earlier stages most of the problems in the marriage were attributed to the alcoholism of the husband, and thus problems in adjustment not related directly to the drinking were unrecognized and unmet. Also, the "sober personality" of the husband was thought of as the "real" personality, with a resulting lack of recognition of other factors involved in his sober behavior, such as remorse and guilt over his actions, leading him to act to the best of his ability like "the ideal husband" when sober. Irritation or other signs of growing tension were viewed as indicators of further drinking, and hence the problems giving rise to them were walked around gingerly rather than faced and resolved. Lack of conflict and lack of drinking were defined as indicating a perfect adjustment. For the wife and husband facing a sober marriage after many years of an alcoholic marriage, the expectations of what marriage without alcoholism will be are unrealistically idealistic, and the reality of marriage almost inevitably brings disillusionments. The expectation that all would go well and that all problems be resolved with the cessation of the husband's drinking cannot be met and this threatens the marriage from time to time.

The beginning of sobriety for the husband does not bring too great hope to the family at first. They have been through this before but are willing to help him along and stand by him in the new attempt. As the length of sobriety increases, so do the hopes for its permanence and efforts to be of help. The wife at first finds it difficult to think more than in terms of today, waking each morning with fear of what the day will bring and sighing with relief at the end of each sober day.

With the continuation of sobriety, many problems begin to crop up. Mother has for years managed the family, and now father again wishes to be reinstated in his former roles. Usually the first role reestablished is that of breadwinner, and the economic problems of the family begin to be alleviated as debts are gradually paid and there is enough left over for current needs. With the resumption of this role, the husband feels that the family should also accept him at least as a partner in the management of the family. Even if the wife is willing to hand over some of the control of the children, for example, the children often are not able to accept this change easily. Their mother has been both parents for so long that it takes time to get used to the idea of consulting their father on problems and asking for his decisions. Often the father tries too hard to manage this change overnight, and the very pressure put on the children toward this end defeats him. In addition, he is unable to meet many of the demands the children make on him because he has never really become acquainted with them or learned to understand them and is lacking in much necessary background knowledge of their lives.

The wife, who finds it difficult to conceive of her husband as permanently sober, feels an unwillingness to let control slip from her hands. At the same time she realizes that reinstatement of her husband in his family roles is necessary to his sobriety. She also realizes that the closer his involvement in the family the greater the probability of his remaining sober. Yet she remembers events in the past in which his failure to handle his responsibilities was catastrophic to the family. . . .

Gradually, however, the drinking problem sinks into the past and marital adjustment at some level is achieved. Even when this has occurred, the drinking problem crops up occasionally, as when the time comes for a decision about whether the children should be permitted to drink. The mother at such times becomes anxious, sees in the child traits which remind her of her husband, worries whether these are the traits which mean future alcoholism. At parties, at first, she is watchful and concerned about whether her husband will take a drink or not. Relatives and friends may, in a party mood, make the husband the center of attention by emphasizing his nondrinking. They may unwittingly cast aspersions on his character by trying to convince him that he can now "drink like a man." Some relatives and friends have gone so far as secretly to "spike" a nonalcoholic drink and then cry "bottoms up!" without realizing the risk of reactivating patterns from the past.

If sobriety has come through Alcoholics Anonymous, the husband frequently throws himself so wholeheartedly into A.A. activities that his wife sees little of him and feels neglected. As she worries less about his drinking, she may press him to cut down on these activities. . . . Also, the wife discovers that, though she has a sober husband, she is by no means free of alcoholics. In his Twelfth Step work, he may keep the house filled with men he is helping. In the past her husband has avoided self-searching; and now he may become excessively introspective, and it may be difficult for her to deal with this. . . .

SUMMARY

The onset of alcoholism in a family member has been viewed as precipitating a cumulative crisis for the family. Seven critical stages have been delineated. Each stage affects the form which the following one will take. The family finds itself in an unstructured situation which is undefined by the culture. Thus it is forced to evolve techniques of adjustment by trial and error. The unpredictability of the situation, added to its lack of structure, engenders anxiety in family members which gives rise to personality difficulties. Factors in the culture, in the environment, and within the family situation prolong the crisis and deter the working out of permanent adjustment patterns. With the arrest of the alcoholism, the crisis enters its final stage. The family attempts to reorganize to include the ex-alcoholic and makes adjustments to the changes which have occurred in him.

▼▼▼▼▼▼▼▼▼▼▼▼▼▼▼▼▼▼▼▼▼▼▼▼▼▼▼▼▼▼

PART VIII

Marital Transitions:
Divorce, Remarriage,
and Widowhood

*H*ardly anyone who gets married *expects* to get divorced. Although couples know that divorce has become common, they do not think that divorce will happen to *them*; it is something that *others* experience. Despite their wishes to the contrary, Americans have become divorce prone.

If divorce comes in spite of their wishes to the contrary and their best intentions, it is likely to bring much pain, for divorce means a wrenching away from the far-reaching adjustments the individuals have made to a coupled life. Divorce brings such extensive change in people's lives that practically nothing remains the same afterward.

Divorce can be viewed as a *reverse image* of the marital process. Like marriage, divorce is the public bestowal of a new identity and the creation of a new legal entity. And like marriage, divorce brings changes in the individual's behavior, relationships with the former spouse, perceptions and evaluations of the former spouse, and relationships with others.

Let us look at each of these changes.

1. In our society, divorce, like marriage, reveals the community's interests in the coupled relationship. The community becomes actively involved by requiring that at least one of the two must formally file papers with a court, official hearings be held, and a judge make a public record of such matters as the distribution of property and arrangements for the custody of children.

Like the marriage ceremony, divorce proceedings result in a new public identity. Our system is very formal, requiring that individuals who wish to divorce give proper notice to the other party and appear before witnesses to give sworn testimony regarding their legal residence, age, financial condition, the date and place of marriage, and children born to the couple. The legal rights of each spouse are protected, for each has the right to enter evidence, to be represented by an attorney, and to give testimony. When the rules are followed, the couple emerges from the courtroom with the new public identity of "single."

Since we view life from our own cultural experiences, it is useful to contrast our formality with a society in which divorce is highly informal. Among the least formal is an Islamic group, the Kanuri. If in front of witnesses a Kanuri man says to his wife, "I divorce you," their marriage is terminated. The double standard operates without mercy among these people, and a wife is not allowed such easy exit from a marriage that she finds intolerable. Among other things, if a Kanuri woman wishes to divorce her husband, she must pay him to obtain her freedom.

2. The divorce judgment also creates a new legal unit. Instead of the two becoming one, the one become two. Among other things, no longer are they able to file tax forms jointly.

3. Divorce alters the behavior of both individuals. Their routines (patterns of work, school, and leisure activities) may change, and their responsibilities are modified (for example, what they do with and for their children).

4. The couple's relationship to one another also changes. Divorce marks a change in the frequency and perhaps quality of their interactions.

5. Like marriage, divorce also changes how each perceives and evaluates the other. To go from husband to ex-husband and from wife to ex-wife changes what each expects of the other. These expectations, emerging out of their own stereotypes of the roles each should play and from their continued interactions, engender new sets of attitudes toward the former spouse. These new perceptions are so radical that they even change the individual's evaluations of the past. What the former spouse

did during the marriage comes to be seen in a new light. For example, a woman might say, "You know, he really *was* a louse all along, only I didn't realize it."

6. Divorce also brings fundamental change in the former couple's relationships with others. Friends find it difficult to invite them both to the same social events, and think that the former couple would also feel uncomfortable. Consequently, divorce tends to divide up their friends, as well as their property.

With exceptions, the general division follows these lines: People who were friends with the husband tend to remain his friends after the divorce, while the wife's friends before the marriage tend to remain loyal to her. The friends they made during marriage generally side with one or the other, with men generally remaining friends of the former husband, and women staying friends with the former wife. Some friends, uncomfortable with the changed identities, are lost to both.

It is understandable why this is so, for friends find it risky to try to remain friends with both parties of a divorce. Such an effort is quickly misunderstood, for neither side seeks a neutral judge. Disputing couples want friends to side with *them.* Anyone who tries to remain friends with both, or even to defend one to the other, runs the risk of being seen as unfaithful, a violation of the basic premise of friendship.

7. Divorce also changes how others are perceived. When others react differently toward the "newly single" individual, that person adopts new sets of attitudes toward them. For example, someone who may have been perceived simply as "friendly" during the marriage may now be seen as "interested," "available," or as a potential date or marital partner. Additionally, the formerly married may develop greater loyalty toward some people for "standing behind me in this trying time," or loathing toward others for "siding" with the former spouse.

8. Divorce also changes self-perceptions. No longer does the individual see the self as part of a "couple." A new self-identity must be sought—and created. Some individuals, coming to see life in terms of a "new chance," grasp newly perceived opportunities for relationships with the opposite sex and friends, or for career, education, leisure pursuits, travel, and so on. They then participate in new settings and situations, their new experiences leading to different reactions from others. When these reactions are internalized, a changed self emerges.

These new perceptions of the self lead to a changed evaluation of the self. Self-scrutiny brings new light on life events as the individual comes to see himself or herself in new terms. The individual is likely to even reinterpret his or her own role in the marriage and the events that led to the divorce. For example, an ex-wife may conclude, "I really was a better wife than I realized—actually, too good for the likes of him." Or, perhaps, as a friend said to me of his former wife (both of whom are sociologists): "I was a fool, and I didn't realize how good I had it. . . . I would take her back in a minute—only I think she's smarter than that." As you can see, when referring to the former marriage, it is difficult to separate the changed evaluations of the self from those of the former spouse. Despite the divorce, the coupled identity lingers.

In Chapter 38, Monica McGoldrick and Elizabeth A. Carter present a model of the major events of family life, including divorce. They identify the stages through which families typically pass, stressing the "developmental tasks" that must be achieved if each succeeding stage is to be adequately traversed. Divorce, as they point out, is a dislocation of the family life cycle that changes these developmental tasks.

In Chapter 39, James M. Henslin stresses that divorce is far from simply a matter of couples not getting along. By identifying ten major reasons why divorce is common in our society, he provides an understanding of *structural* reasons for divorce, that is, factors *built into society* that either increase or decrease the likelihood of divorce.

In Chapter 40, Judith S. Wallerstein and Joan B. Kelly turn to the matter of how children adjust to their parents' divorce. They present findings from a group of children aged six to twelve who used a variety of techniques to try to master their feelings of loss and rejection, of helplessness and loneliness. In Chapter 41, Joan B. Kelly looks at the reactions of adults to divorce. She specifies how men and women react differently, the nature and frequency of their complaints, and the major emotional responses that divorce precipitates.

In Chapter 42, Urie Bronfenbrenner describes the increased responsibilities, reduced income, and increased demands from children that divorced mothers experience. He then reports findings on parenting following divorce, highlighting the importance of support systems and stabilizing third parties for the healthy development of children in mother-headed single-parent homes.

In Chapter 43, Lenore J. Weitzman analyzes why the standard of living improves after divorce for most men, but decreases sharply for most women and children. She summarizes the effects of economic deprivation on the children of divorced parents and reviews suggestions for correcting this inequity.

In Chapter 44, Patricia L. Papernow stresses that stepfamilies begin with built-in problems: a weak couple subsystem, a tightly bounded parent-child alliance, and "interference" in family functioning from the new spouse who is viewed as an "outsider." As they adjust, stepfamilies go through fantasy, assimilation, awareness, mobilization, action, contact, and resolution. Stepfamilies can get "stuck" in a stage, making it difficult for them to function.

In Chapter 45, Robert C. DiGiulio looks at how the loss of a spouse ruptures the survivor's identity. Bereavement entails *encounter*, in which the widowed experience shock, fusion, and searching; *respondence*, characterized by a sense of helplessness, despair, unmet personal needs, and spouse sanctification; *emergence*, when they turn toward the future and experience realization, verification, and the resolution of a critical conflict; and *transformation*, when they develop a new identity. The author's analysis is remarkably sensitive because he also writes from the experience of losing his own wife.

38

▼▼▼▼

The Family Life Cycle—
Its Stages and Dislocations

▼▼▼▼▼

Monica McGoldrick
Elizabeth A. Carter

ABSTRACT: The authors develop a model of the family life cycle to depict major transitions in family life. As they examine its major stages, they identify the "tasks" that must be completed in each stage in order to move successfully to the next. Those stages are (1) the unattached young adult, (2) the newly married couple, (3) the family with young children, (4) the family with adolescents, (5) launching children, and (6) the family in later life.

   With its own patterns of emotional peaks, divorce brings dislocations to the typical cycle. The authors also outline a developmental model of the remarried family.

We now provide a brief outline of the statistically predictable developmental stages of American middle-class families in the last quarter of the twentieth century. Our classification of family life cycle stages highlights our view that the central underlying process to be negotiated is the expansion, contraction, and realignment of the relationship system to support the entry, exit, and development of family members in a functional way. . . .

THE UNATTACHED YOUNG ADULT

In outlining the stages of the family life cycle, we have departed from the traditional sociological depiction of the family life cycle as commencing at courtship or marriage and ending with the death of one spouse. Rather, considering the family to be the operative emotional unit from the cradle to the grave, we see a new family life cycle beginning at the stage of the "unattached young adult," whose completion of the primary task of coming to terms with his or her family of origin will most profoundly influence whom, when, and how he or she marries and carries out all succeeding stages of the family life cycle. Adequate completion of this task requires that the young adult separate from the family of origin without cutting off or fleeing reactively to a substitute emotional refuge. Seen in this way, the "unattached young adult" phase is a cornerstone. It is a time to formulate personal life goals and to become a "self" before joining with another to form a new family subsystem. . . . This is the chance for them to sort out emotionally what they will take along from the family of origin and what they will change for themselves. Of great significance is the fact that until the present generation this crucial phase was never considered necessary for women, who were traditionally handed directly from their fathers to their husbands. Obviously, this tradition has had profound impact on the functioning of women in families, as the current attempt to change the tradition is now having. . . .

We have outlined the shifts in status required for [the] successful accomplishment of life cycle transitions in column 3 of Table 38.1, which outlines the stages and tasks of the life cycle. . . .

In the "unattached young adult" phase, problems usually center on either young adults' or their parents' not recognizing the need for a shift to a less interdependent form of relating, based on their now all being adults complementing each other. Problems in shifting status may take the form of parents encouraging the dependence of their young adult children, or of young adults either remaining dependent or breaking away in a pseudoindependent cutoff of their parents and families. It is our view, following Bowen (1978), that cutoffs never resolve emotional relationships and that young adults who cut off their parents do so reactively and are in fact still emotionally bound to rather than independent of the family "program." The shift toward adult-to-adult status requires a mutually respectful and personal form of relating, in which young adults can appreciate parents as they are, needing neither to make them into what they are not, nor to blame them for what they could not be. . . . An example may clarify the way in which family members can get stuck in a "more of the same" struggle, where the harder they try, the worse it gets. . . .

Table 38.1 **The Stages of the Family Life Cycle**

Family Life Cycle Stage	Emotional Process of Transition: Key Principles	Changes in Family Status Required to Proceed Developmentally
1. Between families: The unattached young adult	Accepting parent-offspring separation	a. Differentiation of self in relation to family of origin b. Development of intimate peer relationships c. Establishment of self in work
2. The joining of families through marriage: The newly married couple	Commitment to new system	a. Formation of marital system b. Realignment of relationships with extended families and friends to include spouse
3. The family with young children	Accepting new generation of members into the system	a. Adjusting marital system to make space for child(ren) b. Taking of parenting roles c. Realignment of relationships with extended family to include parenting and grandparenting roles
4. The family with adolescents	Increasing flexibility of family boundaries to include children's independence	a. Shifting of parent-child relationships to permit adolescents to move in and out of system b. Refocus on midlife marital and career issues c. Beginning shift toward concerns for older generation

| 5. Launching children and moving on | Accepting a multitude of exits from and entries into the family system | a. Renegotiation of marital system as a dyad
b. Development of adult to adult relationships between grown children and their parents
c. Realignment of relationships to include in-laws and grandchildren
d. Dealing with disabilities and death of parents (grandparents) |
| 6. The family in later life | Accepting the shifting of generational roles | a. Maintaining own and/or couple functioning and interests in face of physiological decline; exploration of new familial and social role options
b. Support for a more central role for middle generation
c. Making room in the system for the wisdom and experience of the elderly; supporting the older generation without overfunctioning for them
d. Dealing with loss of spouse, siblings, and other peers, and preparation for own death. Life review and integration |

David G., a 24-year-old computer programmer, applied for therapy with vague complaints of depression and the inability to form close relationships. The picture that emerged was of an isolated young man who had trouble keeping himself motivated at work. He also had trouble feeling connected with friends, especially women. When asked about his parents, he said they were not worth discussing. He described them as critical, cynical, having a poor marriage and little to give. Further questioning revealed that he knew very little about his parents as people. They were Jewish immigrants whose families had struggled through the Depression. As we explored the family relationships, it became clear that David saw his parents as wounded people, felt guilty and resentful that they had not given more to him, and sensed their emptiness as he, the younger of two sons, left home. He did not want to reach back for fear that they would pull him into their depression and bitterness and he would never be able to leave. Yet, by cutting off, he had no sense of who he was or how to make other connections. He was not free to move on as an adult. . . . Questions about his parents' lives gradually helped him to alter his view of them and to redefine his relationship with them as a relationship of adults. Other relatives were called on for information about the family background, and the details they gave David about his parents' lives helped him in making this shift to a different view of his parents and the nature of their hold on him. As he gave up rigidly resisting his parents, he began to get to know them and became freer to make contacts with peers as well. He also found himself having more energy for his work.

It seems clear in this case that the more David tried to cut himself off from his parents and disassociate himself from traits he identified with in them, the less able he became to get on with his own life and to develop a truly personal identity. By reconnecting with them in a new way and shifting his status in relation to them, he became able to move on developmentally.

THE JOINING OF FAMILIES
THROUGH MARRIAGE:
THE NEWLY MARRIED COUPLE

Becoming a couple is one of the most complex and difficult transitions of the family life cycle. However, along with the transition to parenthood, which it has long symbolized, it is seen as the easiest and the most joyous. The positive and romanticized view of this transition may add to its difficulty, since everyone wants to see only the happiness of the shift. The problems entailed may thus be pushed underground, only to intensify and surface later on.

Weddings, more than any other rite of passage, are viewed as the solution to a problem, such as loneliness or extended family difficulties. The event is seen as terminating a process instead of beginning one. The myth "And they lived happily ever after" (with no further effort) causes couples and families considerable difficulty. Weddings, far from resolving a "status problem" of young unmarried adults, come in the middle of a complex process of changing family status.

Marriage requires that a couple renegotiate a myriad of personal issues that they have previously defined for themselves or that were defined by their parents, from when to eat, sleep, have sex, or fight, to how to celebrate holidays or where and how to live, work, and spend vacations. The couple must renegotiate their relationships with their parents, siblings, friends, and other relatives in view of the new marriage, and this will to some degree affect all personal relationships. It places no small stress on the family to open itself to an outsider who is now an official member of its inner circle. Frequently no new member has been added for many years. In addition, marriage involves a shifting of family boundaries for the members on both sides to some degree or other. Not only is the new spouse now a factor for each family, but priorities of both systems must now be negotiated in a complex set of arrangements of each system. As mentioned earlier, relationships with the third generation are of utmost importance in understanding the family life cycle, not only because of their historical importance to the system, but because of their direct, ongoing impact on the life of the next generations' family experiences.

In the animal kingdom, mating involves only the two partners. For mankind, it is the joining of two enormously complex systems. [Furthermore] . . . the fact of having in-laws . . . is surely a complex transition and one that our rituals hardly prepare us for. And, although couples are marrying later and delaying having children more than ever before . . . the birth of the first child [comes], on the average, one and a half years later. This means that there is still a relatively short time in which the couple and both families must adjust to this phase of their life cycle, with its accompanying stresses, before moving on. It may also be worth noting that there seems to be an optimum timing for this phase, with those who fall outside it often having more difficulty. Women who marry before the age of twenty (38 percent of women) are twice as likely to divorce as those who marry in their twenties. Those who marry after thirty (6 percent) are half again as likely to divorce as those who marry in their twenties (Glick and Norton, 1977). Thus it appears that in our culture there is a time for coupling; while it may be better to marry later than sooner, those who fall too far out of the normative range on either end are more likely to have trouble making the transition. A number of other factors appear to make the adjustment to this life cycle transition more difficult:

1. The couple meets or marries shortly after a significant loss.
2. One or both partners wish to distance from family of origin.
3. The family backgrounds of each spouse are significantly different (religion, education, social class, ethnicity, age, etc.).
4. The couple have incompatible sibling constellations (Toman, 1976).
5. The couple reside either extremely close to or at a great distance from either family of origin.
6. The couple are dependent on either extended family financially, physically, or emotionally.
7. The couple marries before age twenty or after age thirty.
8. The couple marries after an acquaintanceship of less than six months or after more than three years of engagement.
9. The wedding occurs without family or friends present.
10. The wife becomes pregnant before or within the first year of marriage (Christensen, 1963; Bacon, 1974).
11. Either spouse has a poor relationship with his or her siblings or parents.
12. Either spouse considers his or her childhood or adolescence as an unhappy time.
13. Marital patterns in either extended family were unstable. . . .

A number of other factors also add to the difficulty of adjusting to marriage in our time. Changing family patterns as a result of the changing role of women, the frequent marriage of partners from widely different cultural backgrounds, and the increasing physical distances between family members are placing a much greater burden on couples to define their relationship for themselves than was true in traditional and precedent-bound family structures. While any two family systems are always different and have conflicting patterns and expectations, in our present culture couples are less bound by family traditions and freer than ever before to develop male-female relationships unlike those they experienced in their families of origin. This is particularly so because of the changing role of women in families. It appears that the rise in women's status is positively correlated with marital instability (Pearson and Hendrix, 1979) and with the marital dissatisfaction of their husbands (Burke and Weir, 1976). When women used to fall automatically into the adaptive role in marriage, the likelihood of divorce was much lower. In fact, it appears very difficult for two spouses to be equally successful and achieving. There is evidence that either spouse's accomplishments may correlate negatively with the same degree of achievement in the other (Ferber and Huber, 1979). Thus, achieving a successful transition to couplehood in our time, when we are moving toward the equality of the sexes (educationally and occupationally), may be extraordinarily difficult. . . .

THE FAMILY WITH YOUNG CHILDREN

The shift to this stage of the family life cycle requires that adults now move up a generation and become caretakers to the younger generation. Typical problems that occur when parents cannot make this shift are struggles with each other about taking responsibility, or refusal or inability to behave as parents to their children. Often parents find themselves unable to set limits and exert the required authority, or they lack the patience to allow their children to express themselves as they develop. Typically, parents with children who present clinically [appear for counseling] at this phase are somehow not accepting the generation boundary between themselves and their children. They may complain that their four-year-old is "impossible to control." Given their relative size, the difficulty here relates to the parents' difficulty exerting authority. From this perspective, whether parents placate and spoil their children, or whether they are endlessly critical, they are reflecting a failure to appreciate the new change in family status required in this stage of the family life cycle. . . .

THE FAMILY WITH ADOLESCENTS

While many have broken down the stages of families with young children into different phases, in our view the shifts are incremental until adolescence, which ushers in a new era because it marks a new definition of the children within the family and of the parents' roles in relation to their children. Families with adolescents must establish qualitatively different boundaries than families with younger children. The boundaries must now be permeable. Parents can no longer maintain complete authority. Adolescents can and do open the family to a whole array of new. values as they bring friends and new ideas into the family arena. Families that become derailed at this stage are frequently stuck in an earlier view of their children. They may try to control every aspect of their lives at a time when, developmentally, this is impossible to do successfully. Either the adolescent withdraws from the appropriate involvements for this developmental stage, or the parents become increasingly frustrated with what they perceive as their own impotence. For this phase the old Alcoholics Anonymous adage is particularly apt for parents: "May I have the ability to accept the things I cannot change, the strength to change the things I can, and the wisdom to know the difference." Flexible boundaries that allow adolescents to move in and be dependent at times when they cannot handle things alone, and to move out and experiment with increasing degrees of independence when they are ready, put special strains on all family members in their new status with one another. This is also a time when adolescents begin to establish their own independent relationships with the extended family, and it requires special adjustments between parents and grandparents to allow and foster these new patterns.

Parents of adolescents often get stuck in attempting to get their children to do what the parents want at a time when this can no longer be done successfully, or they let the children do whatever they want and fail to exert the needed authority. Children may become overly independent and adultlike, or they remain immature and fail to develop sufficient independent functioning to move on developmentally. . . .

LAUNCHING CHILDREN AND MOVING ON

This phase of the family life cycle is the newest and the longest, and for these reasons, it is in many ways the most problematic of all phases. Until about a generation ago, most families were occupied with raising their children for their entire adult lives until old age. Now, because of the low birth rate and the long life span of most adults, parents launch their children almost twenty years before retirement and must then find other life activities. The difficulties of this transition can lead families to hold on to their children or can lead to parental feelings of emptiness and depression, particularly for women who have focused their main energies on their children and who now feel useless and unprepared to face a new career in the job world. The most significant aspect of this phase is that it is marked by the greatest number of exits and entries of family members. It begins with the launching of grown children and proceeds with the entry of their spouses and children. Meanwhile, it is a time when older parents are often becoming ill or dying; this, in conjunction with the difficulties of finding meaningful life activities during this phase itself, may make it a particularly difficult period. Parents must not only deal with the change in their own status as they make room for the next generation and move up to grandparental positions, but they must deal also with a different type of relationship with their own parents, who may become dependent, giving them considerable caretaking responsibilities.

This can also be a liberating time, in that finances may be easier than

during the primary years of family responsibilities and there is the potential for moving into new and unexplored areas—travel, hobbies, new
careers. For some families this stage is seen as a time of fruition and
completion and as a second opportunity to consolidate or expand by
exploring new avenues and new roles. For others it leads to disruption,
a sense of emptiness and overwhelming loss, depression, and general
disintegration. The phase necessitates a restructuring of the marital relationship now that parenting responsibilities are no longer required. As
Solomon (1973) has noted, if the solidification of the marriage has not
taken place and reinvestment is not possible, the family often mobilizes
itself to hold onto the last child. Where this does not happen the couple
may move toward divorce.

The family that fails to appreciate the need for a shift in relationship
status at this stage may keep trying to fill their time with the old tasks,
or the spouses may begin to blame each other for the emptiness they
feel. If they can recognize the new efforts required in this period, they
are much more likely to be able to mobilize the energy to deal with them
than if they go along on the assumptions of the previous phase. . . .

THE FAMILY IN LATER LIFE

As Walsh (1980) has pointed out, few of the visions we are offered in
our culture for old age provide us with positive perspective for healthy
later-life adjustment within a family or social context. Pessimistic views
of later life prevail. The current myths are that most elderly people have
no families; that those who do have families have little relationship with
them and are usually set aside in institutions; or that all family interactions with older family members are minimal. On the contrary, the vast
majority of adults over sixty-five do not live alone but with other family
members. Over 80 percent live within an hour of at least one child
(Walsh, 1980).

Another myth about the elderly is that they are sick, senile, and fee-
ble and can be best handled in nursing homes or hospitals. Only 4 percent of the elderly live in institutions (Streib, 1972), and the average age
at admission is eighty. There are indications that if others did not foster
their dependence or ignore them as functional family members, even
this degree of dependence would be less.

Among the tasks of families in later life are adjustments to retirement,
which may not only create the obvious vacuum for the retiring person
but may put a special strain on a marriage that until then has been balanced in different spheres. Financial insecurity or dependence are also
special difficulties, especially for family members who value managing
for themselves. And while loss of friends and relatives is a particular

difficulty at this phase, the loss of a spouse is the most difficult adjustment, with its problems of reorganizing one's entire life alone after
many years as a couple and of having fewer relationships to help replace
the loss. Grandparenthood can, however, offer a new lease on life, and
opportunities for special close relationships without the responsibilities
of parenthood.

Difficulty in making the status changes required for this phase of life
are reflected in older family members' refusal to relinquish some of their
power, as when a grandfather refuses to turn over the company or make
plans for his succession. The inability to shift status is reflected also
when older adults give up and become totally dependent on the next
generation, or when the next generation does not accept their lessening
powers or treats them as totally incompetent or irrelevant.

Even when members of the older generation are quite enfeebled,
there is not really a reversal of roles between one generation and the
next, because parents always have a great many years of extra experience and remain models to the next generation for the phases of life
ahead. Nevertheless, because valuing older age is totally unsupported
in our culture, family members of the next generation often do not know
how to make the appropriate shift in relational status with their
parents. . . .

DISLOCATIONS IN THE FAMILY LIFE CYCLE
BECAUSE OF DIVORCE

While the statistical majority of the American middle and upper
classes still go through the traditional family life cycle stages as outlined,
. . . the largest variation from that norm consists of families in which
divorce has occurred. With the divorce rate . . . at 38 percent and the
rate of redivorce at 44 percent (Glick and Norton, 1976), divorce in the
American family is close to the point at which it will occur in the majority of families and will thus be thought of more and more as a normative
event.

In our experience as clinicians and teachers, we have found it useful
to conceptualize divorce as an interruption or dislocation of the traditional family life cycle, which produces the kind of profound disequilibrium that is associated throughout the entire family life cycle with shifts,
gains, and losses in family membership. As in other life cycle phases,
there are crucial shifts in relationship status and important emotional
tasks that must be completed by the members of divorcing families in
order for them to proceed developmentally. As in other phases, emotional issues not resolved at this phase will be carried along as hindrances in future relationships.

Therefore, in this view, we conceptualize the need for families in which divorce occurs to go through one or two additional phases of the family life cycle in order to restabilize and go forward developmentally again at a more complex level. Of women who divorce, 25 percent do not remarry. These families go through one additional phase and can restabilize permanently as divorced families. The other 75 percent of women who divorce remarry, and these families can be said to require negotiation of two additional phases of the family life cycle before permanent restabilization.

Our concept of [the] divorce and postdivorce family emotional process can be visualized as a roller-coaster graph, with peaks of emotional tension at all of the transition points.

In divorcing families, emotional tension peaks predictably at these points:

1. at the time of the *decision* to separate or divorce;
2. when this decision is announced to family and friends;
3. when money and custody-visitation arrangements are discussed;
4. when the physical separation takes place;
5. when the actual legal divorce takes place;
6. when separated spouses or ex-spouses have contact about money or children and at life cycle transition points of all family members;
7. as each spouse is making the initial adjustments to rebuilding a new life.

These emotional pressure peaks occur in all divorcing families—not necessarily in the above order—and many of them occur over and over again, for months or years. A more detailed depiction of the process appears in Table 38.2.

The emotions released during the process of divorce relate primarily to the work of *emotional divorce*—that is, the retrieval of self from the marriage. Each partner must retrieve the hopes, dreams, plans, and expectations that were invested in *this* spouse and in *this* marriage. This requires mourning what is lost and dealing with hurt, anger, blame, guilt, shame, and loss in oneself, in the spouse, in the children, and in the extended family.

In our clinical work with divorcing families, we subscribe to the basic systems view that cutoffs are emotionally harmful, and we work to help divorcing spouses continue to relate as cooperative parents and to permit maximum feasible contact between children and natural parents and grandparents. Our experience supports that of others (Hetherington, Cox, and Cox, 1977), who have found that it takes a minimum of two years and a great deal of effort after divorce for a family to readjust to its new structure and proceed to the next developmental stage. Families

Table 38.2 **Dislocations of the Family Life Cycle Requiring Additional Steps to Restabilize and Proceed Developmentally**

Phase	Emotional Process of Transition: Prerequisite Attitude	Developmental Issues
	Divorce	
1. The decision to divorce	Acceptance of inability to resolve marital tensions sufficiently to continue relationship	Acceptance of one's own part in the failure of the marriage
2. Planning the breakup of the system	Supporting viable arrangements for all parts of the system	a. Working cooperatively on problems of custody, visitation, finances b. Dealing with extended family about the divorce
3. Separation	a. Willingness to continue cooperative coparental relationship b. Work on resolution of attachment to spouse	a. Mourning loss of intact family b. Restructuring marital and parent-child relationships; adaptation to living apart c. Realignment of relationships with extended family; staying connected with spouse's extended family
4. The divorce	More work on emotional divorce: overcoming hurt, anger, guilt, etc.	a. Mourning loss of intact family: giving up fantasies of reunion b. Retrieval of hopes, dreams, expectations from the marriage c. Staying connected with extended families
	Postdivorce Family	
A. Single-parent family	Willingness to maintain parental contact with ex-spouse and support contact of children with ex-spouse and his or her family	a. Making flexible visitation arrangements with ex-spouse and his or her family b. Rebuilding own social network
B. Single-parent (noncustodial)	Willingness to maintain parental contact with ex-spouse and support custodial parent's relationship with children	a. Finding ways to continue effective parenting relationship with children b. Rebuilding own social network

in which the emotional issues of divorce are not adequately resolved can remain stuck emotionally for years if not for generations.

At the transition into remarriage, the predictable peaks of emotional tension occur at the time of serious commitment to the new relationship; at the time the plan to remarry is announced to families and friends; at the time of the actual remarriage and formation of the stepfamily; and as the logistics of stepfamily life are put into practice.

The family emotional process at the transition to remarriage consists of struggling with *fears* about investment in a new marriage and a new family: one's own fears, the new spouse's fears, and the children's fears (of either or both spouses); dealing with hostile or upset reactions of the children, the extended families, and the ex-spouse; struggling with the ambiguity of the new model of family structure roles and relationships; rearousal of intense parental guilt and concerns about the welfare of children; and rearousal of the old attachment to ex-spouse (negative or positive). Table 38.3 depicts the process in somewhat greater detail. . . .

In our experience, the residue of an angry and vengeful divorce can block stepfamily integration for years or forever. The rearousal of the old emotional attachment to an ex-spouse, which characteristically surfaces at the time of remarriage and at subsequent life cycle transitions of children, is usually not understood as a predictable process and therefore leads to denial, misinterpretation, cutoff, and assorted difficulties. As in the case of adjustment to a new family structure after divorce, stepfamily integration seems also to require a minimum of two years before a workable new structure permits family members to move on emotionally.

THE FAMILY LIFE CYCLE OF THE POOR

The adaptation of multiproblem poor families over decades and centuries to a stark political, social, and economic context has produced a family life cycle pattern that varies significantly from the middle-class paradigm so often and so erroneously used to conceptualize their situation. Colon (1980) offers a thought-provoking breakdown of the family life cycle of the poor into three phases: the "unattached young adult" (who may actually be eleven or twelve years old), on his or her own virtually unaccountable to adults; families with children—a phase that occupies most of the life span and commonly includes three- and four-generation households; and the phase of the nonevolved grandmother, still involved in a central role in old age—still actively in charge of the generations below. . . .

Table 38.3 **Remarried Family Formation: A Developmental Outline**

Steps	Prerequisite Attitude	Developmental Issues
1. Entering the new relationship	Recovery from loss of first marriage (adequate "emotional divorce")	Recommitment to marriage and to forming a family with readiness to deal with the complexity and ambiguity
2. Conceptualizing and planning new marriage and family	Accepting one's own fears and those of new spouse and children about remarriage and forming a stepfamily Accepting need for time and patience for adjustment to complexity and ambiguity of the following: 1. Multiple new roles 2. Boundaries: space, time, membership, and authority 3. Affective issues: guilt, loyalty conflicts, desire for mutuality, unresolvable past hurts	a. Working on openness in the new relationships to avoid pseudomutuality b. Plan for maintenance of co-operative coparental relationships with ex-spouses c. Plan to help children deal with fears, loyalty conflicts, and membership in two systems d. Realignment of relationships with extended family to include new spouse and children e. Plan maintenance of connections for children with extended family of ex-spouse(s)
3. Remarriage and reconstitution of family	Final resolution of attachment to previous spouse and ideal of "intact" family; acceptance of a different model of family with permeable boundaries	a. Restructuring family boundaries to allow for inclusion of new spouse-stepparent b. Realignment of relationships throughout subsystems to permit interweaving of several systems c. Making room for relationships of all children with biological (noncustodial) parents, grandparents, and other extended family d. Sharing memories and histories to enhance step-family integration

Note: Variation on a developmental schema presented by Ransom, Schlesinger, and Derdeyn (1979).

CONCLUSION

In concluding this chapter, we direct the reader's thoughts toward the powerful (and preventive) implications of family life cycle celebration: those rituals, religious or secular, that have been designed by families in every culture to ease the passage of their members from one status to the next. As Friedman (1980) points out, all family relationships in the system seem to unlock during the time just before and after such events, and it is often possible to shift things with less effort during these intensive periods than could ordinarily be expended in years of struggle.

REFERENCES

BACON, L. Early motherhood, accelerated role transition and social pathologies. *Social Forces*, 1974, 52, 333–341.

BOWEN, M. *Family therapy in clinical practice.* New York: Aronson, 1978.

BURKE, R. J., & WEIR, T. The relationships of wives' employment status to husband, wife and pair satisfaction. *Journal of Marriage and the Family*, 1976, 2. 279–287.

CHRISTENSEN, H. T. The timing of first pregnancy as a factor in divorce: A cross-cultural analysis. *Eugenics Quarterly*, 1963, 10, 119–130.

COLON, R. The family life cycle of the multiproblem poor family. In E. A. CARTER & M. McGOLDRICK (Eds.), *The family life cycle: A framework for family therapy.* New York: Gardner Press, 1980.

FERBER, M., & HUBER, J. Husbands, wives and careers. *Journal of Marriage and the Family*, 1979, 41, 315–325.

FRIEDMAN, E. Systems and ceremonies: A family view of rites of passage. In E. A. CARTER & M. McGOLDRICK (Eds.), *The family life cycle: A framework for family therapy.* New York: Gardner Press, 1980.

GLICK, P., & NORTON, A. J. Marrying, divorcing and living together in the U.S. today. In *Population Bulletin*, 32, No. 5. Washington, D.C.: Population Reference Bureau, 1977.

GLICK, P., & NORTON, A. J. Number, timing, and duration of marriages and divorces in the U.S.: June 1975. In *Current Population Reports.* Washington, D.C.: U.S. Government Printing Office, October 1976.

HETHERINGTON, E. M., COX, M., & COX, R. The aftermath of divorce. In J. J. STEVENS, Jr., & M. MATTHEWS (Eds.), *Mother-child, father-child relations.* Washington, D.C.: National Association for the Education of Young Children, 1977.

PEARSON, W., & HENDRIX, L. Divorce and the status of women. *Journal of Marriage and the Family*, 1979, 41, 375–386.

RANSOM, W., SCHLESINGER, S., & DERDEYN, A. P. A stepfamily in formation. *American Journal of Orthopsychiatry*, 1979, 49, 36–43.

SOLOMON, M. A developmental conceptual premise for family therapy. *Family Process*, 1973, 12, 179–188.

STREIB, G. Older families and their troubles: Familial and social responses. *The Family Coordinator*, 1972, 21, 5–19.

TOMAN, W. *Family constellation* (3rd ed.). New York: Springer, 1976.

WALSH, F. The family in later life. In E. A. CARTER & M. McGOLDRICK (Eds.), *The family life cycle: A framework for family therapy.* New York: Gardner Press, 1980.

39

Why So Much Divorce?

James M. Henslin

ABSTRACT: As they take their wedding vows, most brides and grooms feel love toward one another accompanied by a sincere desire for their marriage to be a success. Why, then, in spite of their best intentions, do so many marriages end in divorce? The author delineates ten major factors that underlie our high divorce rate: (1) incompatible sex roles, (2) the separateness of the sex worlds, (3) the demands of life, (4) the routines of married life, (5) changes in the functions of marriage and family, (6) an emphasis on personality or emotional fulfillment, (7) an emphasis on equality, (8) increased institutional support for divorced people, (9) the social roles of husband and wife, and (10) the changed nature of society itself owing to industrialization and urbanization.

Most newlyweds enter marriage feeling very much in love with one another. Almost always, those feelings of love are accompanied by sincere desires for their marriage to succeed. The realities of married life, however, often undermine the best feelings and intentions. Adjustments from being single to being married usually turn out to be much more difficult than the unmarried ever imagine. What is unanticipated— and often appears to be the consequence of some cruel blow of fate—is that the positive feelings with which a couple begin marriage frequently are replaced by a sense of vague dissatisfaction. Couples sometimes express this feeling of malaise as, "Something is wrong, but I can't put my finger on it."

In a great number of cases, however, the marital partners can put their fingers precisely on the problem—and they point those fingers directly at one another. Each knows that he or she is trying about as hard as anyone ever could, so the problem *must* lie with the partner. Frustrations build up as each blames the other. Initial vague dissatisfactions turn into quarrels over specific frustrations. As the frustrations grow more irksome, the quarrels intensify. With increasing dissatisfaction and frustration, each zeros in on the faults of the other. As this destructive process continues, each may begin to wonder what he or she ever saw in the other in the first place.

It is obvious that the best intentions do not make marriage a success. Feelings of love for the other are not enough to guarantee marital happiness. If such intentions and feelings could ensure a satisfying marriage, almost every marriage would be a success, for such sentiments characterize most brides and grooms at the time they marry.

This scenario of disillusionment—of growing dissatisfactions accompanied by quarreling and faultfinding—is played out in marriage after marriage. Depending on the figures one uses, about a third to a half of American marriages end in divorce. Keep in mind that these figures do not include desertion or those couples who live in various degrees of unhappiness, regret, or downright misery and despair but who, for one reason or another, do not divorce. Add these, and one can see that the promise so blissfully held out by the ideal of marriage is difficult to fulfill.

Why do such positive intentions and feelings so often fail to be translated into marital success? Just what goes wrong? There is no single thing that goes wrong, of course. Many factors contribute to marital problems, each of which takes its toll and all of which increase marital risk.

Yet, there must be some way to pinpoint the causes of our high divorce rate. After all, the commonality of divorce in our society is a *recent* phenomenon, and, sociologically, the causes must be rooted in changes in our society. As we know from our past, as well as from other traditional societies, a high rate of divorce does not necessarily characterize marriage.

Although we could search in a number of places for clues to the components from which divorce is constructed, it is useful to begin with *incompatible sex roles*. The early socialization of almost all couples complicates their adjustment to married life. Much of what the male learns as part of his masculine orientation toward the world and his presumed proper place within that world conflicts with what the female learns about her feminine orientation and with her presumed proper place. During the intensity and idealizing of courtship, the bride and groom minimize the differences in their orientations. As the ideals of marriage give way to the realities of daily life, however, orientational differences can no longer be ignored, and contrasts in their basic approaches to life often end up pitting one against the other.

For many who divorce, there does not have to be a single other factor. Sex-role incompatibility can be enough to signal the destruction of marital hopes. Marriage itself, then, becomes the crucible for the contradictions hidden in their basic socialization into sex roles.

Other social conditions, however, are at work to contribute to the dissolution of marital dreams. The second, highly related to the first, is *the separateness of the sex worlds* in our society. Males and females are placed in different corners of life, with each corner representing unique worlds of experience. This separateness means that even as adults, both husbands and wives undergo continuing socialization during which each learns different ways of handling problems, of evaluating what is important and what is irrelevant, and, in general, of approaching life. Since the husband and wife share the same time/space/relational/income/sexual/emotional dimensions of life space, it is probable that these differences will produce a clash.

We can call the third contributing factor *the demands of life.* It consists of those pressures to which adults in our culture are exposed, those things that demand satisfaction. Bills are high on this list: for their honeymoon trip; for an apartment or a house and its upkeep; for furniture; for a car and its maintenance; for insurance (life, auto, home, accident, and health); for entertainment; for clothing; for alcohol and cigarettes; for doctors' visits and medicines; for taxes and social security; for electricity, gas, and telephone service; and, of course, for food.

This third factor also includes the demands made on the couple's time and energy. Their house or apartment must be cleaned; so must the car. Their own bodies must be washed and groomed. The television set demands to be turned on. The dog or cat must be taken care of.

And so go a thousand and one items, each of which helps sap the couple's energy, enthusiasm, and interest. Of course, if after taking care of all these demands, they have any energy left, they must give at least a little to their employer, who expects something in return for signing a paycheck.

Each of these aspects of modern-day life helps account for the emotional exhaustion so many feel. This modern malaise has a major victim, however, one ordinarily not thought of in this context, and that is marriage. With so numerous, exhausting, and endless demands on the self, often one has little time or energy to direct toward the spouse. Frequently, then, it is the spouse who suffers and, as a consequence, the marriage.

The fourth major factor may be called *the routines of married life*. The newness wears off as a couple live with each other day after day. Before marriage, they spent time together because they wanted to be together. They overcame whatever obstacles they faced to see one another. After several years of marriage (for many, much less than that), some couples perceive their marriage in terms of a monotonous routine.

What has happened? After marriage, the husband and wife see each other daily, no longer from an emotional or rational choice but from the need to share the same living quarters and to meet the demands of the roles thrust on them by marriage itself. As they spend time together, day in and day out, under the intimacies of bed, bathroom, meals, and leisure, they come to know each other extremely well. What at first was pleasant discovery eventually becomes predictability. They come to anticipate each other's words, mannerisms, gestures, and even facial expressions and tone of voice.

Such predictability may be used creatively to build security and dependability into one's relationship. Many people, however, find it leads to boredom, which demands to be relieved. Some couples manage that relief through quarreling (and not knowing why they are quarreling), adultery (and not knowing why they find another person so appealing), and in countless other ways that are destructive to the marital relationship.

The fifth major factor is *changes in the functions of marriage and family*. As traditional functions have been usurped by other social institutions, the forces that keep a couple together *despite* problems have been weakened.

Consider, for example, the many bonds that used to tie a couple to one another. In the typical American farming family until the 1930s, the husband and wife (and the children) shared a large number of *mutually interrelated* tasks or functions. *Each performed jobs that were essential to the support, existence, and welfare of the other* (or, as sociologists tend to say, a married couple or a family at that time were characterized by high integration and high interdependence). The husband's tasks of cultivating the fields and managing the farm are well known. But what was his wife doing while he was in the fields?

In addition to cooking, cleaning, and child care, she baked *from scratch* breads, biscuits, cookies, cakes, and pies. From the berries she picked, she made wine, jams, and jellies. From the large garden that she tended by hand, she provided fresh vegetables during the summer and canned vegetables the rest of the year. She also provided fresh meat and eggs by raising chickens and ducks and a pig, calf, or lamb for the family's table. She joined in milking the cows and made butter, cottage cheese, and most of the family's clothing. In her spare time, she sold eggs and butter to get the cash that was necessary to buy the little clothing that she did not sew and the little food that she and her husband did not produce themselves. (If this listing gives you the idea that the "working woman" who vitally contributes to the family's economic well-being is *not* a recent phenomenon, you are right.)

If one spouse did not feel "emotionally satisfied" by the other, well, that was a fact of life that simply had to be put up with. One married a husband or wife *so each could be a provider for the other:** With life so precarious, one was primarily concerned about producing for survival, not about feeling good.

The contrast should be apparent. With the "functions that bind" so greatly diminished, couples now splinter much more easily when problems arise. Today's husbands and wives depend less on one another for survival. Alternatives to current relationships abound—and beckon.

The sixth major factor is *the replacement of former functions with a heavy emphasis on personality or emotional fulfillment* (commonly called the "companionship marriage"). Increasingly, it has become central to Americans' expectations of marriage that each spouse will fulfill the personality needs of the other. This is an especially onerous expectation, for our personality needs are complicated, ever changing, and unable to be satisfied by any single person. Because our culture emphasizes this expectation as being central to marriage, however, when one spouse feels "unfulfilled," he or she has a built-in tendency to place the blame on the marital partner for failing to meet his or her basic needs.

To depend primarily on one person to satisfy one's needs places tremendous pressures on a relationship. Among those many needs are feelings of security; of comfort; of affection; of love; of appreciation; of encouragement; of knowing you belong; of thinking that the goals you are working for are right and worthwhile; of sensing that you are on the right course in life; of believing you are a good, capable person; of being comforted in sadness, sickness, misfortune; *ad infinitum.*

Who can satisfy all these needs that are basic to a person's deep personality structure? Can any single person accomplish such a gargantuan task? And when the one on whom this burden is placed is so furiously busy meeting the pressing demands of life and has his or her own long list of intricate needs, is it any wonder that contemporary husbands and wives often feel that the other is somehow letting them down?

The seventh major factor is our *emphasis on equality* in marriage. At first glance, to list equality in this context seems wrong. After all, to experience equality is the essence of being an American. We tend to think of equality and happiness as a single term. How, then, could increased equality contribute to divorce?

*"Providing" for one another also included providing children (for oneself and one's spouse).

The ideal of equality pervades our social institutions, and it was only a matter of time until that ideal made its appearance in marriage. Previously, an authority hierarchy was built into marriage. Even though it may have been honored more in the breach than in fact, the husband held the decision-making power. For example, if he said that he was going to move to another house across the street or even across the country, his wife and family had the obligation to move along with him. It was similarly up to him what horse or farm (or car) they were going to buy, and how much of their income they were going to save or to spend. Such things were his decision—certainly a far cry from equality.

Inherent in this patriarchal authority structure, which may strike most modern ears as ludicrous, was a husband's and wife's sense of how they ought to relate to one another. The inequality that characterized their relationship represented guidelines that laid out the basics for their interactions. This authority structure was assumed to be *the* correct way of life. In short, it reduced quarreling because it removed debate about who was responsible for decision making. Even though one might think that a particular decision was not correct, one had the sense that the entire society, as well as one's particular role, supported the *way* the decision was made.

Although equality matches the primary American ideal and brings many benefits to marital relationships, it creates marital problems. Equality makes every decision open to debate. Neither husband nor wife has final authority. To reach decisions jointly, each must have an equivalent right to express desires and to get his or her point across. Yet neither has the authority to make the final decision. Consequently, this structure of equality contains built-in confrontation; to avoid confrontation, each couple must learn how to give and take and defer to the other—a difficult but essential task.

The eighth major factor is *the increased institutional support for divorced women*. Three principal elements are involved: the lessened stigma attached to divorce in our culture; the greater economic independence of women, that is, their greater employability; and a greatly expanded welfare system, unknown only two or three decades ago. Succinctly put, this increased institutional support means that a woman has less need to remain in a marriage with which she is unhappy.

The lessened stigma of divorce also loosens marital ties for men, of course, but perhaps the most applicable support is services traditionally supplied by wives but now easily available outside the family in exchange for cash, such as easy access to laundromats and prepared meals and food.

The ninth major factor, one that many would place at the head of the list, is *the social roles of husband and wife*. For many, to assume the role of husband or wife is to force unthinking demands on the other. Those demands, some of which may lie below the individual's level of awareness, create resentment in the other. This sentiment is captured in the not-uncommon refrain of the wife who laments, "Before we were married, he treated me like someone special. Now he treats me like a *wife!*"

Admittedly, this last factor overlaps with and is difficult to distinguish conceptually from some of the preceding components. Nevertheless, it deserves to be stressed separately because it pinpoints a feature of marital roles that underlies many problems in contemporary marriage. It should also be stressed that such unthinking expectations are not in and of themselves a problem. For them to become problems requires the expectation that something different *ought* to characterize a marital relationship—and that brings us back to the socially rooted expectations of intimacy.

The tenth factor, which is a general condition that makes most of the others possible, is *the changed nature of society owing to industrialization and urbanization.* Industrialization, with all of its technological developments, has allowed us to produce a highly urbanized society. The characteristics of an urban society—especially anonymity; the tendency to displace primary relationships with secondary ones in the form of membership in organizations; the breakdown of traditional authority in all areas of life; the secularization of religion; the debunking of the old ways of doing things; the emphasis on achievement rather than ascribed positions; the expectation of constant social change; mobility; and the focus on hedonism, materialism, and short-term contractual relationships—all militate against lifetime commitments of any sort, including marriage.

Within this context, the flight from relational commitments to the pursuit of pleasure is stressed. The dominant point of view is that pleasure and happiness are the central core of life and, therefore, that one has the right to discard a relationship that fails to bring the requisite degree of pleasure. To select a new spouse when the old relationship becomes tattered, instead of enduring the pains that are required to restructure the old, becomes a natural choice. With the anonymity of urban life, one is able to tear up roots and, just a short distance away, establish new friends and associates and activities to match one's new choice of mate.

CONCLUSION

These ten factors represent only one sociologist's way of computing the components that underlie our high divorce rate. Although other sociologists would stress these components differently and even add or subtract from them, these elements make it evident that divorce is due to much more than such vague factors as "personality problems" or some supposed changed morality. Rather, *our rate of divorce is directly related to the social structure of American society.* That is, the divorce rate of a society is a direct result of relevant social conditions, such as the stigma attached to divorce, the expected social roles of husband and wife, the customary ideas (or ideology) of what one ought to expect from marriage, or any of the other conditions I have analyzed. In short, to change the conditions of society is to change the frequency of divorce—which is the key to understanding why the divorce rate has climbed so sharply in recent years.

From our early socialization into the dominant ethos of our society comes our orientation to marriage, including the marital roles we assume and what we expect to give to and receive from marriage. Those roles and expectations contain built-in inconsistencies that are played out on the personal level, showing up as problems that a couple experiences in their marriage. With their view highly focused on the tensions in their relationship, people tend to see the various misalignments as personality problems, personality incompatibilities, or as personal "mismatches" of various sorts. Remaining largely invisible to them are the *social roots* that underlie such personal difficulties.

40

▼▼▼▼

How Children React to Divorce

▼▼▼▼▼

Judith S. Wallerstein
Joan B. Kelly

ABSTRACT: When children learn of their parents' decision to divorce, they use a variety of techniques to try to master feelings of loss and rejection, helplessness and loneliness. Initially, they cover (layer) their feelings and fears quite well. Some of the older children attempt to cope with their feelings through organized activity and play. After their initial reactions, these children commonly experience anger, fears, and phobias; a shaken sense of identity; loneliness; and conflicts in loyalties. About one-quarter align themselves with one of the parents to the exclusion of the other. After the first year, about half the children have made a good adjustment while half are still troubled.

[T]he decision of divorce frequently ushers in an extended several year period marked by uncertainty and sharp discontinuity which has the potential to move the psychological and social functioning of the latency child* into profound disequilibrium and painfully altered parent-child relationships. Alternatively, these changes can bear the potential

---

*Latency is a psychoanalytic concept referring to school age, around six to twelve, when sexuality is considered "latent" compared to the developmental stages immediately preceding or following.

for promoting development and maturation, as well as the possibility of more gratifying relationships within the post-divorce family structure.

Our data for this [chapter] are drawn from [a] sample [Kelly and Wallerstein, 1976] of 57 latency aged children from 47 families, here focused on the experiences of the 31 children from 28 families who were between nine and ten years old at the time that they were initially seen by us. As elaborated elsewhere [Kelly and Wallerstein, 1976; Wallerstein and Kelly, 1974; Wallerstein and Kelly, 1975], these 31 children from 28 families represent part of a cohort of 131 children from 60 divorcing families referred for anticipatory guidance and planning for their children around the separation, and then seen by us again approximately a year later for the first of two planned follow-up studies.

THE INITIAL RESPONSES

How They Looked When They Came

Many of these children had presence, poise, and courage when they came to their initial interviews. They perceived the realities of their families' disruption and the parental turbulence with a soberness and clarity which we at first found startling, particularly when compared with the younger children who so frequently appeared disorganized and immobilized by their worry and grief. These youngsters were, by contrast, actively struggling to master a host of intense conflicting feelings and fears and trying to give coherence and continuity to the baffling disorder which they now experienced in their lives.

> Robert said, "I have to calm myself down. Everything is happening too fast."

> Katherine told us that a long time ago, when she was little, she thought everything was fine, that her parents really loved each other, and that, "Nothing would happen to them until they got real, real old." She added with the fine perceptions of a latency age child, "Mom and Dad married 12½ years ago. They met 17½ years ago. I always thought love would last if they stayed together that long."

Some children came prepared with an agenda.

> Anna, after a few general comments from the interviewer, designed to put her at ease, interrupted with a brisk, "Down to business," and went on immediately to describe the diffuse feelings of anxiety with which she suffered these days and which made her feel "sick to her stomach."

> Mary volunteered that she was "so glad" her mother brought her to talk about the divorce because, "If I don't talk about it soon I'll fall apart."

For others the opportunity to be with a concerned adult had consider-able significance seemingly unrelated to specific content. Some of these children tried in many ways to continue the relationship.

Janet begged to return the following week. She offered, "I like to talk about my troubles," and drew a heart on the blackboard, writing under it, "I like Miss X."

Mary tried to extend her interview time, saying that her mother had not yet returned to fetch her, and then confessing that she had just lied.

Still others among these children found these interviews threatening and painful, and barely kept their anxiety controlled by keeping them-selves or their extremities in continual motion, the rhythm of which mo-tion correlated with the subject discussed.

Thus, legs moved much faster when Daddy was mentioned to Jim, who was bravely trying to maintain his calm and referred with some disdain to "Mother's divorce problem," adding, "I wonder who she's got now?"

Others maintained their composure by denial and distancing.

Jack stated, "I keep my cool. It's difficult to know what I'm thinking."

David said darkly, "I don't try to think about it."

The Layering of Response

These various efforts to manage—by seeking coherence, by denial, by courage, by bravado, by seeking support from others, by keeping in motion, by conscious avoidance—all emerged as age-available ways of coping with the profound underlying feelings of loss and rejection, of helplessness and loneliness that pervaded these children and that, in most of them, only gradually became visible within the context of the several successive interviews. Actually, the testament of the resourceful-ness of so many of these children is just this capacity to function simul-taneously on these two widely discrepant levels, not always discernible to the outside observer. At times, only information from collateral sources revealed their simultaneous involvement in the mastery efforts of the coping stance and the succumbing to the anguish of their psychic pain. This at times conscious layering of psychological functioning is a specific finding in this age group. It is profoundly useful in muting and encapsulating the suffering, making it tolerable and enabling the child to move developmentally. But it does not overcome the hurt, which is still there and takes its toll.

After his father left the home, Bob sat for many hours sobbing in his dark-ened room. The father visited infrequently. When seen by our project,

Bob offered smilingly, "I have a grand time on his visits," and added unsolicited and cheerily, "I see him enough." Only later would he shame-facedly admit that he missed his father intensely and longed to see him daily.

A few children were able to express their suffering more directly to their parents, as well as to us. This is the more poignant if one bears in mind Bornstein's [1951] admonition that the latency chid is *normally* engaged developmentally in a powerful battle against painful feelings.

Jane's father left his wife angrily after discovering her infidelity, and ceased visiting the children. He moved in with a woman who had children approximately the age of his own children. Jane cried on the telephone in speaking with her father "I want to see you. I want to see you. I miss you. Alice [referring to the child of the other woman] sees you every day. We only see you once a month. That's not enough."

A very few children succumbed more totally and regressively.

Paul responded to his father's departure by lying curled up sobbing inside a closet. He alternated this behavior, which lasted intermittently for several weeks, with telephone calls to his father, imploring him to return.

The suffering of these children was governed not only by the immediate pain of the family rupture, but expressed as well their grief over the loss of the family structure they had until then known, as well as their fears for the uncertain future that lay ahead for their newly diminished family. . . .

Finally, efforts to master inner distress were conjoined at times with efforts to conceal [feelings] from the outside observer because of an acute sense of shame. Feelings of shame did not appear in the younger children in our study, but emerged specifically with this age group. These children were ashamed of the divorce and disruption in their family, despite their awareness of the commonness of divorce; they were ashamed of their parents and their behaviors, and they lied loyally to cover these up; and they were ashamed of the implied rejection of themselves in the father's departure, marking them, in their own eyes, as unlovable. . . .

Attempted Mastery by Activity and by Play

Unlike the younger latency children, so many of whom were immobilized by the family disruption, the pain which the children in this age group suffered often galvanized them into organized activity. This was usually a multidetermined response geared to overcome their sense of powerlessness in the face of the divorce, to overcome their humiliation at the rejection which they experienced, and to actively—and as energetically as possible—reverse the passively suffered family disruption. In some, this was a direct effort to undo the parental separation.

> Marian, with considerable encouragement at long distance from the paternal grandfather, embarked on a frenzied sequence of activities designed to intimidate her mother and force her to return to the marriage. Marian scolded, yelled, demanded, and berated her mother, often making it impossible for her mother to have dates, and indeed almost succeeding in reversing the divorce decision by mobilizing all her mother's guilt in relation to herself and the other children. In one such episode, the child screamed in anger for several hours and then came quietly and tearfully to her mother, saying softly, "Mom, I'm so unhappy," confessing that she felt "all alone in the world." Following this, the harassment ceased.

Several children in this older latency group energetically developed a variety of new, exciting, and intrinsically pleasurable mastery activities which combined play action with reality adaptation. Many of these activities required not only fantasy production but the enterprise, organization, and skill of the later latency child.

> Ann, whose father was a successful advertising and public relations man, designed and issued a magazine with articles and drawings, announcing the impending divorce of her parents, together with other interesting happenings, which she distributed and sold in her school and community.

In her role identification with her public media father, Ann not only overcame the loss of his ongoing presence, at the very same time, through her newspaper publication, she proclaimed her acceptance of the reality of this loss. But central to this maneuver is the psychic gratification in it—Ann transformed pain into pleasure of achievement, and recaptured the center stage of interest. . . .

Anger

The single feeling that most clearly distinguished this group from all the younger children was their conscious intense anger. It had many sources, but clearly a major determinant was its role in temporarily obliterating or at least obscuring the other even more painful affective responses we have described. Although we have reported elsewhere [Wallerstein and Kelly, 1975] a rise in aggression and irritability in the preschool child following parental separation, the anger experienced by these older latency children was different in being both well organized and clearly object-directed; indeed, their capacity directly to articulate this anger was striking.

> John volunteered that most of the families of the kids on his block were getting a divorce. When asked how the children felt, he said, "They're so angry they're almost going crazy."

Approximately half of the children in this group were angry at their mothers, the other half at their fathers, and a goodly number were angry at both. Many of the children were angry at the parent whom they thought initiated the divorce, and their perception of this was usually accurate.

Amy said she was angry at Mom for kicking Dad out and ruining their lives. "She's acting just like a college student, at age 31—dancing and dating and having to be with her friends."

Ben accused his mother, saying, "You told me it would be better after the divorce, and it isn't."

One adopted child screamed at his mother, "If you knew you were going to divorce, why did you adopt us?"

Interestingly, despite detailed and often very personal knowledge of the serious causes underlying the divorce decision, including repeated scenes of violence between the parents, most of these children were unable at the time of the initial counseling to see any justification for the parental decision to divorce. (By follow-up, many had come more soberly to terms with this.) Although one father had held his wife on the floor and put bobbie pins in her nose while their two children cried and begged him to stop, both children initially strongly opposed the mother's decision to divorce.

For some, anger against the parents was wedded to a sense of moral indignation and outrage that the parent who had been correcting their conduct was behaving in what they considered to be an immoral and irresponsible fashion.

Mark said that, "three days before my dad left he was telling me all these things about 'be good.' That hurt the most," he said, to think that his father did that and knew he was going to leave all the time. . . .

The intense anger of these children was variously expressed. Parents reported a rise in temper tantrums, in scolding, in diffuse demandingness, and in dictatorial attitudes. Sometimes the anger was expressed in organized crescendos to provide a calculated nuisance when the mother's dates arrived.

Shortly after the divorce, Joe's abusive, erratic, and rejecting father disappeared, leaving no address. The mother reported that now she had to ask the boy for permission to go out on dates, was reproached by him if she drank, and had her telephone calls monitored by him; when she bought something for herself, he screamingly demanded that the same amount of money be spent on him. Joe used his sessions with us primarily to express his anger at his mother for not purchasing a gun for him. . . .

Other children showed the obverse of all this—namely, an increased compliance and decreased assertiveness following the divorce.

Janet's behavior shifted in the direction of becoming mother's helper and shadow, and showing unquestioning obedience to her mother's orders. She became known throughout the neighborhood as an excellent and reliable baby-sitter despite her very young age (nine years). She was, however, not able to say anything even mildly critical of her rejecting father, and was one of the few children who openly blamed herself for the divorce. When initially seen by us, she was preoccupied with her feelings of inadequacy and her low self-esteem.

Fears and Phobias

Unlike the preschool children and the younger latency group, the children of this sample were not worried about actual starvation, and references to hunger in response to the parental separation were rare. Their fears, however, were nonetheless pervasive. Some, while not entirely realistic, were still tied to reality considerations; others approached phobic proportions. In fact, among this group it was often difficult for us to separate out the reality bases, including their sensitivity to the unspoken wishes of their parents, from the phobic elaboration. Thus, approximately one-quarter of these children were worried about being forgotten or abandoned by both parents. . . .

Martha said to her mother, "If you don't love Daddy, maybe I'm next."

Some of their responses related to their accurate perception of parental feelings that children represent an unwelcome burden at this time in their lives.

Peggy reported that her mother had said to her, "If you're not good I'm going to leave." Although Peggy knew that her mother had said this in anger, she still worried about it.

Ann opined, "If Daddy marries Mrs. S., she has two daughters of her own, and I'll be Cinderella.

Some expressed the not wholly unrealistic concern that reliance on one rather than two parents was considerably less secure, and therefore the child's position in the world had become more vulnerable.

Katherine told us, "If my mother smokes and gets cancer, where would I live?" She repeatedly begged her mother to stop smoking, and worried intensely whenever her mother was late in arriving home.

Some worried, not unrealistically, about emotionally ill parents.

Ann stated about her mother, "I love her very much, but I have feelings. I'm afraid when Mom takes a long time to come home. She once tried to commit suicide. One day she ate a whole bottle of pills. I think of someone dying . . . how I'll be when I'm alone. Mom tried to commit suicide because of my father. It wasn't until after the divorce that she stopped crying. I think of her jumping over the Golden Gate Bridge. Mom thinks no one worries about her, but I do.''

Many of these children experienced the additional concern that their specific needs were likely to be overlooked or forgotten.

> Wendy referred several times through her interviews to the fact that her mother insisted on buying Fig Newtons, when she perfectly well knew that Wendy hated them.

Shaken Sense of Identity

Many of these children experienced a sense of a shaken world in which the usual indicators had changed place or disappeared. For several children, these changed markers were particularly related to their sense of who they were and who they would become in the future. . . . Specifically, the self-image and identity which in latency is still organized around, ''I am the son of John and Mary Smith,'' is profoundly shaken by the severance of the parental relationship. Some children expressed this confusion and sense of ruptured identity with anxious questions, comparing physical characteristics of their parents and themselves, as if trying in this manner to reassemble the broken pieces into a whole.

> Jack, unsolicited, volunteered a long discussion of his physical features. ''My eyes change colors, just like my Mom's. My hair is going to change to light brown, just like my Dad's. Other people say I'm like my Dad. My Dad says I'm like my Mom. I say I'm like a combination.''. . .

Loneliness and Loyalty Conflicts

Children in this older latency group described their loneliness, their sense of having been left outside, and their sad recognition of their powerlessness and peripheral role in major family decisions.

> Betty said, ''We were sitting in the dark with candles. Then they [her parents] told us suddenly about the divorce. We didn't have anything to say, and so then we watched TV.''

These feelings of loneliness, not observed in this way in the younger age groups, reflect not only the greater maturational achievement of these children but also their more grown-up expectation of mutuality, as well as reciprocal support, in their relationships with parents and other adults. They thus felt more hurt, humiliated, and pushed aside by the events visited upon them, over which they had so little leverage.

It should be noted that these children, in their wrestling with this loneliness, realistically perceived the very real parental withdrawal of interest in children which so often occurs at the time of divorce. In addition to the departure of one parent, both parents understandably at such times become preoccupied with their own needs; their emotional availability, their attention span, and even the time spent with the children are often sharply reduced. Moreover, the families in our study were, by and large, nuclear families, unconnected to wider extended families or support systems of any enduring significance to the children. In this sense the children's feelings of loneliness and of loss reflected their realization that the central connecting structures they had known were dissolving.

Perhaps, however, the central ingredient in the loneliness and sense of isolation these children reported was related to their perception of the divorce as a battle between the parents, in which the child is called upon to take sides [Kelly and Wallerstein, 1976]. By this logic, a step in the direction of the one parent was experienced by the child (and of course, sometimes by the parent) as a betrayal of the other parent, likely to evoke real anger and further rejection, in addition to the intrapsychic conflicts mobilized. Thus, paralyzed by their own conflicting loyalties and the severe psychic or real penalties which attach to choice, many children refrained from choice and felt alone and desolate, with no place to turn for comfort or parenting. In a true sense, their conflict placed them in a solitary position at midpoint in the marital struggle. . . .

CHANGES IN PARENT-CHILD RELATIONSHIPS

We turn now to a necessarily abbreviated discussion of some of the new parent-child configurations that emerged as a response to the marital strife and parental separation. These changed relationships constitute a significant component of the total response of children in this age group. The divorce-triggered changes in the parent-child relationship may propel the child forward into a variety of precocious, adolescent, or, more accurately, pseudoadolescent behaviors. They can, on the other hand, catalyze the development of true empathic responsiveness and increased responsibility in the child. And they can also result, as in the case of alignment with one parent against the other, in a lessening of the age-appropriate distance between parent and child. . . .

Alignment

One of the attributes of the parent-child relationship at this particular age is the peculiar interdependence of parent and child, which can become enhanced at the time of the divorce, and which accords the child a significant role in restoring or further diminishing the self-esteem of the parent. Thus the child in late latency, by his attitude, his stance, and his behavior, has independent power to hurt, to reject, to confront, to forgive, to comfort, and to affirm. He also has the capacity to be an unswervingly loyal friend, ally, and "team member," exceeding in reliability his sometimes more fickle and capricious adolescent sibling.

Among the 31 children in this cohort, eight (or 26 percent) formed a relationship with one parent following the separation which was specifically aimed at the exclusion or active rejection of the other. These alignments were usually initiated and always fueled by the embattled parent, most often by the parent who felt aggrieved, deserted, exploited, or betrayed by the divorcing spouse. The angers which the parent and child shared soon became the basis for complexly organized strategies aimed at hurting and harassing the former spouse, sometimes with the intent of shaming him or her into returning to the marriage. More often the aim was vengeance. For many of these parents, these anger-driven campaigns served additionally to ward off depressions, and their intensity remained undiminished for a long time following parental separation. It should be noted that none of these children who participated, many of them as ingenious and mischievous allies, had previously rejected the parent who, subsequent to the alignment, became the target of their angers. Therefore, their provocative behavior was extremely painful and their rejection bewildering and humiliating to the excluded parent.

Our data indicate that, although the flight for allegiance may be initiated by the embattled parent, these alignments strike a responsive chord in the children within this specific age group. . . . A central part of the dynamic of this behavior is the splitting of the ambivalent relationship to the parents into that with the good parent and the bad parent. Moreover, in our findings, these alignments have the hurtful potential for consolidation and perpetuation long past the initial post-separation period, especially in those families where the child is aligned with the custodial parent.

Paul's father was referred to us informally by the court to which the father had gone to complain of his wife's vindictive blocking of his visits with his three children. The father, a successful chemical engineer, expressed sadness and longing for his children, and concern that his children were being systematically turned against him by their mother's unremitting attacks and falsehoods. For example, the children were told by the mother that they had to give up their dog because the father was refusing to purchase food for it, although at that time the family was receiving well over $16,000 a year in support. Paul's mother expressed astonishment and bitterness at his father for the unilateral divorce decision, describing her many years of devoted love and hard work to support the father's graduate education.

Paul's initial response to the parental separation was his regression to sobbing in a dark closet, which we have earlier described, alternating with telephone pleas to his father to return. Later, in recalling this time, the child said to us, "I felt that I was being torn into two pieces." By the time we saw Paul, several months following the separation, he had consolidated an unshakable alignment with his mother. He extolled her as small and powerful, possessed of ESP, and knowledgeable in six languages. Of his father, he stated, "He'll never find another family like us.". . .

Among Paul's activities during the year following our initial contact was his continuing reporting to his mother, and eventually to her attorney, about his father's "lurid" social life and presumed delinquencies, and his continued rejections of his father's increasingly desperate overtures, including gifts and wishes to maintain visitation. Paul also maintained a coercive control over his younger sisters, who were eager to see their father, and he made sure by his monitoring of them that they would not respond with affection in his presence. At follow-up he told us, "We are a team now. We used to have an extra guy, and he broke us up into little pieces." His anger and his mother's anger seemed undiminished at this time. . . .

FOLLOW-UP AT ONE YEAR

A first follow-up on these youngsters took place a year after the initial consultation. By and large, as with the younger latency children, the turbulent responses to the divorce itself had mostly become muted with the passage of the intervening year. In about half the children (15 of the 29 available at follow-up) the disequilibrium created by the family disruption—the suffering, the sense of shame; the fears of being forgotten, lost, or actively abandoned; and the many intense worries associated with their new sense of vulnerability and dependence on a more fragile family structure—had almost entirely subsided. But even these children with apparent better outcomes, who seemed relatively content with their new family life and circle of friends, including stepparents, were not without backward glances of bitterness and nostalgia. In fact, the anger and hostility aroused around the divorce events lingered longer and more tenaciously than did any of the other affective responses. Of the total group, ten (or one-third) of the children maintained an unremitted anger directed at the noncustodial parent; of these, four did so in alignment with the custodial mother, the other six on their own.

Edward, who was doing splendidly in school and in new friendship relationships with his mother and with an admired male teacher, nonetheless said bitterly of his father, "I'm not going to speak to him any more. My dad is off my list now." (This was a father who, prior to the divorce, had had a very warm relationship with his son.)

Although some of these children who were doing well continued to harbor reconciliation wishes, most had come to accept the divorce with sad finality. Some seemed to be unconsciously extrapolating from these reconciliation wishes to plan future careers as repairmen, as bridge builders, as architects, as lawyers. Others, like Jane, were perhaps extending their protective attitudes toward their disturbed parents.

> Asked what she might like to do when she grows up, Jane responded, "You might laugh. A child psychiatrist. You're one, aren't you?" She talked movingly of working someday "with blind children, or mentally retarded children, or children who cannot speak."

By contrast, the other half (14 of the 29 seen at follow-up) gave evidence of consolidation into troubled and conflicted depressive behavior patterns, with, in half of these, *more* open distress and disturbance than at the initial visit. A significant component in this now chronic maladjustment was a continuing depression of low self-esteem, combined with frequent school and peer difficulties. One such child was described by his teacher at follow-up as "a little old man who worries all the time and rarely laughs." In this group, symptoms that had emerged had generally persisted and even worsened. For instance, phobic reactions had in one instance worsened and spread; delinquent behavior such as truancy and petty thievery remained relatively unchanged; and some who had become isolated and withdrawn were even more so. One new behavior configuration that emerged during the first post-divorce year in these nine- and ten-year-olds was a precocious thrust into adolescent preoccupations with sexuality and assertiveness, with all the detrimental potential of such phase-inappropriate unfoldings. And amongst all the children, both in the groups with better and with poorer outcomes, relatively few were able to maintain good relationships with both parents. . . .

[W]e would like to close with the remarks of a ten-year-old sage from our study, whose words capture the salient mood of these children at the first follow-up—their clear-eyed perception of reality, their pragmatism, their courage, and their muted disappointment and sadness. In summarizing the entire scene, she said, "Knowing my parents, no one is going to change his mind. We'll just all have to get used to the situation and to them."

REFERENCES

BORNSTEIN, B. 1951. "On Latency." *Psychoanal. Study of Child*, 6:279–285.

KELLY, J., and J. WALLERSTEIN, 1976. "The Effects of Parental Divorce: Experiences of the Child in Early Latency." *Amer. J. Orthopsychiat.* 46(1):20–32.

WALLERSTEIN, J., and J. KELLY, 1974. "The Effects of Parental Divorce: the Adolescent Experience." In *The Child in His Family: Children at Psychiatric Risk*, J. ANTHONY and C. KOUPERNIK, eds. John Wiley, New York.

WALLERSTEIN, J., and J. KELLY, 1975. "The Effects of Parental Divorce: Experiences of the Preschool Child." *J. Amer. Acad. Child Psychiat.*, 14(4).

41

How Adults React to Divorce

Joan B. Kelly

ABSTRACT: The author summarizes social science research on divorce. Among the findings that she reports are that women most often take the initiative in seeking a divorce, often after contemplating it for a long period; divorced men and women differ in the nature and frequency of their complaints; the major emotional responses precipitated by divorce are anger, depression, changes in self-esteem, regression, anxiety, relief, persisting attachment, and, for women, "new chance" feelings. The author also presents findings on the quality of life after divorce.

[In this overview of how adults adjust to divorce, we shall examine the decision to divorce, the nature of marital complaints, major emotional responses to separation, attitudes toward divorce, restabilization, and the quality of life after divorce. What follows is a summary of the social science literature.]

THE DECISION TO DIVORCE

Who Decides?

. . . Recent research evidence has confirmed that a mutually shared decision to separate or divorce is uncommon. More often one partner wants to terminate the relationship considerably more than does the other, creating a psychological imbalance in which one spouse is actively shutting the door on a marriage while the other continues to be attached to, or dependent upon, the marriage. . . .

There is now convergence in a number of studies . . . which indicate that women more often take the initiative in seeking divorce. . . . Wallerstein and Kelly (1980) in interviewing both divorcing spouses found that women sought the divorce in 75 percent of the couples studied, while 50 percent of the divorces in Ahron's (Note 2) study were initiated by women and 17 percent by men. Hill (1974) and Rubin (1969) also found a similar preponderance of female-initiated breakups in earlier studies of dating couples.

How Was the Decision Made?

Although there are impulsive decisions to divorce, more often the adult contemplates the possibility of divorce for months and sometimes years before there is a firm commitment. The decision is most often the culmination of accumulated grievances, instabilities, and unhappiness, accompanied by the growing recognition that the personal toll that the relationship extracts from the individual is no longer balanced by the security or gratification of being married.

Some studies report a "last-straw" phenomenon in which some specific event precipitated the decision to separate. Two-thirds of the separated men and women interviewed by Bloom and Hodges (Note 3) reported such an event. The three experiences noted most often were infidelity; outside events impinging on the relationship (moving, graduating, a new job); and some variant of the "last straw," such as a second suicide attempt or habitual drinking which was no longer tolerable.

In contrast the majority of the divorced men and women (all parents) interviewed by Fulton (Note 1) denied any specific precipitating factor and described instead a "buildup" or combination of things. This was true as well among the 60 divorcing couples interviewed in the California Divorce Study.[1] These adults, most often the women, verbalized a growing sense of dissatisfaction and emptiness which generated a slow, inexorable move toward the end of the relationship. Once these individ-

---

[1]The California Children of Divorce Project was a five-year longitudinal study of 60 families with 131 children. Family members were first seen shortly after the parental separation (average number of interviews per family was 15) in the context of a preventive intervention focusing on the child's capacity to cope with divorce. Participants returned for subsequent research follow-up at 18 months postseparation and 5 years postseparation. A full report of the five-year study and details of the sample, methodology, and data analysis can be found in Wallerstein and Kelly (1980).

Previously unpublished data included in this chapter will be described as material from the "California Divorce Study." The author was co-principal investigator of the Children of Divorce Project from 1971 to 1980.

uals admitted to themselves that divorce was a viable option, the complex process leading to separation was set in motion, almost always accompanied by turmoil, indecision, and apprehension about the future.
. . .

The Importance of the Decision-Making Role

. . . It appears to be, for most men and women, an extraordinary stressful experience to be told that one is no longer loved or wanted. Most often feelings of humiliation and utter powerlessness overwhelmed the rejected spouse as he or she recognized a helpless inability to make the departing spouse stay married. A common response to this pain and shattered self-esteem was immense anger, depression, and a surprising degree of regressive behavior (Wallerstein and Kelly, 1980; Kelly, Note 5). . . .

Spouses who initiated the divorce often did so with sadness, guilt, apprehension, relief, and sometimes anger, but a clear differentiating feature was their sense of control and the absence of profound feelings of humiliation and rejection. Further they had rehearsed and mentally prepared for their separated status. While they sometimes divorced with the diminished self-esteem characteristic of partners to a failed marriage, their self-esteem at separation was on the upswing, in stark contrast to those feeling shattered by abandonment. The enhanced self-esteem reported by these men and women was in part a result of their active role in deciding to put a miserable relationship behind them and take control of their lives. . . .

THE NATURE OF MARITAL COMPLAINTS

. . . A long-term interaction between two people legally joined in psychological and economic wedlock is complex, likely to be unbalanced in gratifications, and subject to change over the years. The marriage may be dismal for one spouse but nurturing for the other; it may be perceived as a failure by both or only one of the partners. Some men and women were conscious of marital discontent from the outset; others became slowly aware of dissatisfaction over time; and some steadfastly held to the view that the marriage continued to be solid and gratifying even as the divorcing spouse departed. It was apparent that thresholds for pain and unhappiness varied widely from one individual to another and shifted as well within the individual at different times. . . .

Kitson and Sussman (Note 4) found support for their hypothesis that marital complaints varied by education, social class, length of marriage, and income. Men and women of higher social status and married for more years complained more often of a lack of emotional support and deficiencies in the interpersonal relationship. Respondents married for fewer years and of lower social status had more complaints related to the spouse's failings and the performance of tasks, either within the family or outside at work, a finding reported earlier by Levinger (1966). . . .

[The California Divorce Study found] clear sex differences . . . in the nature and frequency of complaints described by men and women, and similar to previously cited studies, women had more complaints about the marriage than did men. Two-thirds of the women complained of feeling unloved (compared to 37 percent of the men). This complaint ranked first in mentioned frequency for women and third for men. Most women associated these feelings with a gradual erosion of affectionate feelings for their spouse and a corresponding feeling of emptiness that led many finally to initiate divorce.

For the men the complaint mentioned most frequently (by 53 percent) was of the wife's being "inattentive," of neglecting or slighting what husbands saw as their needs and wishes. . . .

The second most commonly voiced complaint of the men was that of major incompatibility in interests, values, and goals from the very beginning of the marriage. Three times as many men (39 percent) as women (13 percent) complained of such longstanding incompatibility. . . .

The second and third most frequent complaints of women, almost exclusively female complaints, were closely related to each other. One-third of the women complained that their competence and intelligence were constantly belittled by their spouses, resulting not just in resentment but in the eventual feeling that they could do nothing right. One-third also reported that their spouses were hypercritical of everything about them, including their manner, clothing, physical appearance, ideas, conversations, and child-rearing practices. . . .

Behond these most common complaints there were few differences in the rankings for the next cluster of complaints. Sexual deprivation figured prominently for 34 percent of the men and for almost as many women. Men blamed their spouse's disinterest or frigidity; the women blamed the husband's disinterest or extramarital affairs for the sexual deprivation. Considering that 71 percent of the men had one or more extramarital affairs during the marriage (versus 15 percent of the women), it is surprising that infidelity did not rank higher. A number of couples had not had sexual intercourse for three to five years prior to separation.

Thirty-three percent of the men and 24 percent of the women complained that their spouse was chronically "bitchy" or extremely angry.

Complaints of excessive nagging, or frequent outbursts of excessive anger, or an inability to enjoy anything were included in this category. Another complaint of 31 percent of the women but of very few men was that the spouse was too frequently away from home. Not necessarily "being out with the boys," as described by Goode (1956/1969), these men stayed away because of excessive attention to work and/or lovers.
. . .

MAJOR EMOTIONAL RESPONSES
TO SEPARATION

As would be expected in any event demonstrated to be traumatic and highly stressful, the decision to divorce and subsequent marital separation precipitate intense emotional response (Herman, 1977; Wallerstein and Kelly, 1980; Weiss, 1975, 1979; Bloom and Hodges, Note 3; Kelly, Note 5). The varied psychological reactions are a function of the spouse's role in terminating the marriage, as well as the adult's personality and the presence of other external variables—e.g., a visible lover, the presence of children, support networks, and changed economic circumstances. The major emotional reactions to separation, described by a number of investigators and reviewed briefly in this section, include anger, depression, changes in self-esteem, regression, anxiety, relief, persisting attachment, and "new chance" feelings.

Anger

While most investigators have reported the presence of anger in divorcing spouses, few have focused on the extent or intensity of anger, its duration, or the relationship between anger and adjustment. Most often attention has been directed toward depression, loneliness, unhappiness, and other symptoms of loss. Yet it appears to be quite difficult for spouses to participate jointly in a muted, civilized divorce action. In divorce the ground rules governing behavior shift abruptly and explicitly to self-interest. Whereas the mutual ties of marriage sometimes serve to restrain hostility, in divorce the anger and resentment of the marriage are set free and fully expressed. Encouraged by a legal system which fosters hostility and extreme polarity, aggression, rather than accommodation, is more likely to be rewarded.

Indeed intense anger associated with the failed marriage and separation was one of the hallmarks of the divorce experience for men and women interviewed in the California Divorce Study. For the majority of spouses bitterness and conflict *escalated*, rather than diminished, following separation, and for many the unexpected intensity of anger added significantly to their initial level of stress. . . . Bloom and Hodges (Note 3) [found] that relationships between divorcing parents were considerably more strained, with contacts significantly less pleasant, than were those between divorcing nonparents. They further noted that parents reported more difficulties overall than did nonparents after separation.

Twenty percent of the men and 44 percent of the women in the California Divorce Study were extremely and intensely angry or bitter toward their spouses. An additional 60 percent of the men and 46 percent of the women were rated as having moderate, but not extreme, anger. Thus four-fifths of all the men and even more women were angry at separation, resulting in at least one, if not two, angry parents in each divorcing family. Women were significantly more hostile than were men, despite having initiated the divorce significantly more often.

The intense anger of the separating spouses found expression in a wide range of behaviors around a limited number of issues. Money was one such issue, and the intense hostility which accompanied the economic division of property was a reflection not just of the marital conflict but was related just as strongly to the psychology of the divorce itself for each spouse. The abandoned spouse felt not only devastated and angry at being left but also viewed his/her spouse's ability to take one-half of the community property as a final insult. Such outraged spouses were more likely to fight about every dollar or every piece of furniture in the property settlement and expend thousands of dollars in legal fees in the process. The second issue was the children. Angry parents withheld the children as a punishment or attempted to form an alliance with the child which, if successful, hostilely excluded the other parent from the child's life.

Denigrating the moral character and behavior of the spouse, often with the children as audience, was the most common form of expressing hostility postseparation, with more than half of the women and nearly half of the men openly and extremely critical of their spouses. . . .

. . . Embittered fathers childnapped, used physical violence, and entered into custody battles for children with whom they may have had previously inadequate relationships. They attempted to convince the children and the courts that the mothers were morally bankrupt and unfit. Despite their angry denials, embittered vengeful mothers were intent on destroying the father-child relationship through frequent tirades aimed at convincing the children that the father no longer loved them and by blocking visitings through any means possible. These embittered parents were more likely to turn to the court to seek redress for real or imagined grievances than were the less angry men and women. The endless litigation served to refuel and consolidate their rage, maintaining the anger at a high level of intensity for several years.

Depression

. . . On the basis of spouse and cross-spouse descriptions, ratings of presence, severity, and duration of depression *during* the marriage as well as *after* separation were made for each adult participating in the California Divorce Study. There were significant sex differences, with depression more common in the marriage for women, of greater severity and of longer duration. None of the men had attempted suicide during the marriage, contrasted to 14 percent of the women making one or several attempts. Fifty-four percent of the men and 21 percent of the women were essentially free of depression throughout the marriage. Of the remaining men 10 percent experienced severe, disabling depressions, some requiring hospitalization, and 36 percent were severely depressed, again with some recurrent hospitalizations in this group, and nearly half were moderately depressed at some time in their marriage. Of the women 42 percent (versus 16 percent of the men) had chronic depressions of more than five years' duration, often accompanied by psychosomatic symptoms, including numbness, vague pains, and severe and recurring migraines. . . .

Disequilibrium and Regression

. . . One of the startling findings of the California Divorce Study was the appearance of profoundly regressive and disturbed behavior in a broad range of men and women opposed to the divorce. The shock of rejection, the feeling of helplessness, the sense of dependence on another person for survival—all of these conjoined to cause severe disequilibrium and disorganization of immense and threatening proportions. Generally associated with intense anger and depression, these men and women seemed catapulted into a period of chaos in which primitive, regressed, and uncontrolled behavior erupted unpredictably and for which hospitalization or sedation was sometimes required.

More than a quarter of the men experienced this type of severe disorganization, some over a period of many months, others for one episode, for a few days, or for a week. Some of the men so affected had histories of well-controlled, circumspect behavior throughout the marriage and were successful as businessmen and professionals, and in a few instances they continued to function well in their occupations despite the eruption of primitive behavior outside of work hours. After separating at their wives' insistence, these men engaged in acts of spying, breaking down the doors at night, obscene and frightening phone calls, physical beatings, vandalism, and attempted childnapping.

A similar number of women became severely disorganized from the decision to divorce. Like the men, their wildly fluctuating behavior reflected the severe regression precipitated by the separation. The behavior and thinking of these women [were] irrational and bewildering but were more often expressed verbally or through the children rather than physically.

Equally important, however, were those men and women who did not become particularly disorganized in their personality functioning. While experiencing and acknowledging varying degrees and types of stress, such as intense anxiety, anger, or economic stability, their usual state of equilibrium was not essentially affected. For almost 50 percent of the men (those seeking or not bitterly opposed to the divorce) and 42 percent of the women (all initiators of divorce), there was only mild, if any, disequilibrium generated by the separation. Because 75 percent of the women sought divorce, we can observe that being the party to initiate divorce does not in itself insure stabilized functioning, although these men and women were less likely to experience a state of acute crisis.

Attachment

Weiss (1975, 1979) has described a persisting marital bond in separated spouses which seems unrelated to liking or respect for the spouse. The "separation distress" created by a loss of attachment was seen to be nearly universal after separation, regardless of who precipitated the divorce, and faded only slowly over time if there was no contact with the spouse.

Several recent studies have explored the frequency and type of contacts between separated and divorced men and women. Half of the respondents interviewed by Bloom and Hodges (Note 3), all separated less than six months, described a desire to spend time with their spouses. This occurred significantly more with nonparents than with parents. The majority of respondents were in contact to work out separation details, and parent communications often focused on their children. . . .

Spanier and Castro (1979) explored the issue of continuing attachment in their 50 separated respondents and found 36 percent to have a continuing strong attachment, 36 percent with evidence of mild attachment, and 28 percent showing no evidence of attachment. . . .

Another study (Ahrons, Note 2) examined the nature of the continued coparental interaction at some distance from the separation. Of the couples 85 percent maintained some contact with each other postdivorce (approximately 2 to 2½ years postseparation). Two-thirds of the divorced parents spoke on the phone at least once a month, and their continued relationship involved parental, as well as nonparental, dimensions. Ahrons observed that the majority of the men and women maintained a "kin" or "quasi-kin" relationship with their former spouses which did not produce the stress of persisting marital bonds described by Weiss (1979). Components of the continuing relations, rooted in the past, were identified which, far from being pathological, had positive value for the former spouses and approximated a "normative attachment" involving caring, trust, and friendship.

Relief

As might be anticipated by some of the preceding data, a sense of relief obtained by the separation (and perhaps in making the decision to divorce) was also a major emotional response. . . . Based on ratings of expression of relief, apart from a sense of well-being, no sex differences emerged in the California study. Nearly half of the men and women indicated considerable, if not great, relief after separation. Reported sources of relief included making one of the most difficult decisions of their lives (more difficult by far than the one to marry), as well as relief from the fear and tension that had increased in the time interval between the announced decision to divorce and the actual separation. Some men reporting relief who had not sought the divorce (almost 25 percent) were relieved at their wives' act to terminate a relationship which was more destructive and miserable than had been previously recognized. . . .

The Feeling of a New Chance

Distinct from relief or contentedness with separation, one-fifth of the women in the California Divorce Study described a feeling and conviction that the divorce represented a chance to begin anew. They cautiously articulated their intent to improve the quality of family life for themselves and their children. Not found in women who opposed the divorce, these "new chance" women often felt guilty about the effects that their unhappy marriage may have had on their children, and indeed some had been married to emotionally disturbed men who had dominated the household and family life in erratic and destructive ways. Few of these women had plans to remarry; they intended to strike out on their own and perceived that, even with the anxiety and stress engendered by separating and setting up an independent household, a healthier atmosphere would prevail.

No men expressed this "new chance" phenomenon, in part because they, with one exception, did not have custody of their children. Those who reported a feeling of beginning anew had the immediate intention of remarrying and sought to improve their own lives rather than that of their children's. Some men, in fact, did improve the quality of relationship between themselves and their children in the year following separation, but they had not anticipated this or actively sought to bring about such positive change. . . .

POSTDIVORCE ADJUSTMENT

Attitudes Toward Divorce

In the California Divorce Study the intervening five years between the separation and the second follow-up brought substantial change in attitudes about the divorce (Wallerstein and Kelly, 1980; Kelly, Note 5). Nearly one-half of the men bitterly opposed the divorce at separation, but by five years two-thirds expressed a positive view of the divorce. The significant relationship observed initially between initiating the divorce action, opposition to divorce, and acute stress no longer appeared. Despite a favorable attitude among the majority of men toward divorce and its overall impact on their lives, only 30 percent perceived themselves as content.

Nearly one-fifth of the men had strongly mixed feelings about the divorce, while the remaining 17 percent had a totally negative view of divorce. Five years postseparation these bitter men continued to feel their lives had been ruined by their wives' decision to divorce. Having achieved no insight into their own behavior or possible contributions to the marital failure, their rumination about the divorce and the injustice done to them were strikingly similar to those heard five years earlier. By five years such bitterness and failure to achieve any psychological closure on the divorce experience was significantly linked to serious psychological disturbance.

In contrast to the approving men, whose numbers doubled in the five-year interval, the number of women viewing the divorce favorably had *decreased* in the corresponding time span. Fifty-six percent, equally divided between the remarried and still divorced, felt the divorce had enhanced their lives, including some who originally were shattered by their husband's decision to end the marriage. While many were lonely the majority of this group had made significant shifts in the direction of greater self-esteem. Women, and men, who approved of the divorce at five years most often relegated the divorce to the past. The divorce no longer occupied their thoughts; it had become essentially a dead issue, and for these individuals there was little, if any, remaining hostility toward their ex-spouse.

Nearly one-quarter of the women described strongly mixed feelings about the divorce at five years, most of whom sought the divorce with high hopes. For these women the combined burdens of full-time work and parenting, economic deprivation, social isolation, and loneliness compromised their continuing view that the divorce was a necessary process, and they longed for the remembered and/or fantasized gratifications of the marriage.

Of the women 21 percent viewed the divorce as a totally deplorable event at five years, including a few who initiated the divorce and now viewed their decision as a grave and irretrievable mistake. . . .

Restabilization

Significant sex differences emerged in the length of time it took divorced men and women in the California Divorce Study to restabilize their lives postseparation, a finding noted earlier by Raschke (1974) as well. On the average it took women 3.3 years after separation before their lives assumed a sense of coherence, postdivorce reorganization, and stability, in contrast to 2.2 years postseparation for the men. Older men (43 and older) restabilized significantly earlier than did younger men, but no such difference existed for women. Being a custodial parent appeared to create more turbulence and prolonged the time needed to stabilize, but this relationship warrants further study as to other factors, such as poverty, excessive litigation, and intense bitterness, which were noted to create a sustained period of stressful and unsettled family life.

. . . Thirty-one percent of the men and 42 percent of the women had not achieved a restructured postdivorce stability five years after separation. . . .

The Quality of Life Postdivorce

Contentment and Self-Esteem

Hetherington et al. (1976) reported steady increases in happiness and self-esteem over the two-year period following the final divorce for men and women; yet in comparison to married couples, the divorced men and women were overall less happy and had lower self-esteem. Happiness and self-esteem correlated strongly with intimacy and heterosexual relationships in both samples. The California Divorce Study observed a similar rise in self-esteem, particularly in the women, and a greater sense of contentment with their lives than when initially observed. For 55 percent of the men and two-thirds of the women, life was somewhat, if not significantly, improved, whereas serious problems were created for 15 percent of the men and women. For those individuals with enhanced self-esteem and greater happiness, divorce offered not only a solution to an unsatisfactory marriage but also an opportunity to achieve a healthier and more productive level of psychological adjustment.

Social Interaction

The divorced men studied by Hetherington et al. (1976) were socially quite active in the first year after divorce, but by the second year their social activities had decreased. Divorced mothers complained of social isolation and in fact had significantly less contact with other adults than did divorced men or married couples.

Loneliness was a remaining problem for divorced individuals five years postseparation, but significantly more so for women than for men. The majority of men and women not remarried expressed disillusionment and some distaste for the shallowness of the "singles scene," and women in particular were dissatisfied and depressed by casual sexual encounters (Hetherington et al., 1976; Wallerstein and Kelly, 1980). Those with higher self-esteem preferred their own company to a social and sexual life of continuing disappointment but spoke longingly at five years of their wish for a heterosexual relationship that involved mutual sharing, trust, and affection. Over the intervening years the intensity of loneliness had diminished somewhat as men and women constructed other social networks as alternatives to unsatisfactory dating arrangements. Thus 45 percent of the men and 63 percent of the women were moderately to acutely lonely, and a substantial number of both men and women had no social contacts at all. Severe loneliness was associated significantly more often with unstable psychological functioning in both men and women, and for men, with being in the lower socioeconomic classes. Troubled, lonely women, on the other hand, were more often previously married to upper-class men and, cut adrift from their social moorings and identifications through divorce, seemed unable to reestablish or continue a social life at any level.

CONCLUSIONS

With several million people newly affected each year by divorce, there is compelling need to turn further research attention to this social and psychological phenomenon that has brought far-reaching change to individuals and society at large. Virtually every facet of the divorce experience needs further exploration and replication if we are to understand with greater depth and more certainty both the immediate and longer-range impact of divorce on men and women. The complexities of failed marriages, the divorce decision, the separation period with the intense stress-engendered emotional reactions . . . all of these and more require our continued attention in the coming years.

REFERENCE NOTES

1. Fulton, J. A. *Factors related to parental assessments of the effect of divorce on children: A research report.* Paper presented at the NIMH conference on children and divorce, February 1978. A shortened version of this report was published in *Journal of Social Issues,* 1979, 35, 126–139.
2. Ahrons, C. R. *The continuing coparental relationship between divorced spouses.* Paper presented at the American Orthopsychiatric Association Annual Meeting, Toronto, 1980.
3. Bloom, B. L., & Hodges, W. S. *The predicament of the newly separated.* First report of an NIMH-funded longitudinal investigation.
4. Kitson, G. C., and Sussman, M. B. *Marital complaints, characteristics and symptoms of mental distress among the divorcing.* Paper presented at the Midwest Sociological Society, Minneapolis, Minn., 1977.
5. Kelly, J. B. *Parent attitudes about divorce at separation and five years later.* Paper presented at the American Orthopsychiatric Association Annual Meeting, Toronto, 1980.

REFERENCES

GOODE, W. J. *Women in divorce.* New York: Free Press, 1956. Republished as *Divorce and after.* New York: Free Press, 1969.

HERMAN, S. J. Women, divorce and suicide. *Journal of Divorce,* 1977, 1, 107–117.

HETHERINGTON, E. M., COX, M., and COX R. Divorced fathers. *Family Coordinator,* 1976, 25, 417–428.

HILL, C. T. *The ending of successive opposite-sex relationships.* Unpublished doctoral dissertation. Harvard University, 1974.

LEVINGER, G. Sources of marital dissatisfaction among applicants for divorce. *American Journal of Orthopsychiatry,* 1966, 36, 803–807.

RASCHKE, H. J. *Social and psychological factors in voluntary postmarital dissolution adjustment.* Unpublished doctoral dissertation, University of Minnesota at Minneapolis, 1974.

RUBIN, Z. *The social psychology of romantic love.* Doctoral dissertation, University of Michigan, 1969. (University Microfilms, No. 70–4179)

SPANIER, G. B., and CASTRO, R. F. Adjustment to separation and divorce: An analysis of 50 case studies. *Journal of Divorce,* 1979, 2, 241–253.

WALLERSTEIN, J. S., and KELLY, J. B. *Surviving the breakup: How children and parents cope with divorce.* New York: Basic Books, 1980.

WEISS, R. S. *Marital separation*. New York: Basic Books, 1975.

WEISS, R. S. The emotional impact of marital separation. In G. Levinger & O. Moles (Eds.), *Divorce and separation: Context, causes and consequences*. New York: Basic Books, 1979.

42

Effects of Divorce
on Mothers and Children
▼▼▼▼▼
Urie Bronfenbrenner

ABSTRACT: After describing the vicious cycle that divorced mothers experience—increased responsibilities, reduced income, and greater demands from children—the author reports findings on such aspects of parenting as maturity demands, communication, giving affection, and discipline. Concerning findings that the development of children in mother-headed single-parent homes is disrupted, he notes the importance of support systems and stabilizing third parties.

[In studies in which the cases were matched] scientifically to compare only single mothers with mothers in two-parent families who have the same income to see what single parenthood does by itself, developmental changes are found not only in children but also in parents. . . . [T]he ones who are affected most at the beginning [of divorce] are the husbands. They panic right after divorce and rush about trying on new identities. But they get over it in a year or two, as soon as they find a new female friend.

Recovery is not so quick for the remaining family members. The following summarizes the main research findings about the effects of divorce on the mother and the children. Placed in the unaccustomed posi-

424

tion of family head, the mother often finds its necessary, because of her reduced financial condition, to look for work or for a more remunerative job than the current one. At the same time, she must care for the house and children, not to mention create a new personal life for herself. The result is a vicious cycle. The children in the absence of the father demand more attention, but the mother has other tasks that must be done. In response, the children become more demanding. This spiraling process often leads to an unhappy outcome. The data reveal that in comparison with youngsters in intact families, the children of a divorce are less likely to heed the mother's requests yet are more ready to respond to the father's wishes when he comes around. This can prompt the father to say, "Look, you can't even make him behave. I have no problem. You're not even a decent parent." Ironically, he's right, in a tragic kind of way. Of course, he too is part of the problem. But to a still greater degree, as we shall see, the fault lies with our society; the way we treat single mothers and their children.

Even when the child is responsive to her, the divorced mother is less apt to acknowledge or reward the action. Mavis Hetherington (1978) of the University of Virginia, did one of the best designed, most perceptively and carefully analyzed studies in this area. She found that divorced parents, in comparison with matched groups of married parents, make fewer maturity demands, communicate less well, tend to be less affectionate, and show marked inconsistency in discipline and control of their children. Such poor parenting is more pronounced when divorced parents, particularly divorced mothers, interact with their sons rather than with their daughters. By the way, whenever the going gets tough, it's the truly weaker sex that is most affected: It's males who are undermined more often than females.

Here's a summary of a score of studies: Children living in mother-headed single-parent homes appear at higher risk for disruption in cognitive, emotional, and social development than do children in nuclear families. Children of divorce have difficulty in school, in part because they don't pay attention. Their minds are elsewhere. They are reacting to the stressful situation in which the mother finds herself. In the words of one of the mothers in Hetherington's study, to be a single mother "is like being bitten to death by ducks."

To be sure, the third year after the divorce, the situation improves, but it is still not back to the level of the matched controls from two-parent families. Moreover, the effects of divorce must be viewed in the light of two other important findings:

1. In most research in this area, the comparison is between single-parent families and two-parent families matched on socioeconomic characteristics but not matched on the state of the mother/father relationship. Fortunately, there are a few studies that also have considered the quality of the marriage. Both in Britain and in the United States, these

investigations reveal that children whose parents decide to stay together despite high levels of marital disharmony show even more deleterious effects than do youngsters from father-absent homes. Again, it is the boys who are most affected. So it's not just the one-parent situation. Then what is it? Hetherington (1978:31) sums it up: "These developmental disruptions do not seem attributable mainly to father-absence, but rather to the stresses and the lack of support systems that result in changed family functioning for the single mother and her children."

2. Not all children of divorce exhibit the problems I have described. Why not? The situations in which divorced youngsters were doing fine had one characteristic in common: There was a third party. Somebody acted as the third leg of the stool, giving it stability. It could be a friend, a coworker, more often a relative: the mother's mother, sometimes her mother-in-law. But the most effective, most powerful stabilizing third party was the father, the ex-husband. If he still hung in there, not just in relation to his children but in relation to that family; if he was there to spell the mother; if in an emergency she could call his number; if he dropped by to ask, "Are things OK?"—then nothing terrible happened so far as the children were concerned. Mom may not have been particularly happy, but the kids were able to hack it.

REFERENCE

HETHERINGTON, E. M., M. COX, R. COX. 1978. "The Aftermath of Divorce," in J. H. Stevens, Jr. and M. Mathews, eds., *Mother-Child, Father-Child Relations*. Washington, D.C.: National Association for the Education of Young Children.

43

▼▼▼▼

The Divorce Revolution
and the Feminization of Poverty
▼▼▼▼

Lenore J. Weitzman

ABSTRACT: After divorce, the standard of living of most men increases 42 percent but decreases by 73 percent for women and children. Older and longer-married women suffer the greatest economic decline. This feminization of poverty is a consequence of (1) no-fault divorce laws that have led to inadequate court awards, (2) expanded demands on the former wife's resources after divorce, and (3) the former husband's greater earning capacity and ability to supplement his income. After reviewing suggestions for correcting this inequity and summarizing the effects of deprivation on children of divorce, the author suggests that we may be moving into a two-tier society.

[. . . California pioneered in introducing a "no-fault" divorce law in 1970. The law is based on the modern idea that spouses can agree to divorce rather than fighting an adversarial battle in a court. In interpreting the new law, judges are not so quick to protect women as they once were. They award women alimony even more rarely than in the past. At the same time, the courts continue to give mothers primary responsibility for rearing children. Thus, the new law and its interpretation have contributed to a widening gender gap in income.]

Divorce has radically different economic consequences for men and women. While most divorced men find that their standard of living improves after divorce, most divorced women and the minor children in their households find that their standard of living plummets. This [chapter] shows that when income is compared to needs, divorced men experience an average 42 percent rise in their standard of living in the first year after the divorce, while divorced women (and their children) experience a 73 percent decline.

These apparently simple statistics have far reaching social and economic consequences. For most women and children, divorce means precipitous downward mobility—both economically and socially. The reduction in income brings residential moves and inferior housing, drastically diminished or nonexistent funds for recreation and leisure, and intense pressures due to inadequate time and money. Financial hardships in turn cause social dislocation and a loss of familiar networks for emotional support and social services, and intensify the psychological stress for women and children alike. On a societal level, divorce increases female and child poverty and creates an ever-widening gap between the economic well-being of divorced men, on the one hand, and their children and former wives on the other.

The data reviewed in this [chapter] indict the present legal system of divorce: it provides neither economic justice nor economic equality.

The economic consequences of the current system of divorce emerge from two different types of analysis. In the first analysis we focus on income. Here we compare men's and women's *incomes* before and after divorce. The second analysis focuses on *standards of living*. Here we ask how the husbands' postdivorce standards of living compare with that of their former wives. Since it is reasonable to expect postdivorce incomes and standards of living to vary with the length of marriage and the family income level before divorce, these two factors are controlled in the following analyses. . . .

LONG-MARRIED COUPLES
AND DISPLACED HOMEMAKERS

Economically, older and longer-married women suffer the most after divorce. Their situation is much more drastic—and tragic—than that of their younger counterparts because the discrepancy between men's and women's standards of living after divorce is much greater than for younger couples, and few of these women can ever hope to recapture their loss. . . .

When the courts project the postdivorce prospects for women after shorter marriages, they assume that most of these women will be able to build new lives for themselves.[1] They reason that a woman in her twenties or early thirties is young enough to acquire education or training and thus has the potential to find a satisfying and well-paid job. To be sure, such women will probably have a hard time catching up with their former husbands, but most of them will be able to enter or reenter the labor force. In setting support for these younger women, the underlying assumption is that they will become self-sufficient. (I am not questioning that assumption. What has been questioned is the court's optimism about the ease and speed of the transition. Younger divorced women need more generous support awards for training and education to maximize their long-run job prospects.[2] But their potential for some level of ''self-sufficiency'' is not questioned.)

But what about the woman in her forties or fifties—or even sixties at the point of divorce? What are her prospects? Is it reasonable for judges to expect her to become self-sufficient? This woman's problems of job placement, retraining, and self-esteem are likely to be much more severe.[3] Her divorce award is likely to establish her standard of living for the rest of her life.

The hardest case is that of the long-married woman who has devoted her life to raising children who are now grown. Consider, for example, the hypothetical Ann Thompson, age fifty-three, who was formerly married to a wealthy corporate executive. She is much better off after divorce than the vast majority of divorced women her age because her former husband earns $6,000 a month net. The average Los Angeles judge would award Ann Thompson $2,000 a month in spousal support, giving her a total income of $24,000 a year in contrast to her former husband's $48,000 a year (after alimony payments are deducted from his income). Her former husband will be able to maintain his comfortable standard of living on his $48,000 income (which is likely to rise) and the tax benefits he gets from paying alimony. But Ann, with her house sold, no employment prospects, and the loss of her social status and social networks, will not be able to sustain anything near her former standard of living.

Since Ann Thompson's three children are over eighteen, she is not legally entitled to any child support for them.[4] She is likely, however, to be contributing to their college expenses. In addition, one or more of them is likely to still be living with her, and all probably return from time to time for extended visits. Thus she may well be providing as much if not more for their support than their well-to-do father.*

The combined effects of a less than equal income and a greater than equal share of the children's expenses invariably result in extreme downward mobility for long-married divorced women in California.

---

*When Stanford University students from divorced families were interviewed for a class research project most reported that they first asked their mother for money, even though they knew she had less than their father, because they found her more sympathetic and willing to support them.

They are both absolutely and relatively worse off than their former husbands. Although the courts are supposed to aim at balancing the resources of the two postdivorce households, the data reveal that they do not come near this goal. . . .

The data indicate that men married more than eighteen years have a much higher *per capita* income—that is, they have much more money to spend on themselves—than their former wives at every level of (predivorce family) income. Even where the discrepancy is smallest, in lower-income families, the husband and every member of this postdivorce family have *twice* as much money as his former wife and his children. In higher-income families, the discrepancy is enormous. The husband and each person in his postdivorce household—his new wife, cohabitor, or child—have three times as much disposable income as his former wife and the members of her postdivorce household. When we realize that the "other members" of the wife's postdivorce household are almost always the husband's children, the discrepancy between the two standards of living seems especially unjust.

POSTDIVORCE STANDARDS OF LIVING: IMPOVERISHMENT OF WOMEN AND CHILDREN

. . . We devised a procedure to calculate the basic needs of each of the families in our interview sample. This procedure used the living standards for urban families constructed by the Bureau of Labor Statistics of the U.S. Department of Labor.[5] First, the standard budget level for each family in the interview sample was calculated in three different ways: once for the predivorce family, once for the wife's postdivorce family, and once for the husband's postdivorce family. Then the income in relation to needs was computed for each family. (Membership in postdivorce families of husbands and wives included any new spouse or cohabitor and any children whose custody was assigned to that spouse.) These data are presented in Figure 43.1.

Figure 43.1 reveals the radical change in the standards of living to which we alluded earlier. Just one year after legal divorce, *men experience a 42 percent improvement in their postdivorce standard of living, while women experience a 73 percent decline.**

These data indicate that *divorce is a financial catastrophe for most women:* in just one year [women] experience a dramatic decline in income and

*Detailed information from the interviews provided the researchers with precise income data, including income from employment, intra-family transfers, welfare, and other government programs. Alimony and/or child support paid by the husband was subtracted from his income and added to his wife's postdivorce income. Finally, to facilitate direct comparisons, all income was calculated in constant 1968 dollars so that changes in real income could be examined without the compounding effect of inflation.

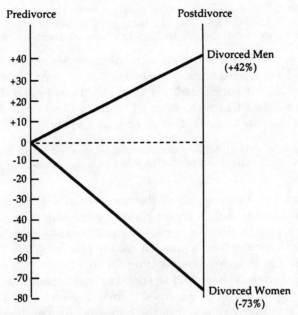

Figure 43.1. **Change in Standards of Living* of Divorced Men and Women (Approximately one year after divorce)**
*Income in relation to needs with needs based on U.S. Department of Agriculture's low standard budget.

Based on weighted sample of interviews with divorced persons. Los Angeles County, California, 1978.

a calamitous drop in their standard of living. It is hard to imagine how they deal with such severe deprivation: every single expenditure that one takes for granted—clothing, food, housing, heat—must be cut to one-half or one-third of what one is accustomed to.

It is difficult to absorb the full implications of these statistics. What does it mean to have a 73 percent decline in one's standard of living? When asked how they coped with this drastic decline in income, many of the divorced women said that they themselves were not sure. It meant "living on the edge" and "living without." As some of them described it:

We ate macaroni and cheese five nights a week. There was a Safeway special for 39 cents a box. We could eat seven dinners for $3.00 a week. . . . I think that's all we ate for months.

I applied for welfare. . . . It was the worse experience of my life. . . . I never dreamed that I, a middle-class housewife, would ever be in a position like that. It was humiliating . . . they make you feel it. . . . But we were desperate and I *had* to feed my kids.

You name it, I tried it—food stamps, soup kitchens, shelters. It just about killed me to have the kids live like that. . . . I finally called my parents and said we were coming . . . we couldn't have survived without them.

Even those who had relatively affluent life-styles before the divorce experienced a sharp reduction in their standard of living and faced hardships they had not anticipated. For example, the wife of a dentist sold her car "because I had no cash at all, and we lived on that money—barely—for close to a year." And an engineer's wife:

I didn't buy my daughter any clothes for a year—even when she graduated from high school we sewed together two old dresses to make an outfit. . . .

Others spoke of cutting out all the nonessentials. For one women it meant "no movies, no ice cream cones for the kids." For another it meant not replacing tires on her son's bike "because there just wasn't the money." For another woman it meant not using her car—a real handicap in Los Angeles—and waiting for two buses in order to save the money she would have had to spend for gas. In addition to scaled-down budgets for food ("We learned to love chicken backs") and clothing ("At Christmas I splurged at the Salvation Army—the only 'new' clothes they got all year"), many spoke of cutting down on their children's school lunches ("I used to plan a nourishing lunch with fruit and juice; now she's lucky if we have a slice of ham for a sandwich") and school supplies and after-school activities ("He had to quit the Little League and get a job as a delivery boy").

Still, some of the women were not able to "make it." Fourteen percent of them moved onto the welfare rolls during the first year after the divorce, and a number of others moved back into their parents' homes when they had "no money left and nowhere to go and three children to feed."

EXPLAINING THE DISPARITY BETWEEN HUSBANDS' AND WIVES' STANDARDS OF LIVING

How can we explain the strikingly different economic consequences of divorce for men and women? How could [no-fault divorce laws] that aimed at fairness create such disparities between divorced men and their former wives and children?

The explanation lies first in the inadequacy of the court's awards, second in the expanded demands on the wife's resources after divorce, and third in the husband's greater earning capacity and ability to supplement his income.

Consider first the court awards for child support (and in rarer cases, alimony). Since judges do not require men to support either their children or their former wives as they did during marriage, they allow the husband to keep most of his income for himself. Since only a few wives are awarded alimony, the only supplementary income they are awarded is child support and the average child support award covers less than half of the cost of raising a child. Thus, the average support award is simply inadequate: even if the husband pays it, it often leaves the wife and children in relative poverty. The custodial mother is expected . . . somehow [to] make up the deficit alone even though she typically earns much less than her former husband.

In this regard, it is also important to note the role that property awards play in contributing to—rather than alleviating—the financial disparities between divorced women and men. Under the old law, when the wife with minor children was typically awarded the family home, she started her postdivorce life on a more equal footing because the home provided some stability and security and reduced the impact of the income loss suffered at divorce. Today, when the family home is more commonly sold to allow an "equal" division of property, there is no cushion to soften the financial devastations that low support awards create for women and children. Rather, the disruptive costs of moving and establishing a new household further strain their limited income—often to the breaking point.

The second explanation for the disparity between former husbands and wives lies in the greater demands on the wife's household after divorce, and the diminished demands on the husband's. Since the wife typically assumes the responsibility for raising the couple's children, her need for help and services increases as a direct result of her becoming a single parent. Yet at the very time that her need for more income and more financial support is greatest, the courts have drastically reduced her income. Thus the gap between her income and her needs is wider after divorce.

In contrast, the gap between the husband's income and needs narrows. Although he now has fewer absolute dollars, the demands on his income have diminished: he often lives alone and he is no longer financially responsible for the needs of his ex-wife and children. While he loses the benefits of economies of scale, and while he may have to purchase some services (such as laundry and cooking) that he did not have to buy during marriage, he is nevertheless much better off because he has so much more money to spend on himself. Since he has been allowed to retain most of his income for himself, he can afford these extra expenses and still have more surplus income than he enjoyed during marriage.

The final explanation for the large income discrepancy between former husbands and wives lies in the different earning capacities and starting points of the two adults at the time of the divorce. Not only do men in our society command higher salaries to begin with, they also benefit from the common marital pattern that gives priority to their careers. Marriage gives men the opportunity, support, and time to invest in their own careers. Thus marriage itself builds and enhances the husband's earning capacity. For women, in contrast, marriage is more likely to act as a career liability. Even though family roles are changing, and even though married women are increasingly working for pay during marriage, most of them nevertheless subordinate their careers to their husbands' and to their family responsibilities. This is especially true if they have children. Thus women are often doubly disadvantaged at the point of divorce. Not only do they face the "normal" 60-percent male/female income gap that affects all working women, they also suffer from the toll the marital years have taken on their earning capacity.

Thus marriage—and then divorce—impose a differential disadvantage on women's employment prospects, and this is especially severe for women who have custody of minor children. The responsibility for children inevitably restricts the mother's job opportunities by limiting her work schedule and location, her availability for overtime, and her freedom to take advantage of special training, travel assignments, and other opportunities for career advancement.

Although the combined income of the former spouses typically increases after divorce, most of the rise is a result of the husband's increased income. Even though women who have not been employed during marriage seek jobs after divorce, and part-time workers take full-time jobs, neither of these factors accounts for as much as the rise in male wages in the first year after divorce. . . .

During the same period, the obligations that these men have for alimony and child support typically remain fixed or diminish: some support obligations have been reduced or terminated by terms of the divorce settlement (and others have been reduced or stopped without the courts' permission). The result, once again, is that divorced men have more "surplus income" for themselves.

The discrepancy between divorced men and women has been corroborated by other research. Sociologist Robert Weiss and economist Thomas Espenshade . . . and Census Bureau data also document the disparities in both income and standards of living of men and women after divorce. In 1979, the median per capita income of divorced women who had not remarried was $4,152, just over half of the $7,886 income of divorced men who had not remarried.[6]

The situation of divorced women with young children is even more grim. The median income in families headed by women with children under six years of age was only 30 percent of the median income for all families whose children were under six.[7] Thus, for the United States as a whole, the "income of families headed by women is at best half that of other families; the income of families headed by women with young children is even less, one-third of that of other families."[8]. . .

SOCIETAL CONSEQUENCES

The rise in divorce has been the major cause of the increase in female-headed families,[9] and that increase has been the major cause of the feminization of poverty. Sociologist Diana Pearce, who coined the phrase "feminization of poverty" was one of the first to point to the critical link between poverty and divorce for women.[10] It was, she said, the mother's burden for the economic and emotional responsibility for child rearing that often impoverished her family.

Contrary to popular perception, most female-headed single-parent families in the United States are *not* the result of unwed parenthood: they are the result of marital dissolution.[11] Only 18 percent of the nearly ten million female-headed families in the United States are headed by an unwed mother: over 50 percent are headed by divorced mothers and the remaining 31 percent by separated mothers.[12]

When a couple with children divorces, it is probable that the man will become single but the woman will become a single parent. And poverty, for many women, begins with single parenthood. More than half of the poor families in the United States are headed by a single mother.[13]

The National Advisory Council on Economic Opportunity estimates that if current trends continue, the poverty population of the United States will be composed solely of women and children by the year 2000.[14] The Council declares that the "feminization of poverty has become one of the most compelling social facts of the decade."[15]

THE RISE IN FEMALE POVERTY

The well-known growth in the number of single-parent, female-headed households has been amply documented elsewhere. (The 8 percent of all children who lived in mother-child families in 1960 rose to 12 percent by 1970[16] and to [22] percent by [1988].[17]) Also well-documented is the fact that these mother-headed families are the fastest growing segment of the American poor.[18]

What has not been well documented, and what appears to be relatively unknown—or unacknowledged—is the direct link between divorce, the economic consequences of divorce, and the rise in female poverty. The high divorce rate has vastly multiplied the numbers of women who are left alone to support themselves and their minor children. When the courts deny divorced women the support and property they need to maintain their families, they are relying, they say, on the woman's ability to get a job and support herself. But with women's current disadvantages in the labor market, getting a job cannot be the only answer—because it does not guarantee a woman a way out of poverty.[19] Even with full-time employment, one-third of the women cannot earn enough to enable them and their children to live above the poverty level.[20] The structure of the job market is such that *only half* of all full-time female workers are able to support two children without supplemental income from either the children's fathers or the government.[21]

In recent years there have been many suggestions for combating the feminization of poverty. Most of these have focused on changes in the labor market (such as altering the sex segregation in jobs and professions, eliminating the dual labor market and the disparity between jobs in the primary and secondary sectors, eradicating the discriminatory structure of wages, and providing additional services, such as child care, for working mothers) and on expanding social welfare programs (such as increasing AFDC benefits to levels above the poverty line, augmenting Medicaid, food stamp, and school lunch programs, and making housewives eligible for Social Security and unemployment compensation).

A third possibility, which has not received widespread attention, is to change the way that courts allocate property and income at divorce. If, for example, custodial mothers and their children were allowed to remain in the family home, and if the financial responsibility for children were apportioned according to the means of the two parents, and if court orders for support were enforced, a significant segment of the population of divorced women and their children would not be impoverished by divorce.

THE RISE IN CHILD POVERTY
AND ECONOMIC HARDSHIPS
FOR MIDDLE-CLASS CHILDREN OF DIVORCE

. . . While the vast majority (82 percent) of all children born in the United States today are born into two-parent families, more than half of these children are likely to experience the disruption of their parents' marriage before they reach age eighteen. As noted above, U.S. Census Bureau data show that close to 60 percent of the children born in 1983 *would not* spend their entire childhood living with both natural parents,[22] while Sandra Hofferth of the National Institute of Child Health and Human Development projected that two-thirds of the children born in wedlock in 1980 would experience a parental divorce before they reach age seventeen.[23]

Whichever figures we use, the statistics suggest that we are sentencing a significant proportion of the current generation of American children to lives of financial impoverishment.

Clearly, living in a single-parent family does not have to mean financial hardship. The economic well-being of many of these children is in jeopardy only because their mothers bear the whole responsibility for their support. That jeopardy would end if courts awarded more alimony, higher amounts of child support, and a division of property that considered the interests of minor children. It would also be greatly reduced if the child support awards that the courts have already made were systematically enforced. Under the present legal system, however, the financial arrangements of divorce foster the financial deprivation of millions of children.

Although the deprivation is most severe below the poverty level, it affects children at every income level. In fact, middle-class children, like their mothers, experience the greatest relative deprivation. The economic dislocations of divorce bring about many changes which are particularly difficult for children: moving to new and less secure neighborhoods, changing schools, losing friends, being excluded from activities that have become too expensive for the family's budget, and having to work after school or help care for younger siblings.

Not surprisingly, the children of divorce often express anger and resentment when their standard of living is significantly less than that in their father's household.[24] They realize that their lives have been profoundly altered by the loss of "their home" and school and neighborhood and friends, and by the new expectations their mother's reduced income creates for them. . . .

The middle-class children of divorce may also feel betrayed by their disenfranchisement in their parents' property settlement. Since the law divides family property between the husband and wife and makes no provision for a child's share of the marital assets, many children feel they have been unfairly deprived of "their" home, "their" piano, "their" stereo set, and their college education. . . . The U.S. Census Bureau data on chid support indicated that even though child support awards are quite modest, less than half of all fathers comply fully with court orders for child support. Another quarter make some payment, and close to 30 percent do not pay anything at all.[25]

Inasmuch as about 1.2 million children's parents divorce each year, the 30 percent who receive no support from their fathers adds up to 360,000 new children each year. Over a ten-year period, this amounts to 4 million children. If we add to these the approximately 3 million over the years who receive only part of their child support (or receive it only some of the time), we find a ten-year total of 7 million children deprived of the support to which they are entitled. Remembering that fewer than 4 million children are born each year helps to put all these figures in perspective.[26]

The failure of absent parents to provide child support has taken an especially severe toll in recent years because of sharp cutbacks in public programs benefiting children since 1979. The Children's Defense Fund shows that children's share of Medicaid payments dropped from 14.9 percent in 1979, to 11.9 percent in 1982, despite a rise in the child proportion among the eligible.[27] The Aid to Families with Dependent Children (AFDC) program has also been sharply cut back. In 1979, there were 72 children in AFDC for every 100 children in poverty, but only 52 per 100 in 1982.[28]

It is not surprising to find a strong relationship between the economic and psychological effects of divorce on children. Economic deprivation following divorce has been linked to increased anxiety and stress among American children.[29] Mounting evidence also shows that children of divorce who experience the most psychological stress are those whose postdivorce lives have been impaired by inadequate income. For example, Hodges, Tierney, and Bushbaum find "income inadequacy" the most important factor in accounting for anxiety and depression among preschool children in divorced families.[30] When family income is adequate, there are no differences in anxiety-depression levels between children in divorced families and those in intact families. However, "children of divorced families with inadequate income had substantially higher levels of anxiety-depression."[31] Hodges, Wechsler, and Ballantine also find significant correlations between income and adjustment for preschool children of divorce (but not, interestingly, for preschool children of intact families).[32]

In summary, the accumulating evidence shows that children in divorced families are likely to suffer a variety of adjustment problems if they experience greater geographic mobility, lower income, and poorer adequacy of income. Unfortunately, these experiences are common to most children of divorce.

CONCLUSION: THE TWO-TIER SOCIETY

The economic consequences of the present system of divorce reverberate throughout our society. Divorce awards not only contribute heavily to the well-documented income disparity between men and women, they also lead to the widespread impoverishment of children and enlarge the ever-widening gap between the economic well-being of men and women in the larger society. Indeed, if current conditions continue unabated we may well arrive at a two-tier society with an underclass of women and children.

Thrust into a spiral of downward mobility by the present system of divorce, a multitude of middle-class women and the children in their charge are increasingly cut off from sharing the income and wealth of former husbands and fathers. Hampered by restricted employment opportunities and sharply diminished income, these divorced women are increasingly expected to shoulder alone the burden of providing for both themselves and their children.

Most of the children of divorce share their mother's financial hardships. Their presence in her household increases the strains on her meager income at the same time that they add to her expenses and restrict her opportunities for economic betterment.

Meanwhile, divorced men increasingly are freed of the major financial responsibility for supporting their children and former wives. Moreover, these men retain more than higher incomes. They experience less day-to-day stress than their ex-wives, they enjoy relatively greater mental, physical, and emotional well-being, and have greater freedom to build new lives and new families after divorce.

The economic disparities between men and women after divorce illuminate the long-standing economic disparities between the incomes of men and women during marriage. In theory, those differences did not matter in marriage, since they were partners in the enterprise and shared the husband's income. As Christopher Jencks observes, ''As long as most American men and women married and pooled their economic resources, as they traditionally did, the fact the men received 70 percent of the nation's income had little effect on women's material well being.''[33] But with today's high divorce rate, the ranks of unmarried women are vastly increased, and the relative numbers of women who share a man's income are greatly diminished.

The result is that the economic gulf between the sexes in the larger society is increasing. Some of this would have occurred even if the traditional divorce law remained everywhere in force. But the new divorce laws—and the way these laws are being applied—have exacerbated the effects of the high divorce rate by assuring that ever greater numbers of women and children are being shunted out of the economic mainstream.

The data on the increase in female poverty, child poverty, and the comparative deprivation of middle-class women and children suggest that we are moving toward a two-tier society in which the upper economic tier is dominated by men (and the women and children who live with them). The former wives of many of these men, the mothers of their children, and the children themselves are increasingly found in the lower economic tier. Those in the first tier enjoy a comfortable standard of living; those in the lower tier are confined to lives of economic deprivation and hardship.

Obviously the two tiers are not totally segregated by sex: professional women for example, whether married or divorced, are more likely to be found in the first tier, and members of many minority groups, both men and women, are more likely to fall into the second. Yet among these groups, and among all families at the lower levels, divorce brings a better economic future for men than for their former wives. . . .

Obviously, membership in the second tier is not necessarily permanent. Some women will find jobs or return to school or obtain training that will enable them to improve their status. Many of those who are under thirty and some of those who are under forty will accomplish the same result by remarrying. But even those women who manage eventually to improve their financial situation will typically spend their early postdivorce years in acute economic hardship. The fact that they are poor only temporarily does not mean that they and their children suffer any the less[34] or that they can ever recapture the losses of those wasted years.

REFERENCE NOTES

1. These assumptions are discussed in Chapters 6 and 7 of *The Divorce Revolution*, on alimony awards, pp. 157, 158, 165, 176, 177 in Chapter 6, and pp. 184–187, 197, 204–206, in Chapter 7.
2. See Chapter 7 of *The Divorce Revolution*, pp. 206, 209, and Chapter 6, 165–169.
3. The special problems that older women face at divorce are discussed in Chapter 7 of *The Divorce Revolution*, pp. 187–194, 198–201, 209–212.
4. The issue of support for dependent children over eighteen is discussed in Chapter 9 of *The Divorce Revolution*, pp. 278–281.
5. We assumed that the basic needs level for each family was the Lower Standard Budget devised by the Bureau of Labor Statistics, U.S. Department of Labor, *Three Standards of Living for an Urban Family of Four Persons* (1967). This budget is computed for a four-person urban family (husband and wife and two children) and kept current by frequent adjustments.
6. Bureau of the Census, U.S. Dept. of Commerce, "Money Income of Families and Persons in the United States: 1979, "*Current Population Reports* Series P-60, No. 129, 1981, p. 23.
7. Bureau of the Census, U.S. Dept. of Commerce, "Families Maintained by Female Householders 1970–79," *Current Population Reports* Series P-23, No. 107, 1980, p. 36.
8. National Center on Women and Family Law, "Sex and Economic Discrimination in Child Custody Awards," *Clearinghouse Review* Vol. 16, no. 11, April 1983, p. 1132.
9. Jane R. Chapman and Gordon Chapman, "Poverty Viewed as a Woman's Problem—the U.S. Case," in *Women and the World of Work*, Anne Hoiberg, ed. (New York: Plenum, 1982).
10. Diana Pearce, "The Feminization of Poverty: Women, Work and Welfare," *Urban and Social Change Review*, Feb. 1978; and Diana Pearce and Harriette McAdoo, "Women

and Children: Alone and in Poverty" (Washington, D.C.: National Advisory Council on Economic Opportunity, September 1981), p. 1 (hereafter cited as Pearce and Mc-Adoo, "Women and Children in Poverty").

11. House Hearings on Child Support Enforcement legislation before the subcommittee on Public Assistance and Unemployment Compensation of the Committee on Ways and Means of the U.S. House of Representatives on July 14, 1983, p. 13 (Washington, D.C.: U.S. Government Printing Office, 1984) (hereafter cited as House Hearings 1983).

12. Ibid.

13. Barbara Ehrenreich and Francis Fox Piven, "The Feminization of Poverty: When the Family Wage System Breaks Down," *Dissent*, 1984, p. 162 (hereafter cited as Ehrenreich and Piven, "Feminization of Poverty").

14. National Advisory Council on Economic Opportunity, *Critical Choices for the '80s*, August 1980, p. 1 (Washington, D.C.: National Advisory Council, 1980).

15. Ibid.

16. Christopher Jencks, "Divorced Mothers, Unite," *Psychology Today*, November 1982, pp. 74–75 (hereafter cited as Jencks, "Divorced Mothers").

17. Ehrenreich and Piven, "Feminization of Poverty," p. 163.

18. Ibid., p. 162; Pearce and McAdoo, "Women and Children in Poverty"; Heather L. Ross and Isabel V. Sawhill, *Time of Transition: The Growth of Families Headed by Women* (Washington, D.C.: The Urban Institute Press, 1975).

19. Pearce and McAdoo, "Women and Children in Poverty," pp. 6, 18.

20. Briefing paper prepared for California Assemblyman Thomas H. Bates for hearings on "The Feminization of Poverty," San Francisco, Calif., April 8, 1983, mimeo, p. 6 (hereafter cited as Bates brief).

21. Ibid. Pearce and McAdoo, "Women and Children in Poverty."

22. Interview with Dr. Arthur Norton, March 1984.

23. Sandra Hofferth, "Updating Children's Life Course," Center for Population Research, National Institute for Child Health and Development, 1983.

24. Judith Wallerstein and Joan Kelly, *Surviving The Breakup: How Parents and Children Cope with Divorce* [New York: Basic Books, 1980], p. 231.

25. See Chapter 9, pp. 283–284, citing Bureau of the Census, "Child Support and Alimony, 1981, *"Current Population Reports*, Series P-23, No. 124.

26. House Hearings 1983, p. 27.

27. Children's Defense Fund, *American Children in Poverty* (Washington, D.C.: Children's Defense Fund, 1984).

28. Ibid.

29. Ann Goetting, "Divorce Outcome Research: Issues and Perspectives," in *The Family in Transition*, Fourth Edition, Arlene S. and Jerome H. Stolnick, eds. [Boston: Little Brown & Co., 1983]; and Nicholas Zil and James Peterson, "Trends in the Behavior and Emotional Well-Being of U.S. Children," Paper given at the 1982 Annual Meeting of the Association for the Advancement of Science, Washington, D.C., 1982.

30. William F. Hodges, Carol W. Tierney, and Helen K. Bushbaum, "The Cumulative Effect of Stress on Preschool Children of Divorced and Intact Families," *Journal of Marriage and the Family*, Vol. 46, no. 3, August 1984, pp. 611–629.

31. Ibid.

32. Ibid., citing their earlier work.

33. Jencks, "Divorced Mothers."

34. Ibid.

44
▼▼▼▼

The Stepfamily Cycle
▼▼▼▼▼

Patricia L. Papernow

ABSTRACT: Stepfamilies begin with built-in problems: a weak couple subsystem, a tightly bounded parent-child alliance, and potential "interference" in family functioning from the new spouse who is viewed as an outsider. Stepfamilies go through seven qualitative stages: fantasy, assimilation, awareness, mobilization, action, contact, and resolution. If a stepfamily gets "stuck" in a stage, it makes it difficult for them to function. Family practitioners should be sensitive to these stages so they can help stepfamilies accomplish their therapeutic tasks.

A REVIEW OF STEPFAMILY STRUCTURE

We know that stepfamilies begin their lives together with a very different history and structure from biological families. Briefly, biological families usually have some time together to develop a couple subsystem, and what Zinker (1981) called a "middle ground"—a solid area of shared interests, values, and rhythms of functioning. Children are added to the system one by one, allowing the couple to slowly resolve differences, create shared values, and evolve a cooperative parenting style.

When a couple divorces, a "double single-parent stage" (Sager et al., 1983) begins in which children become part of two single-parent families. A natural part of this process is the dissolution of intergenerational boundaries, as the single parent turns to his or her children for nourishment and support previously provided by the spouse. These relationships have been variously described in the literature as "overcathexis" (Neubauer, 1960), "pathologically intensified" (Fast and Cain, 1966), "intense overdependence" (Messinger, 1976), and more simply, "exceptionally close" (Visher and Visher, 1979). By whatever name, enmeshment seems to be a normal part of single parent/child relationships!

The stepfamily begins with the stepparent as an outsider to a biological subsystem with much shared history and many unfamiliar rhythms, rules, and ways of operating which have been built over years of connection and often intensified in the single parent stage. This biological subsystem includes an ex-spouse, dead or alive, with intimate ties to the children.

This structure—a weak couple subsystem, a tightly bounded parent-child alliance, and potential "interference" in family functioning from an "outsider"—would signal pathology in a biological family (Minuchin, 1974). It is simply the starting point for normal stepfamily development.

THE STEPFAMILY CYCLE

In analyzing the data from in-depth interviews with stepparents (Papernow, 1980), the Gestalt Experience Cycle proved a useful framework for characterizing qualitative changes in stepparents' experience over time. Seven stages of stepparent development emerged: (1) Fantasy; (2) Assimilation; (3) Awareness; (4) Mobilization; (5) Action; (6) Contact; and (7) Resolution.

Over the past years, data describing the experience of biological parents and of children in stepfamilies have been integrated into the model. In addition, development of the stepfamily system has been more explicitly described. The resulting model, the Stepfamily Cycle, describes the above seven stages of individual development of stepfamily members, interacting with three stages of family development. In the three early stages (Fantasy, Assimilation, and Awareness), the family remains primarily divided along biological lines, with most nourishment, agreement on rules, and rituals and cycle completion happening within the biological subsystem(s).

In the two middle stages (Mobilization and Action), the stepfamily begins the tasks of loosening old boundaries and restructuring itself to strengthen step subunits, with the couple first beginning to complete cycles together in the Action phase. In the two later stages (Contact and Resolution) contact finally becomes regular and reliable within step subsystems, ushering in a period of structural solidification during which a clear stepparent role emerges for the first time.

In the initial interview study (Papernow, 1980), the two "fast" families completed the entire Stepfamily Cycle in about four years. Four "average families" took about seven years. Three "slower" families remained stuck in the early stages after five, eight, and twelve years. (Two of these latter three later divorced. The third moved on to Mobilization in the ninth year and at this writing, several years later, appears to have reached Resolution.)

Early Stages: Getting Started

Stage 1. Fantasy

The fantasies of people beginning a stepfamily and the danger of these myths to stepfamily development have been well articulated in the literature (Goldstein, 1974; Schulman, 1972; Visher and Visher, 1978, 1979), making it enticing for family practitioners to wade in with combat boots to challenge them. While fantasy must give way to reality for stepfamilies to progress, this phase seems to be a universal and a normal part of stepfamily development. It is crucial that stepfamily members be approached with gentleness and empathy about their myths and fantasies. Not only are these myths and fantasies powerful, but their owners almost universally look back upon this phase with a sense of chagrin and self-deprecation bordering on deep shame.

Adult members of stepfamilies ruefully describe shared fantasies: rescuing children from the excesses or inadequacies of the ex-spouse, healing a broken family, stepparents adoring their stepchildren and being welcomed by them; for stepparents, marrying a nurturing parent, and for biological parents, having someone with whom to share the load. For mental health professionals the shared fantasy is: "We understand this so it won't be so hard for us."

Meanwhile the child's fantasies are markedly different: "I thought that maybe if I just didn't pay attention to him, this new guy would go away." Most powerful and most enduring is, "I really hoped for a long time that my parents would get back together."

Stage 2. Assimilation: We're Glad You're Here But Don't Come In

The term "assimilation" captures the intention, not the accomplishment of this phase, as adult stepfamily members join in attempting to carry out the fantasy of the new family. Looking back, one stepmother put it, "I was trying so hard to make these two broken pieces of plate go together. But they were from different plates and they just didn't fit!"

Stepparents, straining to join the intimate biological parent-child unit, find themselves assaulted by unexpectedly powerful and negative feelings: jealousy, resentment, confusion and inadequacy, as they are unable to join the powerful rhythm of cycle completion firmly established in the parent-child relationship. The fantasy of marrying a nurturing parent becomes a bad dream as stepparents find themselves watching their spouses relate more intimately and protectively toward their children than toward their mates.

Acting on their normal eagerness to be liked, most stepparents reach out to their stepchildren, only to find them rejecting or indifferent. "For two whole years Julie would march in the front door for weekend visits, walk right past me and throw her arms around her father." It is now known that for most children every move toward a stepparent places a child in a loyalty conflict (Visher and Visher, 1979) ("If I love my stepfather, have I betrayed my father?"). Furthermore while divorced or widowed adults may be eager to move on, children often struggle for many years with their grief over the breakup of their original family. This original family has been replaced by a single parent family with its intimate parent-child relationship. The stepparent now threatens to dislodge the child once more in order to create a new couple relationship. Unfortunately, all too few stepparents have information about these threats and conflicts, leaving many stepparents straining to make contact, withdrawing in defeat, or alternating between the two.

While the stepparent struggles with rejection and loneliness, the biological parent has a source of nourishment and support in his or her children. In this phase, the biological parent may interpret the stepparent's very different experience of the children, difficulty in joining, and need for withdrawal as a lack of desire to be part of the family—a frightening thought—as it means another failure or loss. Fear, and a very different experience of family functioning, combine so that biological parents may find themselves greeting even the stepparent's tentative expression of negative feelings with disbelief, protectiveness toward children, and even criticism.

For adult stepfamily members, the experience of the Assimilation Stage is much like the sensation phase of the Gestalt Experience Cycle— a strong sense that something's not right, and great difficulty figuring out just what it is. In addition, both members of the stepcouple face powerful forces against moving to awareness. The stepparent's feelings of jealousy, resentment, and rejection and the biological parent's feelings of grief, guilt, and fear of another loss, are nobody's favorite and are more easily denied than acknowledged. Lack of validation from intimate others adds to the confusion for stepparents. For stepparents this confusion is often intensified by the fact that the biological parent's perceptions and sense of "what's normal" are often shared by an extended family of in-laws, aunts, uncles, and friends of the previous marriage.

It is important to note the confusion of the early stages reverberates throughout the extended stepfamily system. For instance, how do grandparents conduct their long established relationship with their now ex-daughter-in-law? Moves to continue the relationship may create acute discomfort in the new stepfamily. To abandon such a long-term relationship is equally impossible.

Stage 3. Awareness: Getting Clear

At first falteringly and then with more confidence, stepfamily members can begin to make more sense out of what is happening to them. For stepparents this means beginning to put names on painful feelings as well as experiencing them more fully, without the self-deprecation of the Assimilation Stage. The increasing clarity includes another qualitative shift for stepparents, as they begin to see patterns to their experience: "I'm jealous and resentful because I'm left out over and over again, not because I'm childish." While the pain doesn't go away, the picture of where it comes from and why it hurts so much gets clearer. As self-acceptance grows, stepparents who continue through the cycle begin to form more definitive statements about their needs from their spouses and stepchildren. Compare these two statements made a year apart by a stepmother named Barbara struggling with an ex-wife's desire to be included in holiday dinners:

> I feel so guilty. It's so hard to put words on the feelings. When she asks to have dinner with us I get so confused. I want two separate families, and when we get together, it feels like one family. And I'm the outsider. (Papernow, 1980, p. 139)

And a year later

> I finally got clear that I don't want her at our family events. It's just too hard for me. I want her to have a separate birthday and a separate Thanksgiving with her kids. I don't think there's any way my husband can understand—it seems natural to him to have her here. But it's just not OK with me any more.

As is implicit in this quote, it is often the stepparent who first becomes aware of a need for change in the stepfamily. This is not surprising, as the old family rules and boundaries continue to be much more supportive and syntonic to the biological parent than they are to the stepparent.

Meanwhile, biological parents report that they begin to gain clarity about the pressure inherent in their central position in the stepfamily structure as the person closest to children, stepparent, and ex-spouse. Biological parents naturally want to protect their children from further hurt and from too much additional change. On the other hand, intimacy with a new partner requires excluding children and imposing new rules. The task of resolving the relationship with the previous spouse may not yet be complete, yet the new couple relationship creates pressure to sever old ties. Many single parents fear that even desirable changes in the ex-spouse relationship could jeopardize their access to their children. While this central position may have created a vague sense of discomfort in the Assimilation Stage, it becomes a clearer source of conflict in the Awareness Stage. As one biological father put it:

> I realized I had this precarious position in the middle. I realized I was always watching: Is this going to work out or isn't it? Will I be able to have a woman I care about and keep my relationship with my kids? Will I have to choose one?

While much internal change is taking place within the adults in the early stages, the awareness process remains fairly private. The lay literature exhorts stepcouples to speed stepfamily integration by talking to each other from the beginning. Observational research at the Gestalt Institute of Cleveland (Zinker and Nevis, 1981) has demonstrated that completed cycles of communication about differences require that each individual be able to articulate his or her own awareness and be heard by the other. In the early stages of stepfamily development, most biological parents and stepparents cannot hear (much less elicit) each other's very different experience of the family. The stepparent remains tentative in the face of what one person called the "biological force field" of established rules and norms. The biological parent is frightened of another failure and protective of his or her children. The combination makes communication about step issues almost impossible at this time. Thus stepfamily structure remains much the same throughout the early stages. Most communication nourishment and completed interaction cycles continue to take place within the biological parent-child subsystem.

It is not surprising that many stepfamilies get stuck in the early stages. A supportive spouse seems to provide the best insurance of speed and ease of movement through the early stages of the cycle. Spouses in the two fast families reported in Papernow (1980) were able to articulate their experience as well as empathize with each other very early in their stepfamily's development. However, stepfamily structure militates against such mutual support in the couple relationship until the Action Stage. Both the initial interview study and subsequent data indicate that average families take two to three years to complete the early stages. Slower families can remain stuck there for many years. Like two-year-old temper tantrums, the problem is not how to avoid the early stages, but how to get through them and on to the next phase of development within two or three years. It is interesting to note that timing of stepparent movement, from Assimilation to Awareness and from Awareness to more active Mobilization, is often related to an infusion of support from someone or something outside the couple relationship: contact with another stepparent who really understood, a book which clarified stepfamily struggles, a therapist who happened to be knowledgeable about stepfamilies, a move from the biological unit's home to a house or community new to the entire family.

Middle Stages: Restructuring

Stage 4. Mobilization: Airing Differences

Many stepparents can mark a specific time when they finally began speaking up with more energy and strength about their perceptions, needs, and feelings. The particular issue around which stepparents mobilize themselves varies: some ask their spouses to restrict phone calls from and to the ex-spouse to particular hours; others finally insist on a door to the parental bedroom. Some more vigorously lobby for support on a particular disciplinary issue. Some overwhelmed stepmothers make their first moves to divest themselves of lopsided parenting responsibilities they had absorbed from an apparently "ineffective" ex-spouse.

While in some families the stepparent's request is met with relieved support by the biological parent ("Finally I know what he needs in order to be part of this family!"), in many families this ushers in a period of conflict and chaos as highly charged differences become aired for the first time. Even couples able to handle differences in other areas of their relationship find conflict over these stepfamily issues deeply polarizing.

It is important for both family practitioners and stepfamily members to know that many fights in this phase appear to be trivial, but are actually major struggles over whether the biological subsystem will continue to function as it has, or the family will change its structure. A stepfamily arguing wildly about the appropriate bedtime for a teenager may actually be struggling over whether the girl and her father will continue to have a special time together in the evening, as they had throughout her childhood (especially in the single parent stage), or the stepmother will have time alone with her husband. At this point in the Stepfamily Cycle the biological parent may begin to feel much more acutely distressed, as the stepparent's demands intensify the biological parent's conflict between meeting the child's needs (or keeping peace with the ex-spouse) and supporting the new couple relationship.

Stepparents often initiate these fights, as they are the excluded and dissatisfied members. In this sense stepparents may often act as change agents to begin the crucial process of loosening the boundaries around the biological subsystem.

Stage 5. Action: Going Into Business Together

The energy and expressiveness of the Mobilization Stage begins what organizational consultants call the "unfreezing" of the old system (Hersey and Blanchard, 1979). The Action Stage marks the beginning of building a new one, as couples begin to work together to resolve their differences.

In Gestalt terms, the couple must now travel together back to the Awareness Stage. In a stepfamily this means articulating the very different perceptions, needs, and feelings experienced by stepparents and biological parents. It also means staying engaged long enough and with enough mutual empathy to create enough shared awareness so that the family can now mobilize and act as a unit to meet their diverse needs. Most workable solutions which result from this mutual effort will leave some of the "old" ways of doing things intact while creating brand new rituals, rules, and boundaries. Thus, father and daughter may establish a "special time" together, but during the daytime on the weekend, leaving evenings after 11:00 P.M. for couple time.

The moves in this phase have in common a quality of firmness, clarity, the shared investment of both spouses, and the fact that they actually change the family structure. Most crucial for stepfamily integration are moves which establish stepcouple boundaries: carving out time alone together, closing the bedroom door, consulting each other on child rearing and visitation issues. Boundaries around the stepparent–stepchild relationship also begin to be built. The process may include the biological parent remaining in the background when stepparent and stepchild interact, especially when they are fighting, and the stepparent beginning to ally with stepchildren against their biological parent at times.

Moves toward establishing firmer family boundaries include creating new stepfamily rituals, and more clearly defining differences between stepfamily and ex-spouse's family. It is crucial to the adjustment of all family members, but particularly that of the children who have loyalties to *two* families, that the differences between their two families be described without connotations of right or wrong: "In this family it's OK to swear, but only three hours of television per day. In your Mom's house you can't swear and you can watch as much television as you like."

Just as the disequilibrium of the early stages reverberated throughout the stepfamily suprasystem, new rules and boundaries established in the middle stages affect the entire extended stepfamily. For instance, a stepfamily decision to initiate a new Christmas ritual may conflict with established extended family rituals, requiring renegotiation not only with the ex-spouse, but with four sets of grandparents, uncles, and aunts. (The numbers involved in stepfamily politics can be overwhelming at times.)

As in all stages, the changes of the middle stages take place little by little over time, with some overlap with other stages. Nonetheless these moves seem to be concentrated in a period of about one to three years.

Movement through the first half of the Stepfamily Cycle is clearly experienced as uphill, until the Action Stage when the couple first begins to function as a unit. While this material provides no hard numbers, data from both the initial study (Papernow, 1980) and subsequent input indicate that most families who make it to the Action Stage seem to do so in a total of about four years. This is consistent with findings in the clinical literature that the first three to four years of stepfamily living seem to be a "critical period" in which the family either makes it or breaks up (Mills, 1980; Visher and Visher, 1978, 1979).

Later Stages: Solidifying the Stepfamily

Development schema in the literature thus far take us solidly into the Middle Stages with some elements of the Contact Stage appearing (McGoldrick and Carter, 1980). However, there is very little describing the Resolution Stage—the experience of stepfamily living after patterns of nourishment have been established in step relationships and after the stepparent role has been solidly established.

Stage 6. Contact: Intimacy in Step Relationships

As the changes of the Action Stage ease children out of the couple relationship and the biological parent out of the stepparent-child relationship, a new phase emerges, the Contact Stage, marked by increasing intimacy and authenticity in steprelationships. In the in-depth interviews reported in Papernow (1980), quotes describing stepparent-child interaction began to run several pages of richly detailed exchanges over what names to call each other, what it was like in the beginning, how the stepparent and child experienced each other, and what they wanted and didn't want from each other.

In this phase, the couple relationship, previously polarized by step issues, is now more often felt as an intimate sanctuary in which to share these issues, including painful or difficult feelings. While couples in the Contact Stage still describe intense struggles over some step issues, these exchanges are now characterized by a quality of freshness and completeness. In Gestalt language, members of step relationships are now able to move through the entire experience cycle together, so that real contact is made, resolution is reached, and exchanges feel satisfying and finished leaving a sense of well-being. In family systems language, step relationships are no longer triadic, ushering in the possibility of real one-to-one exchanges within step subsystems. An appropriate subtitle for this phase might be, "Now that we're alone together, who are you anyway?"

It is not until the Contact Stage, after the major restructuring moves of the middle stages, that stepparents can confidently describe a solid stepparent role. These data support that of others who maintain that the development of a stepparent role is inextricably intertwined with stepfamily restructuring (Waldron and Whittington, 1979).

Many attempts to define the stepparent role appear in the literature (Draughon, 1975; Fast and Cain, 1966; Waldron and Whittington, 1979). Despite many differences in details of the workable stepparent roles described by stepfamily members in this phase, they seem to have in common the following major qualities: (a) the role does not usurp or compete with the biological parent of the same sex; (b) the role includes an intergenerational boundary between stepparent and child; (c) the role is sanctioned by the rest of the stepfamily, particularly the spouse; (d) the role incorporates the special qualities this stepparent brings to this family.

It is interesting to note that differences which had created great discomfort in the early stages and intense conflict in the Mobilization Stage often form the foundation for the stepparent role in this phase. A woman who enters a very hang-loose family becomes "the one who teaches the girls how to take care of their clothes, and how to buy nice things." A very expressive man who enters a fairly polite family becomes "the one who teaches them about feelings."

Stage 7. Resolution: Holding on and Letting Go

As the following quote from a stepfather so eloquently describes, in the Resolution Stage, step relationships now not only provide occasional satisfaction, they begin to feel solid and reliable:

> Deep down I really know now that my stepdaughter and I have a very
> special connection. That can't be threatened by anything. And I know it
> is a lifetime connection. And there is a real bottom line of security there
> where I know I have already made a really big difference to her, and I
> know she's made a big difference to me. (Papernow, 1980, p. 208)

In Gestalt language, step relationships can now, finally, go to the background, and no longer require constant attention and maintenance. In this stage, norms have been established, a history has begun to build, and the family now has a particular and reliable rhythm of cycle completion in which all members can join. Although issues of inclusion and exclusion reappear occasionally as biological ties remain more intense than steprelationships, these have primarily been resolved. In some families this has meant a decision to have a much more distant relationship with one or more stepchildren.

The Resolution Stage is also a time of grieving. It is a cruel paradox of stepparenting that the holding on which becomes possible between stepparents and their children in the Contact Stage how sharpens the sense of loss at sharing this child with another biologically more entitled parent. This is especially acute at visitation times.

For the biological parent, grief centers around the reality of interrupted parenting. This is particularly painful for noncustodial parents of teenagers (often fathers) whose children begin visiting less as peer relationships based in the custodial community become primary. "I feel as if the father part of me has been castrated," said one father. It is as if, in the Resolution Stage, stepfamily members bring to awareness and relinquish the last fantasies of living like a biological family.

Letting go of children, a major life crisis in many biological families, is a regular occurrence in most stepfamilies, and will continue to be as joint custody becomes the norm. Despite the more acute pain involved in facing this reality once more, by the Resolution Stage, stepfamilies have invented ways to make this regularly, and prematurely, occurring crisis of "holding on and letting go" a normative event in their lives: "We always go to MacDonald's on the way to and from the airport." "We always try to have time alone as a couple before and after a visit. When we do that it goes fine. When we don't, it's chaos." "We have no visitors in our house before 2:00 P.M. on the Sunday the kids arrive to spend their week with us." "I finally learned that my stepson needs time alone before he leaves to visit his father, and again after he comes back."

One of the most satisfying aspects of the mature stepparent role experienced during the Resolution Stage is that the stepparent is now solidly established as an "intimate outsider"—intimate enough for children to confide in, and outside enough to share in areas which might prove too threatening to bring up with biological parents. Stepparents may now find themselves a special confidante to stepchildren in such areas as sex, peer relationships, drugs, distress that a biological parent is holding on too tightly during visitations, and unresolved grief about the divorce.

New step issues continue to arise throughout stepfamily life—decisions about childbearing, shifts in visitation arrangements, disagreements between families about money, joint decision making about schools, etc. On particularly stressful issues, families may find themselves reexperiencing the entire Stepfamily Cycle, with some period of confusion and lack of articulation, occasional periods of panicked conflict and polarization along biological lines. However, generally, issues which would have remained as "lumps under the rug" in the Assimilation Stage, or created great disequilibrium in the Mobilization Stage, now occur within the context of a solid couple and stepfamily structure whose members regularly come to resolution together. Tom again captures the feeling of solidarity and reliability of the Resolution Stage:

> I can feel that we've moved. Not easily because it's been a pain in the ass. But I feel very clear that our family works. That is resolved. It's been proven over the years that we could do it and we're doing it. We're happy for the most part. There's a lot of love. You can feel that the family is working. (Papernow, 1980, p. 201)

IMPLICATIONS FOR PRACTITIONERS

Recently, practitioners have advocated family therapy for stepfamily problems (Kaplan, 1977; Ransom et al., 1979; Sager et al., 1983; Schulman, 1972; Waldron and Whittington, 1979). In the early stages it is the stepparent who is most likely to appear to help, complaining of depression, anxiety and a sense of worthlessness. While development from the Mobilization Stage of the Stepfamily Cycle onwards is a family task, the primary tasks of the early stages are individual ones. For the stepparent, the goal is to move from the self-doubt and confusion of the Assimilation Stage to solid enough awareness to engage fruitfully in the stepfamily system. Individual therapy can be very helpful in this differentiation task (see also Visher and Visher, 1979).

The therapeutic tasks of moving from Assimilation to Awareness include: helping stepparents to identify and separate shoulds ("I should love these children") from real experience; education about the stepchild's dilemma; trying powerful and seemingly mysterious feelings like jealousy and resentment to real events; education about the roots of those events in stepfamily structure; support to pursue interests and friendships outside the stepfamily which can provide some of the mastery and nourishment missing for the stepparent in early stepfamily structure; and, finally, identification of a few specific needs from spouse and stepchildren, followed by help generating spousal support. In some families this is enough to launch the restructuring process.

Often intrapsychic issues, for instance chronic difficulty identifying needs or mobilizing to meet them, are intertwined with stepfamily issues. The informed practitioner must treat these without discounting the power of early stepfamily structure to create apparent pathology in the healthiest of us. Furthermore, all individual work with stepparents must be done with an awareness of the entire system's needs. While it is rarely supportive of clients' intimate relationships to side with them against their partners, it is especially enticing and particularly destructive for individual therapists of stepparents to do so. The challenge is to empathize with the stepparent, providing lots of support, while also understanding and empathizing with the struggles of other stepfamily members. Placing these struggles within a developmental framework makes this task easier for both therapist and client.

While individual therapy may be supportive to stepfamily development in the early stages, the difficulties of the Mobilization Stage are systems problems for which individual therapy may be quite destructive and much less effective. Family therapy is suggested as the treatment of choice. Sager et al. (1983) in their seminal work in this field suggest that when possible the entire "suprasystem" (i.e., members of both families) should be involved for best results.

Once the uphill half of the Stepfamily Cycle has been completed, the need for therapeutic intervention will be less intense. The form of assistance in the Resolution Stage may now depend on the locus of the problem. For example, unresolved grief may be adequately handled in individual therapy unless the couple is having trouble supporting each other. Differences in childbearing generations which often become more intense in the Resolution Stage (when the biological parent is "finished" with childbearing and the childless stepparent wants a child) is a couples issue, while a school problem will be most successfully resolved by involving the entire suprasystem.

It is worth stating explicitly that education of stepfamily members about normal stepfamily development is a powerful therapeutic tool in itself. Such education will usually play an important role in successful therapeutic work with stepfamilies and their members.

While support appears crucial for the uphill effort, it is sobering and important for mental health professionals to remember that very few stepfamily members will seek assistance through psychotherapy. Family practitioners will do their best service to stepfamilies by making information about normal stepfamily development available to the general public, offering educational groups (Jacobson, 1979; Messinger, 1976; Messinger, Walker and Freeman, 1978; Visher and Visher, 1983) through churches, PTAs, day care centers, and schools. We also need to encourage colleagues, pediatricians, ministers, lawyers, and others to make lay publications about stepfamily living (Burt and Burt, 1983; Einstein, 1982; Lewis, 1980; Visher and Visher, 1979) available in their waiting rooms; to make photocopied articles from the professional literature available to clients and to post copies of the *Stepfamily Bulletin* visibly on their bulletin boards.

A more detailed and realistic picture of the impact of stepfamily structure on members' experience, as well as an understanding of the awareness tasks of the early stages may help stepfamily members to move more steadily through Assimilation to Awareness. Understanding the normal panic over differences and subsequent hard work and specific Action steps which begin the restructuring process in the middle stages, as well as more vivid and detailed pictures of the fruits this work bears in the later stages, may enable stepfamily members to hang in with more hope and productive effort through the crucial uphill half of the Stepfamily Cycle and coast with more awareness of what has been accomplished over the bumps in the later stages.

CONCLUSION

The Stepfamily Cycle facilitates organization of themes and strains of stepfamily living as stepfamily members experience them over time. This phenomenological approach has created a framework which enables stepfamily members to easily recognize their stage in the cycle.

As an educational tool, the qualitative descriptions upon which the Stepfamily Cycle is built also seem to help stepfamily members empathize across their diverse experience of stepfamily living, as well as enabling family practitioners to use language and examples which join empathetically with all stepfamily members while moving for structural change.

In both therapeutic and educational work with stepfamilies, the Stepfamily Cycle has proven to be very helpful in placing difficult and confusing experiences within a normal chronological developmental framework. It gives clues to areas of difficulty and provides a guide to what kinds of moves might lead onward.

REFERENCES

Burt, M. S., and Burt, R. B. (1983). *What's special about our stepfamily?* Garden City, NY: Doubleday & Co.

Draughon, M. (1975). Stepmother's model of identification in relation to mourning in the child. *Psychological Reports,* **36**(1), 183–189.

456   Patricia L. Papernow

EINSTEIN, S. (1982). Stepfamilies: Living, loving, and learning. New York: Macmillan.

FAST, I., and CAIN, A. C. (1966). The stepparent role: Potential for disturbances in family functioning. *American Journal of Orthopsychiatry,* **36**(3), 485–491.

GOLDSTEIN, H. S. (1974). Reconstituted families: The second marriage and its children. *Psychiatric Quarterly,* **48**(3), 433–440.

HERSEY, P., and BLANCHARD, K. H. (1979). *Management of organizational behavior.* New Jersey: Prentice-Hall.

JACOBSON, D. S. (1979). Stepfamilies: Myths and realities. *Social Work,* **24**(3), 202–207.

KAPLAN, S. L. (1977). Structural family therapy for children of divorce: Case reports. *Family Process,* **16**(1), 75–83.

KESHET, J. K. (1980). From separation to stepfamily: A subsystem analysis. *Journal of Family Issues,* **1**(4), 517–532.

LEWIS, H. C. (1980). *All about families—The second time around.* Atlanta: Peachtree Publishers.

MESSINGER, L. (1976). Remarriage between divorced people with children from previous marriages: A proposal for preparation for re-marriage. *Journal of Marriage and Family Counseling,* **2**(2), 193–200.

MESSINGER, L., WALKER, K. N., and FREEMAN, S. J. (1978). Preparation for remarriage following divorce: The use of group techniques. *American Journal of Orthopsychiatry,* **48**(2), 263–272.

MILLS, D. (1980). *Issues in remarriage: A clinical perspective.* Paper presented at the annual meeting of the National Council on Family Relations, Portland, Oregon.

MINUCHIN, S. (1974). *Families and family therapy.* Cambridge, MA: Harvard University Press.

NEUBAUER, P. D. (1960). The one-parent child and his oedipal development. *Psychoanalytic Study of the Child,* **15**, 286–309.

PAPERNOW, P. (1980). A phenomenological study of the developmental stages of becoming a stepparent: A Gestalt and family systems approach (Doctoral dissertation, Boston University, 1980). *Dissertation Abstracts-International,* **41**, 8B, 3192–3193.

RANSOM, J. W., SCHIESINGER, S., and DERDEYN, A. P. (1979). A stepfamily in formation. *American Journal of Orthopsychiatry,* **49**(1), 36–43.

SAGER, C. J., BROWN, H. S., CROHN, H., ENGEL, T., RODSTEIN, E., and WALKER, L. (1983). *Treating the remarried family.* New York: Brunner/Mazel.

SCHULMAN, G. (1972). Myths that intrude on the adaptation of the stepfamily. *Social Casework,* **53**, 131–139.

VISHER, E. B., and VISHER, J. S. (1979). *Stepfamilies: A guide to working with stepparents and stepchildren.* New York: Brunner/Mazel.

VISHER, E. B., and VISHER, J. S. (1983). *Stepfamily workshop manual.* Palo Alto: Stepfamily Association of America.

WALDRON, J. A., and WHITTINGTON, R. (1979). The stepparent/stepfamily *Journal of Operational Psychology,* **10**(1), 47–50.

45

▼▼▼▼

Beyond Widowhood

▼▼▼▼

Robert C. DiGiulio

ABSTRACT: This analysis is based on the author's own experiences with widow-hood, as well as interviews he conducted with hundreds of widowed men and women. The loss of a spouse is so critical because it ruptures the survivor's identity. Widowed persons go through four stages of bereavement: (1) *encounter*, characterized by shock, fusion, and searching, (2) *respondence*, characterized by a sense of helplessness, despair, unmet personal needs, and spouse sanctifica-tion, (3) *emergence*, during which individuals, turning toward the future, go through realization, verification, and the resolution of a critical conflict, and (4) *transformation*, when they move past the widow role to develop an identity en-riched by both past and present experiences.

Thursday, June 26

Tennis lesson in Woodstock at 9:00 A.M.; almost canceled it because of fore-cast 95-degree heat. At 8:30 A.M. Chrissie came downstairs; I met her on the bottom step. She encouraged me to play, telling me she'd probably take the girls swimming at Stoughton Pond.

"Do you want breakfast?" she asked.

"No thanks. I had some coffee," I replied as I stood to kiss her. She pulled away, teasing in mock shame.

"No! I have 'draa-gon mouth'!" she laughed, imitating the television mouthwash commercial.

I called *"Bye everybody!"* to my mother-in-law, Olga, and my daughter Christine, who were snuggled on the sofa bed in the other room; everyone else was still asleep upstairs, unwilling, I guess, to face the heat.

Chrissie smiled at me as I walked out the door. . . .

I started the car, I waved to her, and I never saw her again.

After tennis I went directly to the office of the superintendent of schools to find out how much money my school could spend on books. I was alone in the office when the phone rang: *"Hello, this is the Vermont State Police calling from Bethel Barracks. I need to locate a Robert—uh—DiGiulio."* . . .

Police? Me? I froze.

"What's wrong, officer?" I interrupted.

My voice shook. He took a deep breath and again identified himself.

Something was wrong; I interrupted him again, needing some instant reassurance.

"My wife. Is my wife okay? What happened? My baby? Tell me!"

"Mister DiGiulio, I need to talk with you in person and. . . . "

He wouldn't reassure me. Something was very wrong. Tears came to my eyes; I wiped them off and wiped off my glasses. My chest hurt.

"Please, officer! Please tell me: Are they all right? Did something happen to my wife? My baby?" . . .

"Sir, our cruiser is on its way to you. Stay there."

. . . I dropped the phone and ran out the door. Incredible heat crashed against me. There—my car is there. Threw briefcase through open window into back seat. Got in. Lit cigarette. Got out of the car and ran out onto U.S. Route 4. Desperate. Nothing. No police cars coming.

Ran back to my car. Two lit cigarettes in ashtray. I began to bargain with God. Pulled out onto Route 4. A car almost hit me. I drove toward Bethel, burning my eyes through the windshield for a police cruiser heading toward me. . . .

The police cruiser! The car was coming toward me; I flashed my lights and blew the horn, waved my arm out the window. He slowed to view this unknown maniac; I screamed my name at him. He nodded and motioned me to pull over. I drove my Rabbit onto someone's lawn, watching him desperately in my rearview mirror. Tore out of the car and dashed back across Route 4. He told me to get into his police cruiser. I got in. . . .

"Mister DiGiulio, there was an accident this morning in Weathersfield. . . . "

"No! Please don't tell me. My wife, my baby . . . "

"It is my duty to tell you . . . "
"Well, I don't care. I don't want to know!"
". . . and your wife . . . "
"Stop! I don't want to hear this!"
". . . and your seven-year-old daughter were killed this morning in Weath-ersfield."
I tried to get away, out of the cruiser. Couldn't see anything but groped for the handle. He put his arm across to restrain me. He told me he was sorry. I sat and cried. . . .

In my solitary movement through grief I gradually became aware that my life was changing; without my wife, daily occurrences took on different meanings, ranging from visits from friends and relatives (Why does everybody leave so quickly now?) to conversations (Nobody mentions her name.) and even choices of food for dinner (more fast food)—all these took on a different texture and meaning. At times there were humorous touches: mail personally addressed to Chris DiGuilio from Ed McMahon promising her a chance to be the envy of her neighbors by winning a Publishers' Clearing House Sweepstakes, or mailings offering her low-cost term life insurance with "no physical exam required." But other mail—from real people—was difficult, including the "how-are-you?-please-write" letters from her more distant friends who hadn't been in touch for a year or so; worst perhaps were the phone calls from those friends or college acquaintances who had not yet heard.

So much had to be changed: I sat at my wife's place at the table, slept on her side of the bed, and moved my clothes to her closet. I also went about trying to tie up loose ends, her "unfinished business" that needed taking care of, ranging from crewel work to painting the dining room—two jobs of many she'd been in the process of completing when she died. I grieved the sadness she would have grieved had she been here; I mourned both her inability to get satisfaction from completing those tasks she had begun, and her no longer being present to enjoy simply being with people she loved and who loved her.

I began to grieve not only for her and for my loss of her as my wife but for the loss of my life—the way it had been. Clinging to those things that did not change (mostly objects and photos), I characterized those things that had (mostly relationships and perceptions) as uniformly bad changes, unwanted evidence that all this was really not a dream. . . .

. . . No event is as powerful as the loss of a spouse. Even for those whose spouses' deaths are not unexpected, widowhood is so profound that it always seems to come too abruptly: "I knew my marriage wouldn't last forever, but I never expected it to end this way. Or so soon." The death of a spouse has such a powerful impact precisely because of its effect on the surviving spouse's sense of personal identity.

The development of that identity begins early in life as the infant perceives his own physiological needs (for food, warmth and safety) and how adequately they are satisfied by the adult(s) on whom he depends for survival. These perceptions provide the basis for the child's initial assessment of who he is and how others value him.

Identity begins as self-esteem: a feeling that one is wanted, and thus, valued. The infant's self-esteem is tenuous, dependent on the sum of messages from the object of primary attachment—usually the parent. These "messages" the infant receives, regarding how wanted he or she is, will naturally be affected by physiological factors (a colicky infant may irritate the parent, who then behaves in a rejecting manner), socioeconomic factors (parents with limited resources and social skills may provide inadequate stimulation or nutrition), and psychological factors (a parent who truly wants an infant will be more likely to show affection and acceptance).

As the child grows, society begins to play a substantial part in the child's developing identity. Through childhood, the child gains experience by engaging in activities alone, as part of a pair, and as part of a group. Messages received at home can now be verified in light of the new ones the child receives from newly significant adults: teachers. They provide assessments of intellectual ("You're a fine student"), physical ("She's the fastest runner in the class"), and social ability ("He's popular").

Early in adolescence, the peer group becomes a more important source of verification than parents, teachers, or other adults. This is a critical time for identity development as adolescents "try on" new roles, sometimes based in imagination, strive to gain peer acceptance, and form new kinds of close friendships. To an adolescent, having a "best friend" implies a deeper closeness and greater sharing of confidences than it did during childhood. Early adolescent cross-sex friendships and romantic relationships ("puppy love") are ways in which adolescents clarify their identities in revealing images of the self to others. We "use" peers to learn about ourselves. What they reflect back to us provides an ongoing validation of what we see ourselves to be. . . .

For an adult, three elements are required for the formation of a stable identity: A sense of "inner sameness and continuity," whereby individuals experience that who we are today is who we were yesterday, last week, and last year. Second, we need to perceive that others whose opinions we value acknowledge our "inner sameness." Social reflection also affirms that we actually are who we perceive ourselves to be. Third, our self-perceptions must be validated in specific life experiences.[1] For example, I may think of myself as being a nurse, and that may have been reinforced by my attending nursing school where others reflected back to me my budding identity as a nurse. That identity is then validated as I gain experience actually working as a nurse. . . .

. . . In the joining of individual identities, intimacy creates a new identity. Without obliterating each individual's identity, this new identity (usually symbolized by marriage) ideally provides a "reciprocal mirroring," a mutual confirmation of each partner's personal identity. By being a part of the valued "we," or marriage identity, each partner's stake in the marital identity is also enriched and enhanced. In the consistent reflection of ourselves, marriage supports and stabilizes personal identity and is the means of ongoing personal "identity renewal"[2]. . . .

GROWING THROUGH WIDOWHOOD

Seen in its broadest perspective, bereavement is an adaptive process that is both a reaction (to the death of a spouse) and an action (a movement toward wholeness of being). Both the reaction to death and the movement toward wholeness are normal and healthy responses to the serious life crisis faced by widowed men and women. Bereavement is the period specifically devoted to the full expression of grief—a normal and healthy reaction to the loss of someone (and something) very important. The expression and dissipation of grief set the stage for the return to wholeness. . . .

The feelings and experiences of widowed people as they proceed through bereavement are predictable. The most intense grief is usually experienced shortly after the death of one's spouse. While all of bereavement is marked by mourning, only early bereavement will bring intense numbness, denial, and anger. These are not normally experienced so powerfully later in bereavement. These predictable phenomena form fairly distinct stages in the transition through bereavement, although there is some overlap from stage to stage and the duration of each varies among individuals. (See Table 45.1, page 468.)

Stage 1. Encounter

Beginning with the death of the spouse, the first stage of bereavement is encounter, the initial confrontation with the new phase of life called widowhood. Encounter is characterized by emotions ranging from numbness to deep sadness to anger. Widowed men and women in encounter may experience depression, shock, rigidity, constant or frequent crying, rage, a desire for revenge, loss of appetite, or insomnia. They must be watched closely, especially if there are expressions of—or wishes for—self-destruction, perhaps wanting to "join" the deceased spouse. The importance of caregiving—watching carefully and sensitively over widowed men and women—cannot be overstated. While three months to one year is the commonly cited amount of time a widowed person needs to move beyond the most intense feelings of grief, there is really no rule of thumb that can suggest how long caregiving must continue. The first days and weeks are certainly critical times. . . .

During encounter, widows may psychologically "fuse" their individual identities to their marriage identities. Even though illusory, retaining the marriage identity can be comforting as it permits the widow to continue to perform *as if still married*. It serves to bolster the widow temporarily, like a bumper jack holding a car for a tire change, until she has moved further in the reformulation of her personal identity. The degree of fusion of widowed men's personal and marital identities is often unclear, because men define and speak of themselves primarily in terms of occupational status instead of their marriage relationships. In addition, their sometimes-marked dependence can be confused with marital closeness.

Fusion allows the widow to postpone addressing the "Who am I?" question. Indeed it prevents that question from fully crystallizing because the fused identity is so powerful that there is no need yet for the widow to fully acknowledge her new status as a single woman. It is not uncommon for widowed women in encounter to speak of their spouses in the present tense, for example, "Harold hates when I go off on tangents like this!"

Widowed women (and sometimes widowed men) show a close identification with the deceased spouse by occupying their spouse's place in bed, taking over his or her seat at the dining table, wearing the spouse's wedding band, or performing roles formerly done by the deceased spouse. Widowed people will defend this behavior by saying, "I couldn't *bear* to stare at his empty seat!" Others make no effort to deny the continuing close identification: British researcher Colin Parkes quoted one widow who claimed, "My husband's in me, right through and through. I feel him in me doing everything." Fusing one's personality to, or closely identifying with the deceased spouse is part of an "equally mystifying . . . loss of self which is reported by many widows.[3]". . .

After the death of a spouse, widowed men and women are driven by the urge to recover the lost "love object," which is characteristic of all human grief. Some will engage in "searching" behavior, emotionally seeking the lost spouse for up to one year following the death.[4] In addition to the cemetery, widowed people can be drawn to visit other places that—to an observer—have no logical purpose. Yet searching can provide the widow with temporarily comforting ties to the life that once was; a college, church, beach, store, city where they first met, or a bar where they first drank with each other. Physical objects, too, can provide those ties, including clothing, books, toiletries, jewelry, and possessions favored by the deceased spouse. People (especially children) can become treasured "objects" because of a favored status they enjoyed with the deceased. . . .

Although fusion fades near the conclusion of encounter, searching may continue through the next stage, because the utterness of death cannot be rapidly internalized by the widowed man or woman. But as bereavement progresses, the widowed person will gradually internalize the death of the spouse, and over the first months of bereavement the deceased spouse's presence will gradually fade, replaced by the demands, tasks, and enjoyments of present life. . . .

Stage 2. Respondence

During encounter the widowed person's behavior is essentially passive: He or she receives the blow dealt by the death. It is primarily a time of impact and immediate, often instinctive, reactions to the blow (sometimes these are life-threatening reactions). As numbness fades, the widowed person begins the first coherent responses to what has happened. This next phase, respondence, is characterized by more active and thoughtful response to the death of a spouse. Respondence marks the beginning of separation of the widowed person's personal identity from the marital identity. In sum, the difference between encounter and respondence is one of degree of active response and comprehension of what has happened. Together, encounter and respondence comprise the widowed person's painful confrontation with—and response to—the movement through widowhood.

In this second stage of grief, as the protection provided by numbness gradually wears off, the reality of being a not-married, widowed adult creeps in—slowly, because widowed men and women who valued their marital identity have great difficulty this soon in the grief process seeing themselves as a single man or single woman. At the beginning of respondence, widowed persons begin responding to and interacting with other people and events, gradually moving away from their obsession with the past in general and with "that day" in particular. . . .

Respondence can be the most emotionally painful phase of widowhood, because the earlier numbness of encounter no longer protects widowed people from the pain of loss. Without the protection of numbness, respondence is an intensely turbulent phase of widowhood. The wrenching experience of grief felt during early bereavement can be especially devastating because it heightens a sense of helplessness; it illustrates our lack of full control over life and leads to feelings of despair. Respondence is also painful because we are fully confronting the personal needs that are now unmet: needs for attachment, social integration, nurturance, alliance, guidance, and reassurance of worth that the widowed person once derived from the marriage relationship.[5] Ultimately, the sense of helplessness coupled with the unmet needs results in an overwhelming sense of loneliness—loneliness that the widowed person still believes can be relieved by only one person, who is no longer alive. . . .

During respondence, the widow engages in spouse sanctification, idealizing the image of the deceased spouse in her memory. Sanctification is a vital step in the bereavement process, because it permits the widow's previously fused identity to become separated. Sanctification initiates a separation that is both comfortable and safe, because by elevating his memory to near or total perfection, the widow is not "casting off" her spouse. Widows who say they have had unsatisfactory marriages are less likely to engage in sanctification of their deceased spouses than those who have had fulfilling marriages and strongly positive memories. For some, sanctification is transitory and hardly noticed, while for others it is a consuming, passionate undertaking that may mark the beginning of sealing themselves off from any future romantic involvements.

When it does not become so extreme, sanctification is not the unhealthy or trivial activity that others may consider it. On the contrary, sanctification can facilitate movement through widowhood. Practically, it provides the widow with a respite, allowing her to go about her business by moving the deceased to "an other-worldly position as an understanding and purified distant observer."[6] The widow is testifying to the goodness not only of her husband but of herself in choosing him.

Sanctification serves as an emotional milestone for the widow, for it opens the way to eventual acceptance of her spouse's death. Although it does not signal her arrival as an unmarried adult, it allows the widow to justify pursuing her own interests because her spouse had gone on to a larger, better, or simply another level of existence. Ultimately, the widow takes comfort in feeling that her spouse is not only not suffering but is in fact "sainted." . . .

The key to moving through respondence comes with the widowed person's understanding that holding on to the past must give way to living in the present. This cannot simply be "told" to the widowed person—it must be personally experienced. Nor can moving through respondence be left to the passage of time, for time by itself does not heal. Instead, the widowed person's understanding must derive from concrete experiences of satisfying human interaction. The majority of widowed women I interviewed felt that other people—family, friends, children, or neighbors—were "most important' in helping them survive since their husband's death. While simply "being there" is important advice for those who wish to help the widowed person in encounter, the widowed person in respondence needs more active social support. That support should be aimed at meeting needs for attachment, social integration, nurturance, alliance, guidance, and reassurance of worth.

Although other individuals cannot replace the lost spouse or meet the widow's needs in exactly the same way, they can meet at least some needs, providing limited but vital respite from the pain. That temporary reprieve can initially bolster the widow, gradually evolving into a more consistent source of support. A widow's loneliness, caused in part by her unmet needs for attachment and reassurance of her worth, can be counteracted by her active involvement in a stable family that loves her. Although family membership cannot provide the especially intense attachment or reassurance of unique worth provided by a marriage relationship, family members can help meet needs that are otherwise unmet. . . .

GROWING BEYOND WIDOWHOOD

Stage 3. Emergence

Stage 3, emergence, is the central goal of bereavement: It is the end of mourning, and it signals the beginning of the growth beyond widowhood.

Questions from the previous stages ("Did this really happen?" or, "Why has this happened to me?") may still be only partially answered. Yet during emergence the widow turns toward a more focused consideration of her future, drawing on the past and present to determine the direction in which she will move. Because of the time that has been spent on grief during the first two stages of bereavement, and as a result of having reflected on and responded to the texture of life without her husband, her life has achieved more equilibrium. . . .

Emergence is a time for "growing out of" the weariness that has become almost routine. It is a time for making contact with the world to a fuller extent than was possible for a numb, angry, and lonely person. This contact with the world is very healing, but it must be gradual and unforced. Trying rapidly to sever ties to the deceased spouse can precipitate symptoms of grief similar to those experienced earlier in bereavement. Enjoying the company of another single adult is very beneficial, but a widower who sees dating as a way of helping himself "get over his wife" is actually highlighting his continuing attachment to her. If the widower (or widow) can say, "I'm looking forward to being with this new person, and I will impose no expectations on her [or him]," then the widowed person may be capable of discovering—and enjoying—new qualities in this "new" person. Otherwise, dating will only serve to emphasize what has been lost, instead of what can be gained by new relationships. The passage of time can help by providing an emotional "distance" between past and present.

As time passes, thoughts and memories of one's spouse become less constant parts of daily life. Early in bereavement widowed people fight against the tendency of memories to fade. But as weeks and months pass, keeping a dim memory in sharp focus takes more and more energy, and it eventually requires more energy than does living in the present. Consequently, it eventually takes greater exertion *not* to grow beyond widowhood—to continue living in the past. . . .

As they move through bereavement, widowed people come to realize that death is a natural outcome of life, one over which we have little control. This realization not only "prepares" the widowed person for future losses, it also facilitates the present movement beyond widowhood. Since they clearly perceive what cannot be controlled (death), what *can* be controlled (where I go, what I do, with whom I spend time) thus becomes clearer, standing out in sharper relief than before, when loss was but an abstraction.

Realization of loss is different from resignation to loss; the latter is a defeated, negative interpretation of the meaning of death on one's life. Resignation is; "I have loved someone who has died. Since death lies at the end of each person's life, there is no point in loving someone who will die." Realization is: "I have loved someone who has died. Even though death lies at the end of each person's life, I am alive and capable of loving and living until I die." With realization, widowed people can make changes they postponed during the early stages of bereavement, such as moving to a new home, making a large purchase, or effecting a career change. Some emerged widows use realization to follow up on activities or interests pursued before marriage, leading to the resumption of a career or the search for professional advancement through study or brushing up on specific skills. Choices made now are usually wiser ones than those made earlier during encounter or respondence. . . .

Acceptance of the death of the spouse is the key issue of emergence, hence it arises frequently in widow's descriptions of their experiences: "Once I accepted the fact that my husband had died, life became clearer to me." Acceptance is the end of a relentless questioning process that begins at the death of the spouse (and sometimes before death, when the spouse is ill), and continues to the point of "verification."

During emergence the widow stops questioning the reality and the meaning of her spouse's death. Verification marks the end of that psychological "searching" that began early in encounter, when the widow set out on an emotional (or actual) search for the deceased spouse. By the time they are in emergence, many widows have become conscious of their "searching" behavior, sometimes dryly sharing stories at coffee breaks in support-group meetings.

There is one final task that must be faced before emergence is complete: A "critical conflict" must be resolved. While acceptance and verification are issues tied to the past relationship, critical conflict is a question rooted in the present. It calls for the widow to take a clear stand on her role as an unmarried person. The widow must now elect to remain defined and confined by her widow identity or to opt out of it. "Am I to be a widow for the rest of my life?" is essentially the question of critical conflict. . . .

Healthy mourning (and successful emergence) demands that the bereaved only temporarily keep the deceased spouse at the customary central place in her life. Fully emerged widows shed widowhood and see themselves as *single, unmarried people,* focused on pursuits and relationships more relevant to the present and future than to the past. A widow can still honor the memory of her deceased spouse without spending so much time dwelling on the memory that it detracts from her present life. Widowed people can keep their spouse's memory alive by establishing philanthropic foundations, scholarship funds, resuming activities they shared with their spouses, or continuing some work their spouses began. Jewish families keep alive the memory of the deceased by customarily naming newborn children after a beloved, deceased relative.

By the conclusion of emergence, an "unmarriage" takes place. Although the marriage physically ended at the moment their spouses died, widowed men and women remain psychologically married through the first two stages of bereavement. Unmarriage is the point of closure to that psychological marriage, and it is the culmination of emergence. Sometimes unmarriage is sought through remarriage, but some widowed men and women and their new spouses have paid the price for engaging in such "psychological bigamy." . . .

Stage 4. Transformation

At the completion of emergence is the fourth stage, more accurately described as a plateau because it signifies an arrival rather than a turning point. The essence of transformation is captured by the French idiomatic expression *l'échapper belle* ("the fortunate escape"), because transformation embodies a departure from and movement beyond widowhood.

Widowed people who experience transformation have moved completely past the widow role and developed a clearer and more enduring identity enriched by past experiences but also by present ones. . . .

As I looked more closely at differences between emerged and transformed widows, I noticed that what distinguished the latter was an additional two-part transition they underwent following emergence: meta-

Table 45.1   Stages of Bereavement in Widowhood

Growing Through Widowhood

Stage 1. Encounter: Characterized by fusion (oneness with deceased spouse), numbness, shock, anger, depression, feelings of guilt, self-blame, sadness, rigidity, lability, denial, rage, physical symptoms, sense of "presence" of deceased spouse, mystical-spiritual experiences, passive or aggressive behavior, searching for lost spouse.

Stage 2. Respondence: Characterized by sanctification (deification of deceased spouse), sadness, hypersensitivity, continued numbness, insomnia, lethargy, first attempts at reaching out, flashes of hope that "it's all a dream," desperate feelings, restlessness, inability to concentrate, beginning of separation of marital identity from self-identity. Searching continues.

Growing Beyond Widowhood

Stage 3. Emergence: Characterized by verification (end of searching), critical conflict (decision to unmarry), conclusion of searching, less intense self-blame, reduced questioning, "emotional roller coaster," anguish more limited, moments of doubt, thoughts of the future, completion of unmarriage.

Stage 4. Transformation: Characterized by metamorphosis and rebirth (*l'échapper belle*), cessation of self-perception as "widow," closure of mourning, concern with present and future, past marriage integrated into flow of life experiences, acceptance of role as single adult.

---

morphosis and rebirth. They went "from grief to growth," as one widow expressed it.

Typically during transformation some widows—fully aware that their intense grief was winding down—began to realize that something was changing in their lives, something they perceived as positive change. Metamorphosis was a time of reflection where the widow "knew" that although life had changed greatly during bereavement, there was still something missing—a question arising not from grief but from an aroused curiosity: "My life is good [again]. I'm not totally sure things will stay this way, but it *won't go back* to the way it was." Metamorphosis is a stepping past emergence.

> I couldn't *wait* to go back to school! All my life I had wanted to graduate with that little white nurse's cap they wear! My family told me to wait until the first year was over, until I was "myself" again. "Myself?" I *knew* what I had to do. I paid my dues by taking good care—and I mean *good* care—of my husband, so I didn't feel one bit guilty about kicking up my heels and going back to college to get my diploma.

These widows were aware of a new direction that their lives had to take; of an exciting new movement toward a fullness of a new, changed persona they had not previously known. . . .

. . . Metamorphosis is not something that happens to some lucky widowed people; it is something that they *do* to bring about positive change in their lives. Occupation and work facilitate metamorphosis because they provide the newly single adult with a facet of identity that, in our society, offers financial and emotional rewards. These will ultimately help her grow toward independence and the fulfillment of her needs that were formerly fulfilled through marriage. She is seeing how much she has—or can potentially have—not only in material terms but in emotional satisfaction.

Completing transformation, metamorphosis ends in a rebirth that is not unlike that of the mythical phoenix arising from the ashes. In fact, one widowed woman used the analogy of being reborn from fire:

> You know, I felt like . . . the animal . . . which rose from the ruins, born again. I looked younger; I felt younger. I lost *tons* of weight . . . you sound like a dear young man and I'd like to talk with you more, but I can't right now. I'm getting packed for an Elderhostel trip to Mexico. Give me a call again next month. . . .

Having unmarried, transformed people are—in the words of one widow—"the same book but a revised edition." Some continue their jobs, some switch careers, others devote their time to family or other pursuits, while still others carry on the work of the deceased spouse. What they all have in common is the fact that their pasts have been put into perspective, neither hindering nor handicapping them, and they have created new identities for themselves. . . .

REFERENCE NOTES

1. E. Erikson. (1963). *Childhood and Society*, 2d ed,. (New York: Norton), 261
2. E. Erikson. (1980). "The Freud-Jung Correspondence, " in E. Smelser and E. Erikson (eds.), *Themes of Work and Love in Adulthood* (Cambridge, Mass: Harvard University Press), 48.
3. C. Parkes. (1975). "Determinants Following Bereavement," *OMEGA: Journal of Death and Dying* 6 (4): 303–23. Parkes, C. (1979). *Bereavement: Studies of Grief in Adult Life* (New York: International Universities Press), 89–90.
4. C. Parkes. (1970). " 'Seeking' and 'Finding' a Lost Object: Evidence from Recent Studies of the Reaction to Bereavement," *Social Science and Medicine* 4 (2): 187–201.
5. J. Smith, quoted in "Samantha Smith's Vision an Inspiration to Mother." (1968). *New York Times* (December 14), p. 68.
6. C. King. (1969). *My Life With Martin Luther King, Jr.* (New York: Holt, Rinehart and Winston), 329.

PART IX
vvvvvvvvvvvvvvvvvvvvvvvvvvvvv

Lasting Relationships

*T*alk shows, situation comedies, and teledramas rivet America's attention on marital problems. Article after article in newspapers and magazines focus on marital spats, spouse abuse, separation, and divorce.

Americans constantly ask what is wrong with marriages today. Not only do they see the television accounts and read the newspaper articles, but they see divorce all around them. Their friends, relatives, neighbors, and associates are getting divorced. And they know that these divorces—and the ominous possibility, perhaps growing likelihood, of their own—are but a reflection of national trends.

If you were to try to pinpoint a single reason for our high divorce rate, what would you choose? You would have many good candidates from which to select. As I discussed in Chapter 39, a candidate that hits at the very heart of the matter is incompatible expectations. This choice encompasses the major problems that couples encounter in the primary areas of money, work, and sex, as well as most other basic disruptions they experience in their marital relationship. I am comfortable with this

471

choice because it allows me to be sociological. That is, as opposed to personal characteristics of individuals (such as their "personalities"), this choice allows me to focus the analysis on *structural* features of American society.

As stressed in that chapter, our society is set up (socially organized) in such a way that it produces and maintains contrasting patterns of male-female orientations to life. In other words, the incompatible expectations that men and women experience in marriage (and, for that matter, in courtship and other interactions) arise largely from their early socialization into their sex roles—as well as from the maintenance of those orientations, of course, in their myriad interactions of later life.

I also like this choice because it does not cause us to neglect people. We are talking about basic differences in men's and women's daily lives. Ultimately, the structural features that sort girls and boys into separate categories produce different types of people. That is, our basic socialization teaches females and males contrasting approaches to life—and those distinctions show up on a very personal level, as problems between an individual wife and her husband. (You may wish to review Chapter 20 by Clayton Barbeau in this regard.)

Certainly our divorce rate is high, but its high visibility, arising from personal observations and media coverage, tends to remove one fundamental fact from our perception: *Most marriages, even today, last throughout a married couple's lifetime.*

What are couples with lasting marriages like? How do they handle the big—and the little—problems of life? Were they just born that way perhaps? Or is it because they have "nice" personalities? After coming this far in this book, you know that inborn characteristics and personalities will never be the answers we shall propose. What, then? How do people in lasting marriages work out adjustments so they are satisfied, content, and even happy with one another?

When we look at such couples, and their entire families, one thing becomes apparent: We find that satisfying relationships don't simply come "naturally." Rather, the couples *work at* their marriages. Successful couples structure their relationships to make them rewarding. They *invest* themselves in their coupled relationship. Simply put, they put the family and its welfare ahead of a lot of other things in life.

It seems worthwhile, then, to pose the question of what is *right* about marriage today. Consequently, we focus on *lasting* relationships in this concluding part of the book to see what we can learn from them.

In Chapter 46, Philip Blumstein and Pepper Schwartz present their findings on how American couples handle money, work, and sex. Most of their findings will not be a surprise. Concerning money, they found that couples who agree on how to manage money are more satisfied with their marriages and tend to stay together. Concerning work, agreement about the wife working and how to divide up the housework increases marital satisfaction. Concerning sex, couples who have more sex are generally more satisfied with their marriage. In addition, spending time together helps couples stay together, and for one of the partners to take the role of caretaker of the marriage also helps to reduce problems.

In Chapter 47, Jeanette Lauer and Robert Lauer report that couples in lasting relationships agree that the two most significant reasons for their marriages being happy are a positive attitude toward the spouse and the belief that marriage is a long-term commitment to something sacred. The couples also agree that sharing the aims and goals of life, feeling that the spouse has grown more interesting, and wanting the relationship to succeed are the next most important reasons.

In Chapter 49, Nicholas Stinnett closes the book with his report on strong families, which he defines as families that are intact and have a high degree of marital happiness, of parent-child satisfactions, and of meeting each other's needs. He found that strong families consistently show six qualities. Based on those qualities, he suggests recommendations designed to help strengthen families.

46

What Makes Today's Marriages Last?

Philip Blumstein
Pepper Schwartz

ABSTRACT: The authors studied a national sample of American couples to see how they handle money, work, and sex. They found that the basic problem with money is not the amount a couple has, but a husband's and wife's conflicting approaches to managing money. In general, couples who agree on how to manage money are more satisfied with marriage and tend to stay together. Major differences about work center on ideas about the wife working and how to divide up the housework. Agreement on these areas increases satisfaction with marriage. If either the husband or the wife serves as a caretaker of the marriage, problems decrease. In contrast, if both are work centered, problems persist. Spending time together helps couples stay together. Finally, in general, the more sex a couple has, the more they are satisfied with their marriage. In contrast, those who have sex outside the marriage are more likely to break up.

American marriage is in trouble. The divorce rate has tripled since 1960, and 41 percent of all presently married couples will see their marriages end by decree rather than by death. For those who take comfort in recent statistics showing a drop in the number of divorces, the fact that lifetime marriage is no longer guaranteed is still sobering. It is a particularly unhappy fact when we realize that second marriages have a slightly higher divorce rate than first marriages indicating that we don't learn from experience.

To better understand the complexity of modern-day relationships, we decided to do a large national study. In the first phase of our study, we asked each member of a couple (our sample included married, cohabitating, and homosexual couples) to fill out separately a 38-page questionnaire. Twelve thousand people did so. From this group we selected 600 people (balancing those in short-, medium-, and long-term relationships) whom we interviewed for several hours in order to ask more intimate questions. Approximately 18 months later we recontacted about one half of the people who had sent in the original questionnaires to see if they were still together as a couple, and if they had broken up, what the reasons were.

We present the results of our investigation in our book, *American Couples*. We concentrate on three specific areas: money, work, and sex. Here we reveal how these three factors affect married couples and what makes marriages work and others falter.

MONEY

In our culture, money is a more taboo topic of conversation than sex. Couples in particular tend to be reticent with each other when talking about money, and this is unfortunate, because if a man and woman don't know each other's financial philosophies, they probably won't discover that they have different values until they are well into the marriage. Indeed, we found that couples fought more about how to spend money than about whether they had enough. If one person's financial philosophy was based on spending while the other's was based on saving, then regular confrontations tended to occur.

Furthermore, when couples told us they argued a lot about how to spend money, they were less likely to be together when we contacted them 18 months later, particularly if they fought in the early years of marriage. The inability to respect each other's financial values opened up the whole question of how well suited the two people were to each other.

Of course, how much money the couple had also was an important element of the relationship. Husbands and wives dissatisfied with the amount of money they had found the entire marriage less pleasing than couples who felt comfortable about income. But having little money did not break them up. It is possible to have a good marriage when a couple is poor—so long as the couple agrees on how to manage the money it has.

There was one area of managing money that often emerged as a problem area for married individuals. When the husband was the only wage earner, or when he earned more money than his wife, he often thought of himself as the provider and his wife as the budgeter. As the budgeter, one of her jobs was to buy the things needed to run the household smoothly. We found if a husband delegated authority to his wife to act as the "purchasing agent" for the couple but really didn't trust her competence, conflict arose.

Interestingly, wives with incomes of their own sometimes did not want to pool all their money with their husbands' because they did not want to be watched over or grilled on personal expenses. Wives with no source of personal income, or with no money to spend as they wanted, often became so frustrated that they resorted to a kind of "guerrilla warfare." For example, one wife said, "I skim a little off the top. Oh, I'll tell him the groceries cost more than they did, or something like that. Nothing spectacular, but it gives me a little breathing room."

Deciding jointly how money should be managed may be tedious, and working out an economic plan may bring up unpleasant issues, but shared control and shared values do seem to predict a happier, calmer, longer-lasting marriage.

WORK

The world of paid work used to be a male domain, but today, while the traditional male provider still exists, the two-paycheck family is becoming more and more common. We discovered that either life-style could work well: Some couples were very happy with the wife staying home; others were happy when she was out in the work force. But if a wife wants to work and her husband will not let her or gripes about the fact that she works, the marriage becomes less stable.

Disagreement could become especially heated if the husband and wife began their marriage with the understanding that the wife would stay home, but she ended up going to work. Even if she did so out of financial necessity or because she needed a new outlet once her children were grown, the husband may have seen this as a disastrous turn of events. Said one man who'd been married for 19 years: "I find it odd that she wants to go out and do somebody else's dirty work when she could stay at home and enjoy the life we worked hard to put together. We argue over this about once a month, especially when she is grouchy because of something someone in the office did or said. I'll tell her again to quit and let me provide, and she'll get huffy and unreasonable."

Our study also showed that when a wife worked, the couple fought more about how the children were being raised. The majority of men and women in our study felt that mothers should be at home during a child's preschool years. Many of the mothers with young children could not, or did not, want to stay at home, and this caused feelings of guilt in both working and nonworking mothers and quarrels between husband and wife.

We did find, however, more wives who wanted to work than husbands who wanted to let them. Husbands were more likely to believe it was unnecessary, because they felt it was the man's duty to provide for the household. When the wives wanted to work despite their husbands' wishes, they sometimes cited the need for the extra income. But just as commonly they indicated that money was not the only—or even the main—reason. Even though many of them spoke of the frustrations of an unwelcoming job market and low pay, they still wanted to work. But when wives were employed outside the home, husbands were more likely to say that they respected their wives' decision-making abilities and were more likely to listen to their opinions. In fact, a man whose wife was successful in the working world was more likely to say she should not have to do housework!

This did not mean, however, that *he* was doing housework. Rather it meant that she did somewhat less than wives who were not employed, and that the couple learned to tolerate more dirt. It was extremely rare for husbands to do the majority of the housework and uncommon for them to do half. Even unemployed husbands did much less housework than wives who worked 40-hour weeks. To be blunt, men hated housework and really wanted women to relieve them of that responsibility, in whatever manner they managed to do it. Husbands' aversion to housework was so intense, our study showed, that the more housework a husband did, the more the couple fought about household duties.

This is not just a harmless disagreement: We found that new marriages are more likely to fail when husbands feel their wives don't do their "fair share" of housework. And her "fair share" is usually well over half. This is clearly a sensitive problem for women who want equal responsibility for tasks in their marriage.

In a healthy marriage there is also a balance of home and work. Marriages need a caretaker, someone who makes sure that the relationship is in good shape, who notices if it's not, who tends to its needs. This caretaker may suggest they have a "date" away from the children or the routine, or that they take the time to discuss a point of contention that has been festering beneath the surface of their daily life. Marriages are best served if both partners take on the caretaker responsibility, but having at least one such person seems essential.

If, however, both partners are "work-centered"—very much bound up in their work and its issues—the marriage may wither from lack of attention. Such couples have a tendency to be less satisfied and less committed to their relationship. While initially they may have been attracted to each other because they admired each other's ambition and commitment to a career, their similarity of outlook, which places their relationship second to their work, tends to undermine their marriage.

Spending enough time together is important. We found that it was not only work that competed with marriage for the individuals' allegiance. If a husband and wife spend too much time apart, for *any* reason—attending to relatives, friends, hobbies, etc.—they're more likely to break up. Some couples told us that they loved each other but had many diverse interests or responsibilities and therefore had to spend a lot of time away from each other. They insisted they were still very happy and committed, precisely because their outside activities gave them rich experiences which made them more interesting spouses.

Nonetheless, people who maintained such a life-style were more likely to break up than couples who spent a lot of time together. In some cases having "separate" lives may have been just a symptom of a husband and wife who didn't enjoy each other's company. But we think it is also true that couples may love each other deeply, yet spend more and more time doing things with other people because they believe their marriage to be so solid that it needs very little constant care to support it. It seems to us that couples should not be too smug. Spending too much time away from each other may make the couple forget what it was that drew them together in the first place.

SEX

Both the quantity and quality of sex are important for the well-being of a marriage. Couples who have sex frequently are more pleased with their sex life. However, frequent sex seems to mean more to men than to women. Married men feel so strongly about having sex regularly that those who told us that sex was infrequent were more likely to be dissatisfied with their entire relationship. Married women may have been unhappy when sex was infrequent, but it was less likely to affect their assessment of the entire marriage. When husbands or wives felt their sex life was not satisfying or was a source of fighting between them, they were more likely to have broken up when we contacted them 18 months later.

How much sex is enough?

We found that the majority of our married couples had sex at least once a week. And even after 10 or more years of marriage, 63 percent had sex at least that often. We found a low sexual frequency in very few couples: Of those married 10 years or more, fewer than 15 percent had sex once a month or less. Thus, while we would say that "enough" sex is a very subjective and personal evaluation, most couples in our study maintained sex as a continuous part of married life. Sex did decline over the length of the marriage and it is less frequent among older people (older people in a new marriage, however, have more sex than those in a long-term marriage).

Couples were more likely to tell us they have a good sex life when they shared responsibility for making it happen. While initiation of sex was generally still the husband's prerogative, couples were particularly pleased when suggesting was shared 50–50. What was disturbing in the couple's relationship was when the wife was the more aggressive initiator and the husband more inclined to veto sex.

Another American tradition that seems firmly in place is monogamy. Or perhaps we should say the *belief* in monogamy. The following statement by a wife of 10 years was a typical opinion:

> Before marriage we discussed monogamy and we both wholeheartedly agree about how important it is. I don't believe in cheating and he doesn't believe in cheating. And that's what it would be—cheating someone out of love and trust. It would make a mockery of marriage.

Nonetheless, more people believed in monogamy than always practiced it. Approximately 26 percent of our husbands and 21 percent of our wives had had sex outside of their marriage (this varied, depending on how long the couple was married). These percentages did not mean changing values about monogamy; most people were quiet about it, and many did it only once, felt guilty and did not wish to repeat the experience.

We didn't find that married people who had extramarital sex were any less satisfied with their sex life together or had sex any less often with their spouse than those who had never had sex outside their marriage. And husbands who were nonmonogamous were not any less committed to the future of their marriage. But wives who had had sex recently with someone else were more inclined to feel their marriage was not going to last. Ultimately, we found that couples in our study were less likely to survive if they had sex outside their relationship in the preceding year.

This is not a complete list of all the things we discovered that can threaten happiness in a marriage and its longevity, but these things are important. These are problems that can gnaw at a marriage. Something like disagreeing about how to spend money may seem just an annoying difference of opinion—until it starts to dismantle the trust and security of the entire relationship. Today's marriages require a new level of awareness and more commitment to problem solving. When marriage was *forever*, issues could be left alone because there was the understanding that the couple had a lifetime together to work them out. Because this is no longer the case, we hope that a little information can help people to spot vulnerabilities and give their marriage the best chance it has to be a satisfying lifetime experience.

47

Marriages Made to Last

Jeanette Lauer
Robert Lauer

ASTRACT: The authors studied 351 couples who had been married for 15 years or more. They found 300 happily married, 32 mixed (only one partner was happy), and 19 unhappily married. Happy couples agreed that the two most significant reasons for their happy marriages were a positive attitude toward the spouse (liking that person as a friend) and the belief that marriage is a long-term commitment to something sacred. They also agreed that sharing the aims and goals of life, feeling that the spouse has grown more interesting, and wanting the relationship to succeed were the next important reasons. The authors discuss such other factors as the couples' laughing together, philosophy of life, showing affection, sex, and exchanging ideas.

. . . We recently completed a survey of couples with enduring marriages to explore how marriages survive and satisfy in this turbulent world. Through colleagues and students we located and questioned 351 couples married for 15 years or more.

Of the 351 couples, 300 said they were happily married, 19 said they were unhappily married (but were staying together for a variety of reasons, including "the sake of the children"), and among the remaining 32 couples only one partner said he or she was unhappy in the marriage.

Each husband and wife responded individually to our questionnaire, which included 39 statements and questions about marriage—ranging from agreement about sex, money and goals in life to attitudes toward spouses and marriage in general. We asked couples to select from their answers the ones that best explained why their marriages had lasted. Men and women showed remarkable agreement on the keys to an enduring relationship (see box).

The most frequently named reason for an enduring and happy marriage was having a generally positive attitude toward one's spouse: viewing one's partner as one's best friend and liking him or her "as a person."

As one wife summed it up, "I feel that liking a person in marriage is as important as loving that person. Friends enjoy each other's company. We spend an unusually large amount of time together. We work at the same institution, offices just a few feet apart. But we still have things to do and to say to each other on a positive note after being together through the day."

It may seem almost trite to say that "my spouse is my best friend," but the couples in our survey underscored the importance of feeling that way. Moreover, they told us some specific things that they liked about their mates—why, as one woman said, "I would want to have him as a friend even if I weren't married to him." For one thing, many happily married people said that their mates become more interesting to them in time. A man married for 30 years said that it was almost like being married to a series of different women: "I have watched her grow and I find her more fascinating now than when we were first married."

A common theme among couples in our study was that the things they really liked in each other were qualities of caring, giving, integrity, and a sense of humor. In essence, they said, "I am married to someone who cares about me, who is concerned for my well-being, who gives as much or more than he or she gets, who is open and trustworthy and who is not mired down in a somber, bleak outlook on life." The redemption of difficult people through selfless devotion may make good fiction, but the happily married people in our sample expressed no such sense of mission. Rather, they said, they are grateful to have married someone who is basically appealing and likable.

Are lovers blind to each other's faults? No, according to our findings. They are aware of the flaws in their mates and acknowledge the rough times, but they believe that the likable qualities are more important than the deficiencies and the difficulties. "She isn't perfect," said a husband of 24 years. "But I don't worry about her weak points, which are very few. Her strong points overcome them too much."

A second key to a lasting marriage was a belief in marriage as a long-term commitment and a sacred institution. Many of our respondents

What Keeps a Marriage Going?
Here are the top reasons
respondents gave, listed in order of frequency.

Men	Women
My spouse is my best friend.	My spouse is my best friend.
I like my spouse as a person.	I like my spouse as a person.
Marriage is a long-term commitment.	Marriage is a long-term commitment.
Marriage is sacred.	Marriage is sacred.
We agree on aims and goals.	We agree on aims and goals.
My spouse has grown more interesting.	My spouse has grown more interesting.
I want the relationship to succeed.	I want the relationship to succeed.
An enduring marriage is important to social stability.	We laugh together.
We laugh together.	We agree on a philosophy of life.
I am proud of my spouse's achievements.	We agree on how and how often to show affection.
We agree on a philosophy of life.	An enduring marriage is important to social stability.
We agree about our sex life.	We have a stimulating exchange of ideas.
We agree on how and how often to show affection.	We discuss things calmly.
I confide in my spouse.	We agree about our sex life.
We share outside hobbies and interests.	I am proud of my spouse's achievements.

thought that the present generation takes the vow, "till death us do part" too lightly and is unwilling to work through difficult times, Successful couples viewed marriage as a task that sometimes demands that you grit your teeth and plunge ahead in spite of the difficulties. "I'll tell you why we've stayed together," said a Texas woman married for 18 years. "I'm just too damned stubborn to give up."

Some of the people in the survey indicated that they would stay together no matter what. Divorce was simply not an option. Others viewed commitment somewhat differently. They saw it not as a chain that inexorably binds people together despite intense misery but rather as a determination to work through difficult times. "You can't run home to mother when the first sign of trouble appears," said a woman married for 35 years.

"Commitment means a willingness to be unhappy for a while," said a man married for more than 20 years. "I wouldn't go on for years and years being wretched in my marriage. But you can't avoid troubled times. You're not going to be happy with each other all the time. That's when commitment is really important."

In addition to sharing attitudes toward the spouse and toward marriage, our respondents indicated that agreement about aims and goals in life, the desire to make the marriage succeed, and laughing together were all important. One surprising result was that agreement about sex was far down the list of reasons for a happy marriage. Fewer than 10 percent of the spouses thought that good sexual relations kept their marriage together. Is sex relatively unimportant to a happy marriage? Yes and no.

Although not many happily married respondents listed it as a major reason for their happiness, most were still generally satisfied with their sex lives. Seventy percent said that they always or almost always agreed about sex. And indeed for many, "satisfied" seems too mild a term. A woman married for 19 years said: "Our sexual desire is strong, and we are very much in love." One man said that sex with his wife was like "a revival of youth." Another noted that for various reasons he and his wife did not have sex as frequently as they would like, but when they do "it is a beautiful act of giving and sharing as deeply emotional as it is physical."

While some reported a diminishing sex life, others described a relatively stable pattern and a number indicated improvement over time. "Thank God, the passion hasn't died," a wife said. "In fact, it has gotten more intense. The only thing that has died is the element of doubt or uncertainty that one experiences while dating or in the beginning of a marriage."

On the other hand, some couples said they were satisfied despite a less-than-ideal sex life. A number of people told us that they were happy with their marriage even though they did not have sex as frequently as they would like. Generally, men complained of this more than women, although a number of wives desired sex more than did their husbands.

There were various reasons for having less sex than desired, generally involving one partner's exhaustion from work or family circumstances ("We are very busy and very involved," reported a husband, "and have a teenager who stays up late. So we don't make love as often as we would like to.")

Does this dissatisfaction with sex life lead to affairs? We did not ask about fidelity directly, but the high value that most of our subjects placed on friendship and commitment strikes us as incongruous with infidelity. And in fact only two of those we questioned volunteered that they had had brief affairs. One husband's view might explain the faithfulness of the group: "I get tempted when we don't have sex. But I don't think I could ever have an affair. I would feel like a traitor."

Such treason, in fact, may be the one taboo in enduring relationships. A wife of 27 years said that although she could work out almost any problem with her husband given enough time, infidelity "would probably not be something I could forget and forgive." The couples in our sample appear to take their commitment to each other seriously.

Those with a less-than-ideal sex life talked about adjusting to it rather than seeking relief in an affair. A woman married 25 years rated her marriage as extremely happy even though she and her husband had had no sexual relations for the past 10 years. "I was married once before and the marriage was almost totally sex and little else," she said. "So I suppose a kind of trade-off exists here—I like absolutely everything else about my current marriage."

Many others agreed that they would rather be married to their spouse and have a less-than-ideal sex life than be married to someone else and have a better sex life. As one wife put it, "I feel marriages can survive and flourish without today's emphasis on sex. I had a much stronger sex drive than my husband and it was a point of weakness in our marriage. However, it was not as important as friendship, understanding, and respect. That we had lots of, and still do."

We found a few beliefs and practices among our couples that contradict what some therapists believe is important to a marriage. One involves conflict. Some marriage counselors stress the importance of expressing feelings with abandon—spouses should freely vent their anger with each other, letting out all the stops short of physical violence. According to them, aggression is a catharsis that gets rid of hostility and restores harmony in the marital relationship. But some social scientists argue that intense expressions of anger, resentment, and dislike tend to corrode the relationship and increase the likelihood of future aggression.

Happily married couples in our survey came down squarely on the side of those who emphasize the damaging effects of intensely expressed anger. A salesman with a 36-year marriage advised, "Discuss your problems in a normal voice. If a voice is raised, stop. Return after a short period of time. Start again. After a period of time both parties will be able to deal with their problems and not say things that they will be sorry about later."

Only one couple said that they typically yelled at each other. The rest emphasized the importance of restraint. They felt that a certain calmness is necessary in dealing constructively with conflict.

Another commonly held belief that contradicts conventional wisdom concerns equality in marriage. Most social scientists note the value of an egalitarian relationship. But according to the couples in our sample, the attitude that marriage is a 50–50 proposition can be damaging. One husband said that a successful marriage demands that you "give 60 percent of the time. You have to be willing to put in more than you take out." A wife happily married for 44 years said she would advise all young couples "to be willing to give 70 percent and expect 30 percent."

In the long run, the giving and taking should balance out. If either partner enters a marriage determined that all transactions must be equal, the marriage will suffer. As one husband put it, "Sometimes I give far more than I receive, and sometimes I receive far more than I give. But my wife does the same. If we weren't willing to do that, we would have broken up long ago."

Finally, some marriage experts have strongly advocated that spouses maintain separate as well as shared interests. It is important, they argue, to avoid the merging of identities. But those in our survey with enduring, happy marriages disagree. They try to spend as much time together and share as many activities as possible. "Jen is just the best friend I have," said a husband who rated his marriage as extremely happy. "I would rather spend time with her, talk with her, be with her than with anyone else."

"We try to share everything," said another. "We even work together now. In spite of that, we often feel that we have too little time together."

We did not detect any loss of individuality in these people. In fact, they disagreed to some extent on many of the questions. Their intense intimacy—their preference for shared rather than separate activities—seems to reflect a richness and fulfillment in the relationship rather than a loss of identity. "On occasion she has something else to do, and I enjoy the time alone. But it strikes me that I can enjoy it because I know that soon she will be home, and we will be together again."

Our results seem to underscore Leo Tolstoy's observation that "Happy families are all alike." Those who have long-term, happy marriages share a number of attitudes and behavioral patterns that combine to create an enduring relationship. For them, "till death us do part" is not a binding clause but a gratifying reality.

48

Five Types of Marriage

John F. Cuber
Peggy B. Harroff

ABSTRACT: The authors studied 211 couples who had been married ten or more years and who felt committed to one another. They found that there is no single type of lasting relationship. Rather, such couples differ markedly in their basic approaches to marriage and in their overall satisfactions and expectations. The five basic marital styles they uncovered are: conflict-habituated, devitalized, passive-congenial, vital, and total.

The qualitative aspects of enduring marital relationships vary enormously. The variations described to us were by no means random or clearly individualized, however. Five distinct life-styles showed up repeatedly and the pairs within each of them were remarkably similar in the ways in which they lived together, found sexual expression, reared children, and made their way in the outside world.

The following classification is based on the interview materials of those people whose marriages had already lasted ten years or more and who said that they had never seriously considered divorce or separation. While 360 of the men and women had been married ten or more years to the same spouse, exclusion of those who reported that they had considered divorce reduced the number to 211. The discussion in this chapter is, then, based on 211 interviews; 107 men and 104 women.

The descriptions which our interviewees gave us took into account how they had behaved and also how they felt about their actions past and present. Examination of the important features of their lives revealed five recurring configurations of male-female life, each with a central theme—some prominent distinguishing psychological feature which gave each type its singularity. It is these preeminent characteristics which suggested the names for the relationship; the *Conflict-Habituated*, the *Devitalized*, the *Passive-Congenial*, the *Vital*, and the *Total*.

THE CONFLICT-HABITUATED

We begin with the conflict-habituated not because it is the most prevalent, but because the overt behavior patterns in it are so readily observed and because it presents some arresting contradictions. In this association there is much tension and conflict—although it is largely controlled. At worst, there is some private quarreling, nagging, and "throwing up the past" of which members of the immediate family, and more rarely close friends and relatives, have some awareness. At best, the couple is discreet and polite, genteel about it in the company of others—but after a few drinks at the cocktail party the verbal barbs begin to fly. The intermittent conflict is rarely concealed from the children, though we were often assured otherwise. "Oh, they're at it again—but they always are," says the high school son. There is private acknowledgement by both husband and wife as a rule that incompatibility is pervasive, that conflict is ever-potential, and that an atmosphere of tension permeates the togetherness.

An illustrative case concerns a physician of fifty, married for twenty-five years to the same woman, with two college-graduate children promisingly established in their own professions.

> You know, it's funny; we have fought from the time we were in high school together. As I look back at it, I can't remember specific quarrels; it's more like a running guerrilla fight with intermediate periods, sometimes quite long, of pretty good fun and some damn good sex. In fact, if it hadn't been for the sex, we wouldn't have been married so quickly. Well, anyway, this has been going on ever since. . . . It's hard to know what it is we fight about most of the time. You name it and we'll fight about it. It's sometimes something I've said that she remembers differently, sometimes a decision—like what kind of car to buy or what to give the kids for Christmas. With regard to politics, and religion, and morals— oh, boy! You know, outside of the welfare of the kids—we don't really agree about anything. . . . At different times we take opposite sides—not deliberately; it just comes out that way.

Now these fights get pretty damned colorful. You called them arguments a little while ago—I have to correct you—they're brawls. There's
never a bit of physical violence—at least not directed to each other—but
the verbal gunfire gets pretty thick. Why, we've said things to each other
that neither of us would think of saying in the hearing of anybody else.
. . .

Of course, we don't settle any of the issues. It's sort of a matter of principle *not* to. Because somebody would have to give in then and lose face for
the next encounter. . . .

There is a subtle valence in these conflict-habituated relationships.
It is easily missed in casual observation. So central is the necessity for
channeling conflict and bridling hostility that these considerations come
to preoccupy much of the interaction. Some psychiatrists have gone so
far as to suggest that it is precisely the deep need to do psychological
battle with one another which constitutes the cohesive factor insuring
continuity of the marriage. Possibly so. But even from a surface point
of view, the overt and manifest fact of habituated attention to handling
tension, keeping it chained, and concealing it, is clearly seen as a dominant life force. And it can, and does for some, last for a whole lifetime.

THE DEVITALIZED

The key to the devitalized mode is the clear discrepancy between
middle-aged reality and the earlier years. These people usually characterized themselves as having been "deeply in love" during the early
years, as having spent a great deal of time together, having enjoyed sex,
and most importantly of all, having had a close identification with one
another. The present picture, with some variation from case to case, is
in clear contrast—little time is spent together, sexual relationships are
far less satisfying qualitatively or quantitatively, and interests and activities are not shared, at least not in the deeper and meaningful way they
once were. Most of their time together now is "duty time"—entertaining together, planning and sharing activities with children, and participating in various kinds of required community responsibilities. They do
as a rule retain, in addition to a genuine and mutual interest in the welfare of their children, a shared attention to their joint property and the
husband's career. But even in the latter case the interest is contrasting.
Despite a common dependency on his success and the benefits which
flow therefrom, there is typically very little sharing of the intrinsic aspects of career—simply an acknowledgment of their mutual dependency
on the fruits. . . .

Judging by the way it was when we were first married—say the first five
years or so—things are pretty matter-of-fact now—even dull. They're dull
between us, I mean. The children are a lot of fun, keep us pretty busy,

and there are lots of outside things—you know, like Little League and the P.T.A. and the Swim Club, and even the company parties aren't always so bad. But I mean where Bob and I are concerned—if you followed us around, you'd wonder why we ever got *married*. We take each other for granted. We laugh at the same things sometimes, but we don't really laugh together—the way we used to. But, as he said to me the other night—with one or two under the belt, I think—"You now, you're still a little fun now and then.". . .

Now, I don't say this to complain, not in the least. There's a cycle to life. There are things you do in high school. And different things you do in college. Then you're a young adult. And then you're middle-aged. That's where we are now. . . . I'll admit that I do yearn for the old days when sex was a big thing and going out was fun and I hung on to everything he said about his work and his ideas as if they were coming from a genius or something. But then you get the children and other responsibilities. I have the home and Bob has a tremendous burden of responsibility at the office. . . . He's completely responsible for setting up the new branch now. . . . You have to adjust to these things and we both try to gracefully. . . . Anniversaries though do remind you kind of hard. . . .

Regardless of the gracefulness of the acceptance, or lack thereof, the common plight prevails: on the subjective, emotional dimension, the relationship has become a void. The original zest is gone. There is typically little overt tension or conflict, but the interplay between the pair has become apathetic, lifeless. No serious threat to the continuity of the marriage is generally acknowledged, however. It is intended, usually by both, that it continue indefinitely despite its numbness. Continuity and relative freedom from open conflict are fostered in part because of the comforts of the "habit cage." Continuity is further insured by the absence of any engaging alternative, "all things considered." It is also reinforced, sometimes rather decisively, by legal and ecclesiastical requirements and expectations. These people quickly explain that "there are other things in life" which are worthy of sustained human effort.

This kind of relationship is exceedingly common. Persons in this circumstance frequently make comparisons with other pairs they know, many of whom are similar to themselves. This fosters the comforting judgment that "marriage is like this—except for a few oddballs or pretenders who claim otherwise." . . .

THE PASSIVE-CONGENIAL

The passive-congenial mode has a great deal in common with the devitalized, the essential difference being that the passivity which pervades the association has been there from the start. The devitalized have a more exciting set of memories; the passive-congenials give little evidence that they had ever hoped for anything much different from what they are currently experiencing.

There is therefore little suggestion of disillusionment or compulsion to make believe to anyone. Existing modes of association are comfortably adequate—no stronger words fit the facts as they related them to us. There is little conflict, although some admit that they tiptoe rather gingerly over and around a residue of subtle resentments and frustrations. In their better moods they remind themselves (and each other) that "there are many common interests" which they both enjoy. "We both like classical music." "We agree completely on religious and political matters." "We both love the country and our quaint exurban neighbors." "We are both lawyers."

The wife of a prominent attorney, who has been living in the passive-congenial mode for thirty years, put her description this way:

> We have both always tried to be calm and sensible about major life decisions, to think things out thoroughly and in perspective. Len and I knew each other since high school but didn't start to date until college. When he asked me to marry him, I took a long time to decide whether he was the right man for me and I went into his family background, because I wasn't just marrying him; I was choosing a father for my children. We decided together not to get married until he was established, so that we would not have to live in dingy little apartments like some of our friends who got married right out of college. This prudence has stood us in good stead too. Life has moved ahead for us with remarkable orderliness and we are deeply grateful for the foresight we had. . . .
>
> I don't like all this discussion about sex—even in the better magazines. I hope your study will help to put it in its proper perspective. I expected to perform sex in marriage, but both before and since, I'm willing to admit that it's a much overrated activity. Now and then, perhaps it's better. I am fortunate, I guess, because my husband has never been demanding about it, before marriage or since. It's just not that important to either of us. . . .

People make their way into the passive-congenial mode by two quite different routes—by default and by intention. Perhaps in most instances they arrive at this way of living and feeling by drift. There is so little which they have cared about deeply in each other that a passive-congenial mode is a deliberately intended arrangement for two people whose interests and creative energies are directed elsewhere than toward the pairing—into careers, or in the case of women, into children or community activities. They say they know this and want it this way. These people simply do not wish to invest their total emotional involvement and creative effort in the male-female relationship. . . .

The passive-congenial mode . . . enables people who desire a considerable amount of personal independence and freedom to realize it with a minimum of inconvenience from or to the spouse. And it certainly spares the participants in it from the need to give a great deal of personal attention to "adjusting to the spouse's needs." The passive-congenial menage is thus a mood as well as a mode.

Our descriptions of the devitalized and the passive-congenials have been similar because these two modes are much alike in their overt characteristics. The participants' evaluations of their *present situations* are likewise largely the same—the accent on "other things," the emphasis on civic and professional responsibilities, the importance of property, children, and reputation. The essential difference lies in their diverse histories and often in their feelings of contentment with their current lives. The passive-congenials had from the start a life pattern and a set of expectations essentially consistent with what they are now experiencing. When the devitalized reflect, however, when they juxtapose history against present reality, they often see the barren gullies in their lives left by the erosions of earlier satisfactions. . . .

THE VITAL

In extreme contrast to the three foregoing [types of relationships] is the vital relationship. The vital pair can easily be overlooked as they move through their worlds of work, recreation, and family activities. They do the same things, publicly at least; and when talking for public consumption say the same things—they are proud of their homes, love their children, gripe about their jobs, while being quite proud of their career accomplishments. But when the close, intimate, confidential, empathic look is taken, the essence of the vital relationship becomes clear: the mates are intensely bound together psychologically in important life matters. Their sharing and their togetherness is genuine. It provides the life essence for both man and woman.

> The things we do together aren't fun intrinsically—the ecstasy comes from being *together in the doing*. Take her out of the picture and I wouldn't give a damn for the boat, the lake, or any of the fun that goes on out there.

The presence of the mate is indispensable to the feelings of satisfaction which the activity provides. The activities shared by the vital pairs may involve almost anything: hobbies, careers, community service. Anything—so long as it is closely shared.

It is hard to escape the word *vitality*—exciting mutuality of feelings and participation together in important life segments. The clue that the relationship is vital (rather than merely expressing the joint activity) derives from the feeling that it is important. An activity is flat and uninteresting if the spouse is not a part of it.

Other valued things are readily sacrificed in order to enhance life within the vital relationship.

> I cheerfully, and that's putting it mildly, passed up two good promotions because one of them would have required some traveling and the other

would have taken evening and weekend time—and that's when Pat and I *live*. The hours with her (after twenty-two years of marriage) are what I live for. You should meet her. . . .

People in the vital relationship . . . find their central satisfaction in the life they live with and through each other. It consumes their interest and dominates their thoughts and actions. All else is subordinate and secondary.

This does not mean that people in vital relationships lose their separate identities, that they may not upon occasion be rivalrous or competitive with one another, or that conflict may not occur. They differ fundamentally from the conflict-habituated, however, in that when conflict does occur, it results from matters that are important to them, such as which college a daughter or son is to attend; it is devoid of the trivial "who said what first and when" and "I can't forget when you. . . ." A further difference is that people to whom the relationship is vital tend to settle disagreements quickly and seek to avoid conflict, whereas the conflict-habituated look forward to conflict and appear to operate by a tacit rule that no conflict is ever to be truly terminated and that the spouse must never be considered right. The two kinds of conflict are thus radically different. To confuse them is to miss an important differentiation.

THE TOTAL

The total relationship is like the vital relationship with the important addition that it is more multifaceted. The points of vital meshing are more numerous—in some cases all of the important life foci are vitually shared. In one such marriage the husband is an internationally known scientist. For thirty years his wife has been "his friend, mistress, and partner." He still goes home at noon whenever possible, at considerable inconvenience, to have a quiet lunch and spend a conversational hour or so with his wife. They refer to these conversations as "our little seminars." They feel comfortable with each other and with their four grown children. The children (now in their late twenties) say that they enjoy visits with their parents as much as they do with friends of their own age.

There is practically no pretense between persons in the total relationship or between them and the world outside. There are few areas of tension, because the items of difference which have arisen over the years have been settled as they arose. There often *were* serious differences of opinion but they were handled, sometimes by compromise, sometimes by one or the other yielding; but these outcomes were of secondary importance because the primary consideration was not who was right or who was wrong, only how the problem could be resolved without tarnishing the relationship. When faced with differences, they can and do dispose of the difficulties without losing their feeling of unity or their sense of vitality and centrality of their relationship. This is the mainspring.

The various parts of the total relationship are reinforcing, as we learned from this consulting engineer who is frequently sent abroad by his corporation.

> She keeps my files and scrapbooks up to date. . . . I invariably take her with me to conferences around the world. Her femininity, easy charm and wit are invaluable assets to me. I know it's conventional to say that a man's wife is responsible for his success and I also know that it's often not true. But in my case I gladly acknowledge that it's not only true, but she's indispensable to me. But she'd go along with me even if there was nothing for her to do because we just enjoy each other's company— deeply. You know, the best part of a vacation is not *what* we do, but that we do it together. We plan it and reminisce about it and weave it into our work and other play all the time.

The wife's account is substantially the same except that her testimony demonstrates more clearly the genuineness of her "help."

> It seems to me that Bert exaggerates my help. It's not so much that I only want to help him; it's more that I want to do those things anyway. We do them together, even though we may not be in each other's presence at the time. I don't really know what I do for him and what I do for me.

This kind of relationship is rare, in marriage or out, but it does exist and can endure. We occasionally found relationships so total that all aspects of life were mutually shared and enthusiastically participated in. It is as if neither spouse has, or has had, a truly private existence. . . .

[T]he five types [are not] to be interpreted as *degrees* of marital happiness or adjustment. Persons in all five are currently adjusted and most say that they are content, if not happy. Rather, the five types represent *different kinds of adjustment* and *different conceptions of marriage*. This is an important concept which must be emphasized if one is to understand the personal meanings which these people attach to the conditions of their marital experience.

Neither are the five types necessarily stages in a cycle of initial bliss and later disillusionment. Many pairings started in the passive-congenial stage; in fact, quite often people intentionally enter into a marriage for the acknowledged purpose of living this kind of relationship. To many the simple amenities of the "habit cage" are not disillusionments or even disappointments, but rather are sensible life expectations which provide an altogether comfortable and rational way of having a "home base" for their lives. And many of the conflict-habituated told of courtship histories essentially like their marriages.

While each of these types tends to persist, there *may* be movement from one type to another as circumstances and life perspectives change. This movement may go in any direction from any point, and a given couple may change categories more than once. Such changes are relatively infrequent however, and the important point is that relationship types tend to persist over relatively long periods. . . .

Whether examining marriages for the satisfactions and fulfillments they have brought or for the frustrations and pain, the overriding influence of life-style—or as we have here called it, relationship type—is of the essence. Such a viewpoint helps the observer, and probably the participant, to understand some of the apparent enigmas about men and women in marriage—why infidelities destroy some marriages and not others; why conflict plays so large a role for some couples and is so negligible for others; why some seemingly well-suited and harmoniously adjusted spouses seek divorce while others with provocations galore remain solidly together; why affections, sexual expression, recreation, almost everything observable about men and women are so radically different from pair to pair. All of these are not merely different objectively; they are perceived differently by the pairs, are differently reacted to, and differently attended to. . . .

49

▼▼▼▼

Strong Families

▼▼▼▼

Nicholas Stinnett

ASTRACT: To improve family life, it is more helpful to look at what makes families strong than at what is wrong with them. Using state, national, and international samples, the author studied "strong" families: intact families that have a high degree of marital happiness and high parent-child satisfactions and that do a good job of meeting each other's needs. Strong families consistently show appreciation of one another, spend time together, are committed to one another, use good communications, are religious, and take a constructive approach to crises. On the basis of these six qualities, the author suggests recommendations designed to help strengthen families.

The quest for self-fulfillment during the twentieth century has developed into a major goal in American culture (Yankelovich, 1981). However, in our preoccupation with this objective we have neglected the family and lost sight of the fact that so much of the foundation necessary to facilitate the life-long process of individual self-fulfillment (such as the development of interpersonal competence, self-confidence, self-esteem, respect for self and others, and the vision and knowledge that life can be enriched) is developed within strong, healthy families.

We have considerable evidence that the quality of family life is extremely important to our emotional well-being, our happiness, and our mental health as individuals. We know that poor relationships within the family are very closely related to many problems in society (such as juvenile delinquency and domestic abuse).

As we look back in history we see that the quality of family life is very important to the strength of nations. There is a pattern in the rise and fall of great societies such as ancient Rome, Greece, and Egypt. When these societies were at the peak of their power and prosperity, the family was strong and highly valued. When family life became weak in these societies, when the family was not valued—when goals became extremely individualistic—the society began to deteriorate and eventually fell.

Obviously, it is to our benefit to do what we can to strengthen family life; this should be one of our nation's top priorities, but unfortunately it has not been.

So much of what is written about families has focused on problems and pathology. On the newsstand we see many books and magazine articles about what's wrong with families and the problems that families have. There are those who like to predict that the family will soon disappear and that it no longer meets our needs.

Certainly we need information about positive family models and what strong families are like. We need to learn how to strengthen families. We don't learn how to do anything by looking only at what *shouldn't* be done. We learn most effectively by examining how to do something correctly and studying a positive model. We have not had this positive model as much as we need it in the area of family life. Understanding what a strong family is provides educators, counselors, and families with a positive model. Getting this knowledge first-hand from those who have created a successful family situation gives us a good picture of how families become strong.

We have many strong families throughout this nation and the world. There has been little written about them because there has been very little research focusing on family strengths. It was with this in mind that we launched the Family Strengths Research Project, a search that has taken us throughout our nation as well as to other parts of the world. This research was inspired in part by the pioneer work in family strengths of Otto (1962, 1964).

Our search began in Oklahoma where we studied 130 families identified as strong. More recently, we have completed a national study of strong families representing all regions of the nation, an investigation of strong Russian immigrant families, a study of strong black families, and an examination of strong families from various countries in South America.

The research method varied. For example, one approach was represented by the Oklahoma study. In this project we had the assistance of the Cooperative Extension Service to help identify the strong families. We asked the Home Economics Extension Agent in each of the counties of Oklahoma to recommend a few families that the agent considered particularly strong. The Home Economics Extension Agents were suited to this task for three reasons—their background training in family life, their concern for improving family life as part of their work, and the great amount of contact they have with families in the community. Also, we gave the agents some guidelines for selecting the families. The guidelines were that the families demonstrated a high degree of marital happiness, a high degree of parent-child satisfaction as perceived by the Extension Agent, and that the family members appeared to meet each other's needs to a high degree.

For purposes of this study, all the families were intact with husband, wife, and at least one child living at home. The first requirement for inclusion in this sample of strong families was the recommendation of the Extension Agent. The second requirement was that the families rate themselves very high in terms of marriage satisfaction and parent-child relationship satisfaction. The 130 families that met these two conditions were included in the sample. Both urban and rural families were represented in the sample, although there were more families from small cities, towns, and rural areas than from large urban areas. In most instances, we found very little difference between the urban and rural families.

A second research technique was demonstrated by the national study. The strong families in this study responded to an article sent to various daily and weekly papers across the nation. The 41 newspapers asked to run the article were selected to ensure a sample from all regions of the country, and from both rural and urban areas. The news release described the national study and asked families who felt they qualified as strong families to send their names and addresses to the researchers. The philosophy behind this approach can be debated almost endlessly. In short, we believed that rather than we as professionals defining what a strong family is, we would let families make the decision themselves.

The response to the news release was tremendous. Each family that responded was sent copies of the Family Strengths Inventory for the husband and wife. Many families also sent elaborate stories describing their family and its characteristics and activities in detail. The inventory focused on both the husband-wife and parent-child relationships and collected demographic information. Only families that rated themselves very high on marriage happiness and parent-child satisfaction were included in the final sample. This was similar to the screening procedure used in the Oklahoma study. The final sample size for the national study was 350 families.

In summary, we researched 130 families in the Oklahoma study, 350 families in the National Project, and 180 families in the South American study. In addition, smaller studies of Russian immigrant families and black families have been completed. In all of these research projects the families completed questionnaires and later a few of them were interviewed. Our questions covered a broad range of factors concerning their relationship patterns. For example, we asked how they deal with conflict, about communication patterns, and about power structure. When we analyzed the vast quantity of information, we found six qualities that stood out among these strong families. Six qualities they had in common seemed to play a very important role in their strength and their happiness. It is interesting that the same six qualities were found to characterize strong families in all of the research studies we conducted.

THE SIX QUALITIES OF THE STRONG FAMILIES

Appreciation

The first quality of the strong families was certainly one of the most important. It emerged from many different questions and in many ways that we were not expecting. The results were permeated by this characteristic. That quality is appreciation. The members of these families expressed a great deal of appreciation for each other. They built each other up psychologically, they gave each other many positive psychological strokes; everyone was made to feel good about themselves.

All of us like to be with people who make us feel good about ourselves; we don't like to be with people who make us feel bad. One of the tasks of family counselors who are working with family members who make each other feel terrible is to get them out of that pattern of interaction and into a pattern where they can make each other feel good. William James, considered by many people to be the greatest psychologist our country has ever produced, wrote a book on human needs. Some years after that book was published he remarked that he had forgotten to include the most important need of all—the need to be appreciated. There are so many things that we do for which we receive no reward other than appreciation; perhaps we all need to work on our ability to express appreciation. One difficulty in this is that we sometimes fear that people will think we're not sincere or that it's empty flattery. This need not be a concern. We *can* be sincere. Every person has many good qualities, many strengths. All we have to do is look for them, and be aware of them.

There are many ways in which we can develop the ability to express appreciation and thus make our human relationships better and certainly improve the quality of our family life. One widely used technique is one that Dr. Herbert Otto, Chairman of the National Center for Exploration of Human Potential, has used and written about a great deal. It has also been a tool for many counselors and is now being used by families on their own. This is called the "strength bombardment" technique. Here is the way it operates: The entire family comes together. There may be a group leader or counselor, or some member of the family can act as a leader. One person in the family is designated as the target person. For example, the mother may begin as target person. She is asked to list the strengths that she feels she has as a person. If she lists only two or three because she's modest, the leader can urge her to list others. After she has finished the list, her husband is asked to add to her list of strengths. Or he may elaborate on the strengths that she has already listed. When he has finished, each of the children is asked to add to mother's list of strengths. When this process is finished, the husband becomes the target person. The same procedure is repeated for him. Then each of the children becomes the target person.

The "strengths bombardment" technique is very simple, but the results have been amazing. When families do this exercise, they become more aware of each other's strengths, and more aware of their strengths as a family. They get into a pattern of looking for each other's good qualities and they also get into the habit of expressing appreciation. The result of this with so many families is that it makes their interaction with each other more positive. Some follow-up studies done with families who have gone through this activity show that the increased level of positive interaction is maintained for a period of time after the exercise has been completed. Many families are now using this technique periodically on their own.

Spending Time Together

A second quality found among strong families is that they did a lot of things together. It was not a "false" togetherness or a "smothering" type of togetherness—they genuinely enjoyed being together. Another important point here is that these families structured their life-styles so that they could spend time together. It did not "just happen"; they *made* it happen. And this togetherness was in all areas of their lives—eating meals, recreation, and work.

One interesting pattern which has emerged from our research is the high frequency with which the strong families participate in outdoor activities together such as walking, jogging, bird watching, camping, canoeing, horseback riding, and outdoor games. While there are many strong families who are not particularly fond of outdoor activities, the finding in our research that so many strong families employed this as an important source of enjoyment and of their strength as a family raises the question of how the participation in outdoor activities as a family might contribute to family strengths. One logical possibility is that when families are participating in outdoor activities together they have fewer distractions—the family members are away from the telephone and the never-ending array of household tasks—and can concentrate more upon each other, thus encouraging a good communication experience. Another possibility is that physical exercise is often one benefit of participation in outdoor activities and the exercise itself contributes to personal feelings of well-being, health, and vitality.

Commitment

A third quality of these strong families was a high degree of commitment. These families were deeply committed to promoting each other's happiness and welfare. They were also very committed to the family group, as reflected by the fact that they invested much of their time and energies in it. We have not had very much research on commitment, and perhaps in recent years it has not been fashionable to talk about it. Yet, Yankelovich (1981) observes that our society is now in the process of leaving behind an excessive self-centered orientation and moving toward a new "ethic of commitment" with emphasis upon new rules of living that support self-fulfillment through deeper personal relationships. Also, as David and Vera Mace (1980) have noted, only if you have produced a commitment to behavior change have you done anything to improve the life of a person or the life of a marriage or family. Some of the best research on commitment has been done in communes.

Some communes have been successful and others have not. One of the main differences found between the two groups is commitment. Those communes that are the most successful, that last the longest, and that are the most satisfying in terms of the relationships, are those in which there is a great deal of commitment—among individuals and to the group. Again, commitment in the communes was reflected in the amount of time the members spent together. The same was true with the strong families.

All of us are busy and we sometimes feel that we have so many things to do that we are pulled in a thousand different directions at the same time. Strong families experience the same problem. One interesting action that these families expressed was that when life got too hectic—to the extent that they were not spending as much time with their families as they wanted—they would sit down and make a list of the different activities in which they were involved. They would go over that list critically and inevitably there were some things that they really did not want to be doing, or that did not give much happiness, or that really were not very important to them. So they would scratch those activities and involvements off their lists. This would free time for their families and would relieve some of the pressure. As a result they were happier with their lives in general and more satisfied with their family relationships.

This sounds very simple, but how many of us do it? We get involved too often and it's not always because we want to be. We act so often as if we cannot change the situation. We *do* have a choice. An important point about these families is that they took the initiative in structuring their life-style in a way that enhanced the quality of their family relationships and their satisfaction. They were on the "offensive." We may have talked too much about families as simply reactors in society, being at the mercy of the environment. In fact, there is a great deal that families can do to make life more enjoyable. These strong families exercised that ability.

Good Communication Patterns

The fourth quality was not a surprise. Strong families have very good communication patterns. They spend time talking with each other. This is closely related to the fact that they spend a lot of time together. It's hard for people to communicate unless they spend time with each other. One of the big problems facing families today is not spending enough time together. Dr. Virginia Satir, a prominent family therapist, has stated that often families are so fragmented, so busy, and spend so little time together that they only communicate with each other through rumor. Unfortunately, too often that is exactly what happens.

Another important aspect of communication is that these families also listen well. They reported that their family members were good listeners and that this was important to them. The fact that family members listen to one another communicates a very important message—respect. They are saying to one another, "You respect me enough to listen to what I have to say. I'm interested enough to listen too."

Another factor related to communication is that these families do fight. They get mad at each other, but they get conflict out in the open and they are able to talk it over, to discuss the problem. They share their feelings about alternative ways to deal with the problem and in selecting a solution that is best for everybody. These strong families have learned to do what David and Vera Mace (1980) have reported to be essential for a successful marriage—making creative use of conflict.

High Degree of Religious Orientation

The fifth quality that these families expressed was a high degree of religious orientation. This agrees with research from the past forty years that shows a positive relationship of religion to marriage happiness and successful family relationships. Of course, we know that there are persons who are not religious who have very happy marriages and good family relationships. Nevertheless a positive relationship between marriage happiness and religion exists according to the research of many years. These strong families went to church together often and they participated in religious activities together. Most of them, although not all of them, were members of organized churches. All of them were very religious.

There are indications that this religious quality went deeper than going to church or participating in religious activities together. It could most appropriately be called a commitment to a spiritual life-style. Words are inadequate to communicate this, but what many of these families said was that they had an awareness of God or a higher power that gave them a sense of purpose and gave their family a sense of support and strength. The awareness of this higher power in their lives helped them to be more patient with each other, more forgiving, quicker to get over anger, more positive, and more supportive in their relationships. Many of the values emphasized by religion, when put into action, can certainly enhance the quality of human relationships. Dr. Herbert Otto has observed that we could spend more time looking at the spiritual aspect of developing human potential, and perhaps we could benefit by exploring more about the spiritual aspects of developing family strengths. For these strong families, religion played a major role.

Ability to Deal with Crises in a Positive Manner

The final quality that these families had was the ability to deal with crises and problems in a positive way. Not that they enjoyed crises, but they were able to deal with them constructively. They managed, even in the darkest of situations, to see some positive element, no matter how tiny, and to focus on it. It may have been, for example, that in a particular crisis they simply had to rely to a greater extent on each other and a developed trust that they had in each other. They were able to unite in dealing with the crisis instead of being fragmented by it. They dealt with the problem and were supportive of each other.

CONCLUSIONS AND RECOMMENDATIONS

The qualities that characterized the strong families in our research coincide with what other researchers examining healthy families have reported (Otto, 1964; Lewis et al., 1976; Lewis, 1979; Nelson and Banonis, 1981). It is interesting that most of these qualities that we found to characterize strong families have been found to be lacking in families that are having severe relationship problems and in families broken by divorce. This fact supports the validity of the finding and suggests the importance of these qualities in building family strength. How can we translate this information into practical help to strengthen families? What kind of recommendations can we make? What can we do?

1. One recommendation is that we help families develop some of these skills, such as the ability to express appreciation and good communication patterns. If we were able to do that, relationships and the quality of family life could be improved. This can be done—in fact, it is being done. One example is the research project we instituted at the University of Nebraska, the Family Strengths Enrichment Program. This was an eight-week program in which couples were assisted in developing skills and competencies found to be characteristic of strong families. Pre- and post-tests were administered to the couples. The results indicated significant, positive increases in marriage and family satisfaction. Substantial positive change was found in the ability of the couples to communicate, to deal effectively with conflict, and to express genuine appreciation.

Also, considering the emphasis by these strong families on outdoor activities, recreational areas could be expanded and developed more for family units. For example, having special family days and outdoor seminars specifically for families might encourage them to do more as a unit.

2. Communities, in order to be strong and healthy, must have strong and healthy families. Therefore, we need to devise more research projects which relate family strengths to community needs. We then need to follow through to help the communities use the information we obtain through the research. An example can be found in Lincoln, Nebraska, where a very interesting demonstration project called the Willard Community Family Strengths Project was established. The project was developed in response to a pressing community need. This particular section of Lincoln—the old Willard School District—had a disturbingly high vandalism and delinquency rate. It was the imaginative thesis of Lela Watts, a Ph. D. student at the University of Nebraska, that

the most effective way to meet the delinquency problem was a total family approach. So a program, beginning in 1980, was conducted to build the strengths and skills of the families of the youth in the neighborhood. Building self-esteem [and] communication skills and expanding the scope of activities which the entire family enjoyed were among the areas of focus for the Willard Family Strengths Program. Some excellent research data were collected, but most importantly the delinquency and vandalism rates were reduced by 83 percent within a six-month period. This program is ongoing and at the time of this writing the delinquency and vandalism rates had been reduced almost to the point of elimination.

3. Another recommendation that we could make is to have a comprehensive human relationships education program incorporated at the preschool, elementary, secondary, and college levels. Isn't it amazing that we have not already done that? Good human relationships are basic and vital to our happiness, our well-being, and our mental health.

4. Also, if we are truly serious about strengthening family life, we might make more of a concerted effort to improve the image of family life. Perhaps we need to make commitment more fashionable as we are so much influenced by it. Some psychologists have stated that if we are really serious about strengthening family life, we are going to have to build much more prestige into being a family member, in being a good father, mother, wife, or husband. We are influenced tremendously by what we think we are rewarded for.

Perhaps we could improve the image of family life through some television spots like public service announcements. The Mormon Church, for example, has . . . some very effective television spots. These short announcements could communicate messages about the importance of expressing appreciation or the importance of parents listening to their children, for example.

5. Another thing that we are going to have to do is reorder our values and priorities. We will have to make family life and human relationships a top priority, and apply this commitment in terms of the way we spend our time and our energy.

6. Finally, in order to build stronger families in the future we must change our remedial services, as David and Vera Mace (1980) have urged. We must turn from our preoccupation with pathology and the commonly accepted practice of spending all our energies doing "patchwork" and "picking up the wrecks." This approach is more expensive—both financially and in terms of human suffering. In order to be most effective we must make preventive services and programs available early in the lives of individuals and families to provide them with skills, knowledge, motivation, and positive models that can help develop family strengths. Just one example of how this might be done is through

more family life education and enrichment programs in the community, which could be organized through such groups as churches, schools, YMCA, YWCA, and local Family Service Association Organizations. Secondary and primary schools could place more emphasis on family life education in the curriculum and encourage, if not require, all students to participate. College curriculum could also be improved by placing more emphasis on family strength in marriage and family classes and designing whole courses specifically for teaching ways to develop family strengths.

Strong families are the roots of our well-being as individuals and as a society. The dream of facilitating strong families that produce emotionally and socially healthy individuals can be realized. The positive potential for the family is great.

Editor's note: Stinnett's findings also contain the basis for additional "conclusions and recommendations." To apply the empirical findings that he reports concerning what makes families strong, we also ought to pay attention to the role of religion. One of the main characteristics of strong families that Stinnett reports in this chapter is their high degree of religious orientation. In fact, he found that *all* the strong families were "very religious." Highly concerned with the spiritual aspects of life, they expressed "an awareness of God or a higher power that gave them a sense of purpose"; this provided these families with "a sense of support and strength."

To use this finding as a basis for recommendations for strengthening families would be to encourage the spiritual development and religious participation of entire families. If Stinnett's findings are generalizable, as they appear to be, to encourage the religious involvement of families would strengthen not only families but the communities in which they live.

—J. M. H.

REFERENCES

Lewis, J. M. (1979) How's Your Family? New York: Brunner/Mazel.

——R. W. Beavers, J. T. Gosset, V. A. Phillips (1976) No Single Thread: Psychological Health in Family Systems, New York: Brunner/Mazel.

Mace, D. and V. Mace (1980) "Enriching Marriages: The foundation stone of family strength," in N. Stinnett et al. (eds.) Family Strengths: Positive Models for Family Life. Lincoln: Univ. of Nebraska Press.

Nelson, P. T., and B. Banonis (1981) "Family concerns and strengths identified in Delaware's White House Conference on families," in N. Stinnett et al. (eds.) Family Strengths 3: Roots of Well-Being. Lincoln: Univ. of Nebraska Press.

Otto, H. A. (1964) "The personal and family strength research projects: Some implications for the therapist." Mental Hygiene 48: 439–450.

———.(1962) "The personal and family resource development programs: A preliminary report." Int. J. of Social Psychiatry 8:185–195.

Yankelovich, D. (1981) New Rules: Searching for Fulfillment in a World Turned Upside Down. New York: Random House.

APPENDIX

Correlation Chart

The following chart correlates this anthology with 18 basic marriage and family texts. The chapter numbers of the texts are located in the column to the left of the boxes. The numbers within the boxes refer to the readings in *Marriage and Family in a Changing Society*.

Because some readings contain more than one theme, they can be correlated with basic texts in a number of ways. Depending upon your particular approach to teaching this course and the sociological principles that you intend to emphasize, you may want to rearrange the ordering that I have suggested in this correlation chart.

The numbers within the boxes refer to selection numbers in Marriage and Family in a Changing Society.

The numbers directly below refer to chapters in the marriage and family texts:	Bahr, Family Interaction, 1989	Cargan, Marriages and Families, 1991	Collins and Coltrane, Sociology of Marriage and the Family, 1991	Cox, Human Intimacy, 1990	Dickinson and Leming, Understanding Families, 1990	Eshleman, The Family, 1991	Galvin and Brommel, Family Communication, 1991	Havemann and Lehtinen, Marriages and Families, 1990	Kephart and Jedlicka, The Family, Society, and the Individual, 1991
1	1-4	1-4	1	6, 7, 49	1	1, 2, 4	1, 3, 9	1	1
2	38	20	3	1-4	3, 12		2	2-4	3
3	5-7	10, 34	4	12-15		3	4, 6, 7, 12, 13, 15	6, 7, 9, 20	2, 28
4	8, 9, 34	12-15	16	8-10	2, 4, 13	28-33	17	5	4
5	12-15	16-19, 35-37	2, 28	17, 18	20	7	5, 14, 16, 19	14, 34	7
6	16, 17, 46-48	28-33	5, 37	5, 19, 20	6, 7, 10	6	10, 20, 48	8, 10, 12, 13, 15	6
7	18, 19	11, 23	6, 7	16	5	5	8, 34	18, 35-37	5
8	21-24	21, 22, 24-26	10, 12-15	28	8, 14	12	11	16, 17, 28-33	13
9	25, 26	6, 7, 9	8, 9, 24, 34	30-33	9, 24	13-15	18	11, 19, 20	12, 14, 15
10	28-33	5	17-20, 31-33	24, 34	15-20, 28-33	8-10	24-27, 38	21-24	
11		27, 38	35, 36	11, 23, 29	11, 21-25	24	35-37, 39-43, 45	25-27	8-10, 34

12		8, 9		21, 22	26, 38	16-20	44	38-45	
13	37	39-45	11, 21-23	25-27	27	11	28-33	46-49	11, 16-20
14	49	46-49	25, 26, 29, 30	38	39-44	21-26	49		21-26
15	35, 36		27, 38-45	35-37, 39-43, 45	45	27			35-44
16	39-43		46-49	44	34-37	34-37, 45			27, 45
17	10, 11, 44			46-48	46-49	38-44			29-33
18	20					46-49			
19	27, 45								46-49
20									
21									
22									
23									
24									

The numbers within the boxes refer to selection numbers in Marriage and Family in a Changing Society.

The numbers directly below refer to chapters in the marriage and family texts:

	Strong and DeVault, The Marriage and Family Experience, 1989	Strinnett, Walters, and Strinnett, Relationships in Marriage and the Family, 1991	Steinmetz, Clavan, and Stein, Marriage and Family Realities, 1990	Saxton, The Individual, Marriage, and the Family, 1990	Rice, Intimate Relationships, Marriages, and Families, 1990	Leslie and Korman, The Family in Social Context, 1989	Lauer and Lauer, The Quest for Intimacy, 1991	Lasswell and Lasswell, Marriage and the Family, 1991	Lamanna and Riedmann, Marriages and Families, 1991
1	1	1-4, 48, 49	1, 3	1-7	1, 3, 4	1, 2	1-4	1-4	1-7
2	2, 4	10, 12-14	2, 4, 28	5, 20, 28, 31-32	5-7	3	14	20	20
3	5-7, 9	6, 7	6, 7	13, 15	46-49		8	13-15	14
4	16-20	8, 15, 16, 33, 46, 47	9, 10	9, 14	2	8-10	13, 15	9, 34	9, 24
5	12-15	5, 31, 32, 34	20	8, 24, 34	10	4	12	8, 10	8, 10
6	8, 10	17-19	8, 12-15	16-19, 35-37	34	13	10	6, 7, 12	12, 13, 15
7	24	20	16-19	12	12-15	5	20	5, 16-19, 46-49	16, 46-49
8	3	35-37	11, 21-23, 25, 26, 29	10	9	6	34	28-33	17-19
9	21-23	9	27	33, 46-49	24	7	16, 17	23	31-33
10	27, 38	11, 21-23, 29		29, 38	8		19	21, 22, 24, 26	11, 21-23
11	11, 25, 26	24	24	39-43	16, 17	49	18	11, 25	25-27

12	28-30		28-33	14, 34, 38	20	44, 45	5	25, 30	28-33
13		35-43	11, 21-26	12, 15	28, 29	11, 21-23, 25-27, 29		28	
14	34-37, 45	44	38	16-20, 28, 34-37, 47, 48	30		30-37, 46-49	26	37, 45
15	38-43	27, 45	46	46			38-45	27, 45	35, 36
16	44		5-7, 9	11, 21-26, 29	31-33			38-44	39-43
17			27, 35-37, 45	27, 30-33	18, 19				44, 46-49
18			39-43	39-43	11, 23				
19			44, 47-49	44, 45	21, 22				
20				27	25				
21					26, 27				
22					37, 45				
23					35, 36, 39-43				
24					44, 46-49